Get the eBook FREE!

(PDF, ePub, Kindle, and liveBook all included)

We believe that once you buy a book from us, you should be able to read it in any format we have available. To get electronic versions of this book at no additional cost to you, purchase and then register this book at the Manning website.

Go to https://www.manning.com/freebook and follow the instructions to complete your pBook registration.

That's it!
Thanks from Manning!

Acing the CCNA Exam

VOLUME 2
ADVANCED NETWORKING AND SECURITY

JEREMY MCDOWELL

MANNING
SHELTER ISLAND

For online information and ordering of this and other Manning books, please visit www.manning.com. The publisher offers discounts on this book when ordered in quantity.

For more information, please contact

> Special Sales Department
> Manning Publications Co.
> 20 Baldwin Road
> PO Box 761
> Shelter Island, NY 11964
> Email: orders@manning.com

Manning Publications Co.
20 Baldwin Road
PO Box 761
Shelter Island, NY 11964

Development editor:	Connor O'Brien
Technical editor:	Jeremy Cioara
Review editor:	Kishor Rit
Production editor:	Kathy Rossland
Copy editors:	Alisa Larson and Kari Lucke
Proofreaders:	Melody Dolab and Katie Tennant
Technical proofreader:	Munish Kaushal
Typesetter:	Tamara Švelić Sabljić
Cover designer:	Marija Tudor

ISBN 9781633435780
Printed in the United States of America

brief contents

contents

preface

In 2018, as a junior high school English teacher in the city of Kobe, Japan, I found myself at a crossroads. What I had originally intended to be a brief teaching stint in Japan had stretched into four years, and I was reaching the limit of my stay. I was in Japan on the Japan Exchange and Teaching (JET) Programme, a program sponsored by the Japanese government to bring recent university graduates to Japan to teach English for up to 5 years. As my tenure neared its end, I pondered my next step.

Being fascinated with computers since childhood, I found the field of IT a natural choice. I was no computer wizard—I had no experience in programming or anything of the sort—but after some searching, I stumbled upon the Cisco Certified Network Associate (CCNA) certification. If the stories were to be believed, getting CCNA certified was the gateway to a promising career in IT with a decent salary and plenty of room for growth. After a bit of studying, I was hooked! Peering under the hood of networks like the internet—an ubiquitous part of the modern world—was (and still is) endlessly fascinating.

Fast forward a year to 2019, and I was a network engineer at the world's leading colocation data center and interconnection provider! I share my personal story here to emphasize that, with no formal education or previous experience on the topic, I was able to self-study, get certified, and make a 180-degree career change to enter the IT industry. And my story is no exception; I hear such stories from students all over the world on a daily basis.

You will occasionally encounter naysayers who downplay the value of the CCNA these days. One common argument is that, with the rise of cloud services like Amazon Web Services (AWS) and Microsoft Azure, there is less demand for network engineers; students should pursue cloud providers' certifications instead. I couldn't disagree more;

connecting the complex multicloud infrastructure used by many modern enterprises is no simple task, and we need network professionals more than ever.

Studying a particular cloud service provider's solutions before learning the fundamentals of networking is simply putting the cart before the horse—a house built on sand. The same can be said of pursuing the field of cybersecurity before grasping basics like networking. Network fundamentals are foundational knowledge for any IT professional, and the CCNA exam tests and certifies not only that you understand the fundamentals, but also that you have the skills to apply them in real networks. In our increasingly interconnected world, such knowledge and skills are invaluable—my story, and countless others' stories, prove that.

This book—consisting of two volumes—is the culmination of insights gained from countless interactions with many thousands of students of my CCNA video course, refined and expanded to offer a comprehensive resource. For countless people— including myself—becoming CCNA certified has been truly life changing. There will be struggles and setbacks, but if you're looking to make a change in your life and career, I can't recommend the CCNA enough, and I hope that this book will inspire and empower you to pursue and achieve your CCNA certification.

acknowledgments

Writing and publishing a book is a major undertaking—certainly not something I could have done on my own! I'd like to thank everyone who contributed to this book in one way or another, directly or indirectly.

Thank you, everyone at Manning who has worked hard on this book; there is a lot of behind-the-scenes work that goes into publishing a book. I'd like to thank my editor Connor O'Brien most of all for his valuable feedback on each chapter of this book. The book has turned out far better than it ever could have without his detailed reviews and guidance.

Thank you, Andy Waldron, acquisitions editor at Manning, for giving me a chance to write this book. I reached out to a few publishers about writing a CCNA book, and Andy was quick to respond and express his interest. After a few quick calls, the contract was signed, and the rest is history!

Thank you, to Jeremy Cioara, for your contributions as technical editor for the book. Jeremy Cioara is an author, educator, and business owner known for his ability to simplify complex technical concepts into entertaining and practical explanations. He brings more than two decades of experience, a love of learning, and a keen eye for detail.

Thank you, to all of the reviewers, for your time and valuable feedback at each stage of the process: Amit Lamba, Andrea Cosentino, Casey Burnett, Eder Andrés Ávila Niño, Emanuele Piccinelli, Emilio Grande, Gavin Smith, George Gyftogiannis, Glen Thompson, Greg MacLean, Jeremy Chen, John Bisgrove, John Guthrie, Jose Apablaza, Narayanan Seshan, Nghia To, Paul Love, Pedro Seromenho, Raghunath Mysore, Simone Sguazza, Sushil Singh, Vladislav Bilay, and Zachary Manning. Special thanks go to Munish Kaushal, my technical proofreader, for your careful reviews of the many (very many!) figures, commands, and examples in this book.

I'd also like to thank everyone who has supported Jeremy's IT Lab during the past five years. It's because of all of you that I can pursue my dream as a job—for that, I am forever grateful. Writing a CCNA book would never have crossed my mind without your support. Special thanks go to those on the Jeremy's IT Lab Discord server for being a totally awesome and supportive group, always willing to lend a hand and lift each other up (without forgetting to have fun).

Finally, thank you, my friends and family who have supported me in my personal life during this process; writing a book is a major time commitment and often means neglecting the more important parts of life. Thank you, Miki, for your understanding and constant encouragement during my long work hours throughout the whole process, and thanks, Mom and Dad, for your support and encouragement as always.

about this book

Acing the CCNA Exam was written with one goal in mind: to help you prepare for and successfully pass the CCNA exam. It begins from zero and assumes no previous knowledge, covering network fundamentals and every CCNA exam topic step by step.

Who should read this book

As an exam study guide, this book is for anyone who wants to pass the CCNA exam and attain their CCNA certification. If that's you (good choice, by the way), you've come to the right place! Even for those who already have their CCNA or are already working in the field, this book will be a useful resource for reference, covering key network protocols and how to configure them on Cisco routers and switches.

How this book is organized

The CCNA exam is quite wide in scope, and as a result, this book is divided into two volumes. This is volume 2, consisting of 25 chapters arranged across 5 parts.

Part 1 details essential network services and protocols that support network operation, including time synchronization, name resolution, logging, and monitoring:

- Chapter 1 explains the roles of Cisco Discovery Protocol (CDP) and Link Layer Discovery Protocol (LLDP) in network discovery and troubleshooting.
- Chapter 2 introduces Network Time Protocol (NTP), essential for synchronizing clocks across network devices.
- Chapter 3 covers Domain Name System (DNS), a protocol that plays a key role in the internet by translating domain names to IP addresses.

- Chapter 4 focuses on Dynamic Host Configuration Protocol (DHCP), which automates the IP configuration process of hosts like PCs.
- Chapter 5 introduces Secure Shell, a protocol used to securely connect to the CLI of network devices for configuration and management.
- Chapter 6 discusses Simple Network Management Protocol (SNMP), which is primarily used for monitoring network devices.
- Chapter 7 covers Syslog, a standard for message logging on network devices.
- Chapter 8 explains the use of Trivial File Transfer Protocol (TFTP) and File Transfer Protocol (FTP) for file transfers over a network.
- Chapter 9 delves into Network Address Translation (NAT), a method of translating private IP addresses into public IP addresses to enable communication over the internet.
- Chapter 10 introduces Quality of Service (QoS), which minimizes the effect of network congestion on sensitive applications by prioritizing and de-prioritizing certain traffic types.

Part 2 addresses fundamental security measures for protecting network infrastructure, focusing on how to implement security protocols on Cisco switches—the point where users connect to the network:

- Chapter 11 introduces foundational concepts related to network security.
- Chapter 12 covers Port Security, a feature that limits which devices can access a switch port.
- Chapter 13 discusses DHCP Snooping, a security feature that mitigates against DHCP-related network attacks.
- Chapter 14 explains Dynamic ARP Inspection (DAI), which prevents attacks that exploit Address Resolution Protocol (ARP).

Part 3 explores local and wide area network (LAN and WAN) architectures—the big picture of how real-world networks are designed—as well as the virtualization technologies and cloud services that underpin modern IT infrastructure:

- Chapter 15 focuses on LAN architectures, ranging from small office/home office (SOHO) networks to large campus and data center LANs.
- Chapter 16 covers WAN architectures, detailing the technologies and services that connect networks over long distances.
- Chapter 17 discusses virtualization technologies and cloud services, two key elements of many modern enterprise networks.

Part 4 provides an overview of wireless networking, ranging from the behaviors of electromagnetic waves to the architectures and security protocols used in wireless LANs, as well as how to configure them:

- Chapter 18 introduces the fundamentals of wireless LANs, including the standards and concepts that underpin wireless networking.
- Chapter 19 covers wireless LAN architectures, detailing the components and design considerations of wireless networks.
- Chapter 20 discusses wireless LAN security, addressing the challenges of securely communicating over the airwaves.
- Chapter 21 demonstrates how to configure a wireless LAN using a Cisco wireless LAN controller (WLC).

Part 5 looks toward the future of network management through automation, covering the various tools that streamline and automate network tasks:

- Chapter 22 introduces the concept of network automation and how software-defined networking (SDN) facilitates the programmatic control of network functions.
- Chapter 23 covers REST APIs, which are the software interfaces used to facilitate communications between applications.
- Chapter 24 delves into standard data formats like JSON, XML, and YAML, which are crucial for providing a shared language through which applications can share data.
- Chapter 25 discusses tools like Ansible and Terraform, which are used to automate various tasks related to the deployment and management of device configurations.

Additionally, there are four appendixes, each of which should prove helpful in your exam preparation:

- Appendix A is a reference table that lists the CCNA exam topics and which chapters of each volume cover each topic.
- Appendix B is a reference table that lists the Cisco IOS CLI commands covered in each chapter of this volume, with a brief description of each.
- Appendix C consists of several quiz questions for each chapter of this volume. I recommend using these questions to test your understanding after studying each chapter, and then doing the same for review as necessary.
- Appendix D lists the correct answers to the chapter quiz questions in appendix C and gives a brief explanation for each answer.

If you are just beginning your CCNA studies, I highly recommend starting from volume 1 and reading the chapters in order before beginning volume 2 (this volume); each chapter builds upon the previous ones, assuming familiarity with all preceding material. However, if you are using this book as a secondary resource (having already completed another course of study, such as my video series), feel free to treat the book more as a reference guide. In this case, you can directly consult chapters that address specific areas you want to focus on. Appendix A will be particularly useful for this targeted study, as it lists which chapters in which volume address each CCNA exam topic.

About Cisco CLI commands and output formatting

This book contains many examples of Cisco command-line interface (CLI) commands and output in examples and in line with normal text. These examples are formatted in a `fixed-width font like this` to separate it from ordinary text, using the syntax conventions shown in the following table. Code annotations accompany many of the code examples and highlight important concepts. Where necessary, the code has been reformatted to accommodate the available page space, and where code wraps, we've used line-continuation markers (➡).

Table 1   CLI syntax conventions

Convention	Description
Standard text	Command prompts and CLI output not typed by the user.
Bold text	Commands and keywords as typed by the user.
Italic text	Arguments in a command for which you supply values.
[**x**]	Square brackets indicate optional elements, such as optional keywords.
. . .	An ellipsis indicates that output has been abbreviated/omitted.
|	Pipes (vertical bars) are used to separate mutually exclusive elements, as shown in the following two conventions (square brackets and curly braces).
[**x** | **y**]	Optional alternative elements are enclosed in square brackets and separated by pipes.
{**x** | **y**}	Mandatory alternative elements are enclosed in curly braces and separated by pipes.

Each command in this book will be explained as it is introduced, but you can refer to this table as needed for clarification. The following examples demonstrate some of these different syntax conventions:

- **show ip interface** *[interface]*
  - You must type **show ip interface** and then optionally provide a value for the *interface* argument.
- **vtp version** {1 | 2 | 3}
  - You must type **vtp mode** and then the keyword **1**, **2**, or **3**.
- **switchport trunk allowed vlan** [**add** | **remove** | **except**] *vlans*
  - You must type **switchport trunk allowed vlan**, optionally specify one of the listed keywords, and then specify a value for the *vlans* argument.
- R1(config-if)# **interface g0/1**
  - The command prompt R1(config-if)# was displayed, and the user typed the command **interface g0/1**.

liveBook discussion forum

Purchase of *Acing the CCNA Exam* includes free access to liveBook, Manning's online reading platform. Using liveBook's exclusive discussion features, you can attach comments to the book globally or to specific sections or paragraphs. It's a snap to make notes for yourself, ask and answer technical questions, and receive help from the author and other users. To access the forum, go to https://livebook.manning.com/book/acing-the-ccna-exam-advanced-networking-and-security/discussion. You can also learn more about Manning's forums and the rules of conduct at https://livebook.manning.com/discussion.

Manning's commitment to our readers is to provide a venue where a meaningful dialogue between individual readers and between readers and the author can take place. It is not a commitment to any specific amount of participation on the part of the author, whose contribution to the forum remains voluntary (and unpaid). We suggest you try asking him some challenging questions lest his interest stray! The forum and the archives of previous discussions will be accessible from the publisher's website as long as the book is in print.

Other online resources

There is no shortage of helpful resources for CCNA students online. I have collected some of my recommended resources (video courses, practice exams, etc.) on my website at https://www.jeremysitlab.com/ccna-resources.

Another page that every CCNA candidate should have bookmarked is the official exam topics list at https://learningnetwork.cisco.com/s/ccna-exam-topics. This is where you can find what Cisco expects you to know to pass the CCNA exam.

Finally, I recommend bookmarking Cisco Certification Roadmaps at https://learningnetwork.cisco.com/s/cisco-certification-roadmaps. This page will give you information about Cisco's yearly certification review process. If there are any scheduled changes coming to the CCNA exam, they will be listed on this page well in advance.

about the author

JEREMY MCDOWELL is a senior network engineer from Canada, living and working in Japan for over 10 years. After graduating with a bachelor of music degree from the University of Toronto, he taught English in Japan for five years before entering the networking industry in 2019.

Combining his knowledge of networking with his teaching skills, Jeremy has helped thousands of students study for and pass the CCNA exam through his YouTube channel Jeremy's IT Lab, which currently has over 340,000 subscribers.

about the cover illustration

The figure on the cover of *Acing the CCNA Exam*, titled "Maître d'école," or "Teacher," is taken from a book by Louis Curmer published in 1841. Each illustration is finely drawn and colored by hand.

In those days, it was easy to identify where people lived and what their trade or station in life was just by their dress. Manning celebrates the inventiveness and initiative of the computer business with book covers based on the rich diversity of regional culture centuries ago, brought back to life by pictures from collections such as this one.

Part 1

Network services

Part 1 covers a range of essential network services that play pivotal roles in the operation and management of modern networks. We start with Cisco Discovery Protocol (CDP) and Link Layer Discovery Protocol (LLDP) in chapter 1, protocols that enable you to discover how devices are connected to each other, playing a critical role in troubleshooting and network documentation. Chapter 2 introduces Network Time Protocol (NTP), a crucial service for synchronizing the clocks of network devices, ensuring accurate time-stamping for logging, security, and other time-sensitive operations.

Chapter 3 covers the Domain Name System (DNS)—a cornerstone of the internet that translates domain names into IP addresses. Any time you type a URL like youtube.com to access a website, you can thank DNS for translating that name to the correct IP address. Dynamic Host Configuration Protocol (DHCP)—the topic of chapter 4—simplifies IP address management by automating the assignment process. In chapter 5, we move on to Secure Shell, which provides a secure, encrypted method for remotely accessing the CLI of network devices to configure and manage them.

Chapters 6 and 7 cover Simple Network Management Protocol (SNMP) and Syslog, respectively. These protocols facilitate network monitoring and event logging, playing crucial roles in the management of networks of all sizes. Chapter 8 covers Trivial File Transfer Protocol (TFTP) and File Transfer Protocol (FTP); as their names imply, these protocols enable file transfers—one of the primary functions of networks since their beginning. Chapter 9 dives into Network Address Translation (NAT), a key tool for enabling hosts in a private network to communicate over the public internet. Finally, chapter 10 covers Quality of Service (QoS), which is essential for prioritizing network traffic to ensure optimal performance for critical applications.

Part 1, consisting of 10 chapters, is the largest in this book. However, each of these services plays an important role in networks of all sizes and is essential knowledge for the CCNA exam and for any modern network professional.

Cisco Discovery Protocol and Link Layer Discovery Protocol

This chapter covers

- The purpose of Layer 2 discovery protocols
- How neighboring Cisco devices use Cisco Discovery Protocol to share information
- CDP's industry-standard equivalent: Link Layer Discovery Protocol

In a perfect world, all networks would be perfectly documented, with up-to-date network diagrams and other documents detailing the routers, switches, firewalls, and other devices that make up the network infrastructure, how they are connected, their IP addresses, etc. In reality, that's often not the case: people cut corners, changes go undocumented, or perhaps the network was never properly documented in the first place.

In either case, the result is often that the network documentation doesn't accurately reflect the current state of the network; this is not an ideal state of affairs. Fortunately, *Layer 2 discovery protocols*—the topic of this chapter—can help you remedy this situation. Layer 2 discovery protocols, such as *Cisco Discovery Protocol* (CDP) and *Link Layer Discovery Protocol* (LLDP), enable devices to share information about themselves with their directly connected neighbors. Using this information, you can map out the network by identifying the devices in the network, their hardware models, how they are connected to each other, their IP addresses, and other information.

Layer 2 discovery protocols are CCNA exam topic 2.3: Configure and verify Layer 2 discovery protocols (Cisco Discovery Protocol and LLDP). This is one of the more straightforward CCNA exam topics. In this chapter, we will primarily examine some **show** commands that allow you to view the information that devices share with CDP/ LLDP, as well as some basic configuration commands to enable, disable, and fine-tune the protocols.

1.1   Cisco Discovery Protocol

CDP is a Cisco-proprietary Layer 2 discovery protocol that runs on Cisco network devices such as routers and switches. CDP is enabled by default; unless you want to modify the default settings, you don't need to do any configuration to use CDP in your network. Using CDP, devices periodically send advertisement messages out of their interfaces, informing directly connected neighbors about various aspects of the local device. They also listen for similar advertisements from those same neighbors. Figure 1.1 illustrates this: R1 and SW1 exchange CDP advertisements with each other.

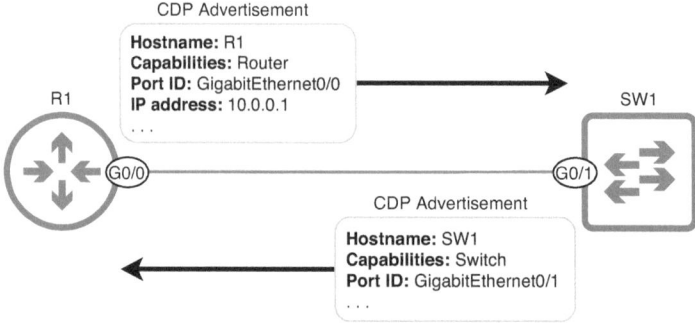

Figure 1.1   Two neighboring Cisco devices share information about themselves via CDP. The shared information includes hostname, capabilities (device type), port ID, IP address, and much more.

CDP messages are sent to the multicast MAC address 0100.0ccc.cccc. However, when a switch receives a CDP message, it does not flood the message like it would with regular multicast frames; the switch receives the frame for itself. Using figure 1.1's example, SW1 will receive R1's CDP message and add R1 to its CDP neighbor table.

NOTE   Most CLI examples in this chapter will be from a router's CLI. However, CDP (and LLDP) commands and their output are identical on Cisco routers and switches.

1.1.1   Viewing CDP neighbors

When using CDP, the **show** command you are most likely to use is **show cdp neighbors**; this command lists basic information about each of the device's CDP neighbors— devices from which it has received CDP messages. In the following example, I use the command on R1:

Codes used in the Capability column

```
R1# show cdp neighbors
Capability Codes: R - Router, T - Trans Bridge, B - Source Route Bridge
                  S - Switch, H - Host, I - IGMP, r - Repeater, P - Phone,
                  D - Remote, C - CVTA, M - Two-port Mac Relay
Device ID       Local Intrfce     Holdtme    Capability  Platform  Port ID
SW1             Gig 0/0           158               R S I  WS-C2960C Gig 0/1
```

SW1 is R1's CDP neighbor.

After a legend listing the different codes that can appear in the Capability column, there is a table listing the device's CDP neighbors—neighbors from which the device has received CDP messages. The Device ID column lists the hostname of each neighbor; in our example, R1 has one neighbor: SW1.

The Local Intrfce column lists the interface on the local device that the neighbor is connected to. The value of Gig 0/0 in this column means that SW1 is connected to R1 G0/0. Don't confuse this with the final column, Port ID, which lists the interface of the neighboring device. The value of Gig 0/1 here means that R1 is connected to SW1 G0/1.

The third column is Holdtme, which states the current *holdtime*—how long until R1 will remove SW1's entry from the neighbor table. The default timer is 180 seconds; each time the device receives a CDP advertisement from the neighbor, this time is reset to 180 and starts counting down. The value of 158 in this column means that 22 seconds have elapsed since R1 received a CDP message from SW1. If this counts down to 0, R1 will remove SW1's entry from the CDP neighbor table. We'll cover this timer more in the next section.

The fourth column is Capability, which identifies the type of device. S means Switch, as indicated in the Capability Codes at the top of the output; SW1 is a switch. However, it also has the R code (for Router), because it has some Layer 3 capabilities, and I (for IGMP), meaning it supports the *Internet Group Management Protocol*—a topic beyond the scope of the CCNA exam.

The next column is Platform, which indicates the hardware model of the neighbor. WS-C2960C is a model in the Catalyst 2960 series of switches, which is no longer being manufactured (but is a great option if you want a switch for a home lab at a low price).

EXAM TIP Make sure you're comfortable reading the output of **show cdp neighbors**. Particularly, remember that Local Intrfce is the port of this device (R1), and Port ID is the port of the neighbor device (SW1).

However, the output of **show cdp neighbors** lists only a fraction of the information learned from the neighbor. To view even more information about each neighbor, you can use **show cdp neighbors detail**. In the following example, I show the output of the command and highlight the same information we saw previously in **show cdp neighbors**. Take a look through the rest of the output to get an idea of what information is conveyed, but focus on the main information shown at the top of the output:

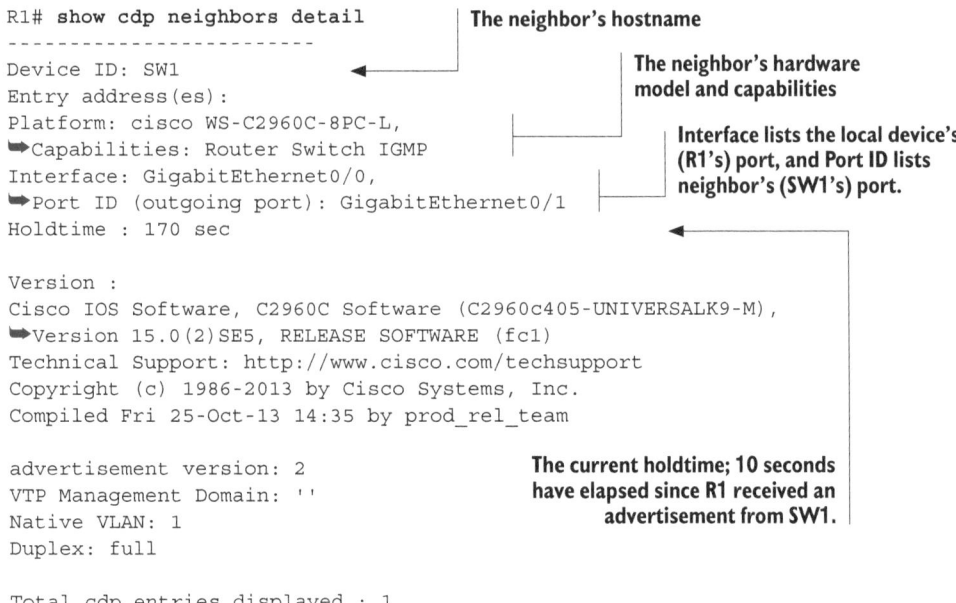

```
R1# show cdp neighbors detail
------------------------
Device ID: SW1
Entry address(es):
Platform: cisco WS-C2960C-8PC-L,
➥Capabilities: Router Switch IGMP
Interface: GigabitEthernet0/0,
➥Port ID (outgoing port): GigabitEthernet0/1
Holdtime : 170 sec

Version :
Cisco IOS Software, C2960C Software (C2960c405-UNIVERSALK9-M),
➥Version 15.0(2)SE5, RELEASE SOFTWARE (fc1)
Technical Support: http://www.cisco.com/techsupport
Copyright (c) 1986-2013 by Cisco Systems, Inc.
Compiled Fri 25-Oct-13 14:35 by prod_rel_team

advertisement version: 2
VTP Management Domain: ''
Native VLAN: 1
Duplex: full

Total cdp entries displayed : 1
```

The neighbor's hostname

The neighbor's hardware model and capabilities

Interface lists the local device's (R1's) port, and Port ID lists neighbor's (SW1's) port.

The current holdtime; 10 seconds have elapsed since R1 received an advertisement from SW1.

NOTE You can use the **show cdp entry** *name* command (i.e., **show cdp entry SW1**) to view the same information as **show cdp neighbors detail** for only the specified neighbor; this is helpful when the device has multiple neighbors.

1.1.2 *Mapping a network with CDP*

As an exercise in reading the CDP neighbor table, let's practice mapping a network using CDP. This is not just an arbitrary exercise—you may have to do this in the real world at some point. Imagine that you have entered a networking role at an organization with less-than-ideal documentation. Although you don't have physical access to the devices, you have remote access to the CLI of several devices via Secure Shell—the topic of chapter 5. However, you don't have access to an up-to-date network diagram. Your task is to fix that, and CDP is a great tool for doing so.

The following five examples show the output of **show cdp neighbors** on five devices. Grab a pen or pencil, and try to draw out the network using the information in the Local Intrfce and Port ID columns of this output:

```
R1# show cdp neighbors
. . .
Device ID       Local Intrfce     Holdtme    Capability  Platform  Port ID
SW1             Gig 0/2           163          R S I                Gig 0/1
SW2             Gig 0/1           151          R S I                Gig 0/2
R2              Gig 0/0           132          R B                  Gig 0/1

R2# show cdp neighbors
. . .
Device ID       Local Intrfce     Holdtme    Capability  Platform  Port ID
```

```
SW3                   Gig 0/0          160           R S I                  Gig 0/1
R1                    Gig 0/1          150           R B                    Gig 0/0

SW1# show cdp neighbors
. . .
Device ID             Local Intrfce    Holdtme       Capability  Platform   Port ID
SW2                   Gig 0/2          168           R S I                  Gig 0/1
R1                    Gig 0/1          178           R B                    Gig 0/2

SW2# show cdp neighbors
. . .
Device ID             Local Intrfce    Holdtme       Capability  Platform   Port ID
SW1                   Gig 0/1          124           R S I                  Gig 0/2
R1                    Gig 0/2          157           R B                    Gig 0/1

SW3# show cdp neighbors
. . .
Device ID             Local Intrfce    Holdtme       Capability  Platform   Port ID
R2                    Gig 0/1          157           R B                    Gig 0/0
```

Figure 1.2 shows the network diagram. Don't worry if the arrangement of the devices in the network you drew is different (i.e., R1 on the right instead of the left); it's how the devices are connected that matters.

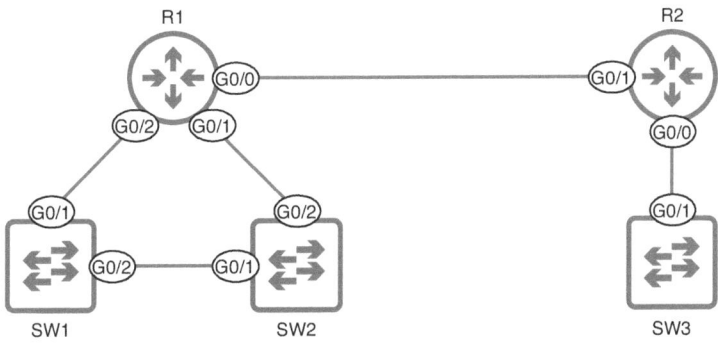

Figure 1.2 The network mapped out using show cdp neighbors

1.1.3 Configuring and verifying CDP

As mentioned previously, CDP is enabled by default. You can confirm that CDP is enabled on the device with **show cdp**. If it is enabled, you will see output like in the following example:

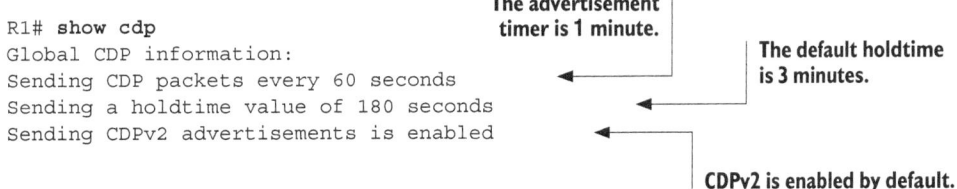

```
R1# show cdp
Global CDP information:
Sending CDP packets every 60 seconds
Sending a holdtime value of 180 seconds
Sending CDPv2 advertisements is enabled
```

The advertisement timer is 1 minute.

The default holdtime is 3 minutes.

CDPv2 is enabled by default.

In addition to confirming that CDP is enabled on the device, the output gives us three pieces of information. The line `Sending CDP packets every 60 seconds` shows the CDP *advertisement timer*—how often the device sends CDP messages out of each interface—which is 60 seconds by default.

The second line, `Sending a holdtime value of 180 seconds`, indicates the holdtime, which is 180 seconds by default. The CDP holdtime determines how long the neighbor will keep this device (R1) in its CDP neighbor table after ceasing to receive CDP messages from this device. A value of 180 seconds means that R1 is telling SW1, "If you don't get a CDP message from me for 3 minutes, remove me from your neighbor table."

The final line, `Sending CDPv2 advertisements is enabled`, indicates that R1 is sending CDP version 2 messages. The differences between CDPv1 and CDPv2 are outside of the scope of the CCNA exam, and unless the neighboring device is very old and only supports version 1, you can leave version 2 enabled. Although there is usually no reason to change the advertisement timer, holdtime, and version, in the following example, I demonstrate the commands to modify them:

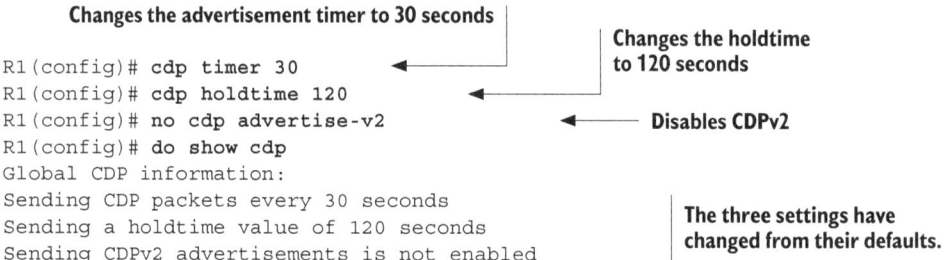

```
R1(config)# cdp timer 30
R1(config)# cdp holdtime 120
R1(config)# no cdp advertise-v2
R1(config)# do show cdp
Global CDP information:
Sending CDP packets every 30 seconds
Sending a holdtime value of 120 seconds
Sending CDPv2 advertisements is not enabled
```

If you wish to disable CDP on the device, you can do so with the **no cdp run** command in global config mode. In the following example, I use the command on R1; notice how the output of **show cdp** changes:

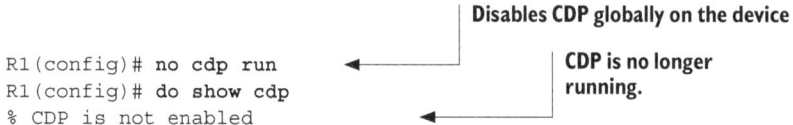

```
R1(config)# no cdp run
R1(config)# do show cdp
% CDP is not enabled
```

NOTE   You can use **cdp run** to reenable CDP after disabling it.

no cdp run disables CDP globally—on the entire device. However, you can also disable CDP on a per-interface basis with the **no cdp enable** command. This prevents the specific interface both from sending CDP advertisements and from processing CDP advertisements it receives—it will discard them. In the following example, I reenable CDP on R1, use **no cdp enable** on one of R1's interfaces, and confirm with a new command:

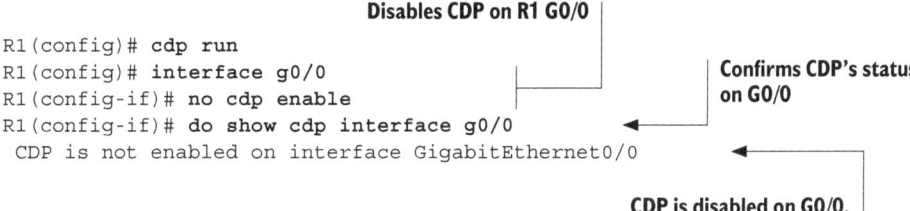

```
R1(config)# cdp run
R1(config)# interface g0/0
R1(config-if)# no cdp enable
R1(config-if)# do show cdp interface g0/0
 CDP is not enabled on interface GigabitEthernet0/0
```

Disables CDP on R1 G0/0

Confirms CDP's status on G0/0

CDP is disabled on G0/0.

To reenable CDP on the interface, use `cdp enable`. I do so in the following example and then confirm with `show cdp interface g0/0` once again; notice how the output of the command changes:

```
R1(config-if)# cdp enable
R1(config-if)# do show cdp interface g0/0
 Encapsulation ARPA
 Sending CDP packets every 30 seconds
 Holdtime is 120 seconds
```

Reenables CDP on R1 G0/0

Information about G0/0's Layer-2 encapsulation and CDP timers is displayed.

NOTE If CDP is disabled globally, CDP won't be active on any interfaces, regardless of the status of the [no] `cdp enable` command.

Why disable CDP?

CDP is quite a useful protocol, so why would you want to disable it globally or on individual interfaces? One reason is that CDP shares a lot of information about the local device, which can be a security concern. A malicious user could, for example, learn the software version of the device, search for known security vulnerabilities of that particular version, and launch targeted attacks to exploit those vulnerabilities. Therefore, it may be advisable to disable CDP either globally (with `no cdp run`) or on specific interfaces (with `no cdp enable`) where it is not strictly necessary for network operations.

One final CDP show command that can be helpful is `show cdp traffic`, which displays statistics about how many CDP messages the device has sent and received. The following example shows the output of the command on R1:

```
R1# show cdp traffic
CDP counters :
     Total packets output: 319, Input: 246
     Hdr syntax: 0, Chksum error: 0, Encaps failed: 0
     No memory: 0, Invalid packet: 0,
     CDP version 1 advertisements output: 164, Input: 4
     CDP version 2 advertisements output: 155, Input: 242
```

The total number of CDP messages sent/received

The number of CDPv1 messages sent/received

The number of CDPv2 messages sent/received

In sections 1.1.1 and 1.1.2, we've covered plenty of CDP configuration and verification commands. Table 1.1 summarizes the verification (`show`) commands we covered; make sure you're familiar with how to read the output of these commands.

Table 1.1   CDP `show` commands

Command	Information displayed
`show cdp neighbors`	CDP neighbors and basic information about each
`show cdp neighbors detail`	More detailed information about CDP neighbors
`show cdp entry` *name*	The same information as **`show cdp neighbors detail`** but for the specified neighbor only
`show cdp`	Basic information about CDP (timers, version)
`show cdp interface` [*interface*]	Information about CDP-enabled interfaces
`show cdp traffic`	The number of CDP messages sent/received

Table 1.2 summarizes the configuration commands. In general, CDP is a fairly hands-off protocol; you can leave it at the default settings in most cases. However, I recommend being familiar with the configuration commands we covered for the CCNA exam.

Table 1.2   CDP configuration commands

Command	Description
R1(config)# **cdp timer** *seconds*	Configures the CDP advertisement timer
R1(config)# **cdp holdtime** *seconds*	Configures the CDP holdtime
R1(config)# **[no] cdp advertise-v2**	Enables/disables CDP version 2 advertisements
R1(config)# **[no] cdp run**	Enables/disables CDP globally
R1(config-if)# **[no] cdp enable**	Enables/disables CDP on a specific interface

1.2   *Link Layer Discovery Protocol*

The Link Layer Discovery Protocol (LLDP) was developed by the IEEE as a vendor-neutral equivalent to CDP (and other vendor-proprietary Layer 2 discovery protocols). Defined in IEEE 802.1AB, LLDP serves a similar purpose as CDP, but as an industry standard, it can be freely implemented by any vendor. This includes Cisco; Cisco routers and switches support both CDP and LLDP. Figure 1.3 shows a Cisco router and switch sharing information about themselves using LLDP.

Whereas CDP messages are sent to the multicast MAC address 0100.0ccc.cccc, LLDP messages are sent to the multicast MAC address 0180.c200.000e. However, like a CDP message, when a switch receives an LLDP message, it does not flood the message; the switch receives the frame for itself.

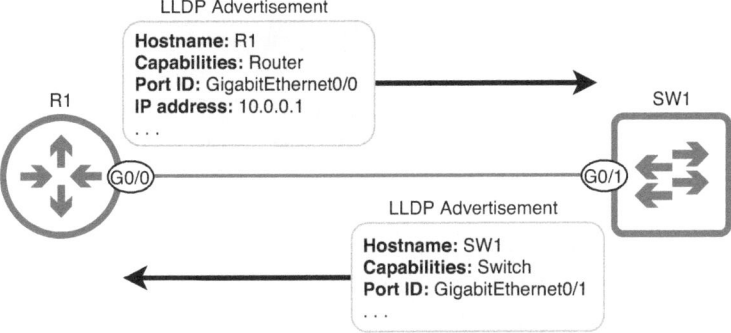

Figure 1.3 **Two neighboring Cisco devices share information about each other via LLDP. The shared information is similar to that shared via CDP.**

CDP or LLDP?

Cisco devices support both CDP and LLDP, so why would you choose one over the other? The main difference is that CDP is Cisco proprietary, whereas LLDP is vendor neutral. If your network uses only Cisco devices, the default CDP is fine. If your network uses a mix of vendors, you should enable LLDP. Note that a device can run both CDP and LLDP at the same time, although it is a bit redundant; they share mostly identical information.

1.2.1 Configuring and verifying LLDP

Although Cisco network devices support LLDP, it is not enabled by default. For that reason, let's first look at how to configure LLDP before analyzing the information that devices share via LLDP. In the following example, I use `show lldp` to confirm that LLDP is disabled on R1, enable LLDP with `lldp run`, and then confirm that it is enabled:

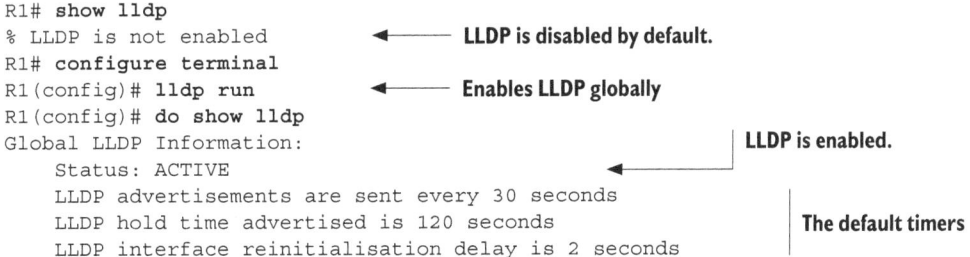

After enabling LLDP, `show lldp` displays similar information about LLDP as `show cdp` does about CDP. The default LLDP advertisement timer is 30 seconds—half that of CDP. The default holdtime is also shorter: 120 seconds. As with CDP, this is the holdtime that the local device is telling neighbors to use; R1 is telling its neighbor SW1, "If you don't get an LLDP message from me for 2 minutes, remove me from your neighbor table." The commands to modify these timers are similar to CDP's—just replace `cdp` with `lldp`: `lldp timer` *seconds* and `lldp holdtime` *seconds*.

LLDP has one additional timer shown in the previous output: the *reinitialization delay*, which is 2 seconds by default. This means that after LLDP is activated on an interface, the device will wait 2 seconds before starting to send LLDP messages. This is beneficial in situations where an interface is *bouncing* (alternating) between up and down states due to an unstable connection or other problem. This delay provides time for the port to stabilize before sending LLDP messages. You can configure this timer with `lldp reinit` *seconds*, but in most cases, the default is fine.

Like CDP, you can also enable/disable LLDP on a per-interface basis. However, there is a major difference: whereas CDP uses only one command (`[no] cdp enable`), LLDP uses two commands: `[no] lldp transmit` and `[no] lldp receive`. This allows you to control the transmission and reception of LLDP messages separately. For example, an interface with transmission enabled but reception disabled will send LLDP messages but will discard any LLDP messages it receives. Likewise, an interface with transmission disabled but reception enabled will not send LLDP messages but will process any LLDP messages it receives and update the LLDP neighbor table as appropriate.

> **NOTE** Disabling only one of either LLDP transmission or reception is rare. One possible use case is that you may want to leave reception enabled to learn about connected devices but disable transmission for security purposes.

LLDP's equivalent to `show cdp interface` is `show lldp interface`. In the following example, I use the command to view the status of R1 G0/0. If LLDP is globally enabled, LLDP transmission and reception will be enabled on all interfaces by default. If needed, you can then disable them on an interface with `no lldp transmit` and/or `no lldp receive`:

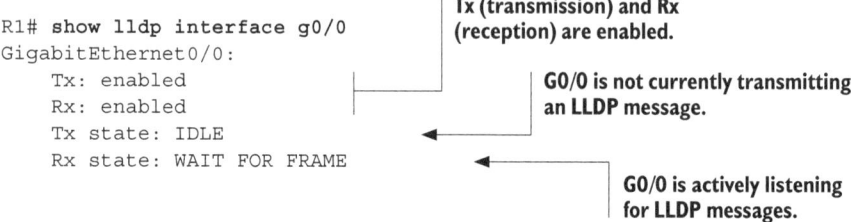

```
R1# show lldp interface g0/0
GigabitEthernet0/0:
    Tx: enabled
    Rx: enabled
    Tx state: IDLE
    Rx state: WAIT FOR FRAME
```

Tx (transmission) and Rx (reception) are enabled.

G0/0 is not currently transmitting an LLDP message.

G0/0 is actively listening for LLDP messages.

> **NOTE** As shown in the previous example, `Tx` is often used as a shorthand for transmission, and `Rx` is often used as a shorthand for reception.

The final LLDP verification command we'll look at in this section is `show lldp traffic`, which is equivalent to `show cdp traffic`. It can be handy when troubleshooting to verify whether the device is actually sending and receiving LLDP messages. The following example shows the output of this command:

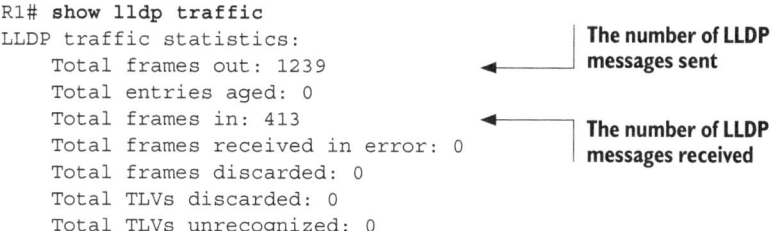

```
R1# show lldp traffic
LLDP traffic statistics:
    Total frames out: 1239                    ◀──┐ The number of LLDP
    Total entries aged: 0                        │ messages sent
    Total frames in: 413                      ◀──┐
    Total frames received in error: 0            │ The number of LLDP
    Total frames discarded: 0                    │ messages received
    Total TLVs discarded: 0
    Total TLVs unrecognized: 0
```

1.2.2   Viewing LLDP neighbors

Now that we've enabled LLDP and checked out some of its settings, here's the most important part: the LLDP neighbor table. The commands are the same as in CDP, replacing **cdp** with **lldp**. The following example shows the output of **show lldp neighbors** on R1:

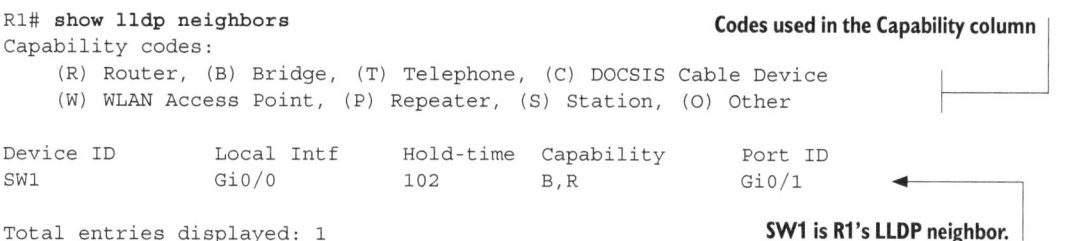

```
R1# show lldp neighbors                          Codes used in the Capability column ┐
Capability codes:                                                                    │
    (R) Router, (B) Bridge, (T) Telephone, (C) DOCSIS Cable Device                   │
    (W) WLAN Access Point, (P) Repeater, (S) Station, (O) Other                      │

Device ID        Local Intf     Hold-time  Capability     Port ID
SW1              Gi0/0          102        B,R            Gi0/1        ◀──┐
                                                                         │
Total entries displayed: 1                             SW1 is R1's LLDP neighbor. ┘
```

The top of the output shows a legend of the different codes that can be used in the `Capability` column. The codes `B,R` in SW1's entry indicate that it has both routing and switching capabilities—`B` for `Bridge` is equivalent to CDP's `S` for `Switch`. The `Local Intf` and `Port ID` columns are the same as in **show cdp neighbors**; this output means that R1's G0/0 interface is connected to SW1's G0/1.

You can view more detailed information about all LLDP neighbors with **show lldp neighbors detail**. The following example shows the output of that command on R1, highlighting the same information we saw in the previous example. This command shows plenty of additional information, not all of it relevant to the CCNA exam; just make sure you can identify the highlighted information:

```
R1# show lldp neighbors detail
-------------------------------------------------
                                                        ┌─ The interface of the
Local Intf: Gi0/0                              ◀────────┘  local device (R1)
Chassis id: 0cf5.a452.b100
Port id: Gi0/1                                 ◀──┐
Port Description: GigabitEthernet0/1              │ The interface of the neighbor (SW1)
System Name: SW1                               ◀──┘
                                                  The neighbor's hostname
System Description:
Cisco IOS Software, C2960C Software (C2960c405-UNIVERSALK9-M),
➥Version 15.0(2)SE5, RELEASE SOFTWARE (fc1)
Technical Support: http://www.cisco.com/techsupport
Copyright (c) 1986-2013 by Cisco Systems, Inc.
```

```
Compiled Fri 25-Oct-13 14:35 by prod_rel_team
                                                    ┌──── The current holdtime
Time remaining: 118 seconds          ◄─────────┘
System Capabilities: B,R
Enabled Capabilities: B,R                    ┌──── The neighbor's capabilities
Management Addresses - not advertised
Auto Negotiation - not supported
Physical media capabilities - not advertised
Media Attachment Unit type - not advertised
Vlan ID: 1

Total entries displayed: 1
```

NOTE   You can use the **show lldp entry** *name* command (i.e., **show lldp entry SW1**) to view the same information as **show lldp neighbors detail** for only the specified neighbor.

Table 1.3 summarizes the LLDP **show** commands we covered in this section. Make sure you can interpret the output of these commands for the CCNA exam.

Table 1.3   LLDP show **commands**

Command	Information displayed
show lldp neighbors	LLDP neighbors and basic information about each
show lldp neighbors detail	More detailed information about LLDP neighbors
show lldp entry *name*	The same information as **show lldp neighbors detail** but for the specified neighbor only
show lldp	Basic information about LLDP (status, timers)
show lldp interface [*interface*]	Information about LLDP-enabled interfaces
show lldp traffic	The number of LLDP messages sent/received

Table 1.4 summarizes the LLDP configuration commands we covered. In most cases, enabling LLDP with **lldp run** is sufficient, but there are cases in which you might want to fine-tune LLDP with the other commands.

Table 1.4   LLDP configuration commands

Command	Description
R1(config)# **lldp timer** *seconds*	Configures the LLDP advertisement timer
R1(config)# **lldp holdtime** *seconds*	Configures the LLDP holdtime
R1(config)# **lldp reinit** *seconds*	Configures the LLDP reinitialization timer
R1(config)# **[no] lldp run**	Enables/disables LLDP globally
R1(config-if)# **[no] lldp transmit**	Enables/disables LLDP Tx on a specific interface
R1(config-if)# **[no] lldp receive**	Enables/disables LLDP Rx on a specific interface

Summary

- Layer 2 discovery protocols such as Cisco Discovery Protocol (CDP) and Link Layer Discovery Protocol (LLDP) allow devices to share information about themselves with their directly connected neighbors.

- The shared information includes hostnames, capabilities (device type), port ID, IP address, and much more.

- CDP is Cisco proprietary and runs on Cisco network devices such as routers and switches. It is enabled by default.

- CDP-enabled devices periodically send CDP advertisement messages out of their interfaces and listen for CDP advertisements from neighboring devices.

- CDP messages are sent to multicast MAC address 0100.0ccc.cccc but are not flooded by switches.

- Use `show cdp neighbors` to view information about CDP neighbors, such as which neighbor is connected to which interface.

- Use `show cdp neighbors detail` to view more detailed information.

- Use `show cdp entry` *name* to view the same information as `show cdp neighbors detail` but for just a single neighbor.

- Use `show cdp` to view basic information about CDP such as the advertisement timer, the holdtime, and the advertisement version.

- The advertisement timer determines how often the device sends CDP advertisement messages. The default is 60 seconds. Use `cdp timer` *seconds* to modify it.

- The *holdtime* tells the neighbor how long to keep this device in its neighbor table after ceasing to receive CDP messages from this device. The default is 180 seconds. Use `cdp holdtime` *seconds* to modify it.

- There are two versions of CDP: CDPv1 and CDPv2. Modern Cisco devices send CDPv2 advertisements by default, but you can use `no cdp advertise-v2` to enable CDPv1 advertisements (e.g., if the device is connected to a very old device).

- You can globally disable CDP with `no cdp run` and use `cdp run` to reenable it.

- You can use `[no] cdp enable` in interface config mode to enable/disable CDP on individual interfaces. It is enabled on all interfaces by default.

- Use `show cdp interface` [*interface*] to view the status of CDP on each interface.

- Use `show cdp traffic` to view statistics about CDP messages sent/received.

- Link Layer Discovery Protocol (LLDP) is an industry-standard (IEEE 802.1AB) Layer 2 discovery protocol that can be implemented by any vendor, including Cisco.

- CDP and LLDP are very similar, as are their commands. In most cases, you can just replace **cdp** with **lldp** to get the equivalent command.

- LLDP messages are sent to multicast MAC address 0180.c200.000e. Like CDP messages, they are not flooded by switches.

- Cisco routers and switches support both CDP and LLDP, but LLDP is disabled by default. You can enable it globally with **lldp run**.

- Use **show lldp** to view basic LLDP information such as the advertisement timer, holdtime, and reinitialization delay.

- The default LLDP advertisement timer is 30 seconds, the default holdtime is 120 seconds, and the reinitialization timer is 2 seconds. You can modify them with **lldp timer** *seconds*, **lldp holdtime** *seconds*, and **lldp reinit** *seconds*.

- The LLDP advertisement timer and holdtime function the same as CDP's timers. The reinitialization timer determines how long an interface will wait to send LLDP messages after LLDP is activated on it (i.e., after the interface is enabled).

- LLDP can be enabled/disabled on a per-interface basis. **[no] lldp transmit** enables/disables LLDP transmission (Tx) on an interface, and **[no] lldp receive** enables/disables LLDP reception (Rx).

- If LLDP is globally enabled, it is enabled on each interface by default. You can then use **no lldp transmit** and/or **no lldp receive** to disable Tx and/or Rx.

- Use **show lldp interface** [*interface*] to view the LLDP status of interfaces.

- Use **show lldp traffic** to view statistics about LLDP messages sent/received.

- Use **show lldp neighbors** to view a list of the device's LLDP neighbors, such as which interface each neighbor is connected to.

- Use **show lldp neighbors detail** to view more detailed information.

- Use **show lldp entry** *name* to view the same information as **show lldp neighbors detail** but for a single neighbor (instead of all neighbors).

Network Time Protocol

This chapter covers

- The importance of date and time on network devices
- Manually setting the date and time on Cisco routers and switches
- How NTP enables devices to synchronize their clocks over a network
- Configuring and securing NTP on Cisco routers and switches

When you think of the most important functions of a router or switch, keeping accurate date and time information is probably not among the first things that come to mind. However, timekeeping that is accurate and consistent across all devices is critical for a variety of functions and services in a network, from security protocols to logging. So how can we achieve accurate timekeeping on our network devices?

The answer is *Network Time Protocol* (NTP), the topic of this chapter. Using NTP, devices across a network can synchronize their clocks to a common time source. NTP isn't limited to just network infrastructure devices like routers and switches; it's used by all kinds of network-connected devices, including smartphones, PCs, and servers. In this chapter, we'll cover CCNA exam topic 4.2: Configure and verify NTP operating in a client and server mode.

2.1   *Date and time on network devices*

Accurate date and time information on network devices is more important than you might expect. In this section, we'll look at a few reasons why that is. We'll also cover how to manually configure the date and time on Cisco IOS devices before covering NTP itself in section 2.2.

2.1.1   *The importance of date and time*

Devices must have accurate date and time information for several reasons. For example, many security protocols (such as *Transport Layer Security*—TLS) rely on time-based mechanisms to function correctly. From a CCNA perspective, however, the main reason is event logging. When events occur on a network device, the device keeps logs of what happened. Log entries can be created for countless kinds of events, but here are a few examples:

- An interface going up or down
- An OSPF neighbor moving to the Full state or Down state
- A user logging in to the CLI of the device

Each log entry is given a timestamp, indicating when the event occurred. You can use **show logging** to view the log entries saved on the local device. The following example shows a couple of log entries on a Cisco router:

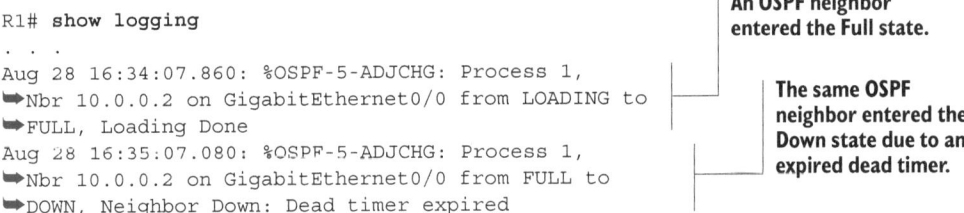

```
R1# show logging
. . .
Aug 28 16:34:07.860: %OSPF-5-ADJCHG: Process 1,
➡Nbr 10.0.0.2 on GigabitEthernet0/0 from LOADING to
➡FULL, Loading Done
Aug 28 16:35:07.080: %OSPF-5-ADJCHG: Process 1,
➡Nbr 10.0.0.2 on GigabitEthernet0/0 from FULL to
➡DOWN, Neighbor Down: Dead timer expired
```

An OSPF neighbor entered the Full state.

The same OSPF neighbor entered the Down state due to an expired dead timer.

> **NOTE**   We will cover logging in detail in chapter 7, which is about Syslog.

The first log message shows that, at about 16:34, R1's OSPF relationship with neighbor 10.0.0.6 moved to the Full state. Then, 1 minute later, the neighbor relationship moved to the Down state due to an expired dead timer. One essential step in identifying the cause of such events is correlating log entries between devices. However, in this case, there is a problem. The following example shows the output of **show clock**, which displays the current date and time, on the two OSPF neighbors (R1 and R2):

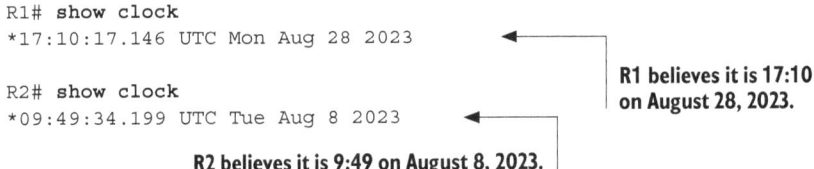

```
R1# show clock
*17:10:17.146 UTC Mon Aug 28 2023
```

R1 believes it is 17:10 on August 28, 2023.

```
R2# show clock
*09:49:34.199 UTC Tue Aug 8 2023
```

R2 believes it is 9:49 on August 8, 2023.

NOTE   The .146 and .199 after the hours, minutes, and seconds indicate milliseconds.

Because the clocks of the two devices are not synchronized, correlating log entries between them is much more difficult. If the problem involves more than two devices, all with clocks set to different dates and times, you'll definitely be wishing that you had configured NTP.

2.1.2 Setting the date and time

All Cisco routers and switches have an internal software clock for keeping the time; that's the clock that you can view with the **show clock** command. By adding the **detail** keyword to the end, you can also get information about how the device learned the current date and time, as shown in the following example:

```
R1# show clock detail
*08:56:18.831 UTC Mon Aug 28 2023
Time source is hardware calendar
```

The asterisk (*) indicates that the time is not authoritative.

R1 learned the date and time from its hardware calendar.

Some devices, like R1 in the example, also have a battery-powered hardware clock called the *calendar* that keeps the time even if the device is shut off. When R1 booted up, its software clock learned the time from the hardware calendar. However, note the asterisk (*) before the time in the previous example, which means that the time is not *authoritative*—not considered to be accurate; this will disappear after setting the time.

SETTING THE CLOCK AND CALENDAR

The command to set the software clock is **clock set** hh:mm:ss month day year. Note that this command is executed from privileged EXEC mode, not global config mode. In the following example, I set R1's software clock:

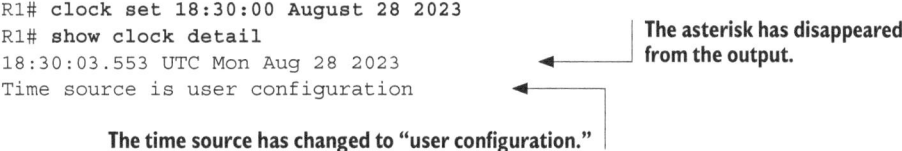

```
R1# clock set 18:30:00 August 28 2023
R1# show clock detail
18:30:03.553 UTC Mon Aug 28 2023
Time source is user configuration
```

The asterisk has disappeared from the output.

The time source has changed to "user configuration."

NOTE   The order of the month and day in the **clock set** command can be reversed—**August 28** and **28 August** are both valid.

The hardware calendar can also be viewed and set separately with the **show calendar** and **calendar set** commands. In the following example, I set R1's calendar:

```
R1# calendar set 18:35:00 August 28 2023
R1# show calendar
18:35:02 UTC Mon Aug 28 2023
```

However, an easier way to ensure that the software clock and the hardware calendar have the same date and time is to use one of the following commands in privileged EXEC mode:

- Sync the calendar to the clock's time—`clock update-calendar`.
- Sync the clock to the calendar's time—`clock read-calendar`.

Note that both commands perform a one-time synchronization; they don't ensure that the clock and calendar remain in sync (unless you use the command again).

CONFIGURING THE TIME ZONE

The default time zone on Cisco devices is *Coordinated Universal Time* (UTC)—you may have noticed the UTC output in previous examples. Actually, UTC is not strictly considered a time zone but rather a time standard—the difference doesn't matter for our purposes.

The command to change the time zone of the device is `clock timezone` *name hours-offset minutes-offset*. Note that this command, unlike the previous commands, is configured in global config mode. The *hours-offset* and *minutes-offset* arguments refer to the offset relative to UTC. For example, my time zone (Japan Standard Time) is UTC+9—9 hours and 0 minutes ahead of UTC. I configure that in the following example:

```
R1(config)# clock timezone JST 9 0
R1(config)# do show clock
03:50:09.104 JST Tue Aug 29 2023
```

The JST time zone is 9 hours and 0 minutes ahead of UTC.

The time zone has changed to JST.

> **NOTE** Changing the time zone will adjust the clock forward or backward according to the specified offsets. If you previously configured the time in UTC, you may have to reconfigure it in the new time zone.

CONFIGURING DAYLIGHT SAVING TIME/SUMMER TIME

Some countries adjust their clocks forward 1 hour in the spring; this is called *daylight saving time* (DST) or *summer time*, depending on the country. They then adjust their clocks back in the fall. In a country that observes DST, you should configure your network devices to adjust their clocks to match.

The command to configure DST is `clock summer-time` *name* `recurring` *start -date-time end-date-time* in global config mode. Figure 2.1 shows the specifics of the syntax, using the time zone of my hometown (Toronto) as an example (my current home of Japan doesn't observe DST). Toronto's time zone is called *Eastern Daylight Time* (EDT) while DST is in effect, and it begins at 02:00 on the second Sunday of March and ends at 02:00 on the first Sunday of November.

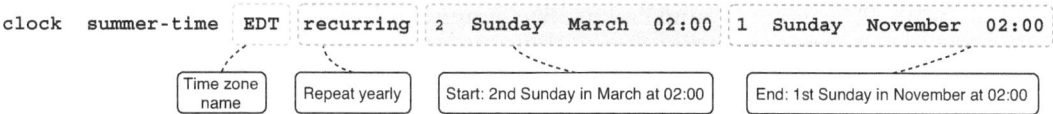

Figure 2.1　The syntax of the `clock summer-time` command. The example specifies that EDT begins at 02:00 on the second Sunday of March and ends at 02:00 on the first Sunday of November.

2.2　How NTP works

When it comes to ensuring that all devices in a network operate with synchronized, accurate date and time, manual configuration simply doesn't cut it. Even if you configure the date and time on all devices, their clocks will drift over time, resulting in inaccurate and inconsistent time. NTP is a much more scalable solution that allows devices to automatically sync their clocks over a network.

The devices you use in your daily life, such as a PC or smartphone, are almost certainly NTP clients. Windows PCs, for example, sync their time with Microsoft's NTP servers by default. Using NTP, *NTP clients* (i.e., Windows PCs) learn the time from *NTP servers* (i.e., Microsoft's NTP servers) by sending NTP requests to UDP port 123—memorize that port!

> **NOTE**　NTP allows accuracy of time within 1 millisecond if the NTP server is in the same LAN as the client or within about 10–100 milliseconds if connecting to the server over a WAN or the internet.

NTP uses a hierarchical model. At the top are *reference clocks*—usually these are very accurate timekeeping devices such as atomic clocks or GPS clocks. The "distance" of an NTP server from a reference clock is called *stratum*—a server with a lower stratum value is closer to a reference clock, and NTP clients will prefer it over a higher-stratum server. "Closer" doesn't mean physically closer in this case but closer in the NTP hierarchy.

Figure 2.2 demonstrates the NTP hierarchy. Reference clocks are stratum 0 in the NTP hierarchy, and NTP servers that learn the time directly from a reference clock are stratum 1. Then NTP servers that learn the time from stratum 1 servers are stratum 2, servers that learn the time from stratum 2 servers are stratum 3, etc.

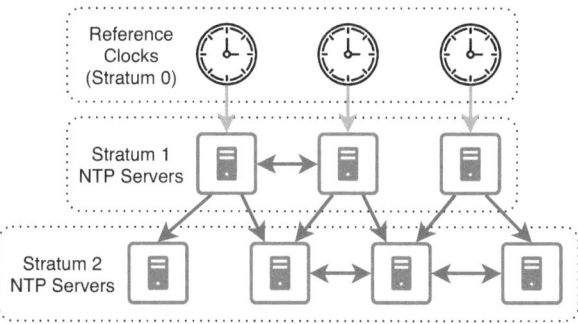

Figure 2.2　The NTP hierarchy. Reference clocks (stratum 0) are high-precision timekeeping devices such as atomic clocks. Stratum 1 NTP servers connect directly and sync to reference clocks. Stratum 2 NTP servers sync to stratum 1 NTP servers. Servers can peer with devices at the same stratum.

> **NOTE** The upper stratum limit is 15. A stratum of 16 indicates a time source that is not considered reliable; devices will not sync to a stratum 16 time source.

Figure 2.2 also demonstrates a few important points about NTP. First, a device can be both an NTP server and an NTP client at the same time. For example, the stratum 2 servers are clients of the stratum 1 servers but are also capable of providing the time for their own clients (such as stratum 3 NTP servers or end devices like PCs). However, note that stratum 1 servers are not NTP clients of the reference clocks; instead, they directly connect to and sync with these highly accurate time sources via specialized hardware and protocols rather than by using NTP.

> **NOTE** An NTP server that gets its time directly from a reference clock is also called a *primary server*. An NTP server that gets its time from another NTP server is called a *secondary server*; a secondary server is both an NTP client and an NTP server.

Second, a device can be a client of multiple NTP servers—actually, this is recommended. In addition to the redundancy and fault tolerance benefits of having multiple time sources (if one server goes down, the client can still learn the time from another server), the clients use algorithms to analyze and consider the time reports of each server, discard outliers, and select the best time source.

Third, two NTP servers can form a *peer* relationship that allows them to exchange time information with each other; these are represented by the bidirectional horizontal arrows. Unlike the typical client–server relationship where the client syncs its time solely based on the time provided by the server, peering allows for a bidirectional exchange between the two peers.

Like a client that learns the time from multiple servers, peering provides similar benefits. Each peer can use the other's time data as an additional reference point, improving the overall accuracy of timekeeping. Furthermore, peering provides an additional layer of redundancy and fault tolerance; if one peer loses connectivity with its servers, it can still sync to its peer.

2.3   *Configuring NTP*

Cisco routers and switches can function as NTP clients, NTP servers, and NTP peers. In this section, we'll examine how to configure all three of these modes in Cisco IOS, as well as how to secure NTP by configuring authentication.

2.3.1   *NTP client mode*

You can configure a Cisco IOS device to become a client of an NTP server with the command `ntp server` `ip-address` [`prefer`]. In figure 2.3, I configure a Cisco router as an NTP client of two servers: Google's and Microsoft's.

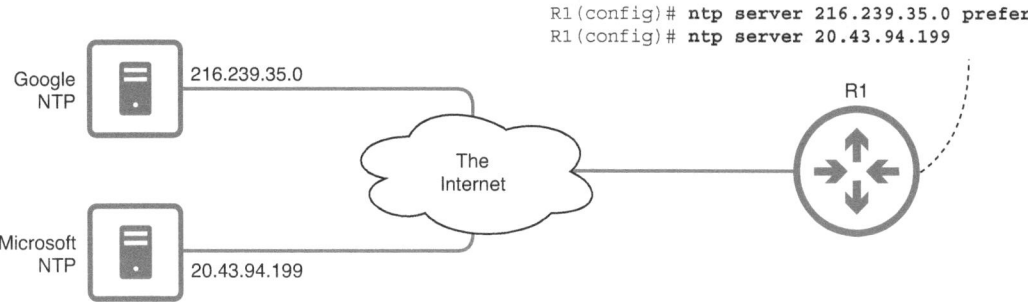

Figure 2.3 Configuring R1 as an NTP client of two NTP servers: Google's (216.239.35.0) and Microsoft's (20.43.94.199). The optional `prefer` keyword tells the router to favor Google's server when deciding which server to sync to.

By adding the optional **prefer** keyword to the end of the command, you can tell the device to favor the specified server when deciding which server to sync to. Note that this doesn't guarantee that the client will select that server; other factors, like the server's stratum, are still taken into account (a lower stratum value is typically preferred). In the following example, I configure R1 as a client of Google's and Microsoft's NTP servers and then confirm with `show ntp associations` and `show clock detail`:

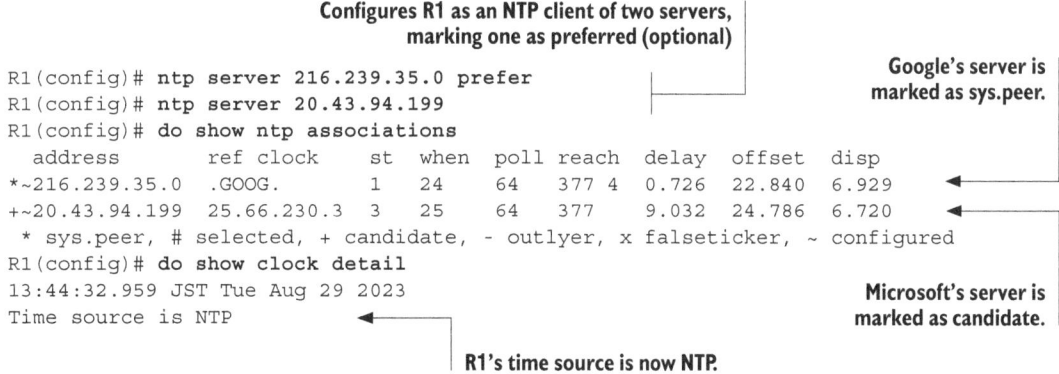

NOTE NTP synchronization can be quite slow, sometimes taking up to 15–20 minutes, depending on a variety of factors. One tip to speed up the process is to manually configure the correct time before configuring NTP.

After configuring R1's two NTP servers, both appear in the output of `show ntp associations`. The * next to the Google server, `sys.peer`, indicates that this is the NTP server R1 is currently synced to. The + next to the Microsoft server, `candidate`, indicates that R1 considers the server as a reliable time source, but it is not currently being used; this is because R1 has selected Google's server instead.

Various columns are shown in the output, but you only need to know the first three: `address`, `ref clock`, and `st`. The `address` column is self-explanatory; it's the NTP server's IP address. `ref clock` shows the server's time source. The Google server lists `.GOOG.`—Google's own reference clock. The Microsoft server lists `25.66.230.3`—another NTP server. So, whereas the Google NTP server in this example gets its time directly from a reference clock (and is, therefore, a primary server), the Microsoft server gets its time from another NTP server (and is, therefore, a secondary server).

The different time sources are reflected in the next column, `st`; this indicates the NTP stratum of the server. Because Google's server gets its time directly from a reference clock (stratum 0), its stratum is 1. Microsoft's server is stratum 3, meaning that it gets its time from a stratum 2 NTP server.

Another useful NTP verification command is **show ntp status**. This command shows a lot of output; for the CCNA, just focus on the top line. In the following example, I use the command on R1. Notice that because R1 is synced to a stratum 1 NTP server, it is now at stratum 2 in the NTP hierarchy:

R1 is synced to a stratum 1 server and is, therefore, stratum 2.

```
R1(config)# do show ntp status
Clock is synchronized, stratum 2, reference is 216.239.35.0
nominal freq is 1000.0003 Hz, actual freq is 1000.0003 Hz, precision is 2**16
ntp uptime is 7500 (1/100 of seconds), resolution is 1000
reference time is E897F742.5E14162D (13:49:06.367 JST Tue Aug 29 2023)
. . .
```

> **NOTE** NTP syncs only the software clock by default, not the hardware calendar. You can use **ntp update-calendar** in global config mode to make NTP periodically update the calendar to ensure that it is accurate.

2.3.2 NTP server mode

A Cisco router that is an NTP client doesn't need any additional configuration to become an NTP server. Now that R1 is a client of the Google and Microsoft NTP servers, other devices can use R1 as their NTP server. Figure 2.4 demonstrates this: R1 gets its time from two NTP servers and provides the time for clients of its own.

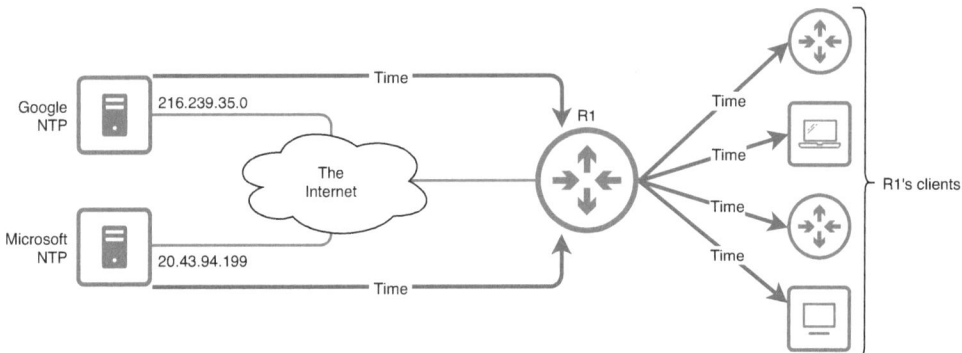

Figure 2.4   R1, a client of two NTP servers, is an NTP server for clients of its own.

EXAM TIP Remember that although the `ntp server` command makes the device an NTP client, it also makes it an NTP server; this is sometimes called *client/server mode*. Later in this section, we'll cover how to make the device an NTP server without it being an NTP client.

One recommended practice when using a Cisco router as an NTP server is to configure a loopback interface on the router and configure clients to use the IP address of the loopback interface as their NTP server. We covered loopback interfaces in chapter 18 of volume 1; their benefit is that they provide a stable, reliable interface that isn't dependent on the status of any particular physical port. Figure 2.5 shows how you can configure this.

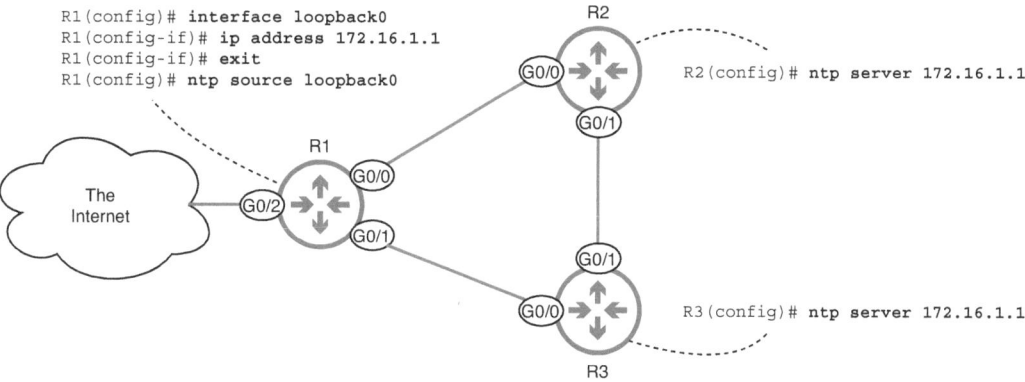

Figure 2.5   Using a loopback interface to provide a reliable NTP server address. The `ntp source` **command specifies that R1 should source NTP messages from its Loopback0 interface.**

Configuring the IP address of R1's Loopback0 interface (172.16.1.1) as the NTP server of R2 and R3 causes them to send their NTP requests to that address. If one of R1's G0/0 or G0/1 ports goes down, R2 and R3 will still be able to sync their clocks to R1 via the loopback interface. The `ntp source loopback0` command then makes R1 use the IP address of the Loopback0 interface as the source of its NTP messages—this is optional but recommended. In the following example, I configure NTP on R2 and confirm its status. Note that R2, a client of a stratum 2 server (R1), is now at stratum 3 of the NTP hierarchy:

```
R2(config)# ntp server 172.16.1.1                              R2 is synced to R1.
R2(config)# do show ntp associations
  address        ref clock      st  when  poll reach  delay  offset   disp
*~172.16.1.1    216.239.35.0    2   15    64    1     1.494  0.695    187.55   ◄
 * sys.peer, # selected, + candidate, - outlyer, x falseticker, ~ configured
R(config)# do show ntp status
Clock is synchronized, stratum 3, reference is 172.16.1.1   ◄
. . .
                            R2 is now a stratum 3 NTP server.
```

Although a Cisco router is automatically able to function as an NTP server if it's a client of another NTP server, you can also use the **ntp master** command to make the router a primary NTP server with its own internal clock acting as the reference clock—the source of time that the router (and its NTP clients) sync to. This allows the device to act as an NTP server even if it's not an NTP client of another server.

However, while the **ntp master** command allows the router to function as an NTP server, it's not meant to replace the **ntp server** command. Instead, the two commands should be used together. The **ntp server** command should be the first choice for time synchronization because it links your device to external NTP servers that get their time from highly accurate reference clocks. But what happens if those external servers become unavailable?

In the example network we've been using in this chapter, R1 is an NTP client of two external NTP servers, and R2 and R3 are clients of R1. However, if R1 loses connectivity to both external NTP servers, R1 will no longer be able to provide time to R2 and R3. The **ntp master** command allows R1 to use its own clock as a backup time source in case it loses connectivity to its servers; it can then provide that time to its clients R2 and R3. Although R1's internal clock isn't as accurate as an atomic clock, at least the time will be consistent across the devices in the network—this is better than having no time synchronization at all. In the following example, I use the command on R1 and confirm:

Configures R1 to use its own clock as an NTP time source

```
R1(config)# ntp master
R1(config)# do show ntp associations
  address        ref clock    st  when   poll reach  delay    offset   disp
*~216.239.35.0   .GOOG.        1   22     64   1      43.221   -1.699   437.57
 ~127.127.1.1    .LOCL.        7   15     16   1      0.000    0.000    7937.5
+~20.43.94.199   25.66.230.5   3   22     64   1   9.397    1.251   437.54
 * sys.peer, # selected, + candidate, - outlyer, x falseticker, ~ configured
```

127.127.1.1 is added as a time source with stratum 7.

Let's examine a few important points about that output. First, notice that the address column lists 127.127.1.1—an address in the reserved loopback address range (127.0.0.0/8) that represents the local device; R1 is listing itself as a time source. Then the ref clock column lists .LOCL.—the clock of the local device.

The final point worth covering is 127.127.1.1's stratum of 7. This means that R1, when using 127.127.1.1 (its local clock) as a time source, will be a stratum 8 NTP server. This is the default value when using the **ntp master** command and reflects the fact that R1's internal clock is not a true reference clock like an atomic clock, which would have a stratum of 0. The stratum value of the local clock is purposefully made higher by default so that R1 views it as a less desirable time source than external NTP servers (such as Google's, which gets its time from a real reference clock). However, you can optionally specify a stratum value at the end of the command. I do that in the following example and confirm:

Specifies a stratum of 5

```
R1(config)# ntp master 5
R1(config)# do show ntp associations
  address         ref clock   st    when  poll reach  delay   offset  disp
*~216.239.35.0   .GOOG.       1     45    64   37     40.890  20.622  2.240
 ~127.127.1.1    .LOCL.       4     3     16   1      0.000   0.000   7937.5
+~20.43.94.199    25.66.230.5 3     169   512    7    8.585   15.092  4.220
```

The stratum of the local clock is 4.

The output may be a bit different than expected; even though I specified a stratum of 5 in the **ntp master** command, the stratum of 127.127.1.1 in the output is 4. That's because the stratum you specify in the command is not the stratum of 127.127.1.1 (the local clock) but rather the stratum of the device when it is synced to that clock. The command **ntp master 5** means that R1, when synced to the local clock, will be at stratum 5 of the NTP hierarchy. However, in this case R1 is still synced to the Google server; it will only use its local clock as a backup.

> **NOTE** In addition to providing a backup time source, you can use **ntp master** to make a Cisco IOS device an NTP server when no external server is available, such as in an isolated network without internet access. This is called *server mode*, as opposed to the client/server mode we configured with the **ntp server** command. Just keep in mind that the device's local clock is not a truly accurate time source—it doesn't keep time accurately like an atomic clock.

Symmetric active mode

Although not covered in the CCNA exam topics list, in addition to client and server, there is a third mode called *symmetric active* mode; this is the NTP peering I mentioned in section 2.2. To configure NTP peers in symmetric active mode, use the **ntp peer** *ip-address* command on each device, specifying the other device's IP address. Unlike a client–server relationship, each peer acts as a time source for the other. To summarize, here are the three commands/modes we covered:

- **ntp server**—*client/server mode*—The device becomes a client of an NTP server and a server for other clients.
- **ntp master**—*server mode*—The device becomes a primary NTP server, using its local clock as a reference clock.
- **ntp peer**—*symmetric active mode*—The two devices become NTP peers, each using the other as a time source.

2.3.3   *NTP authentication*

Public NTP servers like Google's and Microsoft's are open; any client is free to sync their time to those servers, and there are no security checks on the part of either the clients or the servers. However, in more secure environments with private NTP servers, that approach may not be acceptable.

For example, a malicious server could exploit NTP to provide incorrect time data, which could disrupt the operation of time-sensitive applications and protocols. In such an environment, we should ensure that our client devices don't sync to unauthorized NTP servers. In this section, we'll look at how to protect our NTP clients with authentication.

Authentication is the process of verifying someone's—or something's—identity. In the context of NTP, that means verifying that a server really is the server that it claims to be—not an attacker using a *spoofed* (falsified) IP address. Figure 2.6 shows how to configure NTP authentication between an NTP server (R1) and client (R2).

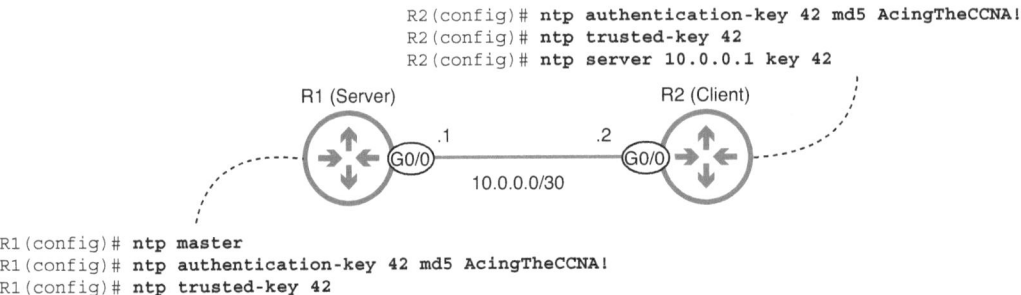

Figure 2.6   **Configuring NTP authentication between a server and client. This ensures that R2 will only sync its time to R1 and not to a malicious NTP server.**

Let's walk through the configuration of both devices. In the following example, I configure the server, R1:

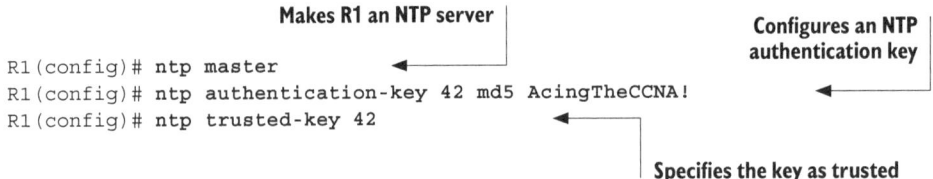

After using `ntp master` to make R1 an NTP server, the first step to configuring authentication is to create an authentication key (password) with the `ntp authentication-key` *key-number* `md5` *key* command. The *key-number* argument is simply a numerical identifier for the key; the *key* argument is the key itself—the actual password.

NOTE   Newer versions of IOS support hashing protocols beyond **md5**, which is no longer considered secure. You can use the IOS context-sensitive help feature (the question mark: `ntp authentication-key` *key-number* `?`) to view the available protocols on the device you are configuring.

However, creating an authentication key alone is not enough; you then have to use the **ntp trusted-key** *key-number* command to specify that the key is a *trusted key*. Without this command, the key cannot be used.

In the following example, I configure the client, R2:

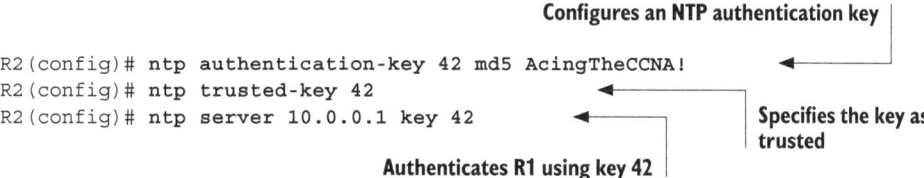

Configures an NTP authentication key

```
R2(config)# ntp authentication-key 42 md5 AcingTheCCNA!
R2(config)# ntp trusted-key 42
R2(config)# ntp server 10.0.0.1 key 42
```

Specifies the key as trusted

Authenticates R1 using key 42

First, I create the same authentication key as on R1 and also specify it as a trusted key. Here's an important point: both the key number (42) and the key itself (AcingTheCCNA!) have to match; it's not enough for just the key itself to match. Then, in the final command, I configure R2 as a client of R1 (10.0.0.1), specifying that R2 should authenticate R1 using key 42. The command syntax is **ntp server** *ip-address* **key** *key-number*.

The result of this configuration is that R2 will include key 42 in its NTP messages to R1, and R1 will include the same key in its NTP messages to R2. Because the key number and the key itself match, R2 will accept R1's time and sync to it; if either parameter does not match, R2 will refuse to sync to R1.

> **NOTE** You can use a nearly identical configuration to authenticate NTP peers: just replace **ntp server** *ip-address* **key** *key-number* with **ntp peer** *ip-address* **key** *key-number*. Make sure to configure it on both peers!

The ntp authenticate command

You'll often see the **ntp authenticate** command included on both the client and the server in NTP authentication configuration examples—this is usually a mistake. Although it's fine to include this command (it doesn't do any harm), it's not necessary when you configure the **ntp server** *ip-address* **key** *key-number* command on the client.

The **ntp authenticate** command is necessary to authenticate servers or peers when using the **ntp passive, ntp broadcast client**, or **ntp multicast client** commands on the client—all beyond the scope of the CCNA exam. For all of the scenarios presented in this chapter, the **ntp authenticate** command is not necessary to achieve authentication.

Summary

- Keeping an accurate date and time is very important for network infrastructure devices and network-connected devices. For example, many security protocols rely on time-based mechanisms.

- Correlating logs between devices is often an essential step in troubleshooting issues, and accurate timestamps facilitate that process.

- A device keeps its time using a software clock. You can view it with **show clock**. Adding the **detail** keyword shows additional information about the time source.

- Some devices also have a hardware clock called the *calendar*. You can view its time with **show calendar**.

- You can set the software clock with **clock set** hh:mm:ss month day year.

- You can set the hardware calendar with **calendar set** hh:mm:ss month day year.

- The **clock update-calendar** command syncs the calendar to the clock's time, and the **clock read-calendar** syncs the clock to the calendar's time.

- The default time zone is Coordinated Universal Time (UTC). You can change that with **clock timezone** name hours-offset minutes-offset in global config mode.

- You can configure daylight saving time (DST) with **clock summer-time** name **recurring** start-date-time end-date-time in global config mode.

- Maintaining accurate date and time information is not feasible with manual configuration. Network Time Protocol (NTP) is the solution, allowing devices to automatically sync their time over a network.

- NTP clients send NTP requests to UDP port 123 on NTP servers.

- NTP uses a hierarchical model. At the top are *reference clocks*—usually very accurate timekeeping devices such as atomic clocks or GPS clocks.

- The "distance" of an NTP server from a reference clock is called its *stratum*.

- An NTP server that learns the time directly from a reference clock is stratum 1— this type of server is called a *primary server*.

- Stratum 2 servers learn the time from stratum 1 servers, stratum 3 servers learn the time from stratum 2 servers, etc. These are called *secondary servers*—they are NTP clients and NTP servers at the same time.

- A device can be a client of multiple NTP servers. This provides improved redundancy and fault tolerance and improves the accuracy of the client's timekeeping.

- Two NTP servers can form a *peer* relationship that allows them to exchange time information with each other. This provides similar benefits to a client learning the time from multiple servers.

- You can configure a Cisco IOS device to be a client of an NTP server with **ntp server** ip-address [**prefer**]. The **prefer** keyword is optional but increases the likelihood that the client will sync its time to the specified server.

- The `ntp server` command puts the device in *client/server mode*. The device becomes an NTP client of the specified server but can also function as an NTP server for clients of its own.

- Use `show ntp associations` to view information about each of the device's NTP time sources. Use `show ntp status` to view information about the device's NTP status, such as its stratum in the NTP hierarchy.

- When a Cisco IOS device is functioning as an NTP server, it is recommended that you configure a loopback interface and specify that address as the client's NTP server. This provides a stable interface that isn't dependent on a physical port.

- You can use `ntp source` *interface* to specify which interface NTP messages should be sourced from.

- Use the `ntp master` [*stratum*] command to make the device function like an NTP primary server, using its own software clock as a reference clock. This is called *server mode*, as opposed to *client/server mode*.

- The `ntp master` command makes the device a stratum 8 NTP server by default, but you can optionally specify the *stratum* argument to change this behavior.

- You can configure *symmetric active* mode with the `ntp peer` *ip-address* command. Configure it on both devices to make them NTP peers.

- You can configure NTP authentication to ensure clients only sync to authorized servers. *Authentication* is the process of verifying someone's/something's identity.

- On both the client and server, use `ntp authentication-key` *key-number* `md5` *key* to create an authentication key. Both the *key-number* and *key* arguments must match between the client and server.

- On both the client and server, use `ntp trusted-key` *key-number* to specify that the key is a *trusted key*; without this step, the key can't be used.

- On the client, add `key` *key-number* to the standard `ntp server` *ip-address* command to specify that the server should be authenticated with the key. The complete syntax is `ntp server` *ip-address* `key` *key-number*.

- You can configure authentication between NTP peers by following the same steps, replacing `ntp server` *ip-address* `key` *key-number* with `ntp peer` *ip-address* `key` *key-number*. Make sure to configure it on both peers.

Domain Name System

This chapter covers

- How Uniform Resource Locators identify a resource and how to access it
- The hierarchical structure of the Domain Name System
- The DNS name resolution process
- Implementing a DNS on Cisco IOS devices

"What's in a name?" Ask that to a computer, and you'll learn that the answer is a number. Although we humans like to use memorable names to refer to the resources we access over a network (i.e., websites), computers use numbers—IP addresses—to identify each other. So when you type a name like "www.google.com" into a web browser's address bar, how does your computer learn the IP address of the server that hosts Google's website?

The answer is the *Domain Name System* (DNS). Using DNS, your computer *resolves*—or translates—the name "www.google.com" into the IP address of the appropriate server. DNS is one of the foundational protocols of the internet and is necessary knowledge not just for network engineers but for professionals in nearly any area of IT. DNS is the second half of CCNA exam topic 4.3: Explain the role of DHCP and DNS within the network. In this chapter, we'll delve into the mechanics of DNS, its significance in network operations, and how to implement it on Cisco IOS.

3.1 How DNS works

Before looking at the Cisco-specific details of how to configure and verify DNS in IOS, let's examine the protocol itself. DNS is an industry-standard protocol that is defined in a series of RFCs, and in this section, we'll cover the fundamentals of how DNS works.

3.1.1 Uniform resource locators

To access a particular website, you can type the website's address into the address bar of a web browser. For example, you might type https://www.google.com/maps to access Google Maps. An address like this is called a *Uniform Resource Identifier* (URI) or *Uniform Resource Locator* (URL); I'll use the latter term.

URI, URN, and URL

A Uniform Resource Identifier (URI) is a unique sequence of characters that identifies a resource; that resource could be a file on a computer or a physical object like a book. URIs can be classified into two main types: Uniform Resource Names (URNs) and Uniform Resource Locators (URLs).

A URN is a unique identifier of a particular resource, without indicating its location or how to access it. An example is a book's International Standard Book Number (ISBN); ISBN 9781633435780 identifies this volume but doesn't tell you anything about where to buy it.

A URL, on the other hand, identifies both the resource itself and how to locate it. A web address like https://www.google.com/maps is an example of a URL; it identifies the resource (the Google Maps website) and tells your computer how to access it.

A URL consists of multiple elements; most URLs you encounter will include a scheme, authority, and path, as shown in figure 3.1. The *scheme* indicates the protocol that the browser will use to send its request to the web server—HTTPS, in this case. The *authority* indicates the name of the web server that the browser should send the request to; in this case, it's Google's web server at www.google.com. This name is called a *domain name*—more on domains and their names in section 3.1.3. The final element is the *path*, which identifies the specific resource on the server; in this case, it's the /maps web page.

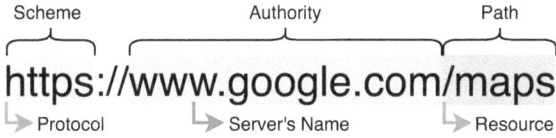

Figure 3.1 Elements of a URL. The scheme identifies the protocol, and the authority identifies the server's name; they are separated by ":// ". The path identifies the resource on the server.

Typing https://www.google.com/maps into the address bar and pressing Enter instructs the browser to use the HTTPS protocol to request the /maps resource on the www.google.com server. This is where DNS comes into play: your computer now has to translate the www.google.com domain name into an IP address that it can send packets to.

> **NOTE**   If you don't specify a URL's scheme when using a web browser, the browser will assume the default scheme—usually HTTPS. If you don't specify the resource, you will be shown a default page, such as index.html or index.php. You can try it on my website: https://www.jeremysitlab.com/index.php should show the same page as www.jeremysitlab.com.

3.1.2   *Name resolution*

After you type a URL in a browser's address bar and press the Enter key, your device will first check its *DNS cache* for a matching entry; the DNS cache temporarily stores previously resolved names and their corresponding IP addresses. If there is a matching entry in the DNS cache, the process is complete; your device knows the destination IP address, and there is no need to ask a DNS server.

> **NOTE**   A device's DNS cache exists at multiple levels; the operating system (i.e., Windows) maintains its own cache, but many applications like web browsers maintain their own DNS cache as well.

If there isn't a matching entry, your device has to send a DNS query to its DNS server asking the server to resolve the name to an IP address. Figure 3.2 shows a high-level overview of this process. PC1 uses DNS to resolve www.google.com to an IP address and then uses HTTPS to access the web server.

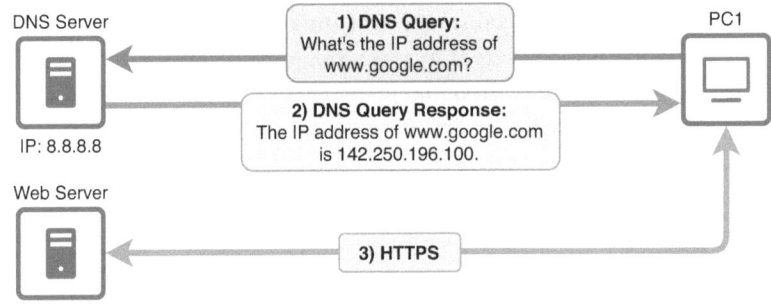

Figure 3.2   DNS name resolution. (1) PC1 sends a DNS query to its DNS server (8.8.8.8) asking for the IP address of www.google.com. (2) The DNS server replies, informing PC1 of the IP address. (3) PC1 communicates with the web server via HTTPS (for example, to retrieve a web page).

NOTE A device learns the IP address of its DNS server via either *Dynamic Host Configuration Protocol* (DHCP)—the next chapter's topic—or manual configuration.

After successfully resolving the name www.google.com to an IP address, PC1 stores this mapping in its DNS cache. This means that it doesn't have to send a new DNS query every time it wants to access the same website; it can use the cached information instead. The following example shows the entry for www.google.com in my PC's DNS cache; on a Windows PC, you can view the DNS cache with the `ipconfig /displaydns` command in the Command Prompt:

```
C:\Users\jmcdo> ipconfig /displaydns
. . .
    www.google.com
    ----------------------------------------
    Record Name . . . . . : www.google.com
    Record Type . . . . . : 1
    Time To Live  . . . . : 267
    Data Length . . . . . : 4
    Section . . . . . . . : Answer
    A (Host) Record . . . : 142.250.196.100
. . .
```

DNS queries are sent to port 53 on the DNS server. However, DNS is different from most other protocols in that it can use both TCP and UDP as its Layer 4 protocol. While UDP is the most common Layer 4 protocol for standard DNS queries and responses (like the one in figure 3.2), TCP is used in certain situations, such as when the server's response exceeds a certain size.

EXAM TIP Don't expect questions on the CCNA exam about whether DNS will use TCP or UDP in a particular situation. Just know that DNS can use both TCP and UDP and that DNS servers listen on port 53 in either case.

The hosts file

Many devices have a file that contains mappings of IP addresses to hostnames; for example, on my Windows 11 PC, the file is located in the C:\Windows\System32\drivers\etc folder and is called *hosts*. Before sending a DNS request, the device will check the hosts file to see if there is a mapping; this is entirely separate from the DNS resolution process. Before DNS existed, devices relied on this file for name resolution, but the lack of scalability led to the creation of DNS. Although the hosts file is still present on many devices, its use is limited.

3.1.3 *The DNS hierarchy*

In the previous section, we took a high-level look at how a host uses DNS to translate a name—such as the authority of a URL—to an IP address. However, within DNS, the name itself also consists of multiple elements, and knowing them is essential to understanding how DNS works.

DNS is a hierarchical naming system for computers connected to the internet. The DNS hierarchy is organized in a tree-like structure, and a *domain* is a subtree of that structure, under the administrative control of a particular organization or individual. Figure 3.3 illustrates a small portion of the DNS hierarchy, highlighting Google's domain under "com."

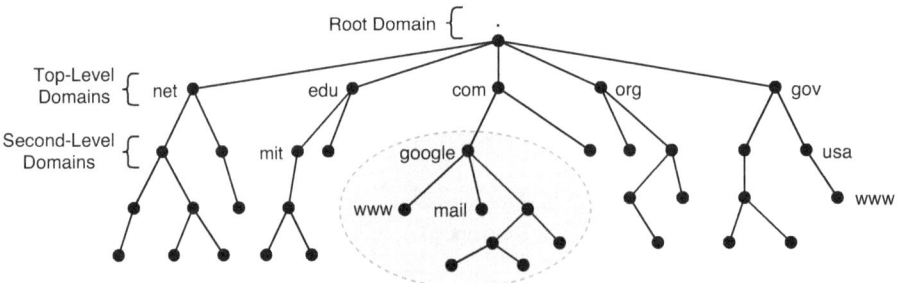

Figure 3.3   The DNS hierarchy. All domains are under the root domain, represented by ".". Under the root domain, there are various top-level domains. Under each top-level domain, there are various second-level domains. The "google" domain, a subtree under the "com" top-level domain, is highlighted.

At the top of the DNS hierarchy, there is the *root domain*, which is usually represented by a single dot (.). Under the root domain, there are various *top-level domains* (TLDs). The most common TLD is com, but you're likely familiar with other TLDs such as net and org. Likewise, under each TLD there are various *second-level domains* (SLDs), such as google or my own jeremysitlab. Then, under each SLD, there can be various third-level domains, fourth-level domains, etc. Each domain is a *subdomain* of the domains above it in the hierarchy. For example, in figure 3.3, google is a subdomain of com, which is a subdomain of the root domain.

The www domain name

You might be aware that WWW stands for World Wide Web, a global system that allows computers to share web pages over the internet. Given that meaning, you might expect www to be at the top of the hierarchy, encompassing all of the web. However, in this context, www doesn't represent the entire web but is just a name that has been conventionally used for the server hosting the main website of an organization. This is not a technical standard, but rather a long-standing conventional practice. Many websites these days do not use www at all.

You may also notice that some websites can be accessed both through www.example .com and simply example.com. Technically, these could be two different addresses, but most organizations configure their DNS to redirect one to the other, making them effectively the same website for the end user.

A host's complete name on the internet is called a *fully qualified domain name* (FQDN); an FQDN is written with a dot separating each part. One example of an FQDN is "www. google.com.". You may have noticed an extra dot at the end of that FQDN; that represents the root domain. The final dot is often omitted, such as when typing a URL in an address bar—we usually write "www.google.com". However, strictly speaking, a domain name without the final dot is not an FQDN but a *partially qualified domain name* (PQDN).

NOTE Strictly speaking, the dot at the end of an FQDN doesn't actually represent the root domain; it's a delimiting character between the TLD and the root domain, which has no name. For the rest of this chapter, I will omit this final dot.

The DNS hierarchy is a global system, and the same FQDN can be used to refer to the same host anywhere in the world. However, there are situations in which we refer to a host by a PQDN—a domain name that doesn't include all of the information about the host's location in the DNS hierarchy. For example, www could be the hostname of a business' main web server, and its FQDN might be www.business.com. In the context of DNS, the hostname www is a PQDN—it identifies the www server within its domain business.com but doesn't provide enough information to identify the host globally; there are countless other servers named www in different domains.

NOTE Domain names are not case-sensitive, but all lower-case is standard.

Domain name vs. hostname

These two familiar terms are frequently confused, and both can refer to different things (or the same thing) depending on the context. Let's clarify them:

- *Domain name*—This term refers to a region of administrative control within the DNS hierarchy, such as example.com, and includes any subdomains under it, such as www.example.com. Alternatively, this term can also specify a particular node within a domain; srv1.example.com is the domain name of a server within that domain.

  In some cases, the same domain name can have both meanings. For example, google.com refers to Google's realm of administrative control within the DNS hierarchy but also to a particular web server. If you access google.com in a web browser, your device will be directed to a web server that hosts Google's website; this server's domain name is google.com.

- *Hostname*—This is an identifier for a specific device on the network. It could be a simple name like srv1 or an FQDN like srv1.example.com. Of course, an FQDN is also an example of a domain name (hence the name "fully qualified *domain name*"). So keep in mind that these terms can have different meanings depending on the context and can often be used interchangeably.

3.1.4   *Recursive and iterative lookups*

Now that you have a basic understanding of the DNS hierarchy, we can dig deeper into the DNS name resolution process by looking at two types of DNS lookups: recursive and iterative. Figure 3.4 shows how a combination of recursive and iterative DNS lookups are used to resolve mail.google.com to an IP address.

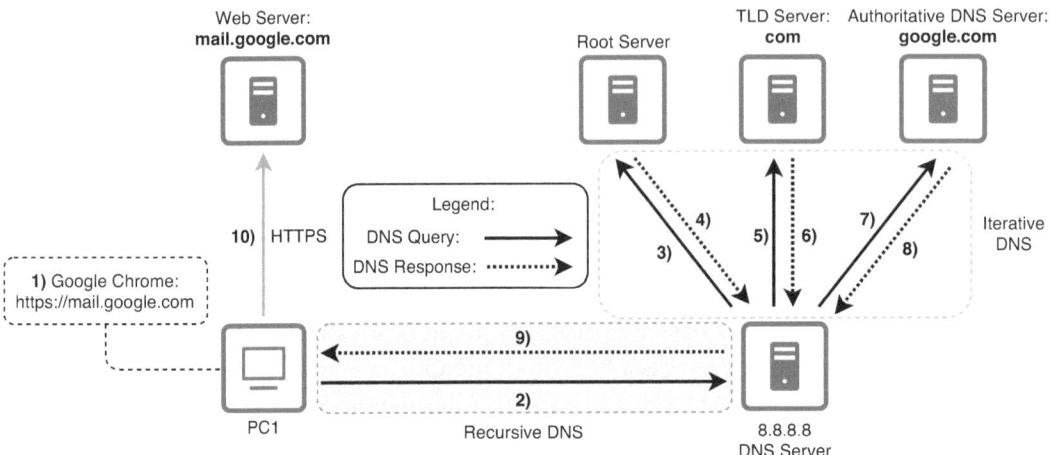

Figure 3.4   Recursive and iterative DNS requests resolve a domain name. In step 1, PC1 attempts to access mail.google.com. Steps 2 and 9 are a recursive DNS exchange between PC1 and the 8.8.8.8 DNS server. Steps 3 through 8 are iterative DNS exchanges between 8.8.8.8 and other DNS servers. Step 10 is an HTTPS exchange between PC1 and mail.google.com.

In step 1 of the diagram, a user tries to check his Gmail by accessing mail.google.com. In step 2, PC1 sends a recursive DNS query to its configured DNS server: 8.8.8.8 (a public DNS server run by Google). A *recursive DNS query* asks the DNS server to give the client a definite answer: either the IP address or an error message stating that the domain name could not be resolved. This is where the second type of DNS query comes into play; 8.8.8.8 will now query other DNS servers to find the answer for PC1. To do so, it will start at the top of the DNS hierarchy.

> **NOTE**   If 8.8.8.8 has a cached entry for mail.google.com, it will reply to PC1 with that information, and the name resolution process will be complete. Caching is used at every step of the name resolution process to reduce the number of DNS queries needed. However, for this demonstration, assume that each device's cache is empty.

In step 3, 8.8.8.8 sends an iterative DNS query to a *root DNS server*—a DNS server at the top of the DNS hierarchy. 8.8.8.8 asks the root DNS server to resolve mail.google.com. However, instead of replying with an IP address, in step 4, the root DNS server replies with a referral to another DNS server. This is how *iterative DNS queries* work; they can be answered with an IP address or with a referral to another DNS server that might have the answer. Basically, the root DNS server is saying, "I don't know the IP address of mail.google.com, but I know another server that might."

The root DNS server refers 8.8.8.8 to a *TLD server*—specifically, a server responsible for the com TLD. In step 5, 8.8.8.8 sends an iterative query to the TLD server. The TLD server also doesn't know mail.google.com's IP address, so in step 6, the TLD server replies with a referral to another DNS server—the authoritative DNS server for the google.com domain. An *authoritative DNS server* holds the definitive set of records for a specific domain and, therefore, can give a definite answer in reply to queries about the domain.

> **NOTE** Although 8.8.8.8 is a public DNS server operated by Google, it's not the authoritative DNS server for the google.com domain. 8.8.8.8 is an example of a *recursive resolver*—a DNS server that resolves clients' recursive DNS queries. It does so by sending iterative queries to other DNS servers, which may include root servers, TLD servers, and authoritative servers for the specific domain.

In step 7, 8.8.8.8 queries the authoritative server and receives a reply in step 8. In step 9, 8.8.8.8 finally replies to PC1's recursive query, informing PC1 of mail.google.com's IP address. Then, in step 10, PC1 initiates its HTTPS communication with mail.google.com.

> **EXAM TIP** Remember the general sequence of events in this process: a client sends a recursive query to a DNS server, and the server iteratively queries other DNS servers (starting at the root DNS server) to resolve the query.

3.1.5 DNS record types

DNS maps domain names to IP addresses, and each of these mappings is called a *DNS record*. However, there are various types of DNS records that can contain information other than IP addresses. In this section, we'll briefly look at some different DNS record types that you should know for the CCNA exam. Table 3.1 summarizes the record types we'll cover.

Table 3.1 DNS record types

Record type	Description	Example
A	Points to an IPv4 address	example.com -> 192.0.2.1
AAAA	Points to an IPv6 address	example.com -> 2001:db8::1
CNAME	Points to another domain name	www.example.com -> example.com
MX	Specifies the domain's mail server(s)	example.com -> mail1.example.com
NS	Specifies the domain's authoritative DNS server(s)	example.com -> ns1.example.com
PTR	Used for reverse DNS lookups, mapping an IP address back to a domain name	192.0.2.1 -> example.com
SOA	Provides administrative information such as admin contact details, a serial number, etc.	example.com -> Admin: admin.example.com; Serial: 123456789; etc.

NOTE   You can look up DNS records for different domain names at https://www .whatsmydns.net/dns-lookup. You can view all of the available records or filter by type (A, AAAA, CNAME, etc.).

A DNS *A record* (address record) maps a domain name to an IPv4 address. All of the examples in this chapter so far have been A records. For another example, the A record for manning.com points to the IP address 35.166.24.88 (at the time of writing).

AAAA records (quad-A records) are similar to A records, except they map a domain name to an IPv6 address, not an IPv4 address. IPv6 addresses are quadruple the length of IPv4 addresses, hence the name.

A *CNAME record* (canonical name record) is used to create an alias for a domain name; it maps one domain name to another. One common use is to map www.example. com to example.com. For example, no A record exists for my website www.jeremysitlab .com. Instead, there is a CNAME record pointing to jeremysitlab.com. This means that you will be taken to the same page, regardless of whether you visit www.jeremysitlab .com or jeremysitlab.com.

An *MX record* (mail exchange record) is used to specify the domain's mail servers. For example, I use Gmail as my email service, so my domain's MX records point to Google's email servers.

An *NS record* (name server record) is used to specify the domain's authoritative DNS servers. For example, I use Bluehost to host my website, so my domain's NS records point to Bluehost's DNS servers.

A *PTR record* (pointer record) is unique; instead of mapping a domain name to an IP address, it maps an IP address to a domain name. This allows for *reverse DNS lookups*, which allow you to find the domain name that is associated with a particular IP address.

The final record type we'll cover is the *SOA record* (start of authority record). An SOA record stores administrative information about the domain. Some example information stored is the contact information of the person or company responsible for the domain and a serial number that is used to keep track of updates to the domain's records. The contact information will be listed, like admin.example.com, but the first dot should be replaced with an @ symbol to make an email address, such as admin@ example.com.

EXAM TIP   You should know these different record types for the CCNA exam. There's no need to know all the details; the level of depth covered in this section is fine.

DNS propagation delay

DNS propagation delay is the time it takes for changes to DNS records to be reflected across the internet, generally taking anywhere from a few minutes to 48 to 72 hours. One factor determining this is the *time to live* (TTL) value of the DNS records. Each record has a TTL value that specifies how long the record should be cached by DNS servers—the lower the value, the more frequently the record will be refreshed. Although the name is the same, this is a different concept than an IPv4 packet's TTL.

If you change a DNS record (for example, to reflect your website's new IP address) without considering propagation delay, visitors might be directed to the old IP address until the update fully propagates, leading to potential downtime or accessibility problems. One option to minimize the effect is to reduce the TTL values for the DNS records you plan to change well in advance of making the changes, allowing enough time for the previous TTL to expire before making the change.

3.2   *DNS on Cisco IOS*

You may have noticed something missing from this chapter up to this point—any mention of Cisco routers and switches! That's because DNS is an exchange between a client and its DNS server; the role of the network infrastructure devices like routers and switches is simply to forward the messages between the communicating hosts.

Figure 3.5 demonstrates this point. PC1 uses DNS to learn the IP address of youtube.com and then uses HTTPS to access youtube.com. R1's role in these exchanges is to forward packets between the communicating hosts: PC1 and 8.8.8.8 (the DNS server) and PC1 and youtube.com. SW1's role is to forward frames between PC1 and R1.

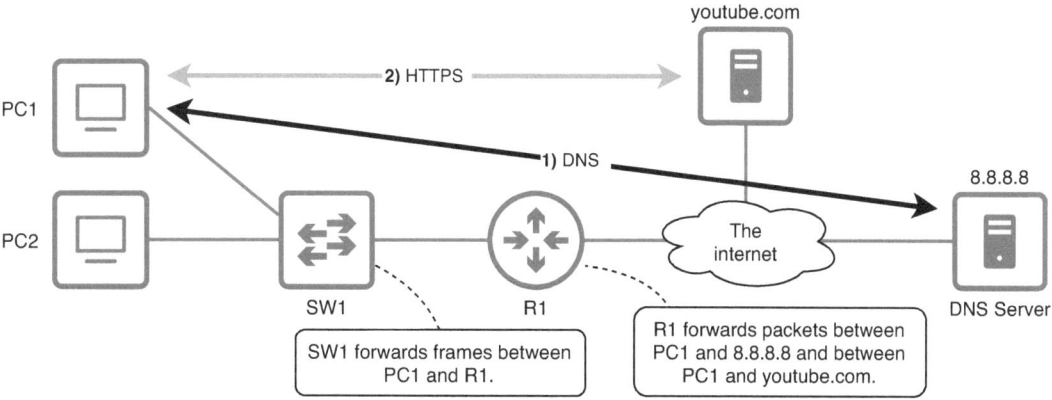

Figure 3.5   The roles of R1 and SW1 in PC1's DNS and HTTPS exchanges. R1's role is to forward packets between the communicating hosts, and SW1's role is to forward frames.

However, Cisco network devices themselves can be DNS clients and are also capable of functioning as DNS servers. In this section, we'll take a look at various DNS-related configurations on R1; figure 3.6 shows the configurations we'll cover.

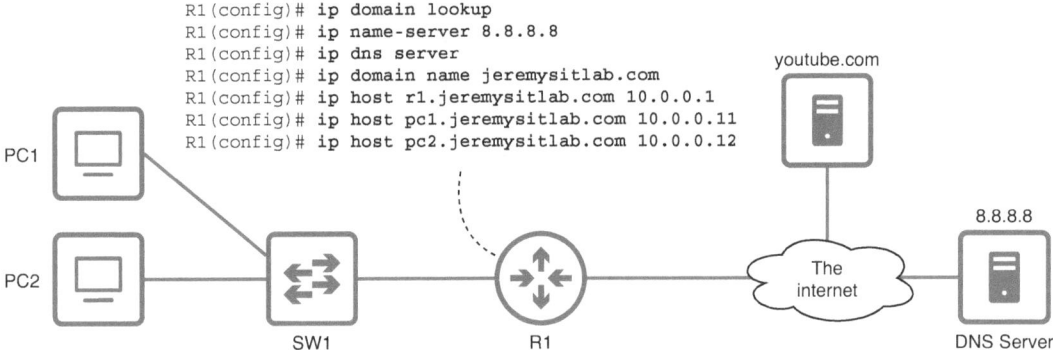

Figure 3.6   DNS configurations on R1, enabling it to function as a DNS client and server and configuring manual name-to-IP-address mappings

3.2.1   Cisco IOS as a DNS client

For a Cisco IOS device, such as a Cisco router, to function as a DNS client—for it to be able to query a DNS server to resolve domain names to IP addresses—two commands are needed. The first command is `ip domain lookup` (it can also be configured with a hyphen: `ip domain-lookup`). This command enables the router to perform DNS queries, whether it is solely as a DNS client or as a DNS server querying other DNS servers.

> **NOTE**   The `ip domain lookup` command is enabled by default, so configuring it is actually unnecessary; I included it here to demonstrate the command. You can use `no ip domain lookup` if you want to disable DNS queries on the router.

The second command is `ip name-server` *ip-address,* which allows you to configure the router's DNS server—the server it will send DNS queries to (*name server* is another name for a DNS server). In the following example, I attempt to ping google.com from R1 before configuring this command, but it fails. However, after configuring 8.8.8.8 as R1's DNS server, the second ping succeeds:

R1 fails to resolve google.com.

```
R1# ping google.com
Translating "google.com"...domain server (255.255.255.255)
% Unrecognized host or address, or protocol not running.
R1# configure terminal
R1(config)# ip name-server 8.8.8.8
R1(config)# do ping google.com
Translating "google.com"...domain server (8.8.8.8) [OK]
Type escape sequence to abort.
Sending 5, 100-byte ICMP Echos to 172.217.161.46, timeout is 2 seconds:
!!!!!
Success rate is 100 percent (5/5), round-trip min/avg/max = 8/8/9 ms
```

Configures 8.8.8.8 as R1's DNS server

The domain name is successfully resolved.

The ping works.

NOTE You can specify multiple DNS servers (up to six) with the `ip name -server` command, either with a single command (i.e., `ip name-server 8.8.8.8 1.1.1.1`) or with separate commands. If the first server fails to resolve the domain name, the router will query the other server(s).

R1 is now a DNS client, capable of resolving domain names to IP addresses by querying its DNS server. To relate this to the previous chapter's topic, we can configure R1 as an NTP client by specifying an NTP server's domain name instead of its IP address. I demonstrate that in the following example by configuring R1 as an NTP client of one of Google's NTP servers, time1.google.com:

Specifies the domain name of Google's NTP server

```
R1(config)# ntp server time1.google.com          ◄
R1(config)# do show ntp associations
  address          ref clock   st   when   poll   reach   delay    offset    disp
*~216.239.35.0    .GOOG.       1     1      64      1      44.273   59.769    1937.5   ◄
 * sys.peer, # selected, + candidate, - outlyer, x falseticker, ~ configured
```

R1 resolved the domain name to an IP address.

3.2.2 Cisco IOS as a DNS server

A Cisco router can also be configured as a DNS server to be used by hosts in your network, and there are some advantages to doing so. One advantage is performance; the router can cache queries for commonly accessed websites. For example, if one host in the LAN accesses youtube.com, the router will cache the DNS mapping and use it to respond to other hosts' queries for the same name. This means that an external DNS server doesn't have to be queried every time another host wants to access the same website.

The command to configure a router to become a DNS server is `ip dns server`. With that command configured, the router will be able to respond to clients' DNS queries. Of course, it's not expected that the router will be able to resolve all DNS queries itself; it will query other DNS servers (as configured with the `ip name-server` command) to do so. Figure 3.7 shows how a Cisco router, R1, queries its own DNS server (8.8.8.8) to resolve a query it receives from a DNS client, PC1.

NOTE Both DNS queries shown in figure 3.7—PC1's query to R1 and R1's query to 8.8.8.8—are recursive queries. 8.8.8.8 will perform iterative queries to resolve the domain name if needed. Basically, R1's role is to forward clients' DNS queries on to 8.8.8.8 and cache the responses, allowing R1 to quickly respond to other clients who send DNS queries for the same domain names.

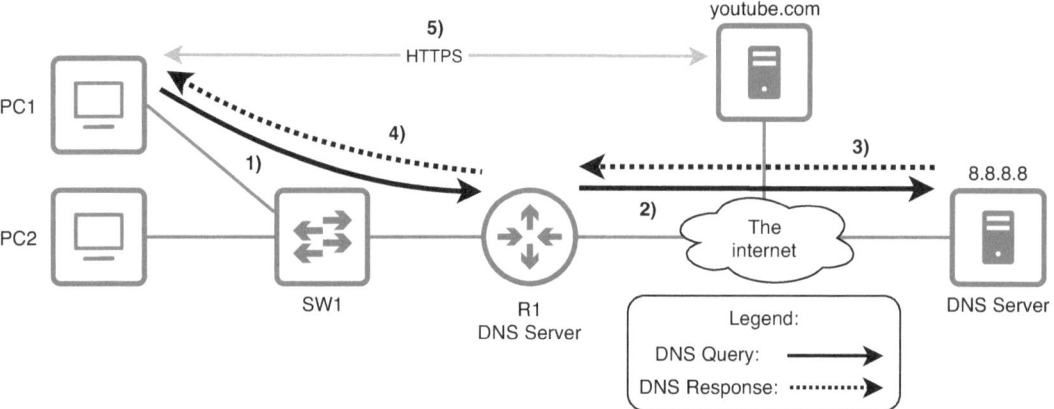

Figure 3.7   R1 is a DNS server for hosts in its connected LAN. (1) PC1 queries R1 to resolve the domain name youtube.com. (2) R1 can't resolve the name itself, so R1 queries 8.8.8.8. (3) 8.8.8.8 responds to R1, informing it of youtube.com's IP address, and then (4) R1 responds to PC1. In step 5, PC1 communicates with youtube.com via HTTPS.

You can also manually configure name-to-IP-address mappings on a router; creating such mappings for hosts in the internal network allows them to communicate with each other via hostnames instead of IP addresses. In the following example, I demonstrate the necessary configurations and verify:

> **Defines a default domain name**

```
R1(config)# ip domain name jeremysitlab.com
R1(config)# ip host r1.jeremysitlab.com 10.0.0.1
R1(config)# ip host pc1.jeremysitlab.com 10.0.0.11
R1(config)# ip host pc2.jeremysitlab.com 10.0.0.12
```

> **Configures manual name-to-IP-address mappings**

The first command is **ip domain name** *name*, which can also be configured as **ip domain-name** *name* (with a hyphen). This command defines a default domain name that R1 will append to DNS queries that specify only a hostname instead of a full domain name. For this example, I used the domain name jeremysitlab.com.

The **ip domain name** command is optional but useful: users will be able to use hosts' hostnames without having to specify each host's full domain name. For example, a user on PC1 can ping PC2 with **ping pc2** instead of **ping pc2.jeremysitlab.com**; R1 will append the domain name itself.

> **NOTE**   The **ip domain name** command is also a step in configuring *Secure Shell* (SSH) on a device to enable remote access to its CLI; SSH is the topic of chapter 5.

The command to manually configure a name-to-IP-address mapping is **ip host** *name* *ip-address*. I configured three: one for R1 itself, one for PC1, and one for PC2. To confirm the mappings, you can use the **show hosts** command; this shows both the manually configured mappings as well as mappings that the device learned via DNS. The following example shows the output. Notice that R1 has an entry for youtube.com, which it resolved via DNS (figure 3.7's example), and the three manually configured entries:

```
R1# show hosts
Default domain is jeremysitlab.com
Name/address lookup uses domain service
Name servers are 8.8.8.8

Codes: UN - unknown, EX - expired, OK - OK, ?? - revalidate
       temp - temporary, perm - permanent
       NA - Not Applicable None - Not defined

Host                      Port  Flags      Age Type  Address(es)
youtube.com               None  (temp, OK)  0  IP    142.251.42.174
r1.jeremysitlab.com       None  (perm, OK)  0  IP    10.0.0.1
pc1.jeremysitlab.com      None  (perm, OK)  0  IP    10.0.0.11
pc2.jeremysitlab.com      None  (perm, OK)  0  IP    10.0.0.12
```

Dynamically learned mapping for youtube.com

Manually configured mappings for R1, PC1, and PC2

In the following example, I ping PC2 from PC1 (a Linux host) with the **ping pc2** command, resulting in PC1 sending a DNS query to R1 to learn PC2's IP address. Although R1 doesn't have a mapping for pc2, R1 appends the default domain name jeremysitlab .com, resulting in pc2.jeremysitlab.com, for which R1 does have a mapping. R1 then responds to PC1's DNS query, and as the example shows, PC1's ping is successful:

```
jeremy@PC1:~$ ping pc2
PING pc2 (10.0.0.12): 56 data bytes
64 bytes from 10.0.0.12: seq=0 ttl=255 time=5.825 ms
64 bytes from 10.0.0.12: seq=1 ttl=255 time=2.962 ms
. . .
```

Summary

- *Domain Name System* (DNS) is a protocol that *resolves* (i.e., translates) names like www.google.com to IP addresses.

- An address like https://www.google.com/maps is called a *Uniform Resource Identifier* (URI) or *Uniform Resource Locator* (URL)—a URL is a type of URI that identifies both the resource (the web page) and how to locate it.

- A URL consists of multiple elements, such as the *scheme*—the protocol that should be used to access the resource (https); the *authority*—the server that hosts the resource (www.google.com); and the *path*—the specific resource on the server (/maps).

- When you type a URL into a web browser, your computer will use DNS to translate the authority (the domain name of the server) into an IP address.

- DNS lookups consist of a *DNS query* from the client and a *DNS query response* from the server. The client will then store the name-to-IP-address mapping in temporary storage called the *DNS cache* for future use.

- Client devices learn the IP address of their DNS server either via *Dynamic Host Configuration Protocol* (DHCP) or manual configuration.

- DNS queries are sent to port 53 on the DNS server. Standard queries and responses use UDP, but TCP is used in certain situations.

- DNS is a hierarchical naming system, organized in a tree-like structure. A *domain* is a subtree of that structure.

- The *root domain* (.) is at the top of the DNS hierarchy, and there are various *top-level domains* (TLDs) under it, such as com. Each TLD has various *second-level domains* (SLDs) under it, such as google.com, and each SLD can have various *subdomains*, such as www.google.com.

- A domain name that specifies its exact location in the DNS hierarchy is called a *fully qualified domain name* (FQDN). The dot at the end of an FQDN is a delimiter between the TLD and the root domain, which has no name; the dot is often omitted.

- A domain name that only includes partial information, such as only the hostname configured on the device, is a partially qualified domain name (PQDN).

- When a host sends a DNS query to its DNS server, it sends a *recursive query*—a query that asks for a definite answer: an IP address or an error message stating that the domain name could not be resolved. The DNS server responsible for resolving recursive queries is called a *recursive resolver*.

- The recursive resolver will then send a DNS query to a *root DNS server*—a DNS server at the top of the DNS hierarchy. This is an *iterative query*—a query that can be answered with an IP address or with a referral to another DNS server.

- The root server will refer the recursive resolver to a *TLD server*—a DNS server responsible for the relevant TLD.

- The TLD server will refer the recursive resolver to an *authoritative DNS server*—a server that holds the definitive set of records for the specific domain and can, therefore, give a definite answer in reply to queries.

- After receiving a response from the authoritative server, the recursive resolver will reply to the client's recursive query.

- Caching is used at every step of the name resolution process to reduce the number of DNS queries required. For example, if the recursive resolver had a cached entry for the domain name that the client queried, it would reply with that information.

- *DNS records* can contain information other than IP addresses. Some record types include A, AAAA, CNAME, MX, NS, PTR, and SOA:

  – *A records* map a domain name to an IPv4 address.

– *AAAA records* map a domain name to an IPv6 address.

– *CNAME records* map a domain name to another domain name.

– *MX records* specify the domain's mail servers.

– *NS records* specify the domain's authoritative DNS servers.

– *PTR records* map an IP address back to a domain name.

– *SOA records* provide administrative information such as admin contact details and a serial number.

■ Beyond forwarding packets and frames, network devices like routers and switches don't participate in DNS exchanges between DNS clients and servers. However, Cisco IOS devices themselves can be DNS clients and servers.

■ Cisco IOS devices need the `ip domain lookup` (or `ip domain-lookup`) command to be able to send queries to DNS servers; this command is enabled by default.

■ Use `ip name-server` `ip-address` to specify the device's DNS server—the server it will send DNS queries to.

■ Use `ip dns server` to configure the device as a DNS server to allow it to respond to clients' DNS queries.

■ Use `ip domain name` `name` (or `ip domain-name` `name`) to configure the device's default domain name. It will automatically append this domain name to DNS queries that don't specify a domain name.

■ Use `ip host` `name ip-address` to manually configure name-to-IP-address mappings. This is useful for hosts in the internal network.

■ Use `show hosts` to display all name-to-IP-address mappings, including manually configured mappings and those learned via DNS.

Dynamic Host Configuration Protocol

This chapter covers

- How Dynamic Host Configuration Protocol (DHCP) automates the configuration of network hosts
- Configuring Cisco IOS devices as DHCP servers and clients
- Using DHCP relay to enable centralized DHCP servers
- Viewing IP settings on Windows, macOS, and Linux

Dynamic Host Configuration Protocol (DHCP) is a protocol that automates the assignment of IP addresses, default gateways, and other network configuration information to hosts. But what exactly is a host? A host is any device that sends and receives packets over a network—put in other terms, any device with an IP address. Manually configuring thousands (or tens of thousands) of hosts in a large network is simply not feasible. Even in a small network—for example, a home network—automating host configuration makes using the network much simpler for end users who might not be tech savvy (or even if they are, would rather not have to manually configure all of their devices).

Hosts can also include network infrastructure devices like routers and switches—as we'll see in the next chapter on *Secure Shell* (SSH), even a Layer 2 switch can have an IP address to allow remote management. However, DHCP is most often used to automate the configuration of end hosts, such as PCs, smartphones, tablets, etc., and is almost ubiquitous in modern networks. In this chapter, we will cover the following CCNA exam topics:

- 1.10: Verify IP parameters for Client OS (Windows, Mac OS, Linux)
- 4.3: Explain the role of DHCP and DNS within the network
- 4.6: Configure and verify DHCP client and relay

4.1 The basic functions of DHCP

For a host to communicate over a network, it needs certain settings to be configured. In most cases, the following four are the bare minimum:

- *IP address*—Acts as the host's identity on the network, providing an address to send and receive packets
- *Netmask*—Allows the host to determine which IP addresses belong to its LAN and which do not
- *Default gateway*—Enables the host to communicate with devices in different LANs
- *DNS server address*—Translates human-readable domain names into IP addresses

While it is possible to manually configure these settings on each host, this approach is not scalable. In a large network, manually configuring all of these parameters on thousands of hosts would be both time consuming and error prone; occasional typos are inevitable, and more typing means more typos.

Furthermore, manual configuration isn't flexible. In dynamic environments where hosts frequently move between networks—think of a smartphone or laptop—manual configuration quickly becomes impractical. DHCP, on the other hand, automates host configuration in a way that is both accurate (less error prone) and scalable.

DHCP uses a client–server model in which clients send requests to a DHCP server, which then leases an IP address to each client, along with providing other settings such as the client's default gateway. Figure 4.1 shows a router using DHCP to lease IP addresses to clients in a LAN—in small networks, it's common for a router to function as a DHCP server.

NOTE DHCP is *stateful*, meaning the DHCP server keeps track of the addresses it leases to clients. This is in contrast to SLAAC (as covered in chapter 21 of volume 1), which is *stateless*—no server keeps track of each device's IP address.

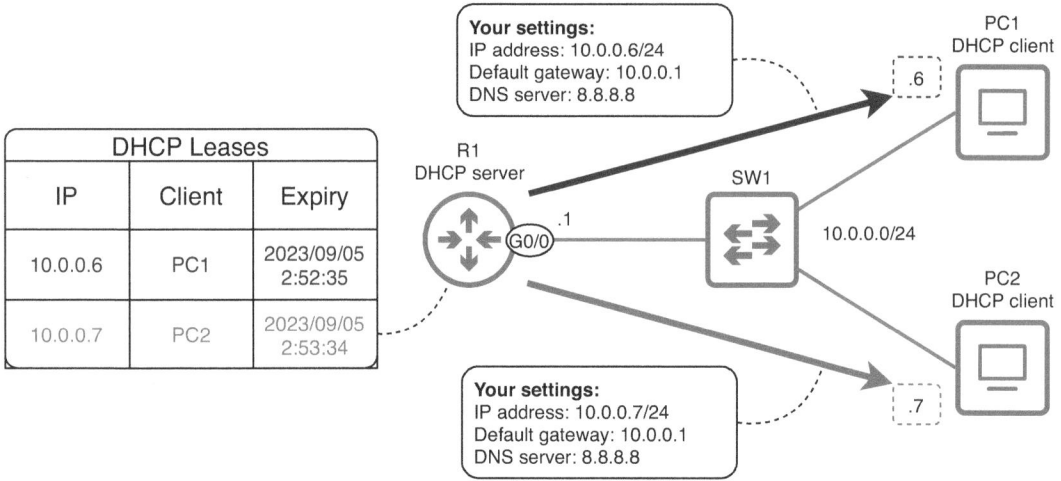

Figure 4.1 **R1, a DHCP server, leases IP addresses to clients PC1 and PC2. In addition to IP addresses, clients learn their netmask, default gateway, and DNS server addresses. R1 keeps track of leases and when they expire.**

In this section, we'll examine the DHCP leasing process step by step. Then, we'll examine how to configure a Cisco IOS device to function as both a DHCP server and a DHCP client.

4.1.1 Leasing an IP address with DHCP

For a DHCP client to lease an IP address from a DHCP server, there is a four-step process that you can remember as DORA, for the first letter of each message type involved:

- *DISCOVER*—Client locates DHCP servers and announces that it needs an IP address
- *OFFER*—Server offers the client an IP address (and other settings)
- *REQUEST*—Client accepts the offered IP address
- *ACK (Acknowledgment)*—Server confirms and finalizes the lease

NOTE The four message types are actually named DHCPDISCOVER, DHCPOFFER, DHCPREQUEST, and DHCPACK in RFC 2131, which defines DHCP. I'll keep the uppercase lettering but leave out DHCP from each message's name.

DHCP uses UDP as its Layer 4 protocol. However, unlike most other protocols in which only the server uses a reserved port (and the client uses an ephemeral port), in DHCP both use reserved ports. DHCP servers source their messages from and listen on UDP port 67, and DHCP clients source messages from and listen on UDP port 68.

EXAM TIP Memorize those ports! DHCP server = UDP 67, DHCP client = UDP 68.

Bootstrap Protocol

DHCP is based on an older protocol called *Bootstrap Protocol* (BOOTP). DHCP features many improvements over BOOTP, which is now considered obsolete. Like DHCP, BOOTP also used UDP ports 67 and 68. In fact, when specifying these port numbers in an extended ACL, the keywords in the command are `bootps` (BOOTP server, UDP 67) and `bootpc` (BOOTP client, UDP 68), even though DHCP supplanted BOOTP many years ago.

Figure 4.2 outlines the four-message DORA process. PC1 (a DHCP client) broadcasts a DISCOVER message. Then, R1 (a DHCP server) responds with an OFFER message. PC1 replies with a REQUEST message, again destined for the broadcast IP address 255.255.255.255. Finally, R1 replies with an ACK message.

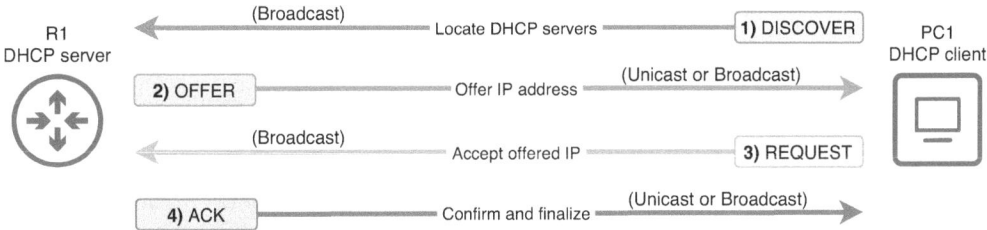

Figure 4.2   Leasing an IPv4 address via DHCP (the DORA process): (1) DISCOVER from client to server, (2) OFFER from server to client, (3) REQUEST from client to server, (4) ACK from server to client.

The DHCP process begins when a client first connects to a network; for example, after a PC boots up or after it is connected to a router/switch with a cable. To communicate over the network, the client needs to know its network configuration—IP address, netmask, etc.—so it will initiate the DHCP leasing process.

A DISCOVER message is sent by the client to locate any DHCP servers on the LAN and let those servers know that the client wants an IP address. Because the client doesn't have an IP address yet, it sources this packet from 0.0.0.0—the all-zeros IP address, which is reserved for a few uses, such as DHCP. The client also doesn't know the IP address of any DHCP servers, so it sends the packet to 255.255.255.255—the reserved broadcast address.

> **NOTE**   When a host first connects to a switch port, it takes 30 seconds for the switch port to move through the Spanning Tree Protocol (STP) listening and learning states to the forwarding state; this will block the client's DISCOVER messages, preventing it from getting an IP address via DHCP. However, you can configure PortFast to allow the switch port to skip to the forwarding state.

After receiving the DISCOVER message, the DHCP server will reply with an OFFER message, which offers an IP address to the client. This message is usually sent as a unicast packet destined for the IP address offered to the client; to offer PC1 10.0.0.6, R1 will address the OFFER message to 10.0.0.6. However, because the client technically doesn't have an IP address configured yet, some client devices will be unable to accept unicast packets until the DHCP leasing process is complete; such clients will indicate so in the initial DISCOVER message, and the server will broadcast the OFFER message instead.

> **NOTE**   If there are multiple DHCP servers in the LAN, all will send OFFER messages to the client. In this case, the client will typically accept the first OFFER it receives. However, this situation is rare; usually, there will be just one server.

To accept the offered IP address, the client will send a REQUEST message, again sourced from 0.0.0.0. Although the client now knows the server's IP address (because it received the OFFER from the server), the client broadcasts this message to all hosts in the LAN. The reason is to accommodate situations where multiple DHCP servers sent OFFERs—if a server sees that another server's OFFER was accepted, it knows that its own OFFER was not. A server whose OFFER was not accepted will free up its offered IP address to be leased to other clients.

To confirm and finalize the lease, the server will send an ACK message. Like the OFFER message, this can be unicast or broadcast, depending on the capabilities of the client. After receiving the ACK, the lease process is complete; the client can start using the assigned IP address (and other parameters) to communicate over the network.

> **NOTE**   An IP address learned via DHCP is called a *dynamic IP address*, whereas a manually configured IP address is called a *static IP address*.

Lease renewal

DHCP leases are typically not permanent. Lease time can vary from a few hours (or even a few minutes) in public Wi-Fi networks to 24 hours or more for home networks. To maintain network connectivity, a client must renew its lease. To do so, the client will send a REQUEST message to the server it is leasing the address from; unlike the REQUEST in the DORA process, this is a unicast message. Typically, a client starts this renewal process when 50% of its lease time has expired. Upon receiving the REQUEST, the DHCP server responds with an ACK message, effectively renewing the lease.

4.1.2   *Cisco IOS as a DHCP server*

In small networks, the router usually serves as the DHCP server for hosts in its connected LANs. Home routers, for example, are typically preconfigured as DHCP servers; a user only has to connect their devices to the router to use the network—no need to understand how to configure IP addresses or even what an IP address is.

In this section, we'll look at how to configure a Cisco IOS router as a DHCP server, including how to configure a *DHCP pool*—a group of IP addresses that can be leased to clients—and how to exclude particular addresses from that pool. Figure 4.3 shows the configurations we'll cover.

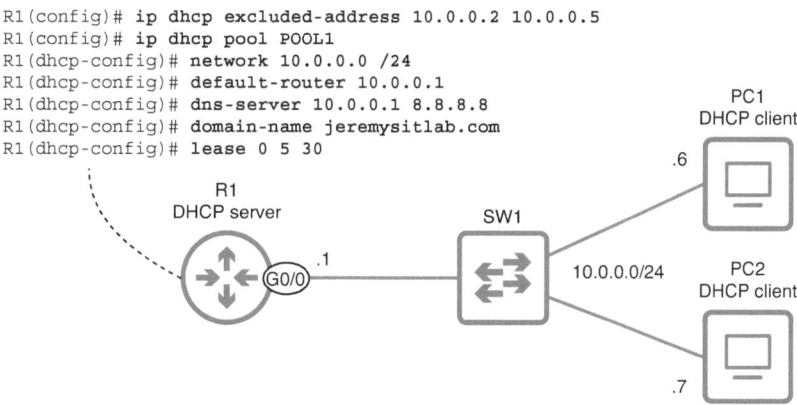

```
R1(config)# ip dhcp excluded-address 10.0.0.2 10.0.0.5
R1(config)# ip dhcp pool POOL1
R1(dhcp-config)# network 10.0.0.0 /24
R1(dhcp-config)# default-router 10.0.0.1
R1(dhcp-config)# dns-server 10.0.0.1 8.8.8.8
R1(dhcp-config)# domain-name jeremysitlab.com
R1(dhcp-config)# lease 0 5 30
```

Figure 4.3 Configuring a Cisco IOS router as a DHCP server, specifying a range of excluded addresses, and then creating a pool of addresses to lease to clients

CONFIGURING THE DHCP POOL

The first command we will cover is `ip dhcp excluded-address` *low-ip high-ip*, which specifies a range of IP addresses that will not be leased to clients. This command is optional, but it's common to reserve some IP addresses for hosts whose IP addresses you plan to statically assign. For example, a server's IP address should be manually configured in most cases rather than leased via DHCP—the server's IP address should remain constant so clients can easily connect to it. In the following example, I reserve the first few addresses from the 10.0.0.0/24 subnet:

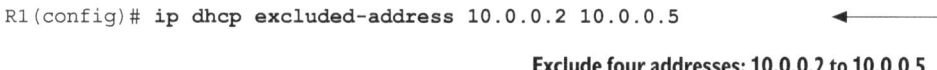

```
R1(config)# ip dhcp excluded-address 10.0.0.2 10.0.0.5
```

Exclude four addresses: 10.0.0.2 to 10.0.0.5

> **NOTE** There is no need to exclude the network address (10.0.0.0), the broadcast address (10.0.0.255), or any IP addresses configured on the router itself (10.0.0.1)—the router knows not to lease them to clients.

The next step is to create a DHCP pool for the 10.0.0.0/24 subnet—the range of IP addresses that will be leased to hosts. The following example shows how to create a DHCP pool and specifies a range of IP addresses and various other parameters:

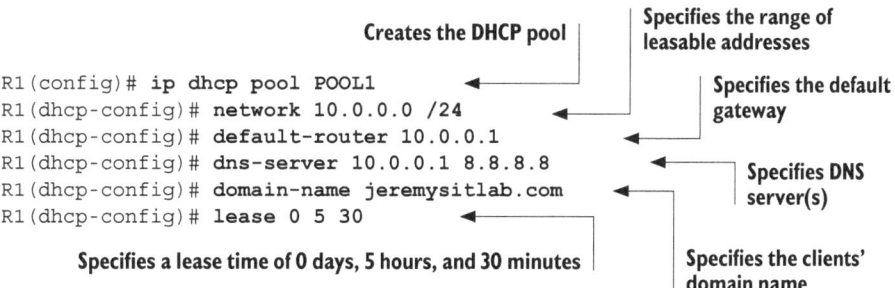

Creates the DHCP pool

Specifies the range of leasable addresses

```
R1(config)# ip dhcp pool POOL1
R1(dhcp-config)# network 10.0.0.0 /24
R1(dhcp-config)# default-router 10.0.0.1
R1(dhcp-config)# dns-server 10.0.0.1 8.8.8.8
R1(dhcp-config)# domain-name jeremysitlab.com
R1(dhcp-config)# lease 0 5 30
```

Specifies the default gateway

Specifies DNS server(s)

Specifies a lease time of 0 days, 5 hours, and 30 minutes

Specifies the clients' domain name

The command to create a DHCP pool is `ip dhcp pool` `name`. That brings you to DHCP config mode, where you can configure the various parameters that will be leased to clients, including the range of IP addresses.

The `network` `network-address` {`netmask` | `/prefix-length`} command configures the range of IP addresses to lease to clients. Note that you can either specify a netmask (i.e., `255.255.255.0`) or a prefix length (i.e. `/24`). In the example, I configured `network 10.0.0.0 /24`, specifying that clients should be leased addresses from the 10.0.0.0/24 range—`network 10.0.0.0 255.255.255.0` would have the same effect.

As mentioned previously, the router won't lease the network address or broadcast address to clients, nor will it assign the router's own address or any addresses in an excluded range (10.0.0.2–10.0.0.5), even if they fit within the range specified in this command (10.0.0.0/24).

> **EXAM TIP**   Although the `network` command is configured in DHCP config mode, the `ip dhcp excluded-address` command is configured in global config mode. Don't mix those up!

I then used the `default-router` `ip-address` command, which specifies the default gateway clients should use. In this case, I specified 10.0.0.1—R1's own IP address—as the default gateway. Note that although the more common term is *default gateway* (*gateway* is an old term for a router), this command is `default-router`.

The next command is `dns-server` `ip-address`, which allows you to specify the DNS server(s) that clients should send DNS queries to. You can specify up to eight DNS servers with this command, with a space between each. In the example, I specified two with `dns-server 10.0.0.1 8.8.8.8`—R1 itself and Google's public DNS server.

Those first three commands—`network`, `default-router`, and `dns-server`—are the essentials you should specify when configuring a DHCP pool. With those parameters, hosts will be able to communicate with local and remote destinations and will be able to resolve domain names to IP addresses. However, there are many more settings that you can configure, and in the example I used two more: `domain-name` and `lease`.

The `domain-name` `domain-name` command tells the clients their domain name. For example, PC1 will know its full domain name is pc1.jeremysitlab.com. This makes it easier for computers in the same domain to communicate using just hostnames instead of FQDNs. When you ping another computer from PC1, you can simply type `ping pc2`; PC1 will automatically add the domain name, making it pc2.jeremysitlab.com.

The final command we'll look at is `lease` `days hours minutes`, which allows you to specify the duration of leases. The default is 24 hours, but in the example, I used `lease 0 5 30` to specify a lease time of 5 hours and 30 minutes. The default of 24 hours is usually fine, but you might want to reduce it for networks that have lots of clients coming and going (i.e., public Wi-Fi networks) to ensure that addresses remain available for new clients, instead of being reserved for clients that have long left the network.

> **NOTE**   You can also configure `lease infinite` to specify an unlimited lease duration.

R1 is now a DHCP server! In the following example, I use `show ip dhcp binding` on R1 to confirm that PC1 and PC2 have successfully leased IP addresses from R1:

```
R1# show ip dhcp binding
Bindings from all pools not associated with VRF:
IP address    Client-ID/              Lease expiration       Type
              Hardware address/
              User name
10.0.0.6      0152.5400.172f.da       Sep 06 2023 01:50 PM   Automatic
10.0.0.7      0152.5400.1792.08       Sep 06 2023 01:51 PM   Automatic
```

PC1 leased 10.0.0.6 from R1.

PC2 leased 10.0.0.7 from R1.

NOTE In section 4.3, we will look at how to verify the IP settings directly on clients, specifically on Windows, macOS, and Linux devices.

In some cases, you may need to manually clear some or all of the addresses in the server's binding table—for example, to free up addresses bound to clients that have already left the network or when testing DHCP in a lab environment. You can clear the DHCP binding table with `clear ip dhcp binding` {`*` | `ip-address`}; specifying `*` clears all bindings, and specifying `ip-address` clears only the specified binding.

The DHCP client ID

The `Client-ID/Hardware address/User name` column in the output of `show ip dhcp binding` can be a bit confusing. In DHCP, it's important that each client has a unique identifier so the server can differentiate between clients. The client typically indicates its client ID in its DISCOVER message (and every message thereafter).

Although the formatting in the previous output makes the client IDs look like MAC addresses with two extra hexadecimal digits at the end (`da` and `08`), they are actually MAC addresses with two extra hexadecimal digits at the beginning. Both PC1 and PC2 use a client ID format consisting of the prefix `01`, which indicates the interface hardware type (Ethernet), plus the interface's MAC address. For example, PC1's MAC address is `5254.0017.2fda`, but when the prefix `01` is added, IOS formats the client ID as `0152.5400.172f.da`.

Don't expect all client IDs to look like this—there are other formats that you might encounter. The details of the client ID and its possible formats are beyond the scope of the CCNA exam, but I remember being curious about the meaning of this column when I first saw the output of `show ip binding`, and I'm guessing that you might have been curious too.

ADDRESS CONFLICTS

Before a DHCP server leases an IP address to a client, it should check to make sure that the address is unique—that another device isn't already configured with that IP address. Although the DHCP server should keep track of which IP addresses have been leased, it's possible that another device has been manually configured with an IP address that is in the server's range of leasable addresses; you might have forgotten to exclude that IP address with the `ip dhcp excluded-address` command. This is called an *address conflict*. Figure 4.4 outlines how a router detects address conflicts.

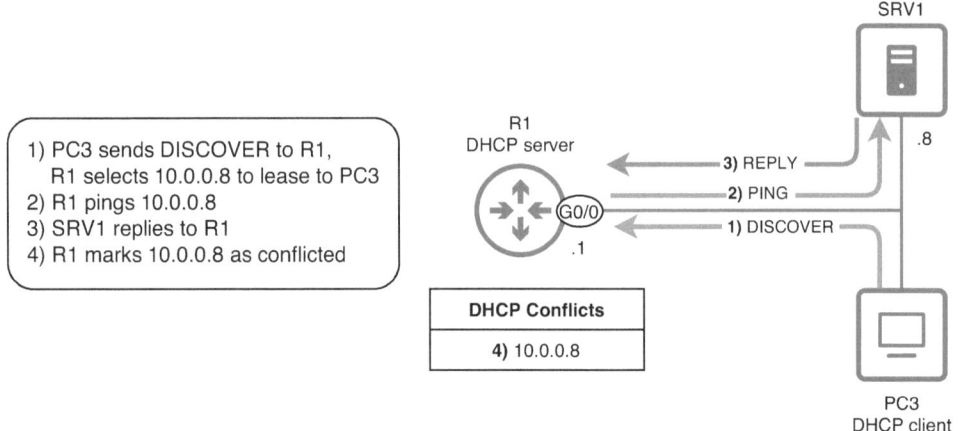

Figure 4.4   R1 detects an address conflict. (1) PC3 sends a DISCOVER message, and R1 selects 10.0.0.8 to lease to PC3. (2) Before sending an OFFER, R1 pings 10.0.0.8 to verify it's not in use. (3) SRV1's IP address is 10.0.0.8, so it replies to R1. (4) R1 marks 10.0.0.8 as conflicted.

Cisco IOS DHCP servers send pings to detect address conflicts—addresses in the DHCP pool that are already in use by another host. After the server receives a DISCOVER message from a client, it will decide which address to lease to the client. However, before sending the OFFER message, the server will ping the IP address it intends to lease to the client; if there is no reply, the address is unique. However, if there is a reply, it means the address is not unique; another host is already using it. You should then see a message like this:

```
%DHCPD-4-PING_CONFLICT: DHCP address conflict:  server pinged 10.0.0.8.
```

The address is marked as a conflict and is removed from the DHCP pool. The server will then select a different IP address to lease to the client and use the same process to determine whether that address is unique. You can confirm IP address conflicts with the `show ip dhcp conflict` command, as in the following example:

```
R1# show ip dhcp conflict
IP address       Detection method   Detection time           VRF
10.0.0.8         Ping               Sep 06 2023 08:40 AM
```

R1 won't assign 10.0.0.8 to any clients until the conflict is resolved—for example, by changing SRV1's IP address. After resolving the conflict, you must also clear it from the conflict table. You can use `clear ip dhcp conflict` *ip-address* to clear the specific conflict from the table or `clear ip dhcp conflict *` to clear all conflicts.

4.1.3   *Cisco IOS as a DHCP client*

Network infrastructure devices like routers and switches typically use static (manually configured) IP addresses instead of dynamic IP addresses learned via DHCP. One
reason is to simplify device management; if devices' IP addresses remain constant, it's
easier to identify and connect to each device for remote management. Changing a
router's IP addresses could also affect other routers' routes; next-hop IP addresses
might need to change. For those and other reasons, you should usually manually configure the IP addresses of network devices.

However, one common use case for configuring a router as a DHCP client is for a
connection to an Internet Service Provider (ISP). An ISP-connected interface can be
configured as a DHCP client, allowing the router to learn its IP address from the ISP
and automatically install a default route with the ISP's router as the next hop. Figure 4.5
shows how to configure a Cisco router's interface as a DHCP client.

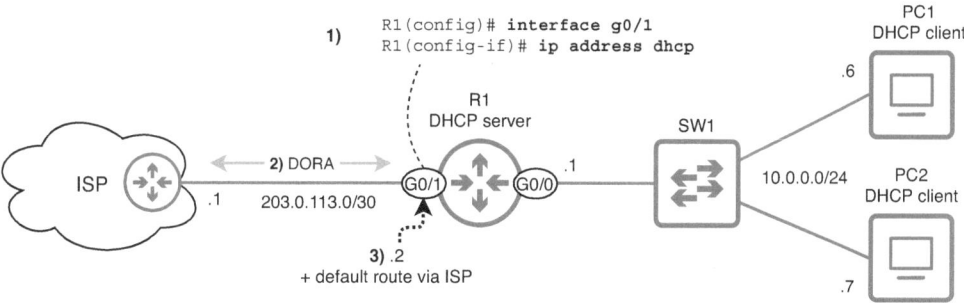

**Figure 4.5   R1 is a DHCP client of the ISP. (1) Configure G0/1 to learn its IP address via DHCP.
(2) DORA exchange between R1 and the ISP router. (3) R1 configures the learned IP on G0/1, and adds
a default route via the ISP router.**

Configuring a Cisco IOS device as a DHCP client is simple: just use the `ip address
dhcp` command on the appropriate interface. In the following example, I configure
R1's G0/1 interface as a DHCP client and then confirm that it has learned both an IP
address and a default route via DHCP:

```
R1(config)# interface g0/1
R1(config-if)# ip address dhcp
R1(config-if)# no shutdown
*Dec 28 05:11:37.351: %LINK-3-UPDOWN: Interface GigabitEthernet0/1,
➥changed state to up
*Dec 28 05:11:38.351: %LINEPROTO-5-UPDOWN: Line protocol on Interface
➥GigabitEthernet0/1, changed state to up
*Dec 28 05:11:45.611: %DHCP-6-ADDRESS_ASSIGN:
➥Interface GigabitEthernet0/1 assigned DHCP address
➥192.168.255.50, mask 255.255.255.0, hostname R1
R1(config-if)# do show ip interface g0/1
GigabitEthernet0/2 is up, line protocol is up
  Internet address is 192.168.255.191/24
  Broadcast address is 255.255.255.255
```

Configures RI G0/1 as a
DHCP client and enables it

A log message indicates that
G0/1 was assigned an IP
address via DHCP.

Confirms G0/1's IP
settings

```
  Address determined by DHCP                  R1 learns its IP
. . .                                         address via DHCP.      R1 learns a default route
R1(config-if)# do show ip route                                      with the ISP's router as
. . .                                                                the next hop.
Gateway of last resort is 203.0.113.1 to network 0.0.0.0
S*    0.0.0.0/0 [1/0] via 203.0.113.1
. . .
```

Notice that the code S is shown next to the default route. Normally, this code indicates a route that was manually configured with the **ip route** command. However, this code is a bit misleading in this case; this route was learned dynamically via DHCP, not statically configured. This can be considered a quirk of Cisco IOS; DHCP-learned routes use the code S instead of their own unique code (like OSPF's O or EIGRP's D).

4.2   DHCP relay

Although a Cisco router can act as a DHCP server for clients in its connected LANs, networks above a certain size will likely use a centralized approach; instead of having each LAN's router function as a DHCP server, a centralized DHCP server is used. A centralized DHCP server simplifies the management of DHCP pools, helps maintain a consistent set of DHCP policies and configurations, and reduces the total number of DHCP servers required. Furthermore, dedicated DHCP servers, which are designed specifically for DHCP services, typically provide more advanced features that are not supported by Cisco IOS.

However, there is a problem: DHCP relies on broadcast messages, which only remain within the local subnet—routers don't forward broadcast messages to other networks. So, how can a client's DISCOVER and REQUEST messages reach a centralized DHCP server that is not in its local subnet?

The answer is *DHCP relay*, in which a router acting as a *DHCP relay agent* forwards DHCP clients' broadcast DISCOVER and REQUEST messages as unicast packets to a remote DHCP server. Figure 4.6 demonstrates the concept and also shows how to configure a Cisco router as a DHCP relay agent.

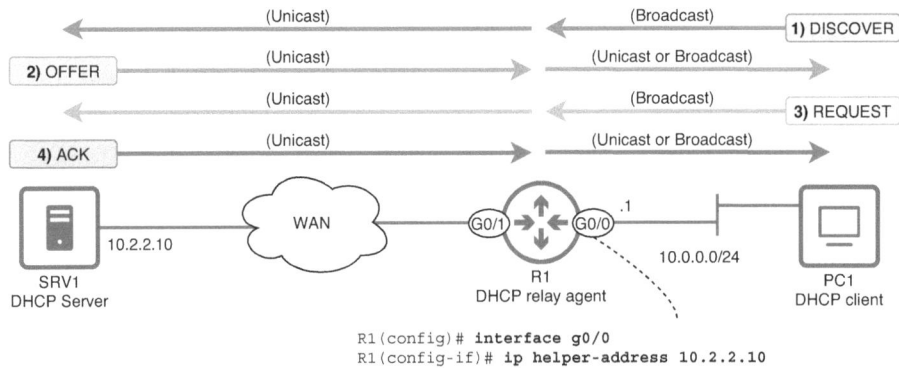

Figure 4.6   The `ip helper-address` command makes R1 a DHCP relay agent, forwarding clients' DHCP messages to the specified server.

To configure a Cisco router as a DHCP relay agent, use the `ip helper-address server-ip` command on the interface connected to the clients. This is very important! The command must be configured on the correct interface; the interface that will actually receive the clients' broadcast messages. Using figure 4.6's example, when PC1 broadcasts a DISCOVER message, R1 will receive it on its G0/0 interface, so the `ip helper-address` command must be configured on that interface.

> **NOTE** A *helper address* is an IP address of a server that the router can relay clients' broadcast messages to. Although most frequently used in the context of DHCP relay, the concept is not exclusive to DHCP—other protocols can use a helper address, too.

With the command configured, R1 acts as a middleman between PC1 (a DHCP client) and SRV1 (a DHCP server). R1 receives PC1's broadcast DISCOVER and REQUEST messages and forwards them as unicast packets to SRV1. Likewise, R1 receives SRV1's OFFER and ACK messages and forwards them to PC1. In the following example, I use the `ip helper-address` command on R1 G0/0, and confirm with `show ip interface`:

```
R1(config)# interface g0/0
R1(config-if)# ip helper-address 10.2.2.10        ◄───── Configures R1 G0/0 as
R1(config-if)# do show ip interface g0/0                  a DHCP relay agent
GigabitEthernet0/0 is up, line protocol is up
  Internet address is 10.0.0.1/24
  Broadcast address is 255.255.255.255
  Address determined by non-volatile memory
  MTU is 1500 bytes                                       SRV1's IP address is a
  Helper address is 10.2.2.10        ◄──────────────      helper address.
. . .
```

4.3   Client OS IP settings

Although the CCNA exam is focused on Cisco IOS (as you've probably noticed), Cisco expects you to be able to verify the IP settings of client devices using the Windows, macOS, and Linux operating systems (OSs).

> **NOTE** Linux is technically not an OS, but a family of OSs based on the Linux *kernel* (a program at the core of the OS); each Linux-based OS is called a Linux *distribution*.

From a practical perspective, this is something you might do as part of the troubleshooting process if a client is unable to communicate over the network. In this section, we'll look at some commands on each OS that allow you to verify clients' IP settings.

4.3.1   IP settings in Windows

Windows offers two CLI applications that you can use to interact with it: *Command Prompt* and *PowerShell*. Command Prompt is nice and simple, whereas PowerShell includes more advanced functionality; the commands we will cover here work in both programs. The most basic command that you can use to verify IP settings on a Windows PC is `ipconfig`, as shown in the following example:

```
C:\Users\jmcdo> ipconfig
. . .
Ethernet adapter Ethernet1:
   Connection-specific DNS Suffix  . : jeremysitlab.com
   IPv4 Address. . . . . . . . . . . : 192.168.1.224
   Subnet Mask . . . . . . . . . . . : 255.255.255.0
   Default Gateway . . . . . . . . . : 192.168.1.1
```

My PC's DNS suffix (domain name)

My PC's IP address and netmask (subnet mask)

My PC's default gateway (my router's IP address)

However, `ipconfig` only shows the most basic information about the device's configuration. For more information, use `ipconfig /all`, as in the following example:

```
C:\Users\jmcdo> ipconfig /all
. . .
Ethernet adapter Ethernet1:
   Connection-specific DNS Suffix  . : jeremysitlab.com
   Description . . . . . . . . . . . : Intel(R) Ethernet Controller (3) I225-V
   Physical Address. . . . . . . . . : D8-BB-C1-CC-FF-76
   DHCP Enabled. . . . . . . . . . . : Yes
   Autoconfiguration Enabled . . . . : Yes
   IPv4 Address. . . . . . . . . . . : 192.168.1.224(Preferred)
   Subnet Mask . . . . . . . . . . . : 255.255.255.0
   Lease Obtained. . . . . . . . . . : Thursday, September 7, 2023 9:29:52 AM
   Lease Expires . . . . . . . . . . : Thursday, September 7, 2023 3:29:51 PM
   Default Gateway . . . . . . . . . : 192.168.1.1
   DHCP Server . . . . . . . . . . . : 192.168.1.1
   DNS Servers . . . . . . . . . . . : 192.168.1.1
   NetBIOS over Tcpip. . . . . . . . : Enabled
```

My PC's MAC address

DHCP is enabled on my PC's interface.

My PC's default gateway, DHCP server, and DNS server are all my router.

(Preferred) means my PC requested this IP address (because it used it previously).

You might be surprised that Windows PCs build their own routing table. Although they don't route packets from other hosts, they can use the routing table to ensure that they send their own packets to the correct next hop. You can view the routing table with `netstat -rn`, as in the following example:

```
C:\Users\jmcdo> netstat -rn
. . .
IPv4 Route Table
===========================================================================
Active Routes:
Network Destination        Netmask          Gateway       Interface  Metric
          0.0.0.0          0.0.0.0      192.168.1.1  192.168.1.224     25
. . .
```

A default route to my router

```
    192.168.1.0    255.255.255.0    On-link    192.168.1.224    281
    192.168.1.224  255.255.255.255  On-link    192.168.1.224    281
. . .
```

Routes to my PC's connected subnet and its own IP address

> **NOTE** `netstat` on its own shows active TCP connections. `-r` tells it to show the routing table, and `-n` tells it to display numerical addresses (otherwise, it will attempt reverse DNS lookups to translate the IP addresses to domain names). You can combine `-r` and `-n` into `-rn`, as I did in this example.

4.3.2   IP settings in macOS

In macOS, you can access the device's CLI with the *Terminal* application. The macOS equivalent of Windows' `ipconfig` is `ifconfig`, and it displays similar information. In the following example, I use the command on my MacBook:

```
jeremy@Jeremys-MacBook-Air ~ % ifconfig
. . .
en5: flags=8863<UP,BROADCAST,SMART,RUNNING,SIMPLEX,MULTICAST> mtu 1500
options=6467<RXCSUM,TXCSUM,VLAN_MTU,TSO4,TSO6,CHANNEL_IO,PARTIAL_CSUM,
ZEROINVERT_CSUM>
    ether 00:e0:4c:68:92:ff
    inet6 fe80::1838:d69d:2d7d:7ecf%en5 prefixlen 64 secured scopeid 0x18
    inet 192.168.1.225 netmask 0xffffff00 broadcast 192.168.1.255
    nd6 options=201<PERFORMNUD,DAD>
    media: autoselect (100baseTX <full-duplex>)
    status: active
```

My MacBook's MAC address

My MacBook's IP address, netmask, and subnet broadcast address

> **NOTE** macOS displays the netmask in hexadecimal: 0xffffff00 is equivalent to 255.255.255.0.

macOS devices also build a routing table, like Windows devices. To view it, the command is the same as in Windows (`netstat -rn`), although the output is slightly different. I use that command in the following example to view my MacBook's default gateway:

```
jeremy@Jeremys-MacBook-Air ~ % netstat -rn
Routing tables
Internet:
Destination      Gateway          Flags        Netif Expire
default          192.168.1.1      UGScg          en5
. . .
```

My MacBook's default gateway is 192.168.1.1 (my router).

4.3.3   IP settings in Linux

Because Linux isn't a single OS but rather a variety of OSs built on top of the Linux kernel, there is some variation in how to view the IP settings. Some Linux distributions still support an old set of commands called *net-tools* by default, which include `ifconfig` (to view interface information) and `route` (to view the routing table). The following example shows the output of those commands on a Linux host named `linuxpc`:

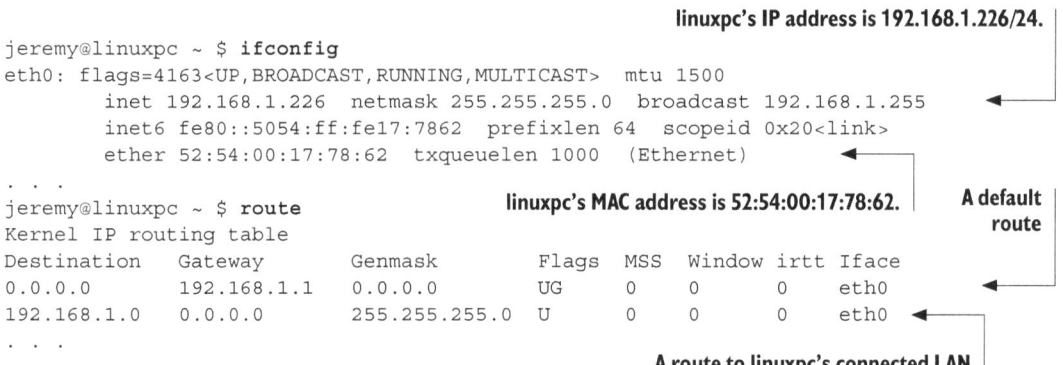

```
jeremy@linuxpc ~ $ ifconfig
eth0: flags=4163<UP,BROADCAST,RUNNING,MULTICAST>  mtu 1500
        inet 192.168.1.226  netmask 255.255.255.0  broadcast 192.168.1.255
        inet6 fe80::5054:ff:fe17:7862  prefixlen 64  scopeid 0x20<link>
        ether 52:54:00:17:78:62  txqueuelen 1000  (Ethernet)
. . .
jeremy@linuxpc ~ $ route
Kernel IP routing table
Destination     Gateway         Genmask         Flags MSS Window irtt Iface
0.0.0.0         192.168.1.1     0.0.0.0         UG    0   0      0    eth0
192.168.1.0     0.0.0.0         255.255.255.0   U     0   0      0    eth0
. . .
```

NOTE `netstat -rn` works in Linux, too.

Other distributions have removed default support for net-tools, instead using a set of commands called *iproute2*. In the following example, I use iproute2's equivalents to **ifconfig** and **route**: **ip addr** and **ip route**:

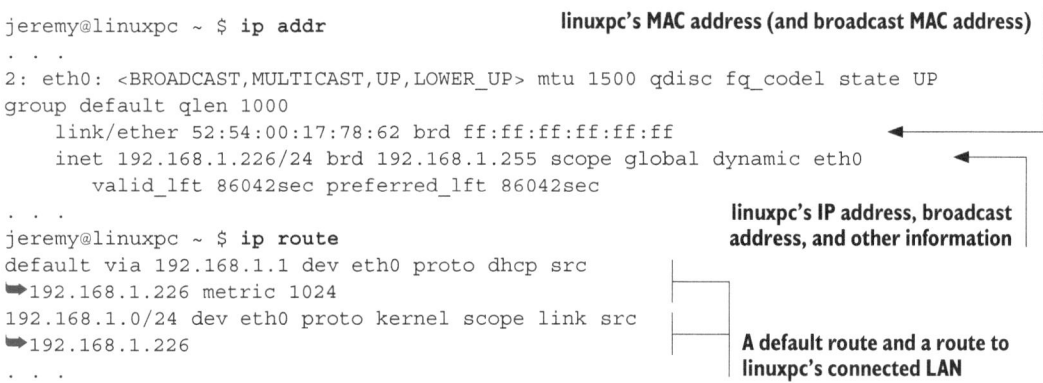

```
jeremy@linuxpc ~ $ ip addr
. . .
2: eth0: <BROADCAST,MULTICAST,UP,LOWER_UP> mtu 1500 qdisc fq_codel state UP
group default qlen 1000
    link/ether 52:54:00:17:78:62 brd ff:ff:ff:ff:ff:ff
    inet 192.168.1.226/24 brd 192.168.1.255 scope global dynamic eth0
       valid_lft 86042sec preferred_lft 86042sec
. . .
jeremy@linuxpc ~ $ ip route
default via 192.168.1.1 dev eth0 proto dhcp src
➥192.168.1.226 metric 1024
192.168.1.0/24 dev eth0 proto kernel scope link src
➥192.168.1.226
. . .
```

EXAM TIP Lots of additional information is shown in the output of the commands we covered. If you can identify the parameters we covered here (IP address, netmask, MAC address, etc.) in the output of each command, you should be ready to answer questions about this topic on the CCNA exam.

Summary

- For a host to communicate over a network, it typically needs an IP address, a netmask, a default gateway, and a DNS server.
- Manually configuring each host with those parameters in a large network isn't feasible and isn't desirable even in small networks. Dynamic Host Configuration Protocol (DHCP) automates the configuration of these parameters on hosts.

- DHCP uses a client–server model in which clients send requests to a DHCP server, which leases an IP address to each client. DHCP is stateful, meaning the server keeps track of the addresses it leases to clients.

- DHCP servers source messages from and listen on UDP port 67, and DHCP clients source messages from and listen on UDP port 68.

- The DHCP leasing process consists of four steps, usually called DORA: DISCOVER, OFFER, REQUEST, and ACK (Acknowledge).

- The DISCOVER message is sent by the client to locate any DHCP servers and announce that the client needs an IP address. It is sourced from 0.0.0.0 and broadcast to 255.255.255.255.

- The OFFER message is sent by the server to offer an IP address (and other configurations) to the client. It is either addressed to the offered IP address (unicast) or broadcast to 255.255.255.255.

- If multiple DHCP servers send OFFER messages, the client typically accepts the first.

- The REQUEST message is sent by the client to accept the server's OFFER. It is sourced from 0.0.0.0 and broadcast to 255.255.255.255.

- The ACK message is sent by the server to confirm and finalize the lease. After receiving this message, the client can use the leased parameters to communicate over the network.

- An IP address learned via DHCP is called a *dynamic IP address*, whereas a manually configured IP address is called a *static IP address*.

- In small networks, the router usually serves as the DHCP server.

- Use **ip dhcp excluded-address** *low-ip high-ip* in global config mode to configure a range of IP addresses that will not be leased to clients. There is no need to exclude the network address, broadcast address, or the router's own address.

- Use **ip dhcp pool** *name* to create a DHCP pool—a set of addresses and other configuration parameters to be leased to clients.

- Use **network** *network-address* {*netmask* | */prefix-length*} to configure the range of addresses to be leased to clients.

- Use **default-router** *ip-address* to configure clients' default gateway.

- Use **dns-server** *ip-address* to configure up to eight DNS servers (with a space between each) that clients should send DNS queries to.

- Use **domain-name** *domain-name* to specify clients' domain name.

- Use **lease** {*days hours minutes* | **infinite**} to configure the duration of leases. The default lease period is 24 hours.

- Use **show ip dhcp binding** to see active DHCP leases.

- Use **clear ip dhcp binding** {***** | *ip-address*} to either clear all bindings (*****) or the specified binding (*ip-address*).

- After receiving a DISCOVER message and selecting an IP address to lease to a client, a Cisco IOS DHCP server will ping the selected address to detect address conflicts—addresses in the DHCP pool that are already in use by another host.

- If the server's ping receives a reply, the address is marked as a conflict and is removed from the pool—it won't be assigned to another host until the conflict is resolved and it is cleared with `clear ip dhcp conflict` {* | *ip-address*}.

- Use `show ip dhcp conflict` to view address conflicts.

- Network infrastructure devices typically use static IP addresses, but it's common for a router's ISP-connected interface to use DHCP to receive a dynamic IP address and default route from the ISP.

- Use `ip address dhcp` to configure a router's interface as a DHCP client.

- Use `show ip interface` *interface* to confirm that the interface's IP address was learned via DHCP, and `show ip route` to confirm that the router has learned a default route.

- Instead of each LAN's router functioning as a DHCP server, in larger networks, it's more common to use a dedicated and centralized DHCP server. This simplifies management and reduces the number of DHCP servers required.

- A DHCP relay agent is able to forward DHCP clients' broadcast DISCOVER and REQUEST messages to a remote DHCP server.

- Use `ip helper-address` *server-ip* on a router's interface to configure it as a DHCP relay agent. Make sure to configure it on the interface that will receive the clients' broadcast messages—the interface connected to the clients.

- Use `show ip interface` *interface-name* to confirm that a helper address has been configured on the interface.

- Use `ipconfig` in the Windows CLI to view basic IP settings (domain name, IP address/netmask, default gateway) and `ipconfig /all` to view more detailed information.

- Use `netstat -rn` to view the routing table in Windows, macOS, and Linux.

- Use `ifconfig` in macOS to view IP settings similar to `ipconfig`.

- Because a variety of distributions are built on top of the Linux kernel, there is some variation in how to view the IP settings.

- Some Linux distributions still support an old set of commands called *net-tools* by default, which include `ifconfig` (to view interface information) and `route` (to view the routing table).

- Other distributions use a set of commands called *iproute2*, which include `ip addr` (equivalent to `ifconfig`) and `ip route` (equivalent to `route`).

Secure Shell

This chapter covers

- Securing access to a device's console port
- Creating local user accounts
- Using Telnet to remotely access a device's CLI
- Using Secure Shell to remotely and securely access a device's CLI

When we first covered the Cisco IOS CLI in volume 1, we looked at how to connect to a device's CLI via the console port. To connect to a device's console port, you must be physically near the device—console cables are typically only a few feet in length. But what if you need to access the CLI of a device in another city or another country? Perhaps you need to troubleshoot a connection between routers that are halfway across the globe from each other. Whatever the situation, you need a better way to access the CLI of your devices.

Secure Shell (SSH), the main topic of this chapter, allows you to securely connect to devices over an IP network such as the internet. SSH is an essential protocol for managing networks, allowing you to remotely configure and verify the devices in your network, and is an important topic on the CCNA exam. In this chapter, we will cover SSH and some related topics. Specifically, we will cover the following CCNA exam topics:

- 4.8: Configure network devices for remote access using SSH
- 5.3: Configure and verify device access control using local passwords

5.1   Console port security

Anyone with a laptop and a console cable can access a network device's CLI via the console port; this is not acceptable from a security standpoint. One important step in securing a device is *physical access control*—controlling who has physical access to the device by, for example, keeping the device in a locked cabinet.

However, physical access control alone is not sufficient. You should also configure security settings on the console port to prevent unauthorized users from accessing the CLI even if they have physical access to the device.

When you connect to a device's console port and access the CLI, you are connecting to the *console line*—a "line" is a logical pathway on a Cisco device that allows you to connect to and manage the device via the CLI. The console line is used when connecting to the CLI via the console port. To secure the device's console port, you should configure the console line by using the `line con 0` command in global config mode, as in the following example:

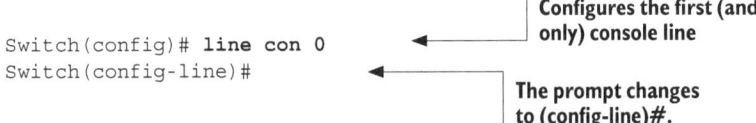

```
Switch(config)# line con 0          Configures the first (and
Switch(config-line)#                only) console line

                                    The prompt changes
                                    to (config-line)#.
```

The `0` at the end of the command indicates that this is the first console line. Actually, devices only have a single console line, meaning that there is only `line con 0`—no `line con 1`, `line con 2`, etc. The significance of having a single console line is that only one user can connect to the console port at once. In this section, we'll cover two methods of securing the console line: line password authentication and user account authentication.

> **NOTE**   The VTY lines used for remote management (i.e., via SSH) are more numerous—typically, there are 16 VTY lines. We'll cover them in sections 5.2 and 5.3.

5.1.1   Line password authentication

The simplest way to secure the console line is to configure a password on it. After a user connects their PC to the device's console port and attempts to access the CLI, they will be required to enter the password. Figure 5.1 outlines the concept.

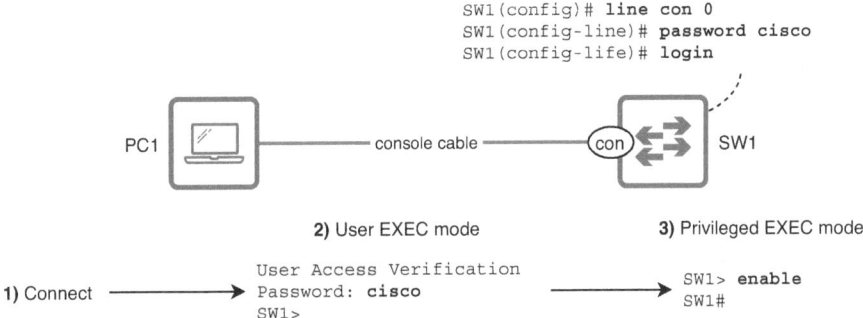

Figure 5.1 SW1's console line is secured with a password. 1) PC1 connects to the console line. 2) The user enters a password to access user EXEC mode. 3) The user issues `enable` to reach privileged EXEC mode.

The following example shows the commands I configured on SW1. Let's walk through each:

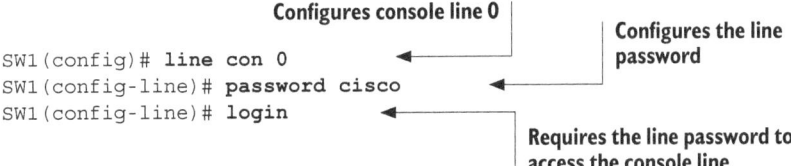

After using `line con 0` to access line config mode, I used the **password** *password* command to configure the line password. However, configuring the password alone is not enough; you also need to use the **login** command. This command specifies that users must enter the line password to access the console line; without this, the password doesn't take effect. The following example shows the process of logging in after these configurations:

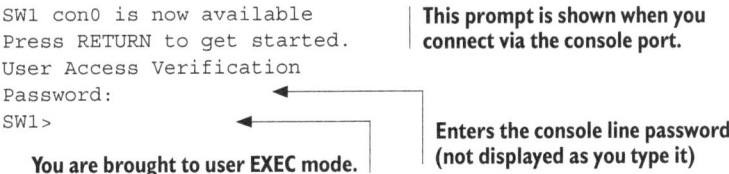

After entering the password, you are brought to user EXEC mode. From user EXEC mode, you can then use the **enable** command to access privileged EXEC mode. Although I omitted it from the example, you should also configure an enable secret to password-protect privileged EXEC mode—we covered the **enable secret** command in chapter 5 of volume 1.

NOTE   By default, users will be logged out of the CLI after 10 minutes of inactivity. You can change this with the **exec-timeout** *minutes* command in line config mode.

5.1.2   *User account authentication*

Instead of configuring a password directly on the console line, you can configure user accounts and require users to log in using one of those accounts. Figure 5.2 shows how to configure this and also demonstrates the login process.

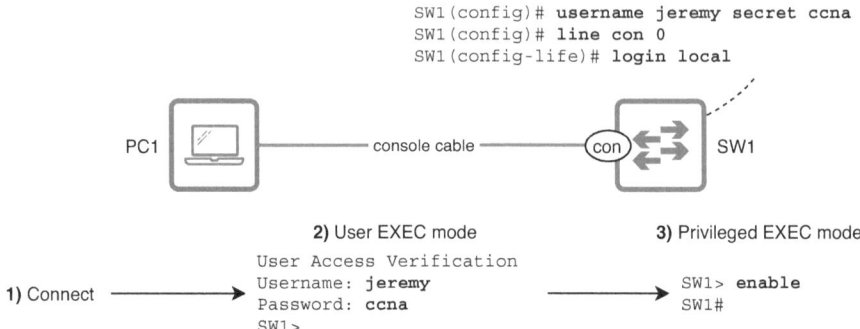

Figure 5.2   SW1's console line is secured with a user account. 1) PC1 connects to the console line. 2) The user enters a username and password to access user EXEC mode. 3) The user issues enable **to reach privileged EXEC mode.**

The command to create an account is **username** *username* **secret** *password* (the password will be saved as a secure hash thanks to the **secret** keyword). However, like the line password in the previous section, creating an account isn't enough on its own. You must use the **login local** command in line config mode to tell the device to require users to log in using one of the accounts on the local device.

NOTE   You can use the **username** *username* **password** *password* command to configure a password that will be saved in cleartext. However, you should always use **secret**—cleartext passwords are not secure. This is the same as the distinction between the **enable password** and **enable secret** that we covered in chapter 5 of volume 1.

The following example shows the login process after creating a user account and then configuring the **login local** command on the console line:

```
SW1 con0 is now available
Press RETURN to get started.
User Access Verification
Username: jeremy
```

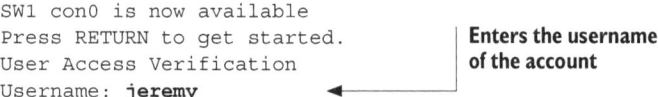

Enters the username of the account

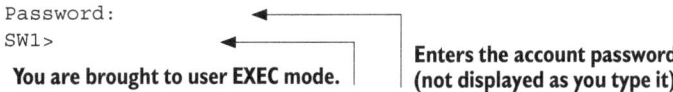

```
Password:
SW1>
```

You are brought to user EXEC mode.

Enters the account password (not displayed as you type it)

EXAM TIP `login` and `login local` cannot be configured at the same time; if you configure one, it will overwrite the other. If `login` is set, users must authenticate with the line password, regardless of any configured user accounts. If `login local` is set, users must authenticate with a user account, even if a line password is set.

In a small network or a low-sensitivity environment such as a lab, a simple line password with the `login` command might be acceptable, but in general, you should opt for user account authentication with the `login local` command. User accounts are more secure than simple passwords, allow for more granular access control, and allow you to track each user's activity on the device. An even better option is to use an Authentication, Authorization, and Accounting (AAA) server that provides centralized control; we will cover AAA concepts in chapter 11, but AAA configuration is beyond the scope of the CCNA exam.

Cisco IOS privilege levels

Cisco IOS uses privilege levels to control a user's access to CLI commands. There are 16 privilege levels: 0 to 15. By default, users connecting to the device via the console or VTY lines have a privilege level of 1; this is also known as user EXEC mode and allows limited read-only access to the device. After using the `enable` command, the user is given privilege level 15; this is also known as privileged EXEC mode and gives full control of the device.

You can specify a user's default privilege level when creating an account: `username` *username* `privilege` *level* `secret` *password*. For example, `username jeremy privilege 15 secret ccna` would grant user jeremy privilege level 15 (privileged EXEC mode) immediately upon logging in; there would be no need to issue the `enable` command.

The remaining privilege levels are not used by default but provide a means of precisely controlling which users can use which commands. You can assign different privilege levels (privilege level 5, 10, etc.) to user accounts and assign different privilege levels to each command. This allows for a high degree of customization, although such detailed configurations are beyond the scope of the CCNA exam.

For example, first-level support staff may only need access to basic commands for information gathering and making simple configuration changes (i.e., enabling/disabling interfaces). If a problem requires more drastic interventions, it can be escalated to a more senior engineer with a higher privilege level. However, there are tradeoffs to overly granular access control, as such setups can become complex and pose problems if a higher-privilege user is needed but not available.

5.2   *Remote management*

The console port is useful for initially configuring a device. However, once the device is set up and connected to the network, remote management is much more convenient; there is no need to be physically near a device to access the CLI to configure the device or check its status. There are two main options for remotely accessing the CLI of a Cisco router or switch: Telnet and SSH. In this section, we'll take a look at the concept of management IP addresses and then cover Telnet as an introduction to remote device management.

5.2.1   *Management IP addresses*

Telnet and SSH both use a client-server model; the user's computer is the client, and the device (i.e., router or switch) that accepts the connection from the client is the server. To be able to communicate, the client and server both need IP addresses. To connect to a router with SSH, for example, you can connect to the IP address of any of its interfaces.

What about switches? When covering VLANs in chapter 12 of volume 1, we looked at Layer 3 switches—switches that, in addition to switching frames, have an internal virtual router that can route packets. To remotely manage a Layer 3 switch, you can use Telnet or SSH to connect to the IP address of one of its switch virtual interfaces (SVIs) or routed ports. But Layer 2 switches operate only at Layer 2, forwarding frames without even considering the IP addresses of the packets they encapsulate. Layer 2 switches can't have IP addresses—right?

Wrong! Although Layer 2 switches can't route packets (can't forward packets between different networks), they can send and receive packets like any other network host. To enable a Layer 2 switch to do so, you can configure one or more SVIs. Figure 5.3 demonstrates the internal logic of Layer 2 and Layer 3 switches.

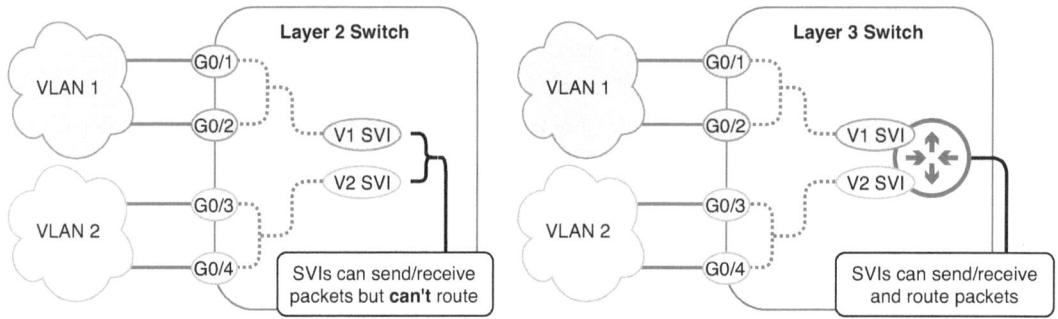

Figure 5.3   The internal logic of Layer 2 and Layer 3 switches. The Layer 2 switch (left) can send and receive packets using its SVIs but can't route packets between them. The Layer 3 switch (right) can send, receive, and also route packets.

Sending, receiving, and forwarding

For a quick refresher, let's review these key terms. *Sending* is the act of originating data and transmitting it over a network. If you ping 8.8.8.8 from your PC, your PC sends the ping to 8.8.8.8. *Receiving* is the act of accepting incoming data from the network. If you ping 8.8.8.8 from your PC, 8.8.8.8 will receive the ping from your PC.

Forwarding is the act of moving data closer to its destination. If you ping 8.8.8.8 from your PC, all of the network infrastructure devices between your PC and the 8.8.8.8 server will forward the ping from your PC to 8.8.8.8. More specifically, *routing* is the act of forwarding packets, and *switching* is the act of forwarding frames.

Layer 2 switches, just like Layer 3 switches, can be configured with SVIs—Layer 3 virtual interfaces that can send and receive packets. SVIs provide the Layer 3 interface (and IP address) necessary to remotely connect to and manage a Layer 2 switch. Figure 5.4 shows how to configure an SVI and default gateway on a Layer 2 switch.

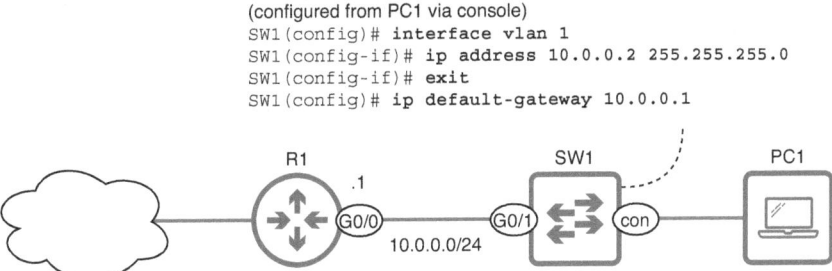

Figure 5.4 Configuring an SVI and default gateway on a Layer 2 switch

Configuring an SVI is the same as we covered when studying VLANs; use the `interface vlan` `vlan-id` command to create the SVI. Then use `ip address` `ip-address netmask` to configure the IP address (like on any other Layer 3 interface).

The next command is new: from global config mode, use `ip default-gateway` `ip-address` to specify the switch's default gateway. A Layer 2 switch doesn't route packets and therefore doesn't need a routing table. However, it does need to know the IP address of the router it should send packets destined for remote hosts to—its default gateway. In the following example, I configure SW1's VLAN 1 SVI and default gateway and then confirm:

```
SW1(config)# interface vlan 1                                    Configures SW1's VLAN 1 SVI
SW1(config-if)# ip address 10.0.0.2 255.255.255.0
SW1(config-if)# exit
SW1(config)# ip default-gateway 10.0.0.1          ◄──── Configures R1 as SW1's default gateway
SW1(config)# do show ip interface brief
Interface          IP-Address      OK? Method Status          Protocol
```

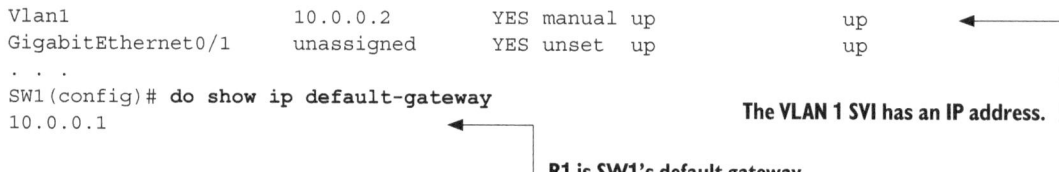

```
Vlan1                    10.0.0.2        YES manual up              up
GigabitEthernet0/1       unassigned      YES unset  up              up
. . .
SW1(config)# do show ip default-gateway
10.0.0.1
```

The VLAN 1 SVI has an IP address.

R1 is SW1's default gateway.

After these configurations, SW1 is now ready to send and receive packets using its VLAN 1 SVI. To send packets to other hosts in its local network (10.0.0.0/24), SW1 will send them in frames destined directly for the destination host. To send packets to hosts in remote networks, SW1 will send them in frames destined for the default gateway (R1).

Management IP address best practices

Any Layer 3 interface's IP address can be used to connect to and manage a device, unless there is a specific reason it cannot be used (such as an ACL blocking certain traffic on that interface). However, it's common to configure a *management IP address*—an IP address configured for the specific purpose of remote management. Let's cover a couple of best practices regarding management IP addresses.

A router's management IP address is usually configured on a loopback interface, providing a stable IP address that isn't dependent on the status of any particular physical port. A switch's management IP address is usually configured on the SVI of a specific VLAN known as the *management VLAN*—a VLAN that doesn't carry regular traffic from network users but is dedicated to the remote management of devices. This is for security purposes; management traffic should be kept isolated from other traffic on the network.

5.2.2   Configuring Telnet

Telnet, which is short for "teletype network," was developed in 1969—quite a long time ago as far as computer networks are concerned. For several reasons, Telnet has largely been replaced by SSH. The main reason is security—Telnet sends data in cleartext, not encrypted text. For example, if you enter a password to log in to a device, that password is sent across the network as is, and any attacker who gets a copy of that packet will now know the device's password.

Although Telnet's use cases are limited, it is still supported on most network devices. And despite not being explicitly mentioned in the CCNA exam topics list, it serves as a useful stepping stone to learn the basics of remote management before learning SSH itself (and I wouldn't be surprised to find a question or two that mention Telnet on the exam). Figure 5.5 shows how to configure Telnet on a Cisco IOS device.

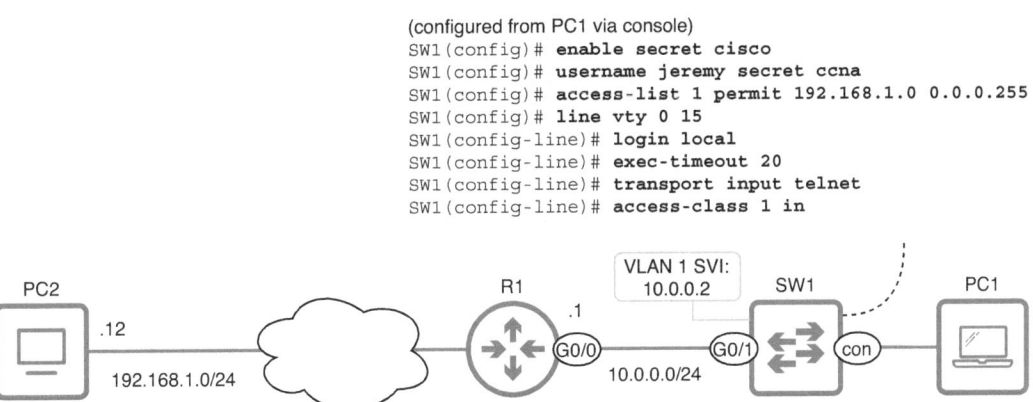

```
(configured from PC1 via console)
SW1(config)# enable secret cisco
SW1(config)# username jeremy secret ccna
SW1(config)# access-list 1 permit 192.168.1.0 0.0.0.255
SW1(config)# line vty 0 15
SW1(config-line)# login local
SW1(config-line)# exec-timeout 20
SW1(config-line)# transport input telnet
SW1(config-line)# access-class 1 in
```

Figure 5.5   Enabling Telnet on SW1. Users must log in with a local user account and will be logged out after 20 minutes of inactivity. Only Telnet can be used to connect to the VTY lines, and only hosts in 192.168.1.0/24 are permitted.

First, I configured an enable secret to password-protect privileged EXEC mode. This is a good idea in any case, but it's essential when configuring Telnet. If there is no enable secret (or enable password), the **enable** command won't work when connected to the device with Telnet (or SSH). Instead, you'll get a message like in the following example:

```
SW1> enable
% No password set
SW1>
```

I then configured a user account: **username jeremy secret ccna**. When using Telnet, you can configure either password-only authentication (**login**) or local user account authentication (**login local**) on the VTY lines; the latter is more secure, so I configured a user account.

In the next command, I configured an ACL, permitting only packets sourced from hosts in 192.168.1.0/24, such as PC2: **access-list 1 permit 192.168.1.0 0.0.0.255**. Although optional, it's generally a good practice to limit which hosts can access the VTY lines of your devices. In a later command, I will apply this ACL to the VTY lines (not to an interface, as we covered in chapters 23 and 24 of volume 1).

Now it's time to configure the VTY lines. Connecting to the CLI via a device's console port uses the console line, but connecting to the CLI via either Telnet or SSH uses the *Virtual Teletype* (VTY) lines. Whereas there is only a single console line (accessed with **line con 0**), there are typically 16 VTY lines; you can access a range of them with **line vty** *first-line last-line*. In most cases, you should configure all VTY lines identically by using **line vty 0 15**.

> **NOTE** The significance of there being 16 VTY lines is that up to 16 users can be connected to the device's CLI at once via Telnet or SSH—one per VTY line.

From line config mode, I first used **login local** to make SW1 require authentication with one of the accounts on the local device—for example, the account that I configured earlier in this example. I then used the **exec-timeout 20** command to modify the default inactivity timeout—this command is optional. In this case, instead of users being logged out after the default 10 minutes of inactivity, they will be logged out after 20.

The next command I used was **transport input** *protocol*. The effect of this command is to allow users to connect to the VTY lines only with the specified protocol(s). In addition to Telnet and SSH, devices may support VTY line connections from a variety of protocols (such as rlogin—remote login). Best practice is to use this command to allow only the necessary protocol(s). In this example, I used **transport input telnet** to allow only Telnet, but in practice, you should most likely use **transport input ssh**—we'll do that in the next section. The following are some different options for this command:

- **transport input telnet**—Allows only Telnet connections
- **transport input ssh**—Allows only SSH connections
- **transport input telnet ssh** (or **ssh telnet**)—Allows both Telnet and SSH
- **transport input all**—Allows connections with all supported protocols
- **transport input none**—Allows no connections to the VTY lines

The final command I used was the **access-class** *acl* **in** command, applying the ACL I previously configured to the VTY lines. By applying an ACL to the VTY lines, you can control connections to the VTY lines without affecting other traffic.

EXAM TIP   Take a minute to review ACL-related commands: **access-list** and **ip access-list** create ACLs, **ip access-group** applies ACLs to interfaces, and **access-class** applies ACLs to the VTY lines.

After completing all of these configurations, let's see how SW1's VTY lines look in the running-config. In the following example, notice that even though I configured all 16 VTY lines at once with **line vty 0 15**, they are split into two separate groups in the configuration file. Older Cisco devices only supported five VTY lines (0–4), so this division maintains backward compatibility with older devices:

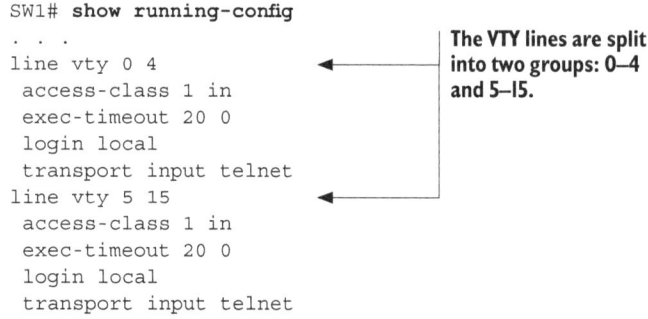

```
SW1# show running-config
. . .
line vty 0 4
 access-class 1 in
 exec-timeout 20 0
 login local
 transport input telnet
line vty 5 15
 access-class 1 in
 exec-timeout 20 0
 login local
 transport input telnet
```

The VTY lines are split into two groups: 0–4 and 5–15.

SW1 is now ready to accept Telnet connections. TCP servers (i.e., routers and switches you connect to and configure via Telnet) listen on TCP port 23—memorize that port! In the following example, I use the `telnet` command from PC2 (a Linux host) to connect to the CLI of SW1:

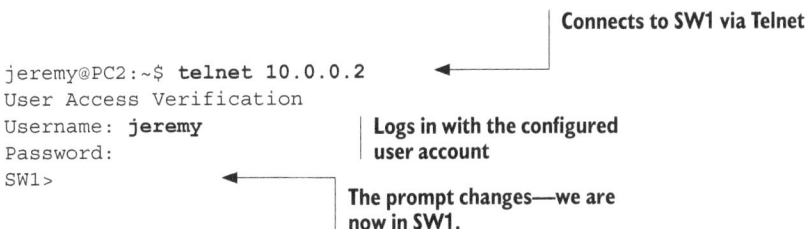

```
jeremy@PC2:~$ telnet 10.0.0.2      ◀─────   Connects to SW1 via Telnet
User Access Verification
Username: jeremy                   Logs in with the configured
Password:                          user account
SW1>                    ◀─────
                                   The prompt changes—we are
                                   now in SW1.
```

5.3 Secure Shell

Let's move on to the main topic of this chapter: Secure Shell (SSH). SSH serves a similar purpose to Telnet; it allows you to remotely connect to the CLI of network devices over a network. However, the major difference is that SSH is secure, as the name implies—it encrypts communications between the client (your PC) and the server (the network device you are connecting to). Even if an attacker gains access to your communications, the messages are encrypted—they will appear as an unintelligible mess to anyone but the intended destination host. SSH configuration consists of two main steps:

1 Generating cryptographic RSA keys
2 Enabling SSH connections on the VTY lines

However, we'll cover some other optional (but recommended) configurations as well. As you'll see, the configurations are very similar to those we have covered previously in this chapter, with just one extra step: generating cryptographic keys. In this section, we'll look at how to generate the cryptographic keys necessary for SSH and how to configure SSH in Cisco IOS.

5.3.1 Generating RSA keys

SSH requires a pair of cryptographic keys to encrypt and decrypt messages. A *cryptographic key* is a piece of information—basically, a string of characters—that is used as input for cryptographic algorithms. Specifically, we need to generate *RSA keys*—cryptographic keys that use the RSA algorithm (RSA stands for Rivest-Shamir-Adleman, the creators of RSA). Using the `show ip ssh` command on a Cisco IOS device without RSA keys gives the following output:

```
SW1# show ip ssh                                              SSH is disabled.
SSH Disabled - version 1.99
%Please create RSA keys to enable SSH (and of atleast 768 bits for SSH v2).  ◀─
. . .
                                              RSA keys are required to enable
                                              SSH (at least 768 bits for SSHv2).
```

So let's generate some RSA keys on the device. The command to do so is `crypto key generate rsa` in global config mode. In the following example, I attempt to use that command but receive an error message:

```
SW1(config)# crypto key generate rsa
% Please define a domain-name first.
```

Generates an
RSA key pair

A domain name is needed
to generate the keys.

The command is rejected because SW1 does not have a domain name. A domain name is needed because the key pair needs a name, and IOS uses the device's FQDN to name the keys. Depending on the device, you may be required to configure a non-default hostname as well; in this case, I have already configured SW1's hostname, but some devices may show an error message like this:

```
Router(config)# crypto key generate rsa
% Please define a hostname other than Router.
```

The default hostname
is rejected.

In the following example, I configure SW1's domain name and then successfully generate the RSA key pair:

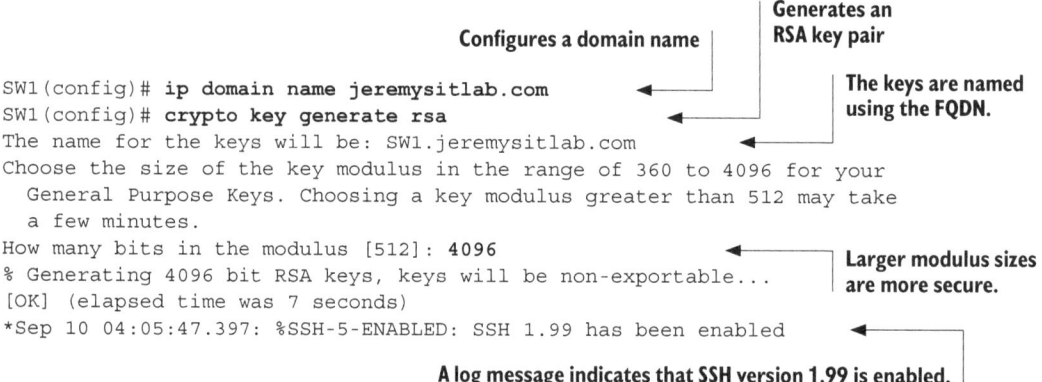

Configures a domain name

Generates an
RSA key pair

```
SW1(config)# ip domain name jeremysitlab.com
SW1(config)# crypto key generate rsa
The name for the keys will be: SW1.jeremysitlab.com
Choose the size of the key modulus in the range of 360 to 4096 for your
  General Purpose Keys. Choosing a key modulus greater than 512 may take
  a few minutes.
How many bits in the modulus [512]: 4096
% Generating 4096 bit RSA keys, keys will be non-exportable...
[OK] (elapsed time was 7 seconds)
*Sep 10 04:05:47.397: %SSH-5-ENABLED: SSH 1.99 has been enabled
```

The keys are named
using the FQDN.

Larger modulus sizes
are more secure.

A log message indicates that SSH version 1.99 is enabled.

> **NOTE**   You can manually specify a name for the key pair with `crypto key generate rsa label` *name*. In that case, an FQDN isn't needed to generate the keys. This also allows you to generate multiple key pairs by giving each pair a unique name, which may be necessary in networks with strict security policies requiring different key pairs for different purposes.

When generating RSA keys, you are asked to specify the size of the key *modulus* (a value that determines the strength of the encryption—larger is more secure). The modulus size is usually referred to as the *key size* or *key length*, although those terms aren't entirely accurate; the keys have other components as well. Cisco recommends modulus sizes of at least 2,048 bits. In fact, in newer software versions, SSH can't even be used with modulus sizes smaller than 2,048 bits.

NOTE You can also specify the modulus size in the original command: `crypto key generate rsa modulus` *bits*.

One more thing to point out about the previous output is `SSH 1.99 has been enabled`. You can also confirm this with **show ip ssh**:

```
SW1# show ip ssh
SSH Enabled - version 1.99          ◄──────  After configuring RSA
. . .                                        keys, SSH is enabled.
```

There are two major versions of SSH: SSH version 1 (SSHv1) and SSH version 2 (SSHv2). So what's SSH version 1.99? It's not actually a separate version of SSH—it just means that the server accepts both SSHv1 and SSHv2 connections from clients. SSHv2 offers security and performance advantages over SSHv1, so in most cases, you should allow only SSHv2; we'll cover how to do that in the next section.

5.3.2 Configuring SSH

Now that SW1 has an RSA key pair, we can configure it to accept SSH connections on its VTY lines. Figure 5.6 shows how to configure SSH on a Cisco IOS device.

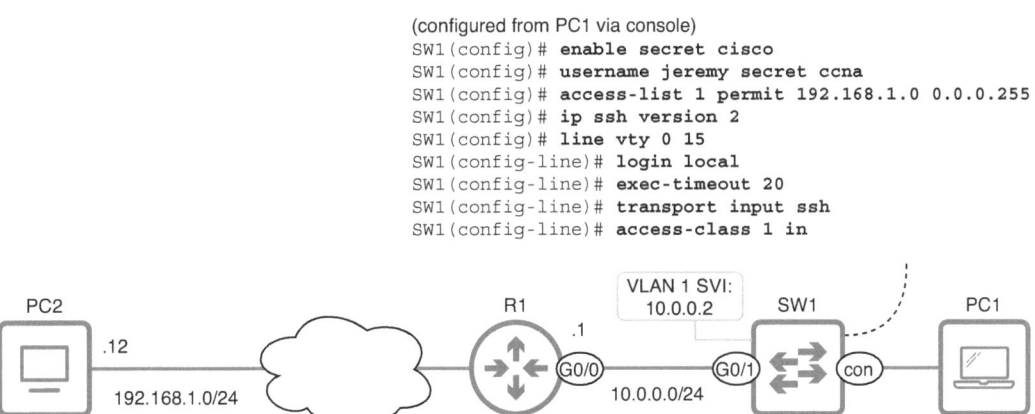

```
(configured from PC1 via console)
SW1(config)# enable secret cisco
SW1(config)# username jeremy secret ccna
SW1(config)# access-list 1 permit 192.168.1.0 0.0.0.255
SW1(config)# ip ssh version 2
SW1(config)# line vty 0 15
SW1(config-line)# login local
SW1(config-line)# exec-timeout 20
SW1(config-line)# transport input ssh
SW1(config-line)# access-class 1 in
```

Figure 5.6 Enabling SSHv2 on SW1. Users must log in with a local user account and will be logged out after 20 minutes of inactivity. Only SSH can be used to connect to the VTY lines, and only hosts in 192.168.1.0/24 are permitted.

The following example shows SW1's configurations:

```
SW1(config)# enable secret cisco           ─┐  Configures an enable secret
SW1(config)# username jeremy secret ccna    │  and user account
SW1(config)# access-list 1 permit 192.168.1.0 0.0.0.255   ◄── Creates an ACL to limit
SW1(config)# ip ssh version 2         ◄────                   access to the VTY lines

                                           Limits connections to SSH version 2 only
```

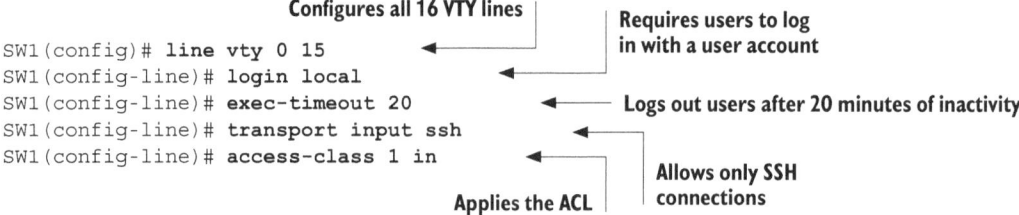

The configurations are nearly identical to the Telnet configurations we covered previously. First, I configured an enable secret, which is necessary to be able to access privileged EXEC mode when connected to the VTY lines. I also configured a user account since I will later configure `login local` on the VTY lines. I configured an ACL this time too; it's considered a best practice to limit which hosts can connect to the VTY lines.

I then issued the `ip ssh version 2` command to allow only SSHv2. SSHv1.99 is enabled by default, meaning SW1 accepts both SSHv1 and SSHv2 connections. However, SSHv2 is more secure than SSHv1, so best practice is to limit connections to SSHv2 only.

NOTE   The device's RSA key pair's modulus size must be at least 768 bits to support SSHv2; otherwise, only SSHv1 can be used.

I then moved on to configure the VTY lines, configuring all 16 at once with the `line vty 0 15` command. The VTY line configurations should look familiar to those in the Telnet section: `login local`, `exec-timeout`, `transport input`, and `access-class`. The only difference is that I configured `transport input ssh` to allow only SSH connections to the VTY lines—not Telnet. This is a best practice in real networks; you should be using SSH instead of Telnet.

SW1 is now ready to accept SSH connections on TCP port 22—another port number to memorize! To connect to a device with SSH, use the `ssh -l` *username ip-address* command, as in the following example:

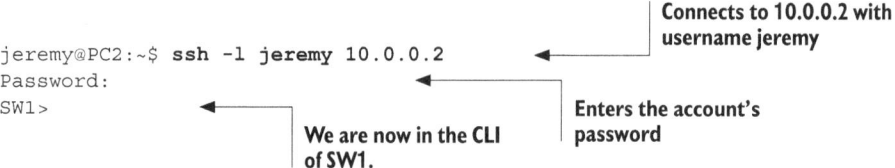

Cisco IOS devices can use SSH to connect too. In the following example, I use SSH on a Cisco router (R1) to connect to the CLI of SW1:

```
R1# ssh -l jeremy 10.0.0.2
Password:
SW1>
```

NOTE   The -l means "login name"—the username you want to log in with. Most systems will support the `ssh  -l` command: Windows, macOS, Linux, Cisco IOS, etc. Another option is `ssh  username@ip-address`—for example, `ssh jeremy@10.0.0.2`. However, only the former option works in Cisco IOS.

Summary

- To secure a network device's console port, *physical access control*—such as locking the device in a cabinet—is essential. However, security settings should also be configured to prevent unauthorized users from accessing the CLI via the console port.
- A *line* is a logical pathway that allows you to connect to and manage the device via the CLI. Console port connections use the console line.
- Use `line con 0` to access line config mode for the console line. There is only one console line, so only one user can connect via the console port at once.
- Use `password` *password* in line config mode to configure a line password and `login` to require users to enter that password to access that line (i.e., the console line).
- By default, users will be logged out of the CLI after 10 minutes of inactivity. Use `exec-timeout` *minutes* to modify this behavior (`exec-timeout 0` disables the timer).
- Use `username` *username* `secret` *password* to configure user accounts.
- Use `login local` in line config mode to require users to log in with one of the user accounts on the device when connecting via the line.
- There are two main options for remotely accessing the CLI of a Cisco router or switch: Telnet and SSH.
- Telnet and SSH both use a client-server model; the user's computer is the client, and the device that accepts the connection from the client is the server.
- The client and server both need IP addresses to communicate.
- Routers and Layer 3 switches, by their nature, have multiple Layer 3 interfaces with IP addresses; you can connect to any of those IP addresses with Telnet or SSH.
- Although Layer 2 switches cannot route packets, they can send and receive packets using switch virtual interfaces (SVIs). To remotely manage a Layer 2 switch, configure an SVI with an IP address.
- To configure a Layer 2 switch's SVI, use `interface vlan` *vlan-id* and assign an IP address with `ip address` *ip-address netmask*. Then configure the default gateway with `ip default-gateway` *ip-address*.
- *Telnet* (teletype network) is a protocol that allows you to remotely connect to the CLI of devices, like routers and switches. However, Telnet is not secure because it sends data in cleartext—no encryption.

- If the device does not have an enable secret (or enable password), users will not be able to use the **enable** command when connected via Telnet or SSH.

- Telnet and SSH connections use the *Virtual Teletype* (VTY) lines. There are usually 16 VTY lines in total (0–15), meaning that up to 16 users can be connected at once.

- The **login**, **login local**, and **exec-timeout** commands work on the VTY lines the same as they do on the console line.

- Use the **transport input** *protocol* command to control which protocol(s) can be used to connect to the VTY lines. **transport input telnet** allows only Telnet.

- Optionally, you can configure an ACL and apply it to the VTY lines with **access -class** *acl* **in**. This controls which hosts can connect to the VTY lines but doesn't affect other traffic entering/exiting the device's interfaces.

- The 16 VTY lines are divided into two groups in the configuration files: **line vty 0 4** and **line vty 5 15**. This is for backward compatibility.

- Telnet servers (i.e., Telnet-enabled routers and switches) listen on TCP port 23.

- *Secure Shell* (SSH) serves a similar function to Telnet, allowing SSH clients (i.e., PCs) to remotely connect to the CLI of SSH servers (i.e., routers and switches). However, SSH is much more secure because it encrypts communications.

- SSH requires a pair of cryptographic keys, specifically *RSA keys*. Use **crypto key generate rsa** in global config mode to generate them.

- By default, the device will name the key pair using the device's FQDN, so a hostname and domain name must be configured first. Or you can use **crypto key generate rsa label** *name* to manually specify the name.

- When generating the RSA keys, you must specify the size of the key *modulus*—a value that determines the strength of the encryption (a larger modulus is stronger).

- Although the modulus is one component of the keys, the modulus size is often called the *key size*.

- Cisco recommends modulus sizes of at least 2,048 bits—in newer software versions, this is the minimum size that can be used with SSH.

- When you use **crypto key generate rsa**, it will ask you the modulus size. Or you can specify it in the original command: **crypto key generate rsa modulus** *size*.

- After creating RSA keys, **show ip ssh** should show that SSH is enabled.

- There are two major versions of SSH: SSHv1 and SSHv2. Version 1.99 is enabled on Cisco devices by default; this means the device accepts both SSHv1 and SSHv2 connections.

- After creating the RSA keys, SSH configuration is nearly identical to Telnet configuration. In global config mode, use **ip ssh version 2** to limit SSH connections to SSHv2 only (optional but recommended).

- The device's RSA key pair's modulus size must be at least 768 bits to support SSHv2.

- Best practice is to use **transport input ssh** to allow only SSH connections to the VTY lines; Telnet is not secure.

- Use **ssh -l** *username ip-address* to connect to a device with SSH. This command works in most operating systems: Cisco IOS, Windows, macOS, Linux, etc.

- **ssh** *username@ip-address* also works in most OSs (but not Cisco IOS).

- SSH servers listen on TCP port 22.

Simple Network Management Protocol

6

This chapter covers

- Managing network devices with Simple Network Management Protocol (SNMP)
- The SNMP network management station and its managed devices
- The three main versions of SNMP
- Securing SNMP with passwords, user authentication, and encryption

Simple Network Management Protocol (SNMP) is, as the name states, a protocol that facilitates the management of networks—specifically, the management of the devices that make up the network. Whether it is simple is perhaps subjective; like most topics, there is plenty of complexity to be found if you dig deep enough!

SNMP allows an admin to centrally monitor the status of devices, trigger alerts for specific events, and even modify device configurations without having to log into a device's CLI. Various types of devices can be managed using SNMP: network devices, like routers and switches; servers; user devices, like PCs and laptops; printers; and many more. For our purposes, we will focus on managing Cisco routers and switches with SNMP.

SNMP is CCNA exam topic 4.4: Explain the function of SNMP in network operations. It's a CCNA exam topic for a good reason: SNMP is widely used in networks of all sizes to provide real-time monitoring and management capabilities that are essential to modern network operations.

6.1 *SNMP operations and components*

The two main components of SNMP are the *network management station* (NMS) and the managed devices. The NMS is a software platform designed for monitoring and managing devices using SNMP; it is usually run on an admin's PC (in smaller networks) or a central server (in larger networks).

Each managed device organizes information about itself into a database called the *Management Information Database* (MIB), and these pieces of information are stored as variables. One variable in a device's MIB could be `GigabitEthernet0/1 status`, and the value of that variable could be `up` or `down`. Some other variables could be the internal temperature of the device, the current CPU utilization, the state of Open Shortest Path First (OSPF) neighbors, and many more; Cisco routers and switches store thousands of these variables.

In this section, we'll examine how devices can use SNMP to interact with the MIB of a device: how the NMS can read and modify MIBs and how the managed devices can notify the NMS of changes to their MIBs. Then, we'll look at the components of the NMS and the managed devices in greater detail.

> **NOTE** Although I will generally refer to the NMS in most examples in this chapter, it is possible for there to be multiple NMSs; this provides the benefit of redundancy.

6.1.1 *SNMP operations*

In this section, let's take the example of the `GigabitEthernet0/1 status` variable to demonstrate SNMP's primary operations. We'll cover how the NMS can read and modify the variables in the MIB and how the managed devices can notify the NMS when certain events occur.

READING THE MIB

The NMS can query its managed devices to get the value of one or more variables. I use the term *get* because that's the name of the SNMP message type used to do so: *Get*. Figure 6.1 demonstrates how an NMS queries a managed device to read the value of one of the variables in its MIB and then receives a Response message from the managed device.

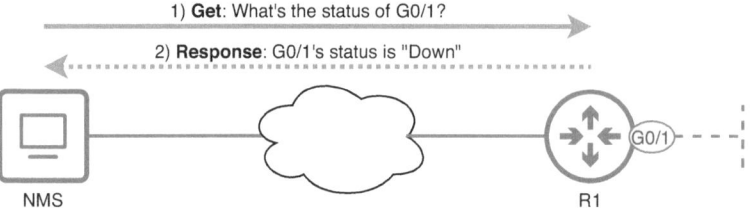

Figure 6.1   An SNMP Get and Response exchange. (1) The NMS sends a Get to R1 to learn the status of R1's G0/1 interface. (2) R1 replies, informing the NMS that G0/1 is down.

The NMS uses a Get message to query the value of one or more variables in the MIB, and the managed device then replies with a Response message, which includes the requested information. Get messages can be manually sent by an administrator as needed, but automation makes them even more powerful. Get messages can be automated from the NMS to periodically check the status of various devices within the network; this allows the NMS to actively monitor the state of the network, gather performance metrics, and collect other information.

> **NOTE**   There are three types of messages used to read the MIB: Get, GetNext, and GetBulk. We'll cover the SNMP message types in greater detail in section 6.2.

MODIFYING THE MIB

In addition to gathering information about managed devices with Get messages, the NMS can modify the values of the MIB's variables with *Set* messages. Figure 6.2 demonstrates the concept: the NMS sends a Set message to R1, instructing it to change the status of one of its interfaces. R1 changes the status as instructed and sends a Response message.

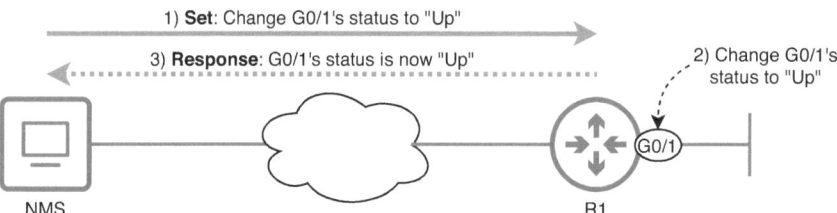

Figure 6.2   An SNMP Set and Response exchange. (1) The NMS sends a Set message instructing R1 to change its G0/1 interface to Up. (2) R1 changes G0/1's status as instructed. (3) R1 sends a Response message to the NMS.

SNMP Set messages allow you to configure the devices in your network centrally from the NMS without logging in to the CLI of each device. For example, if a new DNS server has been added to the network, the NMS can use Set messages to add the new DNS server to each router's configuration; this is simpler than logging in to each router and manually configuring it with the `ip name-server` command.

Other uses for Set messages

The example of changing R1 G0/1's status to Up is equivalent to configuring **no shutdown** on the interface. However, Set messages can be used for more than configuration changes. For example, you can initiate a system reboot or shutdown via a Set message. You can also use Set messages to make devices back up their configuration files to a central file server. This is more efficient than doing so manually via each device's CLI, one by one.

NOTIFYING THE NMS

The final SNMP operation is notifying the NMS. Managed devices can be configured to send notifications to the NMS when specific events occur. Figure 6.3 shows an example: R1's G0/1 interface goes down (perhaps due to a hardware malfunction or a cut cable), and R1 sends a Trap message to the NMS. Whereas Get messages are used to periodically retrieve information from managed devices, Trap messages allow managed devices to immediately notify the NMS when an event occurs, unsolicited by the NMS.

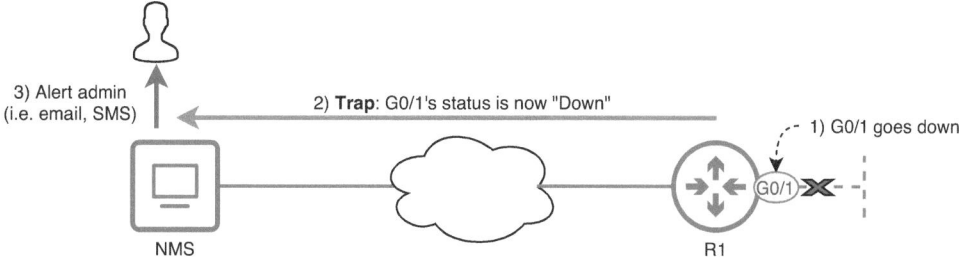

Figure 6.3   Notifying the NMS with a Trap message. (1) R1 G0/1 goes down. (2) R1 notifies the NMS of the event with a Trap message. (3) The NMS notifies an admin via an email or SMS text message.

Figure 6.3 also shows the NMS alerting an admin of the event with an email or SMS text message; this isn't a feature of the SNMP protocol itself but can be implemented in most SNMP applications. Such alerts are very helpful in enabling the admin to respond quickly to serious events that occur on the network.

6.1.2   SNMP components

We've looked at the two main components of SNMP: the NMS and the managed devices. Each device that uses SNMP, whether it's an NMS or a managed device, runs SNMP software that can be called the device's *SNMP entity*. Each device's SNMP entity consists of a couple of components, as shown in figure 6.4.

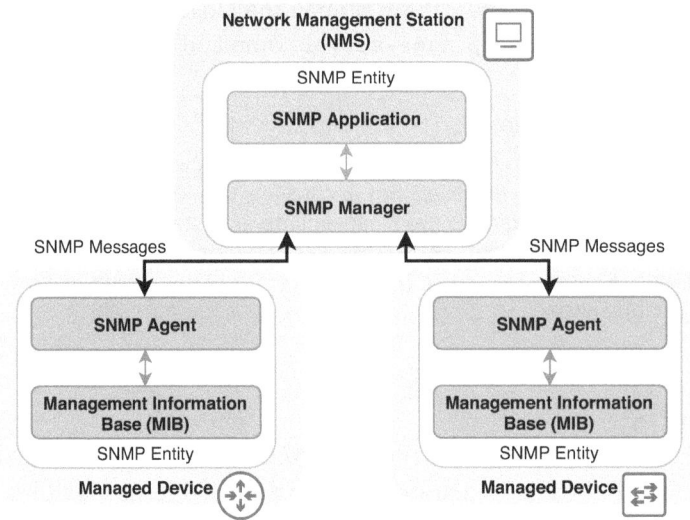

Figure 6.4   The components of the NMS's and managed devices' SNMP entities. The NMS's SNMP entity consists of the SNMP manager and SNMP application(s). The managed devices' SNMP entities consist of the SNMP agent and the MIB.

The SNMP entity on the NMS consists of an SNMP manager and an SNMP application, and the SNMP entity on each managed device consists of an SNMP agent and an MIB. In this section, we'll examine each of these components.

> **EXAM TIP**   Make sure you can identify which components reside on the NMS and which reside on the managed devices.

SNMP MANAGERS AND AGENTS

The SNMP manager and SNMP agent serve as the interface between the NMS and a managed device. The *SNMP manager* runs on the NMS and interacts with the *SNMP agent* that runs on each managed device.

The SNMP manager running on the NMS sends messages (i.e., Get, Set) to the SNMP agent running on each of its managed devices; the agent listens for these messages on UDP port 161 and then responds accordingly (i.e., with the requested information about the device the agent is running on). Similarly, the SNMP agent running on each managed device sends messages (i.e., Response, Trap) to the SNMP manager on the NMS; the manager listens on UDP port 162.

> **EXAM TIP**   Memorize those port numbers! SNMP managers listen on UDP port 162, and SNMP agents listen on UDP port 161.

SNMP APPLICATIONS

An SNMP application is a piece of software that allows a human to interact with SNMP, usually through a graphical user interface (GUI). Through the application, an admin can control how they want to use SNMP to monitor and manage their network devices. Figure 6.5 shows a screenshot from PRTG Network Monitor, a network-monitoring tool that uses SNMP (although it is not exclusively an SNMP application).

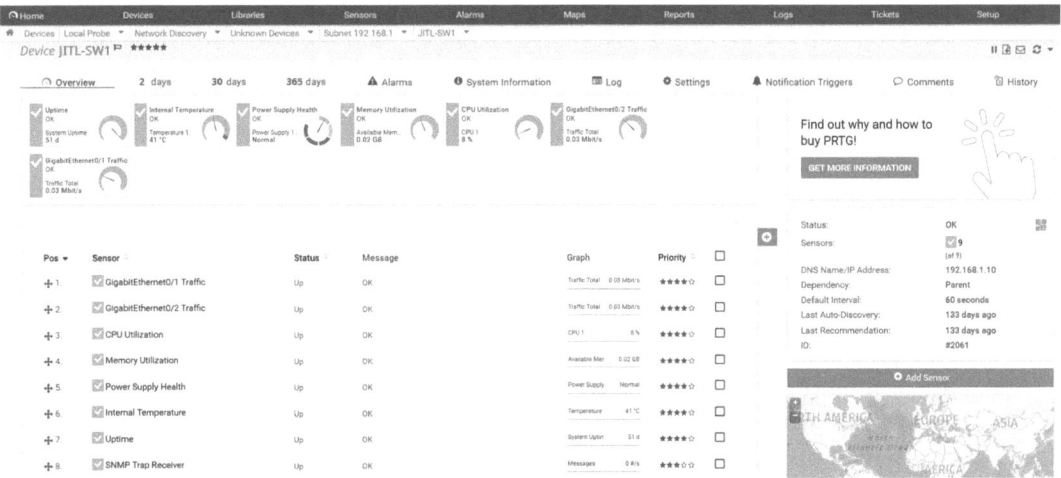

Figure 6.5   The GUI of PRTG Network Monitor, an SNMP application

I have configured PRTG to send SNMP Get messages periodically (every 60 seconds) to the devices in my home network to monitor things like the rate of traffic sent and received by their interfaces, CPU and memory utilization, power supply health, internal temperature, and others. Using PRTG, I can check the current value of each monitored variable and view graphs that display historical data—for example, to view the traffic rate on my router's internet connection for the past day, month, or year.

> **EXAM TIP**   You are not expected to know or be able to set up any particular SNMP application for the CCNA. Just understand its role as SNMP's human interface.

THE SNMP MIB

The Management Information Base (MIB) is the database in which each managed device organizes information about itself; as we covered before, this information is stored as a series of variables. Directly interacting with the MIB is the agent's job; for example, when the agent receives a Get message from the manager, the agent will look up the requested variables, retrieve their values, and send them to the manager in a Response message.

Each variable is given an *object identifier* (OID) that uniquely identifies it. For example, 1.3.6.1.2.1.2.2.1.8 is the OID for interface operational status; the manager can query this OID to learn the status of a particular interface. OIDs are hierarchically organized into a tree-like structure similar to the DNS hierarchy; each number in the OID represents a different level or branch in the tree. Figure 6.6 demonstrates this tree-like structure.

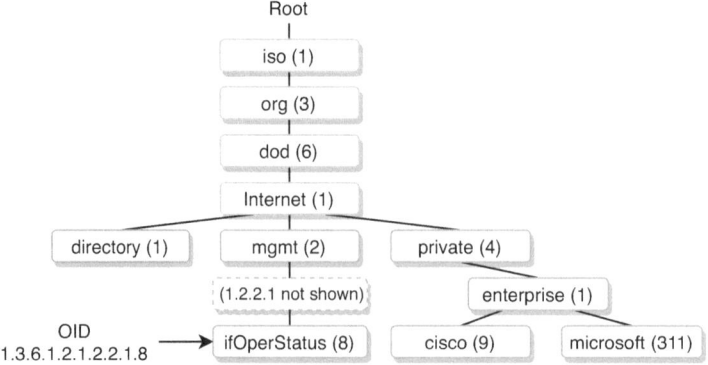

Figure 6.6   A small segment of the SNMP OID hierarchy. 1.3.6.1.2.1.2.2.1.8 is the OID of the `ifOperStatus` variable.

OIDs can be complex and lengthy, making them difficult to remember or work with directly. To simplify this, SNMP applications like PRTG translate these OIDs into user-friendly, descriptive names. So, while the SNMP manager might send a Get for an OID like 1.3.6.1.4.1.9.9.109.1.1.1.1.4, the SNMP application's interface will display this as something more understandable, such as "CPU Utilization." This way, the application removes the need for the user to deal with the intricate details of OIDs.

NOTE   You can explore different OIDs at https://oidref.com/. For example, https://oidref.com/1.3.6.1.2.1.2.2.1.8 and https://oidref.com/1.3.6.1.4.1.9.9.1 09.1.1.1.1.4 are the two example OIDs mentioned in this section.

Vendor-specific OIDs

Vendors can define their own OIDs, and in some cases, the NMS might not be aware of them by default. However, vendors (i.e., Cisco) often provide MIB files for download that define the specific OIDs used by their devices. You can import these MIB files into the NMS to allow it to properly interpret those OIDs when receiving them in Traps and other messages.

6.2   *SNMP messages*

Now that we've covered the basics of SNMP—what it does and its components—let's dig into some more details. In addition to the messages we've covered so far, SNMP includes a few more message types that the NMS and managed devices can exchange with each other. We've already covered four different SNMP message types: Get, Response, Set, and Trap—one message from each class of SNMP message. Table 6.1 lists the four SNMP message classes and the messages included in each category.

Table 6.1 SNMP message types

Message class	Description	Message types
Read	Sent by the NMS to retrieve information from its managed devices	Get, GetNext, GetBulk
Write	Sent by the NMS to modify the values of one or more OIDs	Set
Notification	Sent by the managed devices to alert the NMS of a particular event	Trap, Inform
Response	Sent in response to a previous message	Response

6.2.1 The Read message class

Messages in the Read class are sent by the NMS to retrieve information from its managed devices—to ask for the values of one or more OIDs. The Read class includes three message types: Get, GetNext, and GetBulk. The Get message is the simplest of the three; in a Get message, the NMS specifies one or more OIDs, and the managed device responds with the values associated with those OIDs.

GetNext is used to discover unknown OIDs. When an NMS sends a GetNext request, the managed device returns the next OID in the tree and its value. For example, consider the following three OIDs:

- 1.3.6.1.2.1.1.1
- 1.3.6.1.2.1.1.2
- 1.3.6.1.2.1.1.3

If a managed device sends a GetNext request asking for the OID immediately following 1.3.6.1.2.1.1.1, it would receive the value associated with OID 1.3.6.1.2.1.1.2. This allows the NMS to discover the available information without having to know each specific OID in advance, also called "walking the tree."

The GetBulk message type, which was introduced in SNMPv2, provides the NMS with an efficient way to retrieve lots of information from a managed device without specifying each individual OID. Instead, GetBulk allows the NMS to specify an entire range of OIDs. This message type also allows the NMS to "walk the tree" like GetNext, but in a more efficient manner; whereas GetNext requests OIDs one at a time, GetBulk can request many at once.

6.2.2 The Write message class

The Write message class, containing only the Set message type that we looked at earlier, allows the NMS to modify the value associated with a specified OID. In section 6.1.1, I gave the example of modifying an interface's status, equivalent to issuing the `shutdown` or `no shutdown` commands in the CLI. A few other examples of OIDs you might use Set messages to change are the device's hostname, ACLs, IP addresses, and various other device configurations.

However, it's worth noting that some OIDs are *read-only*—their values can't be modified with Set messages. Some types of OIDs that would likely be read-only are OIDs related to system information (i.e., temperature, system health), resource utilization (i.e., CPU, memory), and interface statistics (i.e., current traffic rate). The NMS might send Get messages to retrieve the values associated with these OIDs, but modifying them with Set messages doesn't make much sense—telling a device "your internal temperature is X degrees" won't actually change the temperature!

6.2.3   *The Notification message class*

Next is the Notification message class, which includes two message types: Trap and Inform. Figure 6.7 demonstrates the difference between these two message types.

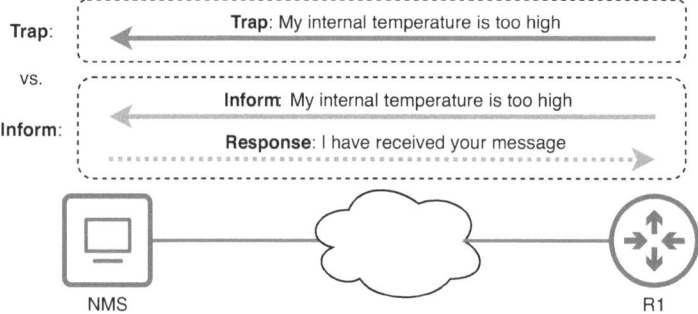

Figure 6.7   The two notification messages: Trap and Inform. Whereas Traps are unacknowledged, the NMS acknowledges each Inform with a Response message.

Traps are simple. When a particular event occurs (i.e., when the device's internal temperature passes X degrees or when an interface goes down), the managed device will send a Trap to the NMS; the NMS is thus considered notified of the event, regardless of whether it actually received the Trap or not. If the NMS successfully receives the Trap, it can then display an alert in the SNMP application, notify an admin, or perhaps just add the Trap to its logs. However, it does not respond to the managed device that sent the Trap.

Informs, introduced in SNMPv2, serve the same purpose as Traps: informing the NMS of a particular event. However, whereas Traps are unacknowledged by the NMS, Informs are acknowledged with a Response message. This provides a more reliable method of notifying the NMS; if the managed device doesn't receive a Response after sending an Inform, it will retransmit the Inform to ensure that the NMS receives it. For this reason, Informs should be preferred over Traps when using SNMPv2 or SNMPv3— if an event is worth notifying the NMS about, it's worth ensuring that the NMS actually received the notification.

EXAM TIP   Traps are unacknowledged notifications, and Informs are acknowledged notifications. Remember this difference between the two! Note that you can configure network devices to send Traps, Informs, or both.

6.2.4   *The Response message class*

The final message class is Response, which consists of a single message type, also called Response; we've already looked at Response messages multiple times in this chapter. Response messages are used by both the NMS and its managed devices:

- Managed devices send Responses to reply to Get, GetNext, GetBulk, and Set.
- The NMS sends Responses to reply to Informs.

Although all of these examples use the Response message type, the exact contents of the message depend on the type of message it is in response to. For example, a Response message sent in response to a Get message includes the requested OIDs and their values. A Response message sent in response to an Inform message, on the other hand, confirms that the NMS received the managed device's Inform message.

6.3   *SNMP versions and security*

Three major versions of SNMP have been widely implemented: SNMPv1, SNMPv2c, and SNMPv3. Table 6.2 summarizes the three versions of SNMP.

Table 6.2   SNMP versions

Version	Message types	Authentication	Encryption
SNMPv1	Get, GetNext, Set, Trap, Response	Community strings	No
SNMPv2c	Get, GetNext, Set, Trap, Response, GetBulk, Inform	Community strings	No
SNMPv3	Get, GetNext, Set, Trap, Response, GetBulk, Inform	Hash-based authentication with username/password	Yes

SNMPv1 was originally defined in three RFCs in 1990: RFCs 1155, 1156, and 1157. It included five message types: Get, GetNext, Set, Trap, and Response—no GetBulk or Inform messages yet. SNMPv1 included very basic security in the form of *community strings*—essentially passwords used to authenticate SNMP operations between an NMS and its managed devices.

SNMPv2 was later introduced, adding two new message types: GetBulk and Inform. However, the standard did not include the community string feature, instead introducing a different system of security. However, industry demand for backward compatibility and the simplicity of community strings led to *SNMPv2c*, also called *community-based SNMPv2*, which uses the same community string system (the "c" in SNMPv2c stands for *community-based*).

SNMPv3 did not add new message types but greatly improved SNMP's security by adding improved authentication and encryption. Security is a major concern when using SNMP because an attacker can use SNMP both to gather information about the devices in your network and also to make changes to them with Set messages. In the rest of this section, let's dig into SNMPv1's and SNMPv2c's community-based security, and SNMPv3's improved security features.

6.3.1   SNMPv1 and SNMPv2c security

SNMPv1 and SNMPv2c use a community-based security model. An SNMP *community* is a group of SNMP managers and agents that share common authentication parameters—a password called a community string. SNMPv1 and v2c define two different community types: *read-only* (RO) and *read-write* (RW). Figure 6.8 demonstrates the difference between them.

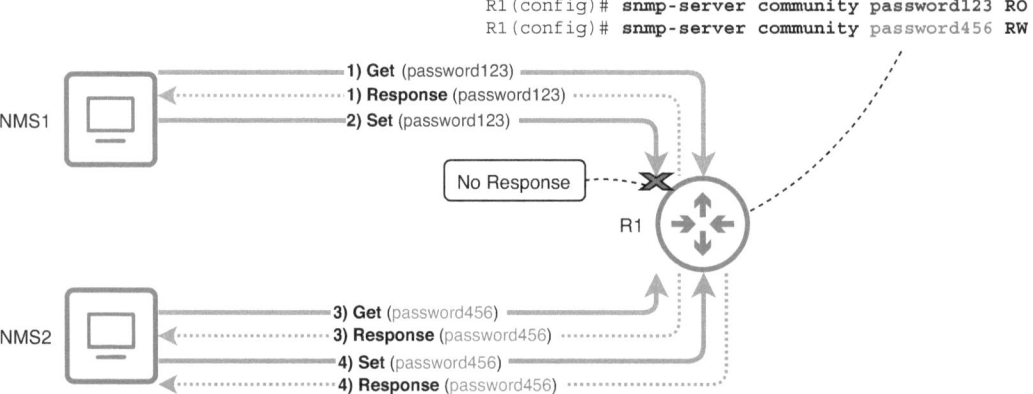

Figure 6.8   The difference between read-only (RO) and read-write (RW) community strings. NMS1 provides the RO string, so its Get (1) succeeds, but its Set (2) fails. NMS2 provides the RW string, so its Get (3) and Set (4) both succeed.

An NMS that provides the RO community string in its messages can only read information from the managed device; it can send Get, GetNext, and GetBulk requests, but it can't modify the managed device with Set messages. In figure 6.8, NMS1 provides the RO community string in its requests to R1. As a result, its Get message succeeds, but R1 rejects NMS1's Set message.

An NMS that provides the RW community string is capable of both reading information from (i.e., with Get) and writing to (with Set) the managed device. In figure 6.8, NMS2's Get and Set requests both succeed because NMS2 provides the RW string.

CCNA exam topic 4.4 states that you must be able to "explain the function of SNMP in network operations"; it doesn't mention SNMP configuration. However, examining a few basic SNMP configuration commands can help you grasp the concepts. The following example shows how I configured the two community strings on R1:

Configures a read-only community string

```
R1(config)# snmp-server community password123 RO        ◄
R1(config)# snmp-server community password456 RW        ◄
```

Configures a read-write community string

These commands alone are sufficient to enable R1 to respond to SNMP Get (including GetNext/GetBulk) and Set messages. R1 will respond to Get messages that specify either the RO community string (password123) or the RW community string (password456). R1 will also respond to Set messages, but only those that specify the RW community string.

> **NOTE** You can also specify an ACL for each community string: `snmp-server community community-string {RO | RW} [acl]`. The device will only respond to messages specifying that community string if the NMS is permitted by the ACL.

To enable R1 to send Traps to an NMS, we need a couple more commands: one to enable traps (`snmp-server enable traps`), and one to specify the IP address of an NMS (`snmp-server host ip-address [version 2c] community-string`). I configure both commands in the following example:

Enables all Traps

```
R1(config)# snmp-server enable traps                              ◄
R1(config)# snmp-server host 192.168.1.10 version 2c password789  ◄
```

Specifies an NMS to send SNMPv2c Traps to with the specified community string

The first command, `snmp-server enable traps`, enables all Trap messages. Alternatively, you can limit traps to specific events; one example is `snmp-server enable traps cpu`, which only sends CPU-related traps (i.e., CPU utilization alerts). There are many different options; if you have access to the CLI of a Cisco device, check some of them out with the IOS context-sensitive help feature (the question mark "**?**").

The second command, `snmp-server host 192.168.1.10 version 2c password789`, tells R1 to send Traps to the specified NMS (192.168.1.10) using SNMPv2c and the specified community string (password789). Notice that I specified a different community string here than those I configured previously.

The RO and RW community strings I configured earlier determine how the device reacts to Get, GetNext, GetBulk, and Set messages from an NMS. However, the community string in the `snmp-server host` command determines the community string the device will send in its Trap (and Inform) messages to the NMS; it doesn't have to match the community string specified in the `snmp-server community` command. You can then configure the NMS to only accept Traps/Informs that include the correct community string.

6.3.2   *SNMPv3 security*

Although community strings, in combination with ACLs, provide some degree of security, remember that community strings are sent in plaintext; they are not encrypted. This is not acceptable in modern networks; any attacker who gets a copy of the SNMP communications will know the community strings. SNMPv3 improves SNMP's security in four main ways:

- *User-based*—Instead of community strings, which are tied to each device, SNMPv3 grants access based on users. For example: "User A can access information X on the managed devices," "User B can access information Y," etc.
- *Message integrity*—SNMPv3 performs checks to ensure that messages weren't altered by an attacker before reaching their destination.
- *Authentication*—Username/password authentication that can be secured with hashing algorithms (like those used by the **enable secret** command), preventing hackers from reading the passwords.
- *Encryption*—SNMPv3 message contents can be encrypted so that only the intended recipient can read them.

All of these features are great for improving SNMP's security, but SNMPv3 offers some flexibility: authentication and encryption are optional. Although most networks should ideally use both for maximum security, SNMPv3 offers three security levels:

- *NoAuthNoPriv*—No authentication and no encryption
- *AuthNoPriv*—Authentication, but no encryption
- *AuthPriv*—Both authentication and encryption

SNMPv3's security features make its configuration a bit more complicated than SNMPv1/SNMPv2c. For example, here's how to configure a device to respond to SNMPv3 Get messages:

```
                                                        Creates a group with
                                                        AuthPriv security
R1(config)# snmp-server group GROUP1 v3 priv         ◄─
R1(config)# snmp-server user USER1 GROUP1 v3 auth sha AuthPW priv aes 256 PrivPW ◄─┐
                                                                                   │
           Creates a user account (USER1) in the GROUP 1 group ───────────────────┘
```

Instead of simply specifying one or more community strings, you must specify a *group* that specifies the security level to be used (**priv** configures the AuthPriv security level) and then assigns one or more users to that group. Figure 6.9 clarifies the syntax of the **snmp-server user** command.

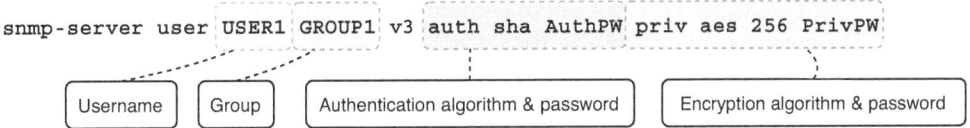

Figure 6.9 The syntax of the `snmp-server user` command. This command configures user USER1 in group GROUP1, the SHA authentication algorithm with password AuthPW, and the AES-256 encryption algorithm with password PrivPW.

After creating one or more groups and assigning users to each group, you can then enable Traps with `snmp-server enable traps` (like in SNMPv1 and v2c), and specify an NMS with `snmp-server host`.

EXAM TIP Don't expect CCNA exam questions about the specifics of configuring SNMPv1/v2c and SNMPv3. It's sufficient to understand SNMPv1/v2c's community-based security model and SNMPv3's user-based security and additional security improvements (integrity, hash-based authentication, and encryption).

Summary

- Simple Network Management Protocol (SNMP) facilitates the management of devices, such as routers and switches, over a network.
- The two main components of SNMP are the network management station (NMS) and the managed devices. The NMS is a software platform designed for monitoring and managing devices using SNMP.
- Managed devices organize information about themselves into a database called the *Management Information Base* (MIB). The pieces of information are stored as variables, such as "interface status," "CPU utilization," etc.
- SNMP operations can be divided into reading the MIB, modifying the MIB, and notifying the NMS.
- The NMS can query a managed device to get the value of one or more variables in the managed device's MIB. *Get* messages are used for this purpose.
- The NMS can modify the value of the MIB's variables with *Set* messages.
- In addition to configuration changes, Set messages can also serve other purposes, such as initiating system reboots and backing up device configuration files.
- Managed devices can notify the NMS when specific events occur, such as an interface going down, using *Trap* messages.
- Each device that uses SNMP runs SNMP software that can be called the SNMP entity.
- The SNMP entity of the NMS consists of the SNMP manager and SNMP application.

- The SNMP entity of a managed device consists of the SNMP agent and MIB.

- The manager and agent serve as the interface between the NMS and a managed device, the manager running on the NMS and the agent on the managed device.

- The manager sends messages (i.e., Get, Set) to the agent, which listens on UDP port 161. The agent sends messages (i.e., Response, Trap) to the manager, which listens on UDP port 162.

- An SNMP application is a piece of software that allows a human to interact with SNMP, usually through a graphical user interface (GUI). Through the application, an admin can control how they want to use SNMP to monitor and manage the network.

- Each variable in the MIB is given an object identifier (OID) that uniquely identifies it. OIDs are hierarchically organized into a tree-like structure, similar to the DNS hierarchy. Each number in the OID represents a different level or branch in the tree.

- OIDs can be complex and lengthy (i.e., 1.3.6.1.4.1.9.9.109.1.1.1.1.4), making them difficult to remember or work with directly. SNMP applications typically translate these OIDs into user-friendly, descriptive names like *CPU Utilization*.

- Vendors can define their own OIDs to use on their devices. You may need to download an MIB file from the vendor and import it into the NMS to allow it to properly interpret the vendor-specific OIDs.

- SNMP messages can be divided into four classes: Read (Get, GetNext, Bulk), Write (Set), Notification (Trap, Inform), and Response (Response).

- *Get* messages retrieve the values associated with one or more OIDs.

- *GetNext* messages retrieve the value of the next OID in the MIB—the OID after the one specified in the message. This allows the NMS to discover the available OIDs.

- *GetBulk* messages provide an efficient way to retrieve lots of information without specifying each individual OID. GetBulk allows the NMS to specify a range of OIDs.

- *Set* messages are used to modify the values associated with one or more OIDs.

- *Trap* messages notify the NMS of a particular event, but the NMS does not send a Response back to the managed device. If the Trap is lost, it is not retransmitted.

- *Inform* messages serve the same purpose as Traps, but the NMS acknowledges receipt of each Inform by sending a Response message to the managed device. If the Inform message is lost, the managed device will retransmit it, making Informs more reliable than Traps.

- *Response* messages are sent by both the NMS (in response to Inform messages) and managed devices (in response to Get, GetNext, GetBulk, and Set messages).

- There are three main SNMP versions: SNMPv1, SNMPv2c, and SNMPv3.

- SNMPv1 uses five messages: Get, GetNext, Set, Trap, and Response.

- SNMPv2c and SNMPv3 add GetBulk and Inform messages to SNMPv1's five messages.

- SNMPv1 and SNMPv2c use a community-based security model. An SNMP community is a group of SNMP managers and agents that share common authentication parameters—a password called a *community string*.

- There are two community types: read-only (RO) and read-write (RW).

- An NMS that provides the RO community string in its messages can only read information from the managed device (Get, GetNext, GetBulk). It cannot use Set.

- An NMS that provides the RW community string in its messages can both read information from (i.e., Get) and write information to (Set) the managed device.

- Use **snmp-server community** *community-string* {**RO** | **RW**} [*acl*] to configure RO and RW community strings on a Cisco IOS device. This enables it to respond to SNMP messages that include the appropriate community string.

- Use **snmp-server enable traps** to enable all Trap messages.

- Use **snmp-server host** *ip-address* [**version 2c**] *community-string* to specify an NMS to send Traps/Informs to. The *community-string* in this command will be sent with all Traps/Informs, and the NMS can use it to authenticate the device.

- SNMPv3 greatly improves SNMP's security with a user-based security system, message integrity checks, hash-based authentication, and encryption.

- Authentication and encryption are highly recommended but optional. The three security levels are NoAuthNoPriv (no authentication and no encryption), AuthNoPriv (authentication, but no encryption), and AuthPriv (authentication and encryption).

- SNMP's user-based system requires you to create groups with **snmp-server group**, and then assign one or more users to each group with **snmp-server user**.

Syslog
7

Syslog is a standard for message logging in computers and is CCNA exam topic 4.5: Describe the use of syslog features including facilities and severity levels. Like SNMP, the topic of the previous chapter, Syslog provides mechanisms to collect information about devices and monitor network health.

Although they do have their similarities, there are significant differences between SNMP and Syslog, and for that reason, most networks make use of both protocols. SNMP is like a network health report, proactively polling devices at regular intervals to gather mostly (but not exclusively) quantitative metrics—numerical statistics like traffic rates, CPU utilization, error rates, etc. SNMP is also often used for event-based alerting using Trap and Inform messages.

Syslog, on the other hand, is like a journal that the device keeps—a logbook that records significant (and not so significant) events that occur on a device. Although there is overlap between the information both protocols gather, Syslog generally focuses on qualitative information—descriptive information that provides context or insight into what's happening on the device; this is especially useful when you need to dive deep into troubleshooting or forensic analysis. SNMP might alert you that a router is down, but Syslog can tell you the sequence of events that led to the failure.

7.1 *Viewing device logs*

As you've practiced configuring Cisco routers and switches throughout your studies, you've certainly seen messages shown in the CLI like this:

```
Sep 18 00:54:27.832: %LINK-3-UPDOWN: Interface FastEthernet0/1,
↪changed state to down
```

This is an example of a Syslog message logging a change in an interface's state. Syslog messages can be displayed in real time to users connected to the CLI of a device. They can also be stored locally on the device or a centralized Syslog server to be viewed later. In this section, we'll examine both aspects of Syslog.

7.1.1 *Real-time logging*

Cisco IOS displays Syslog messages to users connected to the CLI via the console line by default. This can be controlled with the `logging console` command, which is enabled by default. You can disable logging to the console line with `no logging console` if you wish; the device will then stop showing log messages to users connected to the console line.

Similarly, logging to the VTY lines is enabled by default; this applies to users connected to the CLI via Telnet or SSH. This is a result of the `logging monitor` command that is configured by default; you can disable it with `no logging monitor`.

However, despite the `logging monitor` command being enabled by default, when connected to a device's VTY lines via Telnet or SSH, no log messages are displayed by default. This is because an additional command is required to enable VTY line logging for a particular session: `terminal monitor`, which is issued in privileged EXEC mode.

NOTE In this context, a *session* is an individual connection between a user's device and a network device via Telnet or SSH.

I demonstrate this in the following example. I am connected to SW1 via SSH, but disabling GigabitEthernet0/1 shows no Syslog messages. However, after I issue the `terminal monitor` command, reenabling the interface results in two Syslog messages being shown:

No Syslog messages are shown after disabling G0/1.

Enables real-time logging for the session

Reenables the interface

```
SW1(config)# interface g0/1
SW1(config-if)# shutdown
SW1(config-if)# do terminal monitor
SW1(config-if)# no shutdown
Sep 18 02:17:46.867: %LINK-3-UPDOWN: Interface FastEthernet0/3, changed state to up
Sep 18 02:17:47.874: %LINEPROTO-5-UPDOWN: Line protocol on Interface FastEthernet0/3,
changed state to up
```

Syslog messages are displayed.

To view real-time Syslog messages when connected via a VTY line, you must use the `terminal monitor` command every time you connect to the CLI; the command only applies to one session. For example, if you disconnect and then reconnect, you must use the command again if you want to view the real-time messages. Likewise, if multiple users are connected to the VTY lines simultaneously, each user must use the command.

Figure 7.1 demonstrates these concepts. PC1's user, connected to R1's console line, enables R1's G0/1 interface with `no shutdown` and is shown a Syslog message. PC2 and PC3 are both connected to R1 via SSH. PC2's user has issued the `terminal monitor` command and therefore is shown the same log message as PC1's user. PC3's user has not used `terminal monitor`, so no Syslog message is displayed on PC3.

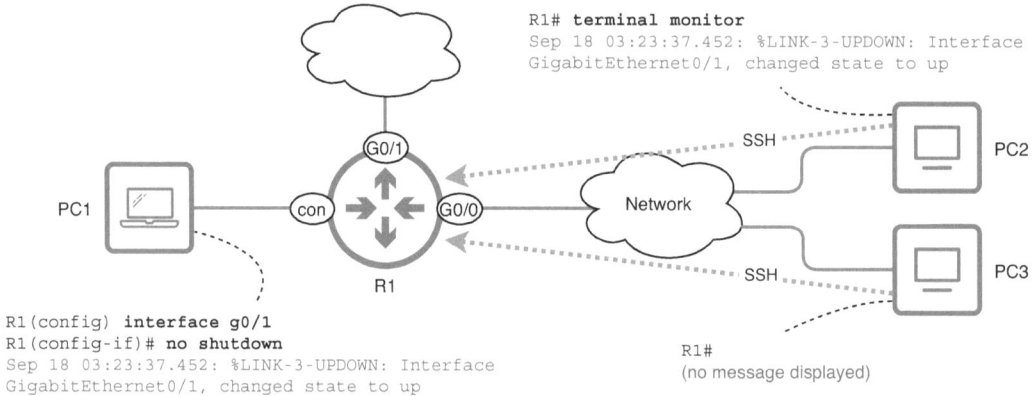

Figure 7.1   Syslog messages displayed when connected to the console line versus when connected to a VTY line

The command to stop displaying messages for a particular session is a bit different than you're used to; it is not `no terminal monitor` but rather `terminal no monitor`. You might choose to use this command if the device is generating a significant number of messages, making it difficult to work in the CLI.

EXAM TIP   Remember the difference between real-time logging to the console and VTY lines. Although logging is enabled for both by default (due to the default `logging console` and `logging monitor` commands), users connected via the VTY lines must also use `terminal monitor` to enable VTY line logging for each session.

7.1.2   *The logging synchronous command*

As you've practiced configuring Cisco routers and switches, you've probably had the frustrating experience of a Syslog message being displayed as you are typing a command, resulting in something like the following example:

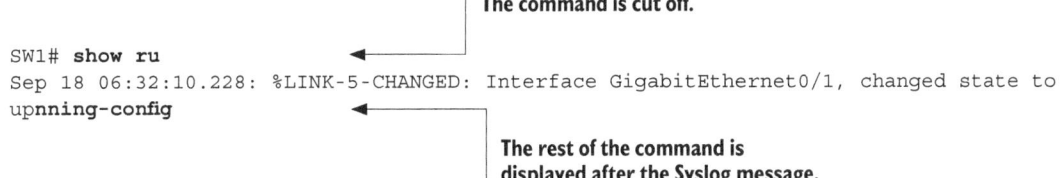

The command is cut off.

```
SW1# show ru
Sep 18 06:32:10.228: %LINK-5-CHANGED: Interface GigabitEthernet0/1, changed state to
upnning-config
```

The rest of the command is
displayed after the Syslog message.

By default, if a Syslog message is displayed as you are typing a command, the command is cut off, and any additional characters you type are displayed on the same line as the Syslog message. If you hit Enter at this point, the command will execute correctly; using the previous example, the command would be executed as **show running-config**.

However, this default behavior doesn't lead to a very good user experience; it can be especially distracting and confusing when using long and complex commands. One solution is to use the Ctrl-l keyboard shortcut, which reprints the command you are currently typing on a new line. However, a better solution is the **logging synchronous** command.

With **logging synchronous** configured on the console and VTY lines, the command you are typing will be automatically reprinted on a new line if it gets cut off by a Syslog message. I demonstrate this in the following example:

```
SW1(config)# line vty 0 15                     Enables synchronous logging
SW1(config-line)# logging synchronous          on the VTY lines
SW1(config-line)# end
SW1# show ru
Sep 18 09:32:59.035: %SYS-5-CONFIG_I: Configured from console by jeremy on vty0
(192.168.1.224)
SW1# show running-config
```

The command is automatically reprinted
on a new line, and I finish typing it.

The command I am typing
is cut off by a Syslog message.

This command is a major quality-of-life improvement when working in the CLI, and I highly recommend configuring it on the console and VTY lines of your devices; this is one command that I wish was enabled by default!

7.1.3 Storing logs

Real-time logging to the console and VTY lines is useful for alerting you to events as you configure devices, but Syslog's ability to provide a historical view is even more valuable. This allows you to review events that occurred and their causes after the fact. To enable this, Cisco IOS provides two main ways to store Syslog messages: the device's memory and an external Syslog server.

THE LOGGING BUFFER

By default, Cisco IOS devices store Syslog messages in RAM; this is called the *logging buffer*. You can control this with the **logging buffered** [bytes] command, which is enabled by default. The optional *bytes* argument allows you to specify how much memory to allocate to the buffer.

The size of the buffer

The default size of the buffer depends on the device. For example, my Catalyst 2960 switch's buffer is 4,096 bytes in size by default—enough for about 35–40 log messages, depending on each message's length. At the default size, the buffer fills up rather quickly. After it fills up, messages are added to and removed from the buffer in a *first in, first out* (FIFO) manner.

A Catalyst 9300 switch—a newer and much more powerful model (that I can't afford to buy for my home lab)—uses a default size of 102,400 bytes (102.4 kilobytes). Whatever the model, the default settings are fairly conservative. In most cases, there will be enough room to expand the buffer to store more messages. However, before increasing the size of the buffer, use **show memory** to view the device's current memory usage and ensure that the device has sufficient memory.

To view the logs stored in the buffer, use the **show logging** command. This command also displays information about the device's Syslog settings in general, as shown in the following example. The output of this command is quite large (especially with a large buffer), so I will leave out some output and show only the two most recent log messages:

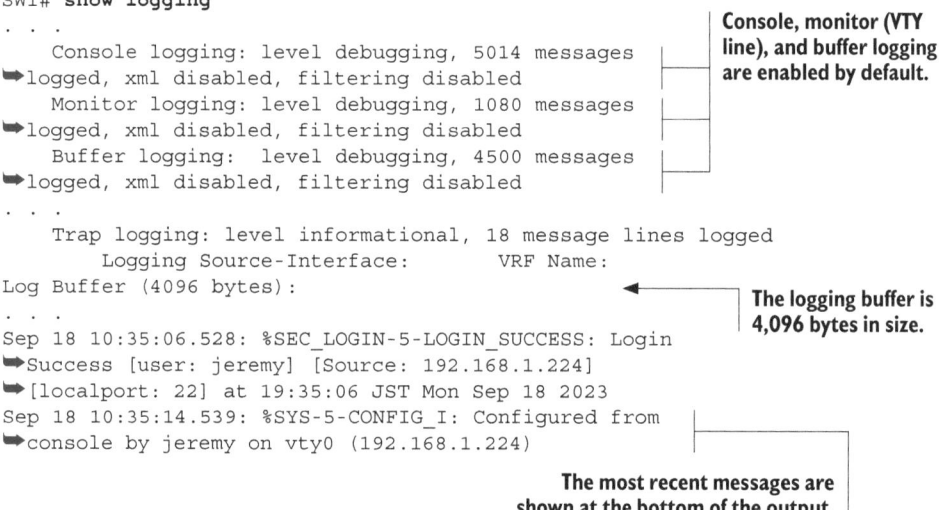

```
SW1# show logging
. . .
    Console logging: level debugging, 5014 messages
➥logged, xml disabled, filtering disabled
    Monitor logging: level debugging, 1080 messages
➥logged, xml disabled, filtering disabled
    Buffer logging:  level debugging, 4500 messages
➥logged, xml disabled, filtering disabled
. . .
    Trap logging: level informational, 18 message lines logged
        Logging Source-Interface:      VRF Name:
Log Buffer (4096 bytes):
. . .
Sep 18 10:35:06.528: %SEC_LOGIN-5-LOGIN_SUCCESS: Login
➥Success [user: jeremy] [Source: 192.168.1.224]
➥[localport: 22] at 19:35:06 JST Mon Sep 18 2023
Sep 18 10:35:14.539: %SYS-5-CONFIG_I: Configured from
➥console by jeremy on vty0 (192.168.1.224)
```

Console, monitor (VTY line), and buffer logging are enabled by default.

The logging buffer is 4,096 bytes in size.

The most recent messages are shown at the bottom of the output.

As the top section of the output shows, console, monitor (VTY line), and buffer logging are all enabled by default, thanks to the **logging console**, **logging monitor**, and **logging buffered** commands that are part of the device's default configuration. If you use **no logging console** to disable console logging, for example, the output will state Console logging: disabled.

While troubleshooting problems on a device (or multiple devices), you will likely use **show logging** quite often. One point to remember is that the most recent logs are displayed at the bottom of the output; if there are quite a few messages stored in the buffer, you may have to press the spacebar quite a few times to get to the most recent messages.

NOTE You can also hold down the spacebar to quickly scroll to the bottom of a command with a lot of output, instead of repeatedly pressing the spacebar.

LOGGING TO A SYSLOG SERVER

In addition to locally saving log messages, you can configure the device to send them to a central Syslog server. This can be very useful, especially in large networks with many devices; storing logs in a central location simplifies the process of viewing and correlating those logs, eliminating the need to log in to each device one by one.

Logging to a Syslog server is governed by the **logging trap** command (not to be confused with the SNMP Trap message type). Like the other commands we've covered, this is enabled by default. However, for a device to actually send Syslog messages to a server, you need to tell the device which server to send the messages to. You can configure this with the **logging [host]** *ip-address* command; the device will then send Syslog messages to UDP port 514 on the specified server, in addition to the other destinations (console line, VTY lines, and buffer).

EXAM TIP Although standard Syslog uses UDP port 514, there is a secure, encrypted version of Syslog called *Syslog over TLS* (Transport Layer Security) that uses TCP (not UDP!) port 6514. Although you don't have to know the details of Syslog over TLS for the exam, be aware that Syslog can use both UDP 514 and TCP 6514.

Note that the **host** keyword in this command is optional; **logging** *ip-address* and **logging host** *ip-address* both have the same effect. However, regardless of which command you configure, it will be saved in the running-config as **logging host** *ip-address*.

Figure 7.2 visually demonstrates a network device logging events to the four destinations we have covered: real-time logging to the console line (PC1) and VTY lines (PC2) and log storage via the logging buffer (in R1's RAM) and a Syslog server (SRV1).

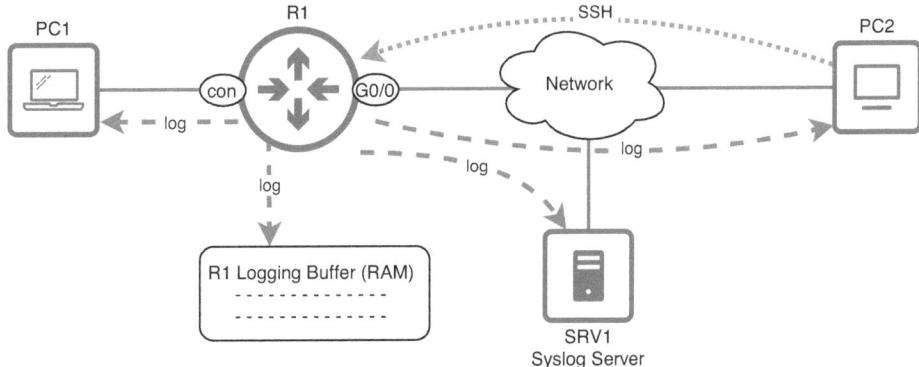

Figure 7.2 R1 logs events to four different destinations: the console line, the VTY lines, the logging buffer, and a Syslog server.

7.2   *The Syslog message format*

Syslog messages in Cisco IOS use a consistent format, as shown in figure 7.3.

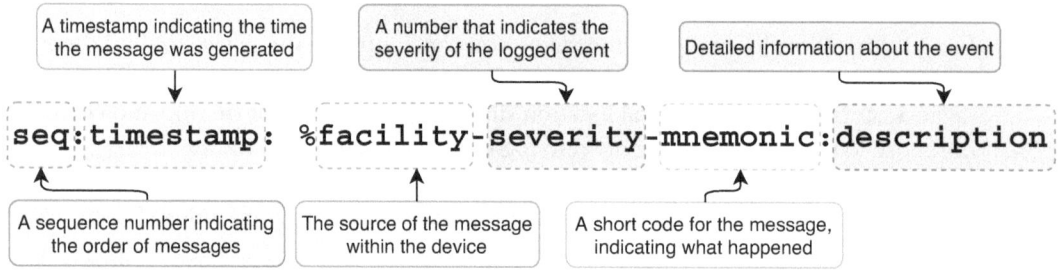

Figure 7.3   Syslog message format. The sequence number and time stamp components are optional.

Let's use the following Syslog message as an example to examine each component:

```
000065: Sep 19 01:01:01.133: %LINK-3-UPDOWN: Interface FastEthernet0/1,
changed state to down
```

The first two fields are a *sequence* number (000065), indicating the order of log messages, followed by a *timestamp* (Sep 19 01:01:01.133), indicating the time each message was generated. These two fields are optional. For example, in the Syslog messages we have looked at previously, there is no sequence number. We will examine these two components more in section 7.2.1.

The first mandatory component is the *facility*—a value that indicates the source of the message within the device. In other words, it specifies the service, application, or other component that generated the message. In the example, the facility is LINK, indicating that the message was generated by one of the device's links—this usually indicates an interface's status changing to up or down.

> **EXAM TIP**   There are various facilities, but there's no need to memorize them for the CCNA exam. Just be sure that you can identify the facility within a Syslog message.

The next component is the *severity*, which is a numerical value indicating how urgent or critical the message is—a lower value is more severe. In our example, the severity is 3; we'll cover severity levels in detail in section 7.2.2.

Next is the *mnemonic*—a short text string that provides a more specific descriptor of the event that triggered the Syslog message. The mnemonic acts as a code that briefly identifies the reason or area within the facility that generated the message. In our example, the mnemonic is UPDOWN, indicating that the message was generated by an interface state changing to up or down.

The final part is the *description*, which provides a more detailed explanation of the event that triggered the message. In our example, the facility LINK and the mnemonic UPDOWN indicate that the message relates to a link's status changing to up or down, and the description `Interface FastEthernet0/1, changed state to down` gives us the details of what really happened.

7.2.1 *Sequence numbers and timestamps*

The first two components of a Syslog message—the sequence number and time-stamp—are optional. Whether they are present or absent by default can vary depend-ing on the device; in many cases, sequence numbers are not included by default, but timestamps are.

You can enable sequence numbers with the **service sequence-numbers** command in global config mode. After issuing this command, sequence numbers will be added to any future Syslog messages generated by the device (but not past messages).

Timestamps can be controlled with the **service timestamps log** command in global config mode. However, this command includes various keywords that allow you to control how timestamps are displayed. The following are two options:

- `service timestamps log datetime`
- `service timestamps log uptime`

With the **datetime** option configured, Syslog messages will be timestamped with the date and time when the event occurred. With the **uptime** option, however, Syslog mes-sages will be timestamped with the uptime of the device (the amount of time since the device booted up) when the event occurred. **datetime** is generally the more useful option of the two, enabling you to identify exactly when events occurred and correlate logs across different devices.

> **NOTE** You can check a device's current uptime in the output of **show version**. For example: `SW1 uptime is 15 hours, 14 minutes`.

The **datetime** keyword has some further options that you can configure. For example, with **service timestamps log datetime localtime**, you can configure the device to timestamp Syslog messages in the local time zone. By default, Syslog messages are timestamped in UTC. In an international network with devices in multiple time zones, this default behavior is generally preferred; it makes correlating logs between devices in different time zones easier. However, you may prefer to have messages timestamped with the local time; the **localtime** option allows you to do this.

You can also add milliseconds to the timestamps with the **service timestamps log datetime msec** command; the format of the timestamps will be `hh:mm:ss.msec`. All of the timestamps shown in this chapter have included milliseconds, but they are optional. If you don't include the **msec** option in the command, they will not be displayed.

> **NOTE** You can combine the **localtime** and **msec** options if you want; **service timestamps log datetime localtime msec** will timestamp Syslog messages using the local time and will also include milliseconds.

7.2.2   *Syslog severity levels*

Syslog messages are categorized by their severity—how urgent or critical the logged event is. There are eight severity levels, and a lower value indicates a more severe event. In addition to a numerical value, each severity level also has a keyword that you can use when configuring severity levels in Cisco IOS. Figure 7.4 outlines the eight Syslog severity levels. Note that some of the keywords are different from those in the Syslog standard (RFC 5424). For the CCNA exam, remembering the keywords as used in Cisco IOS is more useful.

Level	IOS Keyword	Description
0	emergencies	System is unusable
1	alerts	Action must be taken immediately
2	critical	Critical conditions
3	errors	Error conditions
4	warnings	Warning conditions
5	notifications	Normal but significant condition
6	informational	Informational messages
7	debugging	User-requested debug messages

Figure 7.4   **The eight Syslog severity levels. Lower levels are more severe.**

EXAM TIP   Make sure you can identify the severity levels and their keywords for the CCNA exam. You can use a mnemonic such as "Every Awesome Cisco Engineer Will Need Ice Cream Daily," using the first letter of each level's keyword.

The first two severity levels (0–1) are reserved for particularly serious events—system crashes, critical hardware failures, and other events that demand immediate attention. The next three severity levels (2–4), described by RFC 5424 as critical, error, and warning conditions, respectively, are used for events that should be addressed but do not necessarily require immediate action. An example is an interface unexpectedly going down, which IOS categorizes at severity level 3 (LINK-3-UPDOWN).

The next two levels (5–6) are usually used for routine operational status messages or notifications of minor changes that don't typically affect performance or security. For example, a user logging into the CLI is categorized at severity level 5 (SEC_LOGIN-5-LOGIN_SUCCESS), and so is an interface being manually disabled with the **shutdown** command (LINK-5-CHANGED).

The final severity level (7) is unique; it is reserved for messages that are generated as a result of the **debug** command, which allows you to track events in detail as they occur. We will cover the **debug** command in the next section.

You can control the types of events logged to each destination—the console, VTY lines, buffer, and Syslog server—based on their severity levels. For example, to avoid filling up the device's logging buffer, you may want to only store logs for more severe events in the buffer.

Let's first look at the default logging configurations for these different destinations. The **logging console**, **logging monitor**, **logging buffered**, and **logging trap** commands on their own—which are part of the device's default configuration—enable logging to each destination with the default severity levels. To check these defaults, use **show logging**:

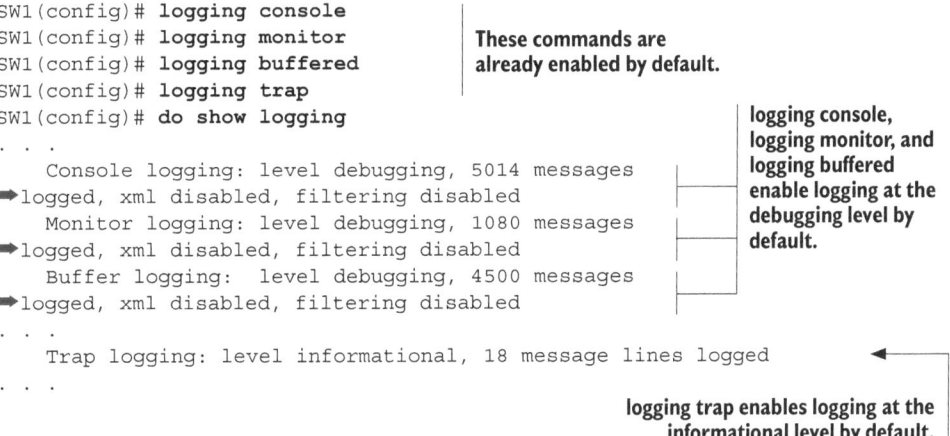

```
SW1(config)# logging console
SW1(config)# logging monitor          These commands are
SW1(config)# logging buffered         already enabled by default.
SW1(config)# logging trap
SW1(config)# do show logging                              logging console,
. . .                                                     logging monitor, and
    Console logging: level debugging, 5014 messages       logging buffered
➡logged, xml disabled, filtering disabled                enable logging at the
    Monitor logging: level debugging, 1080 messages       debugging level by
➡logged, xml disabled, filtering disabled                default.
    Buffer logging:  level debugging, 4500 messages
➡logged, xml disabled, filtering disabled
. . .
    Trap logging: level informational, 18 message lines logged ◄─────┐
. . .
                         logging trap enables logging at the
                            informational level by default.
```

Logging to the console, monitor, and buffer is enabled at level 7 (debugging) by default. This means that events with that severity level or numerically lower (more severe) will be logged; because level 7 is the numerically highest, all events will be logged to the console, monitor, and buffer by default (severity levels 0–7).

However, trap logging (to a Syslog server) is enabled at severity level 6 (informational) by default; this means that events of severity level 6 or lower will be logged to the Syslog server. Level 7 events will not be logged to the server. This choice of default settings minimizes unnecessary network traffic to the Syslog server.

To modify which severity levels are logged to each destination, you can add the optional *level* argument to the end of each command. Note that for this argument, you can specify either the numerical value or the keyword. For example, **logging console 4** and **logging console warnings** both enable console logging for severity levels 4 and lower (0–4). Table 7.1 summarizes the commands we've covered, adding the optional *severity* argument.

Table 7.1 Syslog config ration commands

Destination	Commands
Console line	Device(config)# **logging console** [*severity*]
VTY lines	Device(config)# **logging monitor** [*severity*]
(monitor)	Device# **terminal monitor**
Logging buffer	Device(config)# **logging buffered** [*bytes*] [*severity*]
Syslog server	Device(config)# **logging trap** [*severity*]
(trap)	Device(config)# **logging** [**host**] *ip-address*

EXAM TIP   Remember that specifying a certain severity level enables logging for events at that level and all numerically lower (more severe) levels.

7.2.3   *The* debug *command*

The **debug** command allows you to view detailed real-time information about various operations on a Cisco IOS device, including data about network activity, internal processes, and other specific events. You can use this command to troubleshoot difficult problems or learn more about how the device is functioning.

This command includes countless keywords that allow you to specify what kind of information you want to see. For example, **debug spanning-tree events** can be used to display real-time messages about STP-related events, such as changes in port roles and states. The following example shows some output generated by that command:

```
SW1# debug spanning-tree events
Spanning Tree event debugging is on
Sep 19 05:38:17.003: STP: VLAN0010 new root port Gi0/1, cost 8
Sep 19 05:38:17.003: STP: VLAN0010 Gi0/1 -> listening
Sep 19 05:38:32.003: STP: VLAN0010 Gi0/1 -> learning
Sep 19 05:38:47.003: STP[10]: Generating TC trap for port GigabitEthernet0/1
Sep 19 05:38:47.004: STP: VLAN0010 sent Topology Change Notice on Gi0/1
Sep 19 05:38:47.005: STP: VLAN0010 Gi0/1 -> forwarding
```

NOTE   Debug output does not follow the same format as regular Syslog messages.

The **debug** command is extremely useful for troubleshooting difficult problems, allowing you to get a detailed look at how the device is functioning. Furthermore, it is a great tool for learning. For example, when studying OSPF neighbor relationships, you can use **debug ip ospf adj** to see how the routers transition through the OSPF neighbor states.

NOTE   Debug messages are processed by the device's CPU, and debugging can be quite resource intensive. It is recommended that you be very careful about using this command on a live network to avoid overwhelming the device.

Feel free to experiment with the **debug** command in a lab, but it is beyond the scope of the CCNA exam. You just need to understand its relationship to the Syslog severity levels: debugging-level events will not be logged unless severity level 7 (debugging) is enabled.

Summary

- *Syslog* is a standard for message logging in computers, providing mechanisms to collect information about devices and monitor their health.

- Whereas SNMP provides regular polling of quantitative metrics and event-based alerting, Syslog functions like a logbook that records significant (and not so significant) events that occur on a device.

- Syslog messages can be displayed in real time to users connected to the CLI of a device and stored locally or on a centralized Syslog server for later review.

- Real-time logging to the console line is controlled with the **logging console** command, which is enabled by default.

- Real-time logging to the VTY lines is controlled with the **logging monitor** command, which is also enabled by default.

- A user connected to a VTY line must issue the **terminal monitor** command in privileged EXEC mode to view real-time messages for that session. The command only applies for the individual session.

- The **logging synchronous** command can be configured in line config mode to make the device automatically reprint the command you are typing on a new line if it gets cut off by a Syslog message.

- Cisco devices can store Syslog messages in the *logging buffer* in RAM. Use **show logging** to view the messages stored in the logging buffer.

- Logging to the buffer is controlled with the **logging buffered** [*bytes*] command, which is enabled by default. The optional *bytes* argument lets you specify the size of the logging buffer.

- You can configure a device to send Syslog messages to a central Syslog server. This is especially useful in large networks with many devices to facilitate viewing and correlating their logs.

- Logging to a Syslog server is controlled with the **logging trap** command, which is enabled by default. However, you also must specify the IP address of the Syslog server with **logging** [**host**] *ip-address*.

- Standard Syslog uses UDP port 514. However, the more secure version, Syslog over TLS, uses TCP port 6514.

- The Syslog message format is seq:timestamp: %facility-severity -mnemonic: description.

- The first part is a sequence number that identifies the order of messages, followed by a *timestamp* that indicates when the message was generated. These two components are optional.

- The *facility* indicates the source of the message within the device—the service, application, or other component that generated the message.

- The *severity* is a numerical value indicating how urgent or critical the message is.

- The *mnemonic* is a short text string that provides a descriptor of the event that triggered the Syslog message.

- The *description* is a more detailed description of the event.

- You can control whether sequence numbers are added to Syslog messages with the `service sequence-numbers` command in global config mode.

- You can configure timestamps with `service timestamps log [datetime | uptime]`. The `datetime` keyword timestamps log messages with the date and time of the event. The `uptime` keyword timestamps log messages with the device's uptime when the event occurred.

- The `datetime` keyword has further options like `localtime`, which timestamps logs in the device's local time zone (instead of the default UTC), and `msec`, which adds milliseconds to the timestamps.

- Syslog messages are categorized by their severity—how urgent or critical the logged event is. A lower numerical value is more severe. The eight severity levels and their keywords in IOS are
  - *0*—emergencies
  - *1*—alerts
  - *2*—critical
  - *3*—errors
  - *4*—warnings
  - *5*—notifications
  - *6*—informational
  - *7*—debugging

- Console, monitor, and buffer logging are enabled at level 7 (debugging) by default. This means that all events of severity level or numerically lower (all events) will be logged.

- Trap logging (to a Syslog server) is enabled at severity level 6 (informational) by default. This means that events of severity level 6 or lower will be logged.

- You can control the severity levels that are logged to each destination (console, monitor, buffer, trap) by adding the optional *severity* argument to each command. You can either specify the severity level's keyword or numerical value.

- For example, `logging console 4` and `logging console warnings` both enable console logging for severity levels 4 and lower (0–4).

- The `debug` command allows you to view detailed real-time information about various operations on a Cisco IOS device, including data about network activity, internal processes, and other specific events.

- Debugging-level events will not be logged unless severity level 7 is enabled.

Trivial File Transfer Protocol and File Transfer Protocol

This chapter covers

- Sending files across a network with Trivial File Transfer Protocol and File Transfer Protocol Cisco IOS file systems
- Upgrading Cisco IOS software

A file serves as a digital container in a computer, designed to store a variety of data ranging from text and images to audio, video, and software applications. Files can be of any size, from a few bytes to hundreds of gigabytes or more. Transferring files from one computer to another has been one of the primary functions of networks since their beginning. Over time, this has led to the development of various protocols dedicated to facilitating file transfers over a network.

Trivial File Transfer Protocol (TFTP) and File Transfer Protocol (FTP) are two such protocols that have been widely used for this purpose and still are. While TFTP is a simple protocol that is often used to transfer small files in a controlled environment, FTP offers a robust set of features for secure and versatile file transfers. These two protocols are CCNA exam topic 4.9: Describe the capabilities and functions of TFTP/FTP in the network.

TFTP and FTP can both be used to transfer any kind of file over a network, but we'll focus on one use case that is relevant for anyone working with Cisco routers and switches: transferring IOS files from a file server to upgrade the operating system of a device.

8.1   *Trivial File Transfer Protocol*

Trivial File Transfer Protocol (TFTP) is a protocol used for transferring files over a network. TFTP uses a client–server model, in which one device (i.e., a PC) acts as the client and another (i.e., a file server) acts as the server. It is "trivial" because it is a relatively simple protocol with few features; the client can transfer files to and from the server, but that's about it.

TFTP doesn't use any kind of authentication; a TFTP server will respond to all client requests—no username/password needed. Furthermore, TFTP communications are unencrypted, so all data is sent in plaintext. For these reasons, it would not be wise to use TFTP to send important files over a public network like the internet; TFTP does not provide sufficient security.

However, to transfer files within a controlled environment like a LAN, TFTP is often selected for its simplicity and ease of use. Figure 8.1 shows an example use case for TFTP: an admin uses HTTPS to securely download a Cisco IOS image from Cisco's website and then uses TFTP to transfer the image to a network device. In this case, the network device (SW1) is a TFTP client, and the admin's PC is a TFTP server.

NOTE   An IOS *image* is a complete copy of the Cisco IOS software that is run on a Cisco router or switch.

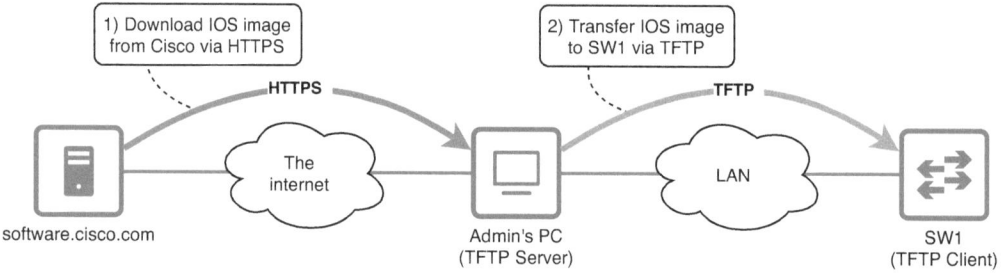

Figure 8.1   Transferring an IOS image to a network device with TFTP. (1) Download the IOS image from Cisco's website via HTTPS. (2) Transfer the image to the network device via TFTP.

NOTE   Instead of transferring the file directly from the admin's PC to the network device, another common setup is to store IOS images in a central file server, from which network devices can use TFTP to download the appropriate image.

8.1.1   *How TFTP works*

A TFTP file transfer is initiated by a client sending either a read request or a write request to a TFTP server. The purpose of a *read request* is to request to download a file from the server, and the purpose of a *write request* is to request to upload a file to the server. For this chapter, we'll focus on read requests, but keep in mind that TFTP supports both functions.

TFTP servers listen for requests on UDP port 69 (memorize that port for the exam). Given the characteristics of TCP and UDP that we covered in chapter 22 of volume 1, this may be unexpected; when transferring files, you want to make sure that the entire file arrives intact, with all of its bytes in the correct order. TCP's reliability and sequencing features make it the usual Layer 4 protocol of choice for transferring files.

However, I also mentioned in chapter 22 of volume 1 that UDP may be preferred when reliability is provided via other means; this is the case with TFTP. TFTP uses *lock-step communication*, meaning that the client and server alternately send a message and then wait for a reply. When a TFTP server transfers a file to a client, it divides the file into ordered blocks. After sending one block, the server won't send another block until it has received an acknowledgment message from the client. Each block must be acknowledged, and messages are retransmitted if needed. Figure 8.2 demonstrates this process.

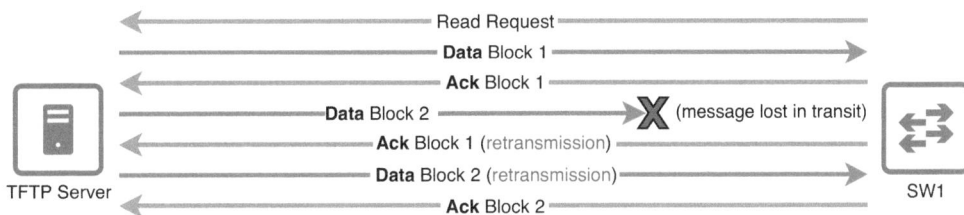

Figure 8.2 TFTP lock-step communication. The client and server alternate between sending and waiting to receive messages. The server divides the requested file into ordered blocks, and the client acknowledges receipt of each block. Lost messages result in retransmissions.

After either device (the client or server) sends a message, it sets a timer. If the timer expires, it retransmits its previous message. Using figure 8.2's example, after SW1 acknowledges block 1, it sets a timer. Although the TFTP server receives SW1's acknowledgment and sends block 2, it is lost in transit. As a result, SW1's timer expires, and it retransmits block 1's acknowledgment. Upon receiving the retransmitted acknowledgment for block 1, the server understands that block 2 did not make it to the client. The server then retransmits block 2.

The TFTP Transfer ID

Although TFTP servers listen for requests on UDP port 69, that only applies to the initial read or write request. After receiving the initial request, the server allocates a new port number in the ephemeral range (49152–65535) to identify that specific session; this port is called the *Transfer ID* (TID). For the remainder of the communication between the server and client, the server will listen on and source messages from the TID port, not port 69. However, for the CCNA exam, just remember that TFTP = UDP port 69.

To summarize, although TFTP uses UDP, which doesn't offer sequencing and reliability features, the TFTP protocol itself uses lock-step communication to provide both sequencing and reliability. It's not as sophisticated as TCP's features, but it's sufficient to allow TFTP to use the lightweight UDP as its Layer 4 protocol.

8.1.2   *Transferring files with TFTP*

Now that you have a basic understanding of how TFTP works, in this section let's take a look at how to use TFTP to transfer a file from a TFTP server to a Cisco IOS device. Specifically, we will copy a Cisco IOS image to our device to upgrade the device to a newer version of IOS; we'll cover the actual upgrade process in section 8.3.

THE CISCO IOS FILE SYSTEM

To transfer files to and from Cisco IOS devices, you need a basic understanding of the Cisco IOS *file system*—the hierarchical structure that IOS uses to store, manage, and organize various types of files, such as configuration files, IOS images, and log files. These files can then be easily accessed and manipulated by both applications and users.

While we commonly refer to "the IOS file system" in a general sense, it's important to note that this term encompasses multiple file systems. These are designed to manage different physical storage locations, such as flash memory, NVRAM (non-volatile RAM), and even remote storage like TFTP or FTP servers. Each of these storage options has its own unique file system. You can view the various file systems with the `show file systems` command. The following example shows some partial output:

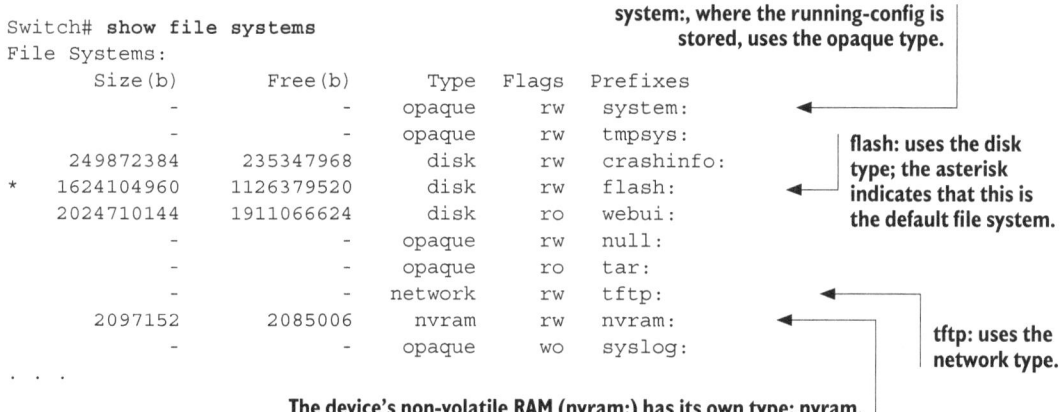

There are a few different types of file systems in that output that you should know:

- *Opaque*—Logical file systems used for internal functions
- *NVRAM*—Used for the device's NVRAM (where the startup-config file is saved)
- *Disk*—Physical storage devices (like flash memory)
- *Network*—Used to access external file systems over a network (i.e., TFTP servers)

Let's look at these four types and some examples of each. Opaque file systems are logical file systems used for the device's internal functions. For example, `system:` is where the device's running-config file is stored; the configuration commands in this file determine how the device actually functions. You can view the contents of a file system with the **dir** command, as in the following example:

```
Switch# dir system:
Directory of system:/
    2  -r--              0        <no date>  default-running-config
    4  dr-x              0        <no date>  memory
    1  -rw-           5369        <no date>  running-config
. . .
```

The running-config file is stored in system.

Previously, we used the **show running-config** command to view this file; this command is basically a shortcut, providing a simple method to view the device's configuration without needing to know the actual location of the file. Alternatively, you can use the **more** command, which allows you to view the contents of a file, and then specify the **system:running-config** file path, as in the following example. The output is the same as **show running-config**:

```
Switch# more system:running-config
!
! Last configuration change at 09:30:41 JST Thu Sep 21 2023
!
version 16.6
. . .
```

The NVRAM file system type is only used for one file system: nvram:. Although it stores other files, this file system is best known for storing the startup-config file that the device loads when booting up. In the following example, I use **dir nvram:** to confirm the contents of the file system, and then **more nvram:startup-config** to view the startup-config file; this is equivalent to using the **show startup-config** command:

```
Switch# dir nvram:                         The startup-config file is stored in nvram:.
Directory of nvram:/
 2049  -rw-     5449        <no date>  startup-config
 2050  ----     3573        <no date>  private-config
. . .
Switch# more nvram:startup-config          Views the contents of nvram:startup-config
!
! Last configuration change at 14:43:55 JST Sat Sep 16 2023 by jeremy
! NVRAM config last updated at 14:43:55 JST Sat Sep 16 2023 by jeremy
!
version 16.6
. . .
```

The Disk file system type is used for physical storage devices. One example is flash:, which is the *default file system*—the primary location where the operating system looks for files during various operations unless another file system is specified. This is the location we'll copy files to with TFTP. If a USB flash drive is inserted, it typically uses the Disk file system type as well.

The Network file system type is used to access remote file systems over a network, such as TFTP servers; the `tftp:` file system is an example. Likewise, there is also an `ftp:` file system. When specifying a network file system in a command, you also have to specify the IP address of the target host—these file systems don't reside on the local device.

TRANSFERRING FILES WITH THE COPY COMMAND

To transfer files to and from a TFTP server, use the **copy** `source destination` command—this creates a copy of the specified source file at the specified destination. My Cisco Catalyst 2960 switch in my home network is not running Cisco's recommended software version, so in this section, let's transfer a newer IOS image from a TFTP server (my PC) to my switch (SW1), and then we'll do the upgrade itself in section 8.3. The following example shows the contents of the `flash:` file system on my switch:

```
SW1# show flash:
Directory of flash:/
    3  -rwx        10152   Mar 30 2011 10:28:53 +09:00   vlan.dat
    4  -rwx         2974   Sep 20 2023 15:32:05 +09:00   config.text
    5  -rwx         3096   Sep 20 2023 15:32:06 +09:00   multiple-fs
    6  -rwx     15208832   Sep 20 2023 13:46:38 +09:00
➡ c2960c405-universalk9-mz.150-2.SE5.bin
  610  -rwx         5058   Sep 20 2023 15:32:06 +09:00   private-config.text
```

The IOS image that my switch currently uses

I have downloaded a newer IOS image from software.cisco.com and set up my PC as a TFTP server. Figure 8.3 shows how my switch will copy the new image from my PC.

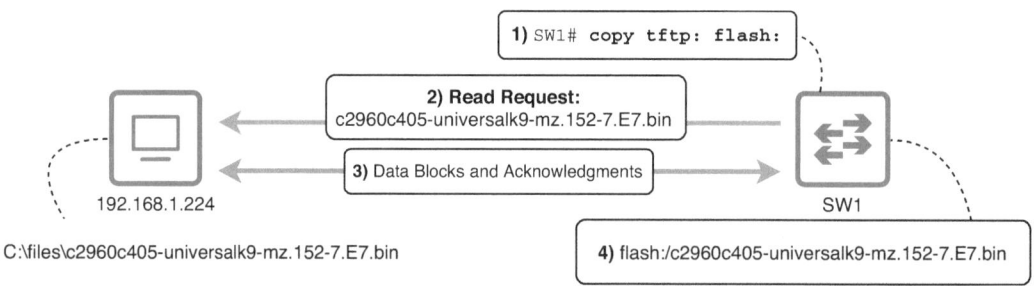

1) SW1# `copy tftp: flash:`

2) **Read Request:**
c2960c405-universalk9-mz.152-7.E7.bin

3) Data Blocks and Acknowledgments

192.168.1.224

SW1

C:\files\c2960c405-universalk9-mz.152-7.E7.bin

4) flash:/c2960c405-universalk9-mz.152-7.E7.bin

Figure 8.3   Copying an IOS image from a TFTP server to a Cisco switch. (1) Copy the file with the `copy tftp:` `flash:` **command. (2) The switch sends a read request for the file. (3) The file is transferred to the switch. (4) The file has been copied.**

NOTE   You need a valid service contract with Cisco to download and use IOS software; this isn't something you need to worry about for the CCNA exam.

In the following example, I use the **copy tftp: flash:** command on my switch, telling it that I would like to copy a file from a TFTP server to the `flash:` file system:

Specifies the IP address of the TFTP server

```
SW1# copy tftp: flash:
Address or name of remote host []? 192.168.1.224
```

Specifies the name of the file on the TFTP server

Specifies the name to save the file as on the local device

```
Source filename []? C2960c405-universalk9-mz.152-7.E7.bin
Destination filename [c2960c405-universalk9-mz.152-7.E7.bin]?
Accessing tftp://192.168.1.224/c2960c405-universalk9-mz.152-7.E7.bin...
Loading c2960c405-universalk9-mz.152-7.E7.bin from 192.168.1.224 (via Vlan1): !!!!!!!
!!!!!!!!!!!!!!!!!!!!!!!!!!!!!!!!!!!!!!!!!!!!!!!!!!!!!!!!!!!!!!!!!!
[OK - 18179072 bytes]
18179072 bytes copied in 200.831 secs (90519 bytes/sec)
```

The file was successfully copied.

> **NOTE**   Setting up a TFTP server is beyond the scope of the CCNA exam.

After issuing the **copy tftp: flash:** command, I am shown a series of prompts. The first prompt asks for the IP address (or name, if DNS is available) of the TFTP server; I specify my PC's IP address of **192.168.1.224**. I am then prompted for the source filename—the name of the file that I want to copy from the TFTP server. I specify **c2960c405-universalk9-mz.152-7.E7.bin**—the IOS image I want to copy to my switch.

> **NOTE**   TFTP does not allow you to view the files on the TFTP server; you must know the name of the file you want to download in advance.

The final prompt is for the destination filename—the name that the file will be saved as on the local device (my switch). By default, the destination filename will be the same as the source filename (as indicated by the value in square brackets); simply pressing Enter at this prompt accepts the default. You can optionally specify a different name, but IOS image names include information about the image type and IOS version, so they're best left as is.

> **NOTE**   To skip the prompts for the TFTP server's address etc., you can specify them in the command itself. The syntax is **copy tftp://**server-ip**/**src -filename **flash:/**dst-filename.

The new IOS image has now been transferred to my switch. The following example shows the new image, as well as the image the switch is currently using, in flash::

```
SW1# show flash:
Directory of flash:/
    2  -rwx    18179072  Sep 21 2023 10:40:22 +09:00
➥c2960c405-universalk9-mz.152-7.E7.bin                        ◄———— The newly copied image
. . .
    6  -rwx    15208832  Sep 20 2023 13:46:38 +09:00
➥c2960c405-universalk9-mz.150-2.SE5.bin    ◄
. . .
```

The currently used image

8.2   *File Transfer Protocol*

Of the two protocols we are covering in this chapter, FTP is the older one, first standardized in 1971. However, FTP is more robust, providing a variety of features that TFTP does not. For example, FTP requires authentication with a username/password, providing greater security than TFTP. However, FTP does not encrypt data; files are transferred as plaintext. For even more security, you can use an encrypted protocol like FTP Secure (FTPS). However, for the purpose of the CCNA exam, we will focus on FTP itself, not its related encrypted protocols.

Encrypted file transfers

Ideally, file transfers should be encrypted for maximum security, especially over a public network like the internet. Here are a couple of options:

- *File Transfer Protocol Secure* (FTPS) uses Transport Layer Security (TLS) to secure FTP communications between the server and client.
- *SSH File Transfer Protocol* (SFTP) is an extension of SSH that enables it to perform encrypted file transfers. Despite the name, this protocol isn't actually related to FTP.

8.2.1   *How FTP works*

Unlike TFTP, FTP uses TCP as its Layer 4 protocol. This means that, whereas a TFTP exchange begins with the client immediately sending a request to the server, an FTP exchange must begin by establishing a TCP connection—the TCP three-way handshake. However, transferring files with FTP requires two TCP connections, not one. Figure 8.4 outlines the process.

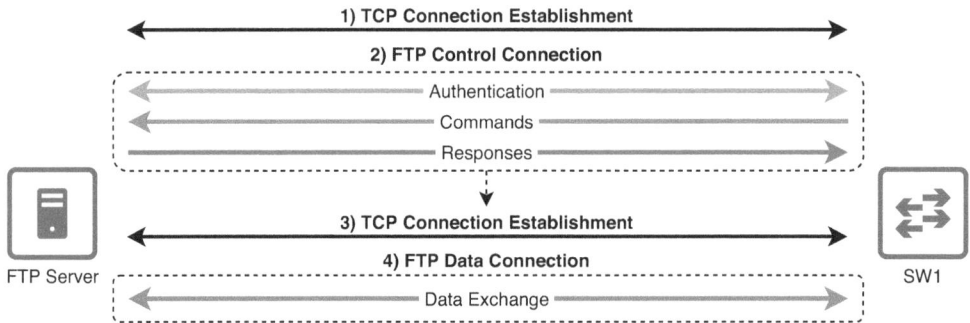

Figure 8.4   An FTP exchange involves two TCP connections: an FTP control connection, and an FTP data connection.

Step 1 in figure 8.4 shows the initial TCP connection establishment. This is a standard TCP three-way handshake: SYN (client to server), SYN-ACK (server to client), and ACK (client to server). Once this three-way handshake is done, the client and server have established the *FTP control connection*—step 2 in figure 8.4. Through this connection, the server will first authenticate the client by checking its username and password. If the authentication succeeds, the client can then send *FTP commands* to the server; it is through these commands that the client can tell the server what it wants to do.

EXAM TIP FTP servers listen for control connections on TCP port 21; memorize that port!

Unlike TFTP, in which a client can only copy files to or from the server, FTP has a variety of commands to support functions like listing the available files and directories, navigating through directories, renaming and deleting files, and various others. In our example, SW1 needs to download a file from the server. SW1 will send a RETR (retrieve) command to get a copy of a specific file; this is equivalent to a TFTP read request.

However, the actual data exchange does not take place over the FTP control connection. Instead, a second TCP connection is established—step 3 in figure 8.4. This second three-way handshake establishes the *FTP data connection*, which is step 4 in figure 8.4. It is over this connection that the server transfers the file to the client. One advantage of having separate control and data connections is that FTP can support multiple data transfers simultaneously; with a single control connection, the client can establish multiple data connections with the server.

EXAM TIP TCP port 20 is reserved for FTP data connections, but modern FTP servers often use an ephemeral port instead—the port that will be used for the data connection is conveyed through the control connection. However, for the CCNA exam, memorize these ports: FTP control = TCP 21, FTP data = TCP 20.

FTP active and passive modes

Although the FTP client initiates the control connection (by sending the first TCP SYN to port 21 on the FTP server), the data connection can be initiated by either the client or the server. In the original FTP standard, it was the server that initiated the data connection; this is called *active mode* (the server is the "active" one).

However, active mode caused problems as firewalls and Network Address Translation (NAT—next chapter's topic) became common, as they could block the incoming data connection from the server to the client. This led to the development of *passive mode*, in which the client initiates the data connection (the server is "passive"), solving the problems with active mode. A Cisco IOS device will use passive mode by default when acting as an FTP client; it does this by sending a *PASV* command to the server.

8.2.2   *Transferring files with FTP*

Transferring files with FTP is largely the same as with TFTP but with the addition of username/password authentication. For this section, we will once again look at how to transfer an IOS image from an FTP server (my PC) to a Cisco IOS device (a switch in my home network)—I erased the one we transferred previously with TFTP (the command to do so is **delete** *file*). In the following example, I use **show flash:** to confirm the contents of my switch's flash drive:

```
SW1# show flash:
Directory of flash:/
    3  -rwx       10152  Mar 30 2011 10:28:53 +09:00  vlan.dat
    4  -rwx        2974  Sep 20 2023 15:32:05 +09:00  config.text
    5  -rwx        3096  Sep 20 2023 15:32:06 +09:00  multiple-fs
    6  -rwx    15208832  Sep 20 2023 13:46:38 +09:00
➥c2960c405-universalk9-mz.150-2.SE5.bin
  610  -rwx        5058  Sep 20 2023 15:32:06 +09:00  private-config.text
```

The IOS image that my switch currently uses

To transfer a file with FTP, we can use the same command as with TFTP: **copy** *source destination*, using **ftp:** instead of **tftp:** for the *source* argument. However, as the following example shows, this doesn't work initially:

```
SW1# copy ftp: flash:
Address or name of remote host []? 192.168.1.224
Source filename []? c2960c405-universalk9-mz.152-7.E7.bin
Destination filename [c2960c405-universalk9-mz.152-7.E7.bin]?
Accessing ftp://192.168.1.224/c2960c405-universalk9-mz.152-7.E7.bin...
%Error opening ftp://192.168.1.224/c2960c405-
➥universalk9-mz.152-7.E7.bin (Incorrect Login/Password)
```

The connection fails due to incorrect credentials.

FTP requires username/password authentication, so we first have to configure an FTP username and password on SW1 with the **ip ftp username** *username* and **ip ftp password** *password* commands; of course, these must match a user account on the FTP server. In the following example, I use these commands on SW1:

```
SW1(config)# ip ftp username jeremy
SW1(config)# ip ftp password password123
```

> **NOTE**   This probably goes without saying, but you should never use a password like "password123." We will cover password best practices in chapter 11.

With these credentials configured, SW1 is able to authenticate to the server and retrieve the file, as shown in the following example:

```
SW1# copy ftp: flash:
Address or name of remote host [192.168.1.224]?
Source filename []? c2960c405-universalk9-mz.152-7.E7.bin
Destination filename [c2960c405-universalk9-mz.152-7.E7.bin]?
```

```
Accessing ftp://192.168.1.224/c2960c405-universalk9-mz.152-7.E7.bin...
Loading c2960c405-universalk9-mz.152-7.E7.bin
!!!!!!!!!!!!!!!!!!!!!!!!!!!!!!!!!!!!!!!!!!!!!!!!!!!!!!!!!!!!!!!!!!!!!!!!!!!!
[OK - 18179072/4096 bytes]
18179072 bytes copied in 157.933 secs (115106 bytes/sec)
```

The credentials specified in the `ip ftp username` and `ip ftp password` commands are the device's default FTP credentials—the credentials that will be used if none are specified in the command. To specify the credentials in the command, the syntax is `copy ftp://`*username:password*`@`*server-ip* `flash:`; for example, `copy ftp://jeremy:password123@192.168.1.224 flash:`.

After the file transfer is complete, I once again use `show flash:` to confirm that the new IOS image is in SW1's flash drive. In the next section, we'll configure SW1 to load that new image instead of its current one after its next reboot:

```
SW1# show flash:
Directory of flash:/
   2  -rwx    18179072  Sep 21 2023 21:18:13 +09:00        │ The newly copied
➡c2960c405-universalk9-mz.152-7.E7.bin          ◀──────────┘ image
. . .
   6  -rwx    15208832  Sep 20 2023 13:46:38 +09:00        │ The currently used
➡c2960c405-universalk9-mz.150-2.SE5.bin         ◀──────────┘ image
. . .
```

8.3   Upgrading Cisco IOS

After transferring a new IOS image to a device, configuring the device to use that new image requires just one configuration command, followed by a system reboot. Regardless of whether you use TFTP, FTP, or another method to transfer the new image to the device, the upgrade process is identical. However, before we do that, let's pause to consider the purpose of upgrading to a new version of IOS in the first place. Here are a few reasons:

- *Security*—New releases often include fixes for security vulnerabilities that have been discovered in previous releases. By keeping your devices up to date, you can protect your network from known security threats.
- *Bug fixes*—New releases often include bug fixes for issues such as memory leaks, crashes, and performance problems that can negatively affect your network.
- *New features and functionality*—New releases often include new features and functionality not present in previous versions, offering more configuration options and networking solutions.
- *Cisco support*—Cisco routinely ends support for older versions, making it challenging to get technical assistance for any issues that may occur.

Security is undoubtedly the most important reason to upgrade to a new version of Cisco IOS. The version of IOS currently running on my switch has 48 security advisories associated with it, 4 of which are marked as "critical"—this would not be acceptable in an enterprise network. To check the current version of IOS running on a device, use the **show version** command, as in the following example:

```
SW1# show version
Cisco IOS Software, C2960C Software (C2960c405-
➡UNIVERSALK9-M), Version 15.0(2)SE5, RELEASE SOFTWARE (fc1)
Technical Support: http://www.cisco.com/techsupport
Copyright (c) 1986-2013 by Cisco Systems, Inc.
. . .
```

The current version is 15.0(2)SE5.

NOTE   To check the latest and recommended versions of IOS available for a particular device, go to software.cisco.com (a Cisco account is required) and search for the device model. From there, you will also be able to find links to release notes, security advisories, etc.

To make the device boot with a different image, use the **boot system** *image-path* command in global config mode. I do so in the following example and confirm before and after with the **show boot** command, which lists various boot settings:

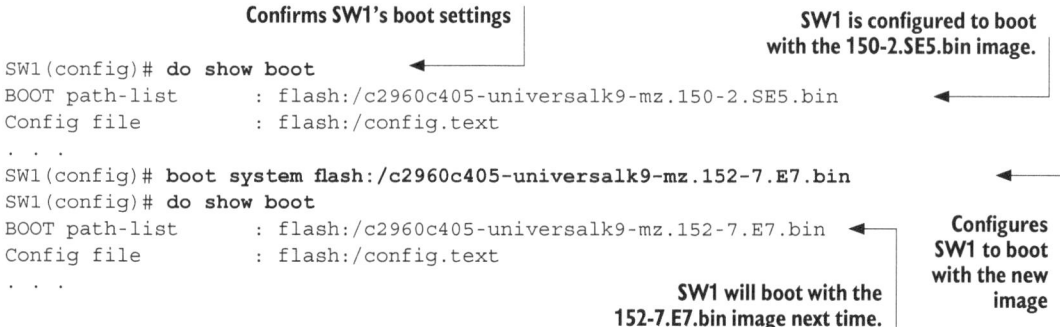

Confirms SW1's boot settings

SW1 is configured to boot with the 150-2.SE5.bin image.

Configures SW1 to boot with the new image

SW1 will boot with the 152-7.E7.bin image next time.

The second **show boot** command indicates that SW1 will load the new image the next time it boots, so now we just have to save the configuration (very important!) and reboot the device with the **reload** command, as in the following example:

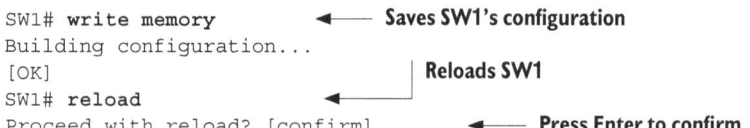

Saves SW1's configuration

Reloads SW1

Press Enter to confirm.

NOTE   Make sure to save the configuration with **write**, **write memory**, or **copy running-config startup-config** before rebooting, or the **boot system** command will not take effect upon reboot.

If you are connected to the device remotely via Telnet or SSH, you will lose connectivity while the device reboots—you won't be able to see the CLI. However, if you are connected via the console port, the device will display its boot sequence in real time. You'll be able to observe the device as it goes through its POST (Power-On Self-Test), loads the specified IOS image, and finally brings you back to the CLI once it has successfully rebooted. This can be particularly useful for troubleshooting issues or verifying that the device is booting correctly. In the following example, I use the **show version** command once again to verify that SW1 is using the new image:

```
SW1# show version
Cisco IOS Software, C2960C Software (C2960c405-
➡UNIVERSALK9-M), Version 15.2(7)E7, RELEASE SOFTWARE (fc10)
Technical Support: http://www.cisco.com/techsupport
Copyright (c) 1986-2022 by Cisco Systems, Inc.
. . .
```

SW1 is now using version 15.2(7)E7.

After the upgrade is complete, you can delete the old IOS image with the **delete** command, for example, **delete flash:/c2960c405-universalk9-mz.150-2.SE5.bin**. However, it's important to verify that the device is functioning properly and there are no network issues before doing so; if any issues arise, you may have to "roll back" to the previous IOS version.

IOS upgrade best practices

You should not carelessly upgrade a device to a newer IOS version. Here are a few best practices to ensure a successful upgrade:

- Back up your configuration before upgrading. This will allow you to restore it if something goes wrong.
- Read the release notes for the new IOS version carefully and ensure you understand the changes.
- Test the new IOS version in a lab before deploying it in a live network to identify any potential problems.
- Have a plan in place for rolling back to the previous IOS version if necessary.

Summary

- A file is a digital container for data such as text, images, audio, video, and software.
- Transferring files between computers is one of the primary functions of networks.
- Trivial File Transfer Protocol (TFTP) is a protocol used for transferring files over a network. It is relatively simple, allowing a client to transfer files to and from a server without additional features.
- TFTP doesn't use authentication and encryption, so it is recommended that you only use it to transfer files within a controlled environment like a LAN.
- A TFTP file transfer is initiated by a client sending either a read request to download a file from a server or a write request to upload a file to a server.

- TFTP servers listen for requests on UDP port 69. Although UDP doesn't provide the reliability and sequencing features desirable when transferring protocols, the TFTP protocol itself provides these features.

- TFTP uses *lock-step communication*, in which the client and server alternately send a message and then wait for a reply. Files are divided into ordered blocks, and each block must be acknowledged by the receiver before the next one is sent.

- If a device doesn't receive a reply to one of its messages after a certain period of time, it will retransmit the message.

- Cisco IOS uses a variety of *file systems* to store, manage, and organize files. Use **show file systems** to view them.

- The opaque file system type indicates logical file systems used for internal functions. For example, the system: file system that stores the running-config.

- The disk type is used for physical storage devices, like the flash file system, which is the default file system.

- The network type is used to access external file systems over a network, for example, the tftp: file system is used to access remote TFTP servers.

- The nvram type is used for the device's NVRAM, where the startup-config is stored.

- Use the **dir** command to view the contents of a particular file system. To view the flash: file system, you can also use **show flash:**.

- Use the **more** command to view the contents of a particular file.

- To transfer files to and from a TFTP server, use **copy** *source destination*, which creates a copy of the specified source file at the specified destination.

- You can specify the full file path of the source and/or destination in the **copy** command: **copy tftp://***server-ip***/***src-filename* **flash:/***dst-filename*.

- File Transfer Protocol (FTP) serves the same purpose as TFTP but is more robust, providing a variety of features that TFTP does not.

- FTP requires username/password authentication. However, it does not encrypt data; files are transferred as plaintext.

- Protocols like File Transfer Protocol Secure (FTPS) and SSH File Transfer Protocol (SFTP) can be used for encrypted file transfers.

- FTP uses TCP as its Layer 4 protocol. FTP exchanges require two TCP connections: one for the FTP control connection and one for the FTP data connection.

- Using the FTP control connection, the server authenticates the client, and the client sends FTP commands to the server. For example, the RETR (retrieve) command is used to retrieve a copy of a specific file on the server, like a TFTP read request.

- FTP servers listen for FTP control connections on TCP port 21.

- The client and server establish a separate FTP data connection for the actual file exchange. TCP port 20 is reserved for FTP data connections, but modern

FTP servers often use an ephemeral port instead. For the CCNA, remember TCP port 20.

- Transferring files from an FTP server requires a username and password. Use `ip ftp username` *username* and `ip ftp password` *password* to configure a Cisco IOS device's default FTP username and password.

- Alternatively, you can specify a username and password in the `copy` command. The syntax is `copy ftp://`*username*`:`*password*`@`*server-ip* `flash:`.

- Regardless of whether you use TFTP, FTP, or another method to transfer a new IOS image to a device, the upgrade process is identical.

- There are various reasons to upgrade a device's IOS software. A few main reasons are security, bug fixes, new features and functionality, and Cisco support.

- Security is the most important reason to upgrade to a new version of IOS. If a particular version has known security vulnerabilities, running it is a risk.

- Use `show version` to confirm the current version of IOS running on a device.

- Use `show boot` to view the device's boot settings, such as which IOS image it will load the next time it boots up.

- Use `boot system` *image-path* to specify the IOS image the device should load the next time it boots up. Remember to save the configuration.

- Use `reload` to reboot the device. If connected via Telnet or SSH, you will lose connectivity during reboot. If connected via the console port, you'll be able to observe the device as it boots up.

Network Address
Translation
9

This chapter covers

- Private IPv4 addresses
- Using NAT to translate between private and public
  IPv4 addresses
- The different types of NAT
- Configuring NAT on Cisco routers

IPv4 address exhaustion is a major problem and has been for a long time. In chapters 20 and 21 of volume 1, we covered the long-term solution: IPv6. However, IPv4 is still dominant to this day thanks to a few solutions that have been very effective in extending IPv4's lifespan. We covered one of these solutions in chapter 11 of volume 1 on subnetting with Classless Inter-Domain Routing (CIDR), which allows more flexibility than the rigid classful addressing system that came before it.

In this chapter, we will cover two more important solutions that, combined, have proven essential in preserving the IPv4 address space: private IPv4 addressing and Network Address Translation (NAT). Three ranges of IPv4 addresses have been reserved for free use in private networks without the need to be globally unique, and NAT provides a way to translate those private addresses into public addresses for communication over the internet. We will cover the following two CCNA exam topics:

- 1.7 Describe the need for private IPv4 addressing
- 4.1 Configure and verify inside source NAT using static and pools

9.1 Private IPv4 addresses

Private IPv4 addresses are IPv4 addresses that can be freely used by any organization or individual for their internal networks; they do not have to be globally unique. Three private IPv4 address ranges are defined in RFC 1918, Address Allocation for Private Internets:

- 10.0.0.0/8 (10.0.0.0–10.255.255.255)
- 172.16.0.0/12 (172.16.0.0–172.31.255.255)
- 192.168.0.0/16 (192.168.0.0–192.168.255.255)

EXAM TIP   Make sure you know the three ranges defined by RFC 1918. Additionally, remember the name *RFC 1918*; memorizing RFC numbers is unnecessary in most cases, but these addresses are often called *RFC 1918 addresses.*

Figure 9.1 shows three LANs connected to the internet. The LANs all use IPv4 addresses from the third private range (192.168.0.0/16). Notice that the three subnets overlap: 192.168.0.0/23 (192.168.0.0–192.168.1.255), 192.168.1.0/24 (192.168.1.0–192.168.1.255), and 192.168.1.0/25 (192.168.1.0–192.168.1.127). This is not a problem because the networks are never directly connected; their addresses don't have to be unique.

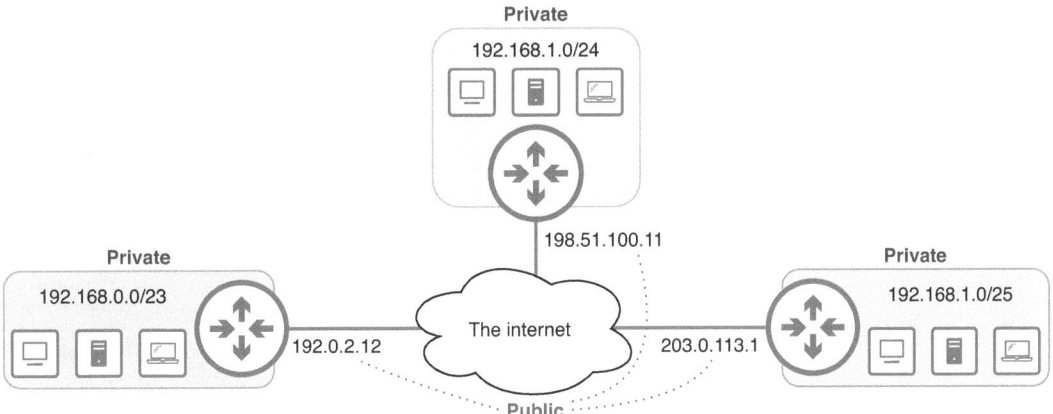

Figure 9.1   Public and private IPv4 addresses. Private IPv4 addresses can be freely used for internal networks and do not have to be globally unique. Public IPv4 addresses, used for communication over the internet, must be globally unique.

IPv4 addresses that are not in the RFC 1918 ranges (or another reserved range) are *public IPv4 addresses*; these addresses must be globally unique because they are used to communicate over the internet. If two internet-connected hosts have the same IP address, other routers won't be able to determine which of the two hosts is the intended recipient of a packet destined for their shared address. Anycast addresses (outlined in chapter 20 of volume 1) are an exception to this rule; they are purposefully assigned to multiple hosts.

> **NOTE** The public IPv4 addresses in figure 9.1 are from reserved ranges too: 192.0.2.0/24, 198.51.100.0/24, and 203.0.113.0/24 are reserved for use in documentation and examples but are often used to represent public addresses.

Private IPv4 addresses are not *routable* over the internet—packets sourced from or destined for private addresses will be discarded by the Internet Service Provider (ISP). If you have a Windows PC, use `ipconfig` to check your PC's IPv4 address (`ifconfig` if you're using macOS/Linux)—it's almost certainly a private address. So how can your PC communicate over the internet despite having a private address? The answer is NAT.

9.2 NAT concepts

Network Address Translation (NAT) is the process of modifying a packet's source and/or destination IP addresses and is typically performed by a router (or firewall) at the network's perimeter—a router that connects the internal network to the internet. By translating private IP addresses to public IP addresses, NAT allows hosts with private IP addresses to communicate over the internet.

9.2.1 The NAT process

Figure 9.2 demonstrates the NAT process. PC1, a host with a private IP address, sends a packet to the server at 8.8.8.8. R1 uses NAT to translate between PC1's private IP address (which is not routable over the internet) and a public IP address.

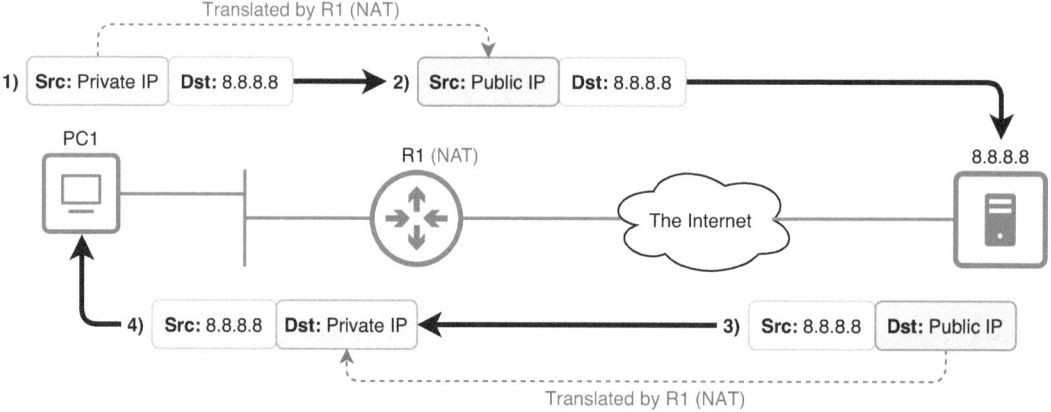

Figure 9.2   R1 translates between PC1's private IP address and a public IP address for use over the internet.

In step 1, PC1 sends a packet sourced from its private IP address—the IP address of its network interface. In step 2, R1 translates the source IP address of PC1's packet to a public IP address before forwarding it over the internet. Then, in step 3, the server at 8.8.8.8 replies by sending a packet destined for the public IP address, which R1 translates back to PC1's private IP address before forwarding the packet to PC1 in step 4.

> **NOTE** NAT was designed to translate between private and public IP addresses, but private–private and public–public translations are technically possible too. However, the use cases for private–private and public–public NAT are more limited than private–public NAT. For the CCNA exam, you can assume that NAT is private–public.

9.2.2 Cisco NAT terminology

When a host in an internal network communicates with a host in an external network via a NAT-enabled router, there are four addresses involved from the standpoint of the router:

1 The IP address of the internal host before NAT (inside local)
2 The IP address of the internal host after NAT (inside global)
3 The IP address of the external host before NAT (outside local)
4 The IP address of the external host after NAT (outside global)

Cisco uses four terms to describe each of these addresses: inside local, inside global, outside local, and outside global. In this section, we'll examine the inside/outside distinction and the local/global distinction and then define these four terms, which are critical to understand for the CCNA exam.

INSIDE AND OUTSIDE

Cisco uses the terms *inside* and *outside* to refer to the internal and external networks, respectively. An *inside address* is the IP address of a host located in the router's inside (internal) network, and an *outside address* is the IP address of a host located in an outside (external) network. Similarly, hosts in the inside network are called *inside hosts*, and hosts in the outside network are called *outside hosts*. Figure 9.3 demonstrates these concepts. R1's G0/0 interface connects to the internal/inside network, and G0/1 connects to the external/outside network—the internet.

> **NOTE** For consistency's sake, I will use the terms *inside* and *outside* from now on since they are the terms that Cisco uses in the context of NAT. Their meanings are the same as *internal* and *external*.

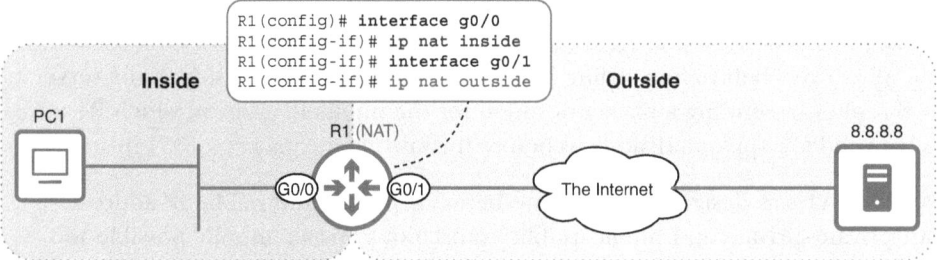

Figure 9.3   The inside/outside distinction from the perspective of R1. The *inside* network is R1's internal network, and the *outside* network is the external network (everything else).

> **NOTE**   All of these terms are dependent on perspective. From R1's perspective, PC1 is an inside host and 8.8.8.8 is an outside host, but from the perspective of 8.8.8.8 and its router (not shown), the opposite is true.

We will cover NAT configuration in section 9.3, but figure 9.3 shows one important step in the process: specifying the router's inside and outside interfaces with the `ip nat {inside | outside}` command. Because R1 G0/0 is configured with the `ip nat inside` command, PC1 is an inside host. And because R1 G0/1 is configured with `ip nat outside`, 8.8.8.8 is an outside host.

LOCAL AND GLOBAL

When PC1 (an inside host) sends a packet to a destination in the outside network, the source IP address of that packet is the IP address configured on PC1—a private IP address. But what about after R1 uses NAT to translate the source IP address of PC1's packet to a public IP address? The address after translation still represents PC1, so it remains an inside address, but another distinction is needed to differentiate between the pre- and post-NAT addresses: the local/global distinction.

A *local address* is an address before the router translates it, and a *global address* is an address after the router translates it. In other words, a local address is a host's address from the perspective of the inside network, and a global address is a host's address from the perspective of the outside network. Figure 9.4 demonstrates the local/global distinction.

Local/global and private/public

Local addresses and global addresses might seem similar to private addresses and public addresses. However, the concepts don't always overlap. For example, in figure 9.4, 8.8.8.8 (a public address) is both a local address and a global address from R1's perspective.

Local and global are NAT-specific terms that have specific meanings. Local addresses are used on the inside of a NAT network, while global addresses are used on the outside of a NAT network. NAT translates local addresses to global addresses when traffic flows from the inside to the outside of the network and vice versa, regardless of whether the addresses are private or public.

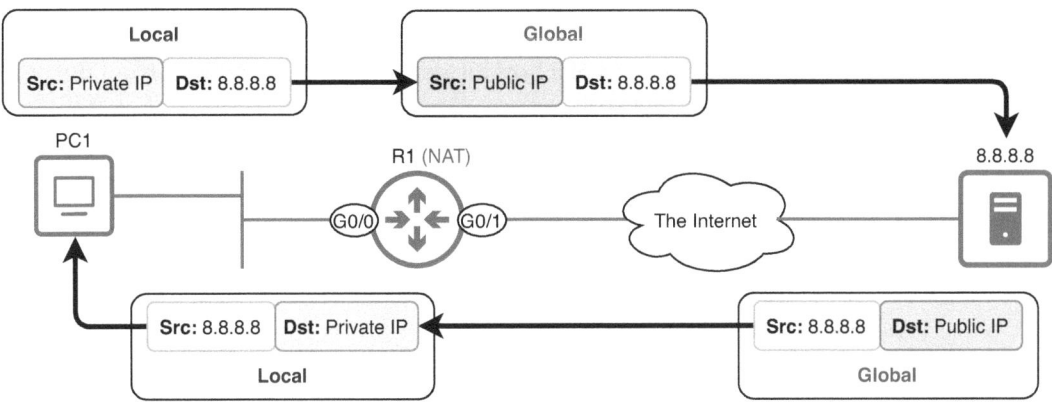

Figure 9.4 The local/global distinction. Local addresses appear in the inside network, and global addresses appear in the outside network.

From PC1's perspective, and from the perspective of other hosts in the inside network, PC1's IP address is a private IP address (i.e., 10.0.0.10). However, from the perspective of any hosts in the outside network, PC1's IP address is a public IP address (i.e., 203.0.113.1). For example, when the server at 8.8.8.8 replies to PC1's packet, it addresses its response to the public IP address, not PC1's private IP address—the server isn't even aware of PC1's private IP address.

When we combine the inside/outside and local/global distinctions, we get the four terms mentioned at the beginning of this section: inside local, inside global, outside local, and outside global. Figure 9.5 illustrates these four addresses.

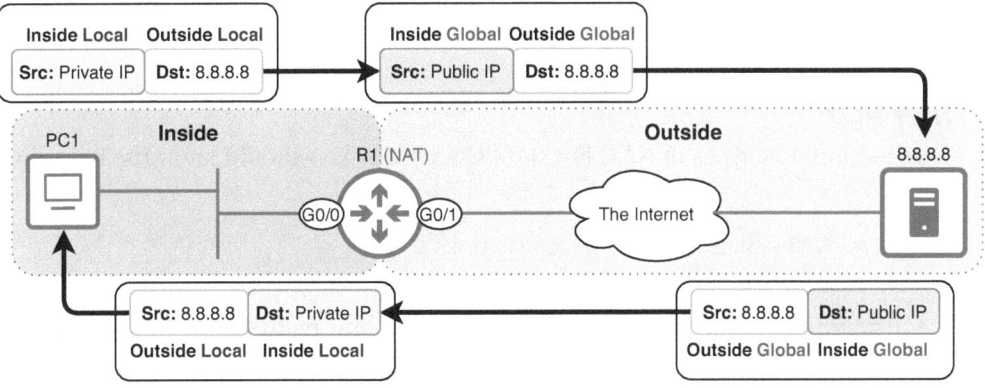

Figure 9.5 Inside local, inside global, outside local, and outside global addresses. The inside/outside distinction differentiates between hosts located in the inside and outside networks, and the local/global distinction differentiates between the perspectives of hosts in the inside and outside networks.

NOTE In our example, R1 doesn't translate the external host's IP address, so the outside local and outside global addresses are identical.

Now we can more accurately define those four terms:

- *Inside local*—The IP address of a host located in the inside network from the perspective of the inside network
- *Inside global*—The IP address of a host located in the inside network from the perspective of the outside network
- *Outside local*—The IP address of a host located in the outside network from the perspective of the inside network
- *Outside global*—The IP address of a host located in the outside network from the perspective of the outside network

As pointed out in the previous note, the outside local and outside global addresses are identical in our example. This is because R1 only performs *source NAT* on PC1's packet—it only translates the packet's source IP address. R1 does not perform *destination NAT* on PC1's packet—it does not translate the packet's destination IP address. Destination NAT is not part of the CCNA exam, so we won't cover it in this book.

It's all about perspective

To repeat what I said in a previous note, these terms are all dependent on perspective; they are relative to R1, the router performing NAT in our example. As far as R1 is concerned, 8.8.8.8 is both an outside local and an outside global address. However, the server at 8.8.8.8 is likely connected to its own router performing NAT as well, with its own perspective on what's inside and what's outside, what's local and what's global. From that router's perspective, 8.8.8.8 is the server's inside global address, and its inside local address is a private IP address that is unknown to R1, PC1, or any other host outside of that network.

9.3   Types of NAT

There are multiple types of NAT. For the CCNA exam, you should know the following three:

- *Static NAT*—Static one-to-one translations
- *Dynamic NAT*—Dynamic one-to-one translations
- *Dynamic PAT* (Port Address Translation)—Dynamic many-to-one translations

Each type has its own use cases, but dynamic PAT is by far the most widely used, potentially allowing thousands of hosts to share a single public IP address. In this section, we'll examine each type and how to configure it on a Cisco router.

9.3.1 Static NAT

The first type of NAT we'll cover is static NAT, which involves statically configuring one-to-one mappings of inside local (private) addresses to inside global (public) addresses. Figure 9.6 demonstrates static NAT and how to configure it in Cisco IOS.

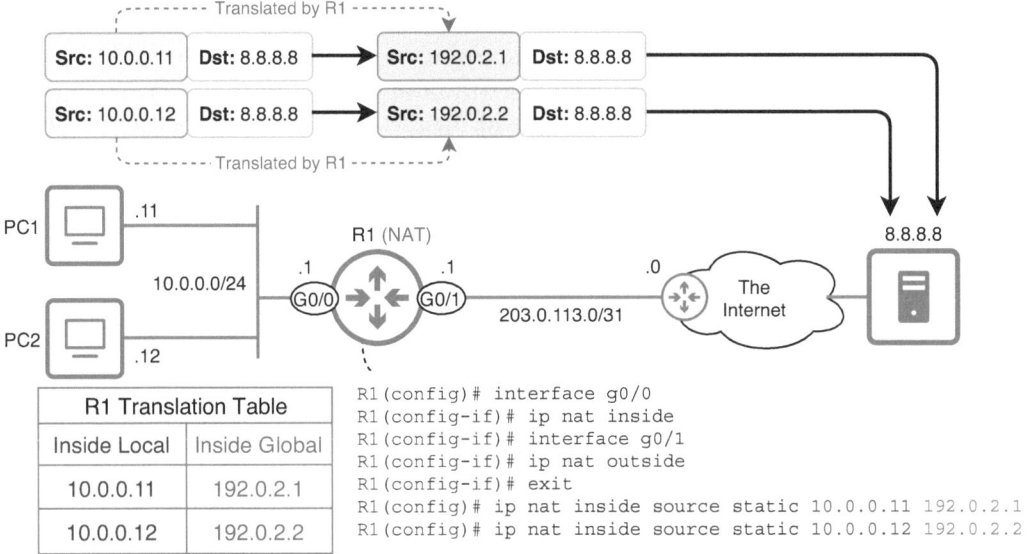

Figure 9.6   Static NAT. Inside local addresses 10.0.0.11 and 10.0.0.12 are statically mapped to inside global addresses 192.0.2.1 and 192.0.2.2, respectively.

NOTE   Figure 9.6 only shows the translations in one direction (from PC1/PC2 to the server), but R1 will translate the server's replies too (as shown in previous figures).

By mapping PC1's private IP address (10.0.0.11) to a public IP address (192.0.2.1), PC1 is able to communicate over the internet. To allow another inside host (PC2) to communicate over the internet, a second public IP address (192.0.2.2) is needed. This is the limitation of static NAT—it is one to one. As such, it does not help with the problem of IPv4 address exhaustion, although it is sometimes used to allow particular hosts to communicate over the internet. In the following example, I demonstrate the configurations:

```
R1(config)# interface g0/0
R1(config-if)# ip nat inside
R1(config-if)# interface g0/1
R1(config-if)# ip nat outside
```

Specifies G0/0 as an inside interface

Specifies G0/1 as an outside interface

Statically maps 10.0.0.11 to 192.0.2.1

```
R1(config-if)# exit
R1(config)# ip nat inside source static 10.0.0.11 192.0.2.1
R1(config)# ip nat inside source static 10.0.0.12 192.0.2.2
```

Statically maps 10.0.0.12 to 192.0.2.2

The first step is to configure the inside and outside interfaces with `ip nat {inside | outside}` in interface config mode, as we covered in the previous section. After that, all that's left to do is create static mappings with the `ip nat inside source static` *inside-local inside-global* command. In the example, I mapped inside local addresses 10.0.0.11 and 10.0.0.12 to inside global addresses 192.0.2.1 and 192.0.2.2, respectively. Figure 9.7 clarifies the meaning of the command's keywords.

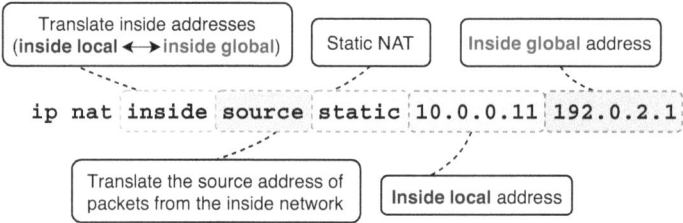

Figure 9.7   Static NAT. Inside local addresses 10.0.0.11 and 10.0.0.12 are statically mapped to inside global addresses 192.0.2.1 and 192.0.2.2, respectively.

The `inside` keyword tells R1 to perform translations for IP addresses originating from the inside network. Specifically, R1 will translate inside local addresses to inside global addresses as packets move from the inside network to the outside network.

The `source` keyword that follows tells R1 to translate the source IP address of packets coming from hosts on the inside network. So when R1 forwards a packet from PC1, it will translate the packet's source IP address from 10.0.0.11 to 192.0.2.1. However, it's important to remember that the reverse is true of the reply from the outside host. When a reply comes from the outside host and is destined for 192.0.2.1, R1 will translate the packet's destination IP address back to 10.0.0.11, allowing the packet to be correctly delivered to PC1.

The CCNA exam topics list states that you must be able to "configure and verify inside source NAT," so all of the NAT statements that we configure will start with `ip nat inside source`. It is the rest of the command that differentiates between static NAT, dynamic NAT, and dynamic PAT. By using the `static` keyword, you can configure static inside local addresses to inside global address mappings, as in this example.

After configuring static NAT, you can use `show ip nat translations` to view the router's translation table, as in the following example. One potentially confusing aspect of this command's output is that the leftmost column is `Inside global`, followed by `Inside local`—I think the opposite makes more sense, but Cisco didn't ask my opinion when they designed this command!

```
R1# show ip nat translations
Pro Inside global      Inside local       Outside local      Outside global
--- 192.0.2.1          10.0.0.11          ---                ---
--- 192.0.2.2          10.0.0.12          ---                ---
```

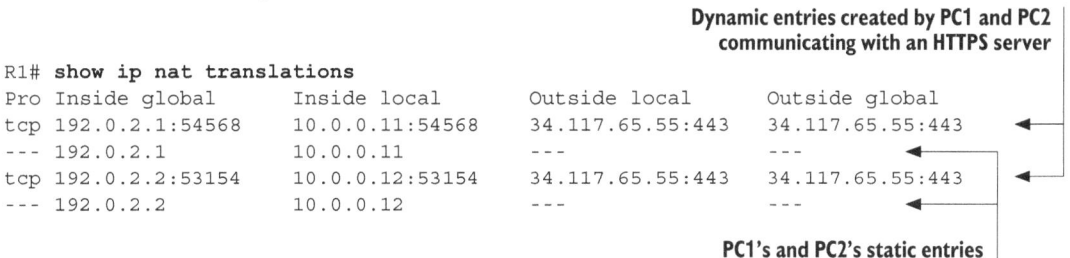

PC1's static mapping

PC2's static mapping

A static entry is created in the table for each mapping: 10.0.0.11 to 192.0.2.1 and 10.0.0.12 to 192.0.2.2—the other columns are empty. To see some information in these columns, I'll open web browsers on PC1 and PC2 and access some websites. When an inside host communicates with an outside host, additional dynamic entries are created in the NAT table. These dynamic entries are tied to the static mapping but track the state of individual communication sessions. The following example shows a small portion of the output afterward:

Dynamic entries created by PC1 and PC2 communicating with an HTTPS server

```
R1# show ip nat translations
Pro Inside global        Inside local         Outside local        Outside global
tcp 192.0.2.1:54568      10.0.0.11:54568      34.117.65.55:443     34.117.65.55:443
--- 192.0.2.1            10.0.0.11            ---                  ---
tcp 192.0.2.2:53154      10.0.0.12:53154      34.117.65.55:443     34.117.65.55:443
--- 192.0.2.2            10.0.0.12            ---                  ---
```

PC1's and PC2's static entries

> **NOTE** The numbers displayed after the IP addresses (separated by colons) indicate the TCP and UDP port numbers used by PC1/PC2 and the external hosts. That's how you can identify that HTTPS (TCP port 443) is being used in the previous example.

Whereas the static entries are permanent, the dynamic entries will be removed after a certain period of inactivity. For example, if PC1 and PC2 stop communicating with the HTTPS server at 34.117.65.55, those entries will be automatically removed, leaving only the static entries. You can also use `clear ip nat translation *` in privileged EXEC mode to manually clear all dynamic entries from the NAT translation table.

> **NOTE** Don't confuse the static/dynamic entries in the translation table with static/dynamic NAT; all of the entries we just examined are the result of static NAT translations.

9.3.2 Dynamic NAT

The next type of NAT we'll cover is *dynamic NAT*. Static NAT and dynamic NAT are similar in that they both involve one-to-one mappings of inside local addresses to inside global addresses. The difference is in how the mappings are assigned. In static NAT, you statically configure each mapping one by one. In dynamic NAT, the router dynamically creates the mappings itself from a pool of available addresses. Figure 9.8

demonstrates dynamic NAT; aside from the configuration commands, the NAT process is similar to that of static NAT.

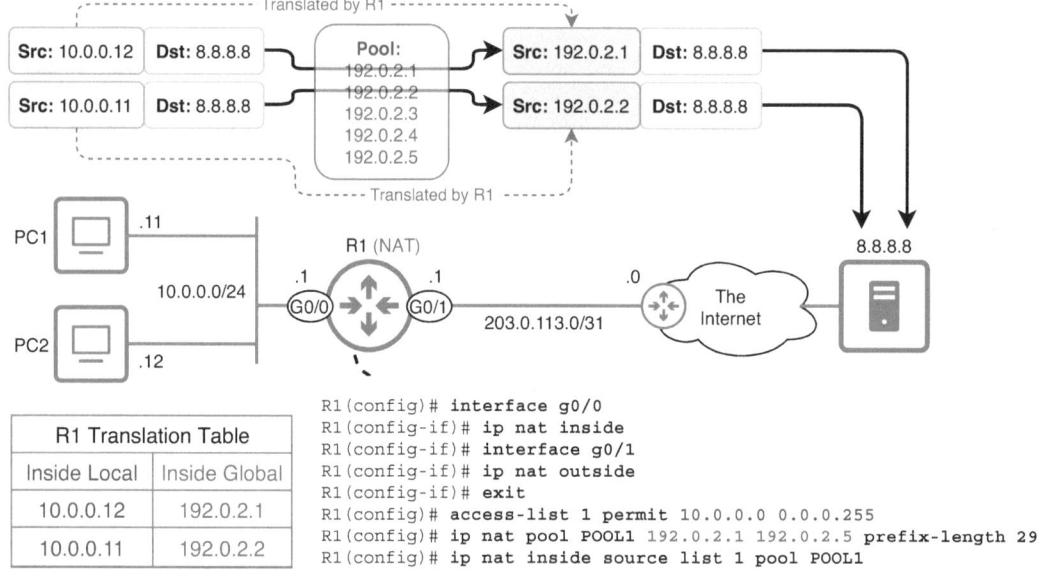

```
R1(config)# interface g0/0
R1(config-if)# ip nat inside
R1(config-if)# interface g0/1
R1(config-if)# ip nat outside
R1(config-if)# exit
R1(config)# access-list 1 permit 10.0.0.0 0.0.0.255
R1(config)# ip nat pool POOL1 192.0.2.1 192.0.2.5 prefix-length 29
R1(config)# ip nat inside source list 1 pool POOL1
```

R1 Translation Table	
Inside Local	Inside Global
10.0.0.12	192.0.2.1
10.0.0.11	192.0.2.2

Figure 9.8   Dynamic NAT. An ACL is used to identify a range of inside local addresses, and a NAT pool is used to identify a range of inside global addresses. Addresses in the pool are assigned on a first come, first served basis.

Dynamic NAT configuration consists of three main steps:

1 Define a range of inside local (private) addresses with an ACL
2 Define a range of inside global (public) addresses with a NAT pool
3 Map the ACL to the NAT pool

When the router forwards a packet from a host with an IP address in the range specified by the ACL, it will translate the source IP address to one of the available inside global addresses on a first come, first served basis. The following example shows the necessary configurations:

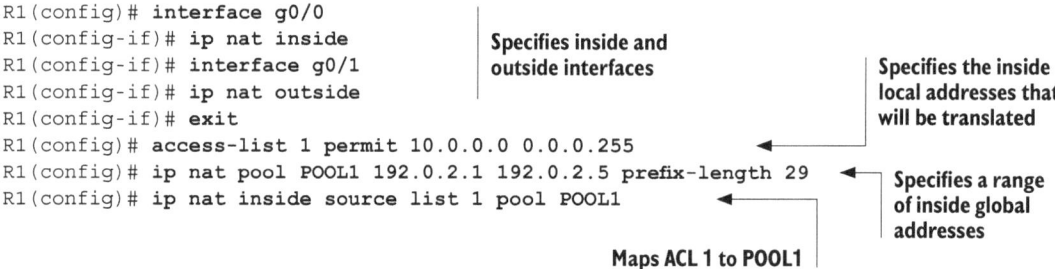

```
R1(config)# interface g0/0
R1(config-if)# ip nat inside          Specifies inside and
R1(config-if)# interface g0/1         outside interfaces
R1(config-if)# ip nat outside                                    Specifies the inside
R1(config-if)# exit                                              local addresses that
R1(config)# access-list 1 permit 10.0.0.0 0.0.0.255             will be translated
R1(config)# ip nat pool POOL1 192.0.2.1 192.0.2.5 prefix-length 29   Specifies a range
R1(config)# ip nat inside source list 1 pool POOL1                  of inside global
                                                                    addresses
                        Maps ACL 1 to POOL1
```

Just like in static NAT, you must use **ip nat {inside | outside}** to specify which interface(s) connect to the inside network and which connect to the outside network. Next, create an ACL to identify a range of inside local addresses to be translated. Packets that are permitted by the ACL will be translated, and packets that are denied by the ACL will not be translated; they will be forwarded as is (however, if their source IP address is a private IP address, they will be dropped by the ISP).

> **NOTE** The ACL isn't being used to decide which packets should be forwarded and which should be blocked; it is only being used to decide which packets should be translated with NAT. This is another common use for ACLs, which are quite versatile.

The ACL I created is **access-list 1 permit 10.0.0.0 0.0.0.255**, which permits all IP addresses from 10.0.0.0 through 10.0.0.255 but denies all other IP addresses via the implicit deny. R1 will use NAT to translate packets with a source IP address in the permitted range, but packets with a source IP address that is not in that range will not be translated.

The next step is to specify a range of inside global addresses—the public IPv4 addresses that will be used for communication over the internet. This is done by creating a NAT pool with the **ip nat pool** *name start-ip end-ip* **prefix-length** *length* command. The *start-ip* and *end-ip* arguments identify the range; I configured **192.0.2.1 192.0.2.5** to specify a range of five public addresses: 192.0.2.1–192.0.2.5.

> **NOTE** In a real network, you cannot freely use any public IPv4 addresses you want. Public addresses must be globally unique, and their assignment is governed by IANA and the RIRs below it (as we covered in chapter 20 of volume 1). To receive a range of public IP addresses, an enterprise must apply to an ISP or directly to an RIR.

In the **ip nat pool** command, you must also specify a prefix length; this is used to ensure that all addresses in the specified range are in the same subnet. I specified the 192.0.2.1–192.0.2.5 range with a /29 prefix length. This implies the 192.0.2.0/29 subnet (all host bits set to 0), which includes all addresses from 192.0.2.0 to 192.0.2.7. The specified range (192.0.2.1–192.0.2.5) is included in that subnet, so the command succeeds. Otherwise, the command would be rejected.

> **NOTE** Instead of **prefix-length**, you can use the **netmask** keyword—for example, **ip nat pool POOL1 192.0.2.1 192.0.2.5 netmask 255.255.255.248**.

The final step is to combine the ACL and pool with a NAT statement, mapping the range of inside local addresses (the ACL) to the range of inside global addresses (the pool). The command is **ip nat inside source list** *acl* **pool** *pool*; I mapped ACL **1** to **POOL1** in the example with **ip nat inside source list 1 pool POOL1**. After that command, the dynamic NAT configuration is complete.

It is worth repeating that dynamic NAT is one to one, just like static NAT. Multiple inside local addresses cannot be translated to the same inside global address at the same time. The inside global addresses are assigned on a first-come, first-served basis, and if the pool dries up, other hosts' packets will not be able to be translated—they will be dropped! Those hosts will have to wait for an inside global address to become available again; this is a major downside of dynamic NAT.

Figure 9.9 demonstrates this. The first five inside local addresses are translated to inside global addresses, but the sixth cannot be translated, resulting in the packet being dropped. The seventh packet, from 10.1.1.2, is forwarded without being translated because its source IP address is denied by ACL 1.

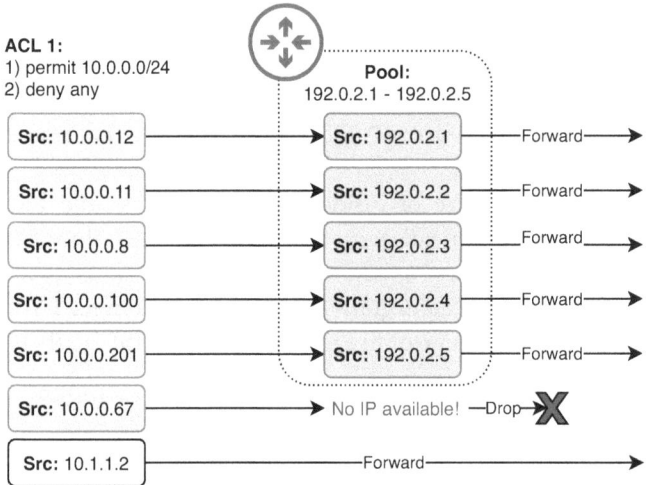

Figure 9.9   The dynamic NAT pool dries up. Packets that match ACL but can't be translated are dropped. Packets that are denied by the ACL are forwarded as is.

EXAM TIP   Packets that are permitted by the ACL but can't be translated due to a lack of addresses in the pool will be dropped. Packets that are denied by the ACL will be forwarded as is, without being translated (likely resulting in them being dropped by the ISP due to their private IP addresses). Remember this distinction!

As with static NAT, you can view the router's translation table with **show ip nat translations**. The output looks the same as when using static NAT. The following example shows a few entries in R1's translation table. For each translation, one entry is added showing only the inside local to inside global mapping, and then additional entries are added for each communication session from an inside host to an outside host—in this case, a DNS session (UDP 53), an HTTPS session (TCP 443), and an HTTP session (TCP 80) are shown:

```
R1# show ip nat translations
Pro Inside global        Inside local        Outside local       Outside global
udp 192.0.2.2:58910      10.0.0.11:58910     8.8.8.8:53          8.8.8.8:53
--- 192.0.2.2            10.0.0.11           ---                 ---
tcp 192.0.2.3:33630      10.0.0.12:33630     142.250.207.14:443  142.250.207.14:443
--- 192.0.2.3            10.0.0.12           ---                 ---
tcp 192.0.2.1:32980      10.0.0.13:32980     34.107.221.82:80    34.107.221.82:80
--- 192.0.2.1            10.0.0.13           ---                 ---
```

Of the types of NAT you need to know for the CCNA exam, dynamic NAT has the fewest real-world use cases. Like static NAT, it only provides one-to-one translations. However, unlike static NAT, it doesn't let you control the translations. If the number of inside hosts is larger than the available pool of inside global addresses, there's no easy way to control which hosts get to access the internet and which have to wait. Obtaining enough public IP addresses to support all inside hosts simply isn't feasible for most enterprises these days, given the state of the IPv4 address exhaustion problem.

9.3.3   *Dynamic PAT*

Dynamic Port Address Translation (PAT) is a type of NAT that translates both IP addresses and TCP/UDP port numbers (if necessary) to provide many-to-one mappings of inside local to inside global addresses. By using a unique port number for each communication session, a single public IP address can be shared by many inside hosts at the same time; the NAT-enabled router uses the port numbers to keep track of each individual session.

There are 65,536 (2^{16}) port numbers in total, meaning that a single public IP address can theoretically support tens of thousands of sessions from inside hosts—the actual number will depend on a number of factors, such as the router's memory capacity. It is this type of NAT that, combined with private IPv4 address ranges, has greatly extended IPv4's lifespan.

> **NOTE** ICMP doesn't use port numbers like TCP and UDP, but many ICMP message types use a 16-bit *Identifier* field for a similar purpose. When translating ICMP packets (i.e., ping), the Identifier plays the role that TCP/UDP port numbers do.

DYNAMIC PAT USING A POOL

One way to configure dynamic PAT is to simply add the **overload** keyword to the end of a dynamic NAT statement; in fact, another name for PAT is *NAT overload*. The following example demonstrates how to configure dynamic PAT in this way:

```
R1(config)# interface g0/0
R1(config-if)# ip nat inside
R1(config-if)# interface g0/1                      Adds the overload keyword
R1(config-if)# ip nat outside                        to the NAT statement
R1(config-if)# exit
R1(config)# access-list 1 permit 10.0.0.0 0.0.0.255
R1(config)# ip nat pool POOL1 192.0.2.1 192.0.2.5 prefix-length 29
R1(config)# ip nat inside source list 1 pool POOL1 overload
```

Figure 9.10 shows how the translations work after these configurations. When the router translates a packet, it will keep the pre- and post-translation port numbers the same if possible. However, if a packet's pre-translation port number is already in use for another session, the router will translate the port number to an available one.

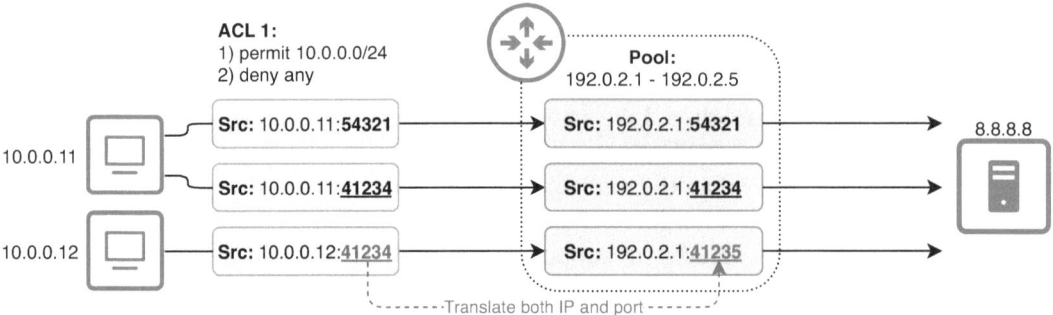

Figure 9.10 **Dynamic PAT using a NAT pool. The router keeps the pre- and post-translation port numbers the same if possible but translates them if needed.**

> **NOTE** Once a session's first packet has been translated, the same port number is used for the rest of the session; each individual packet doesn't need a unique port number.

Notice that in figure 9.10's example, R1 translates all three packets' inside local addresses to the same inside global address, even though the NAT pool has five available addresses. The router will use up all available port numbers for one inside global address (i.e., 192.0.2.1) before translating to the next available address in the pool (i.e., 192.0.2.2).

When the router receives the reply packets, it is able to identify which session the packets belong to, thanks to the unique port numbers. The router can then translate each packet's inside global address back to the appropriate inside local address. Figure 9.11 demonstrates this.

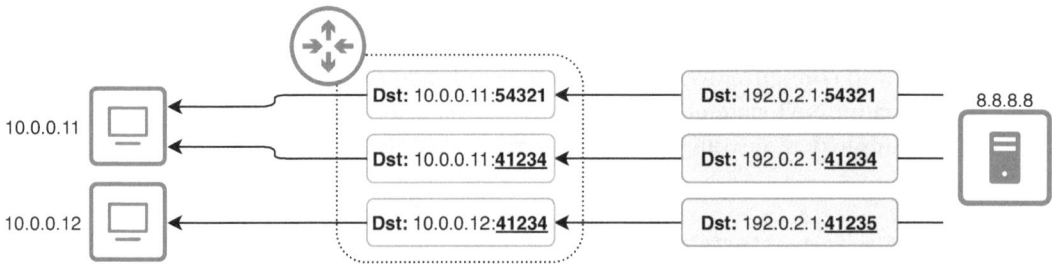

Figure 9.11 **The router tracks each session and translates each reply's destination address back to the appropriate inside local address.**

Dynamic PAT using an interface's IP address

Although dynamic PAT can be configured with a pool, PAT's many-to-one translation capabilities mean that many organizations require only a single public IP address, not a pool of them. And if a router is connected to the internet, the router already has a public IP address assigned to it—the IP address of the internet-connected interface. With PAT, the router can translate inside hosts' IP addresses to the IP address of the router's own interface.

Figure 9.12 shows how to configure this in Cisco IOS. Packets from hosts in R1's internal LAN are translated to the IP address of R1's G0/1 interface: 203.0.113.2.

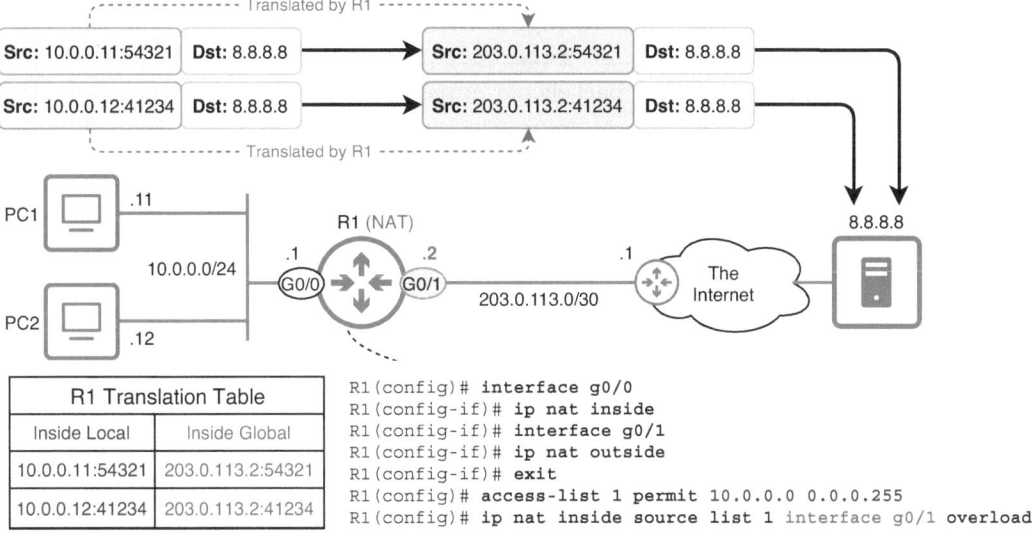

Figure 9.12 Dynamic PAT using an interface's IP address. R1 translates inside local addresses to the IP address of its own G0/1 interface: 203.0.113.2.

This is how dynamic PAT is most often configured because it allows inside hosts to communicate over the internet using the IP address already configured on the router—no additional public addresses are needed. The following example shows the configuration steps; let's walk through each command:

```
R1(config)# interface g0/0
R1(config-if)# ip nat inside
R1(config-if)# interface g0/1
R1(config-if)# ip nat outside
R1(config-if)# exit
R1(config)# access-list 1 permit 10.0.0.0 0.0.0.255
R1(config)# ip nat inside source list 1 interface g0/1 overload
```

Specifies inside and outside interfaces

Specifies the inside local addresses that will be translated

Translates inside local addresses to R1 G0/1's address

As in previous examples, you must first configure the inside and outside interfaces with `ip nat` {`inside` | `outside`} in interface config mode. Then, as in dynamic NAT, configure an ACL to determine which IP addresses should be translated. This ACL functions the same as the ones in NAT configurations we covered earlier: packets that are permitted by the ACL will be translated before being forwarded, but packets that are denied by the ACL will be forwarded as is.

> **NOTE** If a packet is permitted by the ACL but can't be translated due to a lack of addresses or port numbers, the packet will be dropped. However, you likely won't encounter this with dynamic PAT because so many port numbers are available.

All that remains is to configure the NAT statement itself. The syntax in this case is `ip nat inside source list` *acl* `interface` *interface* `overload`. This tells the router to use PAT to translate packets permitted by the ACL to the IP address of the specified interface. Port numbers are used to keep track of each session, including the router's own sessions (when the router sends its own packets using that IP address).

> **NOTE** The `overload` keyword is optional. If you omit it, IOS will automatically add it.

The following example shows R1's translation table after three inside hosts have communicated with an HTTPS server. The three inside local addresses are all translated to 203.0.113.2, but all have unique source ports, allowing R1 to keep track of them:

```
R1# show ip nat translations
Pro Inside global     Inside local      Outside local     Outside global
tcp 203.0.113.2:44578 10.0.0.11:44578   34.117.65.55:443  34.117.65.55:443
tcp 203.0.113.2:33032 10.0.0.12:33032   34.117.65.55:443  34.117.65.55:443
tcp 203.0.113.2:39102 10.0.0.13:39102   34.117.65.55:443  34.117.65.55:443
```

One more useful NAT verification command is `show ip nat statistics`. The following example shows the output on R1:

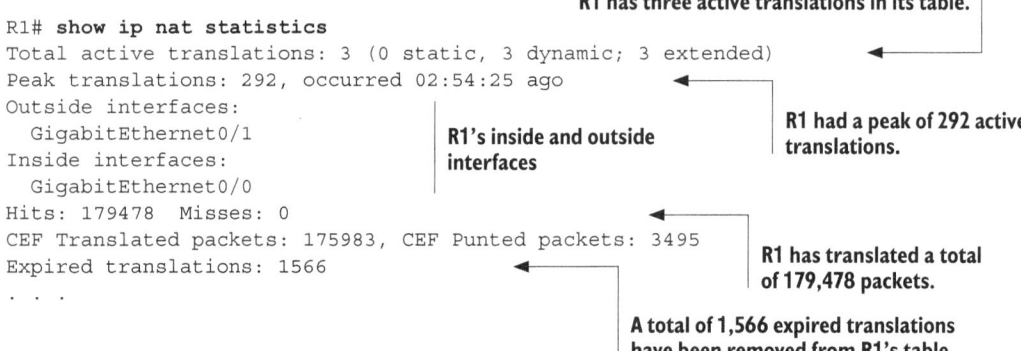

Exam scenarios

NAT is a key technique that is employed in the vast majority of modern networks and is a critical CCNA exam topic. Here are a couple of questions that illustrate how your understanding of NAT might be tested in the CCNA exam:

1   (multiple choice, single answer)
    You create an ACL as part of a dynamic NAT configuration. What is the role of this ACL?

    A   To define which packets should be forwarded and which should be dropped
    B   To define which packets should be translated
    C   To define the range of inside global addresses that will be used for communication over the internet
    D   To create a NAT pool

The key to this question is understanding that an ACL's role in a dynamic NAT (or PAT) configuration is different from an ACL applied to an interface. Instead of determining which packets should be forwarded and which should be dropped, the ACL is used to define which packets should be translated. Packets that are permitted by the ACL are translated, and those that are denied by the ACL are forwarded as is (without translation). So B) is the correct answer.

2   (drag and drop)
    Drag the NAT types on the left to the appropriate characteristics on the right. Each NAT type can be used more than once.

A) Static NAT	One-to-one translations
B) Dynamic NAT	One-to-many translations
C) Dynamic PAT	Automatic translations
	Manual translations

Here are the correct answers:

- One-to-one translations: A) and B)
- One-to-many translations: C)
- Automatic translations: B) and C)
- Manual translations: A)

Static and dynamic NAT both offer one-to-one translations: each inside local address is translated to a unique inside global address. Dynamic PAT, on the other hand, provides many-to-one translations: many inside local addresses are translated to a single inside global address.

Static NAT requires manual configuration of each translation with the `ip nat inside source` *inside-local inside-global* command. Dynamic NAT and PAT, on the other hand, provide automatic translations; you simply need to specify a range of inside local addresses and a range of inside global addresses (or an interface), and the router automatically creates the translations as it forwards packets.

Summary

- IPv6 is the long-term solution to IPv4 address exhaustion, but subnetting/CIDR, private IPv4 addresses, and NAT have greatly extended IPv4's lifespan.

- *Private IPv4 addresses* can be freely used by any organization or individual for their internal networks; they do not have to be globally unique.

- RFC 1918 defines three private IPv4 address ranges: 10.0.0.0/8, 172.16.0.0/12, and 192.168.0.0/16.

- IPv4 addresses that are not in an RFC 1918 range (or another reserved range) are *public IPv4 addresses* and must be globally unique.

- Private IPv4 addresses are not *routable* over the internet—packets sourced from or destined for private addresses will be discarded by the ISP.

- *Network Address Translation* (NAT) is the process of modifying a packet's source and/or destination IP addresses. By translating private IP addresses to public IP addresses, hosts with private addresses can communicate over the internet.

- NAT was designed to translate between private and public IP addresses, but private–private and public–public translations are technically possible too.

- Cisco uses four terms to describe a packet's source/destination addresses before/after NAT: inside local, inside global, outside local, and outside global.

- The terms *inside* and *outside* refer to the internal and external networks, respectively—for example, inside/outside address and inside/outside host.

- Use the `ip nat {inside | outside}` command to specify a router's interfaces as connecting to the inside or outside networks. This step is required for all NAT types covered in the CCNA exam.

- The terms *local* and *global* are used to distinguish between pre- and post-NAT addresses.

- A device's IP address from the perspective of the inside network is local (pre-NAT). A device's IP address from the perspective of the outside network is global (post-NAT).

- *Inside local*—The IP address of a host located in the inside network from the perspective of the inside network

- *Inside global*—The IP address of a host located in the inside network from the perspective of the outside network

- *Outside local*—The IP address of a host located in the outside network from the perspective of the inside network

- *Outside global*—The IP address of a host located in the outside network from the perspective of the outside network

- If a router does not perform *destination NAT* (does not translate the destination IP address of inside hosts' packets), the outside local and outside global addresses will be identical.

- There are three types of NAT to learn for the CCNA exam: static NAT (static one to one), dynamic NAT (dynamic one to one), and dynamic PAT (dynamic many to one).

- *Static NAT* involves configuring static one-to-one mappings of inside local (private) addresses to inside global (public) addresses.

- Use `ip nat inside source static` *inside-local inside-global* to configure a static NAT mapping.

- Use `show ip nat translations` to view the NAT translation table. Permanent entries are made for each static mapping.

- When a static mapping is used, dynamic entries are made to track each communication session between inside and outside hosts. These entries are cleared from the table after a period of inactivity.

- Use `clear ip nat translation *` to manually clear all dynamic entries.

- *Dynamic NAT* is similar to static NAT in that it involves one-to-one mappings of inside local to inside global addresses. However, in dynamic NAT, the router performs the mappings dynamically.

- Dynamic NAT configuration consists of three main steps: (1) Define a range of inside local addresses with an ACL, (2) define a range of inside global addresses with a NAT pool, (3) map the ACL to the NAT pool.

- The ACL's purpose in dynamic NAT isn't to decide which packets are forwarded or dropped. It is only used to decide which packets are translated and which are not.

- Use `ip nat pool` *name start-ip end-ip* `prefix-length` *length* to create a NAT pool. Instead of `prefix-length` *length*, you can also use the `netmask` *netmask*.

- Use `ip nat inside source list` *acl* `pool` *pool* to map the ACL to the pool.

- If a packet is permitted by the ACL, its source IP will be translated to one of the addresses in the pool on a first come, first served basis.

- Dynamic NAT mappings are one to one. Multiple inside local addresses cannot be translated to the same inside global address at the same time.

- A packet that is permitted by the ACL but can't be translated due to a lack of addresses in the pool will be dropped.

- A packet that is denied by the ACL will be forwarded as is, without being translated (although the ISP will probably drop the packet because of its private address).

- *Dynamic Port Address Translation* (PAT) is a type of NAT that translates both IP addresses and TCP/UDP port numbers (if necessary) to provide dynamic many-to-one mappings of inside local to inside global addresses.

- It is this type of NAT that, combined with private IPv4 address ranges, has greatly extended IPv4's lifespan.

- Dynamic PAT can be configured with a pool, like dynamic NAT. Simply add the **overload** keyword to the end of the NAT statement: **ip nat inside source list** *acl* **pool** *pool* **overload**. Dynamic PAT is also called *NAT overload*.

- When translating packets, the router keeps the pre- and post-translation port numbers the same if possible but translates them if needed. Unique port numbers are needed for the router to track each session.

- The router will use up all available port numbers for one inside global address before translating to the next available address in the pool.

- Instead of using PAT with a pool, it is more common to translate inside hosts' IP addresses to the IP address of the routers' own internet-connected interface.

- Use **ip nat inside source list** *acl* **interface** *interface* **overload** to configure this. The router will translate packets that match the ACL to the IP address of the specified interface, using port numbers to track sessions.

- Use **show ip nat statistics** to view statistics such as the total number of active translations, peak translations, packets translated, etc.

Quality of service 10

This chapter covers

- Enabling IP telephony with voice VLANs
- Powering IP phones and other devices with Power over Ethernet
- Prioritizing important network traffic in times of congestion with quality of service

Network resources—bandwidth, in particular—are not unlimited. This means that networks can become congested, and bottlenecks can occur, negatively affecting network performance and the experience of the network's users. Some types of network communications are more sensitive to these problems. For example, users in a voice/video call, due to their real-time nature, are more likely to notice a network slowdown than users communicating via email.

Quality of service (QoS) is a set of technologies that enable the prioritization of more important traffic (and the de-prioritization of less important traffic) in times of network congestion. In this chapter, we will cover QoS and its various components. Before covering QoS itself, we will cover the topic of IP telephony, also called Voice over IP (VoIP)—telephones that communicate over a network using IP packets. Voice traffic is particularly sensitive to poor network performance and is usually prioritized in a QoS policy. We'll also cover Power over Ethernet (PoE), which is used

147

to power IP phones (and other devices) over Ethernet cables. Here are the exam topics we'll cover:

- 1.1.h PoE
- 2.1.a Access ports (data and voice)
- 4.7 Explain the forwarding per-hop behavior (PHB) for QoS such as classification, marking, queuing, congestion, policing, shaping

10.1   IP telephony

Traditional telephones connect to the *public switched telephone network* (PSTN), a network separate from the computer networks that are the subject of this book—this is also called *plain old telephone service* (POTS). *IP phones*, or *VoIP phones*, on the other hand, connect to Ethernet switches and communicate by sending and receiving IP packets.

Many companies have migrated from POTS to IP telephony for a variety of reasons, such as the cost effectiveness and advanced features that IP telephony provides (i.e., voicemail-to-email, integration with other business software, etc.). However, this created its own problems: each desk would now have two end-user devices (a PC and an IP phone), doubling the required number of Ethernet UTP cables that must be installed to each desk and the number of switch ports required. As a solution to this problem, IP phones have a small, internal three-port switch, allowing the IP phone and PC to connect to a single switch port, as in figure 10.1.

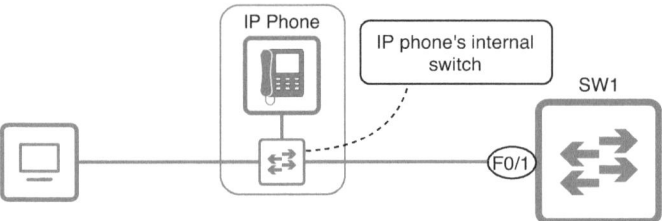

Figure 10.1   An IP phone's internal switch allows both the phone and a PC to connect to a single port on SW1. One port of this mini-switch connects to the PC, one to SW1, and one to the IP phone's internals.

10.1.1   Voice VLANs

Although a PC and IP phone can share a single switch port, their traffic should be kept segmented—kept in separate subnets and separate VLANs. One major reason for this is QoS: voice calls are very sensitive to lost and delayed packets, so voice traffic should be prioritized over regular network traffic from the PCs—also called *data traffic*. By segmenting voice and data traffic into separate subnets and VLANs, you can more easily identify and prioritize each traffic type in QoS policies. This can be achieved using the *voice VLAN* feature, as shown in figure 10.2.

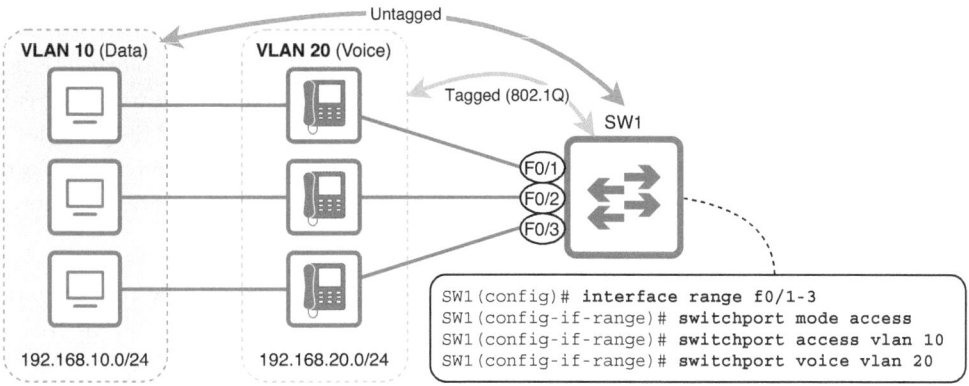

Figure 10.2   **Segmenting voice and data traffic into separate subnets and VLANs**

When covering access and trunk ports in chapter 12 of volume 1, I said that access ports belong to a single VLAN, whereas trunk ports can carry traffic from multiple VLANs, tagging frames with the 802.1Q protocol to differentiate between VLANs. Given that information, the configuration shown in figure 10.2—access ports carrying traffic in two VLANs—might seem incorrect. However, this case is an exception. When an access port is configured with a voice VLAN, it carries traffic in two VLANs:

- One for the data VLAN (also called the *access VLAN*), which is untagged
- One for the voice VLAN, which is tagged

In the following example, I configure SW1's ports as access ports, with VLAN 10 as the data VLAN (`switchport access vlan 10`) and VLAN 20 as the voice VLAN (`switchport voice vlan 20`). I then use `show interfaces f0/1 switchport` to confirm that F0/1 is indeed considered an access port, despite carrying traffic in two VLANs:

```
JITL-SW1(config)# interface range f0/1-3
JITL-SW1(config-if-range)# switchport mode access            Manually configures access mode
JITL-SW1(config-if-range)# switchport access vlan 10         Configures the data
JITL-SW1(config-if-range)# switchport voice vlan 20          (access) and voice VLANs
JITL-SW1(config-if-range)# do show interfaces f0/1 switchport
Name: Fa0/1
Switchport: Enabled
Administrative Mode: static access
Operational Mode: static access                              F0/1 is an access port.
Administrative Trunking Encapsulation: dot1q
Operational Trunking Encapsulation: native
Negotiation of Trunking: Off
Access Mode VLAN: 10 (VLAN0010)                              F0/1's data and voice
Trunking Native Mode VLAN: 1 (default)                       VLANs are listed.
Administrative Native VLAN tagging: disabled
Voice VLAN: 20 (VLAN0020)
. . .
```

10.1.2 *Power over Ethernet*

IP phones often take advantage of a technology called *Power over Ethernet* (PoE), which allows the phones to receive electrical power over the same Ethernet UTP cables that they use to transmit data—no need for separate power cables. This provides reduced costs (fewer power cable runs are required), less desk and office clutter (fewer cables and adapters), and the flexibility to place devices in locations without a power outlet nearby.

> **NOTE**   You may wonder how electrical power and data can be transmitted over the same cable. The short answer is that because of the different frequency ranges used for power and data transmissions, they don't interfere with each other.

Figure 10.3 demonstrates how PoE works. Whereas SW1 and the PCs receive electrical power from wall outlets, the IP phones receive electrical power from SW1 using PoE. SW1 is the *Power Sourcing Equipment* (PSE)—the device that supplies power using PoE—and the IP phones are the *Powered Devices* (PDs).

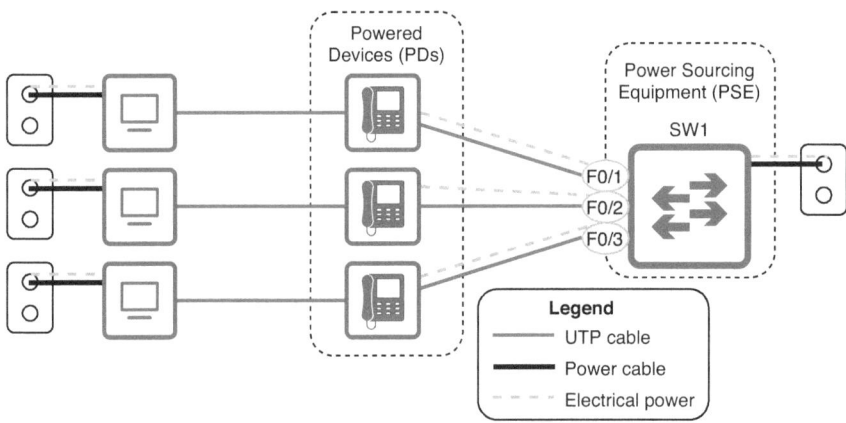

Figure 10.3   SW1, the PSE, supplies electrical power to IP phones (PDs) using PoE.

> **NOTE**   In addition to IP phones, a variety of devices can use PoE: IP cameras, wireless access points, access control devices like badge readers, door locks, and many others.

A PSE must be cautious about sending electrical power over an Ethernet cable; if a PSE were to incorrectly send electrical power using PoE to a device that is not designed to handle it, there is a risk of damaging the device. Similarly, if the PSE were to send too much power to a PD, that could damage the PD. For that reason, a PoE-enabled switch port doesn't immediately send electrical power when a device is connected. Instead, it uses the following process:

1 *Detection*—When a device is connected, the PSE performs an initial check by applying a low voltage to the cable to detect if the device can handle PoE.

2 *Classification*—The PSE assesses the power needs of the connected PD, and allocates the required amount of power from its available supply.

3 *Startup*—The PSE supplies the appropriate voltage to start up the PD.

4 *Normal operation*—The PSE supplies power to the PD and monitors the electrical current to ensure safe and consistent delivery of power.

On a PoE-enabled switch, you can confirm the status of PDs with the `show power inline` command. The following example shows the output:

```
                              Information about the available power budget          The two PDs are
SW1# show power inline                                                              class 3, meaning
Available:124.0(w)  Used:30.8(w)  Remaining:93.2(w)    ◄                            the switch
Interface Admin  Oper   Power   Device              Class Max                       allocates 15.4
                        (Watts)                                                      watts each.
--------- ------ ------ ------- ------------------- ----- ----
Fa0/1     auto   on      15.4   AIR-CAP3502I-E-K9   3     15.4
Fa0/2     auto   on      15.4   AIR-CAP3502E-E-K9   3     15.4
Fa0/3     auto   off      0.0   n/a                 n/a   15.4
. . .
```

NOTE The *class* indicates the power needs of the connected device. The devices in the example are wireless access points. IP phones typically require less power and are often class 1 (in which the switch allocates 4 watts) or class 2 (7 watts).

You can modify the PoE settings of each switch port with the `power inline` command in interface config mode, which has various keywords. By default, the `power inline auto` command is applied. With this command enabled, the switch will automatically allocate power to the port after detecting a device that requires PoE connected to the port. However, power is allocated on a first come, first served basis; if there isn't enough power remaining in the switch's total budget, it will not be able to supply power to the device.

The `power inline static` [`max` *milliwatts*] command can be used to preallocate power to a port, reserving a certain amount of power for the port even when a PD isn't connected. If you don't specify a value in the command, the maximum value is allocated. When a device is connected to the port, the switch still waits to detect the PD, assess its power needs, and supply the appropriate amount of power, but the amount of power specified in this command is always allocated for this port, even when it's not in use.

NOTE You should usually use the default mode of `auto` since it allocates only as much power as needed to each device and doesn't require manual configuration. However, `static` can be used if the power budget is tight and you need to guarantee power to a particular device. Another option is `never`, which disables PoE on the port.

CDP and LLDP's role in PoE

The Layer 2 discovery protocols Cisco Discovery Protocol (CDP) and Link Layer Discovery Protocol (LLDP) can be used to facilitate PoE by allowing devices to communicate their PoE requirements. These protocols help switches determine how much power a connected device, like an IP phone or wireless access point, needs. This negotiation process helps to prevent devices from drawing too much power while ensuring that each device is getting the power it needs.

If a PD draws too much power from the switch, it can damage the switch. One feature to protect against this is *power policing* (also called *power classification override*). You can enable this feature on a switch port with the `power inline police` command in interface config mode. In the following example, I configure it on two switch ports and confirm with `show power inline police`:

```
SW1(config)# interface range f0/1-2
SW1(config-if-range)# power inline police                    ◄────── Enables power policing
SW1(config-if-range)# do show power inline police
Available:124.0(w)  Used:30.8(w)  Remaining:93.2(w)
Interface Admin  Oper   Admin      Oper     Cutoff Oper
          State  State  Police     Police   Power  Power
--------- -----  -----  ---------- -------- ------ -----
Fa0/1     auto   On     errdisable ok        15.4   8.5      | The cutoff power
Fa0/2     auto   On     errdisable ok        15.4   8.5      | is 15.4 watts.
. . .
```

With power policing enabled, if a PD draws too much power (more than the cutoff power), the switch will put the port into an *error-disabled* state (stopping data and power transmission on the port) and generate a Syslog message. To reenable an error-disabled port, you can use `shutdown` to administratively disable the port and then `no shutdown` to reenable it. Make sure to disconnect the device that caused the problem first!

10.2 QoS concepts

Voice traffic from IP phones is particularly sensitive to network congestion; if packets are getting delayed or dropped, the user experience can be severely impacted. The same applies to calls on Zoom and similar apps. However, other types of traffic are less affected. File downloads, for example, may take a bit longer to complete when the network is congested, but the overall user experience remains the same. Using QoS, we can prioritize some types of traffic and de-prioritize others to maintain a positive user experience when congestion occurs. In this section, we'll examine some high-level QoS concepts before diving into the details in the following sections.

10.2.1 Bandwidth

Bandwidth refers to a link's capacity—how much data it can carry per second. We covered this concept in chapter 16 of volume 1 on EtherChannel. Different areas of a network typically have different total bandwidths, which can lead to bottlenecks, as shown in figure 10.4.

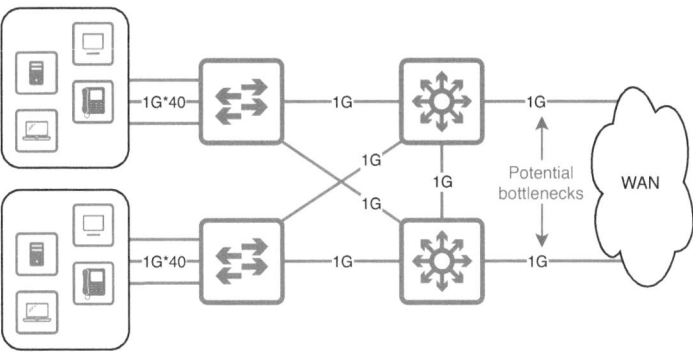

Figure 10.4 Different areas of the network have different total bandwidths. The LAN has two 1 Gbps WAN connections, which are potential bottlenecks.

Whereas each end host typically has plenty of bandwidth over its connection to the network (e.g., a 1 Gbps link per host), wide area network (WAN) and internet connections are common bottlenecks. A significant reason for this is cost; connecting remote sites over a service provider's network is expensive.

Fortunately, it's not necessary to have a 1:1 ratio of bandwidth between end hosts and the WAN. End hosts aren't always communicating over the WAN, and when they are, they usually aren't all communicating at their full capacity at the same time. However, during peak usage, congestion can occur, leading to some negative effects: delay, jitter, and loss.

10.2.2 Delay, jitter, and loss

The purpose of QoS is to minimize the delay, jitter, and loss of important traffic during times of congestion. *Delay* (or *latency*) is the amount of time it takes a packet to travel across the network from its source to its destination. A related term is *round-trip time* (RTT), which is a two-way delay—the amount of time it takes a packet to reach its destination and for the reply packet to be received by the original sender. Figure 10.5 demonstrates these concepts.

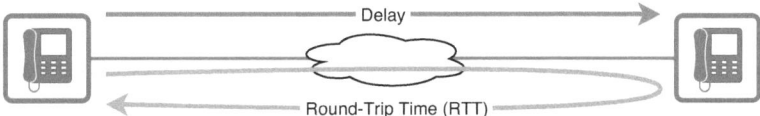

Figure 10.5 Delay and round-trip time (RTT). Delay is the amount of time it takes a packet to go from source to destination. RTT is the amount of time it takes a packet to go from source to destination and for the reply to arrive back at the source.

Delay is usually measured in milliseconds, and Cisco recommends that delay should be 150 ms or less for voice traffic. What happens if the delay gets much higher than that? It's not hard to imagine. Think of a phone call in which the person you're talking to only hears what you say 2 seconds after the fact—not a smooth conversation.

Jitter is the variation in delay in a series of packets. Some delay is inevitable; packets sometimes have to travel quite a long way and through quite a few intermediate devices to reach their destination. However, the delay should ideally remain fairly constant; too much jitter negatively affects user experience in real-time apps like voice and video calls. Like delay, jitter is measured in milliseconds. Cisco recommends that jitter should be 30 ms or less for voice traffic. Figure 10.6 demonstrates jitter.

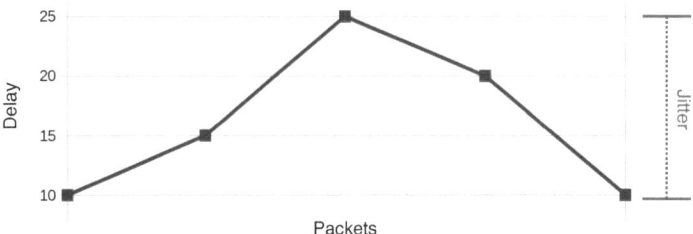

Figure 10.6   Jitter is the variation in delay in a series of packets.

The final concept is *loss*, which is the percentage of packets lost over a period of time—packets that didn't reach their destination. Under normal circumstances, loss should be close to zero. However, in times of congestion, some packets may have to be dropped. Cisco recommends loss of 1% or less for voice calls. TCP-based applications can deal with dropped packets through retransmissions. On the other hand, UDP-based VoIP protocols don't retransmit dropped packets. This is intentional; waiting for a packet to be retransmitted in a voice call would only cause more delay and disrupt the conversation. However, if there are too many drops, users will experience the familiar issue of the call "breaking up," resulting in choppy or interrupted audio.

IP Service-Level Agreement

Cisco IOS devices include a feature called *IP Service-Level Agreement* (IP SLA) that can be used to measure various aspects of network performance, including delay, RTT, jitter, and loss. A *service-level agreement* is a predefined set of performance metrics/standards that a service is expected to meet; this is usually agreed upon between a service provider and a customer. IP SLA helps verify these standards by using mechanisms such as ICMP echo requests (ping) to measure RTT and loss; this can be used to measure the effectiveness of QoS policies. Although IP SLA was part of older CCNA exams, it was removed in the current 200-301 version.

10.2.3 *What QoS does*

So, how does QoS help prioritize certain types of traffic in times of congestion, minimizing their delay, jitter, and loss? QoS consists of several different components that we will cover in the remaining sections of this chapter. Figure 10.7 gives a high-level overview of some of the key components that we will cover.

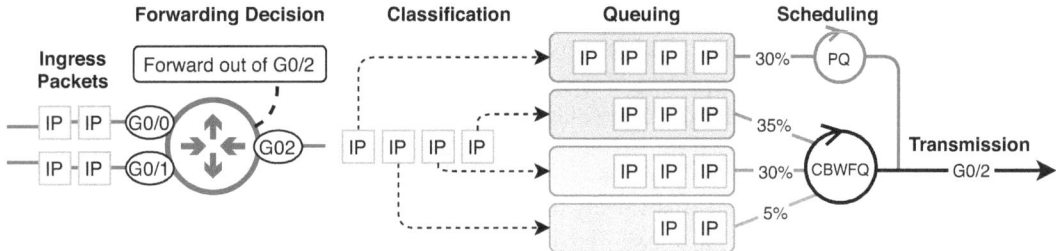

Figure 10.7   The QoS big picture. A router receives packets and makes a forwarding decision for each, classifies the packets based on their type, queues them for transmission, and uses scheduling methods to determine the order of transmission.

When packets arrive faster than the router can forward them out of a particular interface, it queues the packets waiting to be transmitted; this is when QoS is needed. By default, there is only a single queue, and packets are forwarded in a *first in, first out* (FIFO) manner, not prioritizing any packets over others. However, as shown in figure 10.7, QoS allows you to classify packets based on their type, queue them in separate queues, and use advanced scheduling methods such as Class-Based Weighted Fair Queuing (CBWFQ), Priority Queuing (PQ), and Low Latency Queuing (LLQ) to determine the order in which the packets are transmitted.

10.3   Classification and marking

Classification and marking are two components of QoS that are often confused. *Classification* is the process of sorting messages into different classes based on the kind of treatment you want to give them: high priority, low priority, etc. *Marking* is the process of setting the value of certain header fields to make the classification process simpler.

10.3.1   Classification

Classification is essential for QoS; to prioritize certain types of traffic, you have to identify those types of traffic—that is the role of classification. Figure 10.8 demonstrates classification: a device classifies packets into four different classes.

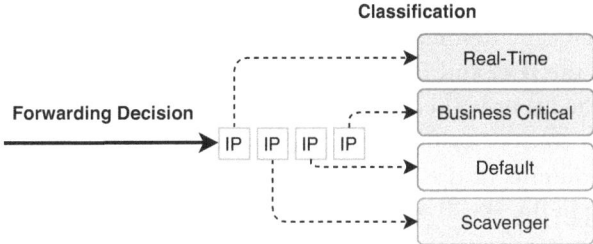

Figure 10.8   After making a forwarding decision, the device classifies each packet into a class: Real-Time (i.e., voice and video), Business Critical (important business apps), Default, and Scavenger traffic (low priority).

NOTE   *Scavenger traffic* is low-priority, noncritical traffic that is left to "scavenge" for leftover bandwidth during network congestion. These packets are the first that should be dropped or delayed to prioritize more critical/delay-sensitive packets. For example, social media browsing would likely be classified as scavenger traffic.

Packets can be classified in a variety of ways. For example, ACLs can be used; packets permitted by one ACL are assigned to one class, and packets permitted by another ACL are assigned to another class. However, ACLs have their limitations—matching based on information in the Layer 3 and Layer 4 headers.

Sometimes, you have to look deeper to determine exactly what kind of packets are being sent. *Network-Based Application Recognition* (NBAR) makes this possible by performing a *deep packet inspection*, examining the actual contents of some of the packets in a particular exchange to accurately classify them.

10.3.2 *Marking*

Complex classification using ACLs/NBAR can be demanding on the device doing the classification and also complex to configure on every device in the network. Ideally, a packet should be classified with these methods early and then marked (using specific fields in the IP/Ethernet headers) to make the classification process simpler for the rest of the packet's life. Figure 10.9 demonstrates this concept.

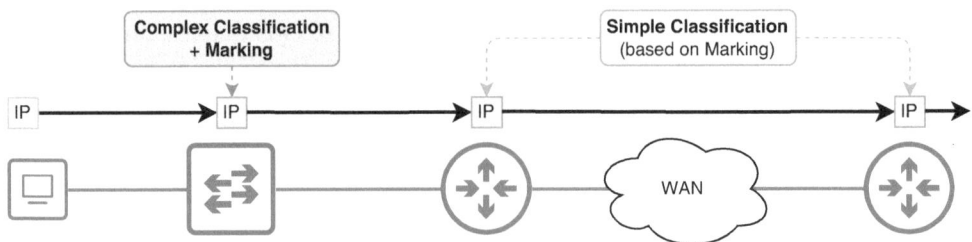

Figure 10.9   Complex classification and marking should be done early in a packet's life. Subsequent devices can then simply classify it based on its marking.

Two fields have been specifically defined for QoS marking: the *Differentiated Services Code Point* (DSCP) field of the IPv4 and IPv6 headers and the *Priority Code Point* (PCP) field of the 802.1Q tag in the Ethernet header. After a packet has been marked, instead of examining the packet's source/destination IP addresses and port numbers with ACLs, or examining the contents of the packet's payload with NBAR, the device can simply look at the marking in the DSCP or PCP fields to make a classification decision. This reduces the burden on the device itself, and on the people who configure it.

NOTE   The PCP field is also called *Class of Service* (CoS), which is commonly confused with QoS as a whole. However, CoS only refers to this specific field in the 802.1Q tag.

The three-bit PCP field can be used to mark 802.1Q-tagged Ethernet frames, allowing them to be easily classified based on the value in this field. For review, figure 10.10 shows the PCP field within the 802.1Q tag.

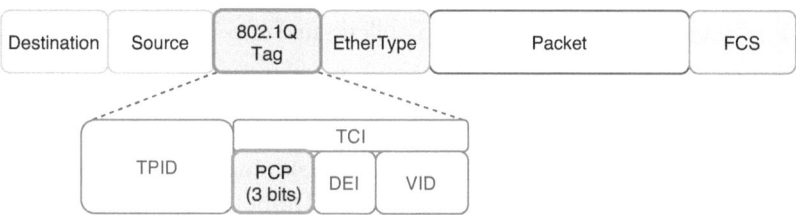

Figure 10.10   PCP is a three-bit field in the 802.1Q tag of the Ethernet header.

As a three-bit field, PCP provides eight possible values ($2^3 = 8$). For example, the standard PCP marking for voice traffic is 0b101 (0d5)—messages with this marking should be treated with high priority. On the other hand, the default value is 0b000 (0d0), meaning "best effort"—regular traffic that should not be given special treatment. For your reference, table 10.1 lists the eight PCP markings and their standard names; don't worry about memorizing these for the exam.

Table 10.1   Standard PCP markings

Decimal value	Traffic type	Decimal value	Traffic type
0	Best effort (default)	4	Video
1	Background	5	Voice
2	Excellent effort	6	Internetwork control
3	Critical applications	7	Network control

The PCP field has one major limitation: it's part of the 802.1Q tag, which is only present in frames traversing trunk links (or the voice VLAN of access links). Frames sent between two routers, for example, don't include 802.1Q tags. Figure 10.11 demonstrates this concept.

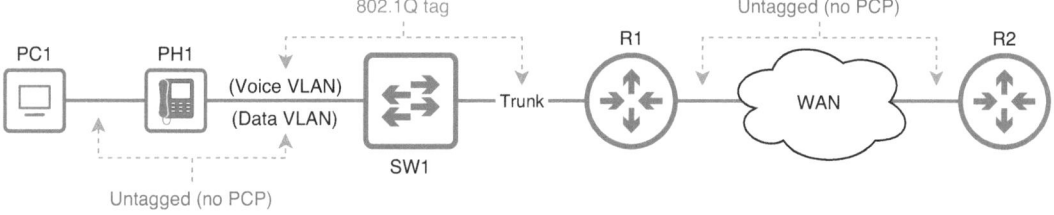

Figure 10.11   The PCP field is in the 802.1Q tag and only present in tagged frames.

If a user is having a phone call on PH1, PH1 can send its packets in 802.1Q-tagged frames marked with a PCP value of 5; this allows SW1 and R1 to recognize them as high priority. However, the 802.1Q tag is only present until the packet reaches R1. When R1 forwards the packets to R2, it forwards them in untagged frames. For this reason, PCP's utility is limited. Instead, most QoS policies make use of the DSCP field in the IP header.

10.3.3   Marking the DSCP field

Both IPv4 and IPv6 headers contain a 6-bit DSCP field. In the IPv4 header, it's part of a byte called Differentiated Services (DiffServ). The DiffServ byte was formerly known as Type of Service (ToS). In the IPv6 header, this byte is called *Traffic Class*; its definition is the same as in IPv4: DSCP (6 bits) and ECN (2 bits). In the past, only 3 bits of this byte were used for QoS marking; this 3-bit field was called IP Precedence (IPP). Figure 10.12 compares the old and current definitions of the ToS/DiffServ byte.

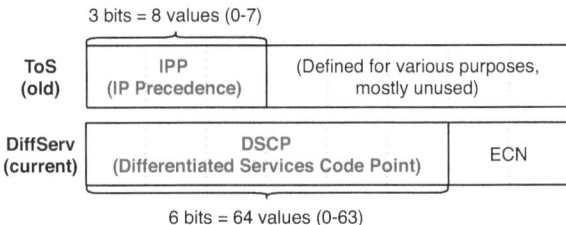

Figure 10.12   The old and current definitions of the ToS/DiffServ byte. The old ToS byte defined the 3-bit IPP field for QoS marking. The current DiffServ byte defines the six-bit DSCP field for QoS marking.

NOTE   The 2-bit Explicit Congestion Notification (ECN) field's purpose is to notify the packet's receiver of network congestion. However, its practical adoption has been somewhat limited, and it's not part of the CCNA exam.

One major benefit of basing your QoS policies on DSCP markings, rather than PCP markings, is that DSCP markings stay with the packet end to end. Once a device marks a packet's DSCP field, that marking will remain with the packet until it reaches its destination (unless another device modifies the marking).

As opposed to IPP and PCP, which are both 3 bits in size, DSCP is 6 bits, providing 64 (2^6) unique values. You are free to use these 64 values as you like in your QoS policies. For example, you could mark voice traffic with the highest value (63), scavenger traffic with the lowest value (0), and everything else with a value in between.

However, it would not be ideal for every network to use a totally different marking scheme; this would overcomplicate things and create challenges in maintaining consistent QoS policies when different networks connect with each other. To address this, standardized markings have been developed and are widely adopted in the industry.

These standards provide a common "language" for QoS across various devices and vendors. Here are two examples of standard markings:

- *Default Forwarding (DF)*—Default marking used for best-effort traffic
- *Expedited Forwarding (EF)*—Used for delay/jitter/loss-sensitive traffic

DF uses a binary value of 000000 in the DSCP field (0 in decimal), and EF uses a binary value of 101110 in the DSCP field (46 in decimal). However, these are just two values; what about the other 62 values DSCP provides? There are two standardized sets of DSCP markings that you should know for the CCNA: Class Selector and Assured Forwarding.

CLASS SELECTOR

Class Selector (CS) is a standardized set of DSCP markings created to be backward compatible with the older IPP system. Both IPP and CS use only the first three bits of the ToS/DiffServ byte, providing eight possible values. Figure 10.13 demonstrates how CS works. The three least-significant bits of the DSCP field are set to 0. Then, the three most significant bits—the same bits used by IPP—are used to create eight possible values.

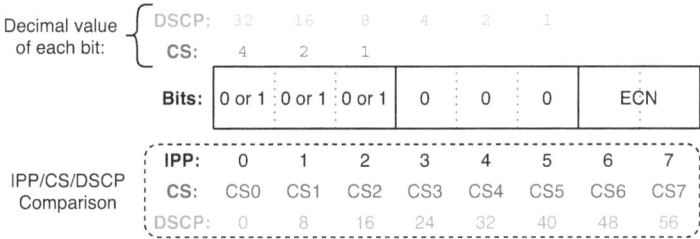

Figure 10.13   The CS marking system. The most significant three bits are used to make eight possible values, and the three least significant bits are set to 0.

Figure 10.13 probably needs some explanation. In the middle, I show the DSCP field of the IP header. Above it, I show the decimal value of each bit. When looking at only the 3 bits used for CS, the decimal values are 1, 2, and 4. However, keep in mind that the DSCP field as a whole is still 6 bits; the decimal value of each of those 6 bits is written at the top (1, 2, 4, 8, 16, 32).

Finally, the figure compares the IPP and CS values, showing how they correspond to specific decimal values within the entire DSCP field. For example, an IPP value of 7 is equivalent to CS7 (0b111). This translates to a value of 56 (0b111000) when looking at the DSCP field as a whole.

The CS marking system is particularly useful when dealing with legacy systems or environments where older IPP values are still in use. Organizations that designed their QoS policies around IPP can simply translate those values to their equivalent CS values. In other words, CS was designed as a way to bridge the gap between the old IPP and the new DSCP (although you can't really call DSCP "new" anymore—it was first defined in 1998).

ASSURED FORWARDING

CS is useful for its backward compatibility with IPP, but it doesn't take advantage of the greater number of possible values that DSCP offers. *Assured Forwarding* (AF) defines 12 additional standardized marking values: four traffic classes, with three levels of *drop precedence* within each class. A packet marked with a higher drop precedence is more likely to be dropped during congestion. Packets are assigned to one of four queues, and within each queue, some packets are more likely to be dropped than others during congestion.

AF uses the five most significant bits of the DSCP field; the least significant bit is set to 0. Furthermore, the 5 bits are divided into a class value (3 bits) and a drop precedence value (2 bits), written as AFXY (X = class, Y = drop precedence). Figure 10.14 demonstrates how AF uses the bits of the DSCP field.

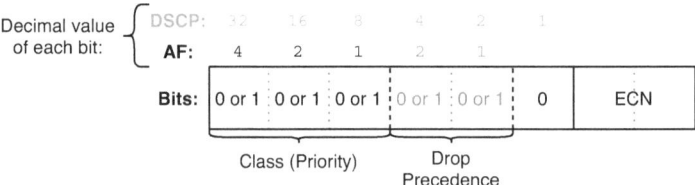

Figure 10.14   The AF marking system. The five most significant bits are divided into the class (3 bits) and drop precedence (2 bits). The sixth bit is always 0.

> **NOTE**   Although 3 bits allow for eight different values (0–7), AF only defines four traffic classes (1–4). Likewise, 2 bits allow for four different values (0–3), but AF only defines three drop precedence levels (1–3).

Figure 10.15 demonstrates the 12 AF markings with their decimal DSCP values in brackets. One counterintuitive thing is that a higher value doesn't necessarily mean better. For example, AF41 (decimal 34) and AF43 (decimal 38) are both in the highest-priority class, but AF41 has a lower drop precedence than AF43.

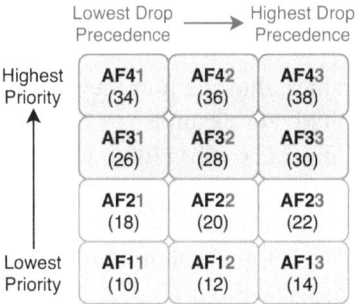

Figure 10.15   The 12 AF markings (decimal DSCP values are in brackets)

A simple shortcut to calculate the decimal DSCP value of a particular AF marking is to multiply the class value by 8 and the drop precedence value by 2 and then add them together. Let's use AF42 as an example:

1 The class is 4: $4 \times 8 = 32$.
2 The drop precedence is 2: $2 \times 2 = 4$.
3 Add them together: $32 + 4 = 36$.

RECOMMENDED MARKINGS

In this section about marking the DSCP field, we've covered DF, EF, CS, and AF. This has probably left you with questions about which marking system should be used and in which situations. You're not alone in that; others had the same questions, which led to RFC 4594. RFC 4594 provides standardized marking recommendations for various kinds of traffic. Table 10.2 lists some of those recommendations.

Table 10.2 RFC 4594 recommended markings

Class name	DSCP name	DSCP value	Examples
Network Control	CS6	48	OSPF, EIGRP, BGP messages
Telephony	EF	46	Voice call traffic
Real-Time Interactive	AF4x	34, 36, 38	Interactive gaming
Multimedia Streaming	AF3x	26, 28, 30	Streaming video/audio
Low-Latency Data	AF2x	18, 20, 22	Client–server interactions
Standard	DF (CS0)	0	Default (best effort)
Low-Priority data	CS1	8	Scavenger traffic, guest Wi-Fi

RFC 4594 includes several more recommendations than those shown in table 10.2. Depending on the needs of the network, differentiating between so many traffic types may be unnecessary. The RFC recommends thinking of them as a toolkit; some tools are necessary for some jobs but unnecessary for others.

> **EXAM TIP** I include table 10.2 to give you a picture of how these different markings can be combined in a holistic QoS policy that differentiates various kinds of traffic. However, I wouldn't expect any CCNA exam questions about these recommended markings, their decimal DSCP values, etc. I recommend knowing DF's role as the default best-effort marking, EF's role in marking delay/jitter/loss-sensitive traffic, CS's use for backward compatibility with IPP, and AF's class/drop precedence system.

10.3.4 Trust boundaries

A *trust boundary* is a logical division in a network. Markings from devices on one side of the boundary are trusted to be accurate, and markings from devices on the other side are not trusted. If a device trusts a marking, the device will forward the packet without modifying the marking. However, if a device doesn't trust a marking, the device will re-mark the packet according to the configured policy. Figure 10.16 demonstrates typical trust boundaries.

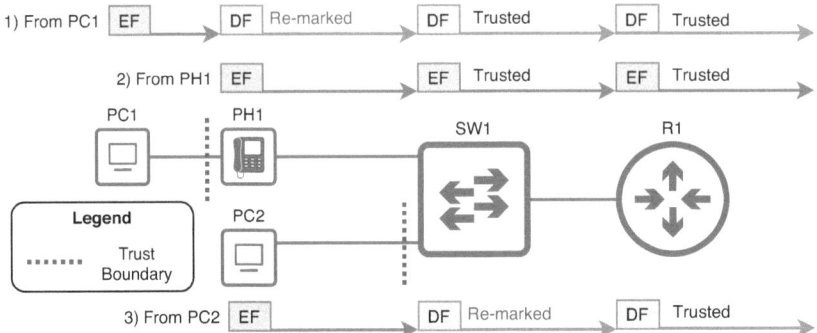

Figure 10.16 Typical trust boundaries. IP phones mark their packets, and it is standard practice to trust them. Markings from PCs should usually not be trusted.

IP phones mark their packets—usually EF for the packets that contain the actual audio data. To simplify things for the switch, it is standard practice to trust the phone's markings. However, markings from PCs are a different story; a tech-savvy user (who is aware of QoS concepts) could configure their PC to mark its packets with EF as well, resulting in the PC's traffic receiving preferential treatment over that of other PCs.

To protect against such a situation, you should ensure that PCs are on the "untrusted" side of the trust boundary; if a packet from a PC is marked, the IP phone or switch should re-mark it to the appropriate value (according to the configured policy).

10.4 *Queuing and scheduling*

In times of congestion, an interface may not be able to transmit packets fast enough to keep up with the rate at which packets are assigned to be transmitted out of the interface. What happens to the excess packets that cannot immediately be transmitted? The answer is *queuing*; the device will store the excess packets in one or more queues as they wait their turn to be transmitted.

Without QoS, each interface uses a single egress queue, and the device will transmit packets in the queue in a first in, first out (FIFO) manner—in the order that they enter the queue. This is called *scheduling*—the process of determining the order in which queued packets are actually transmitted. Figure 10.17 demonstrates FIFO.

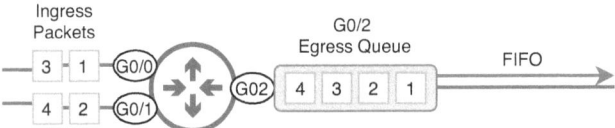

Figure 10.17 Packet forwarding without QoS. G0/2 has a single egress queue, and packets are transmitted in a FIFO manner.

NOTE In this chapter, we are looking at queuing from the perspective of a single interface, but keep in mind that each interface has its own queues.

FIFO is fine for simple networks without a lot of traffic, but to prioritize particular kinds of traffic—the goal of QoS—a different technique is needed. In this section, we will examine three queuing and scheduling techniques: Priority Queuing (PQ), Class-Based Weighted Fair Queuing (CBWFQ), and Low Latency Queuing (LLQ).

EXAM TIP Queuing is the process of storing packets in queues while they wait to be transmitted, and scheduling is the process of deciding in which order the queued packets will be transmitted. Remember this distinction!

10.4.1 Priority Queuing

Priority Queuing (PQ) supports up to four separate queues that are ranked by priority. Packets in a lower-priority queue will only be transmitted if the higher-priority queues are all empty. Figure 10.18 demonstrates PQ.

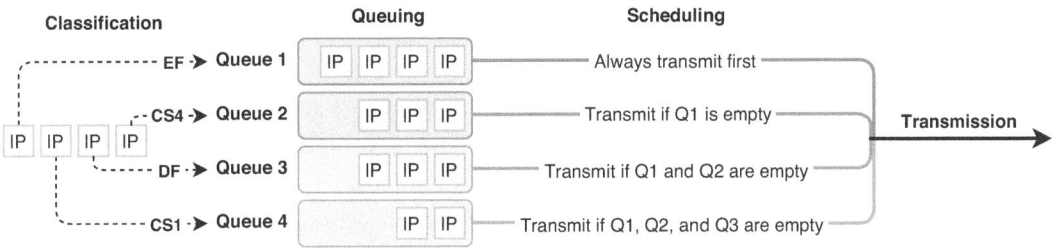

Figure 10.18 Priority Queuing (PQ). Packets are classified based on markings (the example markings in the figure are arbitrary) and added to a queue. The scheduler only services a lower-priority queue if all higher-priority queues are empty.

NOTE To *service* a queue is to transmit a packet (or packets) from that queue.

When the PQ scheduler decides which queue to service next, it scans the queues in order from highest to lowest priority. It makes this decision one packet at a time, scanning the queues in order each time. Depending on the amount of traffic in the higher-priority queues, this could mean that queue 4 is serviced very infrequently; this is called *queue starvation*. For that reason, PQ is rarely used anymore. It's better than simple FIFO, but there are even better options available on modern devices.

10.4.2 Class-Based Weighted Fair Queuing

Class-Based Weighted Fair Queuing (CBWFQ) uses *round-robin* scheduling; it services each queue in cyclical order; for example, if there are four queues: 1, 2, 3, 4, 1, 2, 3, 4, 1, etc. However, simple round-robin scheduling treats all queues equally, which doesn't fulfill the goal of prioritizing certain types of traffic.

Instead, CBWFQ uses *weighted round-robin*, which allows you to specify a guaranteed minimum amount of bandwidth for each queue. In times of congestion, the scheduler will ensure that each queue receives at least the specified amount of bandwidth. Figure 10.19 demonstrates CBWFQ.

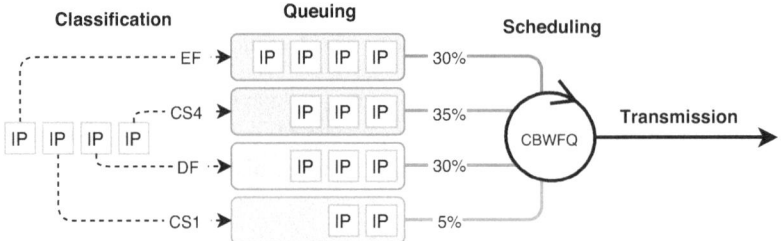

Figure 10.19   Class-Based Weighted Fair Queuing (CBWFQ). Packets are classified and queued. The CBWFQ scheduler ensures that each queue receives at least its guaranteed bandwidth, even if other queues are congested.

NOTE   CBWFQ supports up to 64 queues, although I'll use 4 for the examples.

CBWFQ avoids the problem of queue starvation by guaranteeing a minimum amount of bandwidth to each queue. However, its round-robin scheduler is a problem for delay-sensitive traffic. Even if delay-sensitive traffic is given sufficient bandwidth, packets may have to wait to be transmitted as the scheduler services other queues. The next queuing/scheduling method we'll cover addresses this concern.

10.4.3 *Low Latency Queuing*

Low Latency Queuing (LLQ) combines the strengths of PQ and CBWFQ; in fact, another name for it is PQCBWFQ (not a very elegant name—let's stick with LLQ). To put it simply, LLQ is CBWFQ with a priority queue. Delay-sensitive traffic should be assigned to the priority queue; if packets are waiting in the priority queue, the scheduler will always service them first. If the priority queue is empty, the scheduler will serve the other queues using CBWFQ logic. Figure 10.20 demonstrates how LLQ works; you may recognize this from the QoS big picture in figure 10.7.

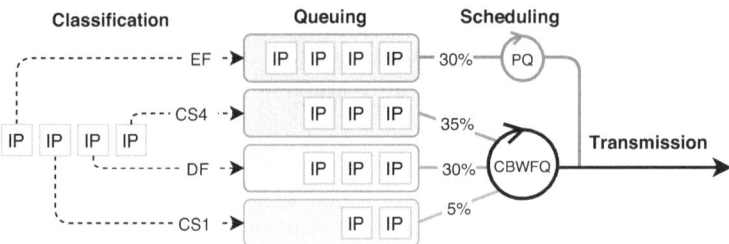

Figure 10.20   Low Latency Queuing (LLQ). Delay-sensitive packets are assigned to a priority queue that is always serviced first. The remaining queues are serviced using CBWFQ logic.

Notice that a bandwidth of 30% is applied to the priority queue at the top of figure 10.20. In the priority queue's case, this isn't the minimum guaranteed bandwidth—it's the maximum. Because the priority queue is always serviced before other queues, there is a risk of queue starvation occurring if lots of packets are assigned to the priority queue.

By limiting the amount of traffic that is allowed to enter the priority queue (30% of the interface's bandwidth in this example), you can avoid queue starvation. In figure 10.20's example, EF-marked packets enter the priority queue. What happens if more than 30% of the bandwidth consists of EF-marked packets? In that case, the excess packets will either be dropped or re-marked and assigned to a lower queue; this is an example of policing, which we will cover in section 10.5.

10.5 *Policing and shaping*

Policing and shaping are two *rate-limiting* techniques—they limit the rate at which an interface sends or receives traffic. Both techniques work by defining a rate limit (e.g., 300 Mbps) and then taking action on traffic that exceeds the configured limit. *Policing* drops traffic that exceeds the rate limit. *Shaping* buffers traffic that exceeds the rate limit to smooth out the flow of data. Instead of dropping the packets, shaping queues them in a separate *shaping queue* and transmits them at a rate that conforms with the configured limit. Figure 10.21 demonstrates policing and shaping.

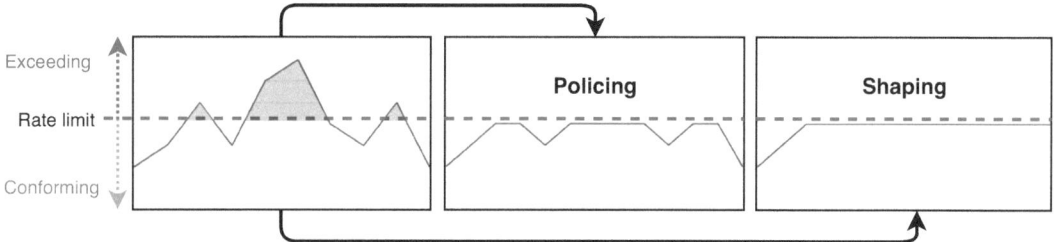

Figure 10.21 Policing and shaping. Policing drops traffic that exceeds the configured rate limit, and shaping buffers it to smooth out the traffic rate.

> **NOTE** Traffic within the rate limit is considered *conforming*, and traffic that surpasses the rate limit is considered *exceeding*.

Instead of dropping packets that exceed the rate limit, policing also provides the option to re-mark them, causing the packets to be classified differently. We covered one example of this in the previous section: LLQ uses policing to limit the rate at which packets enter the priority queue. Excess packets are either dropped or re-marked and assigned to a different queue, depending on the configuration.

Policing and shaping can be configured on a per-class basis, so packets in each class (and, therefore, each queue) are policed/shaped separately. They can also be configured on a per-interface basis, applying to all packets transmitted or received by the interface. Figure 10.22 shows a common use case for shaping and policing.

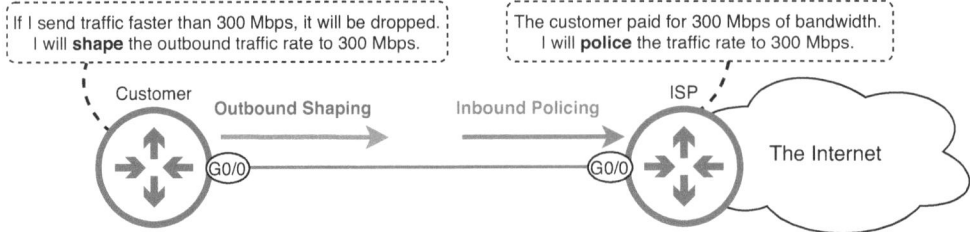

Figure 10.22   A common use case for policing and shaping. The customer shapes outbound traffic to 300 Mbps to ensure that packets don't get dropped by the ISP, which polices traffic to 300 Mbps.

An ISP's customer has paid for a 300 Mbps connection, so the ISP router polices traffic received from the customer to a rate limit of 300 Mbps. Both routers are connected by GigabitEthernet interfaces, but because the ISP router polices incoming traffic, the customer router shouldn't send packets out of G0/0 at full capacity; that would result in dropped packets. To ensure that packets don't get dropped by the ISP's router, the customer uses shaping to control the rate at which packets are sent to the ISP.

NOTE   Policing and shaping can both be configured to allow for *bursts*—temporary spikes in traffic that exceed the configured rate limit.

10.6   *Congestion avoidance*

The QoS techniques we have covered so far are all designed to help devices in the network deal with congestion, minimizing its impact on types of traffic that are particularly sensitive to delay, jitter, and loss. However, interfaces' queues aren't infinite; if the congestion reaches a certain point and the queues start to overflow, packet loss is inevitable. Congestion avoidance techniques attempt to reduce the amount of congestion by taking advantage of TCP's mechanics. In this section, we'll examine the effects of too much congestion and then look at two congestion avoidance techniques that aim to remedy the situation.

10.6.1   *Tail drop and TCP global synchronization*

When a packet is assigned to enter a queue but can't because the queue is full, the packet will be dropped; this is called *tail drop*. Figure 10.23 demonstrates tail drop. Two of the queues are full, resulting in tail drop.

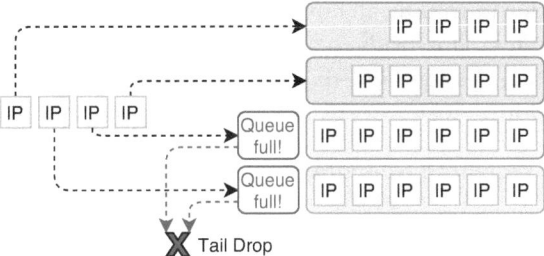

Figure 10.23   Tail drop occurs when queues fill up and cannot contain more packets.

Packet loss on its own isn't such a bad thing; protocols that use TCP as their Layer 4 protocol can recover from dropped messages using retransmissions. However, tail drop in particular can lead to (and result from) an undesirable phenomenon called *TCP global synchronization.* To understand TCP global synchronization, let's review the TCP window size mechanism we covered in chapter 22 of volume 1.

In a TCP exchange between hosts, each host specifies a window size; in effect, this tells the other host how much data to send before waiting for an acknowledgment. This mechanism allows the receiver to control how quickly the sender sends data to ensure that the receiver isn't overwhelmed.

The window size is not static. Each time the receiver receives data, it will specify a larger window size in the acknowledgment message it sends in reply. However, when a segment is lost (e.g., as a result of tail drop), the receiver will immediately reduce the window to a much smaller size. The receiver will then gradually increase the window size again, and the process will repeat. The purpose is to find the optimal transmission rate that doesn't result in packet loss and to dynamically adapt to network congestion.

Global synchronization occurs when many hosts simultaneously reduce and then increase their window sizes in response to packet loss; this is often the result of tail drop. Although packet loss on its own doesn't have such negative effects, the effect is greater when it happens to many hosts at once, leading to the vicious cycle shown in figure 10.24: TCP global synchronization.

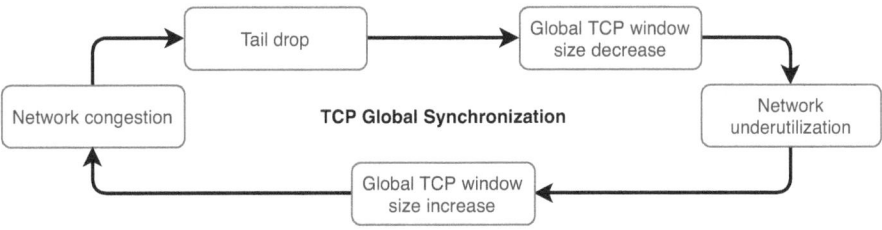

Figure 10.24   The vicious cycle of TCP global synchronization

Network congestion leads to tail drop, which leads to a global TCP window size decrease; all hosts who experience packet loss will immediately reduce their window sizes. This leads to network underutilization; all hosts are using very small window sizes, leading to slow transmission rates. This leads to a global TCP window size increase, which again leads to network congestion, and the vicious cycle repeats; this isn't an efficient use of network bandwidth.

10.6.2 *Random Early Detection and Weighted Random Early Detection*

Instead of waiting for queues to fill up, resulting in tail drop and TCP global synchronization, a better tactic is to start dropping some packets before tail drop happens. That way, instead of all receivers reducing their TCP window sizes simultaneously, only those few hosts that have experienced packet loss will. That's what *Random Early Detection* (RED) and *Weighted Random Early Detection* (WRED) do.

RED drops a percentage of packets once a queue starts filling up beyond a certain point. Hosts that experience dropped packets will reduce their window sizes, and that will hopefully reduce the overall traffic rate and size of the queue. WRED functions in the same manner but allows for more control over which packets are dropped. For example, think back to the AF markings we covered in section 10.3.3. Some AF markings are designated as having a high drop precedence, and some are designated as having a low drop precedence; this is one situation in which those drop precedences can be implemented.

The main advantage of using RED and WRED over simple tail drop is that they provide a more proactive approach to managing congestion. By dropping some packets before a queue is full, RED and WRED aim to prevent the queue from becoming full in the first place and avoid TCP global synchronization.

> **NOTE**   RED and WRED should not be used for traffic types that are sensitive to packet loss; the LLQ priority queue is not a good place to implement RED/WRED.

Per-hop behavior

Exam topic 4.7 specifies the *per-hop behavior* (PHB) of QoS. PHB describes how each device handles QoS individually. All of the QoS concepts we have covered in this chapter, from classifying packets to scheduling them for transmission, apply on a per-device basis. In other words, just because one router is configured to prioritize EF-marked packets, it doesn't automatically mean that the other devices in the network will. Each device needs to be explicitly configured to treat these markings according to your QoS policy; an EF marking (or any other marking) is meaningless unless you tell each device how to treat packets with that specific marking.

When implementing QoS, the policy must be consistently applied across all devices in the network path for it to be effective from end to end. The details of designing and implementing QoS policies, including how to configure QoS on Cisco devices, are beyond the scope of the CCNA exam. However, it's important to understand the per-hop behavior of QoS.

Summary

- *Quality of Service* (QoS) is a set of technologies that enable the prioritization and de-prioritization of certain types of traffic in times of network congestion.

- QoS is often used to prioritize sensitive traffic like voice traffic from IP phones.

- *IP phones*, also called *Voice over IP* (VoIP) phones, connect to Ethernet switches and communicate by sending and receiving IP packets.

- IP phones have an internal three-port switch that allows the IP phone and a PC to share a single switch port.

- Access ports can be configured with a voice VLAN to carry traffic in two VLANs: the data/access VLAN (untagged) and the voice VLAN (tagged).

- Use `switchport voice vlan` *vlan-id* to configure an access port's voice VLAN.

- Power over Ethernet (PoE) is often used to power IP phones and other smaller devices over the same Ethernet cable they use for network communication.

- A switch is the PoE Power Sourcing Equipment (PSE)—the device that supplies power using PoE—and the IP phones are Powered Devices (PDs).

- To avoid damaging a connected device, the PSE waits to detect a PoE-enabled device, assess its power needs, and then supply electrical power to the PD.

- Use `show power inline` to confirm the status of PDs, and `power inline` [`auto` | `static` [`max` *milliwatts*]] to control a port's PoE settings.

- *Power policing* can be used to error-disable a switch port if its connected device draws too much power. Use `power inline police` to enable it on a port, and `show power inline police` to check the status.

- *Bandwidth* refers to a link's capacity—how much data it can carry per second. Not all areas of the network have identical bandwidth; this can lead to bottlenecks.

- The purpose of QoS is to minimize delay, jitter, and loss during network congestion.

- Delay is the amount of time it takes a packet to travel from source to destination (one way), measured in milliseconds. Round-trip time (RTT) is two-way delay. Cisco recommends that delay should be 150 ms or less for voice traffic.

- Jitter is the variation in delay in a series of packets. Cisco recommends that jitter should be 30 seconds or less for voice traffic.

- Loss is the percentage of packets lost over a period of time. Cisco recommends that loss should be 1% or less for voice traffic.

- When packets arrive faster than the router (or switch) can forward them out of a particular interface, it queues the packets that are waiting to be transmitted.

- By default, there is only a single queue, and packets are forwarded in a first in, first out (FIFO) manner, not prioritizing any packets over others.

- Classification is the process of sorting messages into different classes based on the kind of treatment you want to give them.
- Packets can be classified in a variety of ways, for example, by using ACLs or Network-Based Application Recognition (NBAR), which performs a deep packet inspection on packets' contents to accurately classify them.
- Marking is the process of setting the value of certain header fields (802.1Q's PCP/CoS, IP's DSCP) to make classification simpler. Instead of using ACLs/NBAR, the device can simply look at the marking to determine a packet's class.
- The Priority Code Point (PCP) field, also called Class of Service (CoS), is a 3-bit field in the 802.1Q tag of an Ethernet frame used for QoS marking.
- The downside of PCP is that it is only included in 802.1Q-tagged Ethernet frames. It does not stay with the packet for its entire life.
- Previously, a 3-bit field in the IP header called *IP Precedence* (IPP) was used for QoS marking.
- The modern IP header uses the 6-bit Differentiated Services Code Point (DSCP) field for QoS marking. As a 6-bit field, it provides 64 possible values (0–63).
- Several marking schemes have been developed to standardize DSCP markings.
- *Default Forwarding* (DF) uses a binary value of 000000 in the DSCP field (0d0). It is recommended for best-effort traffic—regular traffic that isn't high priority.
- Expedited Forwarding (EF) uses a binary value of 101110 in the DSCP field (0d46). It is recommended for delay/jitter/loss-sensitive traffic like voice traffic.
- Class Selector (CS) is a standardized set of DSCP markings created to be backward compatible with the older IPP system.
- In CS, the three least significant bits of the DSCP field are set to 0. The three most significant bits—the same bits used by IPP—are used for QoS marking.
- Assured Forwarding (AF) defines twelve additional standardized marking values: four traffic classes, with three levels of drop precedence in each class.
- AF uses the five most significant bits of the DSCP field, and the sixth is set to 0.
- The 5 bits are divided into a class value (3 bits) and a drop precedence value (2 bits), written as AFXY (X = class, Y = drop precedence).
- To calculate the decimal DSCP value of a particular AF marking, multiply the class value by 8 and the drop precedence by 2 (i.e., AF32 = 28).
- RFC 4594 provides standardized marking recommendations for each traffic type.
- A trust boundary is a logical division in a network. Markings from devices on one side of the line are trusted to be accurate, and markings from devices on the other side are not trusted.
- If a device trusts a marking, it will forward the packet without modifying the marking. If a device doesn't trust a marking, it will re-mark the packet itself.
- Typically, markings from IP phones are trusted, but markings from PCs are not.

- Queuing is the process of storing packets in queues while they wait to be transmitted, and scheduling is the process of deciding in which order the queued packets will be transmitted.

- Priority Queuing (PQ) uses up to four queues. Packets in a lower-priority queue will only be transmitted if the higher-priority queues are all empty.

- Although PQ is good for prioritizing certain traffic, lower-priority queues can suffer from queue starvation, in which they are serviced very infrequently.

- Class-Based Weighted Fair Queuing (CBWFQ) uses weighted round-robin scheduling. It services each queue in cyclical order while guaranteeing each queue a minimum amount of bandwidth, even in times of congestion.

- CBWFQ is not ideal for delay-sensitive traffic because packets may have to wait to be transmitted as the scheduler services other queues.

- Low Latency Queuing (LLQ) combines CBWFQ with a priority queue. Packets in the priority queue are always serviced first. If the priority queue is empty, the scheduler will serve other queues using CBWFQ logic.

- LLQ limits the rate at which packets can enter the priority queue to avoid queue starvation.

- Policing and shaping are two rate-limiting techniques. Policing drops traffic that exceeds the rate limit, and shaping buffers excess traffic in a separate queue.

- A service provider might police a customer's traffic to provide only the bandwidth the customer paid for, and the customer might shape traffic to avoid exceeding it.

- If a packet can't enter a queue because it is full, tail drop occurs; it is dropped.

- Tail drop can lead to TCP global synchronization, in which many hosts simultaneously reduce and then increase their transmission rates (window size) in response to packet loss.

- TCP Global Synchronization is a vicious cycle: tail drop leads to a global TCP window size decrease, which leads to network underutilization, which leads to a global TCP window size increase, which leads to network congestion, which leads to tail drop.

- Random Early Detection (RED) avoids tail drop by randomly dropping a percentage of packets after a queue fills up beyond a certain point.

- Weighted Random Early Detection (WRED) is similar to RED but allows for more control over which packets are dropped.

- RED and WRED should not be used for traffic types that are sensitive to packet loss.

Part 2

Security fundamentals

In today's world, where seemingly everyone and everything is increasingly connected to the internet, robust network security isn't optional; it's absolutely critical. A data breach can cost an enterprise millions of dollars; according to IBM, the average cost of a breach was 4.45 million US dollars in 2023. And beyond the financial costs, the reputational damage can lead to lower trust from customers, negatively affecting the business for years to come. To put it simply, security cannot be an afterthought when it comes to designing and operating networks. So in part 2 of this volume, we turn our focus to network security.

Chapter 11 begins this part of the book with a selection of various security-related topics: the basic goals of security, common network-based attacks, social engineering attacks that target users, password-related best practices, user access control, firewalls, and more. Then, chapters 12, 13, and 14 cover three specific security features on Cisco switches: Port Security, DHCP Snooping, and Dynamic ARP Inspection. Each of these plays a key role in securing LANs right where user devices connect to them: switches.

Security is a key concern for any network professional, and that's why 15% of the CCNA exam is dedicated to various security-related topics (Domain 5.0: Security fundamentals). The goal of part 2 is to equip you with the foundational knowledge and skills required to address network security challenges, both in the CCNA exam and in the field.

Security concepts

This chapter covers

- Key security concepts and common attacks
- User authentication via passwords and alternatives
- Controlling and tracking user access with AAA
- Securing a network with firewalls and IPS

The most secure network would be a closed system, like a house with no doors or windows. But just like a house with no doors or windows would be uninhabitable, a completely isolated network would be counterproductive. The entire purpose of a network is connectivity—the ability to share, communicate, and access resources both within and outside of its confines.

In the real world, networks need to interact with other networks, applications, and users. But this interconnectivity introduces vulnerabilities from a variety of angles, so security concerns must always be at the forefront of any network design. The CCNA isn't a cybersecurity certification per se. However, just as networking is an essential skill for nearly any IT professional, the same can be said of security. A system is only as secure as its weakest link, and security is everyone's responsibility—including those in non-IT roles. In this chapter, we'll cover a variety of fundamental security concepts. Specifically, we will cover the following CCNA exam topics:

- 1.1.c Next-generation firewalls and IPS
- 5.1 Define key security concepts (threats, vulnerabilities, exploits, and mitigation techniques)
- 5.2 Describe security program elements (user awareness, training, and physical access control)
- 5.4 Describe security password policy elements, such as management, complexity, and password alternatives (multifactor authentication, certificates, and biometrics)
- 5.8 Compare authentication, authorization, and accounting concepts

11.1 Key security concepts

What exactly does it mean to say that a network and its connected devices are "secure"? That's what we'll explore in this section. We will first delve into the CIA triad, a foundational security framework emphasizing the concepts of confidentiality, integrity, and availability. After covering the principles of the CIA triad, we'll define and differentiate some vital terms in security, such as vulnerabilities, exploits, and threats.

11.1.1 The CIA triad

The *CIA triad* (not to be confused with the US Central Intelligence Agency) describes the goals of information security in an organization and stands for

- *Confidentiality*—Systems and data should only be accessible by authorized entities.
- *Integrity*—Systems and data should be trustworthy. For example, data should not be altered during storage or transmission except by authorized entities.
- *Availability*—Systems and data should be accessible and usable by authorized entities when required.

Figure 11.1 shows the three elements of the CIA triad. Note that *data* refers to the information that is stored, processed, or transmitted, whereas *systems* refers to the devices, networks, and infrastructure that facilitate the storage, processing, and transmission of this data.

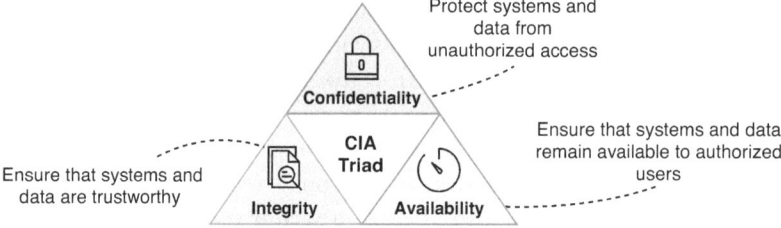

Figure 11.1   The CIA triad. Confidentiality protects systems and data from unauthorized access, integrity ensures that systems and data are trustworthy, and availability ensures that systems and data remain available to authorized users.

Basically, a security program should ensure that systems and data can only be accessed by authorized users, can only be controlled or modified by authorized users, and are available to authorized users when needed. If all three of these elements are ensured, we can say that the systems and data are "secure." As we cover various security concepts in this chapter (and the rest of this part of the book), always keep the CIA triad in mind. For example, consider how a particular attack harms the confidentiality, integrity, or availability of data and how a particular security solution protects them.

11.1.2 Vulnerabilities, exploits, and threats

No system is perfectly secure. Even a closed system with no network connection to the outside world has vulnerabilities that can be exploited. For example, a malicious user with physical access to the devices is one potential threat.

> **EXAM TIP**   Exam topic 5.1 specifically mentions "threats, vulnerabilities, exploits, and mitigation techniques," so make sure you can differentiate between these concepts.

In the previous paragraph, I used three key security terms: vulnerability, exploit, and threat. These terms are related, but each has its own distinct meaning. A *vulnerability* is any potential weakness that can compromise the security (CIA) of a system or data. Using a house as an analogy, a window is a vulnerability that can potentially be used by an intruder to enter the house.

An *exploit* is something that can potentially be used to take advantage of a vulnerability. Continuing with the house analogy, a rock that can be used to break a window is an exploit. And a *threat* is the real possibility of a vulnerability to be exploited; an intruder who intends to use a rock to break a window and enter your house is a threat. Depending on where you live and the likelihood of threats, you may choose to implement a measure like installing metal bars over your house's windows. This is an example of a *mitigation technique*—a measure implemented to protect against threats.

Let's turn away from the house analogy to think of a computer network. Standard network protocols like DHCP contain vulnerabilities that can be exploited using various tools (computer programs). A malicious user who intends to use such tools to harm the CIA of your network is a threat. Fortunately, there are mitigation techniques like DHCP Snooping (the topic of chapter 13) that can be implemented to protect against such threats.

11.2   Common threats

Networks and the devices connected to them face various threats. For example, standard network protocols have vulnerabilities that can be exploited unless appropriate mitigation techniques are in place. To secure a network, it's essential to "know your enemy"—to know what kinds of threats are out there. In this section, we'll cover a variety of threats targeting networks and the devices connected to them, as well as threats targeting the humans who use those devices.

11.2.1 *Technical threats*

In this section, we will cover various types of threats: denial-of-service (DoS), spoofing, reflection, man-in-the-middle, reconnaissance, malware, and password-related attacks. As we go through these threat types and examples of each, consider how they affect one or more aspects of the CIA triad: confidentiality, integrity, and availability.

DENIAL-OF-SERVICE ATTACKS

A *denial-of-service (DoS) attack* is a malicious attempt to disrupt a targeted system, service, or network and render it unusable. Referring to the CIA triad, DoS attacks affect the target's availability. Figure 11.2 shows an example DoS attack that exploits the TCP three-way handshake by flooding a target with SYN messages; this is called a *SYN flood attack.*

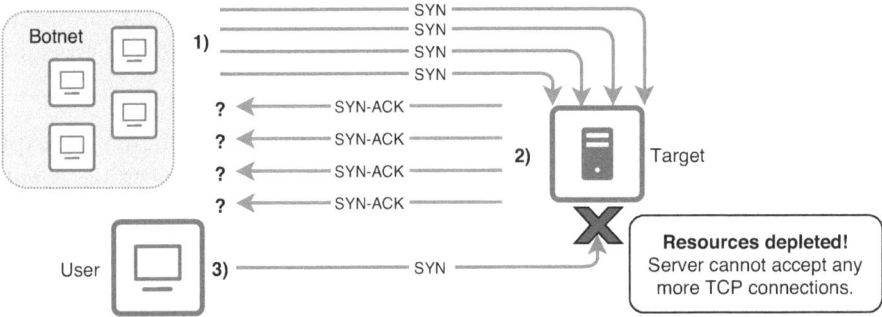

Figure 11.2   A TCP SYN flood attack—an example of a DoS attack. (1) The target is flooded with SYN messages and (2) replies with SYN-ACK messages. (3) The half-open TCP connections prevent the target from accepting legitimate TCP connections.

After being flooded with SYN messages, the target responds to each SYN message with a SYN-ACK message and adds each connection to its TCP connection table. However, the final ACK message required to complete each TCP connection never comes, resulting in the target's TCP connection table being full of these "half-open" connections. As a result, legitimate users are unable to access the target server; the server has reached its maximum capacity and cannot accept any more connections.

> **NOTE**   The attack in figure 11.2 is an example of a *distributed denial-of-service* (DDoS) attack. A *botnet*—a group of devices infected with malware—is used to attack the target in a distributed manner (instead of attacking from a single device).

SPOOFING ATTACKS

A *spoofing attack* is any attack that involves falsifying a device's identity (i.e., by using a fake source IP or MAC address). Spoofing is used in a variety of attacks. For example, SYN flood attacks often involve spoofing; the attacker can spoof their source IP address so that the target's SYN-ACK replies are not sent back to the attacker.

Another example of an attack that involves spoofing is a *DHCP exhaustion attack* (also known as *DHCP starvation*). The attacker sends countless DHCP DISCOVER messages using spoofed MAC addresses to exhaust the DHCP server's address pool, preventing legitimate clients from receiving IP addresses. Figure 11.3 demonstrates DHCP *exhaustion*.

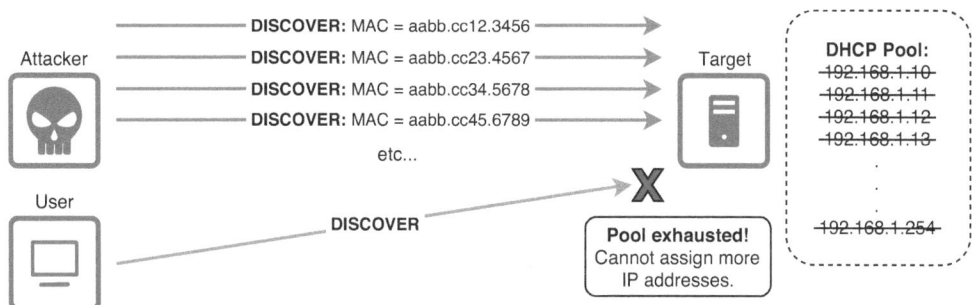

Figure 11.3   A DHCP exhaustion attack. The attacker sends countless DHCP DISCOVER messages with spoofed MAC addresses, exhausting the target DHCP server's pool. As a result, legitimate user devices cannot receive IP addresses.

NOTE   DHCP exhaustion is also an example of a DoS attack, making the network unusable for legitimate users because their devices cannot get IP addresses.

REFLECTION/AMPLIFICATION ATTACKS

In a *reflection attack*, the attacker sends spoofed requests (using the IP address of the target) to third-party servers (called *reflectors* in this context). This triggers the servers to send responses to the target, overwhelming it. Reflection attacks can be particularly effective when a small request triggers large amounts of data to be sent in response; this is called an *amplification attack*. Figure 11.4 shows a reflection/amplification attack.

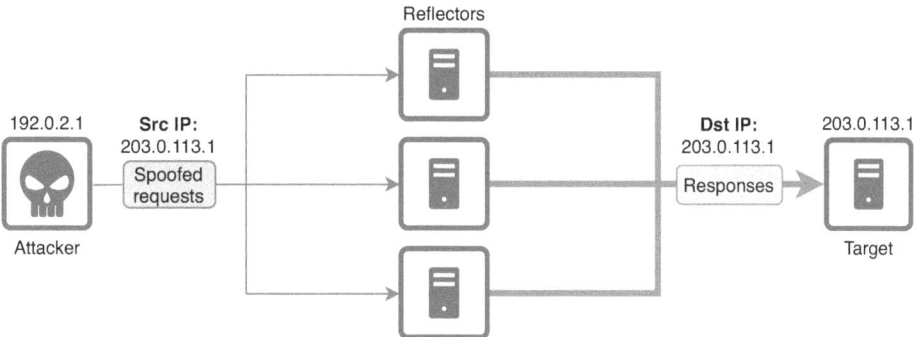

Figure 11.4   A reflection/amplification attack. The attacker sends spoofed requests to third-party servers (reflectors), triggering asymmetrically large responses that are sent to the target, overwhelming it and resulting in a denial of service.

NOTE   The reflection/amplification attack shown in figure 11.4 is an example of both a DoS attack and a spoofing attack. NTP and DNS are two common protocols used for reflection/amplification attacks because small requests can result in large responses.

MAN-IN-THE-MIDDLE ATTACKS

A *man-in-the-middle (MITM) attack* is an attack in which an attacker secretly intercepts communications between two parties, relaying messages between them. The attacker gains access to the contents of the communications and can even alter them without the communicating parties noticing. One example is *ARP poisoning* (or *ARP spoofing*), in which an attacker sends spoofed ARP replies to make communicating hosts send their frames to the attacker instead of directly to each other. Figure 11.5 illustrates ARP poisoning.

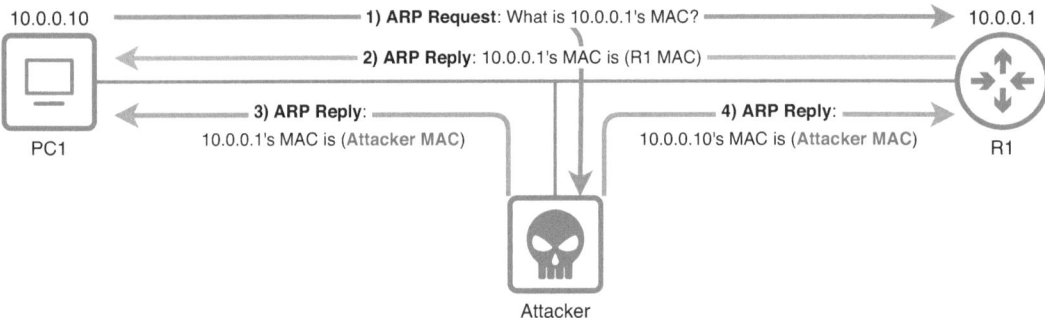

Figure 11.5   An ARP poisoning attack. An attacker sends malicious ARP replies to modify the ARP tables of PC1 and R1, allowing it to intercept their communications.

Steps 1 and 2 of figure 11.5 show a legitimate ARP exchange between PC1 and R1. PC1 broadcasts an ARP request to learn the MAC address of 10.0.0.1 (R1), and R1 replies. Through this exchange, PC1 and R1 learn each other's MAC address. However, in steps 3 and 4, the attacker sends malicious ARP replies to PC1 and R1, overwriting their legitimate ARP table entries with "poisoned" entries that map PC1's and R1's IP addresses to the attacker's MAC address. As a result, the attacker is able to intercept frames sent between PC1 and R1; instead of sending frames to each other's correct MAC address, PC1 and R1 will send frames to the attacker's MAC address.

RECONNAISSANCE ATTACKS

A *reconnaissance attack* isn't an attack in and of itself but is rather used to gather information about a target that can be used for a future attack. Reconnaissance attacks don't necessarily use illicit techniques to gather information; a common part of reconnaissance attacks is *open-source intelligence* (OSINT), which involves collecting and analyzing information that is publicly available. For example, a *WHOIS lookup* can be used to learn the email addresses, phone numbers, physical addresses, etc. of a domain's owners.

NOTE You can go to https://lookup.icann.org/lookup to perform a WHOIS lookup.

MALWARE

Malware, which stands for malicious software, refers to harmful programs that can "infect" a target computer and then perform malicious actions like encrypting files, enabling unauthorized access, stealing personal data, etc. Here are a few examples of malware:

- *Virus*—A type of malware that attaches itself to a legitimate program or file. When the program or file is executed, the virus is also executed. Viruses can spread to other computers by infecting files that are shared between computers.
- *Worm*—A type of malware that can spread without human intervention. Worms often spread across networks by exploiting vulnerabilities in software.
- *Trojan horse*—A type of malware that disguises itself as legitimate software. Trojan horses are often spread through email attachments or malicious websites.
- *Backdoor*—A type of malware that allows unauthorized users to access an infected computer. Backdoors are often installed by Trojan horses or other types of malware.
- *Ransomware*—A type of malware that encrypts files on an infected computer and demands payment (often in cryptocurrency) to decrypt the files. Ransomware is often spread through email attachments or malicious websites.

A common element of most types of malware is that they rely on human intervention to spread. You should always be careful about what email attachments you open and what websites you visit. If you are unsure, it is always best to err on the side of caution and not open it or visit it.

PASSWORD-RELATED ATTACKS

The most common form of user authentication is a username/password combination. Determining a user's username is usually a simple task for an attacker; it's often a publicly displayed username or the user's email address. Therefore, we rely on the strength of the password to provide the necessary security.

Attackers have a few options to learn a user's password. It can be as simple as guessing or making use of information learned about the target through an OSINT reconnaissance attack (such as the target's birthday, pets' names, etc.). Another option is a *dictionary attack*, in which the attacker uses a program that runs through a "dictionary"—a list of common passwords—to find the target's password.

A third option is a *brute-force attack*, in which a program tries every possible combination of letters, numbers, and special characters to find the target's password. To protect against these methods, it's essential to use sufficiently strong passwords; the feasibility of brute-force attacks decreases with the length and complexity of the password. In section 11.3, we'll cover some password-related best practices.

11.2.2 Social engineering

Social engineering is the act of manipulating individuals into divulging confidential information or performing specific actions, typically bypassing traditional security measures. Instead of exploiting software vulnerabilities, social engineering targets the human element of security, which is often the weakest link.

SOCIAL ENGINEERING ATTACKS

There are various ways to target users; you've certainly been the target (but hopefully not the victim) of one or more of these on the internet. One example is *phishing*—perhaps the most widespread form of social engineering. Attackers send deceptive emails, pretending to be from a trustworthy entity, to trick recipients into clicking malicious links, downloading malware, or providing sensitive information. Your email's spam folder is likely full of such emails. Here are some additional types of phishing:

- *Spear phishing*—A more targeted form of phishing, often aimed at employees of a certain company
- *Whaling*—Phishing targeted at high-profile individuals, such as the company CEO
- *Smishing* (SMS phishing)—Phishing via SMS text messages
- *Vishing* (voice phishing)—Phishing performed over the phone

Pretexting is another type of social engineering attack in which the attacker creates a fabricated scenario in an attempt to manipulate the target. For example, the attacker might call an employee and say "Hi, this is Jeremy from the IT department. Due to company policy, we need to reset your password. Can you go to this URL, log in, and change your password?"—this is also an example of vishing.

Tailgating (or *piggybacking*) is a physical method in which an attacker seeks entry into a restricted area by following someone authorized to enter. The attacker exploits the target's courtesy or distraction—people are likely to hold the door for the attacker, even if entering a restricted area.

All of these attacks exploit various aspects of human social behavior. For example, people tend to comply with requests from figures of authority. We also tend to comply with requests from people we like. If someone does something for us, we naturally want to return the favor. And once committed to a certain choice or action, people are more likely to follow through—it's hard to back out. Furthermore, many social engineering attacks also play on creating a sense of urgency to make targets act without thinking.

Social engineering as an exploit

Social engineering is often a precursor or facilitator to the technical threats we covered in section 11.2.1, acting as a "human exploit." For example, an attacker might use phishing to deceive a user into downloading malware; the user is a vulnerability that the attacker exploits with social engineering to enable the malware threat.

SECURITY PROGRAM ELEMENTS

> **EXAM TIP**   Exam topic 5.2 mentions "security program elements (user aware-ness, training, and physical access control)," so remember these concepts!

To defend against social engineering, it's essential to raise awareness and provide train-ing so individuals can recognize and respond appropriately to deceptive tactics. The CCNA exam topics list three essential elements of a security program: user awareness, user training, and physical access control.

User awareness programs are not formal training but are designed to make employees aware of potential security threats and risks. For example, a company might send out false phishing emails to trick employees into clicking a link and signing in with their login credentials. Although the emails themselves are harmless, employees who fall for the false emails will be informed that it is part of a user awareness program and that they should be more cautious about phishing emails and other deceptive tactics. Regular reminders like this keep security at the forefront of employees' minds, which is crucial; as I mentioned at the beginning of this chapter, security is everyone's responsibility.

User training programs are more formal educational programs that are usually man-datory for some or all employees (depending on the topic). Examples are dedicated training sessions educating users on corporate security policies or how to avoid poten-tial threats (such as social engineering attacks).

Physical access control protects systems and data from potential threats by only allowing authorized users into areas such as network closets or data center floors. For example, badge readers can be installed to only allow authorized users to open a door.

Unlike a traditional key, badges are flexible, and user permissions can easily be changed. For example, permissions can be removed when an employee leaves the com-pany. However, for particularly sensitive areas, locks requiring multifactor authentica-tion (such as a badge scan and a fingerprint scan) are preferred—more on that in the next section. Security cameras—monitoring the actions of employees and guests on the premises—are another example of physical access control.

11.3 *Passwords and alternatives*

Passwords—secret strings of characters—are an essential tool for user authentication; only the legitimate user(s) of an account should know the password. In this section, we will cover some best practices related to passwords (including some Cisco IOS-specific best practices), as well as some alternatives that can provide more robust means of authentication.

> **EXAM TIP**   These topics are exam topic 5.4: Describe security password policy ele-ments, such as management, complexity, and password alternatives (multifactor authentication, certificates, and biometrics).

11.3.1 *Password-related best practices*

When using a password as a means of user authentication, it's important that the password is strong, meaning that it's resilient to the password-related attacks we covered in section 11.2. Here are a few best practices regarding passwords:

- *Length*—Use at least 15 characters (although length recommendations vary).
- *Complexity*—Include upper- and lowercase letters, numbers, and special symbols (#, @, !, ?, etc.).
- *Unique*—Don't use the same password for multiple accounts.
- *Hard to guess*—Don't use common words or personal information about you that is publicly available (that an OSINT reconnaissance attack could reveal).

It is often recommended that users be required to change their passwords regularly. However, there is a growing trend against this for a few reasons. First, there is no particular benefit to changing a password that hasn't been compromised (if the current password is already strong). Second, requiring users to regularly change passwords tends to lead to weaker passwords; users will often reuse passwords from other accounts. Instead, it's recommended to change passwords only in certain circumstances, such as after a data breach (in which case the password may have been compromised) or if you discover malware on your device.

PASSWORD MANAGERS

A *password manager* is a software tool that users can use to store and manage passwords. One popular example is Bitwarden, but most modern web browsers have their own built-in password managers too. These days, using a password manager is generally considered a best practice for a variety of reasons. Here are a few:

- *Length and complexity*—Users can generate and store long, complex, and unique passwords for each account, without having to remember each password.
- *Auto-fill*—The password manager can automatically fill in usernames/passwords without requiring any keystrokes from the user. This can prevent passwords from being learned by keylogger malware that reads and logs keystrokes.
- *Encrypted storage*—Password managers encrypt stored passwords, so even if a device is compromised, the passwords in the manager are protected.

Password managers also often support multifactor authentication for additional security—more on that in section 11.3.2.

CISCO IOS PASSWORD HASHING

It's crucial that a password remains secret; if it loses its secrecy, it no longer serves as a valid means of authenticating a user's identity. To that end, it's crucial to protect passwords "at rest"; do not store passwords as cleartext (unencrypted text). Instead, passwords should be stored as hashes. A *hash function* converts an input (a password, in this case) into a fixed-length string—a *hash*—that cannot be reverted to the original input. Hash functions are one-way (irreversible).

In this section, we will cover some best practices regarding the storage of passwords on Cisco IOS devices. We will focus on the **enable password** and **enable secret** commands, but the same concepts apply to the passwords of user accounts created with the **username** command.

For review, you can use **enable password** *password* to configure an enable password that is stored in cleartext; Cisco calls this a type 0 password—not acceptable from a security standpoint. You can use the **service password-encryption** command to make the device encrypt the enable password (and other passwords) with a weak form of reversible encryption; Cisco calls this a type 7 password. Type 7 passwords are also unacceptable, as they can easily be decrypted with free online tools.

NOTE Hashing and encryption are often confused. Whereas hashing is irreversible, encryption is reversible.

Instead of **enable password**, you should always use the **enable secret** command, which stores the configured password as a secure hash using one of multiple supported hashing algorithms; the algorithms supported depend on the device model and IOS version. If you simply configure **enable secret** *password*, without specifying the hash algorithm, the device will use its default hash algorithm, which for many years was MD5 (type 5) but is now scrypt (type 9) in modern devices.

To configure the enable secret and hash it with a particular algorithm, use the **enable algorithm-type** *algorithm* **secret** *password* command. Here are a few options that can be used for the *algorithm* argument:

- **md5** (type 5)
- **sha256** (type 8)
- **scrypt** (type 9)

NOTE The US National Security Agency (NSA) has released a set of recommendations regarding Cisco IOS passwords and how to configure them. You can read it at https://mng.bz/9dyl. The NSA recommends type 8, but type 9 (Cisco's recommendation) is also considered very strong.

The enable secret will be saved in the running-config file as **enable secret** *type hash*, with the algorithm type being indicated by its number. The following example demonstrates this; note how the enable secret appears differently in the running-config than the command used to configure it:

Configures an enable secret and hashes
it with the scrypt algorithm

```
SW1(config)# enable algorithm-type scrypt secret CiscoCCNA    ◄──
SW1(config)# do show running-config | include enable
enable secret 9 $9$h.p1X8KVxbaILq$pNEykQjoAJbKCYfmBL9Hq8yPU/EqDGpoBkCIZ.s9GJA    ◄──
```

The enable secret is saved as a hash, with the
algorithm type indicated before the hash.

Then, if you want to configure the same enable secret on another device, you can simply copy and paste the command as it appears in the running-config; the `enable secret` `type hash` command allows you to configure an already-hashed enable secret without having to retype the cleartext password.

> **NOTE** The equivalent commands for configuring a user account are `username` `username` **algorithm-type** `algorithm` **secret** `password` to create a user account and hash its password with the specified algorithm, and `username` `username` **secret** `type hash` to create a user account with an already-hashed password.

11.3.2 *Multifactor authentication*

No matter how strong a password is, it remains a potential vulnerability. If a malicious actor learns an account's password, they can access the account. Instead of simple username/password authentication, multifactor authentication is becoming increasingly prevalent as a more secure option.

Multifactor authentication (MFA) is the process of verifying a user's identity by requiring multiple forms of authentication before granting access—usually two, in which case it can also be called *two-factor authentication* (2FA). The goal is to enhance security by ensuring that even if one authentication factor is compromised (i.e., an attacker learns your password), unauthorized access is still prevented by the need for additional factors. The "factors" of MFA are usually categorized into three main types:

- *Knowledge*—Something you know
  - Passwords or PINs
  - Security questions and answers
- *Possession*—Something you have
  - An ID badge
  - A smartphone receiving SMS codes or push notifications
  - An app like Google Authenticator that generates one-time codes. To obtain the code, you need access to the specific device where the app is installed.
- *Inherence*—Something you are
  - Biometrics such as a facial, palm, fingerprint, or retinal scan

To truly be considered MFA, factors from different categories must be used. Requiring a password and a PIN is not considered true MFA because both are something you know. An example of true MFA is requiring a user to touch their badge to a badge reader (something you have) and scan their fingerprint (something you are) to enter a restricted area. Another example is logging in with a username/password and receiving an SMS code on your phone; the username/password combination is something you know, and the SMS code, although a password-like code, is dependent on something you have—your smartphone.

11.3.3 Digital certificates

Digital certificates are a key form of authentication, predominantly used by websites. Most modern websites use digital certificates to prove their identity—to prove that the website you are visiting is who it says it is and not a fake website designed to imitate a legitimate website.

When you connect to a website, your browser will check the site's digital certificate, verifying its authenticity with a trusted *Certificate Authority* (CA)—an organization that issues and verifies digital certificates. You can think of CAs as the "passport offices" for digital certificates. If everything checks out, your connection proceeds securely using HyperText Transfer Protocol Secure (HTTPS)—the encrypted and secure version of HTTP. If not, you'll typically receive a warning alerting you to potential risks. In Google Chrome, a website with a valid digital certificate will display a padlock next to the URL (see figure 11.6).

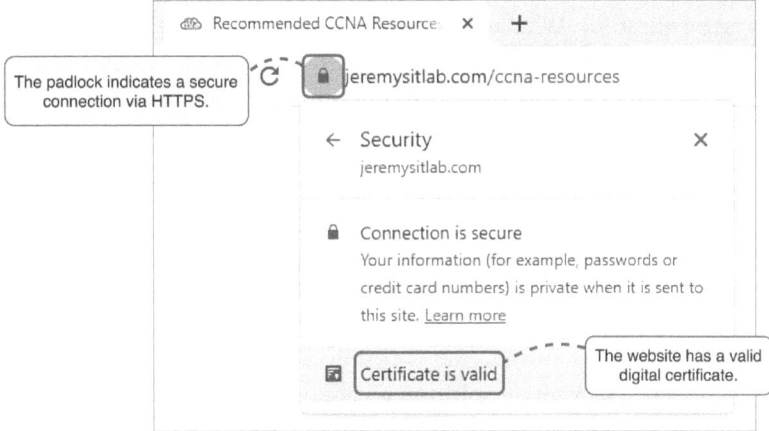

Figure 11.6   Digital certificates are used to verify the authenticity of websites. In Chrome, a padlock next to the URL indicates a secure connection via HTTPS. Clicking on it shows more details, such as information about the certificate.

Digital certificates are an essential part of the modern internet. They help to ensure that users are able to connect to websites securely and that they are not being redirected to fake websites and also play an essential role in enabling secure, encrypted communications via HTTPS.

11.4   User access control with AAA

Authentication, authorization, and accounting (AAA, pronounced "triple-A") is a framework for controlling user access in a network. AAA divides user access control into three components: verifying users' identities (authentication), granting appropriate access (authorization), and recording user activities (accounting). In this section, we'll cover these three components of AAA and two network protocols that use this framework.

EXAM TIP   AAA is CCNA exam topic 5.8: Compare authentication, authorization, and accounting concepts. Make sure you know the differences between them!

11.4.1 AAA components

The AAA framework consists of three components: authentication, authorization, and accounting. Let's break down these three components:

- *Authentication*—This is the process of verifying the identity of a user or system. It answers the question "Who are you?" Ideally, this is performed using MFA.
- *Authorization*—Once authenticated, the next step is to grant the user or device appropriate access. Authorization answers the question "What are you allowed to do?" This could include which files the user is allowed to read or modify, which services the user can access, which Cisco IOS commands they can use, etc.
- *Accounting*—This is the process of keeping track of user activities. Accounting answers the question "What did you do?" Every action a user takes can be logged, from opening or editing a file to making configuration changes to a device. This is crucial for audits, troubleshooting, and understanding user behavior.

By integrating these three components, AAA ensures controlled, secure, and transparent user access to networks and the resources they make available.

11.4.2 AAA protocols

Implementing AAA in a network involves a centralized AAA server that controls user authentication, authorization, and accounting. From this server, you can control user accounts and credentials, what each user is authorized to do, and keep account of each user's activities. Cisco's AAA server solution is called *Identity Services Engine* (ISE).

AAA is typically implemented using one of two protocols: *Remote Authentication Dial-In User Service* (RADIUS) or *Terminal Access Controller Access-Control System Plus* (TACACS+)—I'm not sure if there's a connection between AAA protocols and overly wordy names. Cisco network devices (and ISE) support both protocols. RADIUS and TACACS+ both serve the purpose of providing AAA functionality to control user access, but there are differences between them. Table 11.1 compares RADIUS and TACACS+.

Table 11.1   RADIUS and TACACS+

RADIUS	TACACS+
Open standard	Created by Cisco but now open standard
Combines authentication and authorization into a single operation	Keeps all three AAA components separate
UDP ports 1812 and 1813	TCP port 49
Encrypts passwords only	Encrypts all communications
Typically used for network access	Typically used for device administration

Both protocols are open standards that have been implemented by various vendors, although TACACS+ was originally developed by Cisco. Let's take a look at some of the differences between the two as listed in table 11.1.

One major difference is that whereas TACACS+ keeps all three AAA components separate, RADIUS combines authentication and authorization into a single operation (called the *Access Request*). Because TACACS+ keeps all three components as separate operations, it often provides more granular control. Figure 11.7 demonstrates this difference between RADIUS and TACACS+. A user connects to the CLI of a router, and the router uses RADIUS (left) and TACACS+ (right) to control the user's access to the router.

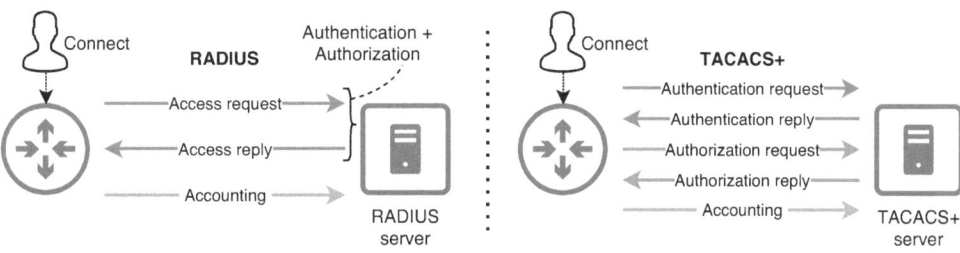

Figure 11.7   A simplified look at RADIUS and TACACS+ communications. Whereas RADIUS combines authentication and authorization into a single operation, TACACS+ keeps them separate.

RADIUS and TACACS+ also differ in the Layer 4 protocols they use. RADIUS uses UDP, and the RADIUS server listens on ports 1812 (for authentication/authorization) and 1813 (for accounting). TACACS+, on the other hand, uses TCP as its Layer 4 protocol, and the TACACS+ server listens on TCP port 49 for all messages.

Whereas TACACS+ encrypts the contents of all messages between the client and server, RADIUS only encrypts the password in the Access Request message. The rest of the Access Request message's content, and the contents of other RADIUS messages, are sent in cleartext.

Although the more robust features of TACACS+ may make it seem the superior choice for an AAA protocol, both are used in different scenarios. TACACS+ is typically used to control device administration, such as an admin configuring a router or switch. TACACS+ provides granular control over which commands a user can use; this can be configured on a per-user or per-group basis (with users assigned to different groups).

RADIUS, on the other hand, is typically used to control network access. This is largely due to the simplicity and efficiency of RADIUS compared to TACACS+, especially when such granular control is not necessary. In the next section, we'll take a look at 802.1X, an example of how RADIUS can be used to control network access.

EXAM TIP   The details of RADIUS and TACACS+ are beyond the scope of the CCNA exam, but I recommend knowing their basic characteristics. Refer to table 11.1 for a summary.

11.4.3 IEEE 802.1X

802.1X (usually pronounced "dot one X") is a standard created by the IEEE for *port-based network access control* (PNAC). Basically, it's a way to secure each port on a switch, allowing only authorized devices to connect to the network. Without 802.1X, a device connected to a switch port can immediately send a DHCP request, lease an IP address, and begin communicating over the network; 802.1X changes that.

When a device first connects to a port secured by 802.1X, the port remains locked until the user successfully authenticates. The only traffic that is allowed is 802.1X authentication traffic, as shown in figure 11.8.

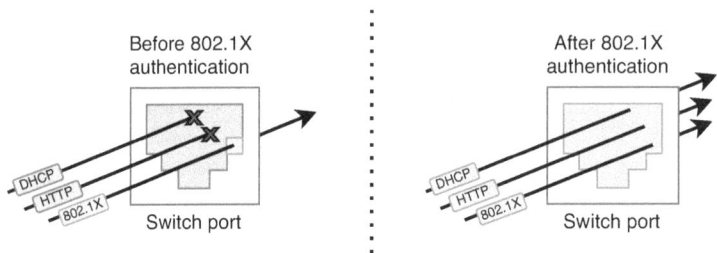

Figure 11.8   An 802.1X-secured port only allows 802.1X traffic until the user has authenticated.

The 802.1X authentication process involves three devices, as shown in figure 11.9:

- *Supplicant*—The client device that wants to connect to the network
- *Authenticator*—The network device that the supplicant connects to
- *Authentication server*—The server that verifies the supplicant's credentials (usually a RADIUS server)

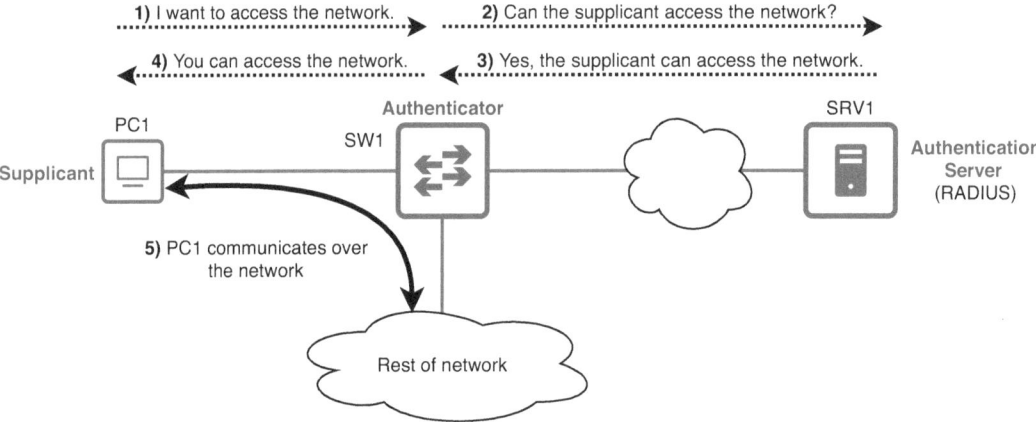

Figure 11.9   802.1X port-based network access control. The authenticator (SW1) only allows the supplicant (PC1) to access the network after PC1 authenticates with the authentication server (SRV1).

802.1X uses a framework called *Extensible Authentication Protocol* (EAP) for the authentication process, which defines various authentication methods and message formats. However, RADIUS is usually employed as the protocol for checking the credentials provided by the supplicant. We will take a closer look at 802.1X and EAP's various authentication methods in chapter 20; 802.1X, paired with RADIUS, is used for both wired and wireless access control.

11.5 Firewalls and IPS

The CCNA exam focuses primarily on configuring Cisco routers and switches. However, the type of network device most synonymous with network security is the firewall. Although firewall configuration is beyond the scope of the CCNA exam, you are expected to have a basic understanding of how firewalls work.

> **EXAM TIP**   These topics are CCNA exam topic 1.1.c: Next-generation firewalls and IPS.

11.5.1 Stateful packet filtering

Routers and switches both have various security features. For example, routers can use ACLs to control which types of traffic are permitted and denied. In fact, ACLs applied to a router's interfaces are a form of *stateless firewall*. They examine each packet on a per-packet basis and decide to permit or deny it, without considering other context, such as the packet's relation to other packets (i.e., whether this packet is a reply to a previously permitted packet).

Most modern firewalls are *stateful firewalls*; they don't just consider individual packets with no other context but also each packet's relationship to other packets. For example, a stateful firewall might block all internet traffic from entering the internal network—generally a good idea, given the public nature of the internet. However, if a host in the internal network initiates communication with a host on the internet (i.e., google .com's web server), the firewall will allow the reply traffic from the internet host.

Figure 11.10 demonstrates stateful packet filtering as done by a firewall and also introduces the concept of *zones*. In addition to considering information like source/ destination ports and IP addresses, firewalls consider how packets move between these zones when determining whether to permit or deny them.

If a host in the Inside zone initiates communication with a host in the Outside zone, the firewall will permit the reply traffic. However, if a host in the Outside zone attempts to initiate communication with a host in the Inside zone, the firewall will block it. Stateless firewalls (like ACLs on a router) are not able to consider the context of packets like this; each packet is considered independently.

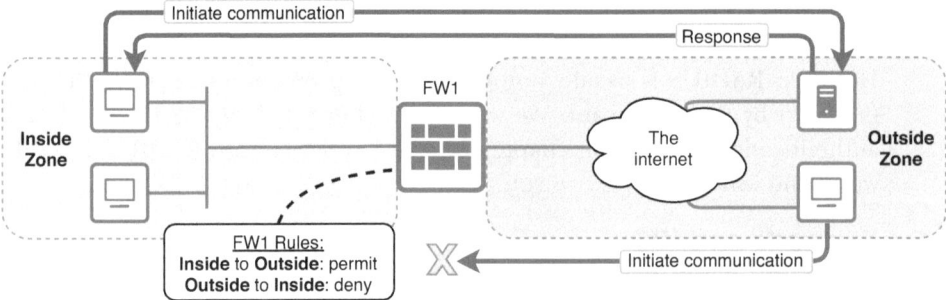

Figure 11.10   Simple firewall rules. Hosts in the Inside zone can initiate communications with hosts in the Outside zone, but hosts in the Outside zone cannot initiate communications with hosts in the Inside zone.

> **NOTE**   Figure 11.10 doesn't show a router. Most firewalls have their own routing capabilities. Depending on the size and requirements of the network, the firewall's routing capabilities may be sufficient, or you may need a separate router.

Figure 11.10 shows two zones, but firewalls can have many different zones, with different policies controlling communication between hosts in each zone. For example, it's common to have a zone called the *demilitarized zone* (DMZ). Servers that need to be reachable from the public internet are placed here so that they can be accessed without compromising the security of hosts in the Inside zone, as shown in figure 11.11.

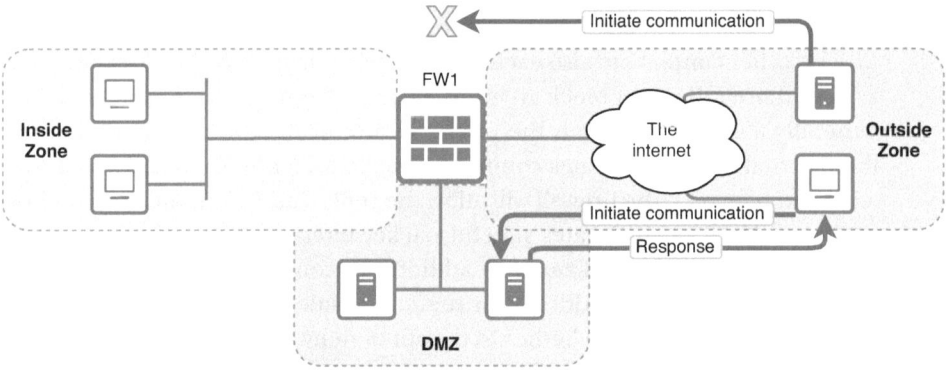

Figure 11.11   Servers that need to accept connections from the internet can be placed in the DMZ without compromising the security of hosts in the Inside zone.

11.5.2 Next-generation firewalls

Next-generation firewall (NGFW) is a bit of marketing lingo that has become the standard terminology for a type of firewall that goes beyond the functionalities of traditional firewalls. While the core remains stateful packet filtering, an NGFW incorporates several advanced security features.

One of those advanced features is *Application Visibility and Control* (AVC). AVC means that the firewall can not only identify traffic based on information like source and destination addresses and ports but can also examine the actual contents of packets to identify the application (similar to NBAR, as we covered in chapter 10).

Cisco NGFWs can also integrate with their anti-malware offering, *Advanced Malware Protection* (AMP). This allows the firewall to inspect files to identify and protect against all types of malware, such as those we covered in section 11.2.

Another common feature of an NGFW is *Intrusion Prevention System* (IPS) functionality. Historically, an IPS was a separate hardware device. However, in modern networks, the IPS feature is typically integrated within an NGFW. This integration simplifies and streamlines the implementation and management of the IPS.

An IPS inspects network traffic for malicious or suspicious activities. Once detected, the IPS takes predefined actions, such as blocking the traffic. Instead of operating based on user-configured rules, an IPS downloads attack "signatures"—identifiable patterns of data that can be used to detect malicious activity—from the vendor (i.e., Cisco). An IPS is also capable of building a picture of typical network activity and looking for anomalies that don't match up with that baseline. The following are some threats that an IPS can protect against:

- DoS and DDoS
- Malware such as viruses, worms, Trojan horses, and ransomware
- Reconnaissance attacks
- SQL injections

Cisco calls their IPS offering a *next-generation IPS* (NGIPS). In addition to traditional IPS functionality (i.e., signature-based threat detection), Cisco's NGIPS includes features such as

- *Contextual awareness*—The NGIPS gathers contextual information about the applications, device types, operating systems, users, etc. The NGIPS uses these details to better understand the actual activity on the network.
- *Talos integration*—Talos is a security research company that's a part of Cisco. The threat intelligence gathered by Talos includes attack signatures and known bad actors (known malicious IP addresses, websites, etc.).
- *Application Visibility and Control* (AVC)—Like Cisco's NGFW, the NGIPS can also examine the contents of packets to identify the application.

EXAM TIP Listing the various features of Cisco's security products can sound like a marketing pitch. You don't have to be able to list all of these features for the CCNA exam. Just understand that an NGFW includes additional features like IPS and anti-malware functionality on top of stateful packet filtering.

Exam scenarios

Here are a couple of questions that illustrate how your understanding of these security concepts might be tested on the CCNA exam:

1 (multiple-choice, single-answer)

   Which of the following commands can be used to configure an enable secret that has been pre-hashed with the scrypt algorithm?

   A `enable algorithm-type scrypt secret` *hash*

   B `enable algorithm-type 8 secret` *hash*

   C `enable secret 9` *hash*

   D `enable secret 5` *hash*

   The key to answering this question is knowing the difference between configuring and hashing the enable secret with `enable algorithm-type` algorithm `secret` password and configuring an already-hashed enable secret with `enable secret` type hash. This question is asking for the latter, so C) is the correct answer. D) is incorrect because it specifies type 5, which is MD5 (not scrypt).

2 (drag-and-drop)

   Drag each authentication method on the left to the appropriate factor type on the right.

(A) Entering a username and password	Something you know
(B) Scanning your fingerprint	Something you have
(C) Entering a one-time password generated by a phone app	Something you are
(D) Automated voice recognition	
(F) Answering a security question	
(F) Scanning an ID badge	

Here are the correct answers:

- Something you know: (A) and (E)
- Something you have: (C) and (F)
- Something you are: (B) and (D)

MFA is widely employed in modern systems to make the authentication process more secure. For the CCNA exam, make sure that you can identify which authentication methods fall into each category: knowledge (something you know), possession (something you have), and inherence (something you are).

Summary

- The CIA triad describes the goals of information security: confidentiality (prevent unauthorized access), integrity (prevent unauthorized alteration), and availability (ensure resources are accessible by authorized entities when required).

- Attacks target one or more components of the CIA triad.

- A vulnerability is any potential weakness that can compromise the CIA of a system or data.

- An exploit is something that can potentially be used to take advantage of a vulnerability.

- A threat is the real possibility of a vulnerability to be exploited, such as an attacker who wants to exploit the vulnerability.

- A mitigation technique is a measure implemented to protect against threats.

- A denial-of-service (DoS) attack is a malicious attempt to disrupt a targeted system, service, or network and render it unusable. An example is a SYN flood attack, in which an attacker floods the target with TCP SYN messages.

- A distributed denial-of-service (DDoS) attack is a DoS attack performed from a group of devices infected with malware, called a *botnet*.

- A spoofing attack is any attack that involves falsifying a device's identity, such as by using a fake source IP or MAC address.

- An example of a spoofing attack is a DHCP exhaustion (or DHCP starvation) attack, in which the attacker sends countless DHCP DISCOVER messages to exhaust a DHCP server's address pool.

- In a reflection attack, the attacker sends spoofed requests (using the IP address of the target) to third-party servers (called *reflectors*). This triggers the servers to send responses to the target. The goal result is a DoS.

- Reflection attacks can be particularly effective when small requests trigger asymmetrically large responses. This is called an *amplification attack*. NTP and DNS are commonly used for reflection/amplification attacks.

- A man-in-the-middle (MITM) attack is an attack in which an attacker secretly intercepts communications between two parties, gaining access to their contents and even altering them without the two parties noticing.

- *ARP poisoning* (or *ARP spoofing*), in which an attacker sends spoofed ARP replies, is an example of an MITM attack.

- A *reconnaissance attack* is used to gather information about a target that can be used for a future attack. Reconnaissance attacks often employ *open-source intelligence* (OSINT), which involves gathering publicly available information.

- *Malware* (malicious software) refers to harmful programs that can infect a target computer and then perform malicious actions. Common types of malware include viruses, worms, Trojan horses, backdoors, and ransomware.

- A few different attacks can be used to learn a target's password. A *dictionary attack* uses a program that runs through a list of common passwords. A *brute-force attack* tries every possible combination of letters, numbers, and special characters.

- *Social engineering* is the act of manipulating individuals into divulging confidential information or performing specific actions.

- Common social engineering attacks include phishing, spear phishing, whaling, smishing, vishing, pretexting, and tailgating/piggybacking.

- To defend against social engineering attacks, it's essential to raise awareness and provide training so individuals can recognize them and respond appropriately.

- *User awareness* programs are not formal training but are designed to make employees aware of potential security threats (i.e., false phishing emails).

- User training programs are more formal educational programs that educate users on corporate security policies, how to avoid potential threats, etc.

- Physical access control protects systems and data from potential threats by only allowing authorized users into restricted areas (i.e., with badge readers).

- Passwords are an essential authentication tool. A password should be of sufficient length (15+ characters) and complexity (upper- and lowercase letters, numbers, and symbols), and be unique (only used for one account) and hard to guess.

- A password manager is software that stores and manages passwords. It allows users to store strong passwords without having to remember each one. It can also protect against keylogger malware by auto-filling in passwords.

- Cisco IOS passwords should be stored as secure hashes. Use `enable algorithm -type` *algorithm* `secret` *password* to configure an enable secret with a specific hashing algorithm.

- Type 5 (`md5`) was the default hash algorithm for many years, but modern Cisco devices use type 9 (`scrypt`). The NSA recommends type 8 (`sha256`).

- Multifactor authentication (MFA), or two-factor authentication (2FA), is the process of authenticating a user with multiple forms (factors) of authentication.

- There are three main categories of factors: knowledge (something you know), possession (something you have), and inherence (something you are). MFA must use factors from different categories.

- A digital certificate is a form of authentication predominantly used by websites. Digital certificates are issued and verified by a Certificate Authority (CA).

- AAA is a framework for controlling user access in a network. AAA divides access control into authentication (verifying users' identities), authorization (granting appropriate access), and accounting (recording user activities).

- Cisco's AAA server solution is Identity Services Engine (ISE).

- Remote Authentication Dial-In User Service (RADIUS) and Terminal Access Controller Access-Control System Plus (TACACS+) are the main AAA protocols.

- RADIUS combines authentication and authorization into a single operation (Access Request), but TACACS+ keeps all three separate.

- RADIUS uses UDP ports 1812 and 1813, and TACACS+ uses TCP port 49.

- RADIUS encrypts only passwords, but TACACS+ encrypts the entire contents of all messages.

- RADIUS is typically used for network access (i.e., clients connecting to a wired or wireless LAN), and TACACS+ is typically used for device administration.

- 802.1X is a standard for port-based network access control (PNAC). Instead of a device being immediately allowed to access the network after connecting to a switch port, the device must authenticate first.

- 802.1X defines three components: the supplicant (the client device that wants to connect), the authenticator (the network device that the client connects to), and the authentication server (the server that verifies the supplicant's credentials).

- 802.1X uses a framework called Extensible Authentication Protocol, which defines authentication methods and message formats. RADIUS is usually employed for checking the supplicant's credentials.

- ACLs applied to a router's interfaces are a form of stateless firewall, meaning they examine each packet independently of context (like its relation to other packets).

- Modern firewalls are stateful firewalls, meaning they can consider the packet's relationship to other packets. For example, traffic from the internet to the internal network might be blocked except if it's in reply to a host in the internal network.

- Firewalls use the concept of zones to differentiate between areas of the network, such as Inside, Outside, and the demilitarized zone (DMZ). Policies can be configured to control how traffic is allowed to flow between zones.

- A next-generation firewall (NGFW) incorporates several advanced security features beyond stateful packet filtering, such as Application Visibility and Control (AVC), Advanced Malware Protection (AMP), and Intrusion Prevention System (IPS).

- Historically, an IPS was a separate hardware device, but it is typically integrated within an NGFW in modern networks.

- An IPS inspects network traffic for malicious or suspicious activities using attack signatures that it downloads from the vendor (as opposed to configured policies). An IPS can protect against DoS/DDoS attacks, malware, and much more.

Port Security

12

This chapter covers

- How Port Security protects against DHCP exhaustion and MAC flooding attacks
- Configuring Port Security on Cisco switches
- Fine-tuning Port Security configurations

Connections to an external network, such as the public internet, are obvious security concerns. However, internal network threats should not be overlooked. It could be a malware-infected device—an external threat from the internet that has taken hold in the internal network. Or it could be a malicious user; no one wants to view their own coworkers with suspicion, but ignoring such possibilities is asking for trouble.

Given these concerns, securing the points where users connect to the network—switches—is paramount. In this and the following two chapters, we will cover CCNA exam topic 5.7: Configure and verify Layer 2 security features. These include DHCP

Snooping, Dynamic ARP Inspection, and Port Security—all of these are security features on switches. This chapter focuses on Port Security, which provides granular control over which devices a switch allows to communicate over the network.

12.1 Port Security basics

Port Security is a feature of Cisco switches that adds a layer of security to a switch's MAC address-learning process. Specifically, Port Security allows you to set a limit on the number of unique MAC addresses that can be learned on each port, and it defines actions to be taken if that limit is exceeded.

By default, the number of MAC addresses that a switch can learn on a port is limited only by the maximum size of the switch's MAC address table—typically in the range of a few thousand to tens of thousands of MAC addresses. However, this default behavior is a vulnerability that can potentially be exploited. In this section, we'll look at a couple of attacks that exploit this behavior and see how to configure Port Security to mitigate those threats.

12.1.1 DHCP exhaustion and MAC flooding attacks

In chapter 11, we briefly looked at a DHCP exhaustion attack as an example of a spoofing attack. In a DHCP exhaustion attack, the attacker sends countless DHCP DISCOVER messages with spoofed MAC addresses to exhaust a DHCP server's pool of available addresses, preventing legitimate user devices from getting IP addresses.

Another type of attack that involves spoofed MAC addresses is a *MAC flooding attack*, which attempts to fill up a switch's MAC address table with spoofed addresses. With a full MAC address table, the switch is unable to learn the legitimate MAC addresses of hosts in the LAN. To understand the effect of this, recall how a switch forwards and floods frames.

When a switch receives a unicast frame (a frame destined for a single host's MAC address), the switch will look for a matching entry in its MAC address table. If it finds a matching entry, it will forward the frame out of the port specified in the entry. However, if the switch doesn't find a matching entry, the switch will flood the frame out of all ports (in the same VLAN) except the port the frame was received on.

If the switch can't learn a host's MAC address because the switch's MAC address table is full, the result is that the switch will always flood frames that are destined for that host. Figure 12.1 demonstrates this. In step 1, the attacker floods thousands of frames with spoofed MAC addresses, resulting in SW1's MAC address table becoming full in step 2. The result is that SW1 can't learn PC1's and R1's MAC addresses, so it floods all frames sent between them, allowing the attacker to receive copies of those frames. With regard to the CIA triad, this harms the confidentiality of communications between PC1 and R1.

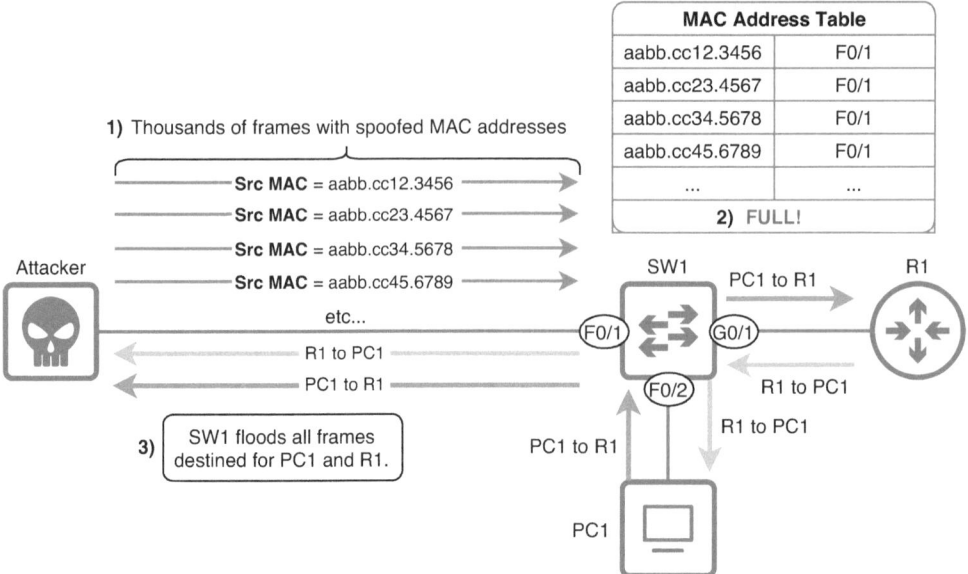

Figure 12.1 A MAC flooding attack. The attacker fills up SW1's MAC address table with spoofed MAC addresses, preventing SW1 from learning PC1's and R1's MAC addresses. As a result, SW1 floods all frames sent between PC1 and R1.

NOTE Although DHCP exhaustion and MAC flooding are separate attacks with different goals, MAC flooding is often a side effect of DHCP exhaustion; the thousands of spoofed DHCP DISCOVER messages can result in MAC flooding.

Port Security can mitigate against both of these attack types by limiting the number of MAC addresses a switch can learn on a port and taking action if that number is exceeded. In the next section, we'll look at how to configure basic Port Security on a Cisco switch.

Tradeoffs: Security vs. flexibility

When setting up network features like Port Security, you're often faced with a balancing act between two elements, both of which are important. One is security—protecting the network from threats that can harm one or more aspects of the CIA triad. The other element is operational flexibility. Strict security policies can be a hindrance in dynamic environments, especially when manual intervention to adjust security settings is not readily available.

Striking the right balance is essential. While it is tempting to lock down your network with the strictest security measures, it's also important to consider the impact on day-to-day operations. In this chapter, we'll cover various ways to configure and fine-tune Port

Security, some leaning toward the security side of the spectrum, and others more toward flexibility. Each network has unique needs and constraints. Therefore, when asked which setting is appropriate, the answer often is "It depends."

Keep this tradeoff in mind as you read this chapter (and the following two, which cover other switch security features). However, the CCNA exam itself focuses mainly on implementation. Questions of network design and security policy are usually left for those in senior roles with the experience necessary to make those high-impact decisions.

12.1.2 Basic Port Security configuration

Port Security, at its most basic, can be configured with a single command in interface config mode: `switchport port-security`. Figure 12.2 shows how to configure Port Security and how it can prevent a MAC flooding attack. Once SW1 detects multiple unique MAC addresses on its F0/1 port, the port transitions to an error-disabled state. This action effectively blocks all incoming and outgoing frames on that port.

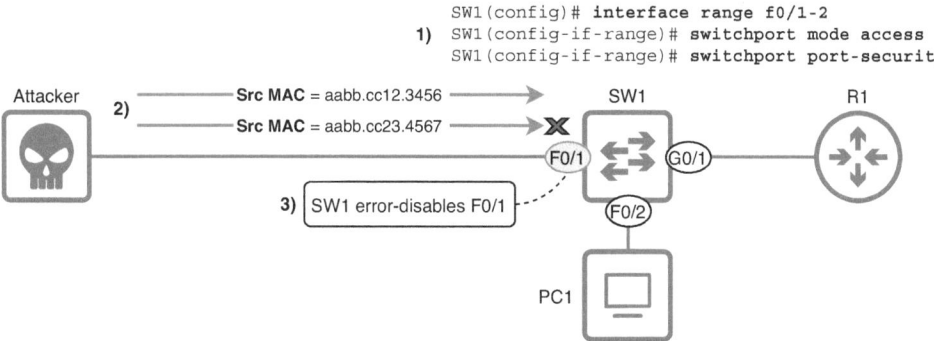

Figure 12.2 Using Port Security, SW1 error-disables F0/1 when it detects more than one unique MAC address on the port, preventing a MAC flooding attack.

If you try to enable Port Security on a switch port with the default settings, the command will be rejected. As shown in the following example, the switch won't allow Port Security on a dynamic port (one that uses DTP—it hasn't been explicitly set to access or trunk mode):

```
SW1(config)# interface range f0/1-2
SW1(config-if-range)# switchport port-security
Command rejected: FastEthernet0/1 is a dynamic port.
```

Enables Port Security

The command is rejected.

To bypass this, specify the mode (access or trunk) before enabling Port Security:

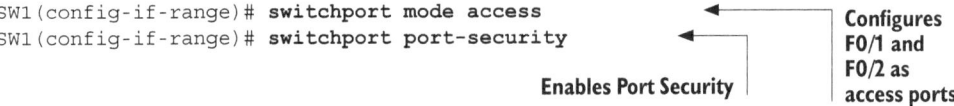

```
SW1(config-if-range)# switchport mode access
SW1(config-if-range)# switchport port-security
```

This time, the command succeeded without any error messages. To confirm the Port Security settings of a port, use the **show port-security interface** *interface* command. In the following example, I confirm F0/1's settings:

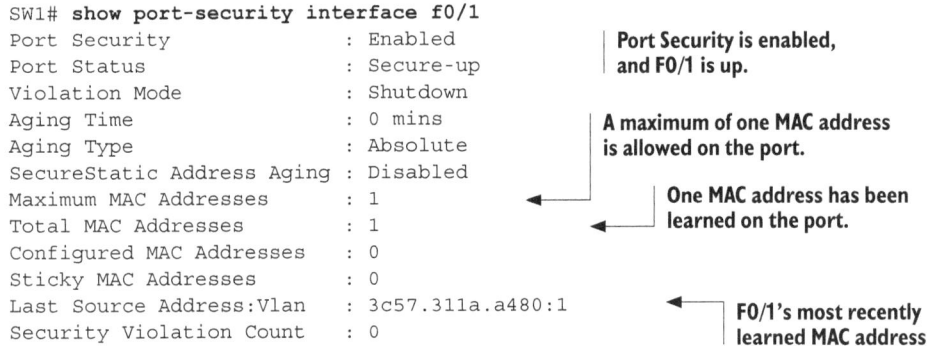

```
SW1# show port-security interface f0/1
Port Security              : Enabled
Port Status                : Secure-up
Violation Mode             : Shutdown
Aging Time                 : 0 mins
Aging Type                 : Absolute
SecureStatic Address Aging : Disabled
Maximum MAC Addresses      : 1
Total MAC Addresses        : 1
Configured MAC Addresses   : 0
Sticky MAC Addresses       : 0
Last Source Address:Vlan   : 3c57.311a.a480:1
Security Violation Count   : 0
```

From that output, you can learn that

- Port Security is active and F0/1 is up.
- Only one MAC address is allowed on F0/1, and it has learned one MAC address.
- The most recently learned MAC address on F0/1 is 3c57.311a.a480.

NOTE   A MAC address learned on a port security–enabled port is called a *secure MAC address.*

Now let's see what happens when the attacker attempts a MAC flooding attack, sending frames with spoofed MAC addresses to SW1. The following output shows what happens when SW1 receives a frame with a different MAC address:

```
%PM-4-ERR_DISABLE: psecure-violation error detected on Fa0/1,
➥putting Fa0/1 in err-disable state
%PORT_SECURITY-2-PSECURE_VIOLATION: Security violation occurred,
➥caused by MAC address 00e0.4c68.92ff on port FastEthernet0/1.
```

As soon as SW1 receives the spoofed frame, a couple of Syslog messages are shown, indicating that a Port Security violation occurred on F0/1. Because SW1 had already learned one MAC address on F0/1, the second MAC address exceeded the limit and triggered the violation. Figure 12.3 demonstrates how the violation was triggered.

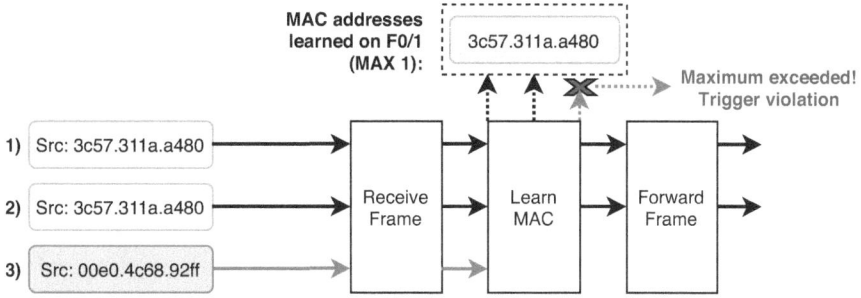

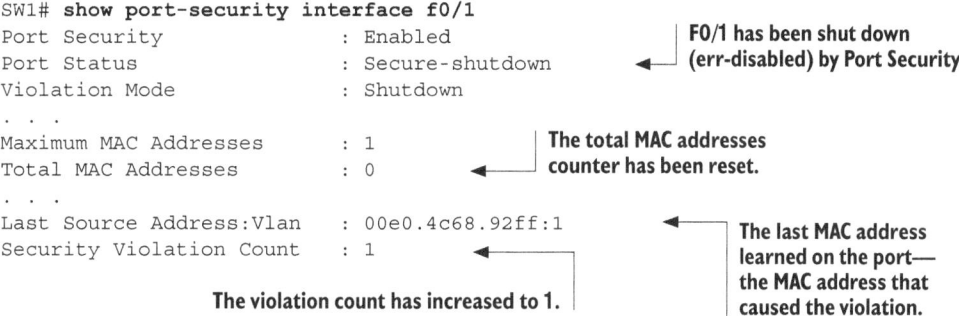

Figure 12.3 Port Security allows SW1 to learn only one MAC address on F0/1. Frames 1 and 2 are from the same MAC address, so they are forwarded normally. Frame 3 makes F0/1 exceed the maximum MAC count, triggering a violation.

The following output of **show port-security interface** shows the results of the violation. SW1 disabled F0/1:

```
SW1# show port-security interface f0/1
Port Security            : Enabled
Port Status              : Secure-shutdown
Violation Mode           : Shutdown
. . .
Maximum MAC Addresses     : 1
Total MAC Addresses       : 0
. . .
Last Source Address:Vlan  : 00e0.4c68.92ff:1
Security Violation Count  : 1
```

F0/1 has been shut down (err-disabled) by Port Security.

The total MAC addresses counter has been reset.

The last MAC address learned on the port— the MAC address that caused the violation.

The violation count has increased to 1.

This time, F0/1's status is `Secure-shutdown`, meaning that it has been disabled by Port Security. Note that the `Total MAC Addresses` count is now 0; when a port is disabled, all dynamically learned MAC addresses on the port are forgotten, including secure MAC addresses.

However, the output still shows the MAC address that was most recently seen on that port in the `Last Source Address:Vlan` row. This is the spoofed MAC address that triggered the Port Security violation. In the bottom row of the output, you can see the `Security Violation Count`. Each time the port is disabled by Port Security, this count will increment by 1.

We have thwarted the attacker! By using Port Security to make SW1 disable a port if too many unique MAC addresses are learned on the port, we prevented the attacker from filling SW1's MAC address table up with spoofed MAC addresses. In this example, Port Security prevented an attack, but it could also interfere with legitimate communications. Port Security simply limits the number of MAC addresses allowed on a specific port but doesn't inherently differentiate between a spoofed frame and a legitimate one.

For example, some devices may legitimately send frames from multiple MAC addresses—one example is a device running virtual machines (which we'll cover in chapter 17). In such a scenario, the default Port Security settings would result in the port being disabled, despite the frames being legitimate. Later in this section, we'll see how to adjust the number of allowed MAC addresses to accommodate scenarios where a switch needs to learn multiple MAC addresses on a port.

REENABLING AN ERROR-DISABLED PORT

This isn't the first time we've seen error-disabled ports in either volume of this book. The first time was in chapter 14 of volume 1, Spanning Tree Protocol (STP), when we covered BPDU Guard—a feature that error-disables a port if it receives STP Bridge Protocol Data Units (BPDUs). And in chapter 10, we covered Power Policing, which disables a port if a PoE-powered device draws too much power.

Just like in those previous examples, you can reenable an error-disabled port by first disabling the port with **shutdown** and then reenabling it with **no shutdown**. In the following example, I do that on F0/1:

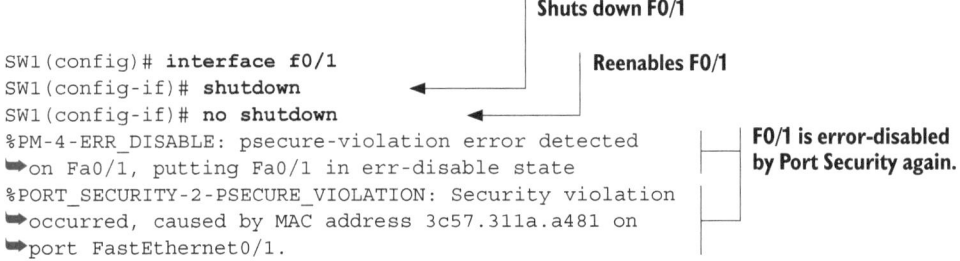

After reenabling F0/1, it was almost immediately disabled by Port Security again. The lesson here is that you should always address the underlying issue causing the error-disabled state before reenabling the port. In this case, the attacker that triggered the violation was still connected to F0/1.

In addition to manually reenabling error-disabled ports, there is a feature called *ErrDisable Recovery* that does it automatically. ErrDisable Recovery is disabled by default, but can be enabled on a per-cause (also called *per-reason*) basis. *Cause* refers to the event that caused the port to be error-disabled (BPDU Guard, Power Policing, Port Security, etc.). You can use **show errdisable recovery** to verify the status of ErrDisable Recovery:

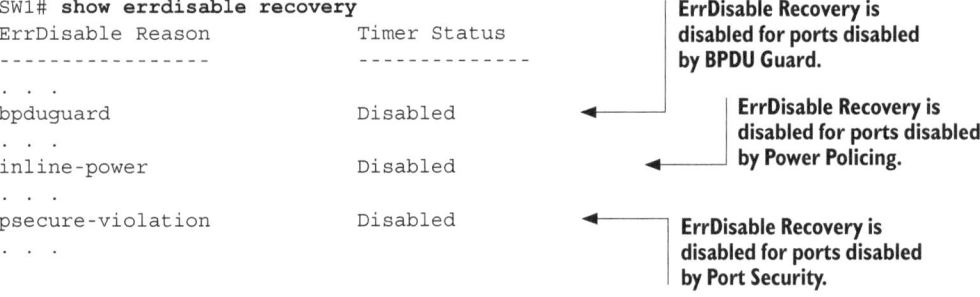

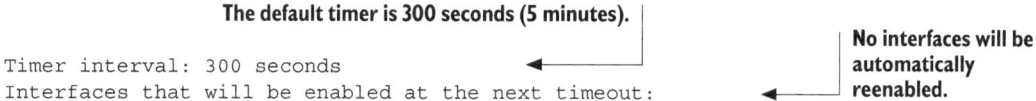

The default timer is 300 seconds (5 minutes).

No interfaces will be automatically reenabled.

```
Timer interval: 300 seconds
Interfaces that will be enabled at the next timeout:
```

ErrDisable Recovery works by automatically reenabling an error-disabled port after a preset duration; the default timer is 300 seconds. To enable ErrDisable Recovery for ports disabled by a particular cause, use the `errdisable recovery cause` *cause* command in global config mode. The keywords for the causes we have covered so far in these volumes are:

- `bpduguard` (BPDU Guard)
- `inline-power` (Power Policing)
- `psecure-violation` (Port Security)

NOTE You can modify the ErrDisable Recovery timer with `errdisable recovery interval` *seconds* in global config mode.

In the following example, I enable ErrDisable Recovery for ports disabled by Port Security and then confirm. Note that F0/1 now appears at the bottom of the output, indicating that it will be automatically reenabled when the timer counts down to 0:

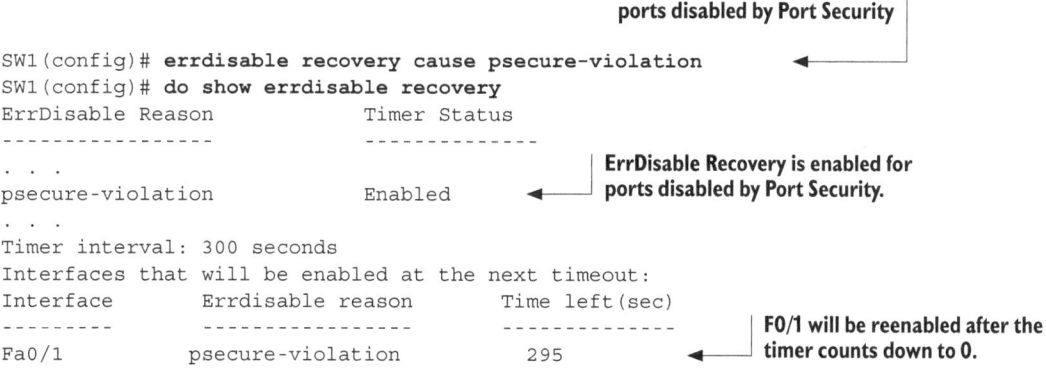

Enables ErrDisable Recovery for ports disabled by Port Security

```
SW1(config)# errdisable recovery cause psecure-violation
SW1(config)# do show errdisable recovery
ErrDisable Reason          Timer Status
-----------------          -------------
. . .
psecure-violation          Enabled
. . .
Timer interval: 300 seconds
Interfaces that will be enabled at the next timeout:
Interface       Errdisable reason       Time left(sec)
---------       ----------------        -------------
Fa0/1           psecure-violation            295
```

ErrDisable Recovery is enabled for ports disabled by Port Security.

F0/1 will be reenabled after the timer counts down to 0.

ErrDisable Recovery is a convenient feature for reenabling error-disabled ports, but keep in mind that you still need to solve the problem that caused the port to be error-disabled in the first place. If not, the port will be disabled again after recovering.

INCREASING THE MAXIMUM **MAC** ADDRESSES

By default, a Port Security–enabled port can only receive frames from one unique MAC address—anything more will trigger a violation. However, there are some scenarios that require a switch port to learn multiple MAC addresses on a single port. Figure 12.4 shows two examples: a port connected to another switch (F0/2) and a port connected to an IP phone and PC (F0/3).

```
SW1(config)# interface f0/1
SW1(config-if)# switchport port-security
SW1(config-if)# interface f0/2
SW1(config-if)# switchport port-security
SW1(config-if)# switchport port-security maximum 8
SW1(config-if)# interface f0/3
SW1(config-if)# switchport port-security
SW1(config-if)# switchport port-security maximum 2
```

Figure 12.4   Allowing multiple MAC addresses on Port Security–enabled ports

NOTE   Figure 12.4 omits the `switchport mode` configurations, but remember that Port Security can only be enabled on manually configured access or trunk ports.

SW1 F0/2 is connected to another switch with its own connected hosts. As those hosts communicate over the network, SW1 will learn their MAC addresses on its F0/2 port; the Port Security default of a single MAC address isn't enough in this situation. I used `switchport port-security maximum 8` to allow SW1 to learn up to eight unique MAC addresses on F0/2, but the appropriate number depends on how many hosts are connected to the other switch.

SW1 F0/3 is connected to an IP phone and a PC, each with its own MAC address. SW1 needs to be able to receive frames from both devices, so the Port Security default of one MAC address doesn't work here either. I used `switchport port-security maximum 2` to increase the maximum number of MAC addresses to two. Let's confirm these settings on SW1 with a new command, `show port-security`:

F0/1 allows a maximum of 1 MAC address and has learned 1.

```
SW1# show port-security
Secure Port  MaxSecureAddr   CurrentAddr   SecurityViolation  Security Action
             (Count)         (Count)       (Count)
-----------------------------------------------------------------------------
   Fa0/1          1              1                0              Shutdown
   Fa0/2          8              5                0              Shutdown
   Fa0/3          2              2                0              Shutdown
-----------------------------------------------------------------------------
. . .
```

F0/3 allows a maximum of 2 MAC addresses and has learned 2.

F0/2 allows a maximum of 8 MAC addresses and has learned 5.

CONFIGURING STATIC SECURE MAC ADDRESSES

The examples we have looked at so far are *dynamic secure MAC addresses*—secure MAC addresses that are dynamically learned. But Port Security allows you to control not only how many MAC addresses are allowed on a port, but also exactly which MAC addresses are allowed. You can do this by manually configuring *static secure MAC addresses.*

You might want to configure static secure MAC addresses to control exactly which devices can connect to which ports. For example, figure 12.5 adds a server to the previous topology. The server is connected to SW1's F0/4 port, and no other devices are allowed to connect to that port.

```
SW1(config)# interface f0/4
SW1(config-if)# switchport port-security
SW1(config-if)# switchport port-security mac-address 0200.0011.1234
SW1(config-if)# interface f0/5
SW1(config-if)# switchport port-security
SW1(config-if)# switchport port-security maximum 2
SW1(config-if)# switchport port-security mac-address 0200.0022.3456 vlan voice
```

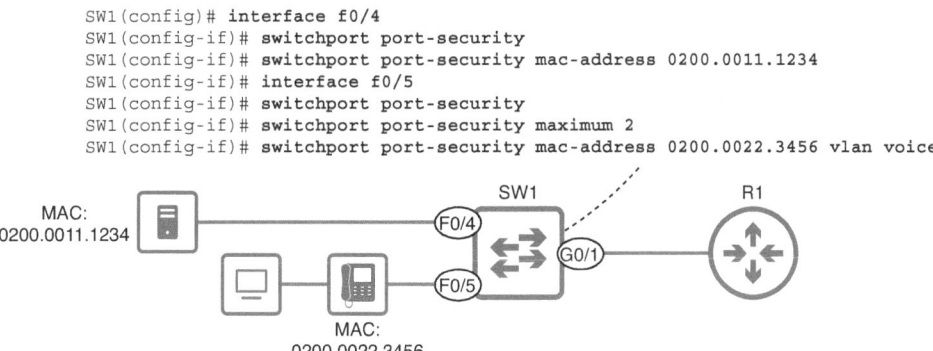

Figure 12.5   Configuring static secure MAC addresses. There can be a mix of static and dynamic secure MAC addresses on a port, as in F0/5's case.

Figure 12.5 also shows an IP phone and a PC connected to SW1's F0/5 port. To accommodate both devices, I raise the maximum number of MAC addresses to two. However, I only statically configure the phone's MAC address, allowing the PC's MAC address to be learned dynamically. Port Security supports this kind of flexibility; on the same port, there can be a mix of static and dynamic secure MAC addresses.

> **NOTE**   Dynamic and static secure MAC addresses both count toward the maximum. If the maximum is two addresses, and you configure one static secure MAC address, that means that only one dynamic MAC address can be learned on the port.

The command to configure a static secure MAC address is `switchport port -security mac-address` `mac-address`. If you issue the command as is, the static secure MAC address will be configured in the access VLAN of the port. However, to configure a static secure MAC address in the voice VLAN—the MAC address of an IP phone—add the `vlan voice` keywords to the end of the command.

Like any other MAC addresses learned by a switch, secure MAC addresses appear in the switch's MAC address table, which you can view with `show mac address-table`. However, to view only secure MAC addresses, you can add the `secure` keyword, as in the following example:

```
SW1# show mac address-table secure
         Mac Address Table
-------------------------------------------
Vlan    Mac Address      Type       Ports
----    -----------      --------   -----
. . .
   1    0200.0011.1234   STATIC     Fa0/4
   1    00e0.423c.f021   STATIC     Fa0/5
   2    0200.0022.3456   STATIC     Fa0/5
```

All secure MAC addresses appear as STATIC in the MAC address table.

That output shows one confusing fact about secure MAC addresses in the MAC address table: they are all listed as STATIC, regardless of whether they were dynamically learned or statically configured. Instead, a better option to view secure MAC addresses is **show port-security address**. This command lists static secure MAC addresses as SecureConfigured and dynamic secure MAC addresses as SecureDynamic:

```
SW1# show port-security address
              Secure Mac Address Table
----------------------------------------------------------------------
Vlan    Mac Address      Type                  Ports     Remaining Age
. . .
   1    0200.0011.1234   SecureConfigured      Fa0/4        -
   1    00e0.423c.f021   SecureDynamic         Fa0/5        -
   2    0200.0022.3456   SecureConfigured      Fa0/5        -
. . .
```

12.2 Port Security configuration options

In the previous section, we covered the basics of Port Security configuration: enabling Port Security, reenabling error-disabled ports, modifying the maximum number of MAC addresses that a port can learn, and configuring static secure MAC addresses. However, Port Security includes some other configuration options that allow you to fine-tune how it operates, and we'll cover those in this section.

12.2.1 Port Security violation modes

By default, a Port Security enabled port will be error-disabled if a violation occurs. This is because of the default *violation mode*: shutdown. However, there are two other violation modes that can be configured on a per-port basis: restrict mode and protect mode. Table 12.1 summarizes each violation mode.

Table 12.1 Port Security violation modes

	Shutdown	Restrict	Protect
Discards violating frames?	Yes	Yes	Yes
Error-disables port?	Yes	No	No
Increments violation counter?	Yes	Yes	No
Generates Syslog/SNMP messages?	Yes	Yes	No

To configure the violation modes, you can use the `switchport port-security violation` *mode* command. In the following example, I configure the restrict mode on F0/2 and the protect mode on F0/3:

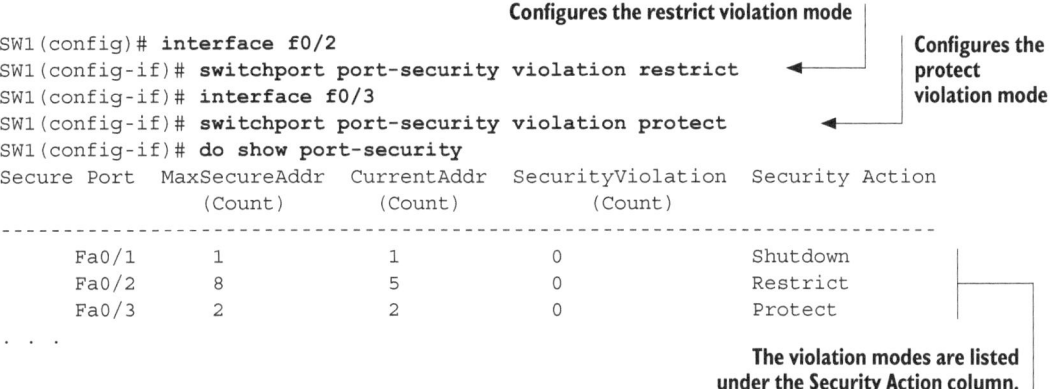

```
SW1(config)# interface f0/2
SW1(config-if)# switchport port-security violation restrict
SW1(config-if)# interface f0/3
SW1(config-if)# switchport port-security violation protect
SW1(config-if)# do show port-security
Secure Port   MaxSecureAddr   CurrentAddr   SecurityViolation   Security Action
              (Count)         (Count)       (Count)
-----------------------------------------------------------------------------
    Fa0/1        1              1               0              Shutdown
    Fa0/2        8              5               0              Restrict
    Fa0/3        2              2               0              Protect
. . .
```

With the default *shutdown* violation mode enabled, the switch error-disables the port if a violation occurs, effectively shutting down the port. In some cases, this reaction might be a bit extreme; the entire port becomes nonoperational. For example, if the port connects to a server providing an essential service, disabling the entire port might not be the ideal choice, despite it being the most secure option. Once again, always keep these tradeoffs in mind.

The *restrict* violation mode is less extreme. Instead of error-disabling the port, it only discards frames that violate the MAC address limit—the port remains up. Figure 12.6 shows how it works. The port in this example can learn a maximum of one MAC address. The first and third frames, which have source MAC addresses matching the port's secure MAC address, are forwarded. The second frame, which has a MAC address that doesn't match the secure MAC address, is discarded (but the port is not error-disabled).

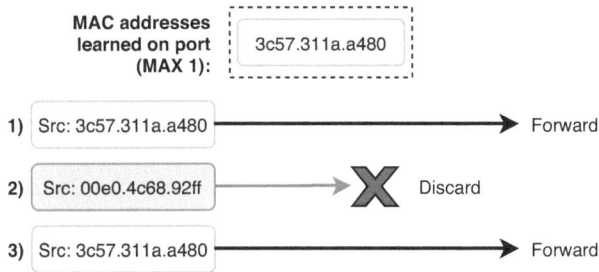

Figure 12.6 The restrict violation mode. Only frames that violate the Port Security rules are discarded. Frames that don't violate the rules are forwarded as normal.

The third mode, *protect*, operates similarly to the restrict mode. A port with protect mode enabled will not be error-disabled if a violation occurs; the port will only discard violating frames, as we saw in figure 12.6. The difference between these two modes is that protect mode silently discards violating frames, but restrict mode increments the violation counter for each violating frame and also generates Syslog messages and SNMP Traps/Informs to notify you of the violation.

> **NOTE**   The shutdown mode also increments the violation counter and generates notification messages, but only when the first violating frame is received. After the port has been error-disabled, all frames are simply ignored.

Protect mode is generally not recommended. If a Port Security violation occurs, it's better to receive a notification (i.e., SNMP Trap) so you can take any necessary action, such as disconnecting the device that triggered the violation. The choice between shutdown mode and restrict mode depends on how drastic an action you want the switch to take when a violation occurs. Shutdown mode is more secure because it prevents all traffic from being sent or received by the port if a violation occurs, but restrict mode is less disruptive to legitimate network traffic.

12.2.2 Secure MAC address aging

We covered the topic of MAC aging in chapter 6 of volume 1. To recap, dynamic MAC addresses are automatically removed (or "aged out") from the MAC address table using a 5-minute timer. This timer resets whenever a frame from the corresponding MAC address is received. But if a frame from that MAC address isn't received for 5 minutes (allowing the timer to count down to 0), the entry is aged out of the table. This ensures that the switch's MAC address table remains up to date and doesn't fill up with stale entries for devices that are no longer connected to the LAN.

> **NOTE**   Static MAC addresses, which are manually configured, don't age out.

However, dynamic secure MAC addresses behave differently. Unlike their regular counterparts, they don't age out by default. The following output shows the default settings for secure MAC address aging:

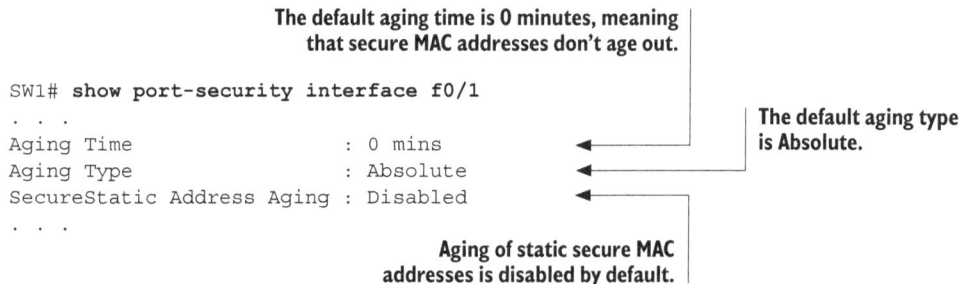

```
                              The default aging time is 0 minutes, meaning
                                 that secure MAC addresses don't age out.

SW1# show port-security interface f0/1
. . .
Aging Time                 : 0 mins        ◄─────────────      The default aging type
Aging Type                 : Absolute      ◄─────────────      is Absolute.
SecureStatic Address Aging : Disabled      ◄─────────┐
. . .
                                  Aging of static secure MAC
                                 addresses is disabled by default.
```

ENABLING SECURE MAC ADDRESS AGING

By default, a secure MAC address remains in the table indefinitely as long as the port it was learned on stays up. Once the port has learned its maximum number of secure MAC addresses, no more MAC addresses will be allowed on that port. You can change this behavior by enabling secure MAC address aging on a per-port basis with the `switchport port-security aging time` *minutes* command. In the following example, I configure an aging time of 5 minutes on SW1 F0/1:

```
SW1(config)# interface f0/1
SW1(config-if)# switchport port-security aging time 5    ◄──────   Enables secure
SW1(config-if)# do show port-security interface f0/1              MAC address aging
. . .                                                             on F0/1 with a
Aging Time                  : 5 mins        ◄───────              5-minute timer
Aging Type                  : Absolute
SecureStatic Address Aging  : Disabled            │ The aging time is now 5 minutes.
. . .
```

With this configuration, secure MAC addresses learned on F0/1 will be removed from the table after 5 minutes, making the port available for learning a new secure MAC address. This means that the port isn't indefinitely "locked" to a specific MAC address, creating a balance between maintaining network security and allowing for dynamic changes in the network environment.

SECURE MAC ADDRESS AGING TYPES

Even with aging enabled, the aging behavior of secure MAC addresses is still different from that of regular MAC addresses—those learned on ports without Port Security. That's because of the default *aging type*, which determines how secure MAC addresses age out.

As the previous example shows, the default aging type is *absolute*. This means that after a secure MAC address is learned, the aging timer starts, and the MAC address will be removed after the timer expires, even if the switch continues receiving frames from the same MAC address. In other words, the timer doesn't reset upon receiving new frames from the same MAC address. However, you can switch to a different aging type—*inactivity*—to change this behavior on a per-port basis. Here's how:

```
SW1(config)# interface f0/1
SW1(config-if)# switchport port-security aging type inactivity    ◄──────
SW1(config-if)# do show port-security interface f0/1                        Enables the
. . .                                                               inactivity aging type
Aging Time                  : 5 mins
Aging Type                  : Inactivity      ◄───────
SecureStatic Address Aging  : Disabled             │ The aging type is
. . .                                              │ now inactivity.
```

In inactivity mode, the aging timer will reset if a frame from the secure MAC address is received, similar to regular dynamic MAC addresses. Figure 12.7 demonstrates the difference between the absolute and inactivity aging types.

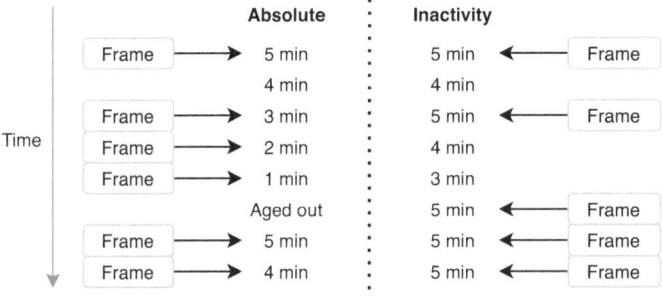

Figure 12.7   Absolute vs. inactivity aging types. With absolute aging enabled, the aging timer does not reset upon receiving new frames from the same MAC. With inactivity aging enabled, the aging timer resets each time a new frame is received.

The absolute aging type forces the switch to regularly relearn its secure MAC addresses. The inactivity aging type, on the other hand, allows the switch to keep secure MAC addresses in its MAC address table as long as it regularly receives frames from those addresses.

STATIC SECURE MAC ADDRESS AGING

As mentioned in a previous note, static MAC addresses, which are manually configured (with the `mac address-table static` command), do not age out. Just as they are manually configured, they must be manually removed. The same is true of static secure MAC addresses by default.

However, this behavior can be changed on a per-port basis with the `switchport port-security aging static` command in interface config mode. In the following example, I enable static secure MAC address aging on SW1 F0/1, configure a static secure MAC address, and then verify that it is removed from the configuration after 5 minutes:

```
SW1(config)# interface f0/1
SW1(config-if)# switchport port-security aging static          ← Enables static secure
                                                                   MAC address aging
SW1(config-if)# switchport port-security mac-address aaaa.bbbb.cccc   ←
SW1(config-if)# do show running-config
. . .                                                     Configures a static secure MAC address
interface FastEthernet0/1
 switchport mode access
 switchport port-security mac-address aaaa.bbbb.cccc   ← The static secure MAC address
 switchport port-security aging time 5                    appears in the running-config.
 switchport port-security aging type inactivity
 switchport port-security aging static   ←  Static secure MAC address
 switchport port-security                   aging is enabled.
. . .
SW1(config-if)# do show running-config   ←  After 5 minutes of inactivity, the
. . .                                        static secure MAC address is
interface FastEthernet0/1                    removed from the configuration.
 switchport mode access
```

```
switchport port-security aging time 5
switchport port-security aging type inactivity
switchport port-security aging static
switchport port-security
. . .
```

Enabling static secure MAC address aging is rare. Generally, if you manually configure a static secure MAC address, you don't want it to be automatically removed. However, static aging could be used to configure a static secure MAC address for a limited time without needing to manually remove the address afterward. The aging type has a major effect on how this works: do you want the static address to be removed after a certain period of time or only after the device stops communicating?

12.2.3 Sticky secure MAC addresses

We've discussed two types of secure MAC addresses in this chapter:

- *Dynamic*—These are learned dynamically when the switch receives frames and are stored only in the MAC address table. They are removed if the port goes down.
- *Static*—These are manually configured and stored in both the MAC address table and the running-config. They remain even if the port goes down.

Dynamic addresses offer a hands-off approach, requiring no manual configuration. Static addresses provide more control, allowing you to specify exactly which addresses are allowed on a port.

However, there is a third option that offers a middle ground: *sticky secure MAC addresses*. These addresses are

- *Dynamically Learned*—Like dynamic addresses
- *Stored in the running-config*—Like static addresses, they are stored in the running-config and retained even if the port goes down.

NOTE Sticky secure MAC addresses cannot be aged out.

Sticky secure MAC addresses can be useful in situations where you want to combine the flexibility of dynamic secure MAC addresses with the persistence of static secure MAC addresses. For example, perhaps the security policy states that only the intended devices can access certain ports; you should not be able to disconnect one device from a port and connect with another. Sticky MAC address learning can facilitate that without requiring the manual configuration of each MAC address on each port, automating the process and reducing administrative overhead.

To enable sticky secure MAC address learning, use the `switchport port-security mac-address sticky` command in interface config mode. This command turns all current and future dynamically learned secure MAC addresses on the port into sticky addresses, automatically adding them to the running-config. I demonstrate the command in the following example:

```
SW1(config)# interface f0/1
SW1(config-if)# switchport port-security mac-address sticky
SW1(config-if)# do show running-config
. . .
interface FastEthernet0/1
 switchport mode access
 switchport port-security mac-address sticky
 switchport port-security mac-address sticky 00e0.4c68.92ff
 switchport port-security
```

Enables sticky secure MAC address learning

A sticky secure MAC address was added to the running-config.

NOTE Disabling sticky learning with `no switchport port-security mac-address sticky` converts all sticky addresses on the port back to dynamic.

Figure 12.8 demonstrates secure MAC address persistence. When a port that has learned dynamic secure MAC addresses goes down, those addresses are forgotten. When the port comes back up, it is free to learn a new dynamic secure MAC address (or addresses, depending on the limit). Static and sticky secure MAC addresses, on the other hand, are retained in the running-config, persisting even when their associated port goes down.

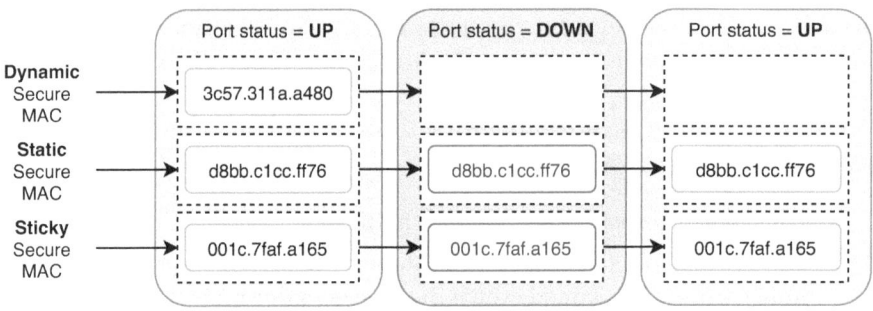

Figure 12.8   Secure MAC address persistence. Dynamic addresses are forgotten when the port goes down, but static and sticky addresses persist.

Summary

- Port Security adds a layer of security to a switch's MAC address-learning process by setting a limit on the number of unique MAC addresses that can be learned on each port and defining an action to be taken if that limit is exceeded.

- By default, the number of MAC addresses that can be learned on a port is limited only by the maximum size of the switch's MAC address table.

- This default behavior makes the switch vulnerable to attacks such as DHCP exhaustion or *MAC flooding*, which attempts to fill up a target switch's MAC address table with spoofed MAC addresses.

- If a switch's MAC address table is full, it can't learn any more MAC addresses. If it can't learn a host's MAC address, the switch will flood frames destined for that host.

- Port Security can be enabled on a port with `switchport port-security`.

- Port Security cannot be enabled on a dynamic port—a port that uses DTP. The port must be configured in access or trunk mode.

- Use `show port-security interface` *interface* to confirm the Port Security settings of a port.

- A MAC address learned on a Port Security–enabled port is called a secure MAC address.

- By default, a Port Security–enabled port can only learn one MAC address. If a frame from another MAC address is received on the port, a Port Security violation occurs. The default action when a violation occurs is to error-disable the port.

- When a port goes down, all dynamically learned MAC addresses on the port are forgotten (cleared from the MAC address table), including secure MAC addresses.

- An error-disabled port can be manually reenabled with `shutdown` followed by `no shutdown`.

- You can use *ErrDisable Recovery* to automatically reenable error-disabled ports.

- Use `show errdisable recovery` to check the status of ErrDisable Recovery.

- ErrDisable Recovery automatically reenables an error-disabled port after a preset duration; the default timer is 300 seconds.

- ErrDisable Recovery is disabled by default, but can be enabled on a per-cause basis with `errdisable recovery cause` *cause* in global config mode.

- You can modify the ErrDisable Recovery timer with `errdisable recovery interval` *seconds* in global config mode.

- Use `switchport port-security maximum` *maximum* to increase the maximum number of MAC addresses allowed on a port before a violation is triggered. For example, this is necessary on a port connected to an IP phone and a PC.

- Use `show port-security` to view information about all Port Security–enabled ports, such as the maximum number of MAC addresses allowed on each port.

- Dynamically learned secure MAC addresses are *dynamic secure MAC addresses*.

- Statically configured secure MAC addresses are *static secure MAC addresses*.

- Use `switchport port-security mac-address` *mac-address* to configure a static secure MAC address on a port. Add the `vlan voice` keywords if necessary to specify that the MAC address is in the port's voice VLAN.

- There can be a mix of static and dynamic secure MAC addresses on a port.

- Use `show mac address-table secure` to view secure MAC addresses in the MAC address table. Secure MAC addresses have the STATIC type.

- You can also use `show port-security address` to view secure MAC addresses.

- There are three Port Security *violation modes* that determine how a port reacts to a Port Security violation: shutdown, restrict, and protect.

- Use `switchport port-security violation` `mode` to configure each port's violation mode.

- The default violation mode is *shutdown*, which error-disables the port.

- The *restrict* violation mode doesn't error-disable the port if a violation occurs; it only discards frames that violate the MAC address limit. If the port's maximum is one MAC address, frames from its learned secure MAC address are allowed, but frames from other MAC addresses are discarded.

- The *protect* violation mode operates similarly to the restrict mode. It only discards violating frames; it doesn't error-disable the port if a violation occurs.

- The difference between the restrict and protect modes is that restrict increments the violation counter for each violating frame. Furthermore, restrict mode generates Syslog/SNMP messages, whereas protect silently discards violating frames without incrementing the counter or generating any messages.

- Secure MAC addresses have an aging time of 0 by default, meaning they don't age out.

- Use `switchport port-security aging time` `minutes` to configure the aging time of secure MAC addresses.

- The default secure MAC address aging type is *absolute.* This means that after a secure MAC address is learned, the aging timer starts, and the MAC address will be removed after the timer expires, even if the switch continues receiving frames.

- The second aging type is *inactivity.* With this mode configured, the aging timer will be refreshed each time the switch receives a frame from the corresponding MAC address. This is similar to the behavior of regular dynamic MAC addresses.

- Use `switchport port-security aging type` `type` to modify the aging type on a per-port basis.

- Regular static MAC addresses do not age out of the MAC address table; they must be manually removed. The same is true of secure static MAC addresses by default.

- Aging of secure static MAC addresses can be enabled on a per-port basis with `switchport port-security aging static.`

- *Sticky secure MAC addresses* offer a middle ground between dynamic and static secure MAC addresses. They are dynamically learned but are automatically inserted into the running-config and retained even if the port goes down.

- Sticky secure MAC addresses cannot be aged out.

- Use `switchport port-security mac-address sticky` to enable sticky address learning on a per-port basis. If you enable it, all current and future dynamically learned secure MAC addresses on the port will become sticky.

- If you disable sticky learning on a port, all sticky addresses on the port will be converted back to dynamic addresses.

DHCP Snooping

This chapter covers

- DHCP-based attacks such as DHCP poisoning
- How DHCP Snooping protects against DHCP-based attacks
- Configuring DHCP Snooping on Cisco IOS switches

DHCP is almost ubiquitous in modern networks, allowing for the automatic configuration of IP addresses, netmasks, default gateways, DNS servers, and other configuration information on hosts; we covered DHCP in chapter 4. However, DHCP contains vulnerabilities that can be exploited if sufficient care is not taken. We looked at one example in chapter 11: DHCP exhaustion, which is a type of DoS attack that prevents legitimate user devices from leasing IP addresses from a DHCP server.

In this chapter, we'll cover *DHCP Snooping*, a security feature on Cisco switches that protects against DHCP-based attacks by inspecting DHCP messages as they are received by the switch. DHCP Snooping is part of CCNA exam topic 5.7: Configure and verify Layer 2 security features (DHCP Snooping, Dynamic ARP Inspection, and Port Security).

13.1   *DHCP-based attacks*

Although DHCP is an essential part of modern networks, attackers can exploit it to harm the confidentiality, integrity, and availability of a network. We have already covered DHCP exhaustion attacks and how Port Security can be used to mitigate against them. In this section, we'll look at how DHCP can be exploited to perform a man-in-the-middle attack: DHCP poisoning.

In a *DHCP poisoning attack*, the attacker configures a *rogue DHCP server* (sometimes called a *spurious DHCP server*) to lease IP addresses to clients. The rogue server leases valid IP addresses, but the point of the attack is to tell the clients to use the rogue server as their default gateway—not the LAN's legitimate router. This allows the rogue server to intercept clients' communications, gaining access to (and possibly altering) their contents before relaying them to the router. Figure 13.1 demonstrates a DHCP poisoning attack.

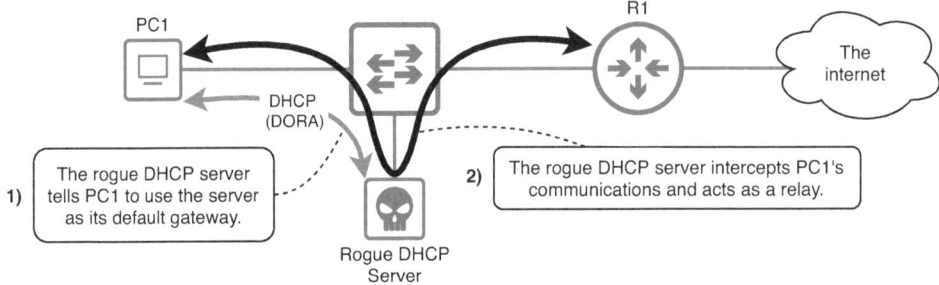

Figure 13.1   A DHCP poisoning attack. The rogue DHCP server replies to PC1's DHCP messages, assigning it an IP address and telling it to use the rogue server as its default gateway. The rogue server then intercepts PC1's communications.

> **NOTE**   DHCP poisoning may remind you of a similarly named attack that we covered in chapter 11: ARP poisoning. Both attacks allow the attacker's device to act as a man-in-the-middle, secretly intercepting targets' communications.

DHCP clients tend to accept the first OFFER message they receive in response to their DISCOVER, so the rogue server's goal is to respond before any legitimate DHCP servers. If both the rogue and legitimate DHCP servers are in the same LAN, it's a race to reply first. But if the legitimate DHCP server is in a different LAN, introducing additional delay between the client and the server, the rogue server's "poisoned" OFFER has a good chance of reaching the client first due to its lower latency.

Port Security, which we covered in chapter 12, doesn't mitigate against DHCP poisoning attacks. The rogue server sends DHCP messages from a single MAC address, so limiting the number of MAC addresses on the port doesn't help. To defend your network against DHCP poisoning attacks, you should use DHCP Snooping.

13.2 *DHCP Snooping*

DHCP Snooping works by examining and filtering DHCP messages received by the switch. That's an important point: DHCP only filters DHCP messages—non-DHCP messages are unaffected by DHCP Snooping. Let's look at how DHCP Snooping works and how to configure it on Cisco switches. Figure 13.2 shows the network we'll configure.

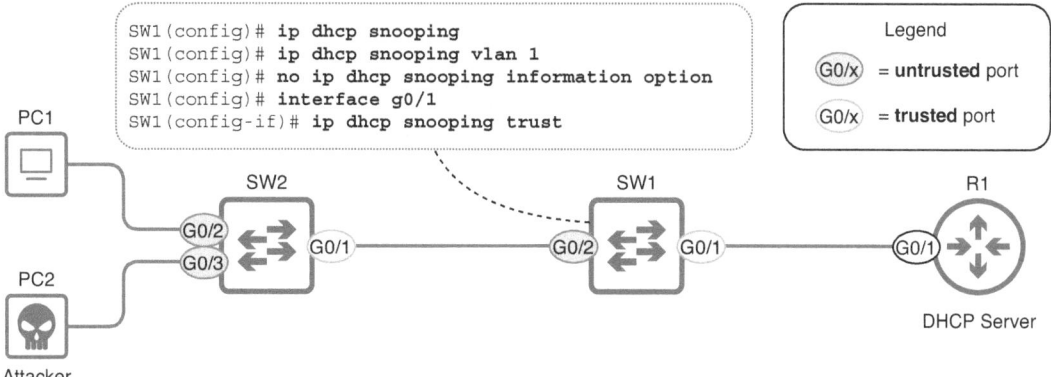

Figure 13.2 Configuring DHCP Snooping on Cisco switches. Ports leading toward the DHCP Server are trusted, and ports leading toward users are untrusted. Only SW1's configurations are shown, but the same commands should be configured on SW2.

The first step in configuring DHCP Snooping is to enable the feature; it is disabled by default. Doing so requires two separate commands:

- Enable DHCP Snooping—`ip dhcp snooping`
- Activate DHCP Snooping on each VLAN—`ip dhcp snooping vlan` *vlans*

`ip dhcp snooping` enables DHCP Snooping, but it won't actually take effect until you use the second command (`ip dhcp snooping vlan` *vlans*) to activate it on each VLAN in the LAN. To keep things simple, the example network we will use in this chapter has a single VLAN (VLAN 1), but in a LAN with multiple VLANs, you should enable it on each VLAN that has hosts using DHCP. You can activate DHCP Snooping on multiple VLANs with a single command by using commas and hyphens in the *vlans* argument—for example:

- All VLANs—`ip dhcp snooping vlan 1-4094`
- VLANs 1, 3, 4, 5, 7, 9, 10, and 11—`ip dhcp snooping vlan 1,3-5,7,9-11`

In the following example, I configure DHCP Snooping on SW2 and verify with `show ip dhcp snooping` (I issued the same commands on SW1 too):

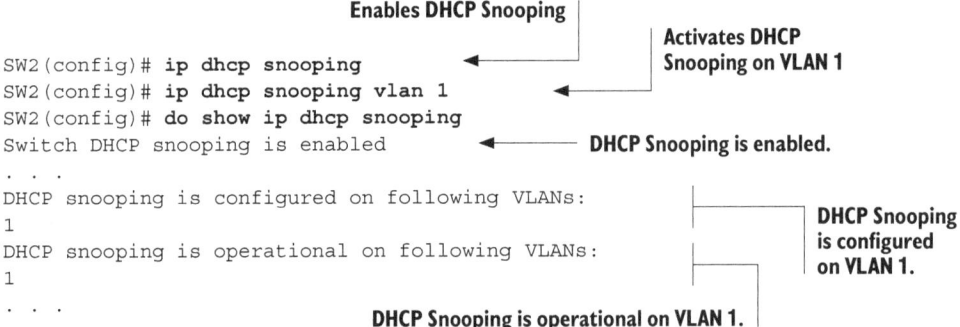

```
SW2(config)# ip dhcp snooping
SW2(config)# ip dhcp snooping vlan 1
SW2(config)# do show ip dhcp snooping
Switch DHCP snooping is enabled
. . .
DHCP snooping is configured on following VLANs:
1
DHCP snooping is operational on following VLANs:
1
. . .
```

NOTE A VLAN might appear as `configured`, but not `operational`, if you enable DHCP Snooping for the VLAN but the VLAN itself is disabled on the switch.

13.2.1 How DHCP Snooping filters DHCP messages

DHCP Snooping works by filtering DHCP messages. However, it doesn't filter DHCP messages received on all ports; it only filters those received on untrusted ports. Messages received on trusted ports are not filtered. In this section, we'll review the different DHCP message types that we covered in chapter 4 (and look at some new ones) and then examine the concepts of trusted/untrusted ports and how DHCP Snooping filters messages.

DHCP MESSAGE TYPES

You should already be familiar with the messages in the DHCP DORA exchange: DISCOVER, OFFER, REQUEST, ACK. However, there are some other DHCP message types that you should know (although not to the same level of detail as DORA). Figure 13.3 lists some of the different DHCP message types.

Figure 13.3   DHCP message types. Client messages include DISCOVER, REQUEST, DECLINE, and RELEASE. Server messages include OFFER, ACK, and NAK.

When DHCP Snooping filters DHCP messages, it differentiates between messages sent by DHCP clients and those sent by DHCP servers. Messages sent by DHCP clients include DISCOVER, REQUEST, DECLINE, and RELEASE. Messages sent by DHCP servers include OFFER, ACK, and NAK. Here's a quick description of each message type we haven't covered yet:

- *DECLINE*—Used to tell the server that the leased IP address is already in use
- *RELEASE*—Used to tell the server that the client no longer needs its IP address
- *NAK* (negative ACK) —The opposite of ACK; used to decline a client's REQUEST

EXAM TIP You don't have to know the details of these additional message types, but you should know which are sent by clients and which are sent by servers. Other DHCP message types exist, but I wouldn't expect to see them on the CCNA exam.

DHCP SNOOPING TRUSTED AND UNTRUSTED PORTS

The concept of trusted and untrusted ports is fundamental to how DHCP Snooping works. DHCP Snooping filters DHCP messages received on *untrusted ports* based on a set of rules, and all ports are untrusted by default. All DHCP messages received on *trusted ports*, however, are allowed. You need to manually specify each trusted port with `ip dhcp snooping trust`. Figure 13.4 demonstrates trusted and untrusted ports.

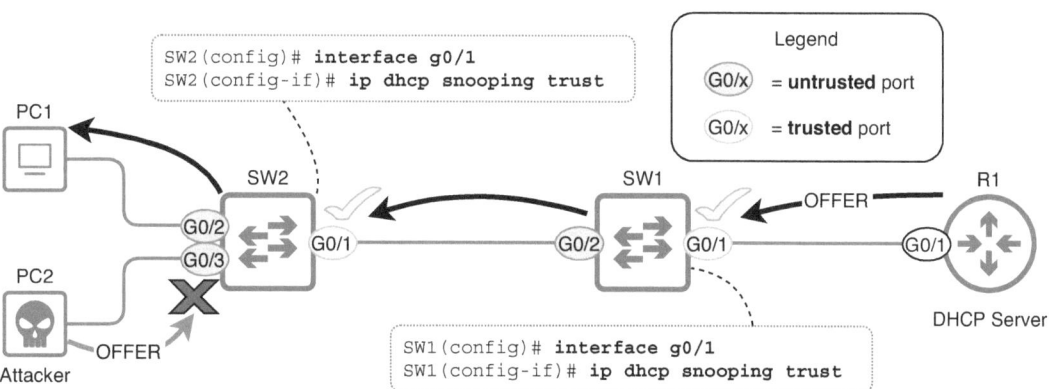

Figure 13.4 DHCP Snooping trusted ports lead toward the DHCP server. Untrusted ports lead away from the DHCP server and block server messages like OFFER.

Ports that lead toward the DHCP server (the G0/1 ports of SW1 and SW2 in figure 13.4) should be trusted. DHCP Snooping forwards DHCP messages received on those ports without any further inspection.

Ports that lead away from the DHCP server—toward end hosts—should remain in the default untrusted state. When a DHCP message is received on an untrusted port, the switch will inspect it and act as follows:

- If it is a DHCP server message (OFFER, ACK, or NAK), discard it.
  - This is why PC2's OFFER is discarded in figure 13.4.

- If it is a DHCP client message (DISCOVER, REQUEST, DECLINE, or RELEASE), inspect it further to determine if it is legitimate.
- If a client successfully leases an IP address, create a new entry in the DHCP Snooping binding table—more on that later in this section.

NOTE   Because all ports are untrusted by default, if you don't configure any trusted ports, DHCP won't work; all messages from DHCP servers will be discarded.

In the following example, I configure SW2 G0/1 as a trusted port and confirm by looking at some more output of `show ip dhcp snooping`:

```
SW2(config)# interface g0/1                        | Configures G0/1 as
SW2(config-if)# ip dhcp snooping trust             | a trusted port
SW2(config-if)# do show ip dhcp snooping
. . .
DHCP snooping trust/rate is configured on the following Interfaces:
Interface               Trusted    Allow option    Rate limit (pps)
----------------------  -------    ------------    ----------------
GigabitEthernet0/1      yes        yes             unlimited         ◄───┐

                                              The Trusted column states yes.
```

INSPECTING CLIENT MESSAGES

Untrusted ports only accept DHCP client messages. However, they don't blindly accept all client messages; they perform additional checks to verify that the message is valid before accepting it. The checks that the switch performs depend on the message type:

- *Messages involved in the DORA process*—DISCOVER and REQUEST. Check that the Ethernet source MAC address and DHCP chaddr match.
- *Messages sent after the client has leased an IP*—RELEASE and DECLINE. Verify the message using the DHCP Snooping binding table.

For the first category, DISCOVER and REQUEST messages, the switch compares two fields: the source MAC address field of the Ethernet header and the *chaddr* (client hardware address) field of the DHCP message (which indicates the client's MAC address). If the addresses in the two fields match, the switch permits the message. If the two addresses don't match, the switch discards the message.

The purpose of the chaddr field

The chaddr field (written in lowercase to align with RFC 2131, which defines DHCP) represents the client's hardware address, typically a MAC address in modern networks (where Ethernet dominates). You might wonder, why have this field when the client's MAC address is already present in the Ethernet frame's source MAC address field?

There are multiple reasons, but a primary one is to support situations where the DHCP client and server are in separate LANs (and a DHCP relay agent is used). In such situations, by the time the client's DHCP message reaches the server, the source MAC address of the Ethernet frame won't be the client's MAC address. Instead, it will be the MAC address of the last router that forwarded the message to the server. The chaddr field ensures that the client's MAC address is still conveyed to the server in such scenarios.

These two fields should match when the client's message reaches the switch; they should only differ if the message is forwarded by a DHCP relay agent. However, an attacker might repeatedly send spoofed DHCP DISCOVER messages from a single source MAC address (to bypass Port Security's MAC address limit), each with a unique address in the chaddr field to perform a DHCP exhaustion attack. Verifying that these fields match protects against such an attack, as shown in figure 13.5.

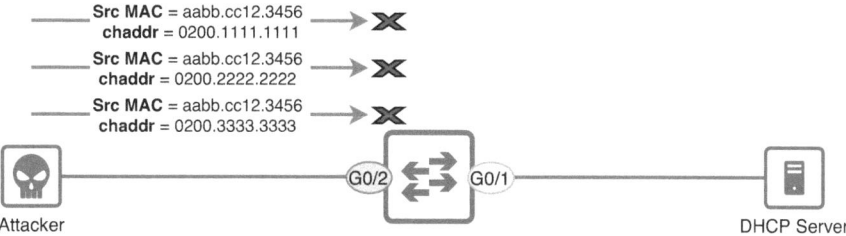

Figure 13.5 DHCP Snooping prevents a DHCP starvation attack by verifying that the source MAC address and chaddr of the attacker's messages match.

The second category of DHCP client messages, RELEASE and DECLINE, are sent after the client has leased an IP address. DECLINE is used if after receiving the final ACK from the server, the client detects that the IP address is already in use by another device. RELEASE is used any time the client decides it no longer needs its leased IP address—for example, if it disconnects from the network.

However, these messages can be exploited by an attacker. For example, the attacker could send a RELEASE message to tell the server to release a particular client's IP address, and then the attacker could attempt to lease that address for itself. To verify that RELEASE and DECLINE messages are legitimate, the switch will verify the message by checking the DHCP Snooping binding table, which we'll cover next.

THE DHCP SNOOPING BINDING TABLE

As a DHCP Snooping-enabled switch observes DHCP exchanges between clients and servers, it builds a table of the clients that have successfully leased an IP address; that table is called the *DHCP Snooping binding table*, and you can view it with **show ip dhcp snooping binding**. The following example shows the DHCP Snooping binding table:

```
SW2# show ip dhcp snooping binding
MacAddress          IpAddress    Lease(sec)   Type            VLAN   Interface
------------------  -----------  ----------   -------------   ----   ---------
52:54:00:08:D3:E0   10.0.0.6     84617        dhcp-snooping   1      Gi0/2
52:54:00:02:F4:E1   10.0.0.7     84623        dhcp-snooping   1      Gi0/3
Total number of bindings: 2
```

The DHCP Snooping binding table includes information like the client's MAC address, the leased IP address and duration of the lease, the VLAN, and the interface (or port—the terms are interchangeable) the client is connected to. When inspecting a RELEASE or DECLINE message received on an untrusted port, the switch ensures that the IP address of the message and the port it was received on match the entry in the binding table.

> **NOTE**   The DHCP Snooping binding table isn't only used for verifying DHCP messages. It also plays a key role in Dynamic ARP Inspection (DAI), the topic of chapter 14.

13.2.2 *DHCP option 82*

If you're following along in a lab as you read this chapter and have correctly enabled DHCP Snooping, activated it on the necessary VLANs, and trusted the appropriate ports, you might be confused as to why hosts are unable to lease IP addresses via DHCP and why your switches have empty DHCP Snooping binding tables. The following output of **show ip dhcp snooping** shows why:

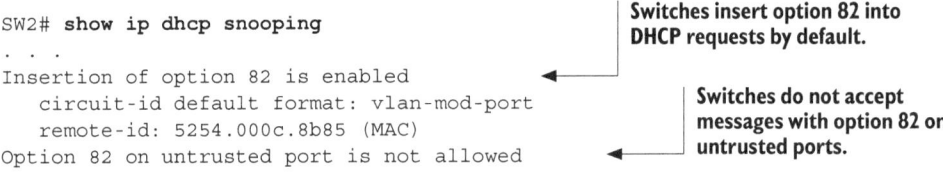

```
SW2# show ip dhcp snooping
. . .
Insertion of option 82 is enabled          ◀——   Switches insert option 82 into
   circuit-id default format: vlan-mod-port        DHCP requests by default.
   remote-id: 5254.000c.8b85 (MAC)
Option 82 on untrusted port is not allowed ◀——   Switches do not accept
. . .                                             messages with option 82 on
                                                  untrusted ports.
```

DHCP defines various optional fields, called *options*, that can be included in its messages. One of those is the *DHCP relay agent information option*, usually called by its number, *option 82*. A DHCP relay agent can insert this option when forwarding DHCP client messages to a remote DHCP server, providing additional information to the server that can inform the IP allocation decision. The details of option 82 are beyond the scope of the CCNA exam, but option 82 is relevant to DHCP Snooping because of some default settings on Cisco routers and switches related to option 82.

Figure 13.6 demonstrates what happens when PC1 sends a DHCP DISCOVER message. SW2 adds option 82 to the message and forwards it to SW1. SW1, receiving a message with option 82 on an untrusted port, discards the message. If you check the CLI of SW1, it will display a Syslog message like the following:

```
%DHCP_SNOOPING-5-DHCP_SNOOPING_NONZERO_GIADDR: DHCP_SNOOPING drop message
with non-zero giaddr or option82 value on untrusted port, message type:
DHCPDISCOVER, MAC sa: 5254.0008.d3e0
```

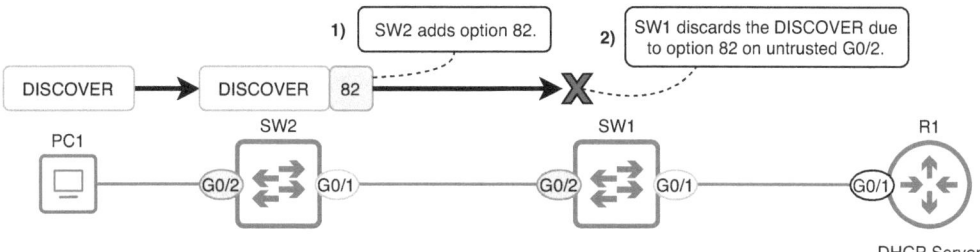

Figure 13.6   SW2 adds option 82 to PC1's DISCOVER. SW2 then discards the DISCOVER after receiving it on an untrusted port.

The previous output of **show ip dhcp snooping** stated Insertion of option 82 is enabled. This means that when DHCP Snooping is enabled, the switch will automatically insert option 82 into DHCP client messages received on untrusted ports. This behavior of inserting option 82 is useful if the switch is a multilayer switch acting as a DHCP relay agent, forwarding client messages to a remote DHCP server. The default settings are configured with this common scenario in mind.

However, if the switch is functioning as a regular Layer 2 switch (not a DHCP relay agent), this default setting can cause headaches; this is the case for SW1 and SW2 in this example. This is because of another default setting shown in the same output: Option 82 on untrusted port is not allowed. These two default settings mean that

- The switch adds option 82 to DHCP messages received on untrusted ports.
- The switch doesn't accept DHCP messages that already have option 82 on untrusted ports.

This might seem contradictory, but there's a reason: a DHCP client has no valid reason to add option 82 to its own messages. If the switch receives a DHCP message that already contains option 82 on an untrusted port, it's likely that a rogue DHCP server or a misconfigured client is at play. For this reason, the switch doesn't accept such messages.

To disable option 82 insertion, use the **no ip dhcp snooping information option** command in global config mode, as in the following example. With this command configured, SW2 will no longer insert option 82 into clients' DHCP messages:

```
SW2(config)# no ip dhcp snooping information option        ◄──── Disables option
SW2(config)# do show ip dhcp snooping                            82 insertion
. . .
Insertion of option 82 is disabled        ◄──── SW2 will no longer
. . .                                            insert option 82.
```

However, in our example network, it's not enough to disable option 82 insertion on SW2 alone. SW1, having received a DHCP client message on an untrusted port, will add option 82 itself before forwarding the message to R1. A Cisco router acting as a DHCP server or relay agent will drop such messages too. So make sure to disable option 82 insertion on SW1 too:

```
SW1(config)# no ip dhcp snooping information option
```

With option 82 insertion disabled on both switches, the client's DISCOVER message will reach R1 as is, and the client will be able to lease an IP address. In figure 13.6's example, R1 is functioning as a DHCP server. But if it were a DHCP relay agent, it could then insert option 82 before forwarding the DISCOVER to the remote DHCP server, providing the server with additional context about the request. This extra context can help the server make an informed IP allocation decision.

> **EXAM TIP**   As far as the CCNA exam is concerned, just know that you should disable option 82 insertion, unless the switch itself is a multilayer switch acting as a DHCP relay agent. This is an often-forgotten step in configuring DHCP Snooping that can lead to frustration. Don't forget!

DHCP options

DHCP options enable the client, server, and sometimes relay agents to exchange additional information that can support the DHCP process and extend its functionality. There are about 100 standard DHCP options defined in various RFCs, although not all are widely used. In addition to option 82, here are a few examples:

- *Option 3 (Router)*—This is a very common option. It is used by the server to tell the client which router to use as its default gateway.
- *Option 6 (DNS Server)*—Another very common option. This tells the client which DNS server(s) to use for name resolution.
- *Option 50 (Requested IP Address)*—A client can include this option if it wants to request a specific IP address from the server (although the server is not obligated to fulfill this request). For example, a Windows PC will typically include this option to request the same IP address it had previously (i.e., before it was last shut down).

We already covered the fact that a DHCP server can inform a client about its default gateway and DNS servers in chapter 4, without mentioning the relevant DHCP options that enable this functionality; that's because DHCP options are generally not something you need to know for the CCNA exam. Option 82 is relevant only due to its effect when DHCP Snooping is enabled.

13.2.3 *Rate-limiting DHCP messages*

The configurations we have covered so far are the minimum essentials for enabling DHCP Snooping without interfering with legitimate DHCP traffic:

1 Enable DHCP Snooping: `ip dhcp snooping`

2 Activate DHCP Snooping on each VLAN: `ip dhcp snooping vlan` `vlans`

3 Trust the appropriate ports: `ip dhcp snooping trust`

4 Disable option 82 insertion: `no ip dhcp snooping information option`

One more optional (but valuable) aspect of DHCP Snooping you can configure is *rate limiting*—limiting the rate at which a DHCP Snooping-enabled switch accepts DHCP messages. The combination of Port Security and DHCP Snooping is able to thwart most DHCP-related attacks like DHCP starvation.

However, inspecting DHCP messages with DHCP Snooping can be demanding of the switch's CPU. This leads to another possible attack: overwhelming the switch's CPU with countless DHCP messages, potentially leading to a denial of service. DHCP Snooping rate limiting can mitigate against such an attack.

You can enable DHCP Snooping rate limiting on a per-port basis with `ip dhcp snooping limit rate` `rate`; the `rate` argument is configured in packets per second (pps). Cisco recommends a rate limit of no more than 100 pps on untrusted ports, but the appropriate rate varies greatly, depending on the port. For example, a port connected to a single PC should receive much less DHCP traffic than a port connected to another switch with 40 of its own connected end hosts.

In figure 13.7, I configure DHCP Snooping rate limiting on SW1's and SW2's untrusted ports at rates of 100 pps and 25 pps, respectively. These numbers are quite generous, given that only two hosts are shown in the network—a single PC, for example, should only generate two messages in the typical DORA exchange. In a real network, it's best to find a balance between protecting against attacks and not blocking legitimate traffic.

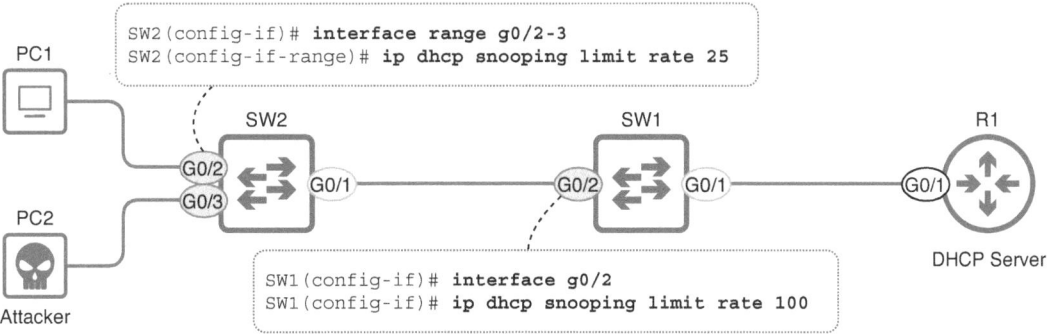

Figure 13.7 Configuring DHCP Snooping rate limiting on untrusted ports

You may be wondering, what happens if a port receives DHCP messages at a faster rate than its configured limit? In the following example, I configure a rate limit of 1 pps on SW2 G0/2 to demonstrate:

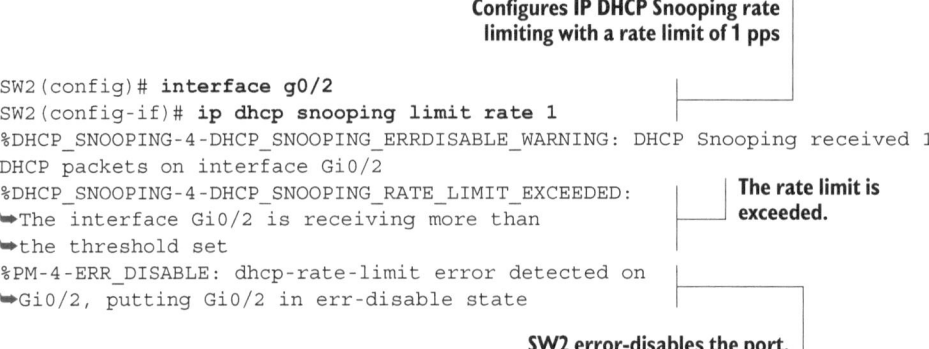

Configures IP DHCP Snooping rate limiting with a rate limit of 1 pps

```
SW2(config)# interface g0/2
SW2(config-if)# ip dhcp snooping limit rate 1
%DHCP_SNOOPING-4-DHCP_SNOOPING_ERRDISABLE_WARNING: DHCP Snooping received 1
DHCP packets on interface Gi0/2
%DHCP_SNOOPING-4-DHCP_SNOOPING_RATE_LIMIT_EXCEEDED:
➥The interface Gi0/2 is receiving more than
➥the threshold set
%PM-4-ERR_DISABLE: dhcp-rate-limit error detected on
➥Gi0/2, putting Gi0/2 in err-disable state
```

The rate limit is exceeded.

SW2 error-disables the port.

NOTE DHCP Snooping doesn't filter DHCP messages on trusted ports, but rate limiting is one aspect that can be configured on trusted ports (although it's rare).

If the rate limit is exceeded, the switch will error-disable the port to prevent any further messages. As with the previous examples of error-disabled ports that we have covered (BPDU Guard, power policing, and port security), there are two ways to reenable a port that was disabled by DHCP Snooping rate limiting:

- *Manual*—Issue shutdown and no shutdown on the error-disabled port.
- *Automatic*—Configure `errdisable recovery cause dhcp-rate-limit` to enable ErrDisable Recovery for ports disabled by DHCP Snooping rate limiting.

Although rate limiting is optional and disabled by default, it's a good idea to configure reasonable rate limits on untrusted ports as an extra layer of protection against threats. Make sure to test rate limits in a controlled environment (a lab) before rolling them out in a live network!

Summary

- *DHCP Snooping* is a security feature on switches that protects against DHCP-based attacks by inspecting DHCP messages as they are received.
- In a *DHCP poisoning attack*, the attacker configures a *rogue DHCP server* (sometimes called a *spurious DHCP server*) to lease IP addresses to clients.
- The rogue server tells clients to use itself as their default gateway, resulting in a man-in-the-middle attack in which the attacker intercepts the clients' communications.
- Port Security doesn't mitigate against DHCP poisoning because the rogue server sends DHCP messages from a single MAC address; DHCP Snooping is needed.
- DHCP Snooping only filters DHCP messages—non-DHCP messages are unaffected.
- Enable DHCP Snooping with `ip dhcp snooping` in global config mode. It also needs to be activated on each VLAN with `ip dhcp snooping vlan` *vlans*.

- Use `show ip dhcp snooping` to verify DHCP Snooping settings.

- DHCP Snooping only filters DHCP messages received on *untrusted ports*. All ports are untrusted by default. It doesn't filter messages received on *trusted ports*.

- DHCP Snooping differentiates between messages sent by DHCP clients and those sent by DHCP servers.

- Messages sent by clients include DISCOVER, REQUEST, DECLINE, and RELEASE.

- Messages sent by servers include OFFER, ACK, and NAK.

- Ports that lead toward the DHCP server should be trusted. Ports that lead away from the DHCP server (toward end hosts) should remain in the default untrusted state.

- Use `ip dhcp snooping trust` in interface config mode to configure a trusted port.

- When a DHCP message is received on an untrusted port, the switch will inspect it and act as follows:

  - If it is a DHCP server message, discard it.

  - If it is a DHCP client message, inspect it further depending on the type.

  - If a client successfully leases an IP address, create a new entry in the DHCP Snooping binding table.

- If the message is a DISCOVER or REQUEST message, the switch will check that the Ethernet source MAC Address and DHCP *chaddr* (client hardware address) match. If they match, it accepts the message. If not, it discards the message.

- The source MAC address/chaddr check protects against DHCP exhaustion attacks in which the attacker sends spoofed DHCP DISCOVER messages from a single source MAC address, each with a unique address in the chaddr field.

- If the message is a RELEASE or DECLINE message, the switch will check the DHCP Snooping binding table to verify the message.

- As a DHCP Snooping-enabled switch observes exchanges between client and servers, it builds a table of the clients that have successfully leased an IP address: the *DHCP Snooping binding table*.

- View the DHCP Snooping binding table with `show ip dhcp snooping binding`.

- When a RELEASE or DECLINE message is received on an untrusted port, the switch ensures that the IP address of the message and the port it was received on match the entry in the binding table.

- DHCP defines various optional fields, called *options*. DHCP options are beyond the scope of the CCNA exam, except for *option 82*, which can impede the DHCP process when DHCP Snooping is enabled.

- Option 82 is the *DHCP relay information option*.

- A DHCP relay agent can insert option 82 when forwarding DHCP client messages to a remote DHCP server, providing additional information to the server.

- By default, a DHCP Snooping-enabled switch will automatically insert option 82 into DHCP client messages received on untrusted ports.

- By default, a DHCP Snooping-enabled switch will discard DHCP messages with option 82 that are received on an untrusted port. A Cisco router acting as a DHCP server or relay agent will drop such messages too.

- To prevent a DHCP Snooping-enabled switch from adding option 82 to client messages, use `no ip dhcp snooping information option` in global config mode.

- You can optionally configure *rate limiting* on a per-port basis to limit the rate at which the port can receive DHCP messages.

- Use `ip dhcp snooping limit rate` `rate` to configure rate limiting. The `rate` argument is configured in packets per second (pps).

- Rate limiting can be configured on both untrusted and trusted ports, although it is rarely enabled on trusted ports.

- If a port receives DHCP messages at a faster rate than its configured limit, the switch will error-disable the port.

- Use `shutdown` and `no shutdown` to manually reenable an error-disabled port or `errdisable recovery cause dhcp-rate-limit` to enable ErrDisable Recovery for ports disabled by DHCP Snooping rate limiting.

Dynamic ARP Inspection

This chapter covers

- Address Resolution Protocol–based attacks such as ARP poisoning
- How Dynamic ARP Inspection protects against ARP-based attacks
- Configuring DAI on Cisco IOS switches

We first covered Address Resolution Protocol (ARP) in chapter 6 of volume 1, and it has come up several times throughout this book. ARP is an essential protocol in IP networks, serving as the bridge between Layer 2 and Layer 3 by mapping IP addresses to their corresponding MAC addresses. However, like many protocols, ARP is susceptible to exploitation that can compromise the security of a network. *Dynamic ARP Inspection* (DAI), the topic of this chapter, is a security feature on Cisco switches that we can use to mitigate such threats.

DAI is part of CCNA exam topic 5.7: Configure and verify Layer 2 security features. (These include DHCP Snooping, Dynamic ARP Inspection, and Port Security.) We have already covered Port Security and DHCP Snooping, so this is the final chapter addressing topic 5.7. As you read this chapter, I'm sure you'll notice similarities between DAI and DHCP Snooping, both in functionality and Cisco IOS configuration. In fact, DAI relies on the DHCP Snooping binding table as one of its key components. Due to their similarities, this chapter will follow a structure similar to the previous one.

12.1   ARP and ARP-based attacks

Although we have covered ARP before, understanding DAI requires a deeper understanding of the contents of ARP messages. Figure 14.1 depicts a standard ARP exchange between two devices, showing some of the fields in each message. Notice that ARP messages include *Sender MAC* and *Sender IP* fields to indicate the MAC and IP addresses of the sender and *Target MAC* and *Target IP* fields to indicate the target's addresses. The Target IP field of the ARP request is particularly important because it's a broadcast message; a switch will flood the message to all hosts in the LAN, so this field is used to indicate the actual intended recipient of the message.

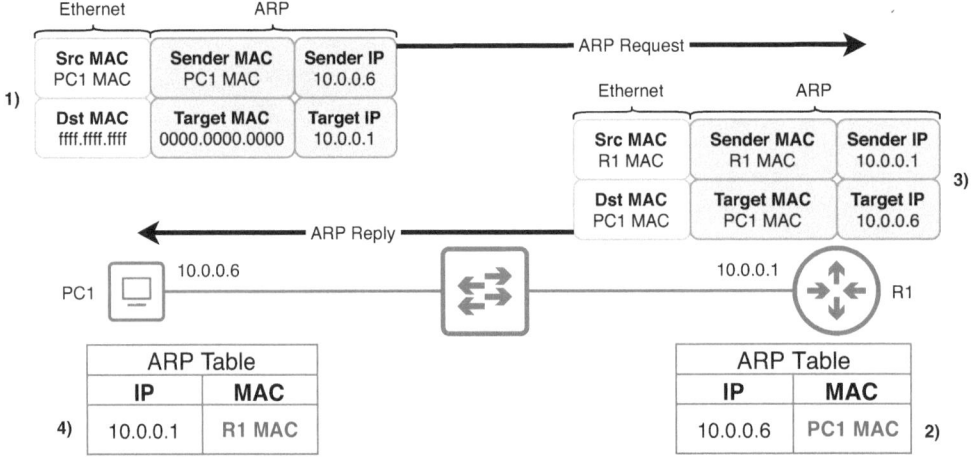

Figure 14.1   A standard ARP exchange. The important fields of each message are shown. The broadcast ARP request's Target MAC is empty (0000.0000.0000) because PC1 doesn't know R1's MAC yet.

NOTE   An ARP message is encapsulated directly in an Ethernet frame—it does not include an IP header. The sender and target IP fields are part of the ARP message itself, not part of an IP header.

In the ARP exchange, both hosts learn each other's MAC address—that is ARP's purpose, after all. Following the flow of figure 14.1, in step 1, PC1 broadcasts an ARP request. In step 2, R1 uses the information in the Sender MAC and Sender IP fields of PC1's request to create an ARP table entry, mapping PC1's IP address to its MAC address.

Then, in step 3, R1 sends a unicast ARP reply message to PC1. After receiving it, PC1 uses the information in the Sender MAC and Sender IP fields to create an entry for R1 in its own ARP table. The ARP process is complete, and both devices know each other's MAC address.

ARP's most significant vulnerability is how simple it is for an attacker to overwrite legitimate ARP table entries with "poisoned" entries—an ARP poisoning attack. Figure 14.2 reviews the process. After PC1 and R1 have learned each other's MAC address, the attacker sends ARP replies to overwrite the legitimate entries with its own MAC address. As a result, PC1 and R1 will send frames to the attacker instead of each other, giving the attacker access to their communications; regarding the CIA triad, this affects the confidentiality of the communications.

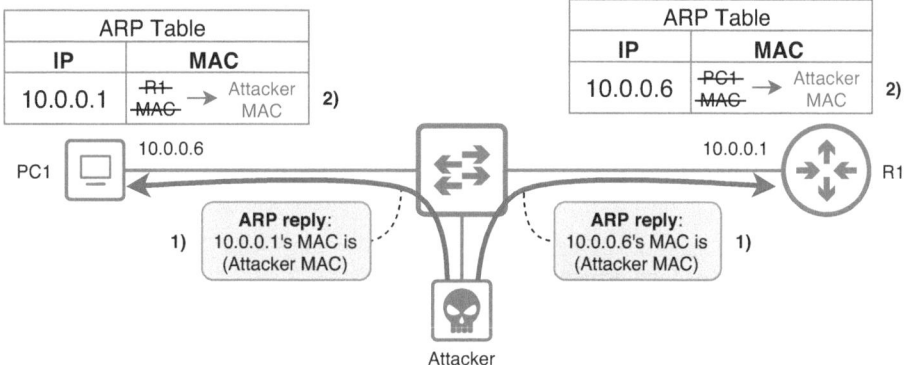

Figure 14.2   An ARP poisoning attack. The attacker sends ARP replies to overwrite PC1 and R1's ARP entries with the attacker's own MAC address.

NOTE   The ARP replies shown in figure 14.1 are gratuitous ARP (GARP) replies—ARP replies that were not prompted by ARP requests. We saw another example of GARP in chapter 19 of volume 1 when covering First Hop Redundancy Protocols.

12.2   *Dynamic ARP Inspection*

The security features we have covered so far (Port Security and DHCP Snooping) don't protect against ARP poisoning attacks. ARP poisoning is performed from a single source MAC address, so limiting the number of MAC addresses on a port with Port Security doesn't help. And DHCP Snooping only filters DHCP messages—not ARP messages.

However, DHCP Snooping does produce a table of hosts who have leased an IP address using DHCP, mapping their IP addresses to their MAC addresses: the DHCP Snooping binding table. DAI uses this table as part of its inspection process. Figure 14.3 shows only the DAI-specific configurations, but the output that follows shows both the DHCP Snooping and DAI configurations for reference.

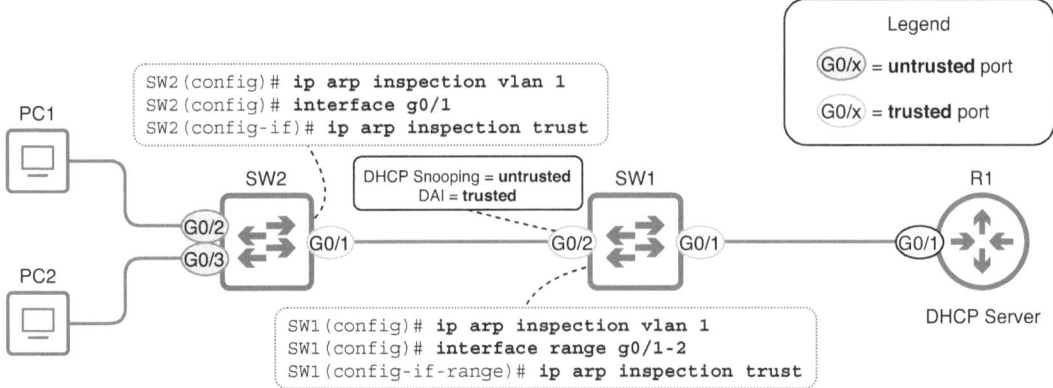

Figure 14.3   Configuring DAI. Note that a port can be untrusted by one feature but trusted by the other, as in SW1's G0/2 case.

```
SW2(config)# ip dhcp snooping
SW2(config)# ip dhcp snooping vlan 1
SW2(config)# ip arp inspection vlan 1
SW2(config)# no ip dhcp snooping information option
SW2(config)# interface g0/1
SW2(config-if)# ip dhcp snooping trust
SW2(config-if)# ip arp inspection trust

SW1(config)# ip dhcp snooping
SW1(config)# ip dhcp snooping vlan 1
SW1(config)# ip arp inspection vlan 1
SW1(config)# no ip dhcp snooping information option
SW1(config)# interface range g0/1-2
SW1(config-if-range)# ip arp inspection trust
SW1(config-if-range)# interface g0/1
SW1(config-if)# ip dhcp snooping trust
```

NOTE   The rest of this chapter will focus on DAI configuration, not DHCP Snooping, but keep in mind that the two features work together. Although DAI can be used without DHCP Snooping, it is rare.

To enable DAI, use the `ip arp inspection vlan` `vlans` command in global config mode. As with the `ip dhcp snooping vlan` command, you can enable DAI on multiple VLANs with a single command. Here are a couple of examples:

- *All VLANs*—`ip arp inspection vlan 1-4094`
- *VLANs 2, 3, 4, 5, 7, 9, and 2028*—`ip arp inspection vlan 2-5,7,9,2028`

NOTE   Enabling DHCP Snooping requires two commands: `ip dhcp snooping` and `ip dhcp snooping vlan`, but DAI only requires one: `ip arp inspection vlan`.

In the following example, I enable DAI on SW2 and confirm with `show ip arp inspection`:

```
SW2(config)# ip arp inspection vlan 1        ◀──────── Enables DAI on VLAN 1
SW2(config)# do show ip arp inspection
. . .
 Vlan     Configuration     Operation   ACL Match              Static ACL
 ----     -------------     ---------   ---------              ----------
    1     Enabled           Active      ◀──────
. . .                                            DAI is enabled and
                                                 active on VLAN 1.
```

NOTE A VLAN might appear as `Enabled` but `Inactive` if you enable DAI for the VLAN but the VLAN itself is disabled (i.e., with the **shutdown** command).

12.2.1 How DAI filters ARP messages

A switch using DAI inspects and filters ARP messages it receives. Much like DHCP Snooping, DAI operates using the concept of trusted and untrusted ports. On a DAI-enabled switch, all ARP messages received on trusted ports are permitted, while ARP messages received on untrusted ports are inspected to determine whether they should be forwarded or discarded. In this section, we'll examine how trusted/untrusted ports work in DAI and then how a DAI-enabled switch uses the DHCP Snooping binding table to filter ARP messages.

NOTE DAI only filters ARP messages. Non-ARP messages are not affected.

DAI TRUSTED AND UNTRUSTED PORTS

When DAI is enabled, all ports are untrusted by default; this means that DAI will inspect ARP messages received on all ports. Figure 14.4 shows which ports should be trusted in our example network.

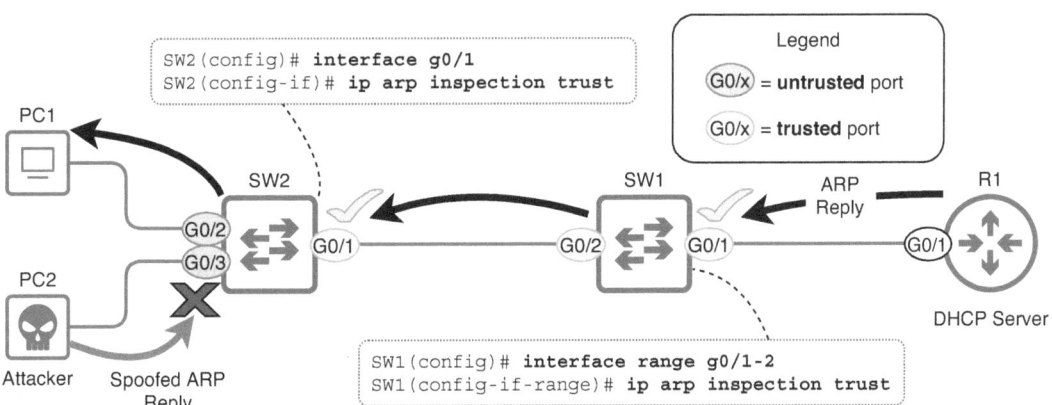

Figure 14.4 Configuring DAI trusted ports. Ports connected to network infrastructure devices (switches, routers) should be trusted, and ports connected to end-user devices like PCs should remain untrusted.

> **NOTE**   Figure 14.4 shows both of SW1's ports as trusted, meaning it will allow all ARP messages—DAI won't filter them. Despite this, enabling DAI is still a valuable security measure. It ensures that any other ports connected to end hosts in the future will be protected against ARP-based attacks from the start.

When configuring DAI, ports connected to end hosts should remain in the default untrusted state. In figure 14.4, PC2's spoofed ARP reply is discarded by DAI because it is received on an untrusted port.

Ports connected to network infrastructure devices, such as routers and other switches, should be trusted. These guidelines are slightly different from those for DHCP Snooping, leading to SW1 G0/2 being untrusted by DHCP Snooping but trusted by DAI. We'll look at the rationale behind this discrepancy in the next section when we look at how DAI inspects and filters ARP messages.

> **NOTE**   The guidelines for DHCP Snooping are to make ports that lead toward the DHCP server trusted, and leave ports that lead toward end hosts in the untrusted state (default).

To make a port trusted, use the `ip arp inspection trust` command in interface config mode. In the following example, I configure SW2 G0/1 as a trusted port and verify with `show ip arp inspection interfaces`:

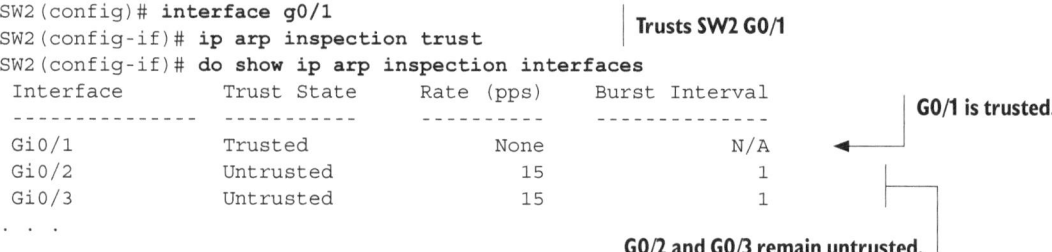

```
SW2(config)# interface g0/1
SW2(config-if)# ip arp inspection trust             Trusts SW2 G0/1
SW2(config-if)# do show ip arp inspection interfaces
 Interface         Trust State      Rate (pps)      Burst Interval
 ---------------   -----------      ----------      --------------        G0/1 is trusted.
 Gi0/1             Trusted               None                 N/A
 Gi0/2             Untrusted               15                   1
 Gi0/3             Untrusted               15                   1
 . . .
                                                 G0/2 and G0/3 remain untrusted.
```

As with DHCP Snooping, trusting the correct ports is critical. Trusting ports that should remain untrusted exposes the network to potential threats (like ARP poisoning). On the other hand, failing to trust ports that should be trusted can disrupt network communications by blocking valid ARP requests. To understand why, let's look at exactly how DAI inspects and filters messages.

INSPECTING ARP MESSAGES

A DAI-enabled switch inspects ARP messages as they are received on untrusted ports; this includes both ARP requests and ARP replies. It then makes a filtering decision: should I forward or discard this message? It does this by examining the Sender MAC and Sender IP fields of the ARP message and comparing them to the DHCP Snooping binding table:

- If there is a matching entry, the message is forwarded.
- Without a matching entry, the message is discarded.

The following example shows SW2's DHCP Snooping binding table with entries for PC1 and PC2:

```
SW2# show ip dhcp snooping binding                              PC1's entry
MacAddress         IpAddress Lease(sec) Type          VLAN Interface
----------------   --------- ---------- ------------- ---- ----------
52:54:00:08:D3:E0  10.0.0.6  84617      dhcp-snooping 1    Gi0/2      ◄
52:54:00:02:F4:E1  10.0.0.7  84623      dhcp-snooping 1    Gi0/3      ◄
Total number of bindings: 2
                                                                PC2's entry
```

NOTE MAC addresses in the DHCP Snooping binding table are formatted differently from how Cisco normally formats them (XX:XX:XX:XX:XX:XX vs. xxxx.xxxx.xxxx).

Given this table, SW2's untrusted ports will only accept ARP messages with

- Sender MAC 5254.0008.d3e0 and Sender IP 10.0.0.6
- Sender MAC 5254.0002.f4e1 and Sender IP 10.0.0.7

Figure 14.5 shows DAI in action. SW2 inspects and filters ARP messages, discarding any suspicious messages, like PC2's message with a spoofed IP address.

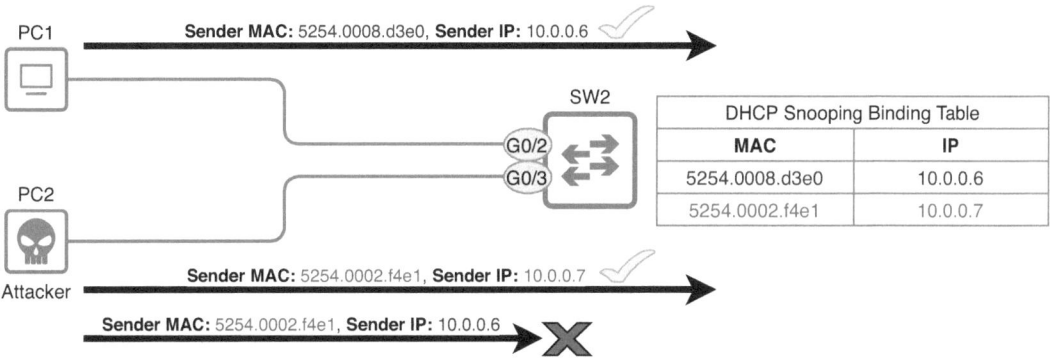

Figure 14.5   A DAI-enabled switch inspects and filters ARP messages. PC2's message with a spoofed IP address is discarded.

SW1's DHCP Snooping binding table has the same entries as SW2's. This is because SW1 also inspected PC1 and PC2's DHCP exchanges with R1. Here's SW1's table:

```
SW1# show ip dhcp snooping binding                              PC1's entry
MacAddress         IpAddress Lease(sec) Type          VLAN Interface
----------------   --------- ---------- ------------- ---- ----------
52:54:00:08:D3:E0  10.0.0.6  68613      dhcp-snooping 1    Gi0/2      ◄
52:54:00:02:F4:E1  10.0.0.7  68613      dhcp-snooping 1    Gi0/2      ◄
Total number of bindings: 2
                                                                PC2's entry
```

With this table, let's consider why SW1's G0/2 port should be trusted by DAI (despite being untrusted by DHCP Snooping). Figure 14.6 shows what happens if SW1 G0/2 is untrusted by DAI.

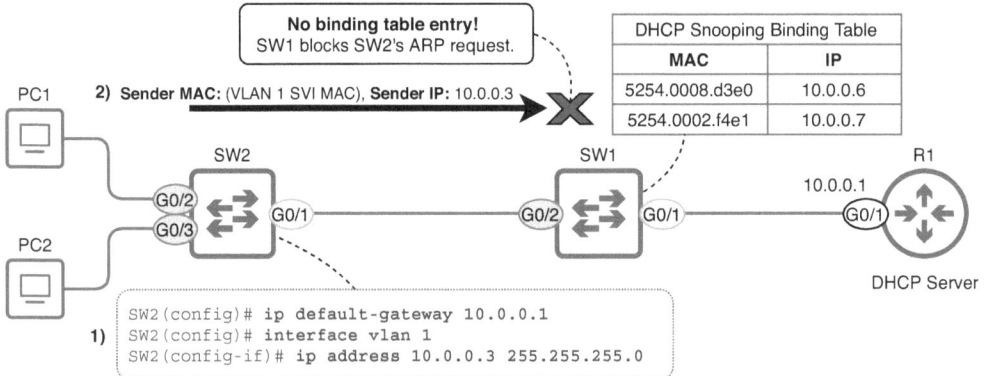

Figure 14.6   SW1 blocks SW2's ARP request because there is no matching entry in SW2's DHCP Snooping binding table.

For remote management via SSH, SW2 uses R1 (10.0.0.1) as its default gateway and has an IP address on its VLAN 1 SVI (10.0.0.3). SW2 sends an ARP request to learn the MAC address of R1, but SW1 blocks it—SW1 doesn't have a matching entry in its DHCP Snooping binding table! The following output is a Syslog message displayed on SW1, indicating that an invalid ARP request was received:

```
%SW_DAI-4-DHCP_SNOOPING_DENY: 1 Invalid ARPs (Req) on Gi0/2, vlan 1.
([5254.000c.8001/10.0.0.3/0000.0000.0000/10.0.0.1/05:16:13 UTC Wed Oct
18 2023])
```

The first two values in square brackets (5254.000c.8001/10.0.0.3) are the Sender MAC and Sender IP of SW2's ARP request. Because SW2's VLAN 1 SVI has a manually configured IP address, SW1 had no opportunity to create a DHCP Snooping binding table entry for it. The same problem would occur for any device with a manually configured IP address; ports connected to such devices should be trusted.

ARP ACLs

In addition to the DHCP Snooping binding table, there is a second source that a DAI-enabled switch can check when deciding to forward or discard an ARP message: ARP ACLs. ARP ACLs can be used to manually configure IP-MAC mappings for devices that don't use DHCP, allowing their ARP messages to pass through untrusted ports without being discarded by DAI. For your reference, the following example shows how to create and apply an ARP ACL to permit SW2's VLAN 1 SVI:

```
SW2(config)# arp access-list ARP-ACL-1
SW2(config-arp-nacl)# permit ip host 10.0.0.3 mac host 5254.000c.8001
SW2(config-arp-nacl)# exit
SW2(config)# ip arp inspection filter ARP-ACL-1 vlan 1
```

ARP ACLs are beyond the scope of the CCNA exam, so this chapter focuses on DAI using the DHCP Snooping binding table. Even though ARP ACLs are an option, the general recommendation is still to trust ports connected to infrastructure devices.

12.2.2 Optional DAI checks

By default, DAI checks that an ARP message's Sender MAC and Sender IP fields have a matching entry in the DHCP Snooping binding table (or ARP ACLs). However, an attacker can easily spoof these addresses. To prevent various kinds of spoofing attacks, you can enable additional checks with the `ip arp inspection validate` command. There are three keywords that can be used at the end of this command:

- `src-mac`—The switch verifies that the Ethernet Source MAC and the ARP Sender MAC of requests and responses match. If they don't match, the message is dropped.

- `dst-mac`—The switch verifies that the Ethernet Destination MAC and the ARP Target MAC of ARP responses match. If they don't match, the message is dropped.

- `ip`—The switch will check for invalid/unexpected IP addresses in the ARP Sender IP or Target IP, such as 0.0.0.0 or 255.255.255.255. These should normally not appear in ARP messages, so their presence would indicate some kind of spoofing.

By default, all of these optional checks are disabled, but you can choose to enable one, two, or all three of them. In the following example, I enable all three on SW2:

Enables source MAC, destination MAC, and IP address validation

```
SW2(config)# ip arp inspection validate src-mac dst-mac ip
SW2(config)# do show ip arp inspection
Source Mac Validation      : Enabled
Destination Mac Validation : Enabled
IP Address Validation      : Enabled
. . .
```

All three optional checks are enabled.

Figure 14.7 visualizes these optional checks, as well as the mandatory check for a matching entry in the DHCP Snooping binding table.

NOTE One potential concern when enabling these additional checks is that they increase the load on the switch's CPU. While this is generally not a concern with modern hardware, it's a good practice to monitor CPU usage, especially in older or resource-constrained environments. Use the `show processes cpu` command to check the CPU load.

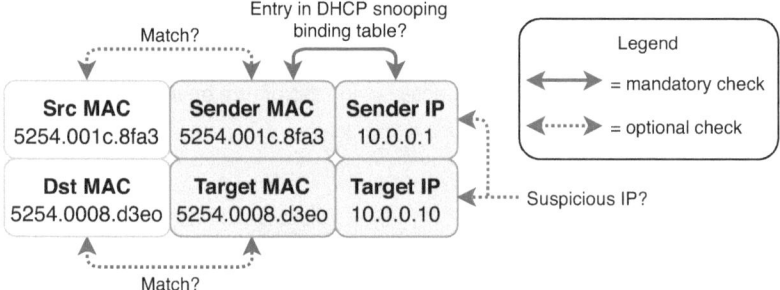

Figure 14.7 The mandatory and optional checks that DAI performs when inspecting ARP messages

12.2.3 *Rate-limiting ARP messages*

Like DHCP Snooping, DAI can be demanding on a switch's CPU. A switch is very efficient at forwarding frames without taxing its CPU. However, when it has to stop and inspect an ARP message with DAI, the CPU gets involved. This means that an attacker can potentially overwhelm the switch with ARP messages, resulting in a denial of service.

To mitigate against such threats, DAI can limit the rate at which a port can receive ARP messages. Whereas DHCP Snooping rate limiting is disabled on all ports by default, DAI has the default rate-limiting settings:

- *Untrusted ports:*—Rate limit of 15 packets per second (pps)
- *Trusted ports*—No rate limit

You might have noticed these settings in the output of `show ip arp inspection interfaces` that we looked at earlier. Here it is again:

```
SW2# show ip arp inspection interfaces
  Interface       Trust State    Rate (pps)    Burst Interval
  ---------------  -----------   ----------   --------------
  Gi0/1           Trusted          None              N/A
  Gi0/2           Untrusted          15                1
  Gi0/3           Untrusted          15                1
  . . .
```

> **G0/1, a trusted port, has no rate limit.**
>
> **G0/2 and G0/3, untrusted ports, have a rate limit of 15 pps.**

You can modify the rate limit on a per-port basis with `ip arp inspection limit rate` *rate* [`burst interval` *seconds*]. Specifying the *burst interval* is optional—the default is 1—but it lets you specify over how many seconds the packet rate is measured. Here are a couple of example commands to demonstrate:

- `ip arp inspection limit rate 20`—Twenty packets per second (equivalent to `burst interval 1`).

- `ip arp inspection limit rate 40 burst interval 2`—Forty packets every 2 seconds

Twenty packets per second and 40 packets every 2 seconds are the same average rate, but the latter allows for larger bursts of traffic (as long as the average rate doesn't surpass 40 packets every 2 seconds). Can you guess what happens if the rate limit is exceeded? If you remember the previous chapter on DHCP Snooping, you probably know: the switch will error-disable the port. To demonstrate, in the following example, I set SW1 G0/2's rate limit to 1 pps:

```
SW1(config)# interface g0/2                       Configures a DAI rate
SW1(config-if)# ip arp inspection limit rate 1    limit of 1 pps on G0/2
%SW_DAI-4-PACKET_RATE_EXCEEDED: 2 packets received in
➥559 milliseconds on Gi0/2.
%PM-4-ERR_DISABLE: arp-inspection error detected on Gi0/2,   The rate limit is
➥putting Gi0/2 in err-disable state                          exceeded.

                                          SW2 error-disables the port.
```

As with all error-disabled ports, those disabled by DAI can be reenabled in two ways: manually or automatically:

- *Manual*—Issue `shutdown` and `no shutdown` on the error-disabled port.
- *Automatic*—Enable ErrDisable Recovery for ports disabled by DAI rate limiting with `errdisable recovery cause arp-inspection`.

Because DAI rate limiting is enabled on untrusted ports by default, you probably won't have to make any changes. Fifteen packets per second is more than enough for most end hosts but low enough to prevent DoS attacks from trying to overwhelm the switch's CPU.

EXAM TIP You should understand how DAI rate limiting works and how to configure it, but identifying an appropriate rate limit is beyond the scope of the CCNA exam.

Summary

- Dynamic ARP Inspection (DAI) is a security feature on Cisco switches that protects against ARP-based attacks by inspecting and filtering ARP messages.
- ARP messages include Sender MAC and Sender IP fields to indicate the MAC and IP addresses of the sender, and Target MAC and Target IP fields to indicate the target's (destination's) addresses.
- ARP's most significant vulnerability is how simple it is for an attacker to overwrite legitimate ARP table entries by sending gratuitous ARP messages—ARP poisoning.

- By telling devices in the LAN to send their frames to the attacker, the attacker gains access to their communications.

- Port Security doesn't protect against ARP poisoning because ARP poisoning is performed from a single source MAC address. DHCP Snooping doesn't protect against ARP poisoning because it only filters DHCP messages.

- DHCP Snooping produces a table of hosts who have leased an IP address using DHCP, mapping their IP addresses to their MAC addresses: the DHCP Snooping binding table.

- DAI uses the DHCP Snooping binding table in its inspection and filtering process.

- Use `ip arp inspection vlan` *vlans* in global config mode to enable DAI.

- Use `show ip arp inspection` to view general information about DAI on the switch.

- DAI uses the concepts of trusted and untrusted ports. All ARP messages received on *trusted ports* are permitted, while ARP messages received on *untrusted ports* are inspected to determine whether they should be forwarded or discarded.

- All ports on a DAI-enabled switch are untrusted by default. Ports connected to end hosts should remain untrusted. Ports connected to network infrastructure devices, such as routers and other switches, should be trusted.

- Use `ip arp inspection trust` in interface config mode to trust a port.

- Use `show ip arp inspection interfaces` to view the DAI trust state and rate limit of each port.

- DAI inspects ARP messages received on untrusted ports by examining the Sender MAC and Sender IP fields and looking for a matching entry in the DHCP Snooping binding table.

- If there is a matching entry, the message is forwarded. Without a matching entry, the message is discarded.

- If a device has a manually configured IP address (not learned via DHCP), the device won't have a matching entry in switches' DHCP Snooping binding tables, leading to the device's ARP messages being discarded if received on an untrusted port.

- For this reason, ports connected to devices with manually configured IP addresses should be trusted.

- In addition to the DHCP Snooping binding table, you can use ARP ACLs to manually configure IP–MAC mappings for devices that don't use DHCP, allowing their ARP messages to pass through untrusted ports without being discarded by DAI.

- In addition to checking an ARP message's Sender MAC and Sender IP fields for a matching entry in the DHCP Snooping binding table, DAI can optionally check other parameters. You can configure it with the `ip arp inspection validate` command.

- The three keywords that can be used with `ip arp inspection validate` are
  - `src-mac`—Checks that the Ethernet Source MAC and ARP Sender MAC of ARP requests and responses match
  - `dst-mac`—Checks that the Ethernet Destination MAC and ARP Target MAC of ARP responses match
  - `ip`—Ensures that invalid/unexpected IP addresses (i.e., 0.0.0.0 or 255.255.255.255) are not present in the ARP Sender IP or Target IP fields
- The three optional checks are all disabled by default, but you can enable one, two, or all three of them.
- DAI inspection can be demanding on a switch's CPU. This means that an attacker can potentially overwhelm the switch with ARP messages, resulting in a denial of service.
- To mitigate against such threats, DAI can limit the rate at which a port can receive ARP messages.
- By default, untrusted ports have a rate limit of 15 packets per second, and trusted ports have no rate limit.
- Use `ip arp inspection limit rate` *rate* [`burst interval` *seconds*] to modify the rate limit on a per-port basis.
- The optional burst interval lets you specify over how many seconds the packet rate is measured (i.e., 40 packets every 2 seconds).
- If a port's rate limit is exceeded, the switch will error-disable the port.
- You can reenable a port disabled by DAI rate limiting in two ways:
  - *Manual*—Issue `shutdown` and `no shutdown` on the error-disabled port.
  - *Automatic*—Enable ErrDisable Recovery for ports disabled by DAI rate limiting with `errdisable recovery cause arp-inspection`.

Part 3

Network architectures

After covering the details of various protocols at all layers of the TCP/IP model and how to configure them in Cisco IOS, let's zoom out and look at the bigger picture. In part 3 of this volume, we will examine various network architectures and how the technologies we have previously covered fit together to form a coherent whole.

Chapter 15 starts with local area network (LAN) architectures, ranging from simple small office/home office (SOHO) networks used by individuals and small businesses to two- and three-tier campus LANs employed by medium and large enterprises and data center networks designed to support the high-performance servers that run modern applications. Chapter 16 then zooms out even further, looking at how LANs can be connected together to form wide area networks (WANs) that can span the globe; in this chapter, we will address the "widest" network of all: the internet. We will also cover two main kinds of virtual private networks (VPNs)—secure connections established over the public internet.

Finally, chapter 17 addresses two key components of most enterprises' IT infrastructure: virtualization technologies, such as virtual machines (VMs) and containers, and cloud computing—better known as "the cloud." Enterprises of all sizes take advantage of cloud computing for its flexibility, scalability, and convenience, and this chapter lays a solid foundation for your understanding of cloud computing's key concepts. The goal of part 3 as a whole is to give you a holistic view of modern network architectures while addressing the specific points that Cisco expects you to know for the CCNA exam.

LAN *architectures*

We have delved into the details of protocols like IPv4 and IPv6, Ethernet, Spanning Tree Protocol, and many others in previous chapters of this volume and volume 1. Now it's time to zoom out. Instead of focusing on individual technologies, let's take a holistic view of real-world network architectures—the blueprints for how computer networks are designed and built.

Although there are standard best practices in network design, many factors such as budget, scale, and specific needs influence the "right" approach; there are few universal correct answers to questions of network design. In the beginning stages of your networking career, you probably won't be designing networks. However, to configure and troubleshoot networks, understanding the architectural principles behind them is essential.

This chapter and the following two align with CCNA exam topic 1.2: Describe characteristics of network topology architectures. This chapter focuses on various types of LANs, from data centers to home offices. Specifically, we will cover the following subtopics:

- 1.2.a Two-tier
- 1.2.b Three-tier
- 1.2.c Spine-leaf
- 1.2.e Small office/home office (SOHO)

15.1   *Common topologies: Star and mesh*

In chapter 14 of volume 1, I defined the term *topology* as "how devices are arranged and connected together in a network." Some common topologies consistently emerge across different networks—common patterns of device connections. Figure 15.1 demonstrates three of those common topologies: star, full mesh, and partial mesh.

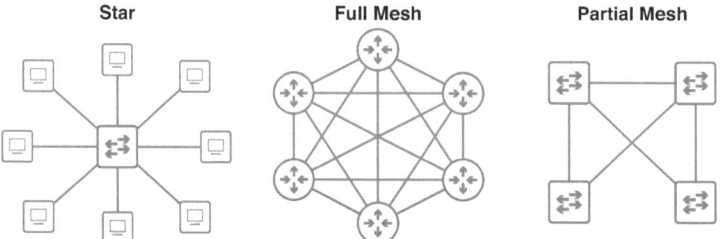

Figure 15.1   Common topologies. In a star topology, all devices connect to a central device. In a full mesh, each device is directly connected to each of the other devices. In a partial mesh, only certain devices are directly connected.

In a *star* topology, all devices connect to one central device. The most common example of a star topology, and the one shown in figure 15.1, is a group of end hosts connected to a switch.

> **NOTE**   Another name for a star topology is *hub-and-spoke* topology. The central device is the hub, and the devices connecting to it are the spokes. *Star* is more commonly used in a LAN context, and *hub-and-spoke* in a WAN context.

In a *full mesh*, each device in the topology is directly connected to each of the other devices. Full-mesh topologies provide high reliability because there are multiple possible paths to each destination; if there is a problem with one path, multiple other paths are available. Figure 15.1 shows six routers connected in a full mesh. Although they appear as direct connections, in reality, these would likely be secure virtual private network (VPN) connections over a service provider's network—we'll delve into VPNs in chapter 16.

> **NOTE** You can calculate the number of connections between devices in a full mesh with the formula *N(N-1)/2*, where *N* is the number of devices. For example, with six devices, there are 15 links.

There is also *partial mesh*, in which certain devices, but not all, are directly connected to each other. You'll see this pattern between the switches in the access layer and distribution layer of a campus LAN—the topic of the next section.

Most networks are a combination of these common topologies and others—a *hybrid* topology. These terms are all commonly used to describe how devices are connected in networks. Keep an eye out for these recurring patterns as we examine different network architectures in this chapter and the next.

15.2 Campus LAN architectures

A *campus LAN* is a network that is designed to serve the networking needs of local users within a certain area. Although the term *campus* evokes the idea of a network spread across multiple buildings in close proximity, like a university campus or office park, in this context, it doesn't imply any particular geographic size. A campus LAN could be a small site with a single switch or a multibuilding campus stretching across an office park.

Cisco campus LANs use a hierarchical design, dividing the network into three modular *layers*, each playing a specific role. The three layers are

- *Access layer*—Provides access to the network for end hosts
- *Distribution layer*—Aggregates connections from the access layer and provides connectivity to the WAN and the internet
- *Core layer*—Aggregates connections between distribution layers in large LANs

Cisco campus LAN architecture is not one-size-fits-all; depending on the site, one, two, or all three layers might be present. Figure 15.2 shows a simplified three-building campus LAN that includes all three layers: access, distribution, and core.

> **NOTE** Figure 15.2 only shows one connection between each layer. This doesn't represent the actual number of physical connections needed to connect all devices. Later diagrams will show the connections in greater detail.

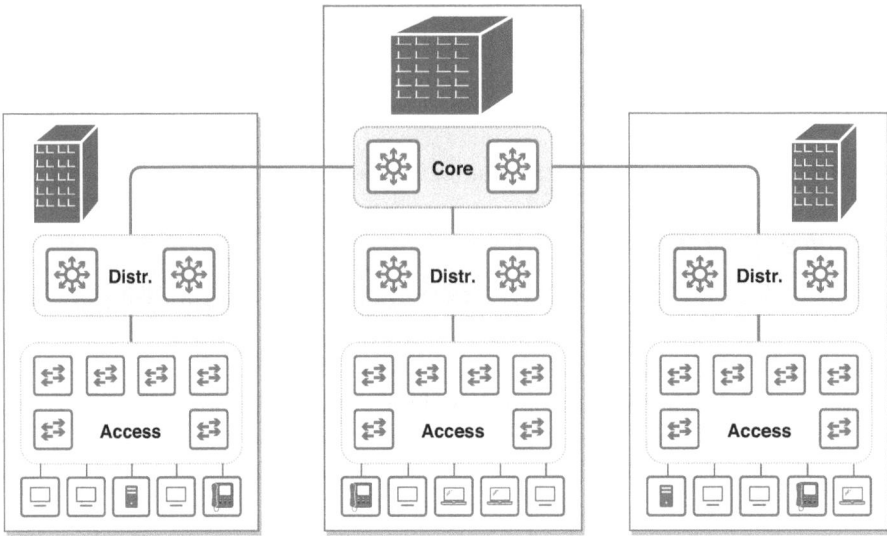

Figure 15.2 A three-tier campus LAN spanning three buildings. End hosts connect to the access layer, the distribution layer aggregates connections from the access layer, and the core layer aggregates connections from the distribution layer.

As mentioned previously, the layers are modular, allowing for flexible scalability; these modular pieces are sometimes called *blocks*. Figure 15.2 shows three access layer blocks, each connected to its own distribution layer block. As the network expands, additional access and/or distribution blocks can be added as needed.

> **EXAM TIP** Two- and three-tier architectures are exam topics 1.2.a and 1.2.b, respectively. For the exam, make sure you know the characteristics of each layer.

15.2.1 *Two-tier (collapsed core) LAN architecture*

The CCNA exam topics list states that you must be able to describe two- and three-tier campus LANs. We will start small, with *two-tier* campus LANs. This kind of design is also called *collapsed core* because the core layer is absent—only the access and distribution layers are present.

> **NOTE** Another way to think of a collapsed core is that core and distribution layers are combined into one. For this reason, the second layer of a two-tier LAN is sometimes called the *core-distribution layer*.

The access layer is typically where end hosts connect to the network. That includes end-user devices like PCs and phones, security devices like security cameras and door locks, servers, and others. Given that, here are some features you can expect to find in the access layer of a campus LAN:

- QoS marking is often done here. As mentioned in chapter 10, marking should be done early in a packet's life.
- Security services such as Port Security, DHCP Snooping, and DAI should be used here to secure the point where users connect to the network.
- The switches will likely support PoE to provide electrical power to devices like IP phones, wireless access points, security cameras, etc.

With more than two or three access switches at a site, directly interconnecting them all quickly becomes impractical. Instead, distribution switches are used to aggregate connections from access switches. The distribution layer also typically connects to the corporate WAN and/or the internet. Figure 15.3 shows an example of a two-tier campus LAN with WAN and internet connections.

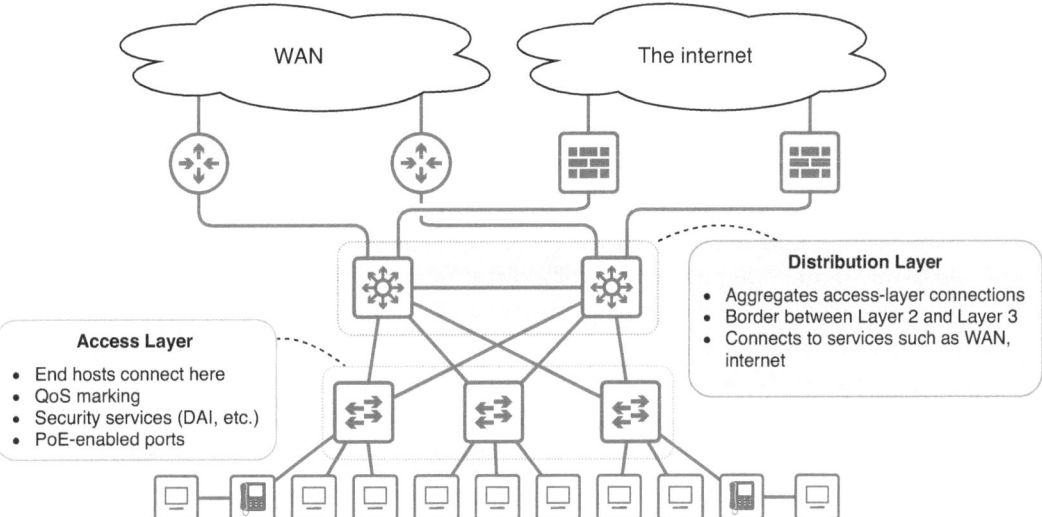

Figure 15.3 A two-tier campus LAN consists of access and distribution layers.

NOTE In figure 15.3, notice that there are two distribution switches, two WAN connections, two internet connections, etc. Redundancy is a critical aspect of an enterprise network.

THE LAYER 2–LAYER 3 BORDER

The distribution layer usually serves as the border between Layer 2 and Layer 3 of the TCP/IP model. Connections from the distribution layer to the access switches are Layer 2 connections (trunk links), but connections to other parts of the network are Layer 3 connections (routed ports configured with **no switchport**). The distribution switches are multilayer switches that support both Layer 2 and Layer 3 features. Figure 15.4 demonstrates this concept.

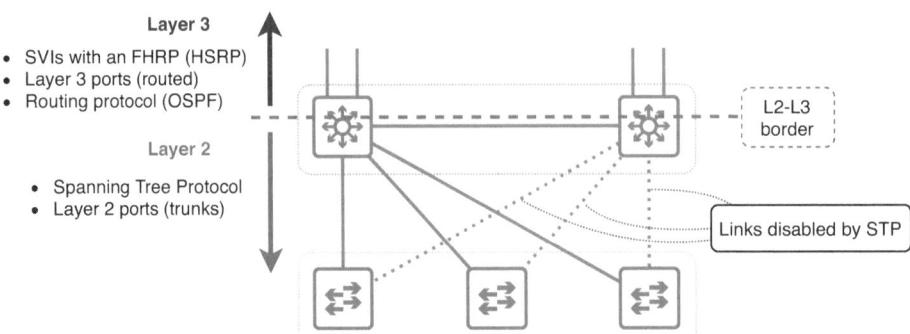

Figure 15.4   The distribution layer typically serves as the border between Layer 2 and Layer 3 of the TCP/IP model.

To provide a redundant IP address that hosts in each VLAN can use as their default gateway, the distribution switches should use a first hop redundancy protocol like HSRP on each of their SVIs. Furthermore, a routing protocol like OSPF can be used to share routing information with the rest of the network. The following example shows how you might configure the SVI of a distribution switch (named DSW1 for distribution switch 1):

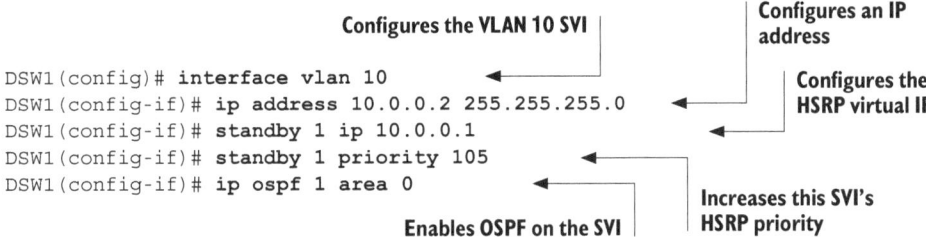

CONNECTING MULTIPLE DISTRIBUTION BLOCKS

As a two-tier campus LAN expands, you may need to add an additional block of distribution switches. Perhaps your company is opening another office in a new building, and the number of access switches is more than the current distribution switches can handle—the current switches don't have enough available ports. Figure 15.5 shows a campus LAN with two access-distribution block pairs.

> **NOTE** The connections between the distribution switches form a full mesh, and the connections between the access and distribution switches form a partial mesh; the access switches connect to each distribution switch but not to each other.

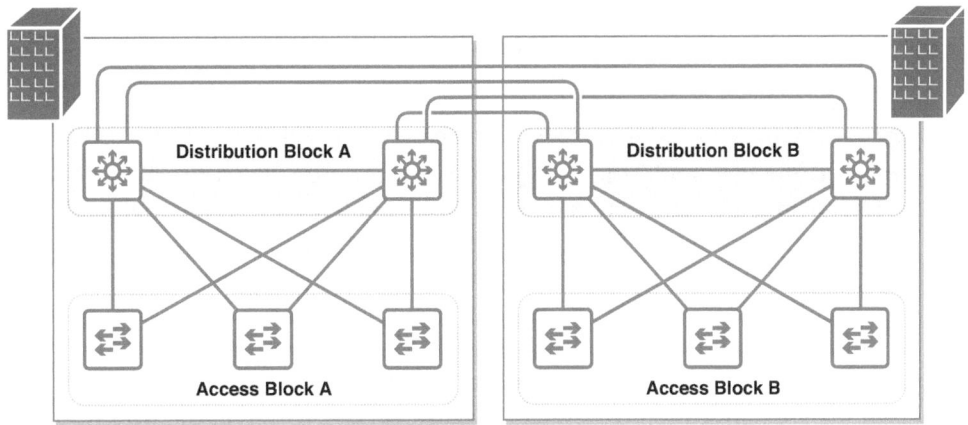

Figure 15.5 A two-tier campus LAN with two distribution and two access blocks

15.2.2 *Three-tier LAN architecture*

Large campus LANs often face the challenge of managing connectivity as they grow. A full mesh between distribution switches, as we saw in figure 15.5, might work well for smaller networks with a couple of distribution blocks. However, with three, four, or even more distribution blocks, this approach quickly escalates in complexity and cost.

In a campus LAN with three or more distribution blocks, you should consider adding a core layer, making a *three-tier* architecture. Figure 15.6 shows how adding a core layer can greatly reduce the number of connections required.

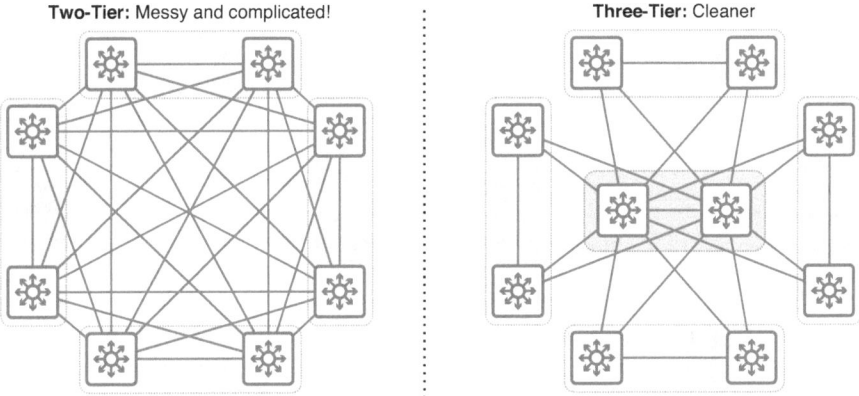

Figure 15.6 Two-tier vs. three-tier architectures with four distribution blocks. In the two-tier LAN, each distribution switch has seven connections. In the three-tier LAN, each distribution switch has only three connections.

NOTE   Another option to reduce the number of connections required is to use a partial mesh between distribution switches instead of a full mesh. However, Cisco's recommendation is to add a core when there are three or more distribution blocks.

Just as the distribution layer aggregates connections from the access layer, the core layer aggregates connections from the distribution layer. Using high-end switches, the focus of the core layer is speed and reliability; it should forward packets as quickly as possible and be able to maintain consistent connectivity throughout the LAN even if failures occur.

CPU-intensive operations like security features (DAI, etc.) and QoS marking, which can slow down the forwarding process, should be avoided at the core layer; the switches in the core layer should trust and forward packets based on the packets' existing QoS markings.

All connections between the core and distribution layers should be Layer 3 connections—we don't want STP disabling links that could otherwise be used to forward packets. A routing protocol like OSPF should be used to share routing information between the distribution and core switches. Figure 15.7 shows a core layer in the context of a whole three-tier LAN. It also shows a wireless LAN controller (WLC) and two wireless access points (WAPs), which are used to enable wireless LANs—a preview of the next part of this book.

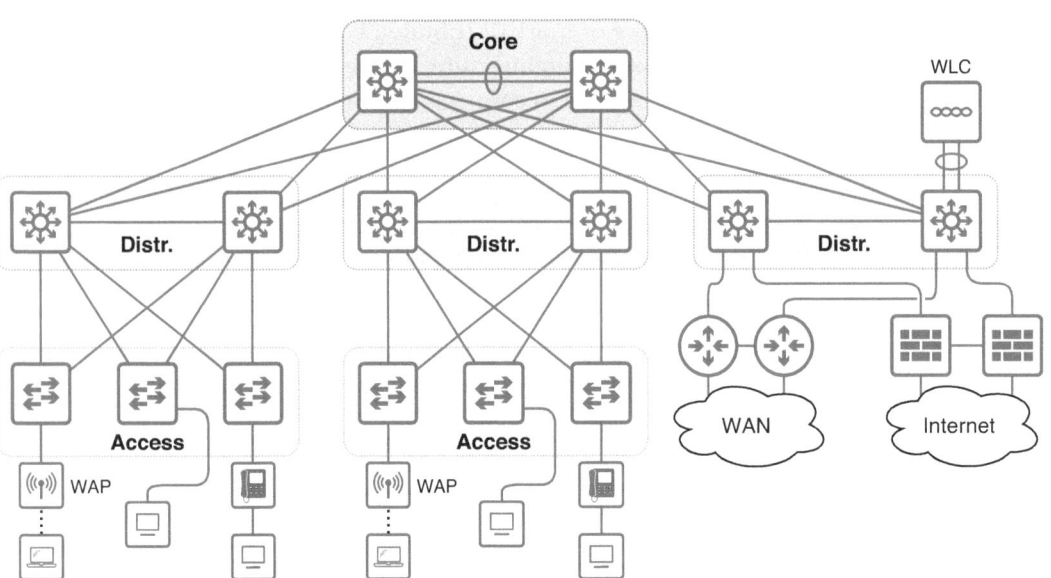

Figure 15.7   A three-tier campus LAN with a core layer connecting three distribution blocks. One distribution block is used to connect to network services like a wireless LAN controller, the WAN, and the internet.

NOTE To avoid cluttering up the diagrams in this chapter, I only show a few access switches and end hosts in each diagram. In a large network, there could be 20+ access switches in each access block, each with 40+ end hosts connected.

15.3 Data center architectures: spine-leaf

A *data center* is a facility—either its own building or a dedicated space in a building—where an organization centralizes its IT infrastructure, particularly servers and the network infrastructure devices that support them. Data centers are vital for many modern enterprise networks, often housing thousands of servers, storage devices, and network devices. A Google search for "data center" will show you images of rows and rows of racks containing countless servers and other devices.

15.3.1 Traditional data center networks

Data center networks traditionally used a three-tier architecture similar to the campus LANs we saw in the previous section; figure 15.8 shows an example. Note that the distribution layer is typically called the *aggregation layer* in a data center context; their function is basically the same.

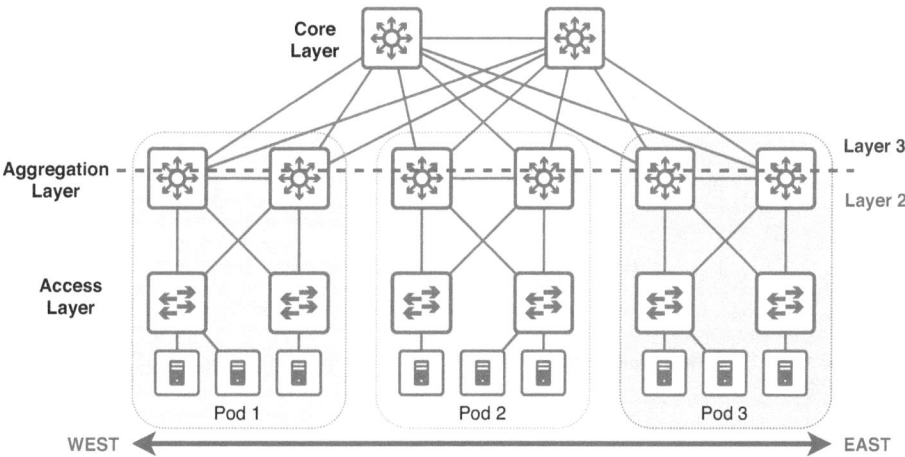

Figure 15.8 A three-tier data center LAN consisting of an access layer, aggregation layer, and core layer

NOTE Each group of servers and the access and aggregation switches that support them are called a *pod*.

However, the rise of virtual servers and distributed applications (applications that run on multiple computers and communicate through the network) led to an increase in the amount of east–west traffic in data centers. *East–west traffic* is traffic flowing between servers within the same data center—for example, communication between a server in pod 1 and a server in pod 3 in figure 15.8.

NOTE   There is a related term—*north–south traffic*—that refers to traffic entering and exiting the data center (via the WAN or the internet).

The traditional three-tier architecture proved to be less than ideal for these kinds of applications, especially if traffic had to traverse multiple layers to reach another server in the same data center. This produces bottlenecks and variability in the server-to-server latency, leading to unpredictability in application performance.

15.3.2   *Spine-leaf architecture*

To better serve modern data center networks, *spine-leaf architecture* (also called *Clos architecture*, named after American engineer Charles Clos) has become the standard. Spine-leaf architecture provides high bandwidth with low and predictable latency for east–west traffic. Figure 15.9 demonstrates spine-leaf architecture, which consists of two layers: a layer of *spine switches* and a layer of *leaf switches*.

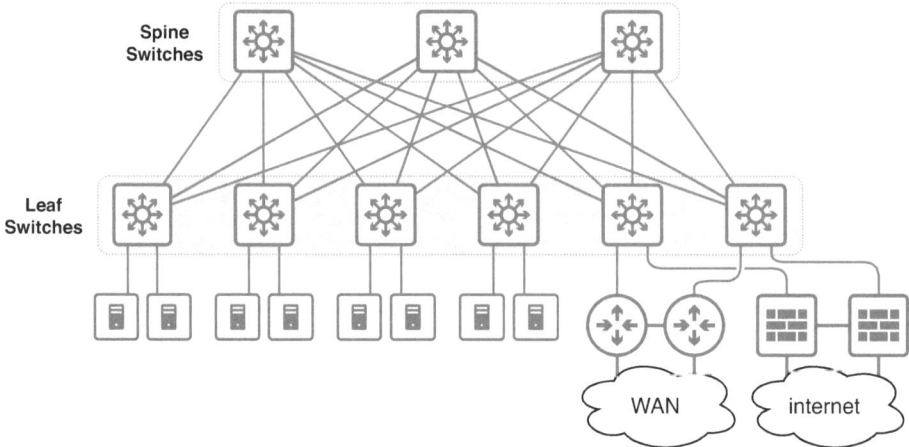

Figure 15.9   Spine-leaf architecture, a two-tier LAN architecture commonly used in modern data center networks

NOTE   Leaf switches that connect to the WAN/internet or other external networks are sometimes called *border leaves*.

Here are some basic characteristics of spine-leaf architecture:

- End hosts (servers) connect to leaf switches.
- Every leaf switch connects to every spine switch.
- Every spine switch connects to every leaf switch.
- Leaf switches do not connect to other leaf switches.
- Spine switches do not connect to other spine switches.

A key result of this architecture is that all leaf switches are the same number of hops apart. This means that the path a packet takes between two servers is always

- Source server
- Leaf switch
- Spine switch
- Leaf switch
- Destination server

The consistent number of hops means that there should be consistent and predictable latency between servers in the network. The one exception is when the two servers are connected to the same leaf switch, in which case there is no need to traverse a spine switch, making the latency even shorter.

Another benefit of spine-leaf architecture is how simple it is to scale it to support large and complex data center networks. If you need to add more servers than the current network can handle, just add more leaf switches, connecting each new leaf to every spine switch.

EXAM TIP Spine-leaf architecture is exam topic 1.2.c. Make sure you know its characteristics and benefits for the exam.

15.4 SOHO networks

In some networks, the complex designs we've looked at aren't necessary. A network with only a few users, each with only a few devices, can often have its needs met by a single network device. A *small office/home office* (SOHO) network—a very small network with about 1 to 10 users—is an example.

NOTE A SOHO network can be a business or nonbusiness network. If your home has a network connected to the internet, it can be considered a SOHO network.

Because of their size and simplicity, it's common for all networking functions in a SOHO to be provided by a single *wireless router* (also called a *Wi-Fi router* or *home router*). Figure 15.10 shows a photo of a simple wireless router.

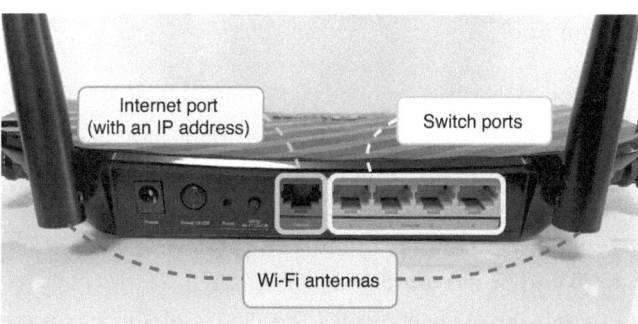

Figure 15.10   A wireless router, including Wi-Fi antennas for wireless clients, switch ports for wired end-user devices, and a port for an internet connection

A wireless router combines the functions of various network devices into one:

- A router that forwards packets between the LAN and the internet
- A switch for wired end-user devices to connect to
- A firewall that blocks connections from the internet
- A wireless access point that allows wireless (Wi-Fi) clients to connect to the network

Figure 15.11 visually demonstrates this. The central gray box represents the wireless router, and the standard icons inside represent each of its functions.

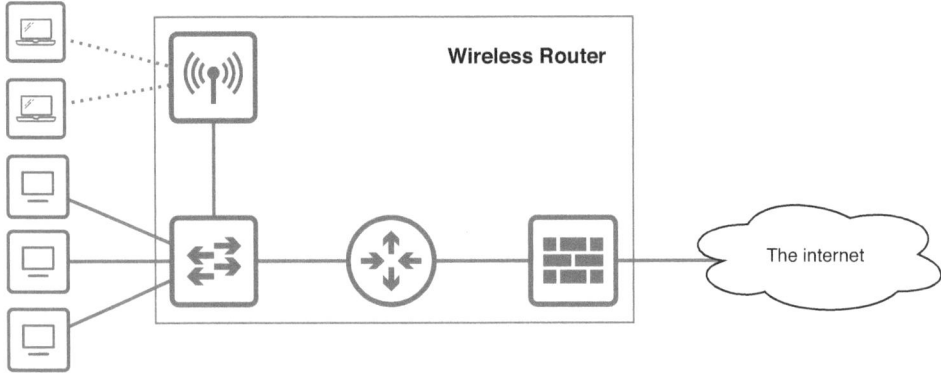

Figure 15.11   **A wireless router functions as a router, a switch, a firewall, and a wireless access point.**

NOTE   Some wireless routers also function as a *modem* (modulator/demodulator). A modem is necessary for some internet connection types. We'll cover internet connections and modems in the next chapter.

In addition to relying on a single wireless router, most SOHO networks have only one internet connection. This lack of redundancy isn't acceptable in enterprise networks like the ones we covered in previous sections. However, given the nature of most SOHO networks, a temporary loss of service would be more of an inconvenience than an emergency. The cost savings of a nonredundant setup are usually prioritized over the reliability of a redundant one.

Summary

- Although there are standard best practices in network design, many factors such as budget, scale, and specific needs influence the "right" approach; there are few universal correct answers to questions of network design.
- In a star topology, all devices connect to one central device. The most common example is a group of end hosts connected to a switch.
- Another name for a star topology is hub-and-spoke topology. Star is more commonly used in a LAN context, and hub-and-spoke in a WAN context.

- In a full-mesh topology, each device in the topology is directly connected to each of the other devices. A full mesh is often seen between the distribution switches of a two-tier campus LAN.

- In a partial-mesh topology, certain devices, but not all, are directly connected to each other. You can find this pattern between the access and distribution switches of a two- or three-tier campus LAN.

- Most networks are a combination of these common topologies and others— a hybrid topology.

- A campus LAN is a network that is designed to serve the networking needs of local users within a certain area. Cisco campus LANs use a hierarchical design, dividing the network into three modular layers: access, distribution, and core.

- The layers are modular, allowing for flexible scalability; these modular pieces are sometimes called *blocks*. Additional blocks can be added as the network expands.

- In a two-tier campus LAN, only the access and distribution layers are present. For this reason, it's sometimes called a *collapsed-core architecture*.

- The access layer is typically where end hosts connect to the network. Some common features implemented at the access layer are QoS, security services (i.e. Port Security, DHCP Snooping, and DAI), and PoE.

- The distribution layer aggregates connections from the access layer and also typically connects to the corporate WAN and/or the internet.

- The distribution layer usually serves as the border between Layer 2 and Layer 3 of the TCP/IP model. Connections to the access switches are Layer 2 connections, but connections to other parts of the network are Layer 3 connections.

- The distribution switches typically use an FHRP (like HSRP) on their SVIs to provide a redundant default gateway to hosts in the LAN and a routing protocol like OSPF to share routing information with the rest of the network.

- In a campus LAN with three or more distribution blocks, you should consider adding a core layer—a three-tier architecture.

- The core layer aggregates connections from the distribution layer, reducing the overall number of connections required.

- The focus of the core layer is speed and reliability; it should forward packets as quickly as possible and be able to maintain consistent connectivity throughout the LAN even if failures occur.

- CPU-intensive operations like security features and QoS marking, which can slow down the forwarding process, should be avoided at the core layer. All connections should be Layer 3.

- A data center is a facility where an organization centralizes its IT infrastructure, particularly servers and the network infrastructure devices that support them.

- Data center networks traditionally used a three-tier architecture similar to campus LANs (with the distribution layer being called the aggregation layer in data center contexts).

- In a data center network, each group of servers and the access and aggregation switches that support them are called a pod.

- The rise of virtual servers and distributed applications led to an increase in the amount of east–west traffic in data centers. East–west traffic is traffic flowing between servers within the same data center.

- North–south traffic is traffic entering and exiting the data center (via the WAN or the internet).

- The traditional three-tier architecture is not ideal for east–west traffic; it can lead to bottlenecks and variability in the server-to-server latency.

- Spine-leaf architecture has become the standard in modern data center networks.

- Spine-leaf architecture consists of two layers: a layer of spine switches and a layer of leaf switches. End hosts (servers) connect to leaf switches.

- Leaf switches that connect to the WAN/internet or other external networks are sometimes called border leaves.

- Every leaf switch connects to every spine switch, and every spine switch connects to every leaf switch.

- Leaf switches do not connect to other leaf switches, and spine switches do not connect to other spine switches.

- The result of this architecture is that all leaf switches are the same number of hops apart; they are all separated by one spine switch.

- The consistent number of hops means that there should be consistent and predictable latency between servers in the network. The only exception is when the two servers are connected to the same leaf switch.

- Spine-leaf architecture can be easily scaled by adding more leaf switches, connecting each new leaf to every spine switch.

- A small office/home office (SOHO) network is a very small network, usually with 1 to 10 users (i.e., a small business or home network).

- It's common for all networking functions in a SOHO network to be provided by a single wireless router (also called a Wi-Fi router or home router).

- A wireless router combines the functions of various network devices into one: router, switch, firewall, wireless access point, and sometimes modem (modulator-demodulator).

- Most SOHO networks prioritize cost savings with a single router and internet connection, trading off the redundancy found in enterprise networks.

WAN architectures 16

This chapter covers

- Connecting remote sites using wide area network technologies
- Different types of internet connections
- Creating virtual private networks over the public internet

In the previous chapter, we covered local area networks (LANs) of various types and scales, from SOHO networks, to two- and three-tier campus LANs and even specialized data center networks that are essential for hosting an enterprise's key servers. But LANs are just one piece of the puzzle; most enterprise networks are not confined to a single physical location.

Take, for example, a multinational corporation that has its headquarters in New York, manufacturing facilities in China, and regional offices scattered across Europe. Each of these locations will have its own local network, tailored for its specific needs. But these dispersed networks need to function as a unified whole, communicating and sharing resources securely and efficiently. Similarly, consider a retail chain with hundreds of stores, each with its own point-of-sale system, security cameras, guest Wi-Fi, and other network-connected devices. These stores also need to be integrated into a centralized system for inventory management, security monitoring, and data analytics.

How can all of these geographically diverse LANs be connected to form a coherent whole? What role does the public internet play in all of this? These are the questions we'll be answering in this chapter, picking up from the previous chapter's coverage of LANs. Here are the exam topics we will cover:

- 1.2 Describe characteristics of network topology architectures.
  - 1.2.d WAN
- 5.5 Describe IPsec remote access and site-to-site VPNs.

16.1   *WAN concepts*

A WAN is a network that extends over a large geographic area, often spanning distances between cities or even countries. Enterprises use WANs to connect their various LANs, whether they are offices, retail stores, data centers, or any other kind of LAN— enterprises of all kinds use WANs. Figure 16.1 shows an enterprise WAN connecting five LANs (four offices and a data center) via a service provider network.

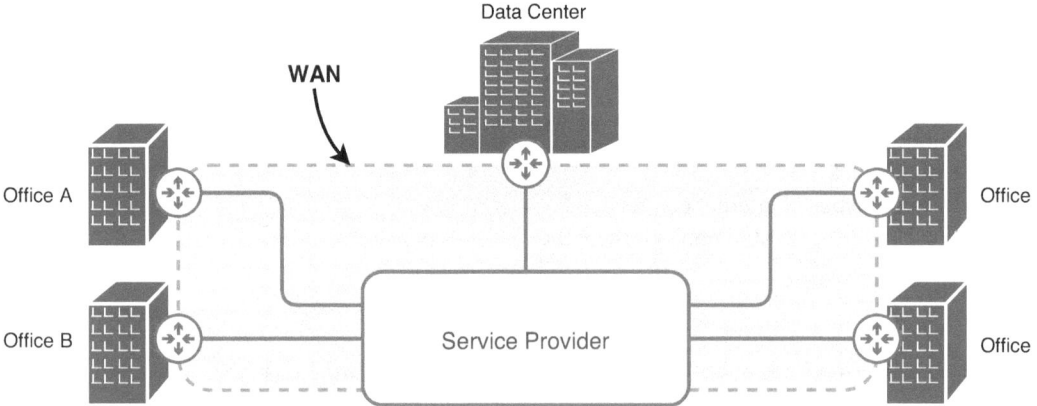

Figure 16.1   An enterprise WAN connecting four offices and a data center via a service provider's network infrastructure

NOTE   Figure 16.1 represents the WAN service provider network as a gray box. The CCNA covers WANs from the perspective of the customer (the enterprise connecting their LANs over the WAN), not the service provider. If you're interested in the details of how service provider networks work, consider the CCNP Service Provider certification in the future.

Using the WAN, hosts in one LAN can communicate with hosts in another LAN. For example, end-user devices in the office LANs can access files and applications hosted on servers in the data center. There are various WAN technologies that make this possible. In this section, we'll cover two: leased lines and Multiprotocol Label Switching (MPLS). Then, we'll move on to examine the public internet and its role in connecting remote sites.

16.1.1 Leased lines

A *leased line* is a dedicated physical connection between two sites, providing fixed bandwidth that is reserved for that specific connection. Figure 16.2 shows an example of leased lines connecting four office sites to a central data center in a hub-and-spoke topology.

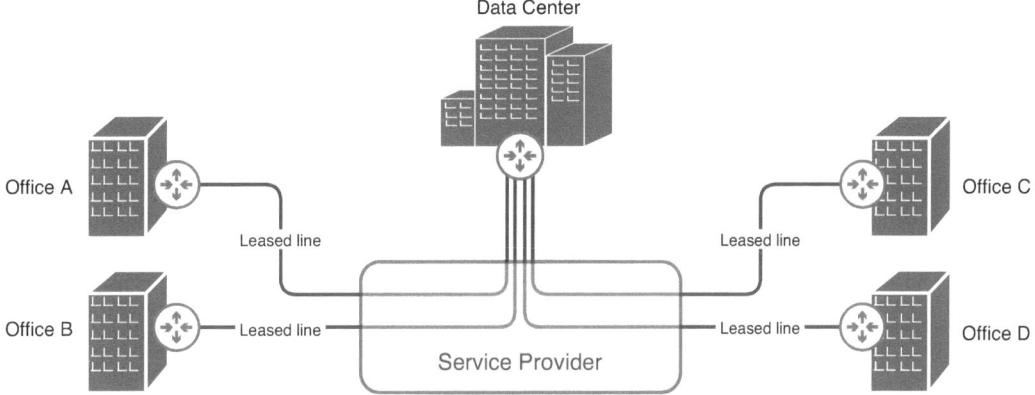

Figure 16.2 Four leased lines providing dedicated connections between each of four office sites and a central data center in a hub-and-spoke topology

> **NOTE** As mentioned in chapter 15, *star* and *hub-and-spoke* both refer to a topology in which all devices connect to one central device. Star is commonly used in a LAN context, and hub-and-spoke in a WAN context.

Because the connection is typically not shared with other customers, the available bandwidth is consistent; the connection won't get clogged up with other customers' traffic. The dedicated nature of a leased line also provides security benefits—it's a truly private connection.

However, leased lines have their downsides compared to more modern solutions: higher cost and lower bandwidth. Due to their price, hub-and-spoke topologies are more common than mesh topologies; the hub-and-spoke topology shown in figure 16.2 requires 4 leased lines, whereas a full mesh would require 10. Considering that each leased line can cost hundreds or even thousands of dollars per month, a full mesh can often be cost prohibitive.

Traditionally, leased lines use serial connections, not Ethernet; I briefly mentioned serial connections in chapter 18 of volume 1 when covering the OSPF point-to-point network type. For reference, table 16.1 lists some different standards of serial leased lines.

Table 16.1   Serial leased line options

North America		Europe (and others)	
Name	Speed	Name	Speed
T1	1.544 Mbps	E1	2.048 Mbps
T2	6.312 Mbps	E2	8.448 Mbps
T3	44.736 Mbps	E3	34.368 Mbps
T4	274.176 Mbps	E4	139.264 Mbps
T5	400.352 Mbps	E5	565.148 Mbps

In many countries, leased lines are considered a legacy technology and have been largely replaced by Ethernet connections. However, leased lines can still be found in networks all over the world.

> **NOTE**   These days, the term *leased line* can be used more broadly to refer to any dedicated connection, such as a fiber-optic Ethernet connection. But from a CCNA perspective, a leased line is specifically a dedicated serial connection.

16.1.2 *Multiprotocol Label Switching*

As you're well aware by now, routers forward packets based on their destination IP address. However, that isn't always the case. Multiprotocol Label Switching (MPLS) is a common WAN technology that uses labels (not IP addresses) to route packets to their destination. The MPLS *label* is an additional header that is added to a message by a router at the edge of the MPLS network—typically, a router belonging to a WAN service provider. Figure 16.3 shows the position of the MPLS label in a message. Due to the label's position between the Layer 2 and Layer 3 headers, MPLS is often called a Layer 2.5 protocol.

Figure 16.3   The MPLS label is inserted between the Layer 2 and Layer 3 headers.

> **NOTE**   *Multiprotocol* refers to the fact that MPLS can encapsulate a variety of packet types—not just IP packets. However, in modern networks, MPLS usually carries IP (IPv4 or IPv6) packets.

MPLS labels offer a more efficient way to route packets through a network, reducing the burden on routers. Instead of examining the entire packet header and performing a lookup in the routing table for each hop, routers simply read the fixed-length MPLS label and forward the packet based on a predetermined path.

Figure 16.4 shows a service provider's MPLS network with four connected LANs belonging to two separate customers. This is an important point about MPLS: as opposed to a leased line, which provides a dedicated connection between two sites, a service provider's MPLS network is a shared infrastructure over which multiple customers can connect.

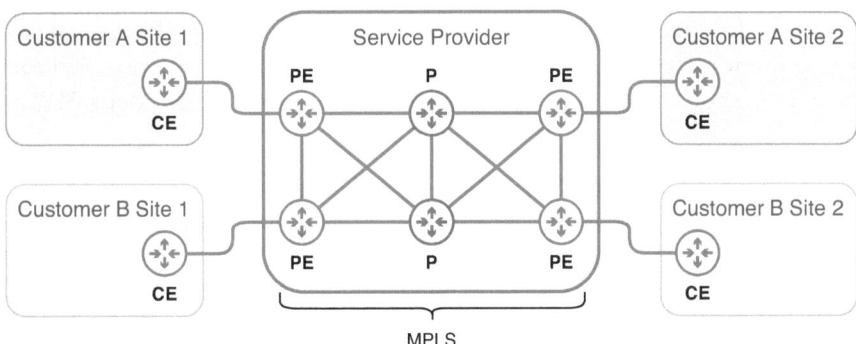

Figure 16.4 **Two customers connect their remote sites via a service provider's MPLS infrastructure.**

Figure 16.4 also introduces three different roles that routers can play in an MPLS WAN: customer edge (CE), provider edge (PE), and provider (P) routers:

- *CE router*—A router located at the customer's premises that connects the customer's network to the service provider's network. This is typically under the control of the customer, not the service provider.
- *PE router*—A router located at the edge of the service provider's network that connects to the customer's network. PE routers are responsible for assigning and removing labels to/from the customer's packets.
- *P router*—A router that is internal to the service provider's network. The router doesn't connect to the customer's network directly but is responsible for forwarding labeled packets across the service provider's network.

NOTE The CE routers don't actively participate in MPLS; they send and receive regular IP packets. MPLS labels are only used by the service provider routers (PE/P).

Although customers connect to the same MPLS infrastructure, MPLS labels offer a secure way to segregate the traffic of each customer through virtual private networks (VPNs). By assigning unique labels to different customer data streams, MPLS ensures that each customer's traffic is kept separate and isolated within their own VPN, despite sharing the same MPLS infrastructure. Let's look at two types of MPLS VPNs: L2VPN and L3VPN.

NOTE   A *virtual private network* (VPN) is a secure virtual connection over shared infrastructure. In this chapter, we'll examine two types of VPNs: MPLS VPNs and internet VPNs.

MPLS LAYER 2 VPNS

In an MPLS Layer 2 VPN (L2VPN), the service provider network is transparent to the CE routers. In effect, the service provider network functions like a giant switch, forwarding frames between each customer's CE routers (hence "Layer 2" in the name). Figure 16.5 shows two customers connected to a service provider's MPLS L2VPN service.

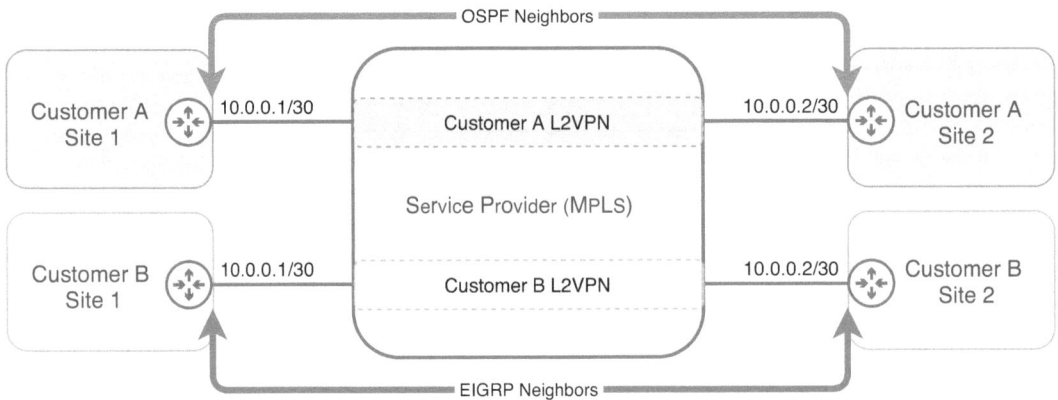

Figure 16.5   Two customers connect their remote sites using a service provider's MPLS L2VPN service. PE and P routers are not shown.

To exchange routing information, each customer's routers form dynamic routing protocol neighbor relationships with each other over the MPLS infrastructure. In figure 16.5's example, Customer A uses OSPF to exchange routing information between its Site 1 and Site 2 routers, and Customer B uses EIGRP between its routers. The service provider network functions like a switch, forwarding the OSPF/EIGRP messages between the routers. Here are a couple of other takeaways from figure 16.5:

- Customers can use private IP addresses for their connections. The service provider's MPLS infrastructure isn't the internet—public addresses aren't necessary.
- Both customers use the 10.0.0.0/30 subnet for their connection. This isn't a problem; it doesn't matter if they overlap. Although they connect to shared MPLS infrastructure, each VPN functions as an isolated, private network.

MPLS LAYER 3 VPNS

MPLS Layer 3 VPNs (L3VPN) take a different approach from L2VPNs. Instead of the service provider network acting like a giant switch connecting CE routers. The service provider routers actively participate in the routing process; the PE routers form dynamic routing protocol relationships with the CE routers. Figure 16.6 demonstrates this.

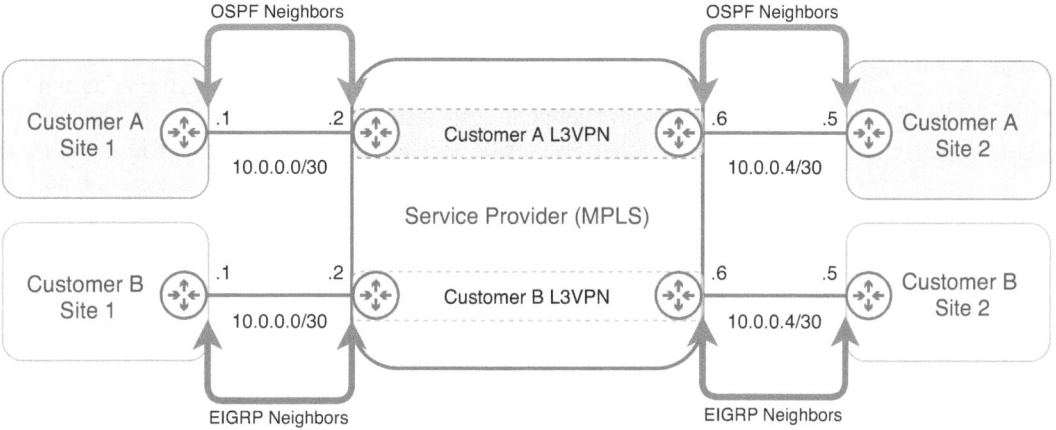

Figure 16.6 **Two customers connect their remote sites using a service provider's MPLS L3VPN service. CE routers form dynamic routing protocol neighbor relationships with PE routers.**

NOTE As in the L2VPN example, the customers use overlapping private addresses in this example. This is not a problem; customer networks are isolated from each other despite connecting to the same MPLS infrastructure.

In MPLS L3VPNs, the service provider routers (specifically, the PE routers) maintain a separate routing table for each customer, ensuring traffic separation and security. This is achieved using Virtual Routing and Forwarding (VRF)—a topic we'll cover in the next chapter.

The customer's CE routers and the service provider's PE routers establish routing protocol adjacencies, allowing for the exchange of routing information. As a result, the underlying infrastructure of the service provider becomes an extension of the customer's IP network, offloading some of the routing complexities to the service provider.

The appropriate MPLS service—L2VPN or L3VPN—depends on the needs and preferences of each customer. If the customer wants to maintain complete control over their routing policies, L2VPN is likely the better choice. For example, security policy might dictate that routing must be strictly controlled, and information about internal networks should not be advertised to the service provider routers. If the customer is comfortable with letting the service provider participate in the routing process (and sharing routing information with the service provider), L3VPN might be appropriate.

NOTE In both cases (L2VPNs and L3VPNs), MPLS is the underlying technology that enables the VPN, although the implementation is different.

Connecting to an MPLS service provider

MPLS is a technology used by WAN service providers to enable customers to connect their remote sites. But how can customers connect their devices (CE routers) to the service provider's MPLS infrastructure (PE routers)? There are various options, such as

- *Ethernet*—This is the most common option, as Ethernet supports high speeds and long distances (especially fiber-optic Ethernet).
- *Leased line*—A serial leased line can be used to connect the CE and PE routers.
- *Wireless (cellular 3G/4G/5G networks)*—This option is convenient for temporary setups, mobile operations, and remote locations where wired access is impractical.

16.2 *Internet connections*

The internet is a vast, interconnected "network of networks" that spans the globe, enabling the exchange of information among billions of devices. It is the foundational infrastructure that supports countless applications and services, such as email, web browsing, and streaming. Figure 16.7 shows a simplified image of the internet.

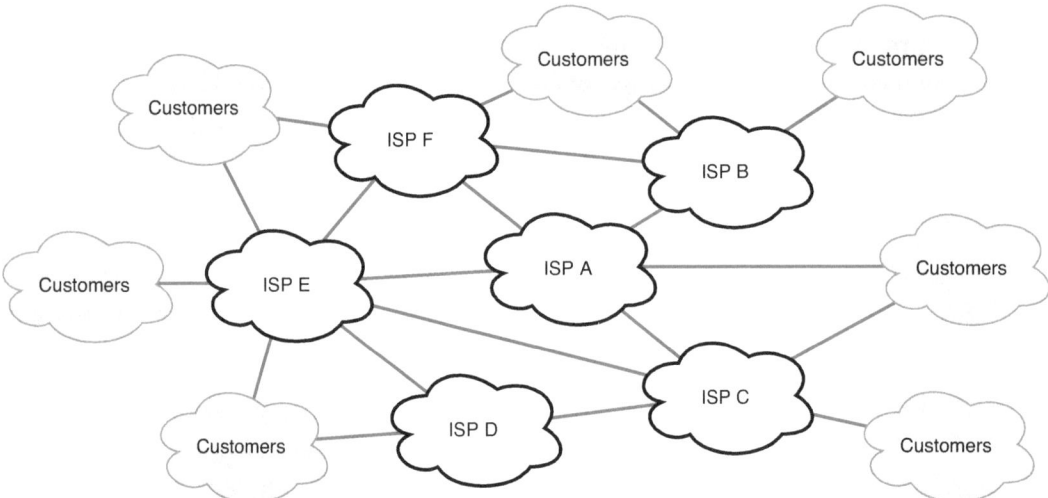

Figure 16.7   The internet is a network of networks—thousands of ISP networks and customer networks connected to share resources.

The internet has become so ubiquitous in most of our lives that we take it for granted. The details of how it works—the inner workings of ISP networks—are beyond the scope of the CCNA exam. However, understanding the internet from the perspective of an ISP's customers (an enterprise or consumer connected to the internet) is essential.

Just as there are numerous ways to connect to a service provider's MPLS infrastructure, multiple methods exist for a customer to connect to their ISP's internet infrastructure.

In this section, we'll look at a few methods of connecting to the internet. Then, in the next section, we'll look at how to use VPNs to create private WAN connections over the internet, similar to the MPLS VPNs we covered in the previous section.

16.2.1 Digital subscriber line

Digital subscriber line (DSL) is a technology that transmits digital data over standard telephone lines and is a common method of connecting to the internet. A DSL *modem* (modulator-demodulator) is required to convert data into a format suitable to be sent over the phone lines. The modem might be a separate device, or it might be incorporated into the wireless home router. Figure 16.8 shows a SOHO network with a DSL internet connection.

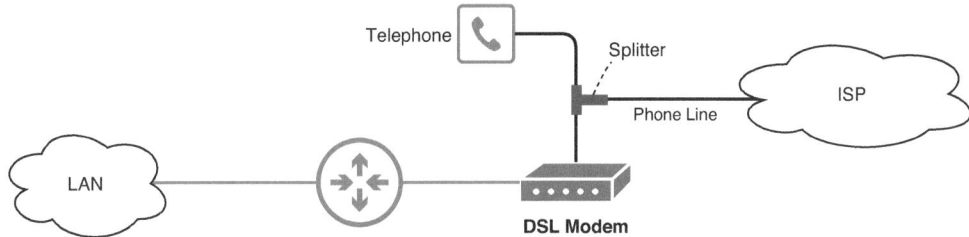

Figure 16.8   A SOHO network connecting to the internet via DSL. A DSL modem translates between Ethernet and the signaling used on telephone lines. A splitter is used to allow both the telephone and modem to connect to a single phone line. The splitter is also called a *DSL filter*, as it serves to filter the DSL and telephone signals to prevent interference between them.

NOTE   The wireless router is represented as a gray box with standard icons representing each of its different functions.

While it's an older technology, DSL is still prevalent in many areas, especially in SOHO networks. One major advantage of DSL is that it uses existing telephone lines, so customers can connect without the need to install new cabling to their premises.

16.2.2 Cable internet

Cable internet, also called *cable TV (CATV) internet*, is similar to DSL in that it takes advantage of preexisting infrastructure—cable TV lines that already connect to many homes—to connect to the internet. As with DSL, a modem is required to translate between Ethernet and the signaling used on the CATV lines. Figure 16.9 shows a SOHO network with a cable internet connection.

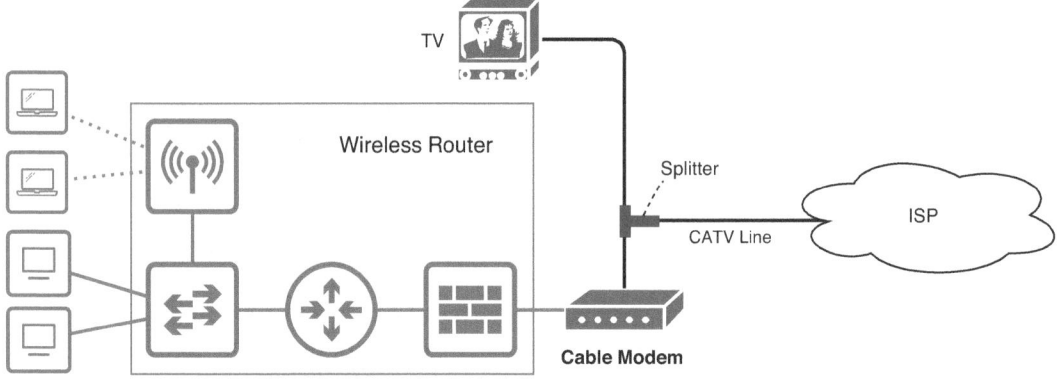

Figure 16.9   A SOHO network network connecting to the internet via the same CATV line used for television. A cable modem translates between Ethernet and the signaling used on CATV lines. A splitter is used to allow both the TV and modem to connect to a single CATV line.

Like DSL, cable internet is still quite common, particularly in SOHO networks. By enabling internet access over existing infrastructure, the financial cost of internet access is greatly reduced.

16.2.3 *Fiber-optic Ethernet*

Another option for internet connectivity that is gaining in popularity is fiber-optic Ethernet. Unlike DSL and cable internet, which use existing telephone and CATV lines, fiber-optic connections require the installation of fiber-optic cables to the customer's premises. Furthermore, a device called an *optical network terminal* (ONT) or *optical network unit* (ONU) is typically needed to convert the light signals from the fiber into the electrical signals used by copper UTP cables. Figure 16.10 shows a SOHO network with a fiber-optic internet connection.

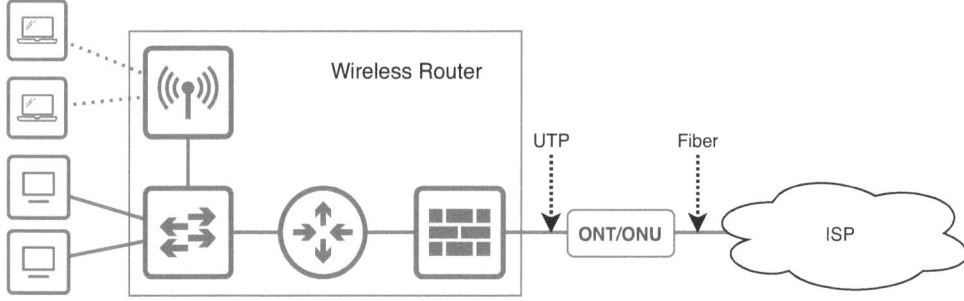

Figure 16.10   A SOHO network connecting to the internet via fiber-optic Ethernet. An ONT/ONU converts between light and electrical signals.

While the installation of fiber-optic cables might seem like a drawback due to the initial investment required, the benefits are significant; fiber-optic connections offer much higher speeds than DSL or CATV. As demand for high-speed internet continues to grow, fiber-optic Ethernet is increasingly popular in both SOHO and enterprise networks. In urban areas and new residential developments, fiber is quickly becoming the standard, with many ISPs offering fiber-to-the-home (FTTH) services.

> **NOTE** Although figures 16.8, 16.9, and 16.10 use a SOHO network as an example, all three of these internet connection options can be used by larger enterprises, too.

16.2.4 Wireless 3G/4G/5G

The final option we'll cover is wireless *3G, 4G,* and *5G*; these stand for third, fourth, and fifth generation, respectively. If you have a mobile phone with a data plan, it likely supports one or more of these technologies for mobile internet access.

> **NOTE** You might have heard of *Long-Term Evolution* (LTE) as well. LTE is considered a part of the 4G family of standards. While initially LTE did not meet the strictest definitions of 4G, advancements in LTE technology have led to its widespread acceptance as a 4G standard, so the terms are sometimes used interchangeably.

Figure 16.11 shows a typical setup where mobile phones connect to the internet via a cell tower, which then connects to the ISP. It also shows another use case for these technologies: a router with the appropriate radio can connect to the internet in the same manner, providing internet access for devices in its connected LAN.

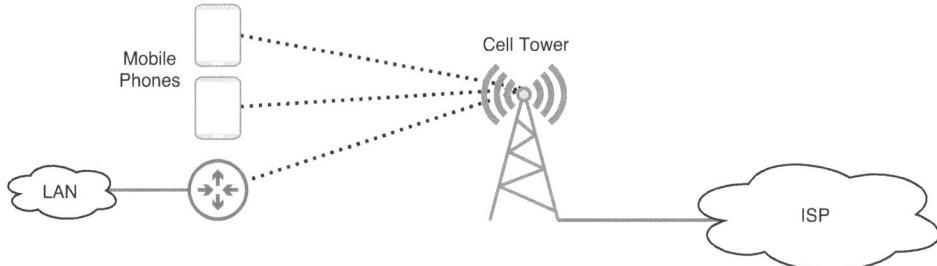

Figure 16.11 Wireless 3G/4G/5G internet access. Devices wirelessly connect to a cell tower, which connects to the ISP infrastructure.

> **NOTE** 3G and 4G are rarely used as a LAN's primary internet connection; they are more common for temporary setups, mobile operations, remote locations, or as a backup connection. However, more recently, the newer 5G standard has gained prominence as a primary internet connection in many networks.

16.2.5 *Redundant internet connections*

In many SOHO networks, temporarily losing access to the internet might be annoying and inconvenient, but it probably wouldn't be a catastrophe. However, this is not the case for larger enterprises, for which even a short outage can have major negative effects in terms of reputation and revenue. In such networks, it is essential to have redundant internet connections. Figure 16.12 introduces some internet connection designs, from *single-homed* (no redundancy) to *dual multi-homed* (high redundancy).

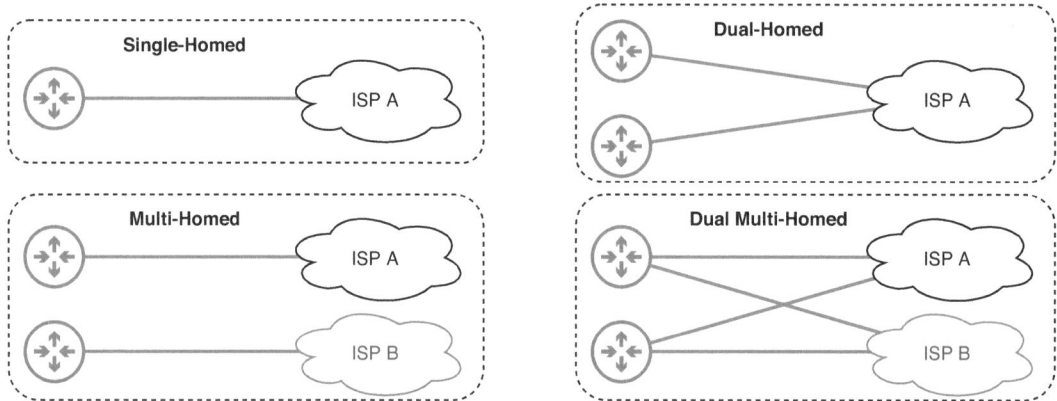

Figure 16.12   internet connection designs. Single-homed = one connection to one ISP. Dual-homed = two connections to one ISP. Multi-homed = one connection to each of two (or more) ISPs. Dual multi-homed = two connections to each of two (or more) ISPs.

In a single-homed design, there is one connection to one ISP. This is common in SOHO networks; if you have internet access at home, it's probably using a single-homed design. A simple way to improve the redundancy of such a design is to add a second connection to the same ISP; if there is a problem with one connection, the other can be used instead. This is called a *dual-homed* design.

> **NOTE**   Figure 16.12's dual-homed design shows two routers, each with one connection to the ISP. Another option is to have two connections from a single router. However, the dual-router design provides better redundancy; if a hardware failure causes one router to go down, the other one is still available.

Although a dual-homed design provides superior redundancy to a single-homed design, it still relies on a single ISP. If that ISP has issues, both connections may be affected. To avoid such situations, you can employ a multi-homed design, which has one connection to each of two (or possibly more) ISPs. If one ISP has issues, the network can still operate via the other ISP's connection.

For most enterprises, a multi-homed design provides sufficient redundancy. However, networks for which continuous internet connectivity is absolutely critical may opt for a dual multi-homed design—two connections to each of two (or more) ISPs. This provides the highest level of redundancy.

NOTE Just as redundancy increases in the order we examined these designs (single-homed, dual-homed, multi-homed, dual multi-homed), so do cost and complexity. Although a dual multi-homed design provides the highest redundancy, its higher cost and complexity mean that it is not always the best choice.

16.3 *Internet VPNs*

So far, we've covered a couple of WAN technologies (leased lines and MPLS) and different types of internet connections. You might be wondering: "Is the internet a WAN?" The answer to that question is "both yes and no."

The definition of WAN I gave earlier in this chapter is "a network that extends over a large geographic area." In that sense, the internet absolutely is a WAN—it extends across the entire globe. However, the term *WAN* is typically used in the context of a private network that connects remote sites (branch offices, data centers, etc.) of a specific organization.

While the internet can serve that purpose, its public nature goes against the private aspect of most WANs. Although you can connect remote sites over the internet, additional steps are necessary to keep communications secure: you should use VPNs. Just as MPLS can create VPNs over shared infrastructure, there are multiple techniques to create VPNs over the public internet.

In this section, we'll examine two types of internet VPNs: site-to-site VPNs and remote access VPNs. Table 16.2 summarizes their characteristics.

Table 16.2 Site-to-site and remote access VPNs

	Site-to-site VPN	Remote access VPN
Common protocol	IPsec	TLS
Use case	Permanent connection between two sites	On-demand access to enterprise resources
How many hosts served?	Serves many hosts within the connected sites	Serves the one host with the VPN client installed

EXAM TIP Internet VPNs are covered in CCNA exam topic 5.5: Describe IPsec remote access and site-to-site VPNs. Make sure you know the characteristics of each type.

16.3.1 *Site-to-site VPNs (Internet Protocol Security)*

A *site-to-site VPN* is a VPN between two devices for the purpose of (as the name suggests) connecting two sites over a non-private network (such as the internet). The most common protocol used for site-to-site VPNs is *Internet Protocol Security* (IPsec), which creates a secure VPN *tunnel*—a virtual pathway—between two devices, allowing for secure, private communications over the public internet. Figure 16.13 demonstrates how an IPsec tunnel works.

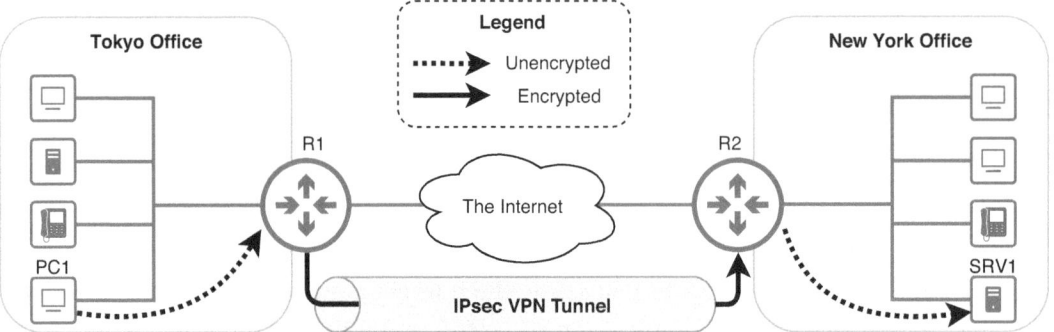

Figure 16.13   A site-to-site IPsec VPN provides a secure virtual pathway between two sites. Traffic is encrypted only when sent over the internet.

> **NOTE**   Although the message is shown going through the IPsec tunnel, keep in mind that the bits still physically pass through the internet connection. A tunnel is a virtual pathway, but it doesn't create a new physical path for bits to travel over.

The concept of tunneling can be hard to wrap your head around at first. Basically, it's the process of encapsulating a packet inside of another packet. Figure 16.14 illustrates how it works, representing a packet as a box:

1   R1 receives a packet destined for SRV1.
2   R1 encrypts the packet, concealing both its intended destination and its contents.
3   R1 encapsulates that encrypted packet inside of another packet that is destined for R2.
4   R1 forwards that packet over the internet toward R2.
5   R2 receives the packet and de-encapsulates it, revealing the encrypted packet inside.
6   R2 decrypts the internal packet.
7   R2 forwards the decrypted packet to its intended destination, SRV1.

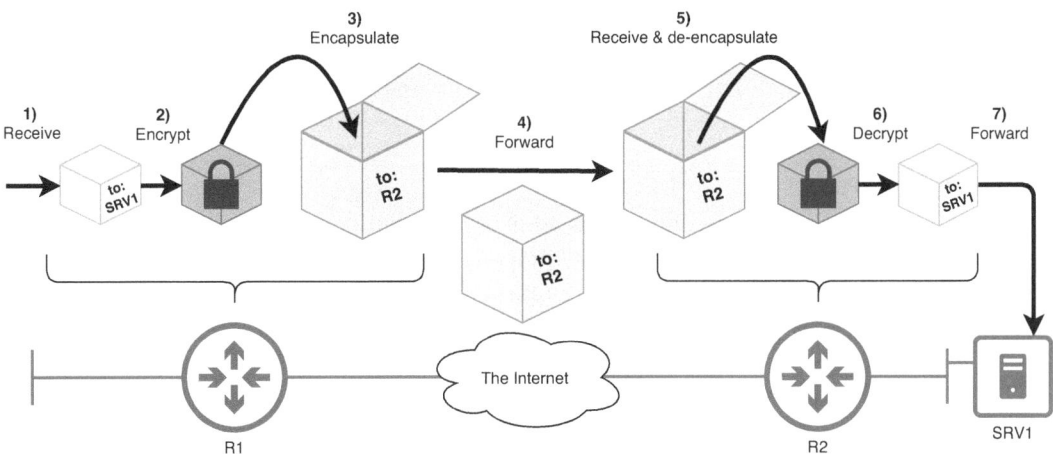

Figure 16.14 A tunnel is created by encapsulating a packet inside of another packet. This outer packet provides a "tunnel" for the inner packet to travel through without being exposed to the internet.

Figure 16.15 provides a more technical image of the encryption and encapsulation process. The original IP packet is first encrypted, then encapsulated with an IPsec header and a new IP header, and then forwarded.

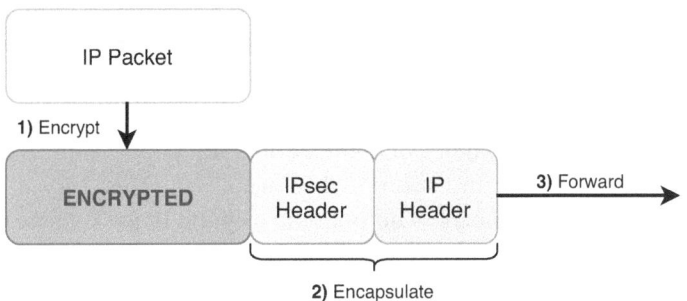

Figure 16.15 Tunneling an IP packet with IPsec. The IP packet is encrypted, encapsulated with an IPsec header and a new IP header, and then forwarded.

A site-to-site VPN tunnel is a permanent virtual connection between two devices; it remains until you remove the relevant configurations. The tunnel allows hosts in remote sites to communicate with each other without the need to create a VPN for themselves. Hosts can send unencrypted data to their site's router, which will encrypt the data and forward it through the tunnel to the remote site. Thanks to the cryptographic technologies employed by IPsec, only the two routers that have formed the tunnel—R1 and R2, in our example—can decrypt packets encrypted by each other; only R2 can decrypt R1's encrypted packets, and only R1 can decrypt R2's encrypted packets.

> **NOTE**   IPsec is actually a suite of protocols, rather than a single protocol. There is some variability in how IPsec works depending on which protocols (and which operational mode) are used, but those details are beyond the scope of the CCNA exam.

GRE OVER IPSEC

IPsec on its own has some limitations. One of those limitations is that it doesn't support broadcast and multicast traffic—only unicast. This limitation can affect routing protocols like OSPF, which rely on multicast messages (sent to multicast addresses 224.0.0.5 and 224.0.0.6, as we covered in chapter 18 of volume 1).

One solution to this limitation is to combine IPsec with another tunneling protocol called *Generic Routing Encapsulation* (GRE). Like IPsec, GRE tunnels packets by encapsulating them with additional headers. However, GRE does not encrypt the original packet, so it is not secure; an attacker who gets access to a message traveling in a GRE tunnel can read the message's contents. However, GRE has the advantage of supporting broadcast and multicast messages.

> **NOTE**   GRE creates tunnels but not VPNs. Because GRE doesn't encrypt messages, its tunnels aren't private or secure on their own.

To take advantage of both the flexibility of GRE and the security of IPsec, you can use *GRE over IPsec*. This does add some extra complexity, but it's a common solution if you need to send multicast packets (i.e., OSPF messages to exchange routing information) over the tunnel.

Figure 16.16 shows how GRE over IPsec works. An IP packet is first encapsulated with a GRE header and a new IP header. Then, the entire GRE packet is encrypted and encapsulated with an IPsec header and additional IP header and then forwarded. Yes, this means that there are three IP headers in total: the original IP packet's header, the IP header added by GRE, and the IP header added by IPsec.

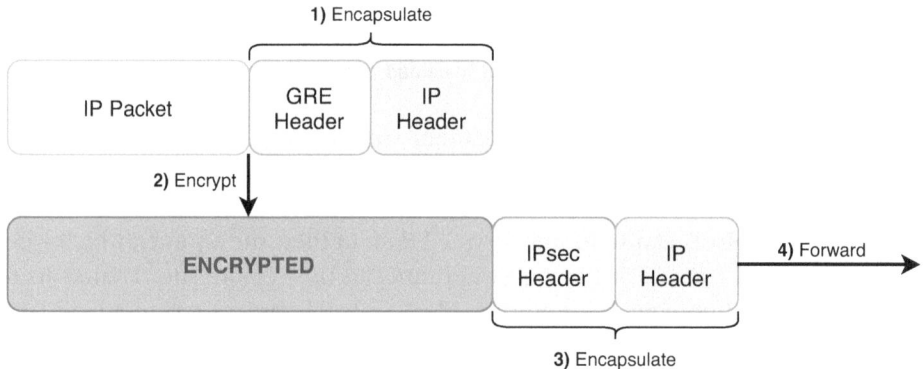

Figure 16.16   GRE over IPsec works by encapsulating an IP packet with GRE and IP headers, encrypting the GRE packet, and encapsulating the encrypted packet with IPsec and IP headers.

NOTE   The interior packet might be unicast, broadcast, or multicast, but the GRE packet itself is always unicast; it's always destined for the router at the other end of the tunnel. This means that GRE can always be encapsulated by IPsec.

GRE over IPsec creates a tunnel within a tunnel. The original IP packet travels in the GRE tunnel, which is contained in the IPsec tunnel. Figure 16.17 illustrates this.

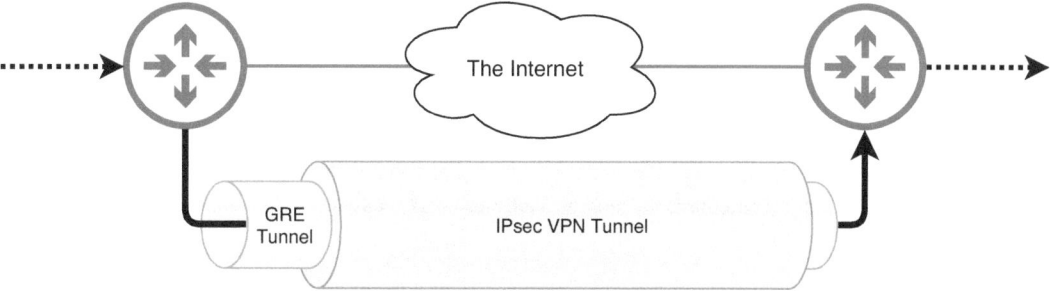

Figure 16.17   GRE over IPsec creates a tunnel within a tunnel. This combines the flexibility of GRE with the security of IPsec.

DYNAMIC MULTIPOINT VPN

A second downside of IPsec is that it can be labor intensive to configure and manage IPsec tunnels, especially with a large number of routers. Each time you add a new branch or location to your network, you have to set up individual VPN tunnels between that new location and all other existing locations, leading to a substantial increase in configuration complexity, and an increased likelihood of configuration errors.

Dynamic Multipoint VPN (DMVPN), developed by Cisco, is a solution that facilitates the creation of a full mesh of tunnels between routers. With DMVPN, you only have to configure a hub-and-spoke topology of tunnels; DMVPN will do the rest to create a full mesh. Figure 16.18 illustrates how DMVPN can help create a full mesh of IPsec tunnels.

NOTE   DMVPN doesn't have to use IPsec; it uses unencrypted GRE tunnels by default. However, IPsec is recommended for secure, encrypted VPN tunnels over the internet; unencrypted GRE tunnels are not secure.

The DMVPN hub router distributes information to each spoke router about how to form IPsec tunnels with the other routers. This allows the routers to create a full mesh of IPsec tunnels without requiring manual configuration of each tunnel.

EXAM TIP   For the exam, just know the basic purpose of DMVPN: it allows routers to automatically create a full mesh of tunnels from a hub-and-spoke configuration.

1) Configure IPsec tunnels to a hub router.

2) The hub router distributes information about how to form IPsec tunnels with the other routers.

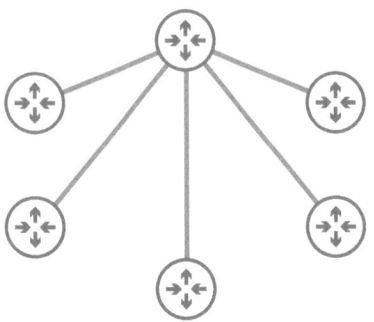
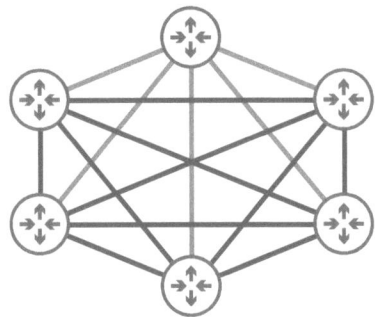

Figure 16.18   DMVPN automatically creates a full mesh of IPsec tunnels after configuring a hub-and-spoke topology.

Hub-and-spoke vs. full-mesh

A full-mesh topology provides a couple of key advantages. The first is redundancy; if a failure causes one tunnel to go down, other tunnels can be used to reach the destination. The second is reduced latency. Because the routers in each site can communicate directly with each other, latency is reduced compared to a hub-and-spoke topology (in which traffic between spoke routers must pass through the hub router).

However, a hub-and-spoke topology has its advantages, too. Because all traffic between two sites has to pass through the hub site, it's easy to implement restrictions on those communications (for example, with a firewall at the hub site). Despite the advantages of full-mesh, security requirements may dictate that a hub-and-spoke topology is appropriate.

16.3.2 *Remote access VPNs (Transport Layer Security)*

A site-to-site VPN is a permanent virtual connection between two routers, providing a secure encrypted communication pathway for hosts connected to each router. A *remote access VPN*, on the other hand, is an on-demand VPN that allows an end user to securely access the company's internal resources over the internet. The protocol of choice is typically *Transport Layer Security* (TLS), but IPsec is also an option. Figure 16.19 demonstrates remote access VPN connections.

> **NOTE**   TLS is often called Secure Sockets Layer (SSL). SSL is the name of a deprecated protocol that was replaced by TLS, but the SSL name is still common.

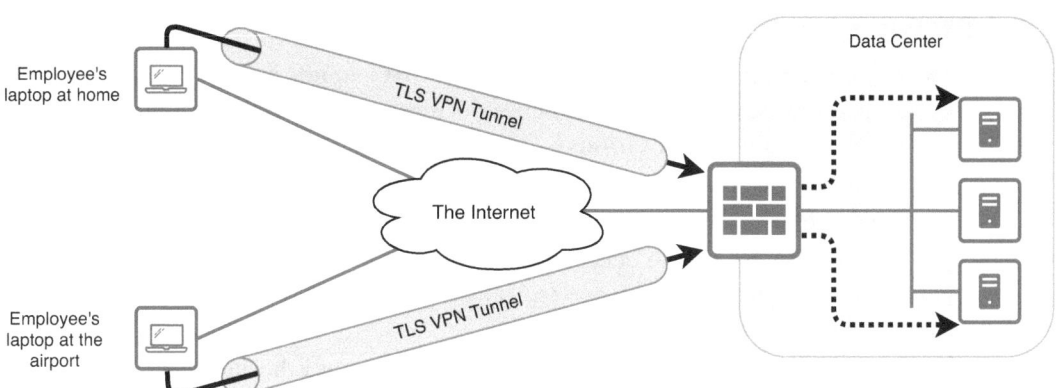

Figure 16.19 Remote access TLS VPNs provide secure access to the company's internal resources over the internet.

Unlike a site-to-site VPN, which provides a virtual pathway for multiple hosts connected to the routers that establish the VPN, a remote access VPN establishes a VPN connection from each individual end-user device to the company's firewall or router. This means that while multiple devices can simultaneously connect via remote access VPN, each device has its own encrypted tunnel that is not shared with other devices.

The end-user device runs a piece of software called a *VPN client*—Cisco's offering is called *Cisco AnyConnect Secure Mobility Client* (usually just "AnyConnect"), but other vendors have their own offerings. This software allows the device to create its own tunnel to the company's firewall or router, providing a secure communication pathway to reach resources on the company's internal network (i.e., file servers). Remote access VPNs are particularly useful in remote work situations, which have become increasingly common.

Transport Layer Security and HTTPS

TLS, commonly used for remote access VPNs, is also the protocol that secures Hypertext Transfer Protocol Secure (HTTPS), which is used to securely access web pages. Whereas a remote access VPN creates a TLS VPN tunnel between your device and a firewall/router, HTTPS creates a TLS VPN tunnel between your device and the web server that hosts the web page you are accessing.

EXAM TIP For the exam, know that a remote access VPN allows a single device to securely access internal resources through a TLS tunnel. The details of the TLS protocol itself are beyond the scope of the CCNA.

Summary

- A wide area network (WAN) is a network that extends over a large geographic area, often spanning distances between cities or even countries. Enterprises use WANs to connect their various LANs.

- A leased line is a dedicated physical connection between two sites, providing fixed bandwidth that is reserved for that specific connection.

- Leased lines are secure because they are private; they are not shared with other customers. However, they are typically more expensive and offer lower bandwidth than more modern solutions.

- Leased lines traditionally use serial connections, not Ethernet. However, service providers sometimes offer fiber-optic Ethernet leased lines.

- Multiprotocol Label Switching (MPLS) is a common WAN technology that uses labels (not IP addresses) to route packets to their destination.

- The MPLS label is an additional header that is added between the Layer 2 and Layer 3 headers of a message.

- Unlike a leased line, a service provider's MPLS network is shared infrastructure over which multiple customers can connect.

- There are three main roles that routers can play in an MPLS WAN: customer edge (CE), provider edge (PE), and provider (P).

- A CE router is located at the customer's premises and connects the customer's network to the service provider's network. It is typically under the control of the customer, not the service provider.

- A PE router is located at the edge of the service provider's network and connects to the customer's network. PE routers are responsible for assigning and removing labels to/from the customer's packets.

- A P router is internal to the service provider's network and doesn't connect to the customer's network directly. P routers are responsible for forwarding labeled packets across the service provider's network.

- Although customers connect to the same MPLS infrastructure, MPLS labels offer a secure way to segregate the traffic of each customer through virtual private networks (VPNs).

- There are two main types of MPLS VPNs: L2VPN and L3VPN.

- In an MPLS Layer 2 VPN (L2VPN), the service provider network is transparent to the CE routers. In effect, the service provider network functions like a giant switch, forwarding frames between each customer's CE routers.

- To exchange routing information, CE routers form dynamic routing protocol neighbor relationships with each other over the MPLS infrastructure.

- In an MPLS Layer 3 VPN (L3VPN), the service provider routers actively participate in the routing process. The PE routers form dynamic routing protocol neighbor relationships with the CE routers.

- In both cases (L2VPNs and L3VPNs), MPLS is the underlying technology that enables the VPN, although the implementation is different.

- The internet is a vast, interconnected "network of networks" that spans the globe, connecting thousands of internet service providers (ISPs) and their customers. There are various methods for connecting to an ISP.

- Digital subscriber line (DSL) is a technology that transmits digital data over standard telephone lines and is a common method of connecting to the internet.

- A DSL modem (modulator-demodulator) is required to convert data into a format suitable to be sent over the phone lines. The modem might be a separate device, or it might be incorporated into the wireless home router.

- One major advantage of DSL is that it uses existing telephone lines, so customers can connect to the internet without the need to install new cabling.

- Cable internet is similar to DSL in that it takes advantage of preexisting infrastructure: cable TV lines that already connect to many homes.

- Just as DSL uses a modem, a cable modem is required to translate between Ethernet and the signaling used on the CATV lines.

- Fiber-optic Ethernet connections are another common internet connection method. Unlike DSL and cable internet, which use existing telephone and CATV lines, fiber-optic connections require the installation of fiber-optic cables.

- Furthermore, a device called an *optical network terminal* (ONT) or *optical network unit* (ONU) is typically needed to convert the light signals from the fiber into the electrical signals used by copper UTP cables.

- As demand for high-speed internet grows, fiber-optic Ethernet is an increasingly common internet connection method in both SOHO and enterprise networks.

- Another option is wireless 3G, 4G/LTE (Long-Term Evolution), and 5G; these stand for third, fourth, and fifth generation, respectively.

- Mobile phones often use 3G/4G/5G for internet access. A router with the appropriate radio can also use these technologies to connect to the internet.

- Redundant internet connections are imperative for enterprises that rely on continuous internet connectivity.

- A single-homed internet connect design involves one connection to one ISP. This does not provide redundancy but is common in SOHO networks.

- A dual-homed design involves two connections to one ISP; this adds some redundancy but is still vulnerable to issues that affect the ISP as a whole.

- A multi-homed design involves one connection to each of two (or more) ISPs, providing resilience to issues that affect one of the ISPs.

- A dual multi-homed design involves two connections to each of two (or more) ISPs. This provides the highest level of redundancy but is not necessary for most networks.

- Is the internet a WAN? Yes and no. The internet is a WAN in that it extends over a large geographic area—the entire globe. However, the term *WAN* is typically used in the context of a private network that connects an organization's sites.

- The public nature of the internet makes it inappropriate for WAN connections without additional security measures: you should use VPNs.

- A site-to-site VPN is a VPN between two devices (routers) for the purpose of connecting two sites over a non-private network (such as the internet).

- The most common protocol used for site-to-site VPNs is *Internet Protocol Security* (IPsec), which creates a secure VPN *tunnel*—a virtual pathway—between two devices, allowing for secure, private communications over the public internet.

- Tunneling involves encapsulating a packet inside of another packet. The outer packet provides a tunnel for the inner packet to travel through without being exposed to the internet.

- IPsec encrypts the original packet before encapsulating it with an IPsec header and a new IP header.

- IPsec only supports unicast traffic. To support broadcast and multicast traffic, you can combine IPsec with Generic Routing Encapsulation (GRE).

- GRE creates tunnels that support various kinds of traffic but doesn't encrypt the contents. By combining GRE with IPsec, you take advantage of GRE's flexibility and IPsec's security; this is called *GRE over IPsec*.

- Configuring a full mesh of IPsec tunnels between routers is labor intensive and prone to configuration errors. Dynamic Multipoint VPN (DMVPN) is a solution that facilitates the creation of a full mesh of tunnels between routers.

- With DMVPN, you only have to configure a hub-and-spoke topology of tunnels. The hub router will then distribute information to the spoke routers, allowing them to form a full mesh of tunnels with each other.

- A remote access VPN is an on-demand VPN that allows an end user to securely access the company's internal resources over the internet. The protocol of choice is typically Transport Layer Security (TLS).

- A remote access VPN establishes a VPN connection from each individual end-user device to the company's firewall or router. While multiple devices can simultaneously connect, each device has its own encrypted tunnel that is not shared.

- The end-user device runs a piece of software called a *VPN client*—Cisco's offering is called *Cisco AnyConnect Secure Mobility Client*, or just *AnyConnect*. This software allows the device to create its own tunnel to the company's firewall or router.

Virtualization and cloud

This chapter covers

- Virtualization with virtual machines and containers
- Dividing a router into multiple virtual routers with Virtual Routing and Forwarding
- Cloud computing and its characteristics, service models, and deployment models

Virtualization and cloud computing are two technologies that have transformed modern IT infrastructure. Virtualization refers to a variety of technologies that enable you to create virtual versions of something—servers, routers, etc.—that are abstracted from the underlying physical hardware. Taking advantage of the flexibility of virtualization, cloud computing provides on-demand computing services that can be accessed remotely over a network and scaled to meet user demands.

In this chapter, we will delve into server virtualization with virtual machines (VMs), a technology that allows multiple virtual servers to run on a single physical server. We will also look at containers, a technology that runs applications in isolated environments offering flexibility, portability, and efficient resource usage. We will then explore Virtual Routing and Forwarding (VRF), which divides a single physical router into multiple virtual routers. Finally, we will cover the concept of cloud computing and the various service models used by modern enterprises of all sizes. Here are the CCNA exam topics we will address:

- 1.2 Describe characteristics of network topology architectures
    - 1.2.f On-premises and cloud
- 1.12 Explain virtualization fundamentals (server virtualization, containers, and VRFs)

17.1   *Virtual machines and containers*

Before we delve into VMs and containers, think back to a technology we previously covered that includes the word "virtual": virtual LANs (VLANs). Figure 17.1 shows how VLANs segment a single physical network into multiple distinct logical networks. Although all six PCs are connected to the same physical switch and are therefore in the same physical LAN, they are grouped into three different VLANs. Hosts in one VLAN cannot communicate directly with hosts in another VLAN, despite being physically connected to the same switch.

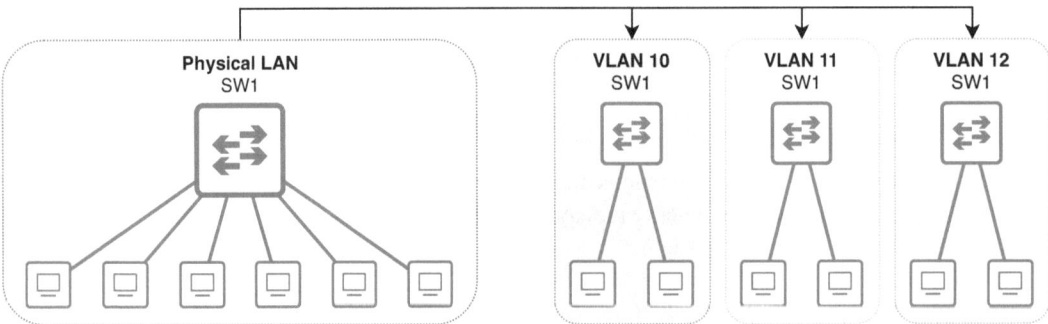

Figure 17.1   VLANs create distinct virtual LANs from a single physical LAN.

We covered another "virtual" technology in the previous chapter: virtual private networks (VPNs). As shown in figure 17.2, VPNs overlay private networks on top of shared infrastructure like the public internet, creating secure tunnels between devices. VPNs are distinct virtual networks that enable secure communication over a shared physical network.

VLANs and VPNs are both examples of network virtualization—creating logically separate networks on shared physical infrastructure. This concept of virtualization extends beyond networking into the realm of computing resources with the topics of this section: VMs and containers. These technologies allow operating systems and applications to run in isolated environments on a single physical server.

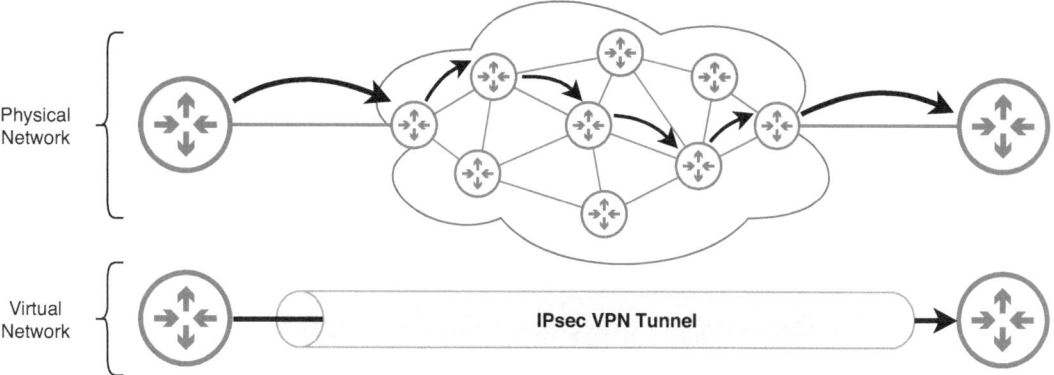

Figure 17.2   A VPN is a secure virtual network created over a physical network.

EXAM TIP   The CCNA, as a networking certification, places less emphasis on VMs and containers than network virtualization technologies. However, they are part of CCNA exam topic 1.12: Explain virtualization fundamentals (server virtualization, containers, and VRFs), so make sure you have a solid grasp of the basics that we will cover.

17.1.1 *Virtual machines*

In the past, a physical server would run a single operating system (OS)—for example, Windows Server or some variety of Linux. This meant that all of the hardware resources—CPU, RAM, storage, etc.—were tied to that one OS and its applications. This often led to resource underutilization, as the dedicated hardware could far exceed the needs of the single OS and its applications—modern server hardware can be very powerful. Figure 17.3 shows this traditional setup: one OS and its apps running on top of the server hardware.

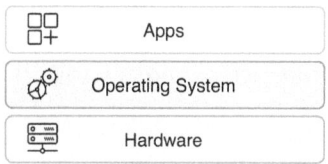

Figure 17.3   A physical server running one OS and its apps

Server hardware is quite expensive, and in addition to the cost of the hardware itself, each server requires physical space, cooling, and electrical power. A data center full of underutilized servers is not an efficient use of these resources. Virtualization addresses inefficiencies like these by consolidating servers and maximizing resource utilization.

Virtual machines break the one-to-one relationship of hardware to OS, allowing multiple OSs to run on a single physical server. This is facilitated by a *hypervisor*, a layer of software that allows multiple operating systems to share a single hardware host. It sits between the hardware and the VMs, managing and allocating the hardware resources (CPU, RAM, Storage, etc.) to each VM. There are two main types of hypervisors:

- *Type 1 hypervisors* run directly on top of the hardware.
- *Type 2 hypervisors* run as an application on a host OS.

NOTE   Another name for a hypervisor is *virtual machine monitor* (VMM).

TYPE 1 HYPERVISORS

A type 1 hypervisor is installed directly on the underlying physical hardware, managing and allocating the physical hardware resources to each VM running on top of it. Figure 17.4 illustrates a type 1 hypervisor running three VMs.

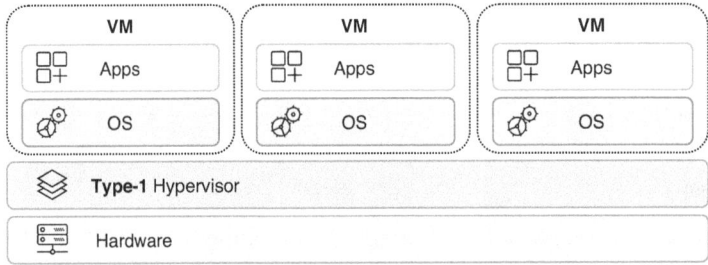

Figure 17.4   A type 1 hypervisor runs directly on the server hardware.

NOTE   Type 1 hypervisors are also called *bare-metal hypervisors* because they run directly on the hardware (the "metal"). Another term is *native hypervisor.* Two common type 1 hypervisors are VMware ESXi and Microsoft Hyper-V.

Type 1 hypervisors are what you'll most often find used for server virtualization in data center environments (including the cloud). By interacting directly with the physical hardware without any intermediaries, they provide very efficient use of hardware resources when compared with type 2 hypervisors.

TYPE 2 HYPERVISORS

Whereas a type 1 hypervisor runs directly on the underlying hardware, a type 2 hypervisor runs as an application on an OS, like a regular computer application. Figure 17.5 shows a type 2 hypervisor running two VMs.

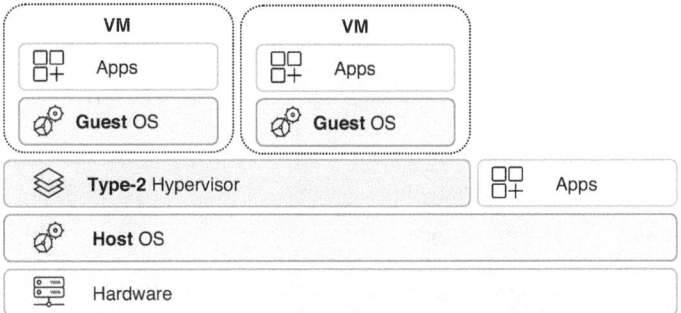

Figure 17.5 A type 2 hypervisor runs as an application on a host OS.

NOTE Another name for a type 2 hypervisor is a *hosted hypervisor*. Two common type 2 hypervisors are Oracle VM VirtualBox and VMware Workstation. Virtual-Box is free, and Workstation has free and paid versions.

The OS running directly on the hardware is called the *host OS*, and an OS running in a VM is called a *guest OS*. Unlike type 1 hypervisors, which have direct access to hardware resources, type 2 hypervisors must go through the host OS to access these resources. Furthermore, the host OS itself consumes hardware resources. Both of these points mean that type 2 hypervisors are less resource-efficient than type 1 hypervisors, making them less suited for resource-intensive applications; type 2 hypervisors are rare in the context of virtual servers in a data center environment.

However, the advantage of type 2 hypervisors lies in their ease of setup and use. A user can install and run a type 2 hypervisor on their PC just like any other application, making it more accessible for those who may not have the technical expertise to set up a type 1 hypervisor. This also means that a type 2 hypervisor can coexist with other applications on the host OS, allowing a PC to be used for virtualization without needing dedicated hardware.

For these reasons, type 2 hypervisors are more common on personal-use devices. For example, if a Mac/Linux user needs to run an app that is only supported on Windows (or vice versa), a type 2 hypervisor can be used to easily run another OS without the need to buy another computer. Type 2 hypervisors are also popular for software development, testing, and educational purposes.

Networking virtual machines

Each VM—whether it is running on a type 1 or type 2 hypervisor—operates as an independent host on the network, much like a physical computer. Although a VM doesn't have its own physical network interface card (NIC) like a standalone physical host, it uses a *virtual NIC* (vNIC). Through this vNIC, the VM can communicate with other hosts, whether they are other VMs on the same physical server or devices on the external physical network.

To manage network traffic to and from VMs, the hypervisor uses a *virtual switch*, which forwards frames between the vNICs of the VMs and the physical NIC (or NICs) of the host machine. Figure 17.6 illustrates how this works.

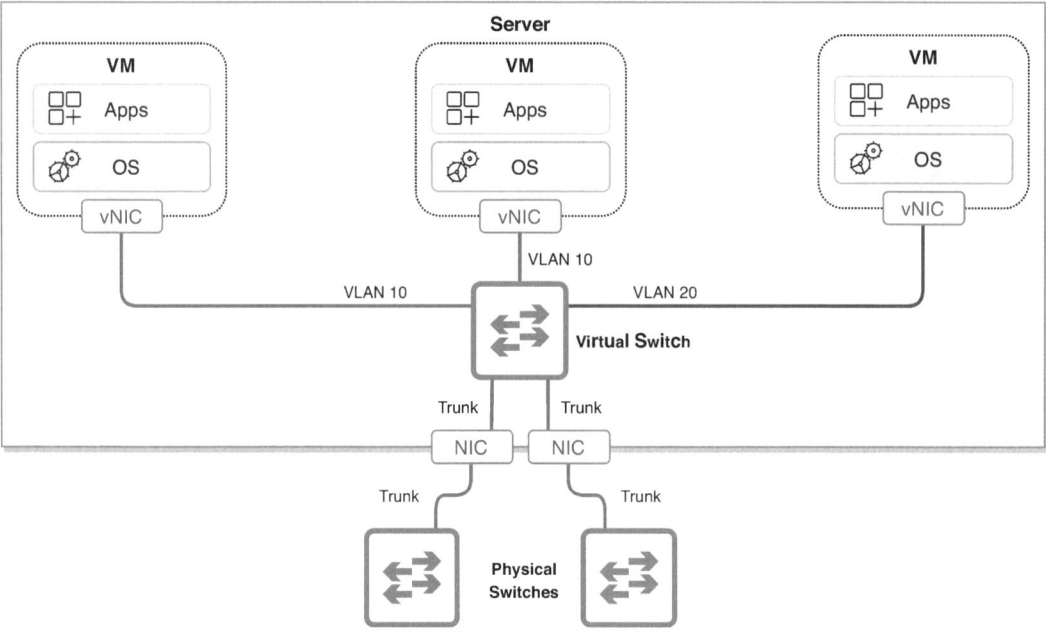

Figure 17.6   VMs connect to each other and the external physical network via a virtual switch. VMs are often segmented into separate VLANs, requiring trunk links.

NOTE   Figure 17.6 shows two NICs on the physical server. It's common for servers to have multiple NICs (each connected to a different physical switch) to provide redundancy, allowing the server to remain accessible if one NIC or switch fails.

Just like a physical switch, a virtual switch's ports can operate in access or trunk mode, enabling the use of VLANs to segment the VMs. To allow VMs in different VLANs to communicate over the network, the virtual switch connects to the physical host's NICs via trunk links. Likewise, the physical host's NICs connect to external physical switches via trunk links. Although switch ports connected to end hosts are almost always access ports, ports connected to servers running VMs are rare examples of trunk ports connected to end hosts; they need to be able to carry traffic to and from VMs in multiple VLANs.

The benefits of virtualization

Virtualization provides a variety of benefits for an enterprise. Here are a few:

- *Reduced costs*—By efficiently using server hardware resources, fewer physical servers are needed, reducing capital expenses (upfront costs). This also reduces the space, cooling, and power demands, reducing operating expenses (ongoing costs).
- *Mobility*—An entire VM can be easily saved as a file. This facilitates easy transfer, duplication, or migration (for example, if a problem occurs on one physical server).
- *Isolation*—Each VM operates independently from the others, providing enhanced security and stability. Problems within one VM, such as crashes or malware infections, do not affect the rest of the system.
- *Faster provisioning*—New VMs can be rapidly provisioned and deployed. This allows the organization to quickly respond to changing business needs, with the ability to roll out new applications and services in minutes rather than the days or weeks required for setting up new physical servers.

17.1.2 *Containers*

While VMs offer full hardware virtualization, providing complete OSs for their applications, a more agile approach is gaining prominence in modern IT infrastructure: containers. A *container* is a lightweight, stand-alone package that includes everything needed to run a particular application. A container is similar to a VM in that it provides an isolated environment for the application but is different in that it's more lightweight (smaller in size), requiring less overhead. Instead of running an independent OS, a container only contains an application and its dependencies (the various files and services it needs to run).

Figure 17.7 illustrates container architecture. Containers run on a *container engine*, a popular example is Docker Engine. The container engine itself runs on a host OS (usually Linux); notice that each container does not run its own OS.

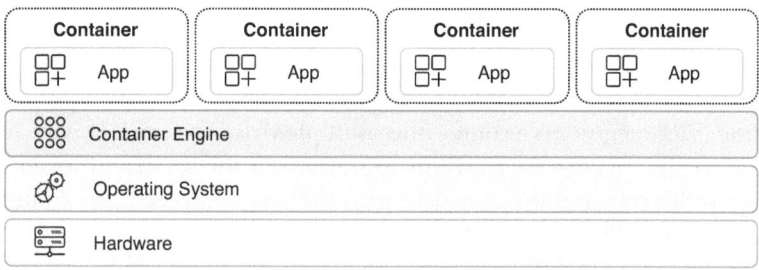

Figure 17.7   Containers run on a container engine, such as Docker Engine. The container engine runs on a host OS, but each container does not run a guest OS.

A software platform called a *container orchestrator* is typically used to automate the deployment, management, and scaling of containers; Kubernetes, originally designed by Google, is the industry standard. In small numbers, manual operation is possible, but large-scale systems can use many thousands (sometimes hundreds of thousands) of containers. This is especially true of applications that employ a *microservices architecture*, which breaks an application into many small, self-contained services. Containers are perfect for this, as they can isolate and manage these services independently.

Comparing VMs and containers

VMs and containers are both methods of virtualization that improve resource utilization and provide isolated environments for applications. Let's briefly compare them:

- *Startup time*—VMs can take minutes to boot up as each runs its own OS. Containers can boot up in milliseconds.
- *Disk space*—VMs take up more disk space (often many gigabytes) due to requiring a full OS. Containers take up relatively little disk space (megabytes).
- *CPU/RAM efficiency*—VMs use more CPU/RAM resources; once again, this is because each VM runs its own OS. Containers share an OS and therefore use fewer CPU/RAM resources.
- *Portability*—VMs are portable across different physical systems running the same hypervisor. Containers offer even greater portability—they are smaller, are faster to start, and can run on any modern container engine with Docker compatibility.
- *Isolation*—VMs offer strong isolation; a problem on one VM won't affect others. Containers run on the same host OS, so a problem on that host OS can affect all containers.

Although there is a major movement toward the use of containers, especially with the rise of microservices, automation, and DevOps (the combination of software development and IT operations), VMs and containers serve different needs, and both are widely used.

17.2   *Virtual Routing and Forwarding*

Let's move away from virtual machines and containers back to network virtualization. Similar to how VLANs segment a switch into multiple virtual switches, *Virtual Routing and Forwarding* (VRF) segments a router into multiple virtual routers. Service providers often use VRF to allow a customer's traffic to travel over the service provider's shared infrastructure while remaining isolated from other customers. As mentioned in the previous chapter, MPLS L3VPNs implement VRF for this purpose.

Figure 17.8 demonstrates VRF in the same manner we saw in the context of VLANs back in figure 17.1. SPR1 (service provider router 1) physically connects to six routers belonging to three customers (C1R1 = customer 1 router 1, C2R1 = customer 2 router 1, etc.). Using VRF, SPR1 is able to act as three independent routers: one for each customer.

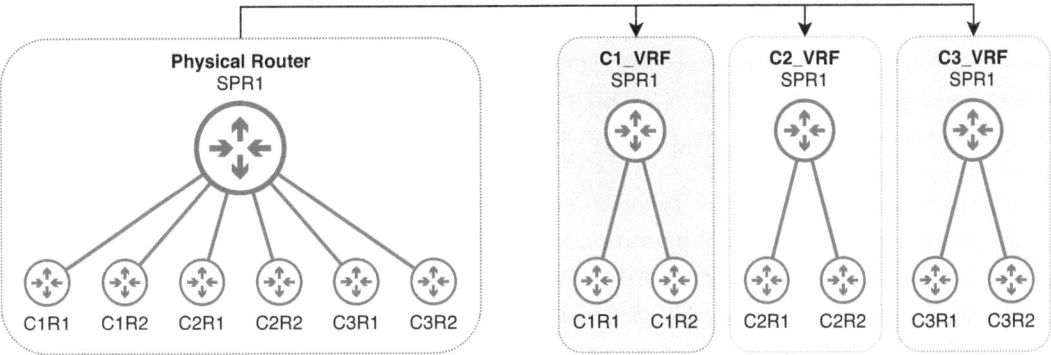

Figure 17.8 VRF segments a physical router into multiple virtual routers.

> **NOTE**   Each VRF virtual router is called a *VRF instance* or simply a *VRF*. Figure 17.8 depicts three VRFs—one for each customer.

Like VLANs, each VRF is isolated from other VRFs; traffic in one VRF cannot be forwarded out of an interface that belongs to another VRF. There is one exception; *VRF leaking* can be configured to allow traffic to pass between VRFs. However, VRF leaking and its use cases are a more advanced topic beyond the scope of the CCNA.

Although VRF configuration itself isn't tested on the CCNA exam, it's a useful tool to demonstrate how VRF works. So let's walk through a basic VRF configuration and examine its effects. Figure 17.9 adds IP addresses and interface IDs to the network shown in figure 17.8. To examine how VRF works, we'll configure SPR1 as shown in this example.

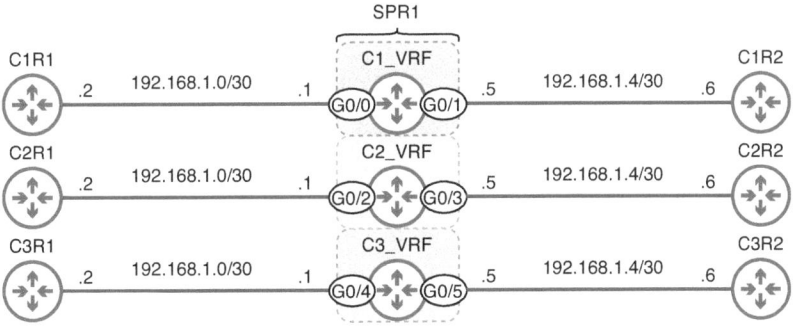

Figure 17.9 SPR1 is divided into three VRFs. Because each VRF functions as an independent router, overlapping IP addresses are not a problem.

> **NOTE**   As mentioned previously, VRF is often used to enable MPLS L3VPNs. VRF without MPLS is called *VRF-lite*, and that's what we're covering in this example; MPLS L3VPN implementation is a more advanced topic.

Basic VRF-lite configuration consists of the following three steps:

1 Create the VRFs.

2 Assign interfaces to each VRF.

3 Configure routing for each VRF.

To create a VRF, use the **ip vrf** *vrf-name* command in global config mode. That will bring you to VRF configuration mode, from which you can configure various VRF-related settings. However, for the most basic VRF-lite configuration, just creating the VRF is sufficient. In the following example, I create three VRFs on SPR1 and verify with **show ip vrf**:

```
SPR1(config)# ip vrf C1_VRF
SPR1(config-vrf)# ip vrf C2_VRF          Creates three VRFs
SPR1(config-vrf)# ip vrf C3_CRF
SPR1(config-vrf)# do show ip vrf
  Name                    Default RD           Interfaces
  C1_VRF                  <not set>
  C2_VRF                  <not set>            Three VRFs exist on SPR1.
  C3_CRF                  <not set>
```

The next step is to assign interfaces to each VRF. In our example network, all three VRFs use overlapping IP addresses in the 192.168.1.0/30 and 192.168.4.0/30 subnets. As the following example shows, this is not possible on a router without using VRFs:

```
SPR1(config)# interface g0/0                            Enables G0/0 and
SPR1(config-if)# no shutdown                            configures its IP address
SPR1(config-if)# ip address 192.168.1.1 255.255.255.252
SPR1(config)# interface g0/2                            Enables G0/2 and
SPR1(config-if)# no shutdown                            configures its IP address
SPR1(config-if)# ip address 192.168.1.1 255.255.255.252
% 192.168.1.0 overlaps with GigabitEthernet0/0
                                G0/2's IP address is rejected because
                                it's in the same subnet as G0/0.
```

Because the purpose of a router is to connect different networks, it can't have multiple interfaces connected to the same network (multiple interfaces in the same subnet). In the previous output, I attempted to configure the exact same IP address on G0/0 and G0/2, but the same problem would occur even if the IP addresses were different (i.e., 192.168.1.1/30 and 192.168.1.2/30); if there is any overlap between the interfaces' subnets, IOS will reject the command.

VRFs, however, are virtually isolated from each other. Interfaces in different VRFs can use overlapping subnets and even identical IP addresses. This allows for different customers to maintain their addressing schemes without worrying about other customers' addressing. In our example, each VRF is used to support a different customer network, and each customer network uses the same subnets.

To assign an interface to a VRF, use the **ip vrf forwarding** *vrf-name* command in interface config mode. In the following example, I assign each of SPR1's interfaces to the appropriate VRF and configure each interface's IP address. To spare some lines, I've omitted the **no shutdown** command from each interface:

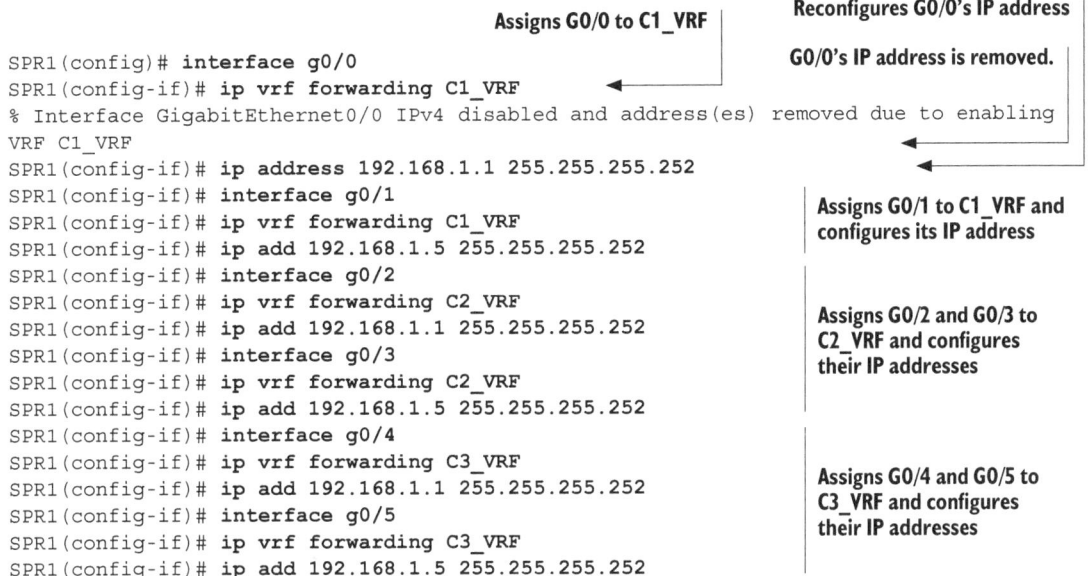

Assigns G0/0 to C1_VRF

Reconfigures G0/0's IP address

G0/0's IP address is removed.

```
SPR1(config)# interface g0/0
SPR1(config-if)# ip vrf forwarding C1_VRF
% Interface GigabitEthernet0/0 IPv4 disabled and address(es) removed due to enabling
VRF C1_VRF
SPR1(config-if)# ip address 192.168.1.1 255.255.255.252
SPR1(config-if)# interface g0/1
SPR1(config-if)# ip vrf forwarding C1_VRF
SPR1(config-if)# ip add 192.168.1.5 255.255.255.252
SPR1(config-if)# interface g0/2
SPR1(config-if)# ip vrf forwarding C2_VRF
SPR1(config-if)# ip add 192.168.1.1 255.255.255.252
SPR1(config-if)# interface g0/3
SPR1(config-if)# ip vrf forwarding C2_VRF
SPR1(config-if)# ip add 192.168.1.5 255.255.255.252
SPR1(config-if)# interface g0/4
SPR1(config-if)# ip vrf forwarding C3_VRF
SPR1(config-if)# ip add 192.168.1.1 255.255.255.252
SPR1(config-if)# interface g0/5
SPR1(config-if)# ip vrf forwarding C3_VRF
SPR1(config-if)# ip add 192.168.1.5 255.255.255.252
```

Assigns G0/1 to C1_VRF and configures its IP address

Assigns G0/2 and G0/3 to C2_VRF and configures their IP addresses

Assigns G0/4 and G0/5 to C3_VRF and configures their IP addresses

NOTE As the previous output shows, if an interface already has an IP address, it will be removed when you assign the interface to a VRF. I configured G0/0's IP address in the example before this one, but I had to reconfigure it after assigning G0/0 to C1_VRF.

Although we won't cover how to configure static and dynamic routing when using VRFs, let's look at the connected and local routes that are automatically added to the routing table after configuring IP addresses on a router's interfaces:

```
SPR1# show ip route
. . .
```

Views SPR1's routing table

No routes are shown.

The **show ip route** command on its own doesn't show any routes. That's because the router builds a unique routing table for each VRF, and you have to specify which VRF's routing table you want to see with **show ip route vrf** *vrf-name*. In the following example, I show the routing table for C1_VRF:

```
SPR1# show ip route vrf C1_VRF          ◄──────── Views the C1_VRF routing table
. . .
C          192.168.1.0/30 is directly connected, GigabitEthernet0/0      Connected and
L          192.168.1.1/32 is directly connected, GigabitEthernet0/0      local routes for
C          192.168.1.4/30 is directly connected, GigabitEthernet0/1      G0/0 and G0/1
L          192.168.1.5/32 is directly connected, GigabitEthernet0/1      are displayed.
```

Other commands require you to specify a particular VRF too. In the following example, I ping 192.168.1.2, which is the IP address of C1R1, C2R1, and C3R1. Note the differing results when I do and don't specify a VRF:

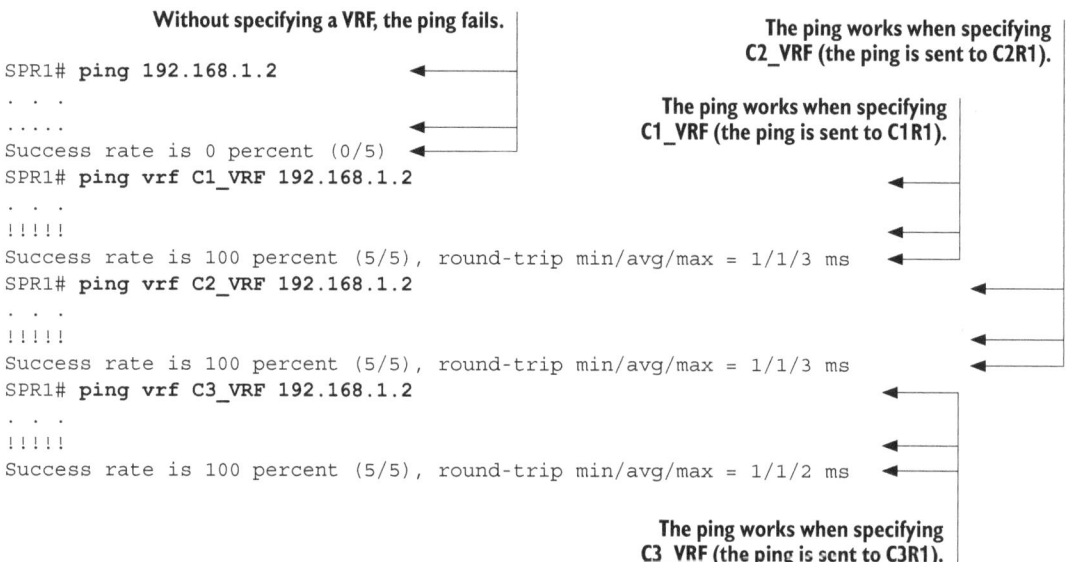

Without specifying a VRF, the ping fails.

The ping works when specifying C2_VRF (the ping is sent to C2R1).

The ping works when specifying C1_VRF (the ping is sent to C1R1).

```
SPR1# ping 192.168.1.2
. . .
.....
Success rate is 0 percent (0/5)
SPR1# ping vrf C1_VRF 192.168.1.2
. . .
!!!!!
Success rate is 100 percent (5/5), round-trip min/avg/max = 1/1/3 ms
SPR1# ping vrf C2_VRF 192.168.1.2
. . .
!!!!!
Success rate is 100 percent (5/5), round-trip min/avg/max = 1/1/3 ms
SPR1# ping vrf C3_VRF 192.168.1.2
. . .
!!!!!
Success rate is 100 percent (5/5), round-trip min/avg/max = 1/1/2 ms
```

The ping works when specifying C3_VRF (the ping is sent to C3R1).

The global routing instance and routing table

Even when using VRFs, the router can have interfaces that aren't assigned to any particular VRF. These interfaces are part of the *global routing instance*, and their associated routes are part of the *global routing table*—this is the "normal" routing table you can view with **show ip route** (without specifying a VRF). If you issue a ping without specifying a VRF, the router will search for the ping's destination in the global routing table. However, in our example network, all interfaces are assigned to specific VRF instances and none to the global routing instance, so the global routing table does not contain any routes.

Although VRF configuration is not included on the exam, remember these key takeaways that we demonstrated with this basic configuration:

- VRF divides a physical router into multiple virtual routers (VRFs), each with its own routing table.

- VRF allows for the use of overlapping subnets on the same physical router (although they must be in different VRFs).
- Traffic in one VRF will only be forwarded within the same VRF, not to different VRFs (or the global routing instance).

17.3 Cloud computing

Now that we've covered the foundational technologies of VMs, containers, and VRF, we're almost ready to ascend into the cloud. These virtualization technologies underpin the vast and scalable architectures of the cloud, enabling the dynamic provisioning, management, and deployment capabilities that are characteristic of cloud computing.

But before we look at cloud computing, let's briefly consider the bedrock of traditional IT infrastructure: on-premises and colocation setups. *On-premises* (often abbreviated as *on-prem*) solutions represent the classic approach in which a company's infrastructure (servers and key network devices) is located within its own facilities, offering complete control over the IT environment. All equipment is purchased and owned by the company using it, and the company is responsible for the necessary space, power, cooling, and physical security.

In contrast, *colocation* services allow a business to rent space in third-party data centers to house its infrastructure. While the business is still responsible for purchasing and operating the servers, the necessary space, power, and cooling are provided by the data center, as well as robust physical security. The proximity to the colocation data center's other customers also has the benefit of facilitating connections between customers, enabling them to share resources efficiently. Figure 17.10 shows such a setup.

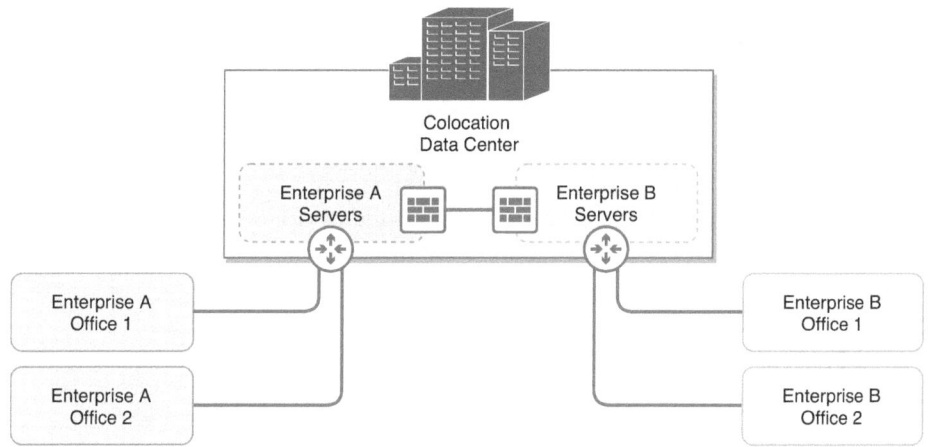

Figure 17.10   Two customers (Enterprise A and Enterprise B) house their servers in a colocation data center. They connect their networks in the data center, allowing them to share resources.

Cloud computing is a third approach that provides on-demand access to shared computing resources over a network. It provides an alternative to on-prem and colocation solutions that is not only hugely popular but is also continuing to grow year on year. In the rest of this section, we'll explore exactly what cloud computing is, covering its essential characteristics, service models, and deployment models.

The NIST definition of cloud computing

In 2011, the American National Institute of Standards and Technology (NIST) published a paper titled "The NIST Definition of Cloud Computing." Despite being published over a decade ago, it remains a cornerstone for understanding cloud computing fundamentals. The PDF file is seven pages in length, but the actual substance of the paper is only the last two pages. In this section, I will mainly expand upon and provide diagrams to help clarify the contents of the NIST's paper, but I highly recommend reading the paper yourself; you can access it for free at https://mng.bz/Y7vB.

17.3.1 *The essential characteristics of cloud computing*

So what exactly is cloud computing? How can you identify if a particular service is cloud computing or not? The NIST defines five essential characteristics of cloud computing:

- On-demand self-service
- Broad network access
- Resource pooling
- Rapid elasticity
- Measured service

These five characteristics are essential to understanding cloud computing, so let's walk through them. *On-demand self-service* means that the customer is able to use the service (or stop using the service) as needed, without direct human interaction with the service provider—for example, via a web portal. Figure 17.11 shows the Amazon Web Services (AWS) web portal; AWS is the most popular public cloud service provider. Some other major players in the business are (in order of market share, with AWS at the top):

- Microsoft Azure
- Google Cloud Platform (GCP)
- Alibaba Cloud
- IBM Cloud

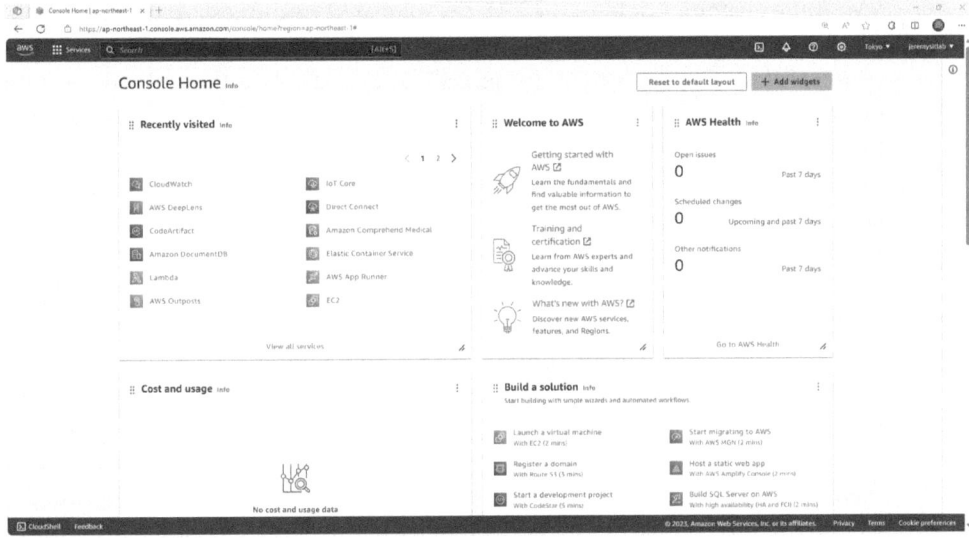

Figure 17.11   The AWS web portal through which customers can access services. Human-to-human interaction with AWS isn't necessary.

Broad network access means that the services should be made available over standard network connections (i.e., the internet or private WAN connections) and should be accessible by many kinds of devices, including mobile phones, desktop PCs, etc. Figure 17.12 shows some ways an enterprise can connect to cloud resources: a private WAN connection, a simple internet connection, or an IPsec VPN tunnel.

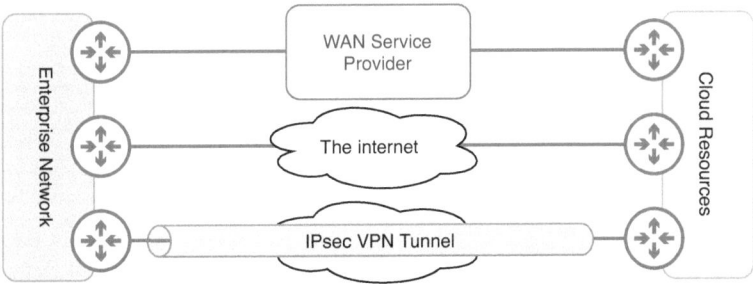

Figure 17.12   Cloud resources are accessible over standard network connections. For example, private WAN connections, simple internet connections, or internet VPNs can be used to access cloud resources.

Resource pooling means that a shared pool of resources is provided to serve multiple customers. When a customer requests a service, the resources to fulfill that request are dynamically allocated from the shared pool. AWS, for example, has data centers all over the world with countless powerful servers. When a customer creates a VM on AWS, a small portion of that huge resource pool is dynamically allocated to the new

VM. If the customer deletes the VM, the allocated resources are released back into the pool.

Rapid elasticity means that customers can quickly scale their cloud resources up or down as needed. This scaling can often be automated, adjusting to resource demands in real time. To understand the utility of rapid elasticity, imagine an e-commerce business gearing up for the Christmas season. Anticipating increased website traffic, the company can easily scale up its cloud resources to accommodate the surge. Once the holiday rush calms down, they can just as easily scale down, ensuring they only pay for the resources they need. Without the cloud, the business would be forced to maintain enough physical servers to support their peak periods year-round, resulting in unnecessary costs for servers that are underutilized most of the year.

The final essential characteristic is *measured service*, which means that the cloud service provider measures the customer's use of cloud resources, providing transparency for both the provider and the customer. The customer is typically charged based on their usage (for example, X dollars per gigabyte of storage per day). Figure 17.13 shows a billing report on GCP, showing the cost increasing and decreasing according to use.

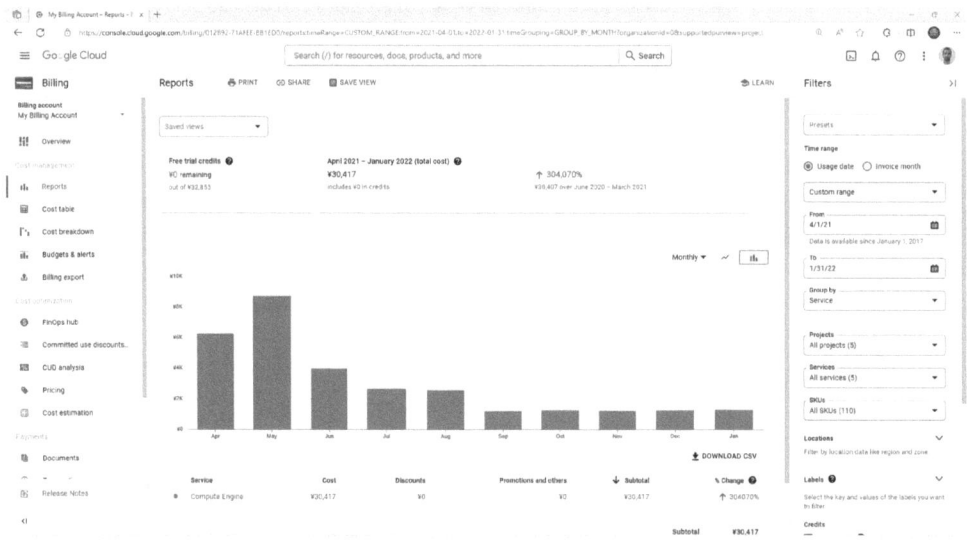

Figure 17.13   A GCP billing report. Cloud providers like GCP measure customers' resource usage and charge according to that usage.

17.3.2 *Cloud service models*

In a traditional on-prem or colocation setup, an enterprise purchases its own resources, using them according to its specific needs. Cloud computing service providers like AWS, Microsoft Azure, and GCP offer these resources—servers, storage, networking, and even entire platforms and applications—as services on a subscription basis. The customer benefits from access to these resources without the responsibilities of ownership and maintenance. But what kinds of services are available through these providers? Cloud service providers offer a variety of different services that can largely be categorized into three main types:

- Software as a Service (SaaS)
- Platform as a Service (PaaS)
- Infrastructure as a Service (IaaS).

Figure 17.14 illustrates what is offered by each of these cloud service models and compares them to colocation and on-prem solutions.

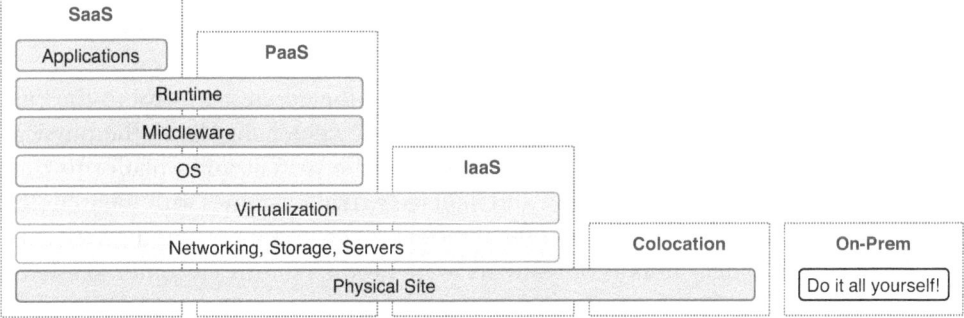

Figure 17.14   **The spectrum of what is offered in each cloud service model in comparison to colocation and on-prem solutions**

> **NOTE**   *Runtime* refers to the environment that executes application code, while *middleware* provides essential services and capabilities, such as database management systems, that enable applications to communicate and manage data.

Software as a Service (SaaS) delivers applications as a service over a network (typically the internet). Instead of installing and using applications on their own devices, users simply access them via the internet. SaaS applications run on the provider's infrastructure and are typically accessible from any device with a web browser. Some popular examples of SaaS are

- Microsoft 365 (formerly Office 365): Word, Excel, PowerPoint, Outlook, etc.
- Google Workspace (formerly G Suite): Gmail, Docs, Drive, Calendar, etc.
- Slack
- Dropbox
- Zoom

> **NOTE**   While some applications are offered primarily as SaaS, others may also provide versions that can be installed locally on individual devices.

Platform as a Service (PaaS) provides a platform for customers to develop, run, and manage applications without the complexity of building and maintaining the infrastructure typically associated with developing and launching an app. As shown in figure 17.14, the service includes everything except the applications themselves, which the customer develops using the provided platform. They don't have the name recognition of famous SaaS products, but some popular PaaS offerings are AWS Lambda, Azure App Service, and Google App Engine.

Infrastructure as a Service (IaaS) offers essential computing resources, storage, and networking capabilities on demand. Customers can create virtual machines, install OSs, run applications, etc., on the provider's infrastructure, customizing the CPU, RAM, and storage for each virtual machine and configuring their interconnections to form a virtual network. Some popular examples are AWS EC2, Azure Virtual Machines, and Google Compute Engine.

Of these three cloud service models, IaaS provides the greatest control to the customer. The service provider is responsible for the data center that hosts the physical infrastructure, the physical infrastructure itself, and the virtualization platforms that enable customers to freely create, run, and manage virtual machines with their choice of OSs and applications. On the other end of the spectrum, SaaS provides the least control; the service provider offers a complete software product for the customer to use.

> **NOTE** In addition to SaaS, PaaS, and IaaS, there are a variety of services with similar *XaaS* names, but for the CCNA exam, you should know these primary three.

17.3.3 *Cloud deployment models*

When you think of "the cloud," cloud service providers like AWS probably come to mind. However, the NIST defines four distinct cloud deployment models, encompassing a variety of cloud environments:

- Public cloud
- Private cloud
- Community cloud
- Hybrid cloud

AWS, Azure, GCP, and similar services fit into the public cloud deployment model—the most common of the four—but understanding all four deployment models is essential. Let's take a look at each of them.

In a *public cloud* deployment, the infrastructure, which is located on the cloud provider's premises, is available for open use by the public (for a fee, of course); anyone who wants to use the cloud resources is free to become a customer. This is by far the most common deployment and is used by individuals and organizations of all sizes. Figure 17.15 shows customers of various sizes connected to different public cloud providers.

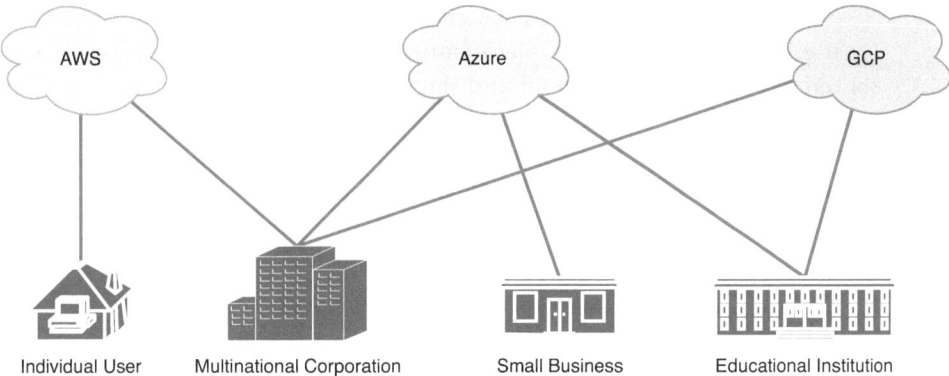

Figure 17.15 Customers of all sizes can connect to and use public cloud resources.

In a *private cloud* deployment, the cloud infrastructure is provided for use by a single organization—typically a very large organization (i.e., government or large business). The cloud resources can be used by different consumers within that organization (i.e., different departments of a business) but are not available for use by those outside of the specific organization.

> **NOTE** Private cloud infrastructure may exist on or off the premises of the organization that uses it. Cloud and on-prem are not always mutually exclusive!

Although the cloud is private—reserved for use by a single organization—it may be owned by a third party. For example, AWS provides private cloud services for the US Department of Defense (DoD). Figure 17.16 depicts the DoD connecting to a private cloud provided by AWS, separate from the AWS public cloud.

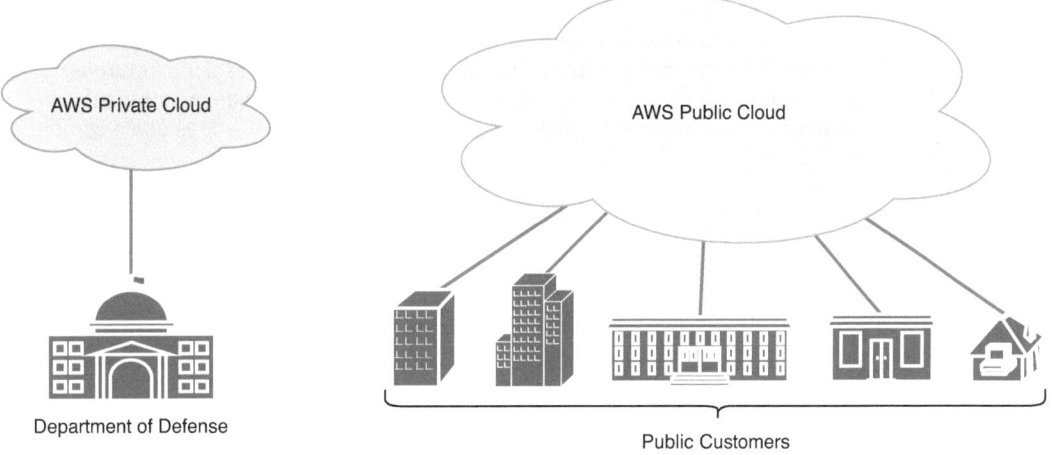

Figure 17.16 AWS provides private cloud services to the US Department of Defense, separate from the AWS public cloud.

A *community cloud* is a collaborative effort where the cloud infrastructure is reserved for use by consumers in multiple organizations. This provides a balance between the shared model of a public cloud and the dedicated resources of a private cloud. The infrastructure itself can be managed by one or more of the organizations or a third-party provider and can exist on or off the premises of any of the member organizations.

The final deployment model is *hybrid cloud*, which is any combination of two or more of the previous models. An example use case for a hybrid cloud is a private cloud that can offload work to a public cloud when necessary when the private cloud does not have sufficient resources.

The advantages of cloud computing

There are various reasons why so many modern enterprises are moving significant portions of their IT infrastructure to the cloud. Here are some advantages of cloud computing:

- *Cost efficiency*—Upfront capital expenditures for hardware, software, and data centers are significantly reduced or even eliminated.
- *Global scaling*—Cloud services can scale globally at a rapid pace. Services can be set up and offered to customers from a geographic location close to them, reducing latency.
- *Speed and agility*—Services are provided on demand, and vast amounts of resources can be provisioned within minutes if needed.
- *Productivity*—By outsourcing physical infrastructure concerns, cloud services reduce the need for labor-intensive tasks associated with hardware setup and other routine IT management chores.
- *Reliability*—Backing up systems in the cloud is simple, and data can be mirrored at multiple sites in diverse geographic locations to support disaster recovery (i.e., if a natural disaster affects one site).

Despite these advantages, moving infrastructure to the cloud is not always the correct answer. If you follow tech-related news, you will occasionally see stories about companies that gained huge savings by moving their infrastructure out of the cloud, returning to on-prem/colocation setups. Each organization should carefully consider whether moving its infrastructure to the cloud will deliver a net benefit; many organizations use a combination of all three.

Summary

- VLANs and VPNs are forms of network virtualization. VLANs segment a physical LAN into separate logical LANs, whereas VPNs create secure, private network connections over shared or public networks like the internet.
- Virtual machines (VMs) and containers are also examples of virtualization, allowing operating systems and applications to run in isolated environments on a server.

- Before virtualization, a physical server would run a single operating system (OS). This meant that all of the hardware resources were tied to that one OS and its applications. This often led to resource underutilization.

- Virtual machines (VMs) break the one-to-one relationship of hardware to OS, allowing multiple OSs to run on a single physical server.

- VMs are facilitated by a *hypervisor* that sits between the hardware and the VMs, managing and allocating hardware resources to each VM. Another name for a hypervisor is a *virtual machine monitor* (VMM).

- A type 1 hypervisor is installed directly on the underlying physical hardware. Other names for this are *bare-metal* or *native* hypervisor.

- Type 1 hypervisors are most often used for server virtualization in data center environments (including the cloud). By interacting directly with the physical hardware, they provide very efficient use of those resources.

- A type 2 hypervisor runs as a program on an OS, like a regular computer application. The OS running directly on the hardware is called the *host OS*, and an OS running in a VM is called a *guest OS*.

- Type 2 hypervisors use hardware resources less efficiently than type 1 hypervisors, but their advantage lies in their ease of setup and use. They are more common on personal-use devices for software development, testing, and educational purposes.

- Each VM operates as an independent host on the network. Instead of a physical network interface card (NIC), it has a virtual NIC (vNIC).

- To manage network traffic to and from VMs, the hypervisor uses a *virtual switch*, which forwards frames between the vNICs of the VMs and the physical NICs of the host machine.

- Just like a physical switch, a virtual switch's ports can operate in access or trunk mode, enabling the use of VLANs to segment the VMs.

- While VMs offer full hardware virtualization, providing complete OSs for their applications, containers provide a more agile approach.

- A *container* is a lightweight, stand-alone package that includes everything needed to run a particular application.

- Containers are more lightweight than VMs, requiring less overhead. Instead of running an independent OS, the container only contains an application and its dependencies. Containers do not run independent OSs.

- Containers run on a *container engine* such as Docker Engine. The container engine runs on a host OS (usually Linux).

- A container orchestrator (such as Kubernetes) is typically used to automate the deployment, management, and scaling of containers.

- Virtual Routing and Forwarding (VRF) segments a router into multiple virtual routers. Service providers often use VRF to allow a customer's traffic to travel over shared infrastructure while remaining isolated from other customers.
- Each VRF virtual router is called a *VRF instance* or simply a *VRF*.
- Each VRF is isolated from other VRFs; traffic in one VRF cannot be forwarded out of an interface that belongs to another VRF.
- VRF is often used to enable MPLS L3VPNs. VRF without MPLS is called *VRF-lite*.
- Use `ip vrf` `vrf-name` to create a VRF and `show ip vrf` to view the existing VRFs.
- Use `ip vrf forwarding` `vrf-name` in interface config mode to assign an interface to a particular VRF.
- The router builds a separate routing table for each VRF. Use `show ip route vrf` `vrf-name` to view the routing table of the specified VRF.
- Before the cloud, traditional IT infrastructure was typically a combination of on-premises and colocation setups.
- *On-premises* (on-prem) means the company's infrastructure (servers and key network devices) are located within its own facilities, offering complete control.
- All equipment is purchased by the company using it, and the company is responsible for the necessary space, power, cooling, and physical security.
- Colocation services allow a business to rent space in third-party data centers to house its infrastructure.
- Cloud computing is a third approach that provides on-demand access to shared computing resources over a network (such as the internet).
- The five essential characteristics of cloud computing are
  - *On-demand self-service*—The customer is able to use (or stop using) the service as needed without direct human-to-human interaction.
  - *Broad network access*—The services should be made available over standard network connections and accessible by many kinds of devices.
  - *Resource pooling*—A shared pool of resources is provided to serve multiple customers. The resources are dynamically allocated as needed.
  - *Rapid elasticity*—Customers can quickly scale their cloud resources up or down as needed.
  - *Measured service*—The cloud service provider measures the customer use of cloud resources and typically charges based on the usage.
- The three main cloud service models are Software as a Service (SaaS), Platform as a Service (PaaS), and Infrastructure as a Service (IaaS).
- SaaS delivers applications as a service over a network (typically the internet). Instead of installing applications on their own devices, users simply access them over the internet. Popular examples are Microsoft 365 and Google Workspace.

- PaaS provides a platform for customers to develop, run, and manage applications without the complexity of building and maintaining the necessary infrastructure.
- IaaS offers essential computing resources, storage, and networking capabilities on demand. Customers can create VMs, install Oss, run applications, etc., on the provider's infrastructure.
- The four cloud deployment models are public, private, community, and hybrid.
- In a public cloud deployment, the infrastructure, which is located on the cloud provider's premises, is available for use by the public. Popular examples are Amazon Web Services (AWS), Microsoft Azure, and Google Cloud Platform (GCP).
- In a private cloud deployment, the cloud infrastructure is provided for use by a single organization. The cloud infrastructure may be owned by a third party and may be on or off the premises of the organization that uses the cloud.
- A community cloud is a collaborative effort where the cloud infrastructure is reserved for use by consumers in multiple organizations. The infrastructure can be managed by one or more of the member organizations or a third party and can exist on or off the premises of any of the member organizations.
- A hybrid cloud is a combination of two or more of the other deployment models (for example, a private cloud that can offload work to a public cloud when necessary).

Part 4

Wireless LANs

In part 4 of this volume, we shift our focus away from wired communications to the world of wireless LANs. Instead of encoding messages into electrical or light signals sent along Ethernet cables, wireless devices encode messages into electromagnetic waves that propagate through the air all around us. Compared to wired LANs, wireless LANs present various challenges but also provide a degree of mobility and flexibility that simply isn't possible when communicating via cables.

Chapter 18 begins this part of the book by introducing wireless LANs, the challenges they present, the characteristics and behaviors of electromagnetic waves, the radio frequency bands used for wireless LANs, and how devices connect to form wireless LANs. In chapter 19, we move on to examine wireless LAN architectures, focusing on autonomous wireless access points (APs)—standalone APs managed on a one-by-one basis—and lightweight APs (LWAPs), which are centrally controlled via a wireless LAN controller (WLC); the latter option is the option of choice for most enterprises.

Chapter 20 covers wireless LAN security, a critical element of any wireless LAN. Unlike wired LANs, wireless signals propagate through the air all around the transmitter and can be received by any device within range, so security measures like encryption are a necessity. Finally, in chapter 21 we will get hands-on, configuring wireless LANs in the graphical user interface (GUI) of a Cisco WLC. Wireless LANs are a major component of the CCNA exam, and they present many new concepts to grasp. Part 4 aims to walk you through these concepts step by step, covering the essential points that Cisco expects you to know for the CCNA exam.

Wireless LAN fundamentals

This chapter covers

- The challenges of using air as a communication medium
- The characteristics of radio frequency
- Wireless LAN standards as defined by IEEE 802.11
- Connecting wireless devices using different kinds of service sets

It's time to break our communications out of their wired constraints and explore a new medium for communication: air. Just as copper twisted-pair and glass fiber-optic cables provide a medium to transmit encoded messages using electricity and light, the air all around us (or, more precisely, the space around us that happens to be filled with air) provides an alternative medium to transmit messages using electromagnetic waves.

In this chapter and the three that follow it, we will cover various aspects of wireless LANs as defined by IEEE 802.11—better known as *Wi-Fi*. This chapter starts by covering the foundational concepts of wireless LANs and how devices communicate with radio frequency waves. We will cover the following CCNA exam topics:

- 1.1 Explain the role and function of network components
  - 1.1.d Access points
- 1.11 Describe wireless principles

18.1   *Wireless communications*

Wired LANs as defined by IEEE 802.3—better known as Ethernet—have been a major focus of both volumes of this book up to this point, and for good reason: Ethernet is the dominant technology used in modern wired network connections and is a key topic of the CCNA exam. Ethernet defines standards at Layers 1 and 2 of the TCP/IP model: physical cables, methods of encoding data signals over these cables, the Ethernet frame format, and various other functions.

Wireless LANs are defined by IEEE 802.11. Like Ethernet, 802.11 defines standards at Layers 1 and 2 of the TCP/IP model: the precise frequencies that can be used for wireless LANs, how to encode data signals in electromagnetic waves over the air, the 802.11 frame format, etc.

> **NOTE**   Wireless LAN is sometimes abbreviated as *WLAN*. *Wired* and *wireless* both start with *W*, so that might seem confusing, but a wired LAN is typically just called a LAN.

Figure 18.1 demonstrates the similar roles of Ethernet and 802.11: they both address how to send a message to another device connected to the same physical medium. Thanks to the modular nature of the TCP/IP model, Layers 3 and above operate identically regardless of which Layer 1/2 protocols are used.

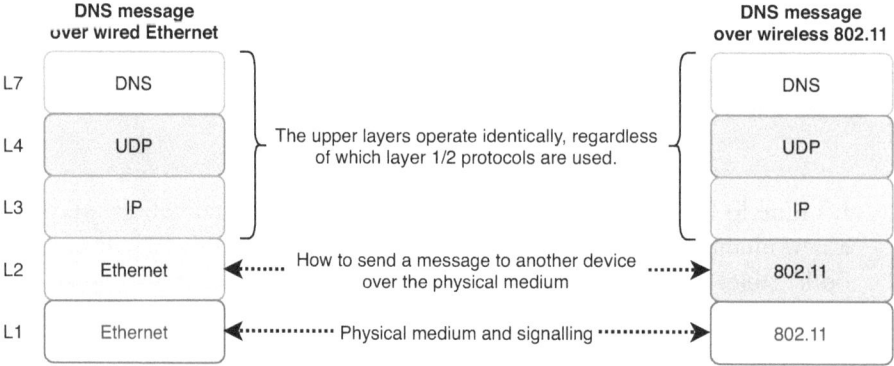

Figure 18.1   Ethernet and 802.11 serve similar functions: how to send a message to another device over a particular physical medium. Layers 3 and above operate identically, regardless of which Layer 1/2 protocols are used.

What's Wi-Fi?

Most people know 802.11 wireless LANs by the name *Wi-Fi*. However, Wi-Fi is not an official name used by the IEEE; it is a trademark of the Wi-Fi Alliance, an organization that tests and certifies equipment for 802.11 standards compliance. An organization whose products pass the testing and certification process can mark their equipment as "Wi-Fi Certified." The goal of this process is to ensure interoperability between different vendors' devices (although a device's lack of Wi-Fi certification doesn't necessarily mean that it is incompatible with other devices). For the sake of accuracy, I will avoid the name Wi-Fi unless specifically referring to the Wi-Fi Alliance's certifications.

18.1.1 *The challenges of wireless communications*

Copper and fiber-optic Ethernet cables are *bounded media*—the signals are confined to the cables, providing a controlled pathway for data transmission. This physical boundary offers some advantages in terms of security (only the device at the other end of the cable receives the signal) and signal consistency (the signal is less susceptible to interference).

In contrast, the air used to transmit wireless signals is an *unbounded medium*. Unlike wired connections, wireless signals propagate freely in open space, radiating in all directions from the source. The unbounded nature of wireless communication introduces both opportunities and challenges. On one hand, it allows for greater mobility and flexibility, as devices don't need to be physically connected with a network cable. However, it also brings various challenges. Here are some key examples:

- All devices within range of a wireless device receive that device's signals.
- Wireless devices must contend for airtime.
- Signal interference can be a major issue.
- Wireless communications are regulated by various international and national bodies.
- Wireless signal coverage area must be considered.

Let's walk through each of these challenges. First, all devices within sufficient range of a wireless device receive that device's signals. In fact, wireless communication is sometimes likened to wired communication via an Ethernet hub—all devices connected to a hub receive all frames from other devices connected to the hub. Figure 18.2 shows this similarity.

This means that data privacy within a wireless LAN is a greater concern than it is in a wired LAN. For this reason, communications are usually encrypted, even within a LAN; we'll cover more about wireless LAN security in chapter 20.

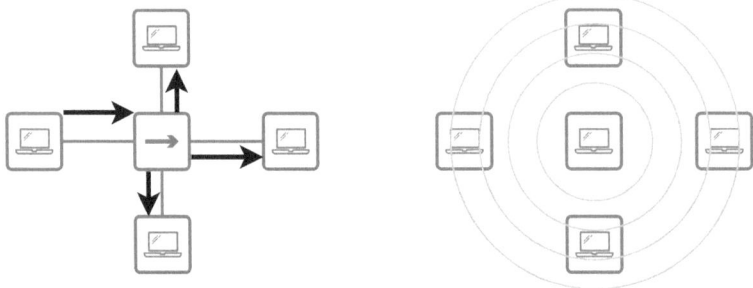

Figure 18.2   Similar to how frames are flooded to all devices connected to a hub, all devices within range of a wireless device receive its signals.

Another consequence of using an unbounded medium is that devices must operate in half-duplex mode; only one device can transmit at a time, or their signals will collide. Wireless devices must contend for airtime—they compete for the chance to transmit data over a shared medium. This half-duplex nature is a significant factor in why wireless networks often do not match the speeds of wired networks using switches (which operate in full-duplex mode).

While wired devices connected to a hub use Carrier-Sense Multiple Access with Collision Detection (CSMA/CD) to detect and recover from collisions, wireless devices use a similar protocol called *Carrier-Sense Multiple Access with Collision Avoidance* (CSMA/CA). Figure 18.3 shows a simplified version of the CSMA/CA process. After preparing a frame for transmission, the device will listen to see if the channel is free. If the channel is busy, the device will wait a random (short) period of time before checking again. The device will transmit the frame only when it senses the channel is free.

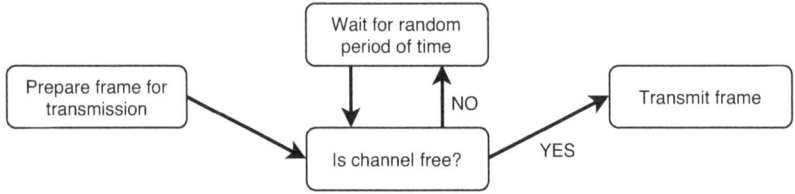

Figure 18.3   The CSMA/CA process. To avoid collisions, a device will listen to ensure the channel is free before transmitting a frame.

NOTE   Although CSMA/CA attempts to avoid collisions, if two devices happen to transmit simultaneously, the frames can still collide, resulting in an incoherent signal. In such a case, the devices will have to retransmit their frames.

The third challenge of wireless communications is signal interference, which can significantly impact network performance. For example, wireless LANs from neighboring offices, homes, or apartments operating on the same or overlapping frequency ranges can cause interference. Interference can disrupt the clarity and integrity of the signal, leading to data transmission errors and reduced network performance in the LAN. Managing interference is a critical aspect of wireless network design, requiring careful channel selection.

NOTE It's not only other 802.11 networks that can cause interference; other devices like microwave ovens, cordless phones, and Bluetooth devices operating in the same frequency range can disrupt wireless LAN communications.

Another challenge stems from the complex landscape of national and international regulations. Each country has its own regulatory body, such as the US Federal Communications Commission (FCC), that governs the use of radio frequencies and sets standards for wireless communication. These regulations are necessary to manage the electromagnetic spectrum and prevent interference between different types of services, such as cellular signals, satellite communications, and wireless LANs.

Although international bodies like the International Telecommunications Union (ITU) work to coordinate the allocation of the radio frequency spectrum across countries to ensure consistent use, there are still differences between countries, and adhering to these regulations is a legal necessity. For this reason, wireless networking equipment used in one country might be legally prohibited in another.

The final challenge we'll consider is the signal coverage area of a wireless LAN. Similar to how cable length must be considered in wired LANs, coverage area is an essential consideration in wireless LANs. As wireless signals propagate through space, they lose strength; this is called *free-space path loss* (FSPL). In addition to FSPL, signals can be influenced by a variety of factors; these include reflection off surfaces, diffraction around obstacles, scattering due to irregularities in the medium, and others.

How far do wireless signals travel?

The real question here is "How far can a wireless signal travel and maintain enough strength for the receiver to effectively distinguish the signal from background noise and decode the information?" Indoors, this is typically up to 150 feet (46 meters). Outdoors, it can extend beyond 300 feet (91 meters), but these distances vary greatly depending on factors like the signal's frequency, transmitter power, antenna type, and environmental conditions such as physical obstructions.

18.1.2 *Wave behaviors*

The electromagnetic waves that are used to encode wireless signals are influenced by the media they pass through and objects they encounter. In this section, we'll examine five phenomena that must be considered in a wireless LAN design, as shown in figure 18.4.

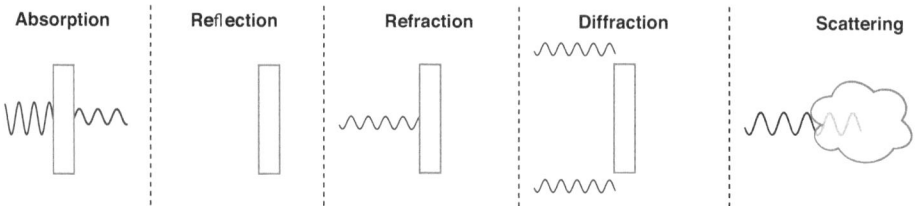

Figure 18.4   Phenomena affecting the behavior of electromagnetic waves include absorption by a medium, reflection off surfaces, refraction (bending) as waves pass through a medium, diffraction around obstacles, and scattering from irregularities.

Absorption occurs when a wave passes through a medium and is converted into heat, weakening the signal. For example, a wireless signal passing through a wall can cause significant attenuation, particularly if the wall is made of a dense material. This can prevent devices on the other side of the wall from receiving a coherent signal.

NOTE   *Attenuation* is the weakening of a signal.

Reflection happens when a wave bounces off a surface rather than passing through it; this is the same phenomenon as light reflecting off a mirror. Metal surfaces are common culprits, as they are highly reflective of radio waves. Reflection is the reason wireless reception is usually poor in elevators; the signal bounces off the metal, and very little penetrates into the elevator.

Refraction occurs when a wave passes from one medium to another one with a different density, altering the wave's speed and causing it to bend. A common everyday occurrence of refraction is the apparent shift in the position of an object in water when viewed from above; this is due to the light waves bending as they move from water to air.

Diffraction is the bending and spreading of waves around the edges of an obstacle, such as a wall. This enables wireless communication even when there isn't a clear line of sight between the transmitter and receiver. In urban environments, diffraction often allows signals to reach street level and indoor areas that are not in direct view of the cell tower or wireless access point.

The final phenomenon is *scattering*, which occurs when a wave encounters a surface or medium with irregularities that cause the wave to spread out erratically. Common causes of scattering are dust, smog, water vapor, and textured surfaces. Scattering can cause signal attenuation as it disperses the signal's energy in various directions.

When designing a wireless LAN, it's essential to account for the various wave behaviors that affect wireless signals. Absorption by walls, reflection from surfaces, refraction through different media, diffraction around obstacles, and scattering due to irregularities all play a role in shaping the coverage and reliability of a wireless network.

EXAM TIP   For the CCNA exam, you are not expected to be able to design a wireless LAN that accounts for these various factors. However, you should have a basic understanding of each.

18.2 Radio frequency

To send a wireless signal, a device applies an alternating electric current to an antenna, which in turn produces fluctuating electromagnetic fields that radiate out as waves; these are called *electromagnetic waves*. Two key measurements of an electromagnetic wave are its amplitude and frequency.

18.2.1 Amplitude and frequency

Amplitude and frequency are two fundamental characteristics of electromagnetic waves. *Amplitude* measures the maximum strength of the electric and magnetic fields of a wave and is associated with how much energy the wave carries; basically, higher amplitude means a stronger signal. If the amplitude of a signal is too low, the receiver won't be able to distinguish a coherent message from the signal. Figure 18.5 shows two waves with different amplitudes: the wave represented by the solid line has a higher amplitude than the dotted one.

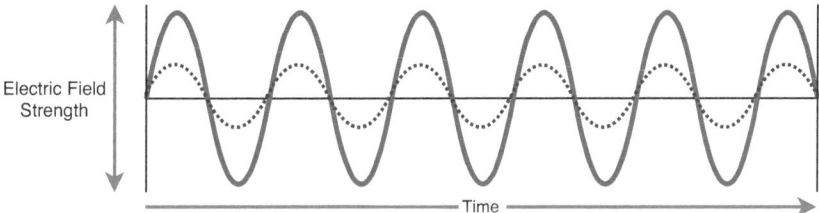

Figure 18.5 **Waves with higher amplitude carry stronger signals, indicated by greater electric and magnetic field strengths.**

> **NOTE** Figure 18.5 only shows the electric field of each wave, but each has an equivalent magnetic field (hence the name *electromagnetic wave*) that oscillates perpendicular to the electric field.

Frequency measures how quickly the strength of the wave's electric and magnetic fields oscillates and is measured in *hertz* (Hz)—the number of oscillations per second. Like bits and bytes, hertz are typically measured in thousands, millions, billions, and trillions (or even greater):

- *kHz (kilohertz)*—1000 cycles per second
- *MHz (megahertz)*—1,000,000 cycles per second
- *GHz (gigahertz)*—1,000,000,000 cycles per second
- *THz (terahertz)*—1,000,000,000,000 cycles per second

Figure 18.6 shows two waves with different frequencies: the wave represented by the dotted line has a higher frequency than the solid one. Notice that, despite having different frequencies, the waves have identical amplitudes.

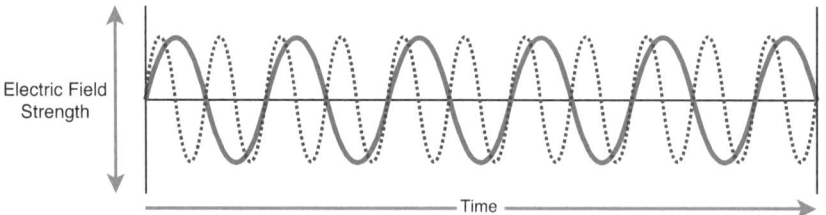

Figure 18.6   Waves with higher frequency oscillate at a greater rate. Frequency is measured in hertz (Hz), which is the number of oscillations per second.

A related concept is *period*, which is the amount of time it takes for one full oscillation. Figure 18.7 shows a wave with a frequency of 4 Hz and, therefore, a period of 0.25 seconds—each oscillation takes 0.25 seconds.

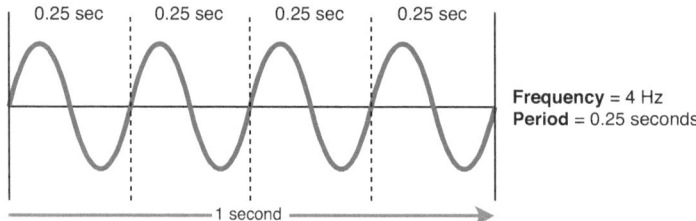

Figure 18.7   A wave with a frequency of 4 Hz. This means it completes four full oscillations every second, resulting in a period of 0.25 seconds per oscillation.

In the context of radio waves, frequency determines a wave's position within the electromagnetic spectrum and has a major effect on how the signal behaves as it propagates through the air and other media. In wireless LANs, higher frequencies can typically support higher data transfer rates and are less crowded with other wireless devices. However, they are also more susceptible to absorption by obstacles. On the other hand, lower frequencies penetrate better through obstacles and can, therefore, cover larger distances. However, lower frequencies typically support lower transfer rates and are more crowded with other wireless devices. In the next section, we'll examine the concepts of the electromagnetic spectrum, radio frequency's position in the spectrum, and the different bands and channels used by 802.11 wireless LANs.

18.2.2   *RF bands and channels*

The *electromagnetic spectrum* is the entire range of electromagnetic radiation, such as AM and FM radio, ultraviolet light, X-rays, and gamma rays. Figure 18.8 shows the electromagnetic spectrum and radio frequency's position within it.

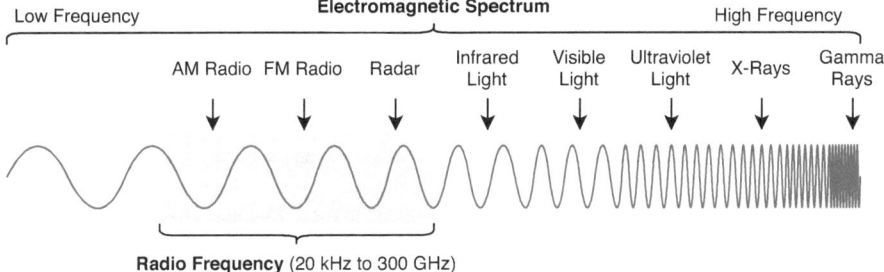

Figure 18.8   The electromagnetic spectrum and examples of different wave types. Radio frequency is from around 20 kHz to around 300 GHz.

NOTE   Figure 18.8 is designed to show a general progression from lower to higher frequencies across the electromagnetic spectrum. The placement of each example doesn't represent its precise frequency value.

Radio frequency (RF) is a segment of the electromagnetic spectrum generally defined as ranging from around 20 kHz to around 300 GHz. RF is used for a variety of purposes, from AM and FM radio to microwaves and radar. However, most relevant to this chapter are 802.11 wireless LANs. Three bands within the RF range are used for wireless LANs: the 2.4 GHz band, the 5 GHz band, and the newer 6 GHz band, introduced to wireless LANs in 2020.

NOTE   A *band* is a specific range of frequencies, such as the AM radio band, FM radio band, and the 802.11 wireless LAN bands.

THE 2.4 GHZ BAND

The 2.4 GHz band spans from 2.4 to 2.495 GHz and is widely used for wireless communications due to its lower frequency, which enables better penetration through obstacles compared to the 5 GHz and 6 GHz bands. However, this band is also used for other technologies, such as Bluetooth, microwave ovens, cordless telephones, and many others. This means that it can sometimes be crowded, leading to congestion and interference.

The 2.4 GHz band is divided into 14 individual channels. Like a band, a *channel* is a specific range of frequencies—you can think of a channel as a smaller division of a band. For wireless communication to occur, both the transmitting and receiving devices must be tuned to the same channel, enabling them to "speak" and "listen" on the same frequency range.

Each channel has a defined center frequency and a standard width of 20 MHz, although older standards use 22 MHz. Wireless devices communicate using these channels, so careful channel selection is critical to minimize interference. Figure 18.9 shows the 14 channels of the 2.4 GHz band (you don't have to memorize the center frequency values).

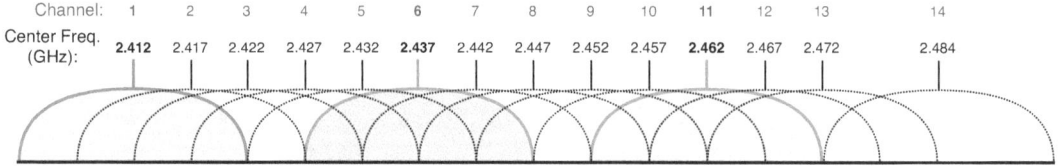

Figure 18.9   Channels in the 2.4 GHz band. There are 14 channels in total. Because many channels in the 2.4 GHz band overlap, channels 1, 6, and 11 should be used to avoid interference.

> **NOTE**   Not all channels in the 2.4 GHz band can be used in all countries. For example, only channels 1 to 11 are commonly allowed in the United States/Canada, while most countries allow 1 to 13. Channel 14 is allowed in Japan, but only when using an older 802.11 standard.

As figure 18.9 shows, there is significant overlap between the 2.4 GHz channels. In a wireless LAN that needs multiple APs for full coverage, it's important to use non-overlapping channels to avoid interference. If adjacent access points use the same channel, devices not only have to contend for airtime with other devices using the same access point but with devices using neighboring access points too. Channels 1, 6, and 11 are recommended, as highlighted in figure 18.9. However, in countries that allow up to channel 13, a layout using channels 1, 5, 9, and 13 is also possible. Figure 18.10 shows both layouts.

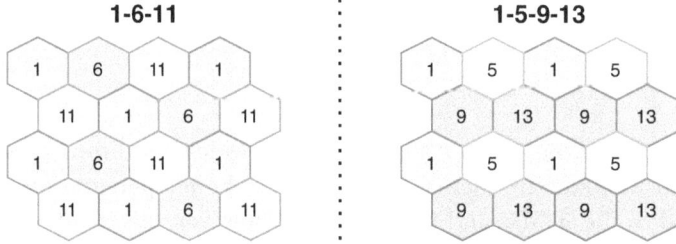

Figure 18.10   Non-overlapping channel layout options in the 2.4 GHz band. Each hexagon represents a wireless access point's coverage area.

> **EXAM TIP**   The key takeaways for the CCNA exam are that the 2.4 GHz band uses overlapping channels and that you should use a 1–6–11 layout to avoid interference (1–5–9–13 is also possible in most countries outside of the U.S./Canada).

THE 5 GHZ BAND

The 5 GHz band, ranging from approximately 5.150 to 5.895 GHz (depending on the country), is the second frequency band widely used for wireless LANs. Compared to the 2.4 GHz band, the 5 GHz is generally less crowded and not as prone to interference from common household devices.

However, signals in the 5 GHz band don't penetrate walls and other barriers as well as the 2.4 GHz band. This can be both a benefit and a drawback. On the upside, it means that 5 GHz signals from neighboring rooms and buildings are less likely to cause interference. On the downside, this can limit the coverage area of 5 GHz signals.

Unlike the 2.4 GHz band, channels in the 5 GHz band are non-overlapping when using the standard 20 MHz width, which simplifies the channel selection process when setting up multiple wireless access points. These channels can be combined to form wider channels of 40, 80, or 160 MHz, supporting higher data transfer rates (although resulting in fewer available channels). Figure 18.11 shows the various 5 GHz channels, demonstrating how they can be combined to make wider channels. The number written in each channel is the *channel number* that identifies it. I include them only for reference; you don't have to memorize them.

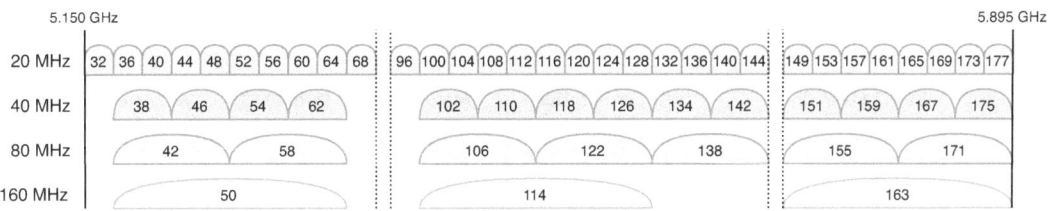

Figure 18.11   Channels in the 5 GHz band. Twenty MHz channels can be combined into wider channels of 40, 80, or 160 MHz to support greater data transfer rates.

NOTE   The available channels in the 5 GHz band can vary greatly depending on the country, so the channels shown in figure 18.11 do not apply everywhere.

THE 6 GHZ BAND

The 6 GHz band is the newest addition to the 802.11 wireless LAN frequency bands, ranging from 5.925 GHz to 7.125 GHz (notably, its low and high ends are both beyond the 6 GHz range). This band provides even more non-overlapping channels than the 5 GHz band. The standard channel width is 20 GHz, but channels can be combined to form wider channels of 40, 80, 160, or even 320 MHz, enhancing data transfer rates. Figure 18.12 shows the different channels in the 6 GHz band.

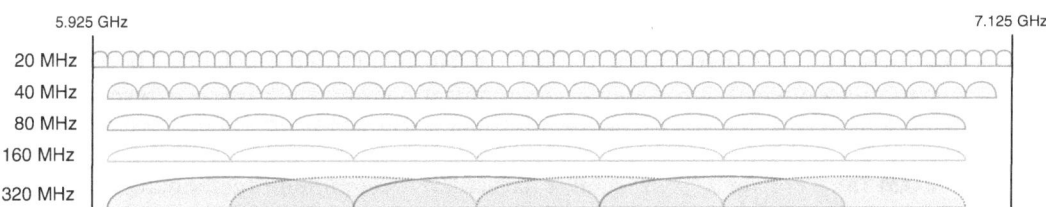

Figure 18.12   Channels in the 6 GHz band. 20 MHz channels can be combined into wider channels of 40, 80, 160, or 320 MHz to support greater data transfer rates. Note that there is some overlap between 320 MHz channels.

The 6 GHz band was adopted in 2020 in the 802.11ax standard, better known as *Wi-Fi 6E*, and also the new 802.11be (Wi-Fi 7) standard. Due to its relatively recent adoption, the 6 GHz band isn't as widely used as the 2.4 and 5 GHz bands. However, it's expected to alleviate the congestion found in the other bands and provide even greater data transfer rates.

18.2.3 IEEE 802.11 standards

Just as there are various 802.3 Ethernet standards designed to accommodate different network environments and objectives, with new ones continually in development to meet evolving demands (such as higher speeds), the same can be said of the 802.11 family of standards. Table 18.1 lists the major generations of 802.11 wireless LAN standards, starting from the original 802.11 standard, which was released in 1997.

Table 18.1   IEEE 802.11 wireless LAN standards

802.11 standard	Wi-Fi generation	Maximum rate (Mbps)	RF band (GHz)
802.11	-	1–2	2.4
802.11b	-	1–11	2.4
802.11a	-	6–54	5
802.11g	-	6–54	2.4
802.11n	Wi-Fi 4	72–600	2.4/5
802.11ac	Wi-Fi 5	433–6933	5
802.11ax	Wi-Fi 6	574–9608	2.4/5
	Wi-Fi 6E		6
802.11be	Wi-Fi 7	1376–46120	2.4/5/6

NOTE   Starting from the 802.11n standard, each new generation has been marketed as *Wi-Fi X*, with 802.11n as Wi-Fi 4. Although not official names, 802.11, 802.11b, 802.11a, and 802.11g are sometimes retroactively called Wi-Fi 0, 1, 2, and 3, respectively.

The maximum transfer rates listed in table 18.1 are theoretical maximums under ideal conditions and don't necessarily reflect the performance that can actually be achieved. Due to the complexities of wireless communications and the various external factors that can have an effect, in real-world applications, actual transfer rates will be lower.

EXAM TIP   For the CCNA exam, I particularly recommend memorizing which standards use which RF bands. For most CCNA exam domains, you don't have to memorize IEEE standard names, but this is an exception.

Exam scenario

Here's an example of how the CCNA exam might test your knowledge of the 802.11 standards. As in this example, CCNA exam questions that require you to select multiple answers will state so explicitly (select two, select three, etc.).

Q: In which of the following 802.11 standards is careful channel selection necessary to avoid interference among neighboring APs? (select two)

A 802.11a
B 802.11b
c 802.11g
D 802.11ac

To correctly answer this question, you need to know two things: which frequency band requires careful channel selection to avoid interference and which 802.11 standards use that band. The 2.4 GHz band consists of channels with significant overlap, so the 1-6-11 or 1-5-9-13 channel patterns should be used to avoid interference among neighboring APs. Of the four options in the question, the two standards that use the 2.4 GHz band are 802.11b and 802.11g, so the correct answers are B and C.

18.3 Service sets

Now that we've covered the basics of electromagnetic waves, RF frequency bands, and 802.11 standards, let's consider how wireless devices can use these tools to communicate. In the 802.11 standards, a *service set* is a group of devices that operate on the same wireless LAN, sharing the same *service set identifier* (SSID)—a human-readable label that identifies the service set. There are four main types of service sets:

- *Independent basic service set (IBSS)*—A peer-to-peer network where devices communicate directly (without an access point)
- *Basic service set (BSS)*—Devices connect through a single access point, forming the basic building block of a wireless LAN
- *Extended service set (ESS)*—Multiple linked BSSs, providing seamless connectivity across a broader area
- *Mesh basic service set (MBSS)*—A network of interconnected APs providing flexible coverage

NOTE When you use 802.11 (Wi-Fi) to connect to a wireless network from your smartphone or laptop, the network name you select is that network's SSID.

18.3.1 *Independent basic service set*

An *independent basic service set* (IBSS), also called an *ad hoc* wireless network, consists of wireless devices (laptops, smartphones, etc.) communicating directly with each other. Figure 18.13 shows a simple IBSS with an SSID of "Jeremy's IBSS" that consists of a smartphone and two laptops.

Figure 18.13   An IBSS of three devices. The devices can communicate directly with each other and share resources.

An IBSS is useful for quick, temporary communication setups. For example, an IBSS can be used for file sharing or gaming (although LAN parties are largely a thing of the past). However, an IBSS doesn't scale beyond a few devices. In most wireless LANs, you will want to employ some network infrastructure: wireless access points.

18.3.2 *Basic service set*

A *basic service set* (BSS) forms the fundamental building block of an 802.11 wireless LAN. In a BSS, wireless clients connect to a *wireless access point* (abbreviated as WAP or AP), which coordinates the communication between the devices and serves as the gateway to other network resources, such as a wired LAN or the internet.

> **NOTE**   A *client* is any device that connects to a wireless LAN via an AP. 802.11 standards use the term *station* to refer to any wireless-capable device (including clients and APs), but it's a more technical term that isn't common in everyday usage. Cisco products call them clients, so that's the term I'd expect on exam questions.

Figure 18.14 shows a BSS consisting of an AP and three clients, all communicating using channel 1 of the 2.4 GHz band. The clients connected to AP1 cannot send frames directly to each other (even if they are in range of each other's signals); they must send their frames to AP1, which will relay the frames to their destination.

> **NOTE**   The area around an AP where clients can successfully communicate with it—the AP's coverage area—is called a *basic service area* (BSA) or *cell*.

The SSID of the BSS, Jeremy's Wi-Fi, is a human-readable name that serves as the network's identifier for users. SSIDs do not need to be unique. Instead, a *basic service set identifier* (BSSID) serves to uniquely identify the BSS. While multiple BSSs may use the same SSID to create an extended service set (ESS) for wider coverage, each BSS will have a unique BSSID; we'll cover ESSs in the next section.

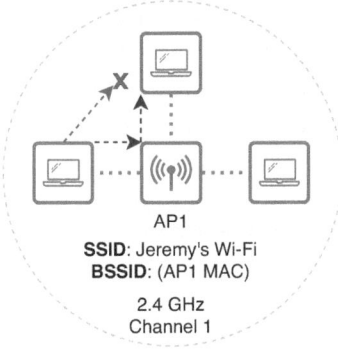

Figure 18.14   A BSS consisting of an AP and three clients. Clients cannot send frames directly to each other; they must communicate via the AP.

NOTE   The BSSID is the MAC address of the AP's radio. MAC addresses are uniquely assigned to the device by the manufacturer; no two devices will have the same MAC.

MULTIPLE BSSs

A single AP is capable of providing more than one BSS. For example, an enterprise may create a BSS for staff and a BSS for guests, applying different security policies to each. However, all of the AP's BSSs must use the same channel—the channel its radio is tuned to. For this reason, creating multiple BSSs won't help to alleviate a congested wireless LAN; all of the AP's clients, regardless of BSS, share the same channel.

Figure 18.15 shows an AP providing two BSSs. Note that, despite both BSSs sharing the same radio, each has a unique BSSID; this is usually accomplished by incrementing the radio's MAC address by 1 for each new BSS.

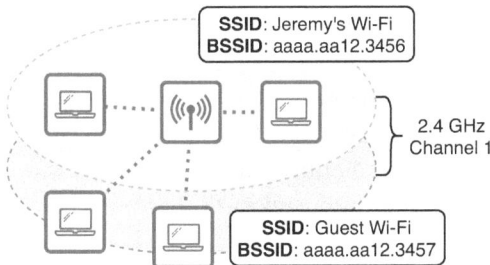

Figure 18.15   An AP providing two BSSs for clients. Both use the same channel. Each BSS requires a unique BSSID. Hosts can only communicate within their BSS.

NOTE   Many modern APs have multiple radios, allowing them to provide BSSs in different channels (typically one in each of the 2.4 and 5 GHz bands).

DISTRIBUTION SYSTEM

Most wireless LANs aren't standalone networks. Rather, wireless LANs are a way for wireless clients to connect to the wired network infrastructure, enabling wireless clients to communicate with hosts in other BSSs, hosts in the wired LAN, in remote sites via the WAN, over the internet, etc. 802.11 calls the wired network infrastructure the *distribution system* (DS). Although the previous diagrams omitted the DS, a wireless LAN without a DS is rare. Without a DS, an AP's wireless clients can only communicate among themselves; they have no gateway to other networks.

In addition to its wireless radio, each AP has an Ethernet port through which it can connect to the DS (usually via a switch). The AP serves as a bridge connecting the two mediums: it translates 802.11 frames from wireless clients to Ethernet frames to be sent over the wired LAN, and vice versa. Figure 18.16 shows an AP connected to a DS (represented by a single switch). The AP maps each wireless SSID to a VLAN on the wired Ethernet network.

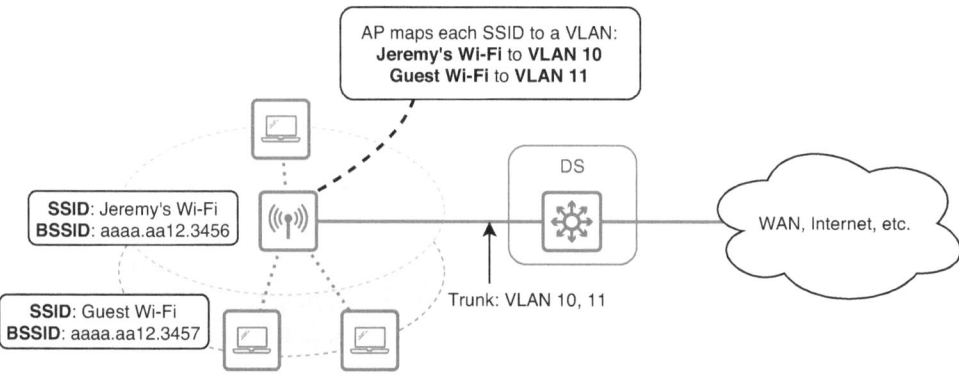

Figure 18.16   The DS connects each BSS to the rest of the network, enabling wireless clients to communicate with hosts outside of their BSSs.

18.3.3 *Extended service set*

In a SOHO network, a single AP (typically a component of a wireless router) is usually sufficient. However, in most enterprise sites (i.e., an office), the range of a single AP isn't enough to provide signal coverage for the entire site. To expand a wireless LAN beyond the range of a single AP, we use an *extended service set* (ESS).

An ESS links multiple BSSs through a DS. Each BSS in an ESS is identified by its own BSSID (the MAC address of the AP), but all operate using the same SSID. Figure 18.17 shows an ESS consisting of three BSSs.

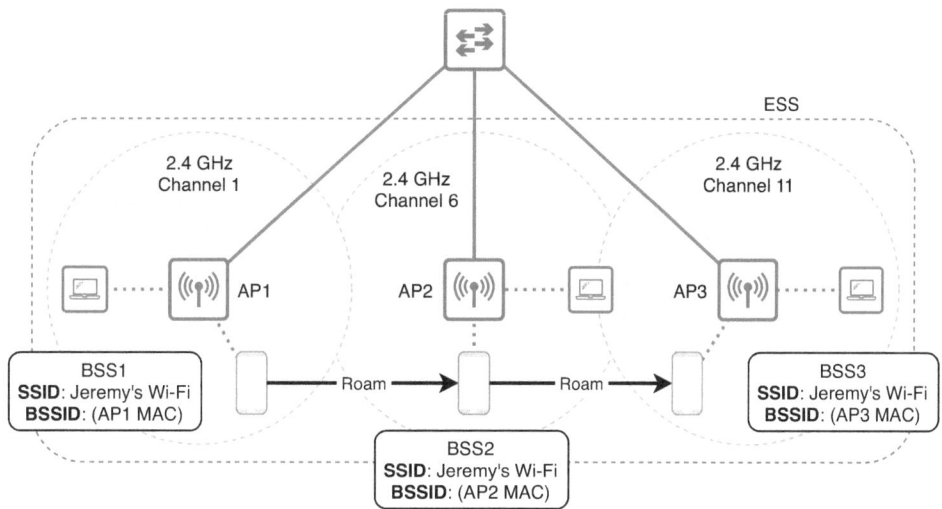

Figure 18.17   An ESS consisting of three BSSs. Each BSS shares the same SSID, but has a unique BSSID. A client can roam seamlessly between BSSs.

NOTE   Notice that each BSS uses a different non-overlapping channel to avoid interference—specifically, the 1–6–11 pattern we covered previously.

To the user, the ESS appears as a single wireless network. Using figure 18.17's example, once a user connects to Jeremy's Wi-Fi, they can move freely throughout the office space without needing to manually reconnect to the network. As the user moves away from the current AP and its signal weakens, the client device will automatically decide to switch to a new AP with a stronger signal, joining its BSS instead of the previous one. This process of passing between BSSs in an ESS is called *roaming*.

NOTE   To provide a seamless roaming experience without temporary loss of connectivity, each AP's cell should overlap by about 10% to 15% (some recommend 20%).

18.3.4   *Mesh basic service set*

In most cases, each AP has its own wired connection to the DS. But in environments where it is impractical or too costly to run an Ethernet cable to each AP, a *mesh basic service set* (MBSS) provides a flexible solution. An MBSS connects multiple APs wirelessly, forming a mesh of APs that can relay data between wireless clients and the DS without each AP requiring a wired connection to the DS. Figure 18.18 illustrates an MBSS.

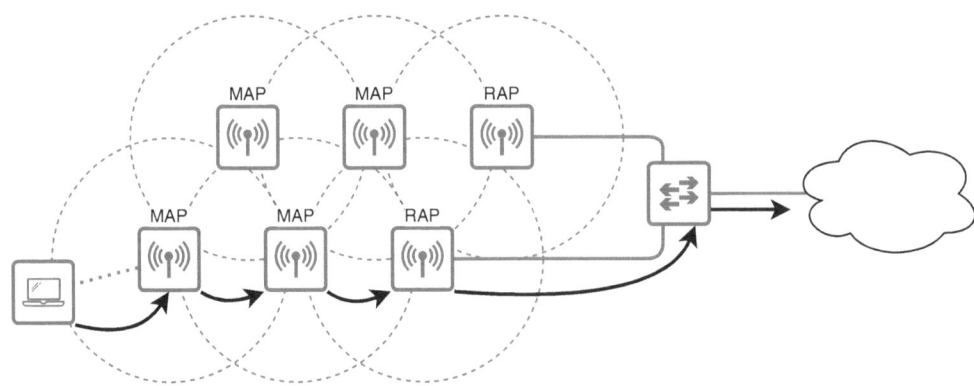

Figure 18.18   An MBSS is a mesh of wireless connections between two types of APs, RAPs and MAPs, that allows them to relay data to and from wireless clients.

> **NOTE**   In an MBSS, an AP connected to the DS is a *root access point* (RAP), and an AP not connected to the DS is a *mesh access point* (MAP).

Ideally, each AP in an MBSS should have two radios tuned to two different channels: one dedicated to providing a BSS to serve wireless clients and one dedicated to relaying frames between wireless clients and the DS over the mesh. A single-radio AP can participate in an MBSS but with greatly reduced performance; its single radio has to perform both jobs.

18.4 *Additional AP operational modes*

APs can operate in various specialized roles outside of simply providing a BSS for wireless clients. An AP participating in an MBSS is an example; in addition to providing a BSS for wireless clients, the AP forms a mesh with other APs to relay frames between them. In this section, we'll look at three more specialized AP operational modes: repeater, workgroup bridge, and outdoor bridge.

18.4.1 *Repeater*

A repeater is an AP used to extend the range of a wireless network. An AP configured as a repeater takes the signal from a main AP and retransmits it to areas outside of the main AP's cell range. This mode is particularly useful in large homes or offices where the coverage of a single AP might not be sufficient. Figure 18.19 shows an AP in repeater mode (AP2) extending AP1's cell.

Repeater APs might remind you of an MBSS. While both repeater APs and APs in an MBSS extend wireless coverage, they serve different network topologies and function differently. A repeater AP is typically a standalone device that extends the range of a single AP without the need for additional configuration or infrastructure. In contrast, a mesh AP is part of a larger mesh network where each AP intelligently routes traffic through the best path within a web of interconnected APs.

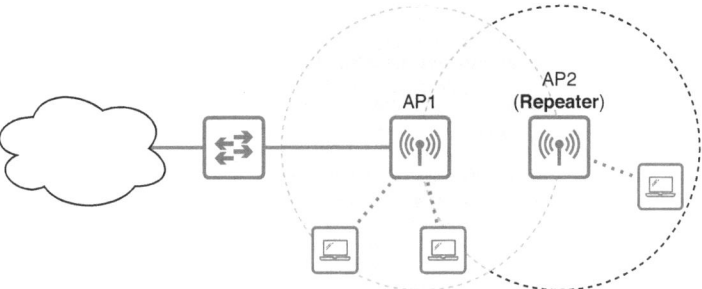

Figure 18.19   AP2, in repeater mode, extends AP1's cell by repeating (retransmitting) wireless signals it receives.

NOTE   A repeater AP can significantly reduce the performance of a wireless LAN. By retransmitting the main AP's signal, the repeater occupies additional airtime for each packet, reducing the network's overall data *throughput*—the rate at which data can be transferred over the network.

18.4.2 *Workgroup bridge*

Not all devices have wireless capabilities. If such a device needs to connect to the network, but running a cable to the nearest switch is not feasible, an AP operating as a *workgroup bridge* (WGB) can be used to connect the wired device to a wireless LAN. The wired device connects to the WGB via an Ethernet cable, and the WGB functions as a client of a main AP on behalf of the wired device, effectively allowing it to participate in the wireless LAN despite having no wireless capabilities. Figure 18.20 shows how it works.

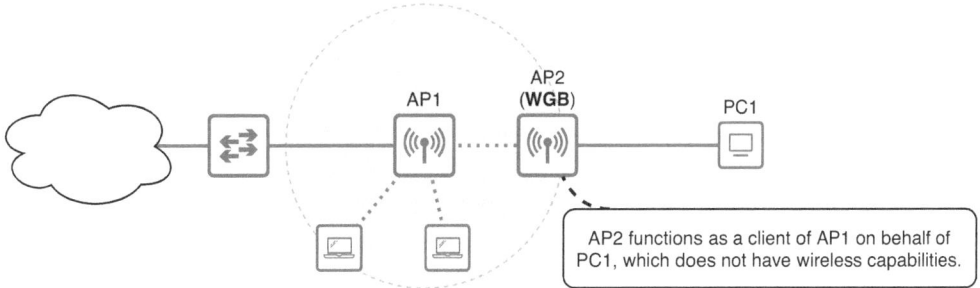

Figure 18.20   AP2, in WGB mode, functions as a client of AP1 to provide network access to PC1, which does not have wireless capabilities.

NOTE   A WGB can support multiple wired devices—not just one. However, if the main AP (AP1 in figure 18.20) is not a Cisco AP, the WGB will have to operate in *Universal WGB* (uWGB) mode, which only supports a single wired device.

18.4.3 Outdoor bridge

Laying cabling between buildings across a campus or city can be quite expensive. An alternative is to connect remote sites wirelessly with APs operating as *outdoor bridges.* Outdoor bridges connect separate LANs over long distances, and are ideal for campus or metropolitan settings, connecting buildings without the need for physical cabling. Figure 18.21 demonstrates a point-to-point outdoor bridge setup connecting two sites. However, a *point-to-multipoint* setup, in which multiple sites connect to a central site, is also possible.

Figure 18.21   APs functioning as outdoor bridges can connect LANs wirelessly over long distances.

NOTE   Outdoor bridges use directional antennas to focus the wireless signal, allowing the signal's strength to be maintained over longer distances than normally possible.

Outdoor bridges can be established over many kilometers. However, the maximum distance varies greatly depending on the hardware and various external conditions; for example, clear line of sight between the two APs is essential.

Summary

- Wireless LANs (sometimes abbreviated as WLANs) are defined by the IEEE 802.11 family of standards. It defines standards at Layers 1 and 2 of the TCP/IP model.
- Copper and fiber-optic cables are bounded media; the signals are confined to the cables, providing a controlled pathway for data transmission.
- The air used to transmit wireless signals is an unbounded medium; the signals propagate freely in open space, radiating in all directions from the source.
- All devices in range of a wireless device can receive its signals, making security a major concern.
- Wireless devices must contend for airtime. If two devices transmit at the same time, a collision occurs. Wireless devices use Carrier-Sense Multiple Access with Collision Avoidance (CSMA/CA) to avoid collisions.
- Wireless signals are vulnerable to interference, for example, from neighboring wireless LANs, microwave ovens, cordless phones, and Bluetooth devices.

- The complexity of national and international regulations means that the same devices can't always be used in different countries.

- Coverage area is an essential consideration in wireless LANs. As wireless signals propagate through space, they lose strength; this is called *free-space path loss* (FSPL). Devices will be unable to receive the signal if it is too weak.

- Electromagnetic waves are influenced by the media they pass through and the objects they encounter.

- Absorption occurs when a wave passes through a medium and is converted into heat, resulting in signal attenuation (weakening).

- Reflection happens when a wave bounces off a surface.

- Refraction occurs when a wave passes from one medium to another with a different density, altering the wave's speed and causing it to bend.

- Diffraction is the bending and spreading of waves around the edges of an obstacle.

- Scattering occurs when a wave encounters a surface or medium with irregularities that causes the wave to spread out erratically.

- To send a wireless signal, a device applies an alternating electric current to an antenna, which in turn produces fluctuating electromagnetic fields that radiate out as waves; these are called *electromagnetic waves*.

- Amplitude is the maximum strength of the electric and magnetic fields of a wave and is associated with how much energy the wave carries; higher amplitude means a stronger signal.

- Frequency measures how often the strength of the wave's electric and magnetic fields oscillates and is measured in hertz (Hz)—oscillations per second.

- 1 kHz (kilohertz) = 1000 Hz, 1 MHz (megahertz) = 1,000,000 Hz, 1 GHz (gigahertz) = 1,000,000,000 Hz, 1 THz (terahertz) = 1,000,000,000,000 Hz.

- Period is the amount of time it takes for one full oscillation. If the frequency is 4 Hz (four oscillations per second), the period is 0.25 seconds.

- In wireless LANs, higher frequencies can typically support higher data transfer rates and are less crowded with other wireless devices, but are more susceptible to absorption by obstacles (i.e. walls). Lower frequencies typically support lower data transfer rates and are more crowded, but penetrate better through obstacles.

- The electromagnetic spectrum is the entire range of electromagnetic radiation.

- Radio frequency (RF) is a segment of the electromagnetic spectrum defined as ranging from around 20 kHz to around 300 GHz. Wireless LANs use three RF bands: the 2.4 GHz band, the 5 GHz band, and the 6 GHz band.

- The 2.4 GHz band spans from 2.4 to 2.4835 GHz and is divided into 14 channels with a standard width of 20 MHz. Not all channels can be used in all countries.

- There is significant overlap among the 2.4 GHz channels, so adjacent APs should use non-overlapping channels (1–6–11 or 1–5–9–13) to avoid interference.
- The 5 GHz band ranges from approximately 5.150 to 5.895 GHz (depending on the country). Channels in this band are non-overlapping when using the standard 20 MHz width, simplifying the channel selection process.
- Channels can be combined to form wider channels of 40, 80, or 160 MHz, supporting higher data transfer rates (although resulting in fewer channels).
- The 6 GHz band is the newest addition to the 802.11 frequency bands, ranging from 5.925 GHz to 7.125 GHz, providing even more non-overlapping channels.
- The standard channel width is 20 MHz, but channels can be combined to form wider 40, 80, 160, or 320 MHz channels.
- New 802.11 standards are constantly in development to meet evolving demands.
- The major generations of 802.11 standards and the RF bands they use are 802.11 (2.4 GHz), 802.11b (2.4 GHz), 802.11a (5 GHz), 802.11g (2.4 GHz), 802.11n (Wi-Fi 4, 2.4/5 GHz), 802.11ac (Wi-Fi 5, 5 GHz), 802.11ax (Wi-Fi 6, 2.4/5 GHz and Wi-Fi 6E, 6 GHz), and 802.11be (Wi-Fi 7, 2.4/5/6 GHz).
- A service set is a group of devices that operate on the same wireless LAN and share the same service set identifier (SSID)—a human-readable label for the service set.
- An independent basic service set (IBSS), also called an *ad hoc wireless network*, consists of wireless clients communicating directly with each other. An IBSS is useful for quick, temporary setups, but doesn't scale beyond a few clients.
- A wireless client is any device that connects to a wireless LAN.
- In a basic service set (BSS), clients connect to a wireless access point (WAP or AP), which coordinates the communication between wireless clients and serves as the gateway to other network resources, such as a wired LAN or the internet.
- Clients in a BSS must communicate via the AP, not directly with each other.
- An AP's coverage area is called a *basic service area* (BSA) or cell.
- A BSS's SSID does not have to be unique. Instead, a basic service set identifier (BSSID) serves to uniquely identify the BSS. The BSSID is usually the MAC address of the AP's radio.
- A single AP can provide more than one BSS. However, if the AP only has a single radio, all BSSs must share the same channel.
- Most wireless LANs serve as a way for wireless clients to connect to the wired network infrastructure (an Ethernet LAN). 802.11 calls the wired network infrastructure the distribution system (DS).
- The AP maps each wireless SSID to a VLAN on the wired Ethernet LAN, serving as a bridge connecting the two mediums.
- An extended service set (ESS) links multiple BSSs through a DS, expanding the coverage area. Each BSS shares an SSID, but has a unique BSSID.

- In an ESS, each AP's cell should overlap by about 10%–15% to allow clients to seamlessly roam among the BSSs without losing connectivity. Neighboring BSSs should use non-overlapping channels.

- A mesh basic service set (MBSS) connects multiple APs wirelessly, forming a mesh of APs that can relay data between wireless clients and the DS without each AP requiring a wired connection to the DS.

- In an MBSS, an AP connected to the DS is a root access point (RAP), and an AP not connected to the DS is a mesh access point (MAP).

- A repeater is an AP used to extend the range of a wireless network. An AP configured as a repeater takes the signal from a main AP and retransmits it to areas outside of the main AP's coverage area.

- An AP functioning as a workgroup bridge (WGB) allows a wired device without wireless capabilities to communicate over a wireless LAN.

- The wired device connects to the WGB via an Ethernet cable, and the WGB functions as a client of a main AP on behalf of the wired device.

- APs operating as outdoor bridges can be used to connect geographically separated LANs wirelessly without the need for physical cabling.

- Outdoor bridges use directional antennas to focus the wireless signal, allowing the signal's strength to be maintained over longer distances than normally possible.

Wireless LAN architectures

This chapter covers

- The structure of 802.11 frames and their types
- Standalone, lightweight, and cloud-based AP architectures
- The various wireless LAN controller deployment options

In the previous chapter, we covered the basic building blocks of wireless LANs, starting with the fundamentals of radio frequency (RF) and connecting devices wirelessly in different types of service sets. In this chapter, we will continue on that theme by examining 802.11 frames and message types. We will then zoom out and look at the bigger picture—the different ways wireless access points (APs) can be deployed and managed to provide wireless access to clients in networks of all sizes. Specifically, we will cover the following CCNA exam topics:

- 1.1 Explain the role and function of network components
  - 1.1.e Controllers
- 2.6 Compare Cisco Wireless Architectures and AP modes
- 2.7 Describe physical infrastructure connections of WLAN components (AP, WLC, access/trunk ports, and LAG)

332

- 2.8 Describe network device management access (Telnet, SSH, HTTP, HTTPS, console, TACACS+/RADIUS, and cloud mnaged)

19.1 802.11 frames and message types

Like Ethernet, 802.11 encapsulates Layer 3 packets in frames before sending them over the physical medium—the air, in 802.11's case. As we covered in the previous chapter, sending frames over the air is quite a bit different from sending them along a cable. For that reason, 802.11 defines its own frame format and a variety of message types necessary to facilitate wireless communications; those are what we'll cover in this section.

19.1.1 The 802.11 frame format

Compared to the Ethernet frame format, the 802.11 frame format shown in figure 19.1 might seem a bit unusual. See if you can tell what's different.

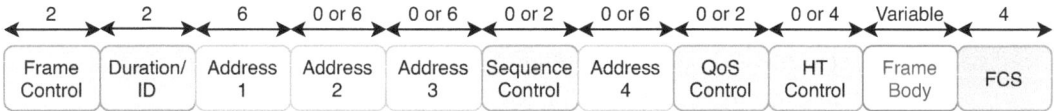

Figure 19.1 The 802.11 frame format. Field sizes in bytes are indicated above each field. Depending on the 802.11 standard being used and the message type, some of the fields might not be present in the frame.

The two major differences between the Ethernet and 802.11 frame formats are

- Depending on the 802.11 standard and message type, some of the 802.11 header's fields might not be present (those with a size of 0 or X bytes in figure 19.1).
- There are up to four address fields instead of the typical two.

Let's focus on the second point. Ethernet connects devices over a bounded medium—cables. Because of this, each frame needs only a source address and a destination address to identify the sender and receiver. Communicating via an AP over the air, an unbounded medium, adds some complexity that requires additional address fields; 802.11 frames contain up to four. These can identify some combination of the following addresses:

- *Basic service set identifier (BSSID)*—The AP's BSSID
- *Destination address (DA)*—The final recipient of the frame
- *Source address (SA)*—The original sender of the frame
- *Receiver address (RA)*—The immediate recipient of the frame
- *Transmitter address (TA)*—The immediate sender of the frame

NOTE Like Ethernet, 802.11 uses MAC addresses.

Figure 19.2 demonstrates one situation in which these addresses play their roles. As mentioned in the previous chapter, clients connected to the same AP must communicate via the AP—not directly with each other—even if they are physically close enough to directly receive each other's signals. So to send a frame to PC2, PC1 must specify AP1 as the immediate recipient (RA) and PC2 as the final recipient (DA).

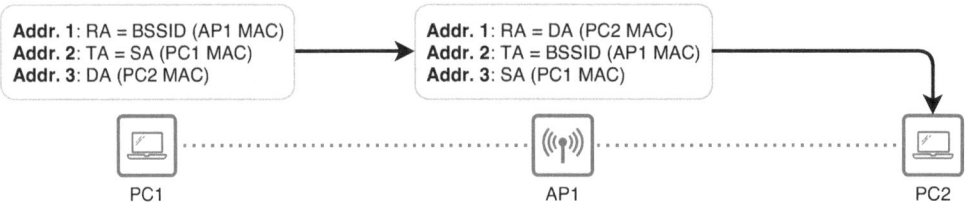

Addr. 1: RA = BSSID (AP1 MAC)
Addr. 2: TA = SA (PC1 MAC)
Addr. 3: DA (PC2 MAC)

Addr. 1: RA = DA (PC2 MAC)
Addr. 2: TA = BSSID (AP1 MAC)
Addr. 3: SA (PC1 MAC)

PC1   AP1   PC2

Figure 19.2   PC1 sends a frame to PC2. By specifying a different immediate and final recipient, PC1 sends its frame via AP1 instead of directly to PC2.

NOTE   RA = BSSID in figure 19.2 means the RA and BSSID are identical: they are AP1's MAC address, and it is specified in the Address 1 field when PC1 sends the frame. The same applies to TA = SA, RA = DA, and TA = BSSID.

Figure 19.2 shows just one example demonstrating that PC1 can specify a different immediate and final recipient. There are various possible patterns, and depending on the message type, there might be one, two, three, or four address fields in an 802.11 frame; such details are well beyond the scope of the CCNA exam.

The other fields of an 802.11 frame

Although not necessary for the CCNA exam, here's a quick description of the remaining fields of an 802.11 frame:

- *Frame Control*—Provides information such as the message type and subtype.
- *Duration/ID*—Depending on the message type, this field can indicate
  - The time (in milliseconds) the channel will be dedicated to transmission of a frame.
  - An identifier for the association (the connection between client and AP).
- *Sequence Control*—Used to reassemble a fragmented message and identify retransmitted frames.
- *QoS Control*—Used in QoS to prioritize certain traffic types.
- *HT (High Throughput) Control*—Used to support the higher data transfer rates of 802.11n, 802.11ac, and later standards.
- *Frame Body*—The message encapsulated inside of the frame.
- *FCS (Frame Check Sequence)*—Like the Ethernet FCS, this allows the receiving device to check if the frame was corrupted in transit.

19.1.2 *The client association process*

In section 19.1.3, we'll take a look at some 802.11 message types. But before that, let's see some of them in action in the client association process. A client's connection to an AP is called an *association*; for a client to send and receive wireless traffic via an AP, the client must be associated with the AP. And before the AP will allow the client to associate with it, it must authenticate the client; it must ensure that it is a valid client.

NOTE We'll cover wireless LAN security, including authentication, in the next chapter.

Figure 19.3 shows a high-level overview of the process. It begins with PC1 sending a *probe request* to discover any APs (and the SSIDs they offer) within range. There are two ways to accomplish this:

- *Active scanning*—The client sends probe requests and listens for probe responses from APs (as shown in figure 19.3). This helps clients discover APs more quickly, although constant active scanning can shorten the client's battery life.
- *Passive scanning*—The client listens for beacon messages from APs; APs send beacon messages periodically to advertise each BSS. This can conserve the client's battery life, but it may take longer for the client to discover available APs.

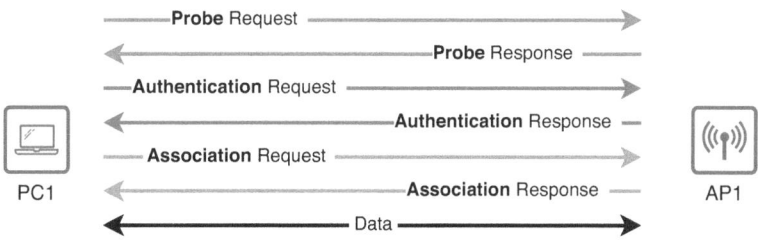

Figure 19.3   The client association process. The probe request/response exchange allows PC1 to discover AP1. PC1 then authenticates and associates with AP1.

After the client discovers an AP, whether through active or passive scanning, it can then request to authenticate and associate with the AP. The client can only send data over the wireless LAN after successfully authenticating and associating with the AP.

A familiar experience

Although 802.11 active scanning and passive scanning are probably new terms to you, you've surely experienced them before. When you connect your phone or laptop to Wi-Fi at a new cafe or someone's house and see a list of available SSIDs, those SSIDs are advertised by APs your device discovered through either active or passive scanning. Your device likely discovers unfamiliar APs/SSIDs even within your own home. If that happens, it means that your device either received beacons from those APs or exchanged probe requests/responses with them.

19.1.3 802.11 message types

802.11 defines three main types of messages:

- *Management*—Used to establish communications in the wireless LAN
- *Control*—Used to facilitate the delivery of frames over the medium
- *Data*—Used to carry data payloads (typically, IP packets)

Let's take a look at some examples of each message type, starting with management. The message types shown in the previous section—probe, beacon, authentication, and association—are all 802.11 management messages. Another example is *disassociation*, which a client sends to end its association with the AP. Management messages are used to establish communications in the wireless LAN and allow the AP to manage the BSS by controlling which clients can participate.

The second type is control, which is used to facilitate the delivery of frames over the medium. Three examples are *request-to-send* (RTS), *clear-to-send* (CTS), and *acknowledgment* (Ack). Figure 19.4 demonstrates how these messages are used.

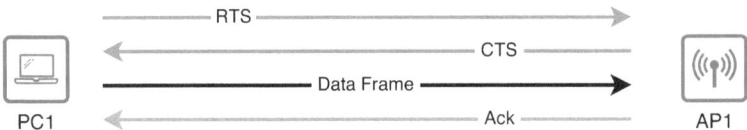

Figure 19.4   RTS, CTS, and Ack messages facilitate smooth communication over the medium. RTS asks for permission to transmit a frame, and CTS grants permission. Ack acknowledges receipt of the frame.

The RTS/CTS mechanism of asking for and granting permission to transmit a frame helps to reduce collisions in the wireless LAN. However, it adds additional overhead: for each data frame to be sent, two extra frames (RTS and CTS) must be transmitted, which can reduce overall network efficiency. Modern networks usually do not use RTS/CTS.

Ack messages, on the other hand, are a necessity. The nature of wireless networks makes frame delivery less reliable than on wired networks, so the Ack mechanism is used to verify that frames have been properly delivered; after a device successfully receives a frame, it must send an Ack back to the sender. If an Ack isn't received, the frame is retransmitted.

Data frames are the final 802.11 frame type; these are frames that carry the actual data to and from wireless clients that are communicating over the network. In most cases, the payload of these frames is an IP packet—IPv4 or IPv6.

19.2   AP architectures

APs can be integrated into a network in multiple ways—for example, as standalone units that you configure and manage individually or centrally managed from a wireless LAN controller (WLC) or SaaS cloud platform. In this section, we will cover the three main AP architectures:

- *Autonomous APs*—Self-contained units that operate independently of other APs, with each requiring individual configuration and management.
- *Lightweight APs*—APs that are centrally managed by a WLC. Complex tasks such as client authentication, security policy enforcement, and RF management are offloaded to the WLC, simplifying AP deployment and management.
- *Cloud-based APs*—APs that are managed remotely over the internet via a cloud service.

Autonomous, lightweight, and cloud based are not simply operational modes that any AP is capable of; they are different types of APs. For example, for an AP to function as an autonomous AP, it requires additional hardware and software capabilities that aren't present in lightweight APs. Some APs can only be autonomous, some can only be lightweight, and some can be either. The same goes for cloud-based APs. A standard Cisco AP cannot operate as a cloud-based AP—only those sold by Cisco Meraki (a company Cisco acquired in 2012).

19.2.1 Autonomous APs

An *autonomous AP* is a self-contained unit. It has the necessary built-in intelligence to handle all aspects of wireless network operations, from client authentication to data encryption—an autonomous AP doesn't rely on an external controller. Each autonomous AP functions as a standalone entity, requiring individual configuration and management. Autonomous APs are useful in small networks or in areas where only a few APs are needed, offering a simple setup without the need for additional centralized control systems. Figure 19.5 shows a LAN with two autonomous APs providing two ESSs for clients.

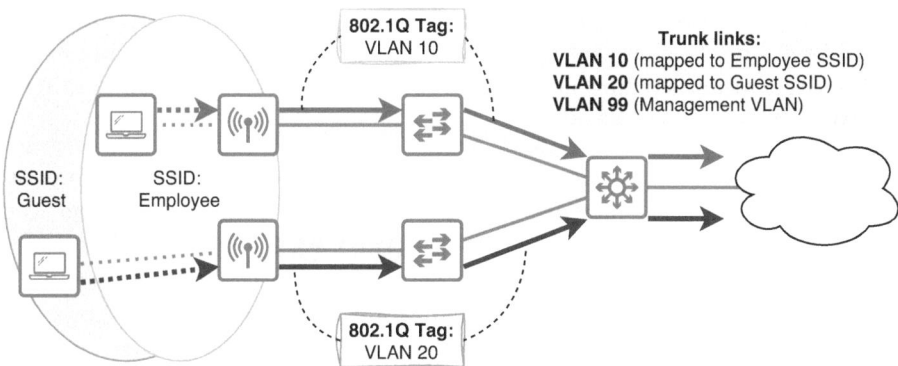

Figure 19.5 Two autonomous APs providing two ESSs for clients. Autonomous APs connect to the wired LAN via trunk links to support multiple SSIDs/VLANs.

Autonomous APs connect to the wired LAN via trunk links. This is because they typically support multiple SSIDs, each mapped to an Ethernet VLAN on the wired LAN.

For example, one SSID may be for employee access while another is for guest access. In figure 19.5, one SSID is mapped to VLAN 10, and the other SSID is mapped to VLAN 20; the AP translates between each SSID and VLAN, serving as the bridge between the wireless and wired LANs. Trunk ports are necessary to support multiple VLANs on the wired network.

Figure 19.5 also lists a management VLAN (VLAN 99)—a VLAN dedicated to managing the APs themselves (and other network devices, like the switches in the LAN). As I mentioned in chapter 5 when covering Telnet and SSH, creating a separate VLAN to isolate management traffic is considered a best practice. This isolation streamlines device management and enhances network security by segregating management traffic from user data.

Autonomous APs require individual configuration, which is done directly through the CLI using the console port, Telnet, or SSH or through the GUI via a web browser using HTTP/HTTPS. Individually managing APs is feasible in a small network with only a few APs, but when the network grows beyond 5 to 10 APs, it becomes inefficient. And in larger networks, which can have thousands of APs spread across many LANs, individually managing autonomous APs is just not practical; centralized management becomes essential.

19.2.2 Lightweight APs

To support larger wireless LANs, a *wireless LAN controller* (WLC) is used to centralize control and simplify operations. An AP that is controlled by a WLC is called a *lightweight AP* (LWAP). LWAPs offload many of their functions to the WLC; this is called *split-MAC architecture*, where real-time media access control (MAC) operations are performed by the LWAPs and more complex, non-real-time functions are handled by the WLC.

> **NOTE** *Media access control* (MAC) is one of the main functions of Layer 2 of the TCP/IP model that manages how devices uniquely identify themselves (MAC addresses) and communicate over a shared network medium, like Ethernet or Wi-Fi.

The WLC is responsible for management functions, such as RF management (setting each LWAP's channel and transmit power), client authentication and association, and QoS and security policy enforcement. The LWAPs handle real-time functions like transmitting and receiving RF signals, encryption of 802.11 frames, sending beacon messages, responding to clients' probe requests, etc. Figure 19.6 shows two LWAPs managed by a WLC. Note that the precise location of the WLC in the network can vary; it could be in a remote data center, connected to a core or distribution switch in the LAN or even incorporated into a switch or AP. Later in this section, we'll examine these different options.

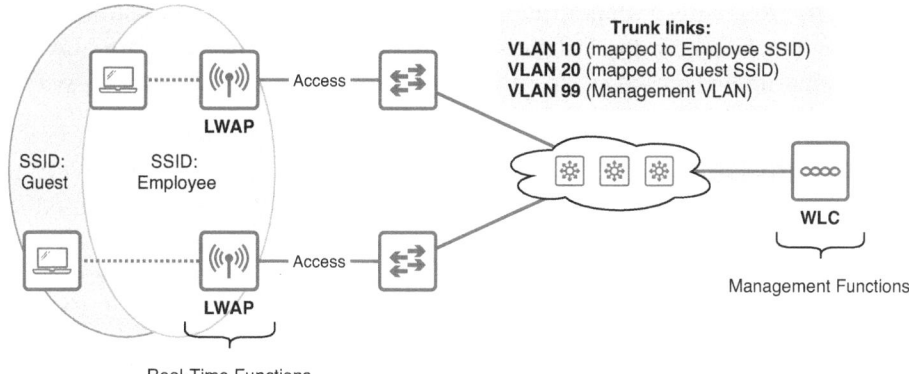

Figure 19.6 Two LWAPs managed by a WLC. The WLC handles management functions, and the LWAPs handle real-time functions.

NOTE Here's a simple way to understand split-MAC architecture: the "intelligence" is centralized in the WLC, and an LWAP's role is simply to handle real-time wireless interactions with clients.

A key difference between autonomous APs and LWAPs is how they connect to the wired network. Autonomous APs use trunk ports to handle multiple VLANs for different SSIDs (plus the management VLAN). In contrast, LWAPs typically connect to the wired LAN using access ports, which only support a single VLAN—the management VLAN, in this case. The job of translating between SSIDs and VLANs is offloaded to the WLC. To achieve this, a protocol called *Control and Provisioning of Wireless Access Points* (CAPWAP) is used to establish tunnels between the LWAPs and the WLC. Figure 19.7 shows how LWAPs tunnel frames from wireless clients to the WLC, which then translates them into Ethernet frames tagged in the appropriate VLAN.

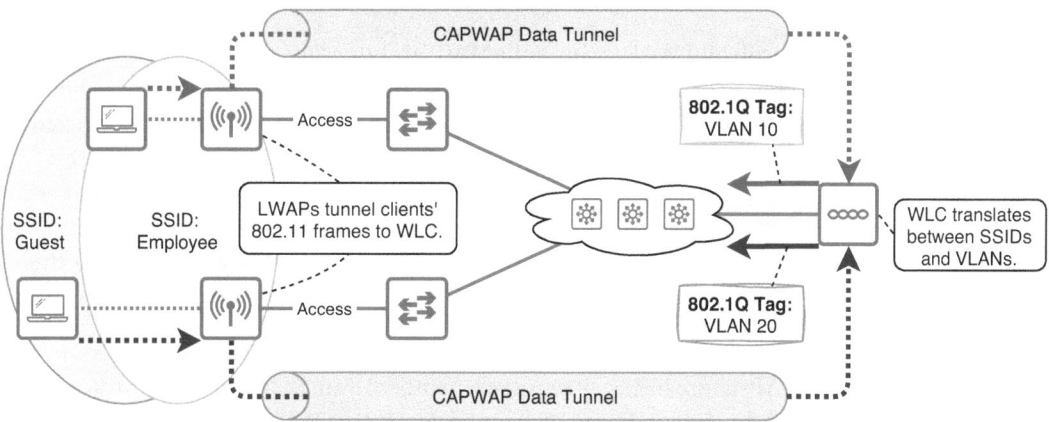

Figure 19.7 LWAPs tunnel client data frames to the WLC, which translates them into Ethernet frames.

NOTE   Remember what a tunnel is: a virtual communication pathway. Tunnels don't make a new physical pathway; the bits still pass over the wired LAN. However, tunneled messages are encapsulated with additional headers, as we covered in chapter 16 when examining VPNs.

CAPWAP doesn't just create one tunnel between each LWAP and the WLC. It creates two: a data tunnel and a control tunnel. The CAPWAP *data tunnel* is used to tunnel traffic sent to and from the wireless clients associated with the LWAP: laptops, smartphones, etc. The CAPWAP *control tunnel* is used to tunnel communications between the LWAP and the WLC; the WLC uses this tunnel to configure the LWAPs and manage their operations. Figure 19.8 illustrates these two tunnels.

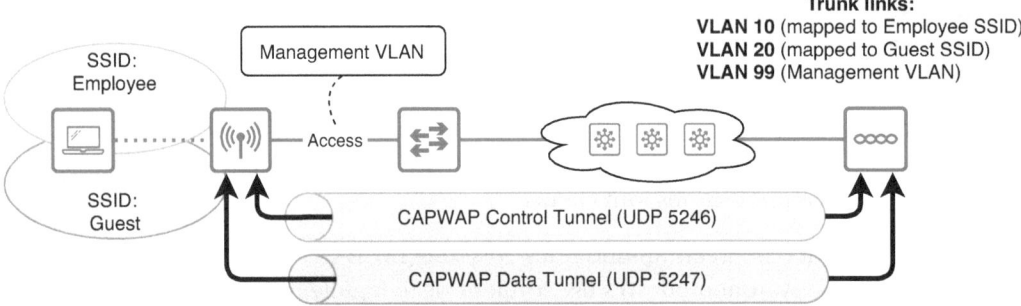

Figure 19.8   CAPWAP creates two tunnels between each LWAP and the WLC: a control tunnel and a data tunnel. The control tunnel uses UDP port 5246, and the data tunnel uses UDP port 5247.

NOTE   The CAPWAP control tunnel is encrypted by default, but the data tunnel isn't; you can enable data tunnel encryption for additional security. CAPWAP encryption uses *Datagram Transport Layer Security* (DTLS)—a type of TLS that uses UDP instead of TCP.

Centralizing control of LWAPs with split-MAC architecture provides several advantages, not just in terms of scalability. For example, the WLC gathers information about the RF environment from the LWAPs it manages and can intelligently make decisions such as which channels each LWAP should use, the optimal transmit power of each AP, etc. This also allows for *self-healing coverage*: if one LWAP stops working, the WLC can make nearby LWAPs increase their transmit power to maintain the coverage area.

Another benefit is the centralization of security and QoS policies. Managing these key functions from a single point ensures consistent standards for access control, encryption, and data prioritization.

NOTE   CAPWAP is an industry-standard protocol but is based on a protocol called Lightweight Access Point Protocol (LWAPP). LWAPP was developed by Airespace, a company that was purchased by Cisco in 2005.

WLC DEPLOYMENT OPTIONS

In a network with more than 5 to 10 APs, you should consider using a WLC to centrally control your wireless LANs. However, there's a big difference between a network with, for example, 20 to 30 APs and a network with thousands of them. For that reason, there is no one-size-fits-all WLC solution; there are a variety of WLC deployment options that meet different needs. Figure 19.9 illustrates four deployment options: unified, cloud, embedded, and Mobility Express.

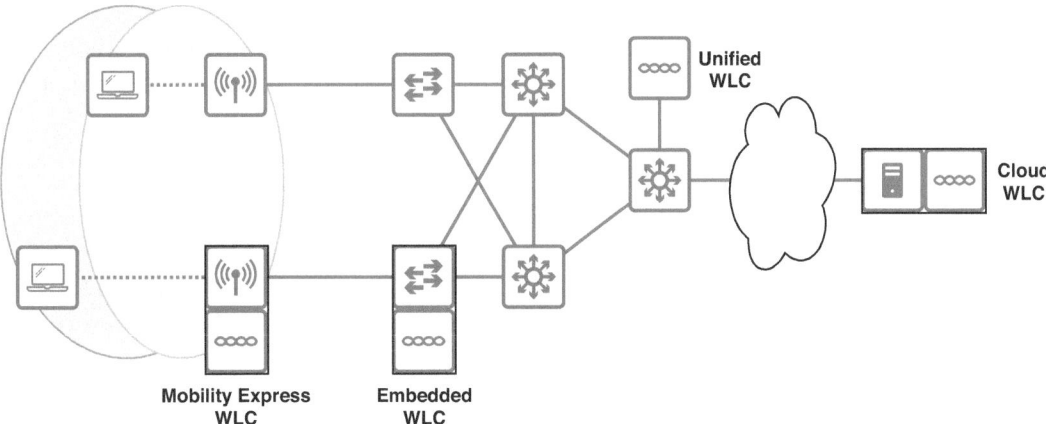

Figure 19.9   WLC deployment options. A unified WLC is a dedicated hardware appliance. A cloud WLC is a VM deployed in a private or public cloud. An embedded WLC is integrated into a switch. A Mobility Express WLC is integrated into an AP.

> **NOTE**   To avoid showing the same network four times with the WLC in different locations, I included all four deployment options in figure 19.9. In practice, a network would typically employ one option suited to its specific needs.

A *unified WLC* is a dedicated hardware appliance; Cisco offers various hardware models that can support anywhere from a few hundred LWAPs to as many as 6,000 LWAPs and 64,000 clients with a single WLC—if your network has to support more WLCs and clients than that, you'll have to deploy a second WLC.

A *cloud WLC* is a virtual machine (VM) deployed on a server in the cloud. It could be, for example, a private cloud in the company's data center or a public cloud platform. Depending on the hardware resources available to the VM, a cloud WLC can support 1,000, 3,000, or even 6,000 LWAPs, and up to 64,000 clients—as much as a unified WLC.

An *embedded WLC* is a WLC integrated into a switch. Embedded WLCs are more suitable for smaller deployments, supporting up to 200 APs and 4,000 clients. For even smaller deployments, *Cisco Mobility Express* integrates the WLC within an AP, supporting up to 100 LWAPs and 2,000 clients. Table 19.1 summarizes these deployment options.

Table 19.1   WLC deployment options

Name	Description	Max LWAPs	Max Clients
Unified	Dedicated hardware appliance	6,000	64,000
Cloud	VM deployed in the cloud	6,000	64,000
Embedded	Integrated into a switch	200	4,000
Mobility Express	Integrated into an AP	100	2,000

NOTE   In Cisco's newer line of WLCs and APs, they have dropped the Mobility Express terminology, using the term *embedded* both for a WLC integrated into a switch and a WLC integrated into an AP; be aware of both terms for the CCNA exam.

CLIENT-SERVING LWAP MODES

In the previous chapter, we looked at a few additional AP operational modes: repeater, workgroup bridge, and outdoor bridge. LWAPs controlled by a WLC can also be configured to operate in various modes. In some modes, the LWAP provides network service to clients, and in others, it is dedicated to a more specialized network management role. First, let's examine the client-serving modes:

- *Local*—The standard operational mode, providing BSSs for clients. The LWAP tunnels all client traffic to the WLC via CAPWAP.
- *FlexConnect*—Similar to Local, but client traffic doesn't have to be tunneled to the WLC; the LWAP can locally switch client traffic between the wired and wireless LANs.
- *Bridge and Flex + Bridge*—Used in mesh deployments.

Local is the default LWAP operational mode that we have covered so far. An LWAP in local mode offers BSSs for clients and tunnels all client traffic to the WLC via the CAPWAP data tunnel. However, this is not always desirable; tunneling all client traffic to the WLC can be inefficient, especially if the WLC and clients aren't located in the same LAN.

FlexConnect offers a more flexible approach (hence the name) in which the LWAP can locally switch client traffic between the wired and wireless LANs—no need to tunnel it to the WLC. This reduces latency for the client traffic because it doesn't have to travel all the way to the WLC and back and also conserves bandwidth on the WAN connections leading to the WLC. FlexConnect can be configured on a per-SSID basis. Figure 19.10 shows how FlexConnect works: FlexConnect is enabled for the Guest SSID but disabled for the Employee SSID.

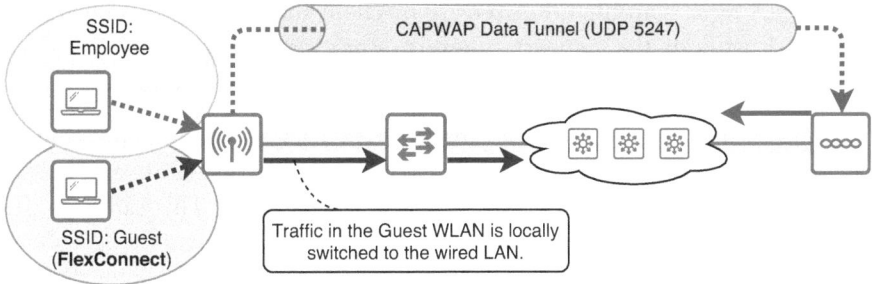

Figure 19.10 With FlexConnect enabled, a LWAP can locally switch traffic between SSIDs and VLANs. FlexConnect can be enabled per SSID.

NOTE If FlexConnect is enabled, the LWAP should connect to the wired LAN via a trunk link; it must support multiple VLANs.

Another benefit of FlexConnect is that the LWAP can locally switch traffic between FlexConnect-enabled SSIDs and the wired LAN even if it loses its connection to the WLC. This allows clients using those SSIDs to maintain connectivity even if such a problem occurs.

An LWAP operating in *Bridge* mode can form a wireless mesh with other LWAPs without directly connecting each LWAP to the wired network infrastructure—an MBSS, as we covered in the previous chapter. LWAPs in Bridge mode can also function as bridges connecting wired LANs (like "outdoor bridge" mode, as covered in chapter 18). *Flex + Bridge* mode adds FlexConnect on top of Bridge mode, allowing the LWAPs to locally switch client traffic without tunneling it to the WLC.

NETWORK MANAGEMENT **LWAP** MODES

Some LWAP operational modes are more specialized; instead of serving wireless clients, the LWAP assists in various network management tasks. The network management LWAP modes are

- *Monitor*—The LWAP doesn't transmit from its radios; it is dedicated to analyzing the RF environment and detecting unauthorized ("rogue") devices.

- *Rogue Detector*—The LWAP's radios are entirely disabled; it is dedicated to analyzing traffic on the wired LAN to detect rogue devices.

- *Sniffer*—The LWAP captures all wireless traffic on a specific channel. The captured messages are then sent to the WLC and can be redirected to analysis software such as Wireshark for detailed inspection and troubleshooting.

- *SE-Connect*—The LWAP is dedicated to RF spectrum analysis on all channels. It feeds data to spectrum analysis software like Cisco Spectrum Expert for in-depth evaluation of the RF landscape.

> **NOTE**   A *rogue* is an unauthorized AP or client that has been connected to the network without the network administrator's permission. Rogue devices can pose a security risk, so identifying and dealing with them is important.

Although these operational modes don't directly serve clients, dedicating LWAPs to specific tasks such as RF spectrum analysis, rogue device detection, and traffic analysis can give important insights into the status of the network. This can help proactively identify and address problems in wireless LANs.

19.2.3 Cloud-based APs

In addition to autonomous and lightweight APs, there is a third option that can be considered a middle ground between the two: *cloud-based.* Cloud-based AP architecture uses a cloud platform to streamline the management of APs; essentially, it's a public SaaS cloud service. Cisco's offering is Cisco Meraki. Figure 19.11 shows how cloud-based APs, such as those offered by Meraki, work.

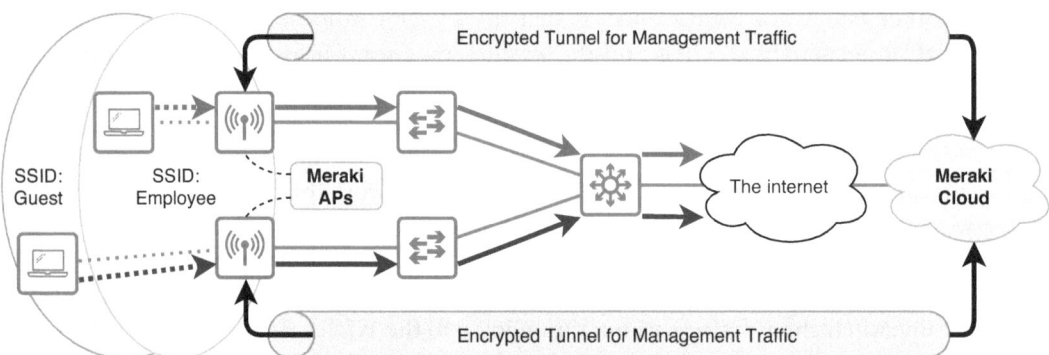

Figure 19.11   Cisco Meraki offers cloud-based APs. Meraki APs are managed using Meraki's cloud platform, which connects to each AP using an encrypted tunnel. User data traffic from clients is not tunneled to the cloud—only management traffic.

Meraki APs communicate with the Meraki cloud platform over the internet in an encrypted tunnel. Each AP sends RF spectrum information, client statistics, and various other kinds of information to the Meraki cloud over this tunnel. The admin can log in to the Meraki dashboard—a web browser-based tool—to centrally manage the APs. User data, however, is not tunneled to the cloud; it goes straight to the wired LAN.

Cloud-based APs use cloud computing to offer a scalable, easy-to-manage wireless network solution. Unlike autonomous APs that are managed individually or lightweight APs that require a WLC, cloud-based APs connect to a SaaS cloud service for configuration and management. This architecture simplifies complex tasks such as deploying new APs, adjusting configurations, monitoring network health, and troubleshooting problems. Although centralized management is common to lightweight and cloud-based APs, the main advantages of the cloud-based approach are simplicity and ease of use.

NOTE   Don't mix up the concepts of cloud-based AP architecture and a cloud WLC deployment. Cloud-based AP architecture manages APs using an SaaS cloud platform. A cloud WLC deployment is a split-MAC architecture with the WLC deployed as a VM in a cloud.

CLOUD-MANAGED NETWORK DEVICES

Although best known for their cloud-based APs, Cisco Meraki offers a variety of network devices that can be managed from their cloud platform: switches, firewalls, Internet of Things (IoT) devices like cameras and sensors, etc. In this section, let's move our focus away from wireless LANs to consider the characteristics and benefits of cloud-based network management platforms like Meraki.

NOTE   For an overview of how Cisco Meraki works, check out https://mng.bz/ z8zB.

Cloud-managed network devices offer a centralized approach to network management, where configuration, monitoring, and troubleshooting are all handled through a cloud-based platform. This centralized approach is the key characteristic of cloud-managed devices; instead of managing devices one by one via the CLI, you can manage all devices from a single web-based dashboard. This offers a variety of benefits for many enterprises:

1 *Rapid and simplified deployment*—Cloud management platforms like Meraki use *zero-touch provisioning* (ZTP) to facilitate the deployment of new network devices without requiring manual configuration of each device. Newly connected devices automatically connect to the Meraki cloud and download their configurations. This is much simpler than the traditional process, which involves manually configuring new devices one by one via the console port before deploying them to the network.

2 *Simplified management*—With a unified interface for managing all devices in the network, adminstrators can spend less time on routine management tasks. Configuration changes can be applied to all devices at once through the cloud, eliminating the need for the manual configuration of each device.

3 *Enhanced visibility and analytics*—Cloud platforms provide detailed analytics and reporting tools that can help administrators understand network usage patterns, identify bottlenecks in the network, and optimize network performance.

4 *Automated updates*—Network device firmware updates and security patches can be automatically deployed to all devices, ensuring they are up-to-date. Out-of-date software can be a serious vulnerability, so this is a critical part of mainting a secure network.

5 *Operational efficiency*—By simplifying the overall process of deploying and managing a network through centralized management and automation, the *operating expenses* (OpEx)—the ongoing costs associated with maintaining the network—are reduced.

The two key takeaways are centralized management and simplicity. Cloud management solutions like Meraki offer a modern, efficient, and scalable approach to network management for many enterprises. However, it might not be ideal for organizations with highly specialized or complex networking requirements, stringent data privacy concerns that mandate keeping all management data on-premises, or those that require deep customization and control beyond what cloud platforms typically offer.

EXAM TIP   Cloud-managed network devices are mentioned in exam topic 2.8, so make sure you can identify the characteristics and benefits of cloud-based management.

Summary

- 802.11 defines a frame format that differs from Ethernet in a couple of key ways. Depending on the 802.11 standard and message type, some fields might not be present, and there are up to four address fields instead of two.
- The 802.11 address fields identify some combination of the following, depending on the message type:
  - Basic service set identifier (BSSID)—The AP's BSSID
  - Destination address (DA)—The final recipient of the frame
  - Source address (SA)—The original sender of the frame
  - Receiver address (RA)—The immediate recipient of the frame
  - Transmitter address (TA)—The immediate sender of the frame
- A client's connection to an AP is called an *association*. For a client to send and receive wireless traffic via an AP, the client must be associated with the AP.
- To discover nearby APs, a client can send a *probe request*. APs will respond with a *probe response*. This is called *active scanning*.
- In *passive scanning*, the client listens for *beacon* messages that APs send periodically to advertise each BSS.
- After discovering an AP, the client must send an authentication request and then, if successful, an association request.
- 802.11 defines three main types of messages: management, control, and data.
- *Management* frames are used to establish and maintain communications in the wireless LAN. Examples include probe, beacon, authentication, and association messages.
- *Control* frames are used to facilitate the delivery of frames over the medium and include *request-to-send* (RTS) and *clear-to-send* (CTS), which are used to request and grant permission to transmit a frame, and *acknowledgment* (Ack), which is used to acknowledge receipt of a frame.
- *Data* frames carry actual data to and from wireless clients communicating over the network.

- APs can be deployed in three main architectures: autonomous, lightweight, and cloud-based.

- An *autonomous AP* is a self-contained unit with the built-in intelligence to handle all aspects of wireless network operations.

- Autonomous APs connect to the wired LAN via trunk links; autonomous APs need to be able to translate each SSID to a VLAN on the wired LAN. Furthermore, a separate management VLAN should be used to connect to and manage the AP itself.

- Autonomous APs require individual configuration, which is done through the CLI (console, Telnet, or SSH) or GUI via a web browser using HTTP/HTTPS.

- Individually managing autonomous APs is not feasible in larger networks. To support larger wireless LANs, a *wireless LAN controller* (WLC) is used to centralize control and simplify operations.

- An AP that is controlled by a WLC is called a *lightweight AP* (LWAP).

- LWAPs offload many of their functions to the WLC; this is called *split-MAC architecture.*

- Real-time operations (sending and receiving RF signals, encrypting frames) are handled by each LWAP, and non-real-time functions (RF management, client authentication and association, QoS and security policy) are handled by the WLC.

- Whereas autonomous APs connect to the wired LAN via trunk ports, LWAPs connect via access ports in the management VLAN. The job of translating between SSIDs and VLANs is offloaded to the WLC.

- The *Control and Provisioning of Wireless Access points* (CAPWAP) protocol is used to establish tunnels between LWAPs and the WLC. LWAPs tunnel frames from clients to the WLC, which translates them into Ethernet frames in the appropriate VLAN.

- CAPWAP establishes two tunnels from each LWAP to the WLC. The *data tunnel* is used to tunnel traffic sent to and from wireless clients. The *control tunnel* is used to tunnel communications between the LWAP and WLC.

- The CAPWAP control tunnel is encrypted by default, but the data tunnel is not. CAPWAP encryption uses *Datagram Transport Layer Security* (DTLS)—a type of TLS that uses UDP instead of TCP.

- There are various WLC deployment options that meet different needs: unified, cloud, embedded, and Mobility Express.

- A *unified WLC* is a dedicated hardware appliance; Cisco offers various hardware models that can support anywhere, from a few hundred LWAPS to as many as 6,000 LWAPs and 64,000 clients.

- A *cloud WLC* is a VM deployed on a server in the cloud. Depending on the hardware resources available to the VM, it can support up to 6,000 LWAPs and 64,000 clients.

- An *embedded WLC* is integrated into a switch. Embedded WLCs are more suitable for smaller deployments, supporting up to 200 APs and 4,000 clients.

- A *Mobility Express WLC* is integrated into an AP, supporting up to 100 LWAPs and 2,000 clients.

- LWAPs can operate in various modes, some of which provide network service to clients and some that play a network management role.

- The default LWAP operational mode is *Local*, in which the LWAP provide BSSs for clients to connect to, tunneling their traffic to the WLC via CAPWAP.

- *FlexConnect* offers a more flexible approach in which the LWAP can locally switch client traffic between the wired and wireless LANs—no need to tunnel it to the WLC. FlexConnect can be enabled on a per-SSID basis.

- An LWAP operating in *Bridge* mode can form a wireless mesh with other LWAPs without directly connecting each LWAP to the wired network. LWAPs in Bridge mode can also form a bridge connecting two wired LANs.

- *Flex + Bridge* mode adds FlexConnect on top of Bridge mode, allowing the LWAPs in the mesh to locally switch client traffic without tunneling it to the WLC.

- In *Monitor* mode, the LWAP doesn't transmit from its radios. It is dedicated to analyzing the RF environment and detecting rogue devices.

- In *Rogue Detector* mode, the LWAP's radios are entirely disabled. It is dedicated to analyzing traffic on the wired LAN to detect rogue devices.

- In *Sniffer* mode, the LWAP captures all wireless traffic on a specific channel and sends it to the WLC for analysis.

- In *SE-Connect* mode, the LWAP is dedicated to RF spectrum analysis on all channels, feeding data to spectrum analysis software like Cisco Spectrum Expert.

- In addition to autonomous and lightweight APs, there is a third option that can be considered a middle ground between the two: *cloud-based.*

- Cloud-based AP architecture uses a cloud SaaS platform to streamline the management of APs. Cisco's offering is Cisco Meraki.

- Meraki APs communicate with the Meraki cloud platform over the internet in an encrypted tunnel. Each AP sends RF information, client statistics, and various kinds of other information to the Meraki cloud over this tunnel.

- The admin can log in to the Meraki dashboard—a web browser-based tool—to centrally manage the APs.

- User data is not tunneled to the cloud; it goes straight to the wired LAN.

- Cloud-managed network devices (e.g., Meraki's APs, switches, and firewalls) offer a centralized approach to network management. Configuration, monitoring, and troubleshooting are all handled through a cloud-based platform like the Meraki dashboard.

- Cloud-based management solutions like Meraki offer simplicity, efficiency, and scalability that is beneficial for many modern enterprises. However, it might not be ideal for organizations with highly specialized or complex networking requirements.

Wireless LAN security

This chapter covers

- Applying the CIA triad to wireless communications
- Authenticating wireless LAN clients before allowing them to communicate
- Maintaining the confidentiality and integrity of communications in a wireless LAN
- The WPA, WPA2, and WPA3 security certification programs

Imagine that you are in a room full of people. You have to communicate a private message to your friend on the other side of the room, but all you can do is shout at the top of your lungs. Basically, that's how communication in a wireless LAN works. Security is a major concern in all networks, but the unbounded nature of the medium means that securing communications in wireless LANs is even more critical.

In this chapter, we will take a high-level overview of wireless LAN security concerns and solutions, covering CCNA exam topic 5.9: Describe wireless security protocols (WPA, WPA2, and WPA3). *WPA* stands for Wi-Fi Protected Access—a set of security certification programs developed by the Wi-Fi Alliance. To earn "Wi-Fi Certified" status, devices must comply with WPA's standards. We will first examine the various elements of wireless LAN security and then see how they all fit together in WPA, WPA2, and WPA3.

20.1 Wireless LAN security concepts

Although wireless LANs introduce unique challenges, the fundamental security concepts we covered in chapter 11 still apply. In this section, we'll consider how the CIA triad applies to wireless LANs and examine the security measures implemented in the original 802.11 standard (before the creation of WPA).

20.1.1 The CIA triad in wireless LANs

For review, the CIA triad describes the goals of information security and stands for

- *Confidentiality*—Data and systems should only be accessible by authorized entities.
- *Integrity*—Data and systems should be trustworthy. For example, data should not be altered during storage or transmission except by authorized entities.
- *Availability*—Data and systems should be accessible and usable by authorized entities when required.

Let's examine each of these goals in the context of wireless LANs. The unbounded nature of wireless LANs makes ensuring the CIA of communications an even greater challenge.

CONFIDENTIALITY

Confidentiality in a wired LAN is largely ensured by the physical characteristics of the medium: the signals are contained within the cables, reducing (although not eliminating) the risk of unauthorized access to communications. Confidentiality is primarily a concern when communicating over public networks like the internet.

However, wireless signals can be picked up by any receiver within range of the transmitter, making it essential to protect information as it travels through the air, even within a private LAN. Figure 20.1 illustrates why encryption of wireless communications is important: a user's unencrypted login information is overheard by an attacker.

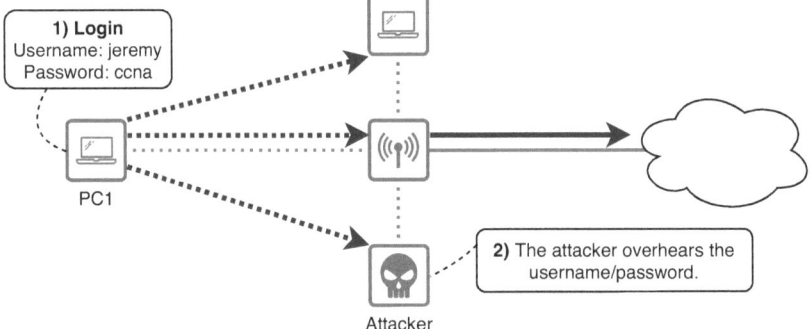

Figure 20.1 Unencrypted communications in a wireless LAN are not secure, as wireless signals can be picked up by nearby devices, allowing malicious users to gain access to confidential information.

To maintain the confidentiality of communications in a wireless LAN, encryption of wireless signals is essential. Encrypting a message converts it into an unintelligible string of text that can only be restored by the intended recipient. Later in this chapter, we will take a look at some encryption methods used in wireless LANs.

> **NOTE** Unencrypted information (that will not be encrypted) is called *cleartext.* Unencrypted information that will be encrypted (but has not yet been fed into the encryption algorithm) is *plaintext,* and encrypted information is called *ciphertext.*

INTEGRITY

Even if a message is encrypted, preventing an attacker from reading its contents, that is no guarantee that the data will not be altered by a malicious user. A *bit-flipping* attack is an attack in which the attacker flips bits (between 0 and 1) in the ciphertext to create predictable changes in the plaintext—even without decrypting the ciphertext.

To protect the integrity of a message before sending it over the air, the sender uses a mathematical function to generate a *checksum*—a small block of data derived from the original message. This checksum is appended to the end of the plaintext message before encrypting and sending it.

Upon receiving the encrypted message, the receiver decrypts it and then calculates its own checksum from the decrypted message. If the newly calculated checksum matches the one sent with the message, the receiver can conclude that the message hasn't been altered. If they don't match, the receiver discards the message. Figure 20.2 demonstrates this process.

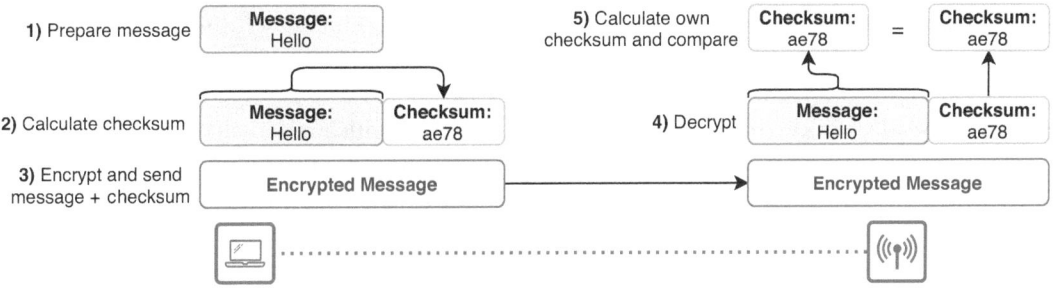

Figure 20.2 **Appending a checksum to the end of a message before encrypting and sending it helps to protect the integrity of wireless communications.**

> **NOTE** It's worth noting that checksums don't prevent data from being tampered with; they only enable a device to identify when data has been tampered with.

AVAILABILITY

Attacks against the availability of a wireless LAN—denial of service (DoS) attacks—are quite simple to carry out by any malicious user with the proper tools. For example, in an *RF jamming attack*, the attacker uses a signal generator to flood the 802.11 frequency bands, preventing legitimate devices from communicating.

An RF jamming attack doesn't require sophisticated hacking skills or deep knowledge of the network, making it an easy choice for a malicious user looking to disrupt the network. Furthermore, preventing such attacks can be challenging; the only solution to an RF jamming attack is to locate and disable/remove the device that is performing the attack. And the only preventative measure is physical security—ensuring that only authorized users have access to the physical premises.

NOTE   Due to the simplicity of wireless DoS attacks, we won't address them any further in this chapter. Instead, we'll focus on protecting the confidentiality and integrity of wireless communications.

20.1.2   Legacy 802.11 security

The original 802.11 standard defined a security protocol called *Wired Equivalent Privacy* (WEP). As the name suggests, WEP promised to provide privacy to wireless communications equivalent to that of wired communications. Unfortunately, it failed to live up to that promise; various vulnerabilities were soon identified, and WEP is now obsolete—it is a *legacy protocol*. However, studying the basics of WEP is crucial for understanding the evolution of wireless security protocols.

WEP OPEN SYSTEM AND SHARED KEY AUTHENTICATION

The definitions I gave for confidentiality, integrity, and availability all mention "authorized entities"—data should only be accessible to and modified by authorized entities and should remain available to those entities. To authorize an entity (a user or device), you must verify that entity's identity—as we covered in chapter 11, the verification process is called *authentication*. WEP defined two methods of authentication: Open System Authentication and Shared Key Authentication.

We already saw an example of Open System Authentication in chapter 19 when covering the association process: the client device sends an authentication request, and the AP sends an authentication response. No credentials are exchanged; the AP simply approves all authentication requests unless there's a problem with the request itself (i.e., invalid formatting)—no questions asked! This verifies that the client and AP are both valid 802.11 devices, but I think it goes without saying that this is not a secure authentication method.

Shared Key Authentication involves the configuration of a static WEP key on the AP and each client—basically, this is the Wi-Fi password. To verify that a client has the correct WEP key, the following process, illustrated in figure 20.3, is used:

1 The client sends an authentication request.
2 The AP sends an authentication response with an unencrypted *challenge phrase*.
3 The client uses the WEP key to encrypt the challenge phrase.
4 The client sends the ciphertext challenge phrase back to the AP.

5 The AP uses the WEP key to decrypt the challenge phrase.

6 The AP compares the original challenge phrase to the one it just decrypted.

7 If the decrypted text matches the original phrase, the AP sends back a response indicating successful authentication (or unsuccessful, if the text doesn't match).

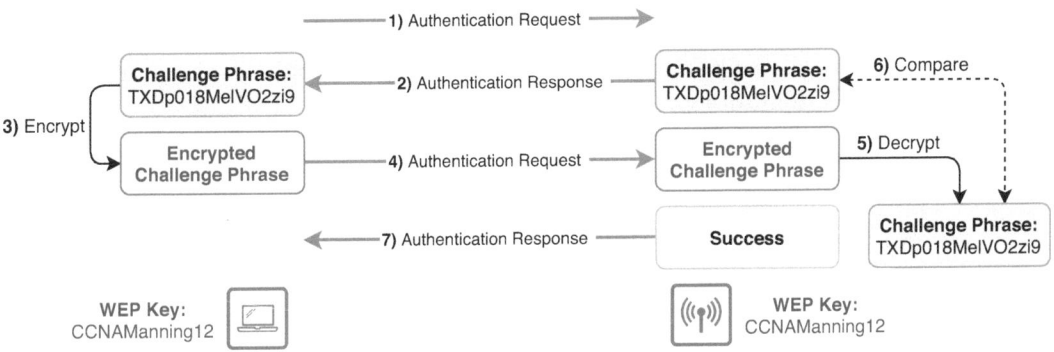

Figure 20.3 WEP Shared Key Authentication involves exchanging a challenge phrase and encrypting/decrypting it with a shared WEP key.

NOTE Diagrams in this chapter omit the probe request/probe response exchange (or beacon messages when using passive discovery) that we covered in chapter 19, but keep in mind that this exchange occurs before any authentication/association processes; the client must discover the AP before it can authenticate.

A static WEP key can be either 40 bits or 104 bits in length. Furthermore, the device generates a random 24-bit number called an *initialization vector* (IV) that is combined with the WEP key. A new IV is generated for each packet; this adds some randomness to the encryption process, making it harder for an attacker to figure out the encryption key.

NOTE As we covered in chapter 19, after the client successfully authenticates (via Open System or Shared Key Authentication), it can send an association request to associate with the AP and start communicating.

WEP ENCRYPTION AND INTEGRITY

In addition to authentication, WEP provides confidentiality via encryption. The same WEP key used in Shared Key Authentication can be used to encrypt data messages to and from wireless clients. The encryption algorithm used by WEP is *Rivest Cipher 4* (RC4); RC4 is no longer considered secure, so newer security standards use different algorithms.

WEP also ensures the integrity of communications as described previously, appending a 32-bit checksum called the *integrity check value* (ICV). This is appended to each plaintext message before it is encrypted, allowing the receiver to verify that the message was not tampered with.

Although WEP seems to have all the bases covered when it comes to wireless security—authentication, confidentiality (encryption), and integrity—it is no longer considered secure. Cryptography, and security in general, is a never-ending arms race, and attackers have known how to exploit WEP for over two decades. As threats evolve and become more sophisticated, so must security protocols.

20.2 *Wireless client authentication*

After WEP's vulnerabilities were discovered, the Wi-Fi Alliance developed the *Wi-Fi Protected Access* (WPA) certification as an interim enhancement until the IEEE could develop a more permanent solution (the 802.11i standard, which was adopted by WPA2). WPA (and its more recent versions WPA2 and WPA3) defines two main authentication methods:

- *WPA-Personal*—A pre-shared key (PSK) is used for authentication. This is similar to WEP Shared Key Authentication but more secure. The most recent WPA3 certification enhances this with Simultaneous Authentication of Equals (SAE).

- *WPA-Enterprise*—Designed to provide more robust authentication in enterprise LANs, WPA-Enterprise uses 802.1X and EAP, replacing the PSK with individual user or device credentials.

20.2.1 *WPA-Personal: PSK and SAE*

WPA-Personal authentication, typically used in SOHO networks, involves configuring a *pre-shared key* (PSK)—a static 256-bit string used to generate secure encryption keys. The same PSK must be configured on all members of the BSS—the AP and its clients—and is used similarly to the key in WEP Shared Key Authentication.

A 256-bit PSK, which is 64 hexadecimal characters, would be difficult for most users to remember (or enter without typos). To simplify things, you can configure an 8- to 63-character passphrase—what most people call the "Wi-Fi password," which is then automatically converted into a 256-bit PSK.

Figure 20.4 demonstrates how WPA-Personal authentication with a PSK works. Interestingly, this authentication occurs after the client has already associated with the AP, beginning with Open System Authentication as we covered earlier; the true authentication occurs after the association.

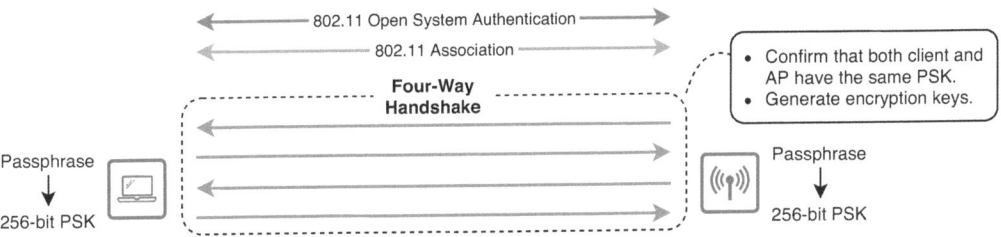

Figure 20.4 WPA-Personal authentication with a PSK. After the client associates with the AP, a four-way handshake is used to confirm that both have the same PSK and to generate unique encryption keys.

After the 802.11 Open System Authentication and association, a *four-way handshake* is used for two main purposes: to confirm that both the client and the AP have the same PSK and to generate unique encryption keys that will be used to encrypt and decrypt data sent to and from the client.

This method of authentication is used in WPA and WPA2 and provides much greater security than WEP Shared Key authentication. However, there are still vulnerabilities. For example, if an attacker manages to capture the four-way handshake, those messages contain enough information for an attacker to attempt a brute-force attack to learn the PSK.

To protect against the vulnerabilities of WPA/WPA2's PSK authentication, WPA3 adopts a new authentication method called *simultaneous authentication of equals* (SAE), which is carried out before 802.11 association (which is then followed by the four-way handshake). Note that SAE still uses a PSK, but the SAE authentication process allows the client and AP to verify that they have matching PSKs without rendering the PSK vulnerable to brute-force attacks. While any password-based system can theoretically be brute-forced with enough time and computational power, the design and implementation of SAE in WPA3 make it practically infeasible. Figure 20.5 illustrates the WPA3-Personal authentication process.

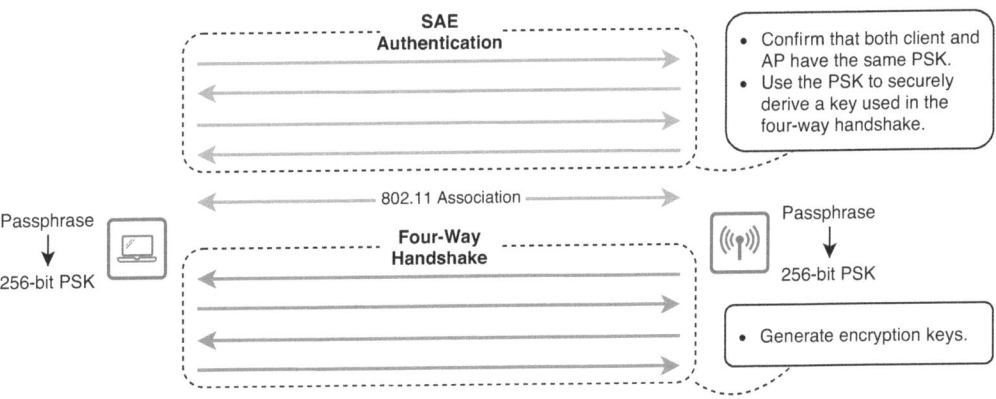

Figure 20.5 WPA3-Personal authentication using SAE. SAE authentication allows the client and AP to confirm they have the same PSK and derive a key used in the four-way handshake. In the four-way handshake, they generate the encryption keys used to encrypt/decrypt data messages.

NOTE   To the user, the experience of using WPA/WPA2/WPA3-Personal authentication is the same: the user just needs to enter an 8- to 63-character passphrase.

Although SAE makes WPA3-Personal more secure than WPA/WPA2 by protecting against brute-force attacks, it still relies on a PSK. The PSK, or the passphrase from which it is derived, could be compromised through a social engineering attack, granting an attacker access to the LAN. Outside of SOHO networks, it's best to opt for a more secure option: WPA-Enterprise.

EXAM TIP   For the CCNA exam, know that WPA-Personal authentication involves configuring a shared passphrase (which generates a PSK) and that WPA3 uses SAE to protect the PSK against brute-force attacks.

20.2.2 *WPA-Enterprise: 802.1X/EAP/RADIUS*

Instead of using a PSK that is shared among all devices in the LAN, the *WPA-Enterprise* authentication mode verifies each individual user's or device's credentials through the IEEE 802.1X standard, which uses the *Extensible Authentication Protocol* (EAP) framework. We briefly covered 802.1X and EAP in chapter 11 in the context of *port-based network access control* (PNAC) for wired hosts connected to switch ports.

WPA-Enterprise uses the same concept, but instead of controlling access to individual switch ports, it controls access to the wireless LAN. To authenticate with WPA-Enterprise, the client first uses Open System Authentication and then associates with the AP. At this point, even though the client is associated with the AP, it cannot communicate over the network; it must authenticate with 802.1X/EAP.

EAP defines various authentication methods and message formats. However, EAP itself doesn't define how those messages should be transported over a network; that's 802.1X's role. 802.1X defines how to encapsulate EAP messages over Ethernet or 802.11 LANs, called *EAP over LANs* (EAPoL). Figure 20.6 shows the 802.1X/EAP "protocol stack"—the set of protocols it uses to enable authentication via EAP.

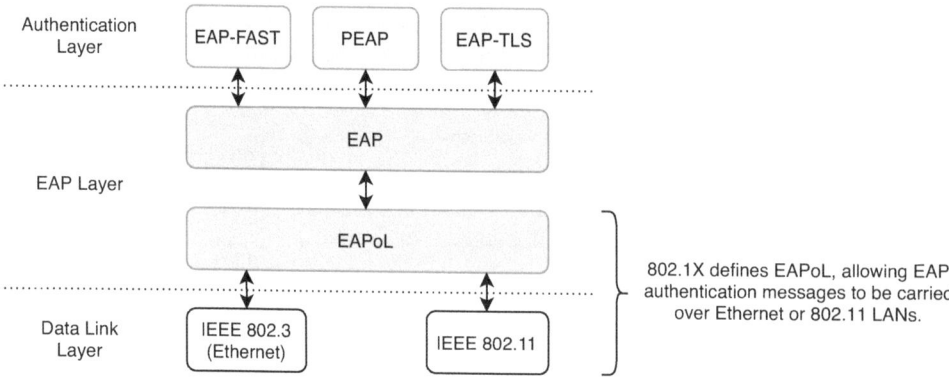

Figure 20.6   The 802.1X/EAP protocol stack. 802.1X defines EAPoL, which allows EAP messages to be transported over Ethernet or 802.11 LANs.

NOTE   The Authentication Layer on top of EAP refers to the various EAP methods that EAP defines. We'll briefly cover a few of them in this section.

EAPoL is designed to transport EAP messages within a LAN between the 802.1X supplicant (client device) and the authenticator (the AP). For review, here are the three devices' roles in 802.1X:

- *Supplicant*—The client device that wants to connect to the network
- *Authenticator*—The network device that the client connects to (the AP)
- *Authentication server (AS)*—The server that verifies the supplicant's credentials (usually a RADIUS server)

NOTE   In a split-MAC architecture, the WLC functions as the authenticator instead of the AP; the AP tunnels clients' EAP messages to the WLC using CAPWAP.

To relay the supplicant's EAP messages to the AS, the authenticator uses RADIUS. Figure 20.7 illustrates this process: EAPoL carries EAP messages between the supplicant and the authenticator, and RADIUS carries the EAP messages between the authenticator and the AS.

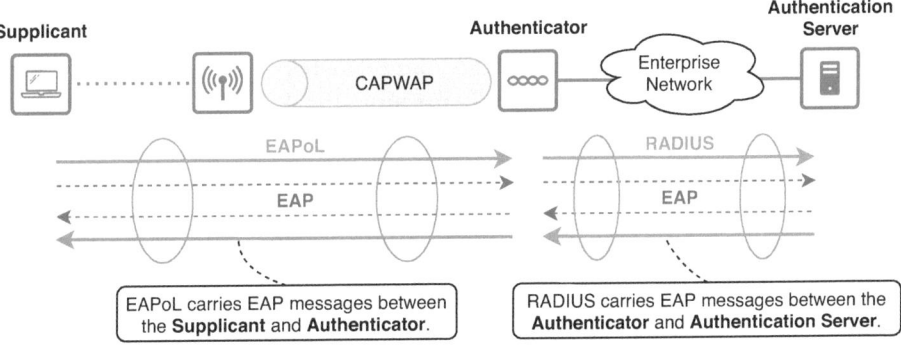

Figure 20.7   EAPoL is used to transport EAP messages between the supplicant and authenticator, and RADIUS between the authenticator and AS.

NOTE   Although previous authentication examples showed a standalone AP, WPA-Enterprise is more common in enterprise networks that would likely use a split-MAC architecture (with a WLC)—not autonomous APs.

EAP isn't a single authentication method. As the name suggests, EAP is extensible, acting as a framework that defines various authentication methods called *EAP methods*. The CCNA exam doesn't expect you to know these EAP methods in detail, but here are a few examples:

- *LEAP (Lightweight EAP)*—Developed by Cisco to address WEP's vulnerabilities. The client authenticates with a username/password combination, and then the supplicant and AS exchange challenge phrases, providing mutual authentication. LEAP uses WEP encryption and is no longer considered secure.

- *EAP-FAST (EAP-Flexible Authentication via Secure Tunneling)*—Developed by Cisco to replace LEAP. It establishes a Transport Layer Security (TLS) tunnel using a Protected Access Credential (PAC)—a shared secret—to authenticate the supplicant and AS. Within this tunnel, user credentials are exchanged for authentication.

- *PEAP (Protected EAP)*—The AS has a digital certificate that the supplicant uses to authenticate the AS and establish a TLS tunnel. In the tunnel, user credentials are provided for authentication.

- *EAP-TLS (EAP-Transport Layer Security)*—The AS and supplicant each have a digital certificate that they use to authenticate each other. EAP-TLS is considered the most secure, but managing certificates on all client devices can be burdensome.

Regardless of which EAP method is used, the same four-way handshake that we outlined in the WPA-Personal section is always used after authentication to generate the encryption keys used to encrypt/decrypt data messages. This handshake is done between the supplicant and authenticator (the client and the AP/WLC).

> **EXAM TIP**   For the CCNA exam, you should understand the basics of 802.1X (supplicant, authenticator, AS), EAP, and RADIUS: EAPoL carries EAP messages between the supplicant and authenticator, and RADIUS carries EAP messages between the authenticator and AS.

20.3   *Wireless encryption and integrity*

WEP defined confidentiality (encryption) and integrity measures that promised to offer privacy equivalent to that of wired LANs. As we already covered, that turned out not to be the case; WEP has various vulnerabilities and should not be used anymore. In this section, we'll examine the encryption and integrity protocols that replaced WEP and were adopted by the Wi-Fi Alliance's WPA, WPA2, and WPA3 certifications.

20.3.1 *Temporal Key Integrity Protocol*

After WEP's vulnerabilities were discovered, a more secure solution was urgently needed. However, there was a major problem: existing hardware was built to use WEP. To address this issue before new protocols and hardware were developed, *Temporal Key Integrity Protocol* (TKIP) was created as an enhancement to WEP. TKIP was included in the Wi-Fi Alliance's first WPA certification.

WEP's fundamental flaw was the fact that it used static encryption keys; all clients used the same encryption key, and it remained unchanged unless an admin manually configured a new passphrase. TKIP solved this by using a process called *per-packet key mixing*, generating a unique encryption key for each packet. This makes it much more difficult for an attacker to decipher the PSK through a brute-force attack. TKIP also added a few more security improvements, such as the following:

- TKIP's data integrity checksum, called a *message integrity check* (MIC), is stronger than WEP's ICV.
- TKIP adds a sequence number to each frame to mitigate against replay attacks.

NOTE   A *replay attack* is when an attacker captures valid messages and retransmits them later. For example, an attacker can gain unauthorized access to a system by replaying a user's valid authentication messages.

20.3.2   *Counter Mode with Cipher Block Chaining Message Authentication Code Protocol*

Although TKIP served as a stopgap to protect against WEP's vulnerabilities, the IEEE 802.11i standard, which formed the basis of WPA2, brought in more advanced security protocols that are still in use in many wireless LANs today. 802.11i/WPA2 uses *Counter Mode with Cipher Block Chaining Message Authentication Code Protocol* (CCMP) to provide message encryption and integrity. That's quite a long name—let's examine it.

Whereas WEP and TKIP use the RC4 encryption algorithm, CCMP uses *Advanced Encryption Standard* (AES), a more robust algorithm that provides much more secure encryption. Specifically, CCMP uses AES *counter mode* encryption, hence the "Counter Mode" in CCMP's name. The details of counter mode aren't necessary for the CCNA exam, but in essence, it involves encrypting a counter value that increments for each block of encrypted data, ensuring that each block of data is encrypted with a unique key.

The second part of the name refers to *Cipher Block Chaining Message Authentication Code* (CBC-MAC); CCMP's CBC-MAC provides a more robust data integrity checksum than TKIP's MIC.

20.3.3   *Galois/Counter Mode Protocol*

The latest security certification from the Wi-Fi Alliance is WPA3, and it uses *Galois/Counter Mode Protocol* (GCMP) for data encryption and integrity. GCMP can be considered an improved version of CCMP, offering improved security as well as greater efficiency—this efficiency is necessary for encryption to keep up with the faster data rates of the latest 802.11 standards.

Like CCMP, GCMP uses AES counter mode encryption. However, it supports greater AES key lengths (128 or 256 bits) than CCMP (128 bits), providing stronger encryption. For its data integrity checksum, GCMP uses *Galois Message Authentication Code* (GMAC)—once again, this provides more secure data integrity than the protocols used in earlier standards.

NOTE   *Galois* is pronounced "gal-wah"—the name of a French mathematician.

20.4   *Wi-Fi Protected Access*

We've covered a lot of different protocols for providing authentication, encryption, and integrity to wireless LANs, referencing the WPA generation that supports each. Table 20.1 summarizes these protocols, including WEP for reference as well.

> **EXAM TIP**   CCNA exam topic 5.9 states that you must be able to "describe wireless security protocols (WPA, WPA2, and WPA3)." In this section, we'll summarize which standards are supported by which WPA certifications; make sure you know them!

Table 20.1   WPA security protocols

	WEP	WPA	WPA2	WPA3
Release Year	1997	2003	2004	2018
Authentication (WPA-Personal)	Open System, Shared key	PSK	PSK	SAE
Authentication (WPA-Enterprise)	N/A	802.1X/EAP	802.1X/EAP	802.1X/EAP
Encryption	RC4	RC4 (TKIP)	AES (CCMP)	AES (GCMP)
Integrity	ICV	MIC (TKIP)	CBC-MAC (CCMP)	GMAC (GCMP)

It's worth noting that table 20.1 isn't complete; it only lists the strongest encryption protocol supported by each WPA certification. For example, WPA2 includes optional support for TKIP to accommodate older client devices that don't support CCMP. Similarly, WPA3 doesn't just support GCMP; it supports CCMP as well. However, for the CCNA exam, I recommend learning the protocols as listed in table 20.1; further details can be left for future studies.

As of 2020, a device must support WPA3 to earn "Wi-Fi Certified" status. WPA2 is still commonly used in enterprise and SOHO wireless LANs, but the move to WPA3 is underway, and WPA3 support is now commonplace for new hardware. In addition to the superior protocols we already covered, WPA3 has some other security benefits:

- *Protected Management Frames (PMF)*—PMF ensures the authenticity and integrity of 802.11 management frames (i.e., authentication and association messages), preventing certain types of spoofing attacks. PMF was supported in WPA2 but is mandatory in WPA3.

- *Forward Secrecy (FS)*—FS, also known as Perfect Forward Secrecy (PFS), ensures that the security of encrypted data remains intact even if the PSK is compromised in the future; a compromised PSK cannot be used to decrypt past communications. This is because the encryption keys used for each session are unique and not solely derived from the PSK.

Summary

- Although wireless LANs introduce unique challenges, fundamental security concepts like the CIA triad still apply.

- Confidentiality in a wired LAN is largely ensured by the medium: the signals are contained within the cables. However, wireless signals can be picked up by any receiver within range of the transmitter, making encryption essential.

- Unencrypted information (that will not be encrypted) is called *cleartext*. Unencrypted information that will be encrypted (but has not yet been fed into the encryption algorithm) is *plaintext*, and encrypted information is called *ciphertext*.

- To protect the integrity of a message before sending it over the air, the sender uses a mathematical function to generate a *checksum*—a small block of data derived from the original message, allowing the receiver to check whether it was altered.

- Attacks against the availability of a wireless LAN are simple to carry out by any malicious user with the proper tools. An example is an *RF jamming attack*, in which the attacker uses a signal generator to flood the 802.11 frequency bands.

- The only solution to an RF jamming attack is to locate and disable/remove the source of the attack, and the only preventative measure is physical security.

- The original 802.11 standard defined a security protocol called *Wired Equivalent Privacy* (WEP). WEP is now obsolete; it is no longer secure.

- WEP defined two methods of authentication: Open System and Shared Key.

- In WEP *Open System Authentication*, the client device sends an authentication request, and the AP sends an authentication response; no questions asked.

- WEP Shared Key Authentication involves the configuration of a static WEP key on the AP and each client—the Wi-Fi password.

- To verify that each client has the correct WEP key, the AP sends an unencrypted *challenge phrase* that the client encrypts with the WEP key and sends back to the AP. The AP then decrypts the challenge phrase and ensures it matches the original.

- In addition to authentication, WEP provides confidentiality with encryption. The same WEP key used in Shared Key Authentication can be used to encrypt messages to and from wireless clients. The encryption algorithm is Rivest Cipher 4 (RC4).

- WEP ensures the integrity of communications using a checksum called the *integrity check value* (ICV).

- After WEP's vulnerabilities were discovered, the Wi-Fi Alliance developed the *Wi-Fi Protected Access* (WPA) certification as an interim enhancement until the IEEE could develop a more permanent solution (802.11i, which was adopted by WPA2).

- WPA, WPA2, and WPA3 define two main authentication methods: WPA-Personal (primarily for SOHO networks) and WPA-Enterprise (for larger businesses).

- WPA-Personal involves configuring a pre-shared key (PSK)—a static 256-bit string that is used to generate secure encryption keys. The same PSK must be configured on the AP and its clients.

- To simplify the experience, you can configure an 8- to 63-character passphrase— what most people call the "Wi-Fi password"—which is then automatically converted into a 256-bit PSK.

- WPA-Personal authentication involves the client and AP performing a *four-way handshake* to verify the PSK and generate encryption keys. This occurs after the client has performed Open System Authentication and is associated with the AP.

- WPA/WPA2's PSK authentication is vulnerable to brute-force attacks if an attacker captures the four-way handshake. To protect against this, WPA3 adopts a new method called *simultaneous authentication of equals* (SAE).

- SAE is carried out before 802.11 association, which is then followed by the same four-way handshake. It still uses a PSK, but in a way that protects against brute-force attacks.

- WPA3 with SAE still relies on a PSK—a single passphrase that can be compromised through a social engineering attack. Outside of SOHO networks, it's best to opt for a more secure option: WPA-Enterprise.

- WPA-Enterprise authenticates each individual user's or device's credentials through 802.1X and EAP. The client first uses Open System Authentication and associates with the AP and then authenticates with 802.1X/EAP.

- 802.1X defines *port-based network access control* (PNAC), controlling whether a host is allowed to communicate via a switch port (or a wireless LAN, in this case).

- EAP defines various authentication methods (EAP methods) and message formats, and 802.1X defines how to encapsulate EAP messages over Ethernet or 802.11 LANS, called *EAP over LANs* (EAPoL).

- 802.1X defines three device roles: supplicant (the device that wants to connect to the network), authenticator (the network devices that the client connects to), and authentication server/AS (the server that verifies the supplicant's credentials).

- EAPoL transports EAP messages within a LAN between the supplicant (the client device) and the authenticator (the AP or the WLC in a split-MAC architecture).

- RADIUS is typically used to transport EAP messages between the authenticator and the AS, which is usually a RADIUS server.

- EAP isn't a single authentication method; it is extensible and defines various EAP methods. Some examples are LEAP (Lightweight EAP), EAP-FAST (EAP-Flexible Authentication via Secure Tunneling), PEAP (Protected EAP), and EAP-TLS (EAP-Transport Layer Security).

- Regardless of which EAP method is used, the same four-way handshake is always used after authentication to generate encryption keys.

- After WEP's vulnerabilities were discovered, Temporal Key Integrity Protocol (TKIP) was created as an enhancement that worked on hardware developed for WEP. TKIP was included in the Wi-Fi Alliance's first WPA certification.

- TKIP uses per-packet key mixing to generate a unique encryption key for each packet, making the PSK less vulnerable to brute-force attacks.

- TKIP's data integrity checksum, called a *message integrity check* (MIC), is stronger than WEP's ICV.

- TKIP adds a sequence number to each frame to mitigate against replay attacks.

- IEEE 802.11i, which formed the basis of WPA2, brought in more advanced security protocols that are still in use in many wireless LANs.

- WPA2 uses Counter Mode with Cipher Block Chaining Message Authentication Code Protocol (CCMP) to provide data encryption and integrity.

- CCMP uses Advanced Encryption Standard (AES) in counter mode as its encryption algorithm, which is stronger than WEP/TKIP's RC4 algorithm.

- CCMP uses Cipher Block Chaining Message Authentication Code (CBC-MAC) to provide a more robust data integrity checksum than TKIP's MIC.

- WPA3 uses Galois/Counter Mode Protocol (GCMP) for data encryption and integrity. GCMP is more secure and more efficient than CCMP, which is necessary for encryption to keep up with the faster data rates of the latest 802.11 standards.

- Like CCMP, GCMP uses AES counter mode encryption, although it supports greater key lengths (128 bits or 256 bits) than CCMP (128 bits).

- GCMP uses Galois Message Authentication Code (GMAC) for its data integrity checksum.

Wireless LAN configuration

This chapter covers

- Preparing a Cisco WLC for configuration via the GUI
- The physical ports and logical interfaces of a Cisco WLC
- Configuring simple wireless LANs with WPA2 PSK authentication

Over the past three chapters, we've covered the fundamentals of wireless LANs, starting with the basics of radio frequency (RF) communications and 802.11 standards, various wireless LAN architectures, and the many protocols used to secure communications over the airwaves. In this chapter, we'll bring it all together and see how to configure basic wireless LANs in the graphical user interface (GUI) of a Cisco wireless LAN controller (WLC). Specifically, we will cover the following CCNA exam topics:

- 2.7 Describe physical infrastructure connections of WLAN components (AP, WLC, access/trunk ports, and LAG)
- 2.8 Describe network device management access connections (Telnet, SSH, HTTP, HTTPS, console, TACACS+/RADIUS, and cloud managed)

- 2.9 Interpret the wireless LAN GUI configuration for client connectivity, such as WLAN creation, security settings, QoS profiles, and advanced WLAN settings
- 5.10 Configure and verify WLAN within the GUI using WPA2 PSK

Wireless LAN configuration is the only CCNA exam topic that requires configuration via the GUI; you could be tested on your knowledge of the WLC GUI via any of the exam question formats (multiple choice, drag-and-drop, lab simulation). When configuring a WLC that potentially manages hundreds or even thousands of lightweight APs (LWAPs), the GUI is usually the tool of choice; it provides a more user-friendly experience, simplifying the configuration, monitoring, and troubleshooting of wireless LANs.

21.1 WLAN initial setup

Before we start looking at how to configure wireless LANs, let's examine the network we will be configuring and do some initial setup. Figure 21.1 shows the simple network topology we will use for this chapter, consisting of one LWAP (AP1), one switch (SW1), and one WLC (WLC1). SW1 functions as a DHCP server, NTP server, and the default gateway for all subnets. Notice that WLC1's ports are labeled P1 and P2; Cisco WLC ports are simply called Port 1, Port 2, Port 3, etc.

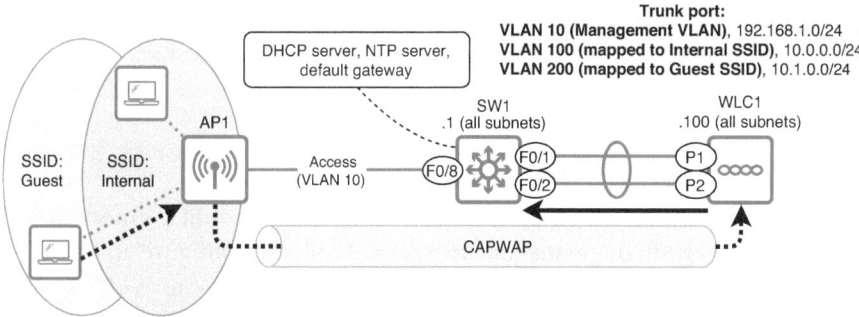

Figure 21.1   This chapter's topology. WLC1 controls AP1, an LWAP. SW1 functions as a DHCP server, NTP server, and the default gateway for all subnets. AP1 tunnels client traffic to WLC1, which translates their 802.11 frames to Ethernet frames.

NOTE   To keep the diagram as simple as possible, no external connections are shown. In a real network, SW1 would likely have connections to the internet, the corporate WAN, a larger wired LAN, etc.

The network consists of two WLANs, each mapped to a VLAN on the wired network. There is also a dedicated management VLAN that is used for remote management of network devices; the CAPWAP tunnels between AP1 and WLC1 use this VLAN. In this section, we'll first configure SW1 to fulfill its role in this LAN. Then we'll perform an initial configuration of WLC1 before moving on to the main topic: configuring the Guest and Internal WLANs in the GUI of WLC1.

What exactly is a WLAN?

Like the term *LAN*, the term *WLAN* can have different meanings depending on the context. For example, it can refer to an entire wireless network with its various APs providing BSSs and ESSs for clients using different SSIDs. In that sense, figure 21.1 depicts a single WLAN consisting of two BSSs, each with a unique SSID. However, a WLAN can also refer to a logical entity within the wireless network—not the wireless network as a whole. By this definition, each SSID is its own WLAN, and figure 21.1 shows two WLANs: one identified by the Internal SSID and one identified by the Guest SSID. We will use this latter definition in this chapter to remain consistent with the wording of the Cisco WLC GUI.

21.1.1   *Switch configuration*

SW1 fulfills some important roles in this LAN: it's the wired infrastructure that AP1 connects to, a DHCP server that AP1 and its wireless clients will lease IP addresses from, an NTP server that enables devices in the LAN to keep consistent time, and the default gateway for hosts in each subnet. To configure SW1, let's start by creating the three VLANs we need:

```
SW1(config)# vlan 10
SW1(config-vlan)# name Management          ◄──────┐   Gives each VLAN a
SW1(config-vlan)# vlan 100                         │   descriptive name
SW1(config-vlan)# name Internal            ◄───────┤
SW1(config-vlan)# vlan 200                         │
SW1(config-vlan)# name Guest               ◄───────┘
```

Because this LAN uses a split-MAC architecture, AP1 should connect to SW1 via an access port (F0/8) in the management VLAN. I will also configure an additional access port (F0/7) for my own PC; this will allow my PC to connect to WLC1's GUI over the network when we configure WLANs later in this chapter. To allow the ports to immediately move to the Spanning Tree Protocol (STP) forwarding state, I will enable PortFast as well:

```
SW1(config)# interface range f0/7-8                    Configures F0/7 and F0/8
SW1(config-if-range)# switchport mode access           as access ports in the
SW1(config-if-range)# switchport access vlan 10        management VLAN
SW1(config-if-range)# spanning-tree portfast   ◄───┐
                                                   │
                                                   Enables PortFast
```

In a split-MAC architecture, the WLC is responsible for translating between VLANs and WLANs (SSIDs), so it must connect to SW1 via a trunk link to support multiple VLANs. For redundancy and additional throughput capacity, it's common to connect the WLC to the network via a Link Aggregation Group (LAG). In the following example, I configure SW1 F0/1 and F0/2 as members of a static LAG and configure it as a trunk.

NOTE Cisco WLCs use the industry-standard terminology *LAG* instead of Ether-Channel—they're the same thing. Also, note that WLCs only support static LAGs (configured with `mode on`); they cannot use the negotiation protocols PAgP or LACP.

Configures F0/1 and F0/2
as members of a static LAG

```
SW1(config-if-range)# interface range f0/1-2
SW1(config-if-range)# channel-group 1 mode on
SW1(config-if-range)# interface port-channel 1
SW1(config-if)# switchport mode trunk
SW1(config-if)# switchport trunk allowed vlan 10,100,200
```

Configures the LAG as a
trunk and allows only the
three VLANs used in the LAN

To function as the default gateway for hosts in each subnet, SW1 needs some switch virtual interfaces (SVIs). Routing also must be enabled to allow SW1 to route packets between subnets. In the following example, I enable routing on SW1 and configure an SVI for each of the VLANs we created previously:

Enables routing

Configures the
Management VLAN's SVI

Configures the
Internal WLAN/
VLAN's SVI

```
SW1(config)# ip routing
SW1(config)# interface vlan 10
SW1(config-if)# ip address 192.168.1.1 255.255.255.0
SW1(config-if)# interface vlan 100
SW1(config-if)# ip address 10.0.0.1 255.255.255.0
SW1(config-if)# interface vlan 200
SW1(config-if)# ip address 10.1.0.1 255.255.255.0
```

Configures the Guest
WLAN/VLAN's SVI

Figure 21.2 illustrates the internal logic of SW1 after configuring these SVIs: three virtual switches (VLANs) connected to a virtual router that can forward traffic between them.

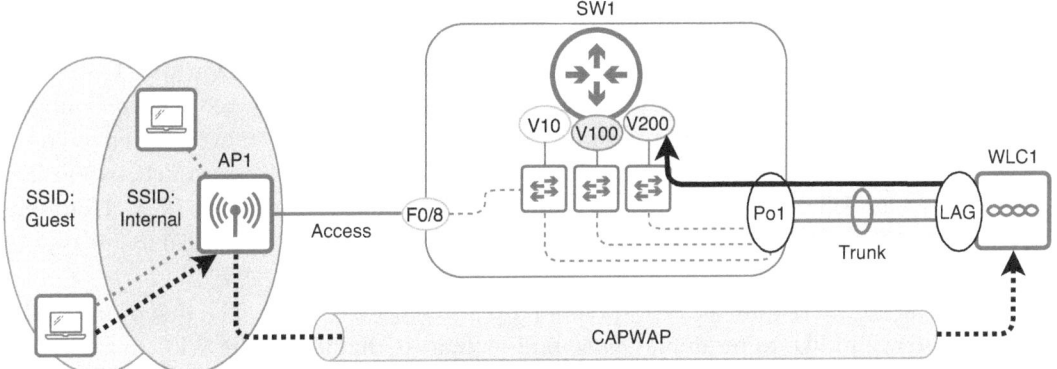

Figure 21.2   The logical internals of SW1, a multilayer switch. Messages from wireless clients are tunneled to WLC1, which sends them over the trunk link to the appropriate SVI on SW1.

Finally, SW1 provides a couple of services to the network: NTP and DHCP. Not only will wireless clients lease their IP addresses from SW1 but so will AP1; LWAPs' IP addresses are usually not manually configured. In the following example, I configure SW1 as an NTP server and create three DHCP pools: the `Management` pool (to lease IP addresses to LWAPs) and the `Internal` and `Guest` pools (to lease IP addresses to wireless clients). Note that I configure two DHCP options: option 42 and option 43. In all three pools, I configure option 42, which can be used to tell DHCP clients which NTP server they should use (SW1 itself, in this case). Option 43 can be used to tell LWAPs the IP address of their WLC:

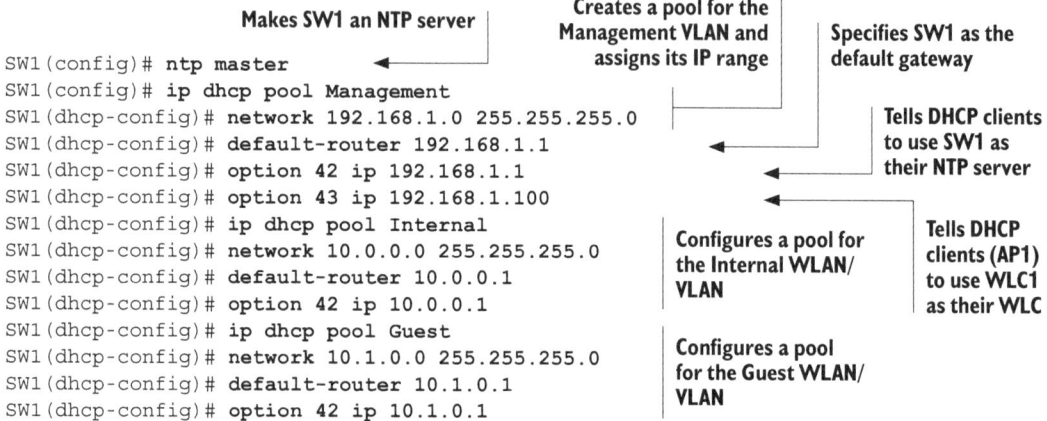

EXAM TIP   Aside from DHCP options 42 and 43, we have covered all of these configurations in previous chapters. The main point to take away is that the WLC only supports static LAG; it can't use PAgP or LACP to negotiate.

21.1.2 *WLC initial configuration*

SW1 is configured and ready to go, but we aren't ready to start configuring WLANs in WLC1's GUI yet. We need to do some initial configurations on WLC1 first. To do so, I will connect my PC to WLC1's console port and go through the Cisco Wizard Configuration Tool—a series of CLI prompts. The exam topics are clear that you need to know how to configure WLANs in the GUI, not how to set up a WLC from scratch, so you can expect any WLC configuration questions to start from an already-setup WLC. However, the steps in this section cover some important concepts and are essential to get a WLC up and running.

The output is quite long, so I'll split it up into several sections. The first prompt asks if you would like to terminate *autoinstall*—a feature that allows the WLC to automatically download its configuration from a server. In the following example, I press Enter to accept the default choice of yes (as indicated in square brackets):

```
Welcome to the Cisco Wizard Configuration Tool
Use the '-' character to backup
Would you like to terminate autoinstall? [yes]:
```

Press Enter to accept the default yes, and terminate autoinstall.

Next, the wizard prompts for the WLC's system name (hostname) and an admin username/password:

Configures the WLC's hostname

```
System Name [Cisco_10:65:64] (31 characters max): WLC1
Enter Administrative User Name (24 characters max): admin
Enter Administrative Password (3 to 24 characters): ***********
Re-enter Administrative Password              : ***********
```

Creates an admin username and password

The next prompt asks if you would like to enable link aggregation. I type yes to enable it; I will connect SW1 and WLC1 via a LAG:

```
Enable Link Aggregation (LAG) [yes][NO]: yes
```

Enables link aggregation on WLC1's ports

The next few prompts ask for information about the management interface—a virtual interface in the WLC that is used to manage it. This is the interface I will connect to later to access WLC1's GUI. The final setting (DHCP Server IP Address) allows you to specify the DHCP server to which the WLC will forward wireless clients' DHCP messages (SW1 in this example):

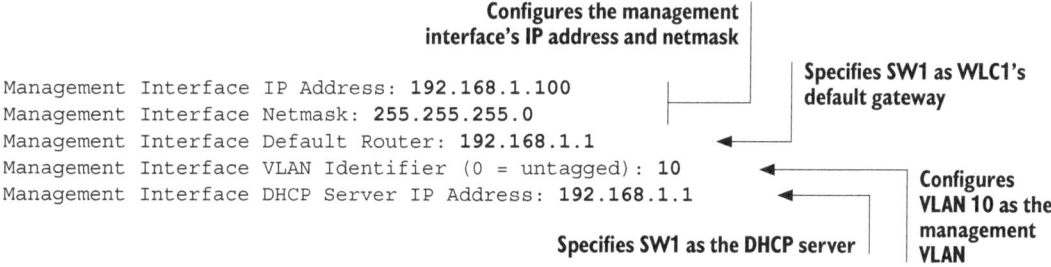

Configures the management interface's IP address and netmask

Specifies SW1 as WLC1's default gateway

```
Management Interface IP Address: 192.168.1.100
Management Interface Netmask: 255.255.255.0
Management Interface Default Router: 192.168.1.1
Management Interface VLAN Identifier (0 = untagged): 10
Management Interface DHCP Server IP Address: 192.168.1.1
```

Specifies SW1 as the DHCP server

Configures VLAN 10 as the management VLAN

NOTE Specifying a VLAN ID for the management interface means that the WLC will tag all traffic sent from that interface with the specified VLAN ID.

The next few prompts cover some settings whose details are beyond what you need to know for the CCNA exam, but you must enter them to complete the initial configuration. The Virtual Gateway IP Address is used in communications between the WLC and wireless clients and is used for specific purposes like relaying DHCP messages. It should be unique in the network but doesn't have to be reachable by any other devices. Cisco recommends using an address in one of the ranges reserved for documentation/ examples (192.0.2.0/24, 198.51.100.0/24, or 203.0.113.0/24):

```
Virtual Gateway IP Address: 192.0.2.1
```

The Multicast IP Address is used by the WLC to send multicast messages to clients. This should be in the multicast (class D) range of 224.0.0.0 to 239.255.255.255. Specifically, it should be in the private ("administratively scoped") multicast range: 239.0.0.0/8:

```
Multicast IP Address: 239.239.239.239
```

The Mobility/RF Group Name is actually two separate settings. The first is the WLC's mobility group, which is used to allow multiple WLCs to coordinate to support clients that roam between APs controlled by different WLCs. The RF group is used to manage and coordinate RF settings like power levels and channel selections across multiple WLCs. These are usually the same group, but you can change them individually from the GUI later:

```
Mobility/RF Group Name: ManningCCNA
```

With those three prompts out of the way, the remaining ones are more familiar. In the next prompt, we have to create a WLAN, specifying its SSID. I'll delete this later and create the Internal and Guest WLANs, so I named it TEST:

```
Network Name (SSID): TEST
```

The following prompt determines how the WLC will handle DHCP traffic from wireless clients. If you type yes to enable *bridging mode*, the WLC will forward clients' DHCP messages as is, simply translating the 802.11 frames to Ethernet frames without any further changes. If you accept the default NO option (the default option is indicated with uppercase letters), the WLC will function in *proxy mode*—basically, it will function like a DHCP relay agent. I pressed Enter to accept the default:

```
Configure DHCP Bridging Mode [yes][NO]:
```

The wizard then asks if you want to allow clients to use static (manually configured) IP addresses or not. If you select no, all clients will be required to lease an IP address via DHCP. I pressed enter at this prompt to accept the default YES:

```
Allow Static IP Addresses [YES][no]:
```

Next up is RADIUS server configuration, which is necessary if using WPA-Enterprise authentication with 802.1X/EAP. The CCNA exam topics state that you need to be able to configure PSK authentication (WPA-Personal), so I'll type **no** here:

```
Configure a RADIUS Server now? [YES][no]: no
```

The wizard then prompts you for a country code. This is necessary because, as we covered in chapter 18, different countries have different laws governing the use of the RF frequency bands. You might be tempted to enter the country you live in, but if you bought secondhand hardware for a home lab like I did, you need to make sure that the country code you enter matches the *regulatory domain* of the APs you are using. The regulatory domain of my APs is "-E," so I entered the code of a country in that regulatory domain: FR (France):

```
Enter Country Code list (enter 'help' for a list of countries) [US]: FR
```

NOTE   The regulatory domain is indicated in the AP model's name, i.e., AIR-CAP3502I-E-K9. To view a list of countries and their regulatory domains, go to https://mng.bz/0GBN. If the WLC's country code isn't in the same regulatory domain as an AP, the WLC won't be able to manage the AP.

The following series of prompts asks if you want to enable each of a series of 802.11 standards. I press Enter to accept the default for each. The final `Enable Auto-RF` option allows the WLC to automatically control each LWAP's transmit power and channel assignment—it's usually a good idea to leave this on:

```
Enable 802.11b Network [YES][no]:
Enable 802.11a Network [YES][no]:
Enable 802.11g Network [YES][no]:
Enable Auto-RF [YES][no]:
```

We've reached the final prompts! In the following prompts, I specify SW1 as WLC1's NTP server, configure its polling interval (how frequently WLC1 will query the NTP server for the time), and then save the configuration, causing WLC1 to reboot:

```
Configure a NTP server now? [YES][no]:
Enter the NTP server's IP address: 192.168.1.1
Enter a polling interval between 3600 and 604800 secs: 3600
Configuration correct? If yes, system will save it and reset. [yes][NO]: yes
```

21.1.3 Connecting to the WLC

EXAM TIP   Connecting to a WLC to manage and configure it is CCNA exam topic 2.8: Describe network device management access connections (Telnet, SSH, HTTP, HTTPS, console, TACACS+/RADIUS, and cloud managed).

Now that WLC1's initial configuration is complete, we can connect to it and configure some WLANs. There are various ways to connect to and configure a WLC. In this section, we'll cover those different methods and also configure a CPU ACL to restrict which devices can manage the WLC.

MANAGEMENT CONNECTIONS

You can configure a Cisco WLC via either the CLI or the GUI using protocols you're already familiar with: Telnet, SSH, HTTP, HTTPS, or a console connection. The WLC also has multiple methods of authenticating users who want to connect to it: its own local user database or a RADIUS/TACACS+ AAA server. Figure 21.3 illustrates these different connection methods.

NOTE   The PC needs network access to the WLC to connect via Telnet/SSH or HTTP/HTTPS. Earlier in this chapter, I configured SW1 F0/7 as an access port in the management VLAN, allowing my PC to connect to the network and access WLC1.

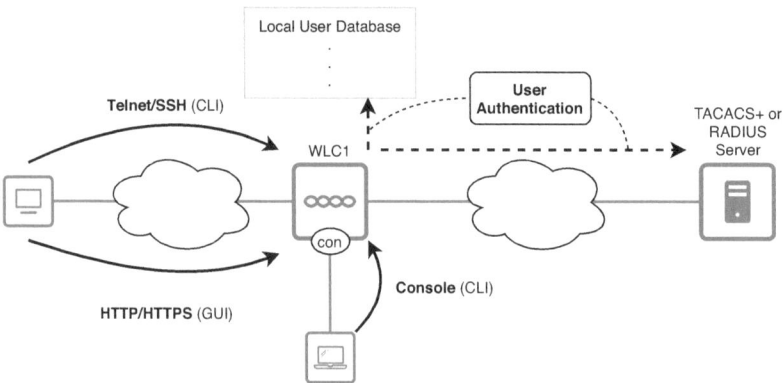

Figure 21.3   WLC management connection methods. The CLI can be accessed via the console port or a network connection (Telnet/SSH). The GUI can be accessed over the network via HTTP/HTTPS. The WLC can authenticate users by checking its local user database or a TACACS+/RADIUS server.

The management connection and authentication methods shown in figure 21.3 apply not only to Cisco WLCs, but to other network devices as well. For example, in addition to the familiar CLI, Catalyst switches (Cisco's line of enterprise-grade switches) have a GUI called the Web User Interface (WebUI) that you can use for configuration and management. However, there's a reason the CCNA doesn't test you on how to configure routers and switches using the GUI: it is quite limited compared to the CLI and is rarely used. Instead, the CLI is usually the tool of choice when configuring routers and switches.

While GUI configuration for devices like routers and switches is less common, the opposite is true of WLC management. To connect to WLC1's GUI, open a web browser, and type the IP address of the WLC's management interface (192.168.1.100) in the address bar. After logging in with the admin username/password, you'll be greeted with a screen like that shown in figure 21.4.

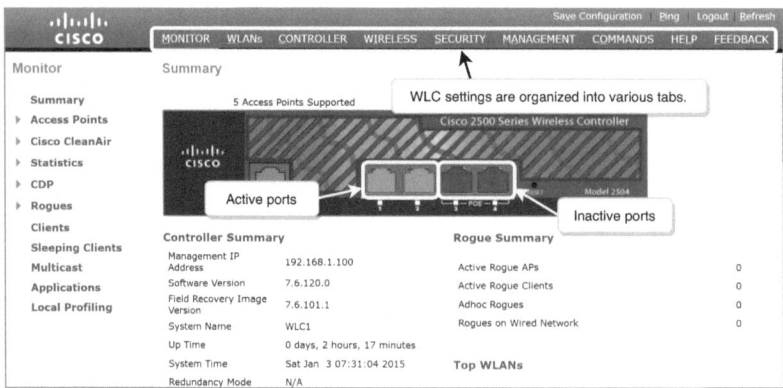

Figure 21.4   The Cisco WLC GUI. An image of the WLC is displayed, showing active and inactive ports. WLC settings are organized into various tabs at the top.

NOTE To more clearly display the relevant sections of the output, I will zoom and crop the screenshots as necessary.

This first screen is the Monitor tab, which shows an overview of the system's status (such as active and inactive ports). The WLC's settings are organized into various tabs at the top of the screen, and we will use six of them:

- Monitor—Provides an overview of system status and client/AP statistics
- WLANs—Manages individual WLAN settings including SSID configuration, security, QoS, and advanced WLAN features
- Controller—Configures global settings for the WLC itself, like network interfaces, IP addresses, NTP, etc.
- Wireless—Settings related to the LWAPs managed by the WLC
- Security—Security settings like ACLs and authentication methods
- Management—WLC management settings like management connections (Telnet, SSH, HTTP, HTTPS, console), SNMP, and Syslog

To configure and verify the WLC's management settings, we'll first click the Management tab at the top of the screen. From the Management tab, you can see which kinds of connections are allowed by default; this is shown in figure 21.5. By default, HTTP, HTTPS, and SSH connections are allowed—Telnet connections aren't. You can change these settings from the HTTP-HTTPS and Telnet-SSH menus on the left. For example, you might want to disable HTTP connections because HTTP isn't a secure protocol; it doesn't encrypt messages.

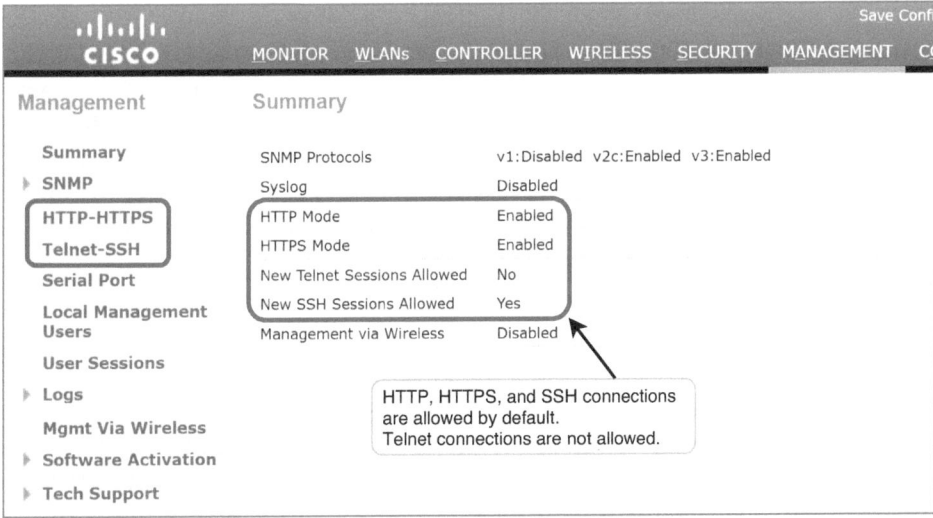

Figure 21.5 The Management tab. HTTP, HTTPS, and SSH connections are allowed by default, but Telnet connections aren't. You can change these settings from the HTTP-HTTPS and Telnet-SSH menus on the left.

The WLC can authenticate users using its local user database (i.e., the admin account created during the initial configuration), a RADIUS server, or a TACACS+ server (or some combination of those three). To check the default settings, click the Security tab, expand the Priority Order dropdown menu, and then select Management User. Figure 21.6 shows the default settings.

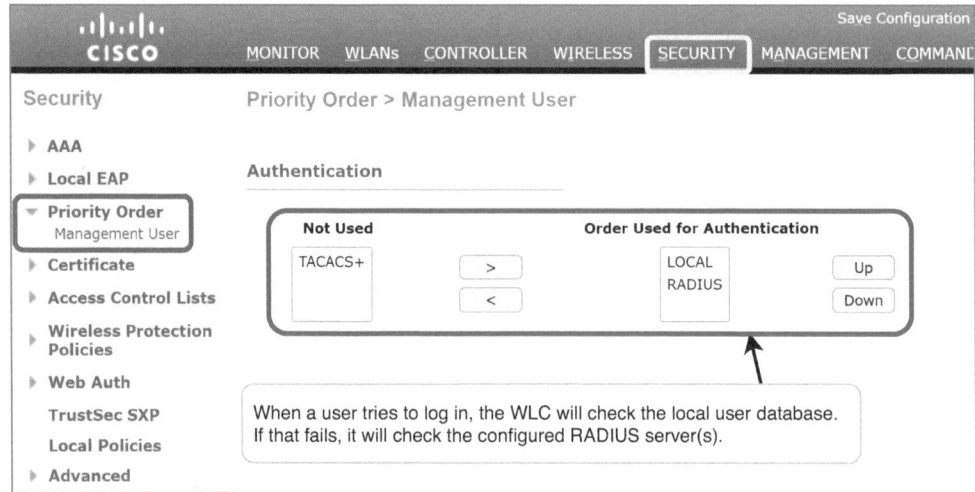

Figure 21.6   The default management user authentication methods. The WLC will authenticate users by checking its local user database and, if that fails, by contacting its configured RADIUS server(s).

When a user tries to log in, the WLC will check the user's credentials against the local user database. If no matching credentials are found, it will check any configured RADIUS servers. If both methods fail, the user won't be able to log in. You can change which authentication methods are used, and in which order, from this screen.

In addition to the Management User menu, the Security tab includes various other security-related menus. Notably, if using WPA-Enterprise authentication, you can configure the relevant RADIUS settings from the AAA dropdown menu. We will stick to the CCNA exam topics, so we won't look at the AAA menu, but let's look at the Access Control Lists dropdown menu to secure access to the WLC with a CPU ACL.

CONFIGURING A CPU ACL

When covering Telnet and SSH in chapter 5, we looked at how to configure an ACL and apply it to the VTY lines of a router or switch to limit which hosts can connect to and configure the device. You can do the same thing on a WLC with a *CPU ACL*—an ACL that filters traffic destined for the WLC itself, such as HTTP/HTTPS/Telnet/SSH management connections. There are two steps to configuring a CPU ACL: create the ACL, and then apply it as a CPU ACL.

> **NOTE**   This two-step process is identical to configuring ACLs on routers/switches. First you create the ACL, and then you apply it (i.e., to an interface or the VTY lines).

Figure 21.7 shows how to create an ACL. From the Security tab, expand the Access Control Lists dropdown menu, and click Access Control Lists. Click New... to create an ACL (you will be prompted for the ACL's name), and then click the ACL's name (MGMT) to edit it and configure some rules.

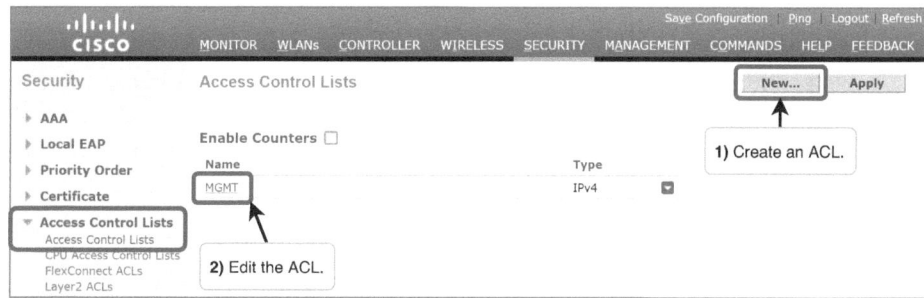

Figure 21.7 Creating a new ACL. Click New... to create and name it, and then click the ACL's name to edit it and configure rules.

Clicking the newly created ACL's name brings you to the Edit page, from which you can create a new rule by clicking Add New Rule at the top right.

NOTE When covering ACLs in chapters 23 and 24 of volume 1, we used the term *access control entry* (ACE) for each of the entries in an ACL—the WLC GUI uses the term *rule*.

Now we can specify the rule's parameters, as shown in figure 21.8. To secure management access to the WLC, let's create a rule permitting only IP addresses in the Management subnet (192.168.1.0/24). To finish configuring the rule, click Apply.

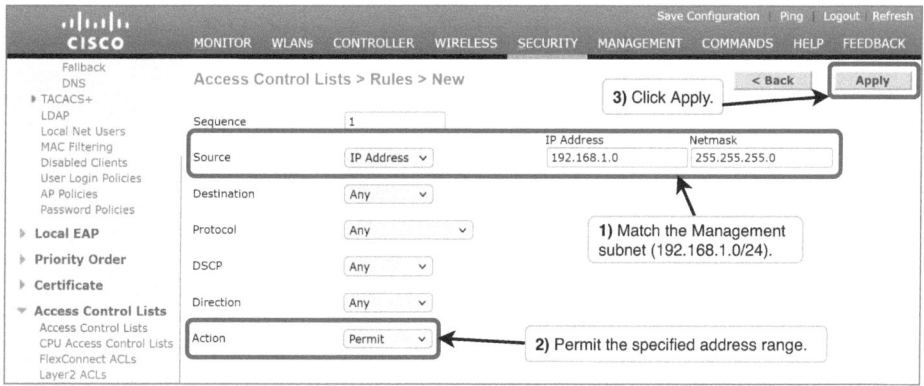

Figure 21.8 Configuring an ACL rule's parameters

Like routers and switches, a WLC's ACLs have an "implicit deny" rule at the end. Any packets not explicitly permitted by the ACL (packets not sourced from the

Management subnet) will be denied, so there's no need to configure any further rules. The one rule we configured permits the Management subnet, and the implicit deny blocks all other traffic.

We have now created the ACL—all that's left is to apply it. To do so, click CPU Access Control Lists under the same Access Control Lists dropdown menu, check the Enable CPU ACL box, select the ACL's name, and click Apply.

> **NOTE** In addition to filtering HTTP/HTTPS/Telnet/SSH management traffic to the WLC, the CPU ACL also filters CAPWAP traffic from LWAPs to the WLC. When configuring a CPU ACL, make sure you don't deny CAPWAP traffic from legitimate LWAPs!

21.2   WLC ports and interfaces

Now that we've connected to WLC1's GUI and secured it with a CPU ACL, we are almost ready to configure the Internal and Guest WLANs—but not quite. Each WLAN needs an interface on the WLC that serves to connect the WLAN to a VLAN on the wired network. In this section, we'll examine the different port and interface types on a WLC and then configure dynamic interfaces to map WLANs to VLANs.

21.2.1   Physical ports and logical interfaces

In chapter 8 of volume 1 on router and switch interfaces, I said that the terms *port* and *interface* are often used interchangeably. This is generally true, but in the context of Cisco WLCs, they are strictly different. A WLC *port* is a physical port—typically an RJ45 port—that cables connect to. A WLC *interface* is a logical entity in the WLC, like an SVI on a switch. Figure 21.9 illustrates some of the physical port and logical interface types that we will cover.

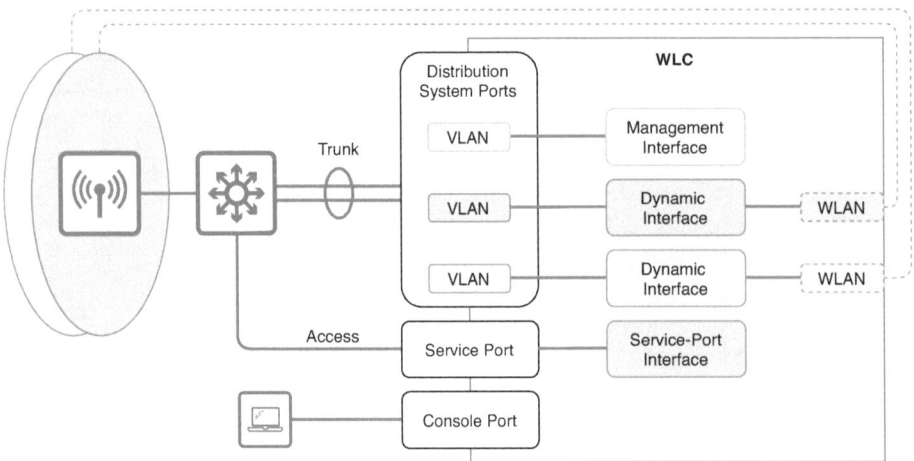

Figure 21.9   WLC ports and interfaces. Ports are physical connectors that connect to other devices, and interfaces are logical entities in the WLC.

NOTE The service port and service-port interface shown in figure 21.9 aren't present in the network we're using for this chapter.

WLC PORTS

There are four types of physical ports on a WLC:

- *Console port*—A standard console port like on a router or switch (RJ45 or USB).
- *Service port*—A dedicated management port. This can be used for out-of-band (OOB) management—connecting to and managing the WLC via a dedicated connection that is separate from the DS ports. The service port doesn't support VLAN tagging; it must connect to an access port on the switch.
- *Redundancy port*—Used to connect two WLCs together to form a redundant pair.
- *Distribution system port*—Standard network ports that connect to the distribution system (DS). DS ports can form a LAG for increased bandwidth and redundancy. WLC1's LAG connection to SW1 in our example uses DS ports (Port 1 and Port 2).

Note that not all WLC models have all of these port types. The WLC model I'm using for this chapter only has one console port and four DS ports—no service or redundancy ports. In section 21.1.1, I connected my PC directly to WLC1's console port to perform the initial configuration. WLC1's two connections to SW1, which form a LAG, are DS ports.

NOTE If you enable link aggregation (as we did in WLC1's initial configuration), all of the WLC's DS ports will be included in the LAG. However, you don't need to use all of the ports; as long as there is at least one functioning physical port in the LAG, it will be operational.

WLC INTERFACES

Whereas ports are physical, interfaces are logical entities. Cisco WLCs have a variety of interface types, each used for specific purposes: connecting to and managing the WLC, mapping WLANs to VLANs, communicating between the WLC and its APs, etc. The different interface types are as follows:

- *Management interface*—This is the default interface for in-band management; it maps to a management VLAN (VLAN 10 in this chapter's network) and sends and receives traffic via the same DS ports as other network traffic.
- *AP-manager interface*—An interface that the WLC uses to communicate with LWAPs via CAPWAP tunnels. The management interface acts as the AP-manager interface by default, but you can optionally configure a separate AP-manager interface to separate CAPWAP traffic from other management traffic (SSH, etc).
- *Redundancy management interface*—When two WLCs are connected by their redundancy ports, one WLC is "active" and the other is "standby." This interface can be used to connect to and manage the standby WLC.

- *Service-port interface*—This interface corresponds to the physical service port and is used for OOB management.
- *Virtual interface*—The Virtual Gateway IP Address we configured during WLC1's initial configuration is applied to this interface. It is used for specific purposes like relaying client DHCP messages.
- *Dynamic interface*—A dynamic interface is similar to an SVI on a switch. Each dynamic interface is mapped to a VLAN and a corresponding WLAN. For example, traffic from the Internal WLAN will be sent to the wired network from the WLC's Internal dynamic interface, tagged in the appropriate VLAN.

21.2.2 Configuring dynamic interfaces

Each WLAN must be mapped to a corresponding dynamic interface. In this section, we'll create the two dynamic interfaces we need: one for the Internal WLAN and one for the Guest WLAN. Figure 21.10 shows how to create a dynamic interface: from the Controller tab, click the Interfaces menu, and then click New… to create a new interface.

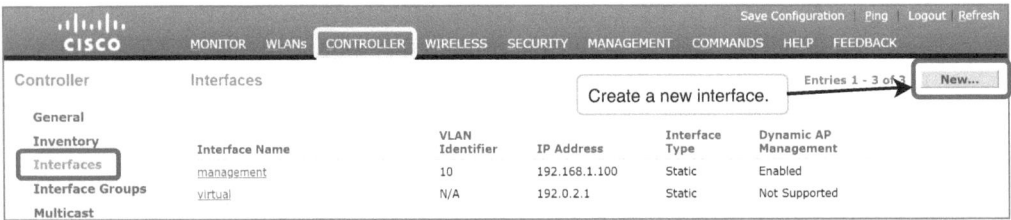

Figure 21.10   Creating a new dynamic interface. From the Interfaces menu in the Controller tab, click New….

> **NOTE**   We will only look at the Interfaces menu, but the Controller tab includes various other settings related to the WLC itself: IP addresses, Ports, DHCP and NTP settings, etc.

The first screen, shown in figure 21.11, prompts you for the interface name and VLAN ID. Although not necessary, I recommend keeping interface, VLAN, and WLAN naming consistent for simplicity's sake. I named this interface Internal and assigned it to VLAN 100. To move to the next screen, click Apply.

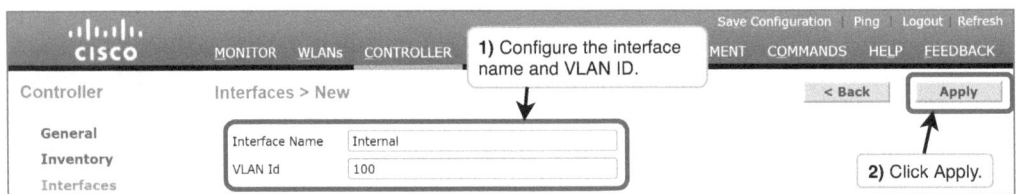

Figure 21.11   Naming an interface and assigning a VLAN ID

Figure 21.12 shows the next screen, where you can configure the interface's IP address, netmask, and gateway—the address of the router (or multilayer switch, in this case) that can be used to reach external destinations. After that, you can specify the DHCP server that the WLC should forward client DHCP messages to. In this case, the gateway and DHCP server are both SW1's VLAN 100 SVI.

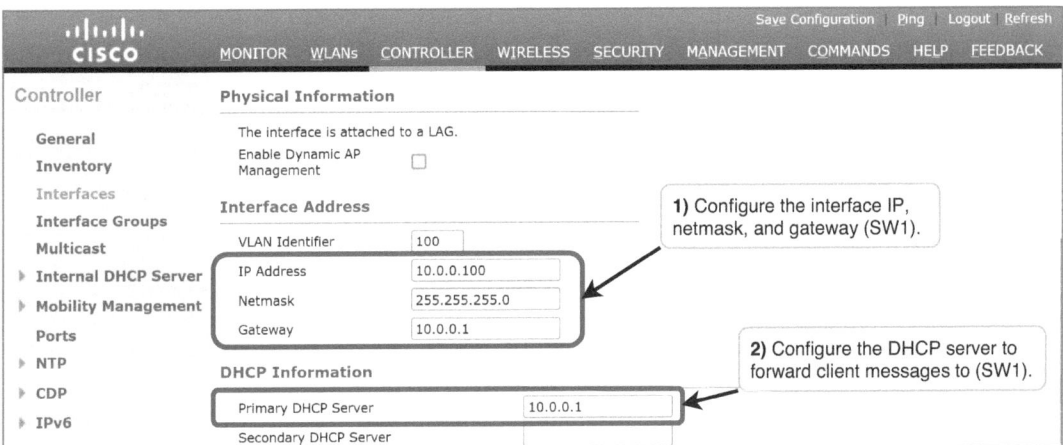

Figure 21.12   Configuring interface details. SW1's VLAN 100 SVI (10.0.0.1) functions as both the default gateway and DHCP server. Afterward, click Apply in the top-right corner (not shown).

After creating the dynamic interface for the Internal WLAN, you can repeat the same process for the Guest WLAN's dynamic interface. When you're done, you'll see both interfaces displayed alongside the Management and Virtual interfaces in the Interfaces menu's list.

21.3   Configuring WLANs

Now that we have created two dynamic interfaces, we can create our two WLANs. When performing WLC1's initial configuration, the wizard prompted us to create a WLAN—I named it TEST. Instead of editing that WLAN, I'll delete it and start from a clean slate. Figure 21.13 shows how to do that: from the WLANs tab, select the TEST WLAN, select Remove Selected from the dropdown menu, and click Go. Then, to create a new WLAN, select Create New, and click Go once again.

> **EXAM TIP**   Configuring WLANs is covered in exam topics 2.9 and 5.10; make sure to familiarize yourself with the basic steps we cover in this section.

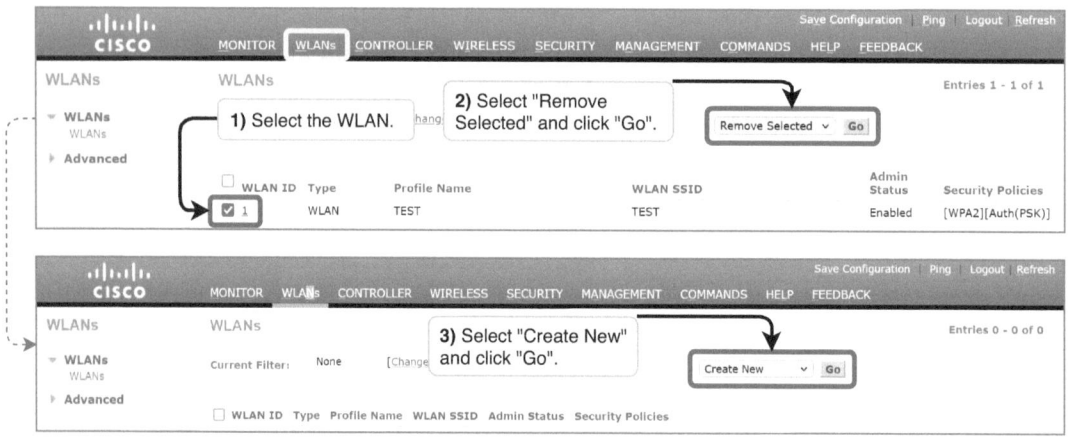

Figure 21.13   Deleting the TEST WLAN (created during initial configuration) and creating a new WLAN

The next page, as shown in figure 21.14, asks for three different identifiers for the WLAN: the Profile Name, the SSID, and the ID. The SSID is the name of the WLAN as seen by clients. The Profile Name and ID aren't seen by clients; they are used only by the WLC. The Profile Name can be any descriptive name—I kept it the same as the SSID. Finally, the ID is a unique numeric identifier. After configuring these three settings, click Apply to move to the next screen.

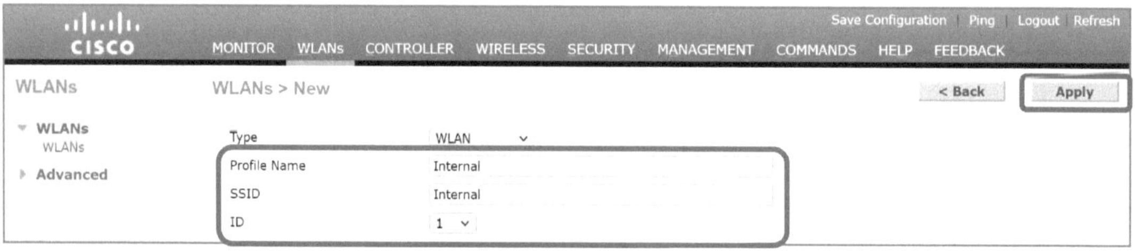

Figure 21.14   Configuring the Profile Name, SSID, and ID of a WLAN

Figure 21.15 shows the next page, with a series of tabs allowing you to configure various aspects of the WLAN, starting with the General tab. There are two main things to point out here. First, make sure to check the Status box to enable the WLAN; if you don't do this, the WLAN will be disabled and clients won't be able to connect to it. Second, make sure to select the appropriate interface. This is the Internal WLAN, so I selected the Internal dynamic interface that we created earlier.

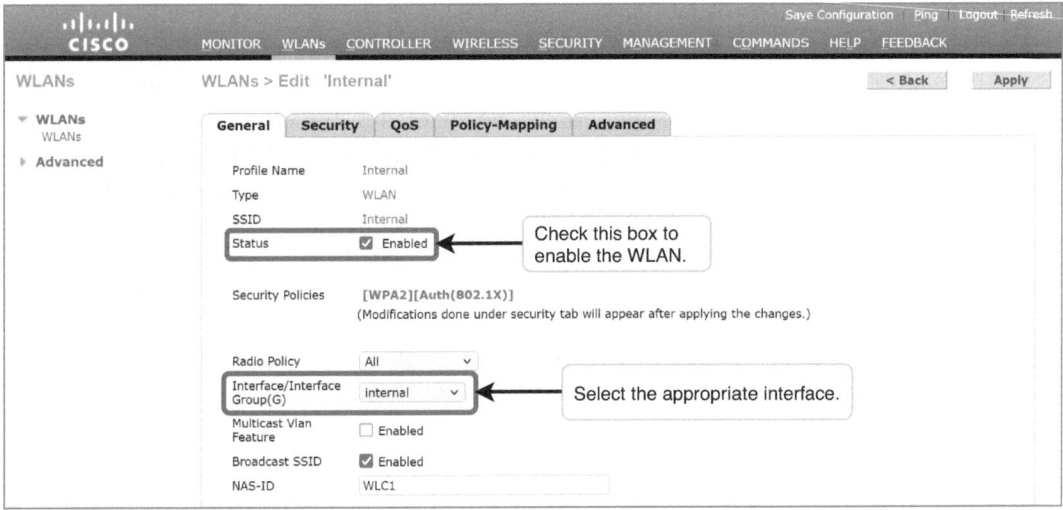

Figure 21.15 The General tab on the WLANs page. Make sure to enable the WLAN, and select the appropriate interface.

21.3.1 WLAN Security settings

Let's configure the Internal WLAN's security settings next. As shown in figure 21.16, the Security tab has its own series of tabs, starting with Layer 2; this is where you configure settings like WPA authentication and encryption. These are considered Layer 2 security settings because they control the client's access to the LAN before the client has its own IP address and is able to participate in Layer 3 communication.

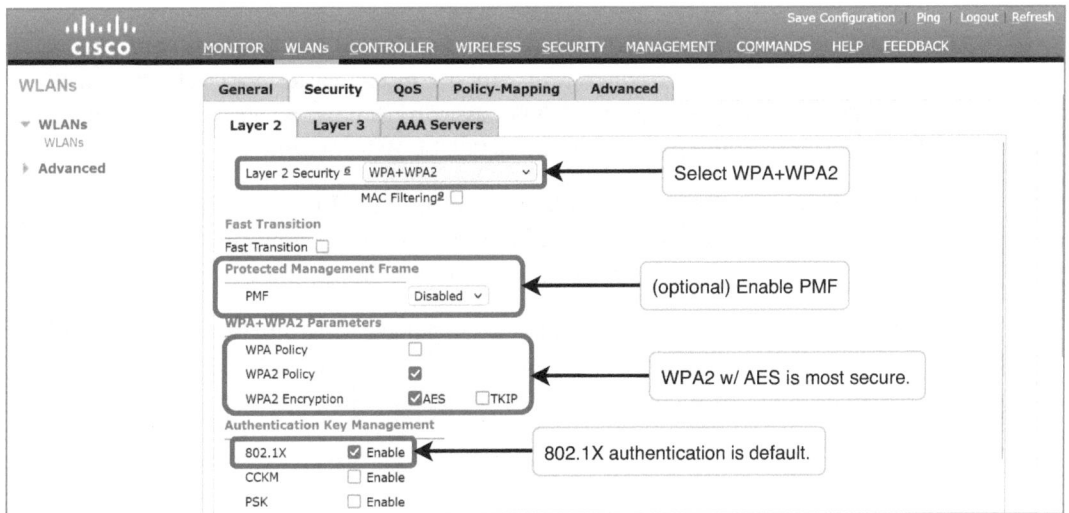

Figure 21.16 WLAN Layer 2 security settings. For the CCNA, you must configure WPA2 with PSK authentication.

CCNA exam topic 5.10 says that you must be able to configure WPA2 PSK authentication, so that's what we'll do. From the top dropdown menu, select WPA + WPA2. I've also highlighted Protected Management Frame (PMF); as I stated in chapter 20, PMF is mandatory in WPA3 but can optionally be enabled in WPA2 to secure management frames—I'll leave it disabled since it's optional. Under WPA + WPA2 Parameters, make sure that WPA2 Policy and AES Encryption are checked. The original WPA is no longer considered secure, and neither is TKIP; leave them disabled. Finally, under Authentication Key Management, notice that 802.1X is enabled by default. The CCNA exam topics list specifies PSK authentication, so I change 802.1X to PSK in figure 21.17.

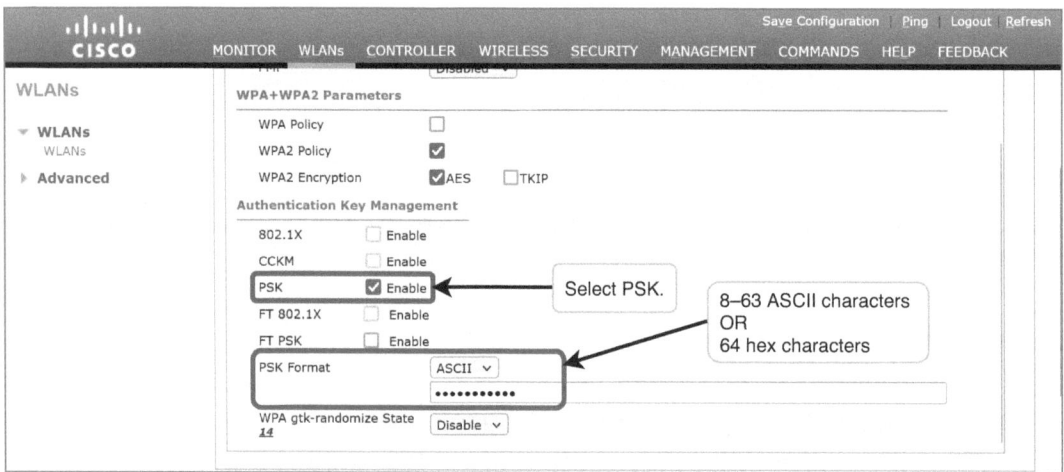

Figure 21.17   Enabling PSK authentication. The PSK can be configured as an 8- to 63-character ASCII passphrase or a 64-character hexadecimal string.

As we covered in chapter 20, the PSK is 256 bits in length. You can configure it as a string of 64 hexadecimal characters, but it's much easier to configure an 8- to 63-character ASCII passphrase—the Wi-Fi password that users will use to authenticate. The WLC will convert the passphrase into a 256-bit PSK for you.

NOTE   *ASCII*, short for American Standard Code for Information Interchange, is a character-encoding standard that represents text in computers. Each ASCII character is 8 bits in length, allowing for 256 (2^8) unique characters.

From the Layer 3 tab, you can configure additional security measures that take place after the client has connected to the network and received an IP address—hence the name Layer 3. Select Web Policy to view the options, as shown in figure 21.18.

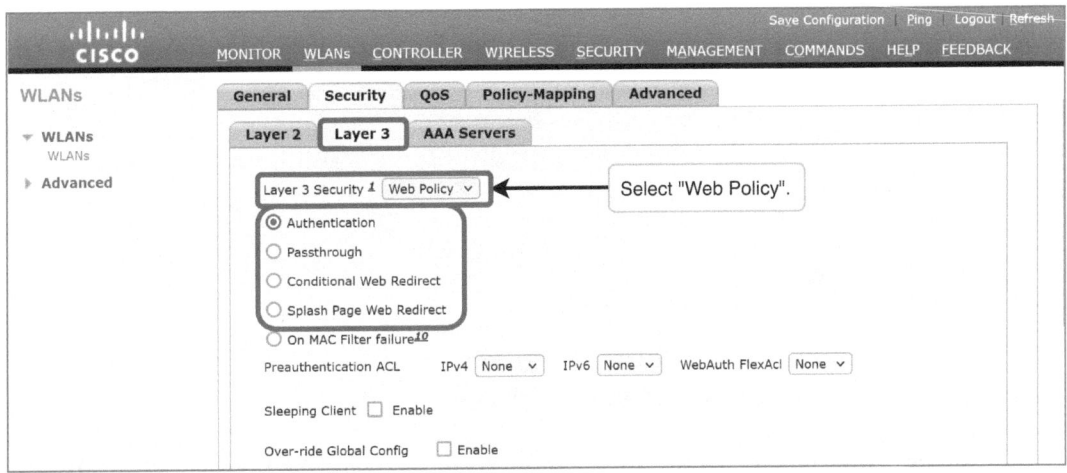

Figure 21.18   **Layer 3 security measures take effect after the client has completed any Layer 2 security measures and has an IP address.**

The following is a brief description of each. Some of them probably sound familiar; they are often used in public Wi-Fi (i.e., at Starbucks):

- *Authentication*—After the client receives an IP address and tries to access a web page, the user will have to enter a username and password to authenticate.
- *Passthrough*—The user can access the network after accepting certain terms and conditions or viewing a mandatory message. No actual authentication is performed (although an email address might be required).
- *Conditional Web Redirect*—The user will be redirected to a specific web page only under certain conditions (i.e., their password has expired or they need to pay a bill to continue using the network).
- *Splash Page Web Redirect*—The client is shown a particular web page upon connecting to the network.

EXAM TIP   Although you don't have to know the details of these Layer 3 security measures, I recommend being able to differentiate between Layer 2 (WPA with PSK or 802.1X) and Layer 3 (web policies like passthrough or redirects) security measures.

21.3.2 *WLAN QoS settings*

The next tab on the WLANs page after Security is QoS. Wireless QoS is its own can of worms that you don't have to open for the CCNA. However, you should know the four QoS levels supported by a Cisco WLC, as shown in figure 21.19.

Figure 21.19   The four QoS levels: Platinum, Gold, Silver, and Bronze

The dropdown menu gives a brief description of each. For the Internal WLAN that we are configuring, the default Silver level is appropriate. For the Guest WLAN, Bronze is appropriate; this gives guest user traffic lower priority than internal user traffic:

- *Platinum*—Used for voice (VoIP) traffic, which is sensitive to delay/loss/jitter.
- *Gold*—Used for video traffic.
- *Silver*—Described as "best effort"; this is the default setting and should be used for standard user data traffic.
- *Bronze*—This is the lowest level of service. It should be used for guest services or other low-priority traffic.

EXAM TIP   Make sure you know the four QoS levels and their descriptions: Platinum = voice, Gold = video, Silver = best effort, and Bronze = background.

21.3.3 *WLAN advanced settings*

After QoS, we will skip Policy-Mapping and move on to the final tab: Advanced. As figure 21.20 shows, many different settings can be enabled here. Let's highlight a few of them:

- *Client Load Balancing*—If a client tries to associate with a busy LWAP (with lots of clients) and another less-busy LWAP is in range, the WLC's response will encourage the client to seek a less-busy LWAP.
- *Client Band Select*—If a client supports both the 2.4 GHz band and the 5 GHz band, LWAPs will delay responses to probes in the 2.4 GHz band, encouraging the client to use the 5 GHz band, which is usually less crowded with devices.

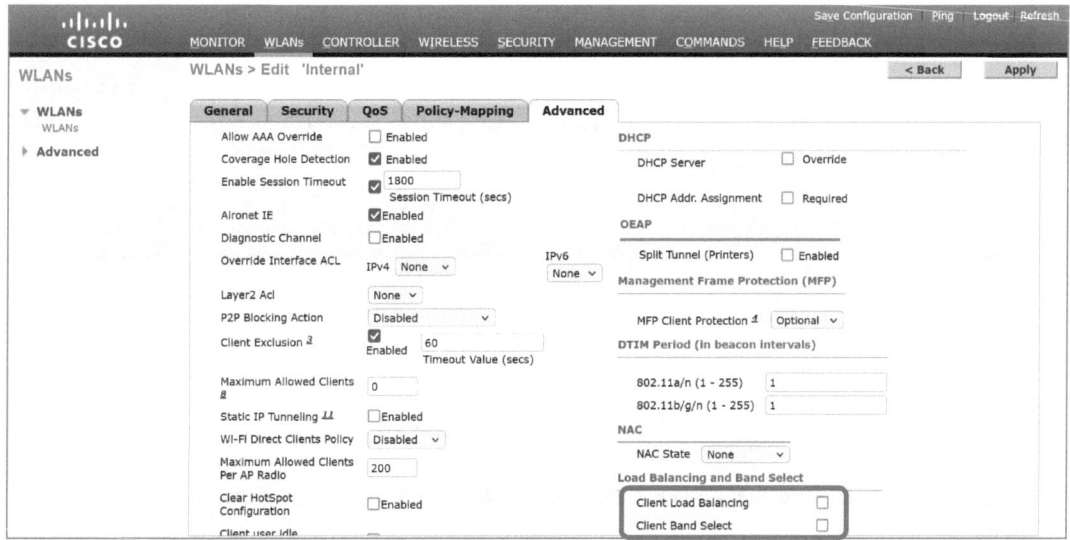

Figure 21.20 The Advanced tab allows you to enable features like Client Load Balancing and Client Band Select.

However, there's more to the advanced tab. Figure 21.21 scrolls down a bit to where you can enable a familiar feature: FlexConnect. As we covered in chapter 19, FlexConnect can be enabled per WLAN. *FlexConnect Local Switching* means that the LWAP can switch client traffic between the wired and wireless networks on its own—no need to tunnel it to the WLC. *FlexConnect Local Auth* allows the LWAP to authenticate clients on its own, instead of relying on the WLC.

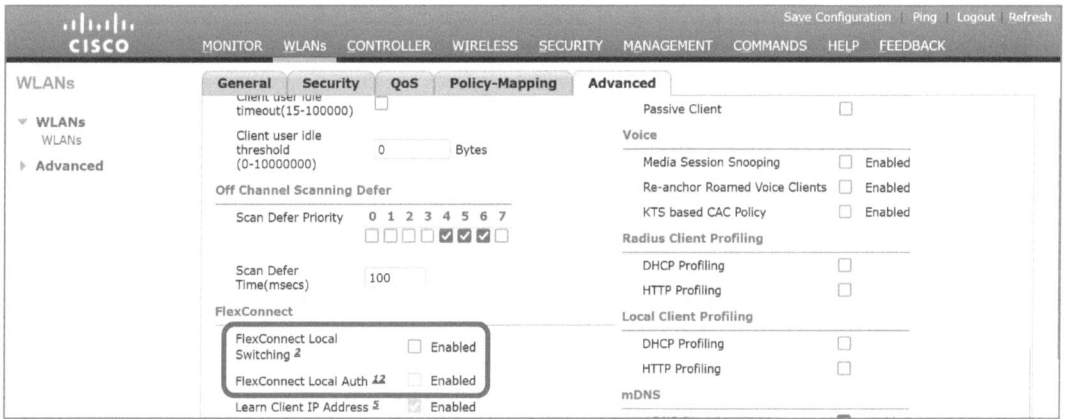

Figure 21.21 FlexConnect features can be enabled on a per-WLAN basis from the Advanced tab.

As you can see in figures 21.20 and 21.21, there are plenty of other features in the Advanced tab, but I recommend knowing the few that we covered. Once all configurations are complete, click the Apply button at the top right (you can see it in figure 21.20).

We've walked through how to configure the Internal WLAN; the process to configure the Guest WLAN is the same. Figure 21.22 shows the WLANs tab again after creating both WLANs.

Figure 21.22   The WLANs tab with the Internal and Guest WLANs, both of which use WPA2 with PSK authentication

21.3.4 Connecting an LWAP

With the Internal and Guest WLANs configured, let's see what happens when I connect an LWAP (AP1) to the network. After connecting AP1 to SW1, I waited for a few minutes for it to boot up. Figure 21.23 shows the result: in the Wireless tab of WLC1's GUI, AP1 is listed. Without any manual configuration of AP1, it joined with and is now managed by WLC1.

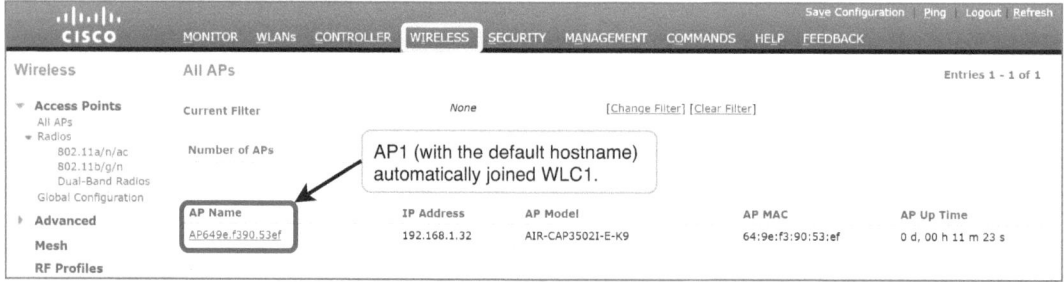

Figure 21.23   AP1 (with its default hostname) automatically joined with and is managed by WLC1 without any manual configuration.

After an AP boots up and gets an IP address, it begins the *WLC discovery process*, in which it attempts to discover any available WLCs. It uses various methods to do this:

- Sending broadcast discovery messages to the LAN
- Contacting any WLCs it had previously joined
- Contacting any WLCs it learned about via manual configuration (in the AP's CLI)

- Contacting any WLCs it learned about via DHCP option 43
- Using DNS to attempt to resolve CISCO-CAPWAP-CONTROLLER.local-domain and contacting any WLCs if the resolution succeeds

After using these methods to discover WLCs, the AP will then decide to join one—the logic it uses to select a WLC isn't important for the CCNA. In our network, there is one WLC (WLC1), and it is located in the same LAN as AP1; this means that WLC1 receives AP1's broadcast discovery messages. Furthermore, we also configured DHCP option 43 in SW1's DHCP pool, so AP1 also learns WLC1's IP address when it leases an IP address from SW1.

> **NOTE**   Because WLC1 is able to receive AP1's broadcast discovery messages in this case, DHCP option 43 is not necessary; I configured it just for demonstration.

Let's change the AP's name from the default name to AP1. To modify an AP's settings, click the AP name to see the screen shown in figure 21.24. In addition to being able to change the AP's name, this is where you can change the AP's operational mode. You should recognize these modes from chapter 19: local, FlexConnect, monitor, etc.

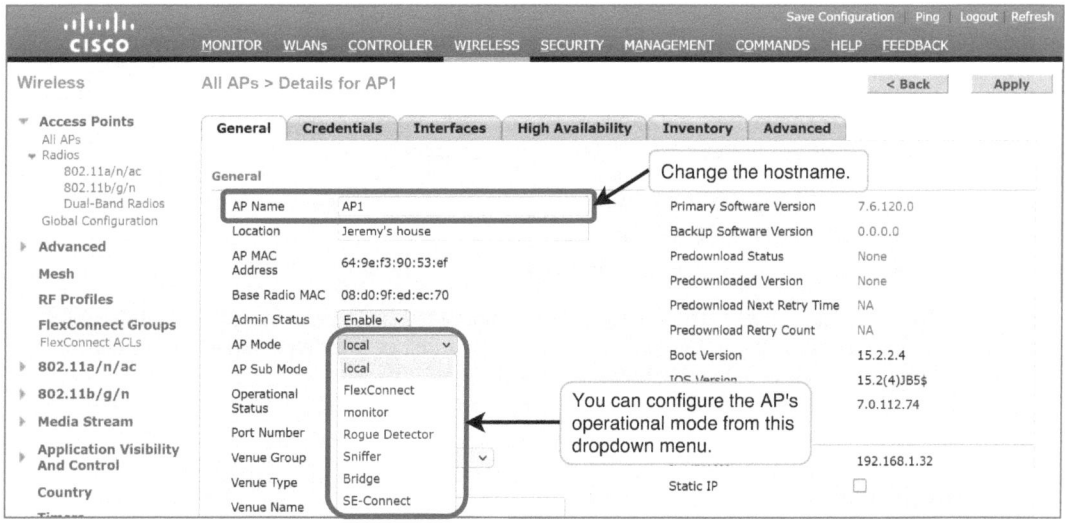

Figure 21.24   The AP configuration screen. From here, you can change the AP's name, configuration mode, and various other settings.

After joining with WLC1, AP1 receives its configuration information from WLC1, including the two WLANs we configured, which bands and channels it should use, its transmit power, etc. AP1 and WLC1 are now ready to accept clients! Figure 21.25 shows WLC1's client list after connecting a client to each of the WLANs; you can view the client list by returning to the MONITOR tab and clicking on the Clients menu on the left.

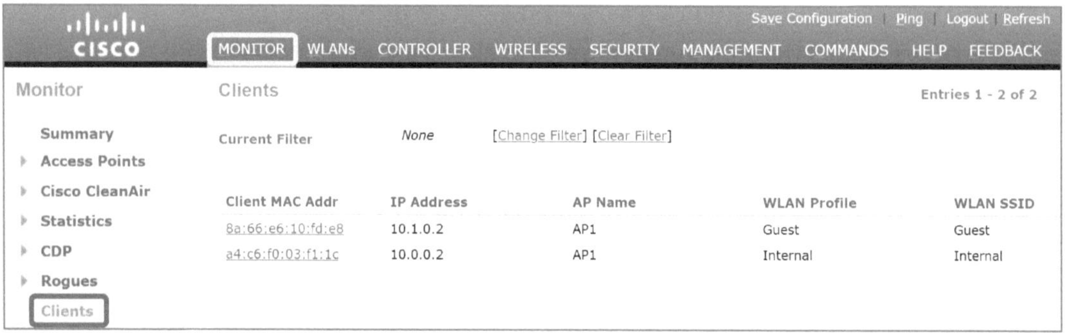

Figure 21.25   WLC1's client list, with one client connected to each WLAN

As you probably noticed when looking through these screenshots of the GUI, there are countless tabs, menus, and settings that you can configure from the GUI, most of which we skipped over. The settings we covered are the essentials that you should know for the CCNA; I recommend spending some time in the GUI familiarizing yourself with them.

Building a wireless home lab

Although Cisco Packet Tracer does offer a simulated WLC, its functionality is extremely limited. If you have the cash to spare, you can buy the same (or similar) equipment that I used off of eBay for about $100. Here is the equipment I used:

- *Switch*—Cisco Catalyst 2960 Series Switch (any model)
- *WLC*—Cisco 2504 Wireless Controller
- *AP*—Cisco Aironet 3502 access point

With that said, the limited configurations supported by Packet Tracer's simulated WLC are sufficient for you to familiarize yourself with most of what we covered in this chapter. A physical lab is nice to have but not necessary.

Summary

- A WLC usually connects to the network via a Link Aggregation Group (LAG)— the industry-standard term for an EtherChannel. Cisco WLCs only support static LAGs; they cannot use the negotiation protocols PAgP or LACP.
- DHCP option 42 can be used to tell DHCP clients which NTP server they should use.
- DHCP option 43 can be used to tell LWAPs the IP address of their WLC.
- Before you can create WLANs via the WLC GUI, you need to perform some initial configurations. You can do so with the Cisco Wizard Configuration Tool in the CLI by connecting to the WLC's console port.

- The initial configuration includes settings like the management interface; this is the interface you can connect to in order to access the WLC's GUI.

- The Virtual Gateway IP Address is used in communications between the WLC and wireless clients, such as when relaying DHCP messages. It should be unique on the network but doesn't have to be reachable by other devices.

- The Multicast IP Address is used by the WLC to send multicast messages to clients.

- The Mobility/RF Group Name configures the mobility group, which is used to allow multiple WLCs to coordinate to support roaming clients, and the RF group, which is used to manage and coordinate RF settings across multiple WLCs.

- If you enable DHCP *bridging mode*, the WLC will forward clients' DHCP messages as is, simply translating the 802.11 frames to Ethernet frames. If you disable bridging mode, the WLC will function in *proxy mode*, like a DHCP relay agent.

- The WLC's country code must match the *regulatory domain* of the LWAPs it manages.

- There are various methods to connect to and manage a WLC. You can access the CLI via the console port or over the network via Telnet/SSH. You can access the GUI over the network via HTTP/HTTPS.

- The WLC can authenticate users with its own local user database or by using a RADIUS/TACACS+ AAA server.

- To connect to the WLC's GUI, open a web browser, and type the IP address of its management interface in the address bar.

- From the Management tab, you can view and modify which kinds of management connections are allowed. By default, HTTP, HTTPS, and SSH connections are allowed, but Telnet connections aren't.

- To view and modify the WLC's management user authentication methods and their order, go to the Security tab, open the Priority Order dropdown menu, and access the Management User menu.

- You can configure a *CPU ACL* in the Security tab to filter traffic to and from the WLC itself, such as management and CAPWAP traffic.

- To configure a CPU ACL, expand the Access Control Lists dropdown menu, create an ACL in the Access Controls Lists menu, and apply it in the CPU Access Control Lists menu.

- A WLC *port* is a physical port, and a WLC *interface* is a logical entity in the WLC.

- The *console port* is a standard console port like on a router or switch.

- The *service port* is a dedicated *out-of-band (OOB) management* port. It doesn't support VLAN tagging, so it must connect to an access port on the switch.

- The *redundancy port* is used to connect two WLCs to form a redundant pair.

- *Distribution system (DS) ports* are the standard network ports that connect to the distribution system.

- If you enable link aggregation, all of the WLC's DS ports will be included in the LAG by default. As long as there is at least one functioning physical port in the LAG, it will be operational.

- The *management interface* is the default interface for in-band management. It maps to a management VLAN and sends and receives traffic via the DS ports.

- The *AP-manager interface* is used by the WLC to communicate with LWAPs via CAPWAP. By default, the management interface functions as the AP-manager interface, but you can configure a separate AP-manager interface.

- The *redundancy management interface* is used to connect to and manage the standby WLC in a redundant pair.

- The *service-port interface* corresponds to the physical service port.

- The *virtual interface* is used for specific purposes like DHCP relay; the Virtual Gateway IP Address is applied to this interface.

- A *dynamic interface* is similar to an SVI on a switch. Each dynamic interface is mapped to a VLAN and corresponding WLAN.

- Before creating WLANs, you must create a dynamic interface for each WLAN.

- You can create dynamic interfaces from the Interfaces menu of the Controller tab.

- You can create WLANs from the WLANs tab. Each WLAN has three identifiers: the SSID is the name as seen by clients. The Profile Name can be any descriptive name (or the same as the SSID), and the ID is a unique numeric identifier.

- When creating a WLAN, the Security tab allows you to configure settings like WPA authentication/encryption, which are Layer 2 security settings.

- You can configure the PSK as 64 hexadecimal characters or an 8- to 63-bit ASCII passphrase.

- The Layer 3 tab allows you to configure web policy security features that require clients to perform additional actions/authentication before accessing the network, such as Authentication, Passthrough, Conditional Web Redirect, and Splash Page Web Redirect.

- The QoS tab allows you to specify the WLAN's QoS level. The levels are Platinum (voice), Gold (video), Silver (best effort, the default), and Bronze (background).

- The Advanced tab allows you to configure various optional features. *Client Load Balancing* encourages clients to associate with less busy LWAPs. *Client Band Select* encourages clients to use the 5 GHz band instead of the 2.4 Ghz band.

- FlexConnect can be enabled from the Advanced tab. *FlexConnect Local Switching* means the LWAP can switch client traffic between the wired and wireless networks on its own—no need to tunnel it to the WLC.

- *FlexConnect Local Auth* allows the LWAP to authenticate clients on its own.

- You can view LWAPs that the WLC controls from the Wireless tab.

- After an AP boots up and gets an IP address, it brings the *WLC discovery* process, in which it attempts to discover WLCs before joining with one.
- Discovery methods include broadcast discovery messages, previously joined WLCs, manual configuration, DHCP option 43, and DNS.
- You can configure an AP's operational mode (local, FlexConnect, monitor, etc.) by clicking on the AP name in the Wireless tab.
- You can view the list of wireless clients from the Clients menu in the Monitor tab.

Part 5

Network automation

In part 5, the final section of this book, our focus moves to the increasingly important topic of network automation. As networks grow in size and complexity, the ability to automate routine operations becomes crucial for efficiency, accuracy, and scalability. Chapter 22 begins with an overview of network automation and its benefits, with a focus on software-defined networking (SDN), an approach to network architecture that centralizes key network functions in an SDN controller, facilitating the programmatic control of the network.

Chapters 23 and 24 cover two key elements in enabling network automation. Chapter 23 focuses on representational state transfer (REST) application programming interfaces (APIs)—software interfaces that facilitate communication between applications. Then, chapter 24 introduces the data formats JSON (JavaScript Object Notation), XML (Extensible Markup Language), and YAML (YAML Ain't Markup Language). Software applications can use these standardized data formats to exchange data in a way both parties understand—key for enabling communication between network devices, SDN controllers, and other applications.

Finally, chapter 25 covers the configuration management tools Ansible and Terraform, used to automate the processes involved in configuring devices and maintaining configuration consistency. Network automation is a paradigm shift from the CLI-focused approach of the rest of the CCNA. As time progresses, network automation is becoming increasingly prevalent in modern networks. While the CCNA exam doesn't test you on the practical application of these network automation tools, it does expect you to have a foundational grasp of a variety of concepts related to network automation, and part 5 covers the key concepts you need to know for the exam.

Network automation

This chapter covers

- Network automation and its benefits
- The three logical planes of networking functions
- Software-defined networking architecture and solutions
- Cisco DNA Center-enabled network management

Enterprise networks can potentially have hundreds, or even thousands, of routers, switches, firewalls, and other network infrastructure devices. In the past, deploying, managing, and maintaining such large networks was very labor intensive, requiring manual configuration of each individual device. However, modern enterprises are increasingly adopting automation to streamline the deployment, management, and maintenance of their networks.

In this chapter, we will take a high-level look at the topic of network automation as a whole and the advantages it offers, allowing networks to scale to meet the needs of modern organizations. We will then move on to look at software-defined networking (SDN), an approach to networking that centralizes network intelligence in one or more controllers, facilitating the management and operation of the entire network with a programmatic approach. We will cover the following CCNA exam topics:

- 1.1.e Controllers
- 6.1 Explain how automation impacts network management
- 6.2 Compare traditional networks with controller-based networking
- 6.3 Describe controller-based and software-defined architectures (overlay, underlay, and fabric)
  - 6.3.a Separation of control plane and data plane
  - 6.3.b North-bound and South-bound APIs
- 6.4 Explain AI (generative and predictive) and machine learning in network operations

22.1   *The benefits of network automation*

What does it mean to automate a network? The term *network automation* doesn't refer to any particular tool or technology but rather a broad category of techniques and methods used to automate network-related tasks. At its core, network automation involves the use of software to create processes that perform various network tasks without the need for manual intervention. This can range from simple scripts for routine tasks to more complex automation platforms that manage multiple interdependent configurations across a variety of devices.

To understand the benefits of network automation, consider this situation. Your company has added a new server that functions as a Syslog server and SNMP manager, gathering logging and status updates from devices in the network. As a junior network engineer, it's your job to add the necessary configurations to each device. That involves connecting to each device one by one using SSH and making the following configurations:

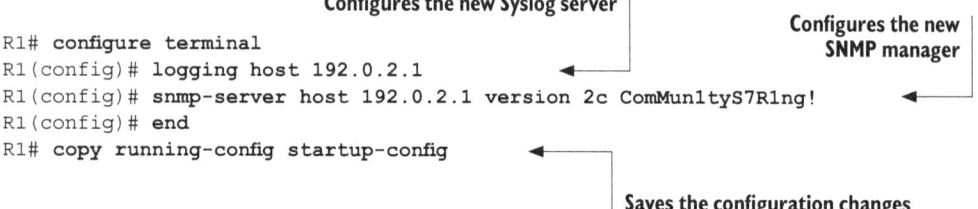

Adding two new commands to and saving a device's configuration isn't such a cumbersome task, and a manual approach is fine if the network has only a few devices. But what if the network consists of thousands of routers and switches? Manually configuring each device one by one would not only take a long time, but it would likely result in mistakes: mistyped IP addresses on some devices, unsaved configurations on others—human error is inevitable. Figure 22.1 shows a better approach: using a Python script, you can reliably and accurately push the necessary configurations to each device in a fraction of the time.

Figure 22.1 Pushing configurations to devices with a Python script. Automating repetitive tasks provides greater accuracy and efficiency.

Writing and interpreting scripts in Python (or any other language) isn't part of the CCNA exam, but for reference, the following example shows how you could accomplish this using Python. Using a *library* (basically, a set of tools) called Netmiko, I wrote a script to log in to a series of devices and apply the specified commands to each:

**Imports the ConnectHandler
class from the netmiko library**

```
from netmiko import ConnectHandler

devices = [
    {"device_type": "cisco_ios", "host": "R1",
➡"username": "admin", "password": "pW12!"},
    {"device_type": "cisco_ios", "host": "R2",
➡"username": "admin", "password": "pW12!"}
]

commands = [
    "logging host 192.0.2.1",
    "snmp-server host 192.0.2.1 version 2c ComMun1tyS7R1ng!"
]

for device in devices:
    print(f"Connecting to {device['host']}...")
    try:
        with ConnectHandler(**device) as net_connect:
            output = net_connect.send_config_set(commands)
            print(output)
            net_connect.save_config()
    except Exception as e:
        print(f"Failed to connect to {device['host']}: {e}")

print("Configuration complete.")
```

**Lists the devices to be configured
(only two shown for brevity)**

**Specifies the configuration
commands**

**Connects to each device,
issues the commands, and
saves the configuration**

**Displays an error message
for each failed connection**

**Displays a message when
the configurations are complete**

As long as the script has been properly written, you can trust it to quickly and reliably make the specified configuration changes—no typos or other mistakes. Automation ensures that configuration changes are made accurately and in a fraction of the time required for manual configuration. By improving the efficiency of network operations, the opex (operating expenses—ongoing costs) of the network are reduced; fewer hours are required for each task.

> **NOTE**   Although automation can reduce opex, it doesn't reduce capex (capital expenses—upfront costs). For example, automation doesn't reduce the amount of hardware a network requires.

Automating configuration changes with Python scripts is just one example of network automation, but the scope of network automation extends beyond just scripting. Network automation encompasses a range of tools and methodologies aimed at making network design, deployment, and management more efficient, reliable, and scalable. In the next section, we'll cover software-defined networking (SDN), a framework that enables and enhances network automation.

22.2   *Software-defined networking*

Software-defined networking (SDN) is a paradigm shift in the way networks are designed, managed, and operated. At its core, SDN is a type of network architecture that separates the network "brains"—the intelligent decision-making processes that determine how the network operates—from the "brawn"—the actual forwarding of messages across the network. In this section, we'll clarify how these different elements work in traditional network architectures and then examine how SDN decouples these processes, centralizing network intelligence in controllers that facilitate the programmatic control of the network.

> **NOTE**   SDN is an example of *controller-based networking*. We looked at another example when covering wireless LANs: split-MAC architecture with a WLC.

22.2.1   *The logical planes of network devices*

A router routes packets and a switch switches frames, but that's not all they do. Although the main purpose of these networking devices is forwarding messages across the network, they have various other functions and responsibilities that contribute to their main purpose. For example, here are some other things that routers do:

- Use a routing protocol like OSPF to share routing information with other routers and build a routing table
- Use ARP to build an ARP table, mapping IP addresses to MAC addresses
- Use Syslog to keep logs of events
- Use NTP to sync its time to a trusted NTP server
- Function as an SSH server, allowing users to connect to and configure it via the CLI

There are many other examples. Think back to the various topics we've covered in this book, and I'm sure you'll be able to list some more. All of these functions can be divided into three logical *planes*:

- *The Data Plane*—Functions that are responsible for the actual forwarding of packets based on predetermined rules, handling the physical transmission of data across the network.
- *The Control Plane*—Functions that control how the Data Plane operates, such as the processes that build a router's ARP and routing tables.
- *The Management Plane*—Functions related to configuring, managing, and monitoring devices.

Figure 22.2 illustrates these planes on three routers.

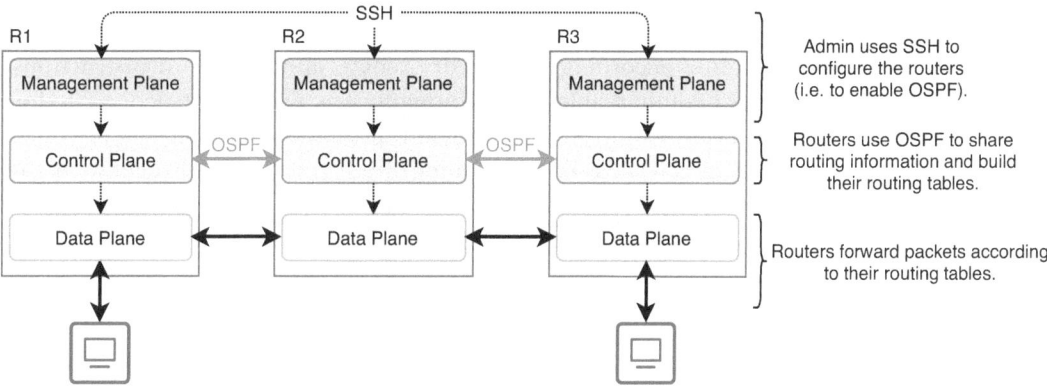

Figure 22.2   The three logical planes. The Data Plane involves forwarding messages, the Control Plane controls how the Data Plane functions, and the Management Plane includes all configuration/management tasks.

THE DATA PLANE

The Data Plane includes all functions directly related to forwarding messages over the network: receiving a message on one interface, performing any necessary processing, and then forwarding it out of another interface. For example, on a switch, the Data Plane includes functions such as

- Forwarding and flooding frames according to their destination MAC address and the switch's MAC address table
- Permitting or denying frames according to security features like Port Security, DHCP Snooping, or DAI
- Tagging frames with 802.1Q before forwarding them over a trunk link

Figure 22.3 lists some equivalent Data Plane functions relevant to routers.

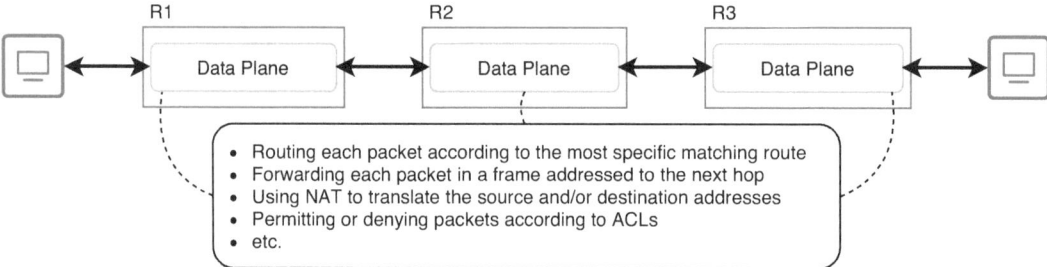

Figure 22.3   Data Plane functions on routers. All tasks directly involved in forwarding packets are part of the Data Plane.

> **NOTE**   The Data Plane is also called the *Forwarding Plane* because it is concerned with forwarding messages over the network.

The Data Plane functions according to a set of predetermined rules or instructions. For example, a router's routing table can be thought of as a set of instructions: to forward a packet toward destination X, encapsulate it in a frame destined for next hop Y, and forward it out of interface Z. Establishing those rules and instructions is the responsibility of the next logical plane: the Control Plane.

THE CONTROL PLANE

The Control Plane, as the name suggests, "controls" the Data Plane. Functions in the Control Plane are not directly involved in the process of forwarding messages but instead perform necessary overhead work to enable the Data Plane's operations:

- OSPF itself isn't involved in the process of forwarding packets, but it allows the router to build its routing table, which is necessary for forwarding packets.
- STP itself isn't involved in the process of forwarding frames, but it informs the switch about which ports should and shouldn't be to forward frames.
- ARP messages don't contain user data but are used to build an ARP table, which is used in the process of forwarding data packets.
- A switch's MAC address-learning process (examining frames' source MAC addresses) is separate from the frame-forwarding process but is necessary to build the switch's MAC address table and enable frame forwarding.

To put it simply, Control Plane functions influence (but aren't directly involved in) the message-forwarding process, whether it is routing packets at Layer 3 or switching frames at Layer 2. Figure 22.4 demonstrates how routers use OSPF and ARP in the Control Plane to facilitate the Data Plane's packet-forwarding capabilities.

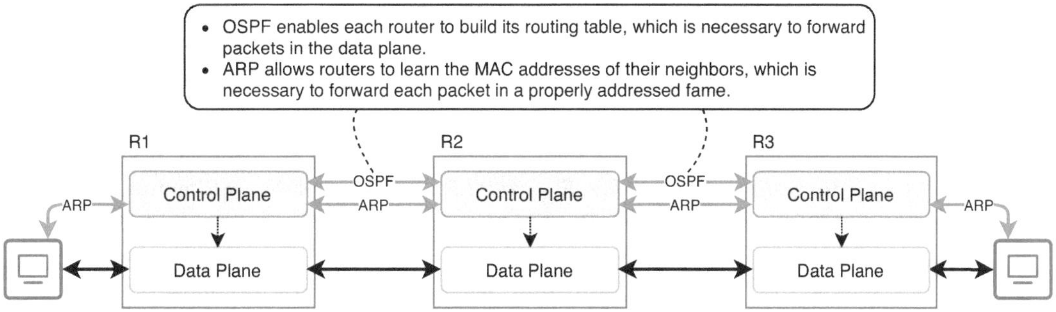

Figure 22.4 Control Plane functions influence (but aren't directly involved in) the message-forwarding process.

Whereas the Data Plane is the "brawn" of the network—the set of processes that actually move messages across the network—the Control Plane is the "brains"—the set of processes that determine how messages should be moved across the network.

THE MANAGEMENT PLANE

The Management Plane includes a variety of functions that don't directly influence the forwarding of messages. Instead, Management Plane functions are related to configuring, managing, and monitoring network devices. Some protocols whose functions are part of the Management Plane include

- *SSH/Telnet*—Used to connect to the CLI of network devices
- *Syslog*—Used to keep logs of events that occur on a device
- *SNMP*—Used to monitor the operations of a device
- *NTP*—Used to maintain accurate time across the network

Although Management Plane functions don't directly influence the forwarding of messages in the Data Plane, actions performed in the Management Plane can influence the Control Plane, thereby having an indirect effect on the Data Plane. For example, OSPF configurations made via a device's CLI (Management Plane) affect how a router shares routing information and calculates routes (Control Plane), influencing how the router forwards packets (Data Plane).

NOTE In the following discussion of SDN, we will focus primarily on the separation of the Data Plane and the Control Plane. Just remember the role of the Management Plane: the configuration, management, and monitoring of the network.

22.2.2 *SDN architecture*

In traditional network architectures, each individual network device contains the necessary intelligence that is required for Control Plane functions. For example, each router runs a routing protocol (such as OSPF), communicates with its neighboring routers, and independently calculates the best route to each destination it learns about. This is called a *distributed Control Plane*—the "brains" of the network are distributed among each individual network device.

However, SDN takes a different approach. Instead of a distributed Control Plane, SDN solutions employ a *centralized Control Plane*, concentrating some or all of the Control Plane functions in a *controller*. Figure 22.5 illustrates SDN architecture's centralized Control Plane: instead of routers communicating with each other using OSPF (or another routing protocol) and independently calculating routes, the controller performs these tasks centrally. The controller has a global view of the network, applies its own routing logic, and distributes the necessary forwarding instructions to each device under its control. Each network device's role is simply to forward messages according to the controller's instructions.

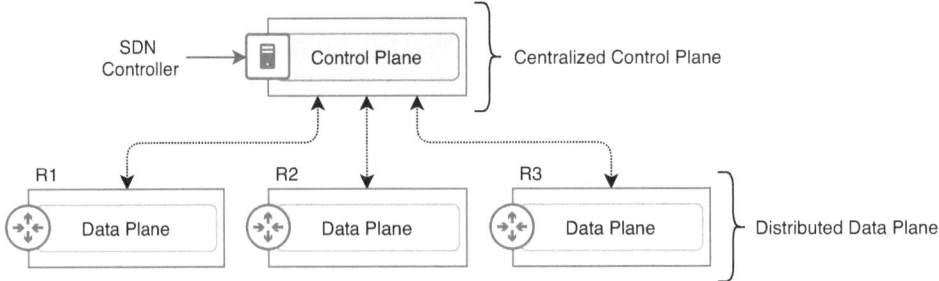

Figure 22.5 SDN architecture centralizes the Control Plane functions in the controller. However, the Data Plane functions (message forwarding) remain distributed among each network device.

SDN facilitates the programmatic control of the network through applications that interact with the SDN controller. This results in a three-layer architecture, as shown in figure 22.6:

- *Application Layer*—Consists of applications that communicate network requirements and desired behaviors to the SDN controller.
- *Control Layer*—Translates the high-level requirements from the Application Layer into actionable instructions for the network devices.
- *Infrastructure Layer*—The network devices like routers and switches that execute the commands received from the Control Layer.

SDN architecture relies on communication between its three layers: the Application Layer must communicate the network requirements and desired behaviors to the Control Layer, and the Control Layer must translate those high-level requirements into instructions that it communicates to the devices in the Infrastructure Layer. This communication is achieved using *application programming interfaces* (APIs)—software interfaces that facilitate communications between different applications—and various communication protocols.

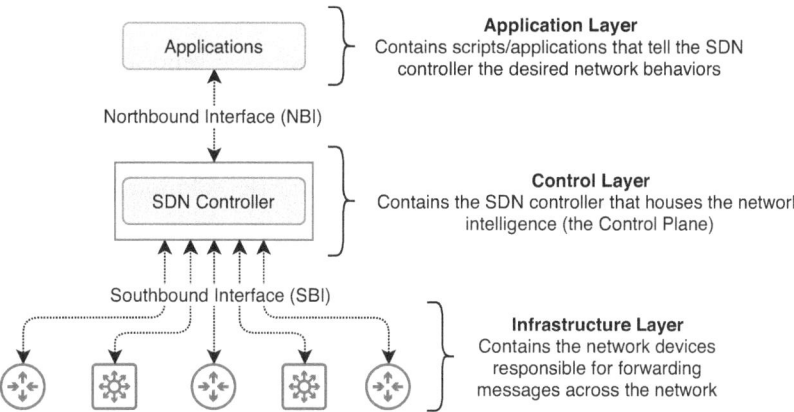

Figure 22.6   The three layers of SDN architecture: Application, Control, and Infrastructure. The NBI facilitates communication between the Application and Control Layers, and the SBI facilitates communications between the Control and Infrastructure Layers.

The interface between the Application and Control Layers is called the *northbound interface* (NBI), and the interface between the Control Layer and the Infrastructure Layer is called the *southbound interface* (SBI). These names simply come from how the SDN architecture is usually depicted in diagrams: the Application Layer on top (north), the Control Layer in the middle, and the Infrastructure Layer at the bottom (south).

The NBI typically uses a *representational state transfer (REST) API* with HTTP messages; we will cover REST APIs (and APIs in general) in chapter 23. A variety of APIs and communication protocols can be used in the SBI, depending on the SDN solution. Here are some examples:

- *OpenFlow*—An open source protocol that allows the controller to directly interact with and control the Data Plane of network devices.
- *NETCONF*—An industry-standard protocol defined by the IETF and used for modifying the configurations of network devices.
- *OpFlex*—Developed by Cisco and used with Application-Centric Infrastructure (ACI), their data center SDN solution.
- *SSH, SNMP*—Traditional protocols such as SSH and SNMP can also be used in the SBI to manage network devices.

EXAM TIP   You don't have to know the details about these different SBI types. For the CCNA exam, know that REST APIs are used in the NBI and protocols like OpenFlow, NETCONF, OpFlex, and traditional protocols like SSH and SNMP are used in the SBI.

22.2.3 *Cisco SDN solutions*

SDN isn't one single solution. Cisco and other networking vendors have developed a variety of SDN solutions based on the principles we have covered so far. In this section, we'll take a high-level look at three SDN solutions from Cisco:

- *Cisco Software-Defined Access (SD-Access)*—Cisco's SDN solution for wired and wireless campus LANs
- *Cisco SD-WAN*—Cisco's SDN solution for WANs
- *Application Centric Infrastructure (ACI)*—Cisco's SDN solution for data center networks

All three of these solutions work by building a virtual network of tunnels (the *overlay*) on top of the underlying physical network (the *underlay*). The combination of the underlay and the overlay—the network infrastructure as a whole—is called the *fabric*.

> **NOTE**   To keep these concepts clear, just remember that the underlay is physical and the overlay is virtual. The fabric is the network as a whole, including all physical and virtual elements.

SD-ACCESS

Software-Defined Access (SD-Access) is Cisco's SDN solution for automating and securing wired and wireless campus LANs, applying the SDN principles we covered previously to automate, streamline, and secure campus LANs. Figure 22.7 illustrates the SD-Access fabric, consisting of a physical network (the underlay) and a virtual network of tunnels (the overlay) using *Virtual Extensible LAN* (VXLAN)—a protocol that allows for the creation of virtual Layer 2 networks over a Layer 3 underlay.

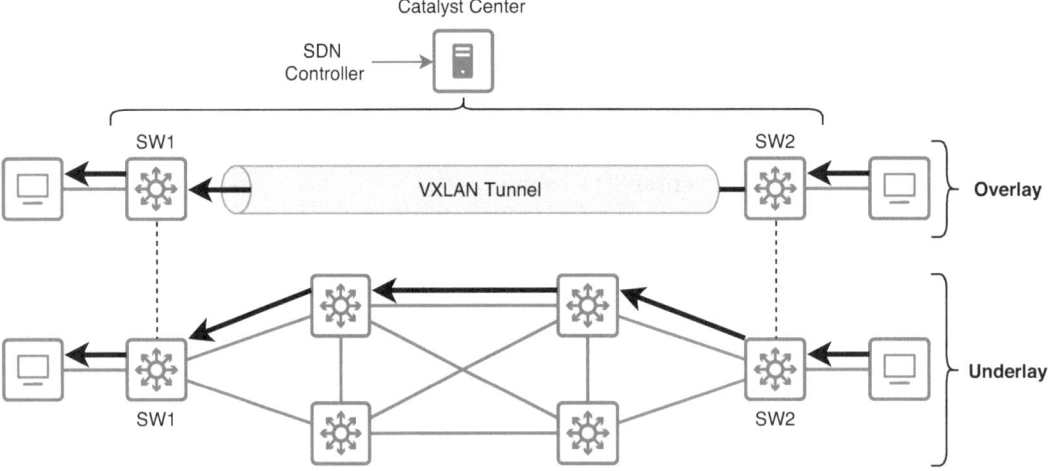

Figure 22.7   The Cisco SD-Access fabric, consisting of a physical underlay of switches and a virtual overlay of VXLAN tunnels. Cisco Catalyst Center is the SDN controller.

Cisco Catalyst Center—often called DNAC—functions as the SDN controller in their SD-Access solution. However, Catalyst Center can also be used in non-SD-Access networks as a network management platform; we'll examine Catalyst Center's management capabilities in section 22.3.

> **NOTE** Catalyst Center used to be called Digital Network Architecture (DNA) Center, but Cisco renamed it in 2023. I recommend knowing both names; you could encounter either on the exam.

SOFTWARE-DEFINED WAN

Software-Defined WAN (SD-WAN) is Cisco's SDN solution for WANs. SD-WAN works by creating an overlay of IPsec tunnels over any physical WAN underlay: the internet, Multiprotocol Label Switching (MPLS), cellular 4G/5G, satellite, etc. This fabric is managed by a few different SDN controllers: one dedicated to onboarding new routers into the fabric, one dedicated to Control Plane functions, and one dedicated to Management Plane functions. Figure 22.8 illustrates the Cisco SD-WAN fabric.

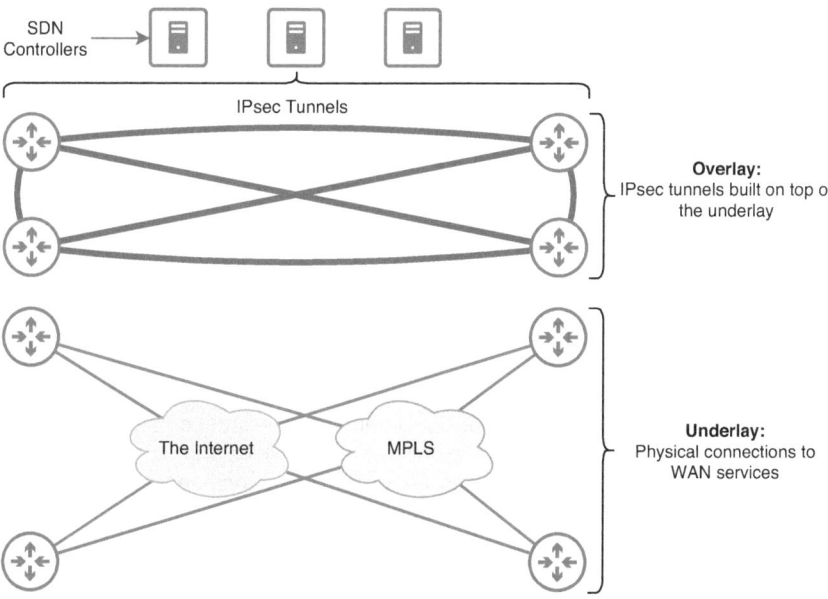

Figure 22.8   The Cisco SD-WAN fabric, consisting of a physical underlay of WAN connections and a virtual overlay of IPsec tunnels. The SD-WAN fabric is controlled by a few different SDN controllers.

APPLICATION-CENTRIC INFRASTRUCTURE

The final Cisco SDN solution we'll look at is *Application-Centric Infrastructure* (ACI)—Cisco's data center SDN solution (see figure 6.9). Like in SD-Access, ACI creates an overlay of VXLAN tunnels over the underlay. In this case, the underlay is a physical spine-leaf network.

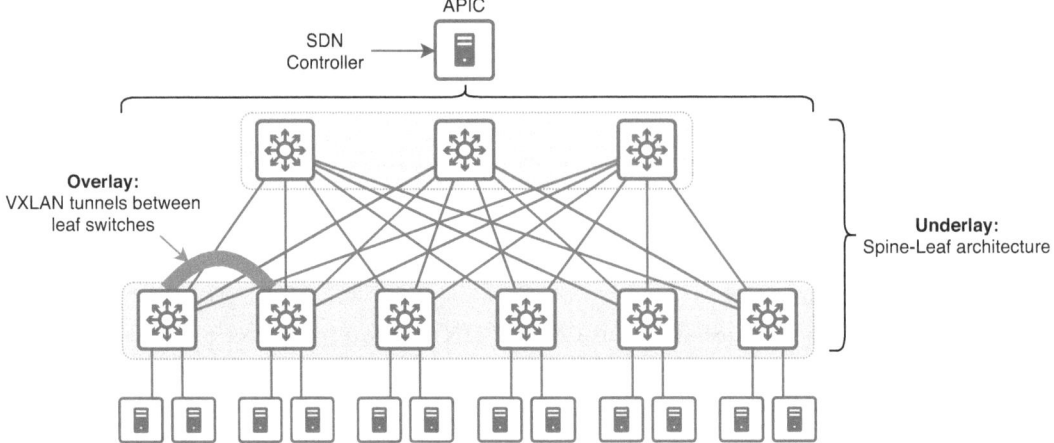

Figure 22.9   The Cisco ACI fabric, consisting of a spine-leaf underlay and an overlay of VXLAN tunnels. The APIC is the SDN controller.

The SDN controller used in ACI is called the *Application Policy Infrastructure Controller* (APIC). The APIC is responsible for translating high-level network policies into specific network configurations and deploying them across the network fabric.

EXAM TIP   For the CCNA exam, you don't need to know the details of these SDN solutions. However, exam topic 6.3 explicitly mentions overlay, underlay, and fabric, so make sure you understand those core concepts.

Intent-based networking

One of the advantages of SDN is that it facilitates *intent-based networking* (IBN). The goal of IBN is to allow the engineer to communicate their intent for network behavior to the controller, which will take care of the details of the actual configurations and policies on the devices. Instead of focusing on individual devices and CLI configurations, IBN allows you to focus on high-level policies. For example, an engineer might state the intent "I want to prioritize video conferencing traffic over other types." The controller will then implement the necessary configurations across the network to make this a reality, without the engineer having to configure QoS settings on each device.

22.3   *Artificial intelligence and machine learning*

Artificial intelligence (AI) refers to the simulation of intelligence in computers, allowing them to exhibit behaviors typically associated with humans such as learning and problem-solving. AI systems are programmed to analyze data, identify patterns, and make predictions or take actions based on those insights. *Machine learning* (ML) is a field within AI that allows computers to learn on their own, without requiring explicit programming.

Ever since the public release of OpenAI's ChatGPT in 2022, AI and ML seem to be on everyone's mind, and for good reason; these technologies, still in their early stages, have the potential to revolutionize many aspects of our private and professional lives. They promise to enhance productivity, automate complex tasks, and provide insights that were previously unattainable. In the realm of network operations, AI and ML are already making significant impacts by enabling more efficiency in network management, improving security through advanced threat detection, and optimizing performance through predictive analytics. As these technologies continue to evolve, their integration into network operations will only continue to grow. In this section we'll examine first examine ML, move on to cover predictive and generative AI, and finally consider their applications in modern network operations.

> **EXAM TIP** AI and ML's applications in network operations are exam topic 6.4, so make sure you have a solid grasp of these concepts.

22.3.1 *Machine learning*

Machine learning (ML) is a subfield of AI that focuses on enabling computers to learn from data and improve without the need for explicit programming. Figure 22.10 shows ML's position within the field of AI, as well as the position of deep learning—a topic we'll explore later—as a further subset of machine learning.

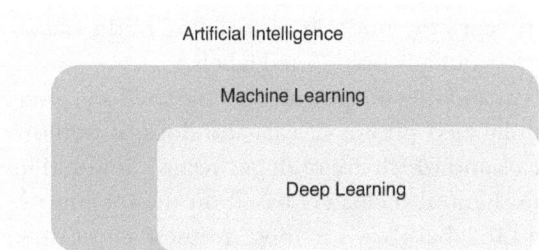

Figure 22.10 **Machine learning is a subfield of artificial intelligence. Deep learning is a further subset of machine learning using artificial neural networks.**

Unlike traditional software that relies on predefined instructions, ML algorithms can identify patterns and relationships within data sets. With ML, computers can learn from vast data sets in a few different ways that we'll look at in this section:

- *Supervised learning*—The ML algorithm is trained on labeled data sets.
- *Unsupervised learning*—The ML algorithm is trained on unlabeled data sets.
- *Reinforcement learning*—The ML algorithm learns by interacting with an environment and receiving positive or negative feedback.

SUPERVISED, UNSUPERVISED, AND REINFORCEMENT LEARNING

Supervised learning involves training an ML algorithm on a labeled data set, meaning that each training example input into the algorithm has a corresponding label. By examining these labeled examples, the algorithm learns the relationships between the data and the given label.

For example, if you want to train an algorithm to recognize images of cats and dogs, you could input thousands of cat and dog photos labelled as such. With enough examples, the algorithm will learn to identify and distinguish cats from dogs in images. Figure 22.11 illustrates how supervised learning works.

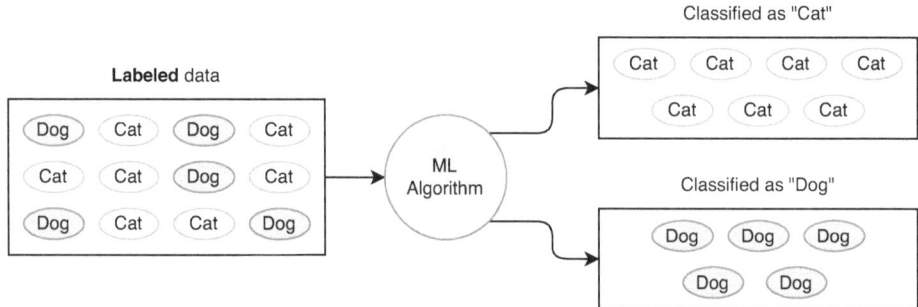

Figure 22.11 Supervised machine learning. Labeled data is input into the ML algorithm, allowing it to learn the relationships between the data and the given label.

Unsupervised learning takes a different approach, training the algorithm on unlabeled data sets. The algorithm tries to learn the underlying structure of the data by identifying patterns and relationships without any predefined labels.

Using the same example of cat and dog images, an unsupervised learning algorithm would analyze a large set of unlabeled photos of cats and dogs. It wouldn't know in advance which images are of cats and which are of dogs. Instead, it would identify patterns in the images and group them into clusters based on these patterns. However, the algorithm wouldn't assign the labels "cat" or "dog" to these clusters—that would require a human to interpret. Figure 22.12 shows how unsupervised learning works.

NOTE   Supervised learning is highly effective when clear and accurate labels are available, enabling precise predictions and classifications. However, unsupervised learning is also powerful for uncovering hidden patterns and relationships in data without predefined labels. There is also a middle ground between supervised and unsupervised learning called *semi-supervised learning* that involves a combination of labeled and unlabeled data, leveraging the strengths of both approaches.

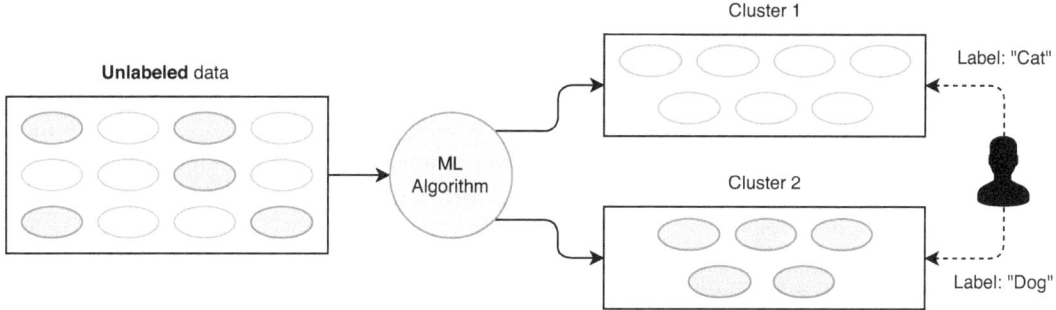

Figure 22.12 **Unsupervised machine learning. Unlabeled data is input into the ML algorithm, allowing it to identify patterns and relationships, categorizing the data into clusters. A human can then assign labels according to their interpretation of the grouped data.**

Reinforcement learning is a distinct approach in which an agent interacts with an environment, receiving positive for actions that lead to desirable outcomes and negative feedback for actions with undesirable outcomes. A classic example of reinforcement learning is training an AI to play a game like chess. The AI learns by playing many games, receiving positive feedback for winning and negative feedback for losing. Over time, it learns to develop strategies that increase its changes of winning.

DEEP LEARNING

Deep learning (DL) is a subset of machine learning that uses artificial neural networks to analyze and learn from large amounts of data. An *artificial neural network* is a computational model inspired by the way biological neural networks in the human brain process information, consisting of many interconnected layers of nodes like the neurons in the human brain.

Just like traditional traditional machine learning, DL's artificial neural networks can be trained using supervised, unsupervised, semi-supervised, and reinforcement learning, but their complex architecture allows them to extract more complex patterns and relationships from data then traditional machine learning algorithms.

DL has gained prominence in recent years due to its success in tackling complex tasks such as image and speech recognition, natural language processing, and autonomous driving. The ability of deep learning models to process vast amounts of unstructured data and uncover intricate patterns has led to significant advancements in AI-driven technologies, such as large language models (LLMs) like OpenAI's GPT-4, Google's Gemini, and Meta's Llama.

> **NOTE** Just as DL's artificial neural networks are many layers deep, DL itself is a very deep topic that the CCNA doesn't dive into. For an interesting look into DL combined with reinforcement learning, check out this video on MarI/O, an AI trained to play the video game Super Mario World: https://www.youtube.com/watch?v=qv6UVOQ0F44.

22.3.2 *Predictive and generative AI*

Predictive and generative AI are two important applications of ML and DL. While ML and DL empower computers to autonomously learn from large data sets, predictive and generative AI apply these techniques to solve specific problems and create new opportunities. In this section, we will examine these two types of AI. Figure 22.13 shows the position of predictive and generative AI within the fields of ML and DL.

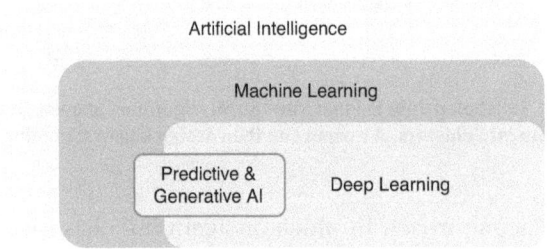

Figure 22.13   Predictive and generative AI are applications of machine learning and deep learning to predict future events and generate new content.

PREDICTIVE AI

Predictive AI uses historical data to predict future events. Using ML and DL to identify patterns and relationships within data sets, predictive AI leverages these insights to make predictions about unseen data, such as forecasting future weather patterns. In addition to weather forecasting, some other common use cases for predictive AI are:

- *Stock market predictions*—Historical stock market data and economic indicators can be used to predict future stock prices and market trends.
- *Customer behavior analysis*—E-commerce platforms use predictive AI to analyze customer purchase history and browsing behavior, enabling personalized recommendations.
- *Healthcare*—Predictive AI can analyze patient data to predict patient outcomes and personalize treatment plans.

GENERATIVE AI

Generative AI leverages ML and DL to create new content. After learning the underlying patterns and relationships within existing data, the AI can then produce novel outputs that resemble the training data. Generative AI tools have become particularly popular within the past couple of years. Two well-known use cases for generative AI are:

- *Text generation*—Chatbots like OpenAI's ChatGPT and Google's Gemini use large language models (LLMs) to generate human-like text based on input.
- *Image generation*—Tools like Midjourney and OpenAI's DALL-E create detailed images from text descriptions.

22.3.3 *Applications in network operations*

We've covered the basics of AI, including machine learning, deep learning, and the predictive and generative AI applications that leverage them. But what does all of this mean for our networks? As modern networks grow in complexity, AI is proving to be a key tool to make networks more efficient, reliable, and secure.

ML and DL can be used to analyze vast amounts of network data to uncover patterns, anomalies, and insights that are not immediately apparent to us humans. By processing and learning from historical and real-time data, these models can make intelligent decisions and predictions that improve network performance, enhance security, and automate routine tasks. Although we're still in the early days of using AI in network operations, I think it's safe to say that AI has the potential to bring network automation to the next level. In this section, let's consider some applications of AI and ML in network operations.

PREDICTIVE AI IN NETWORKS

Predictive AI can use historical network data to forecast future events, enabling proactive management and decision-making. Some applications of predictive AI in network operations are:

- *Traffic forecasting*—AI models can analyze network traffic patterns to predict future network load. With this information, you can proactively provision additional network resources to accommodate anticipated traffic spikes or optimize QoS policies to prioritize important traffic.
- *Predictive maintenance*—By analyzing data from network devices, AI models can identify potential hardware failures before they occur, enabling proactive maintenance scheduling and minimizing downtime.
- *Capacity planning*—Predictive AI can help plan for future network capacity by analyzing trends in traffic and user behavior, allowing an enterprise to scale its network infrastructure to meet increasing demand.
- *Security threat prediction*—By analyzing historical security data and identifying patterns associated with cyber attacks, predictive AI can forecast potential security threats.

GENERATIVE AI IN NETWORKS

In its current state, generative AI has fewer use cases in networking than predictive AI; it's too early to hand off your network to an AI and let it handle everything for you. However, let's consider some uses cases for generative AI that, combined with human oversight, can greatly improve network operations.

- *Automated scipt creation*—Generative AI can assist by generating scripts or templates for network automation tasks. To put that in other words, it can automate network automation!

- *Network diagram generation*—AI tools can gather information about a network and automatically generate network diagrams.

- *Network documentation*—In addition to visual diagrams, AI can analyze information about the network to generate other network documentation about configurations, policies, etc.

- *Device configuration*—AI can generate device configurations based on given requirements, reducing manual effort and improving documentation accuracy.

- *Network design*—Generative AI can assist in creating optimal network designs according to given requirements.

- *Virtual assistant*—Chatbots like ChatGPT can function as a virtual assistant, providing real-time answers to queries. You should always be weary of accepting what a chatbot says as truth, but chatbots' use as a tool is undeniable.

AI in Cisco Catalyst Center

Cisco Catalyst Center—the SDN controller in Cisco's SD-Access solution—can also serve as a general network management platform outside of an SDN context. Catalyst Center includes several AI features such as:

- *AI endpoint analytics*—This feature uses deep packet inspection and other techniques to identify endpoint devices when they access the network. It then classifies these endpoints and assigns policies based on their classification, enhancing network management and security.

- *AI enhanced radio resource management (RRM)*—By analyzing past radio frequency (RF) data, Catalyst Center can predict future network conditions and recommend optimal configurations for wireless LANs. This helps to deliver a consistent user experience across the network without manual tuning.

- *Machine reasoning (MR) engine*—This feature automates network troubleshooting. It uses AI to perform a root cause analysis when network issues arise. Furthermore, it can take corrective actions, potentially resolving problems without requiring manual intervention.

If you want to check out Catalyst Center, Cisco has an always-on sandbox that you can access at https://sandboxdnac.cisco.com with username "devnetuser" and password "Cisco123!". You don't have to be familiar with the Catalyst Center for the CCNA exam, but it's worth eploring a bit to familiarize yourself with DNAC's features.

Summary

- Network automation is a broad category of techniques and methods used to automate network-related tasks, ranging from simple scripts for routine tasks to more complex automation platforms.

- For example, a Python script can be used to reliably perform configuration changes on large numbers of devices in a fraction of the time required for manual configuration.

- Traditional network devices perform a variety of functions on top of forwarding messages, such as building routing/ARP/MAC address tables, using Syslog to log events, and using SSH to accept remote CLI connections.

- The various functions can be divided into three logical planes: the Data Plane, the Control Plane, and the Management Plane.

- The Data Plane includes all functions directly related to forwarding messages over the network: receiving a message on one interface, performing any necessary processing, and then forwarding it out of another interface.

- The Control Plane controls the Data Plane. Functions in the Control Plane are not directly involved in the process of forwarding messages but instead perform necessary overhead work to enable the Data Plane's operations.

- The Management Plane includes a variety of functions that don't directly influence the forwarding of messages—functions related to configuring, managing, and monitoring network devices.

- Traditional network architectures use a distributed Control Plane—the "brains" of the network (the Control Plane) are distributed among each network device. For example, each router uses OSPF to learn routes and build a routing table.

- SDN takes a different approach, centralizing some or all of the Control Plane functions in a controller. This is called a centralized Control Plane.

- In SDN architecture, each network device's role is simply to forward messages according to the controller's instructions. Although the Control Plane is centralized, the Data Plane remains distributed among the network devices.

- SDN facilitates the programmatic control of the network through applications that interact with the SDN controller, resulting in a three-layer architecture consisting of the Application, Control, and Infrastructure Layers.

- The Application Layer consists of applications that communicate network requirements and desired behaviors to the SDN controller.

- The Control Layer translates high-level requirements from the Application Layer into actionable instructions for the network devices.

- The Infrastructure Layer consists of network devices like routers and switches that execute the command received from the Control Layer.

- Communication between the three layers is achieved using application programming interfaces (APIs) and various communication protocols.

- The interface between the Application and Control Layers is the northbound interface (NBI). It typically uses a representational state transfer (REST) API with HTTP messages.

- The interface between the Control and Infrastructure Layers is the southbound interface (SBI). A variety of APIs and communication protocols can be used in the SBI, such as OpenFlow, NETCONF, OpFlex, and traditional protocols like SSH and SNMP.

- SDN isn't a single solution. Cisco's SDN solutions include SD-Access for wired and wireless campus LANs, SD-WAN for WAN networks, and Application Centric Infrastructure (ACI) for data center networks.

- These SDN solutions work by building a virtual network of tunnels (the overlay) on top of the underlying physical network (the underlay). The combination of virtual and physical networks is called the fabric.

- Software-Defined Access (SD-Access) is Cisco's SDN solution for campus LANs. The SD-Access fabric consists of a physical underlay of switches and a virtual overlay of tunnels using Virtual Extensible LAN (VXLAN).

- Cisco Catalyst Center, formerly called Digital Network Architecture (DNA) Center, functions as the SDN controller in SD-Access.

- Software-Defined WAN (SD-WAN) is Cisco's SDN solution for WANs. SD-WAN creates an overlay of IPsec tunnels over any physical WAN underlay: the internet, MPLS, cellular 4G/5G, satellite, etc.

- Application-Centric Infrastructure (ACI) is Cisco's data center SDN solution. Like SD-Access, ACI creates an overlay of VXLAN tunnels over the underlay, which is a physical spine-leaf network.

- The SDN controller used in ACI is called the Application Policy Infrastructure Controller (APIC).

- *Artificial intelligence* (AI) refers to the simulation of intelligence in computers, allowing them to analyze data, identify patterns, and make predictions or take actions based on those insights.

- *Machine learning* (ML) is a field within AI that allows computers to learn on their own, without requiring explicit programming.

- With ML, computers can learn from vast data sets in a few different ways:
  - *Supervised learning*—The ML algorithm is trained on labeled data sets.
  - *Unsupervised learning*—The ML algorithm is trained on unlabeled data sets.
  - *Reinforcement learning*—The ML algorithm learns by interacting with an environment and receiving positive or negative feedback.

- *Semi-supervised learning* is a middle ground between supervised and unsupervised learning that involves a combination of labeled and unlabeled data.

- *Deep learning* (DL) is a subset of machine learning that uses artificial neural networks to analyze and learn from large amounts of data. These neural networks can extract more complex patterns and relationships from data than traditional ML algorithms.

- Predictive and generative AI are two important applications of ML and DL.

- *Predictive AI* uses historical data to predict future events, such as weather forecasts and stock market predictions.

- *Generative AI* leverages ML and DL to create new content, such as text and image generation.

- ML and DL can be used to analyze vast amounts of network data to uncover patterns, anomalies, and insights.

- Predictive AI has applications in network operations such as traffic forecasting, predictive maintenance, capacity planning, and security threat prediction.

- Generative AI has applications in network operations such as automated script creation, network diagram generation, network documentation, deug-and-play deployments, and intent-based networking (IBN).

REST APIs

This chapter covers

- How applications communicate and share data
- HTTP requests and responses
- REST API architecture
- Making REST API calls to Cisco Catalyst Center

Programming and automating networks require seamless communication between software running on various devices—from network equipment like routers and switches to servers, controllers in an SDN architecture, and the network administrator or engineer's own PC. There are two essential elements that facilitate communication between these software applications: an interface that opens up each application's data to external applications and standard data formats for exchanging information efficiently.

In this chapter, we'll cover the first piece of the puzzle: *application programming interfaces* (APIs). APIs are software interfaces that enable two or more software applications to communicate with each other. Specifically, we will examine representational state transfer (REST) APIs, which are commonly used in network automation contexts, such as the northbound interface (NBI) of an SDN controller. Specifically, we will cover CCNA exam topic 6.5: Describe characteristics of REST-based APIs (authentication types, CRUD, HTTP verbs, and data encoding).

23.1 The purpose of APIs

Enabling two applications to communicate and share data is no simple task, especially when they are written by different developers in different programming languages. Without APIs, achieving communication between applications often requires building custom integrations between each pair of applications—a time-consuming and expensive process that results in a tangled web of point-to-point connections between applications. A custom integration between app A and app B wouldn't help either communicate with app C.

An API is a software interface that opens up an application's data in a way that allows other applications to access it in a uniform manner. Figure 23.1 illustrates how an API facilitates communications between applications.

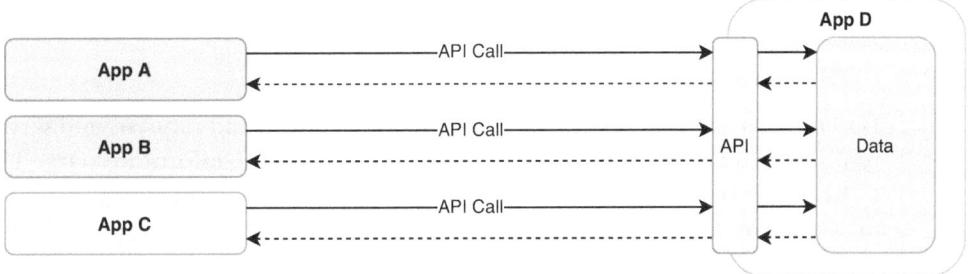

Figure 23.1 An API on app D provides a uniform interface for external apps to access app D's internal data.

Apps A, B, and C don't need to know the intricate details of app D's inner workings; they can simply make an *API call* (request) to app D's API. The API interprets and fulfills the request, returning the relevant information in a response. Basically, APIs simplify and standardize the way applications communicate, making an otherwise complex and costly process manageable and scalable.

23.2 HTTP

APIs can be used to facilitate communications between applications, whether they're running on the same system or remote systems. For applications on different machines to communicate over a network, a suitable communication protocol is required; for most REST APIs, HTTP is the protocol of choice. Figure 23.2 illustrates an API call in the form of an HTTP request, receiving a response in the form of an HTTP response.

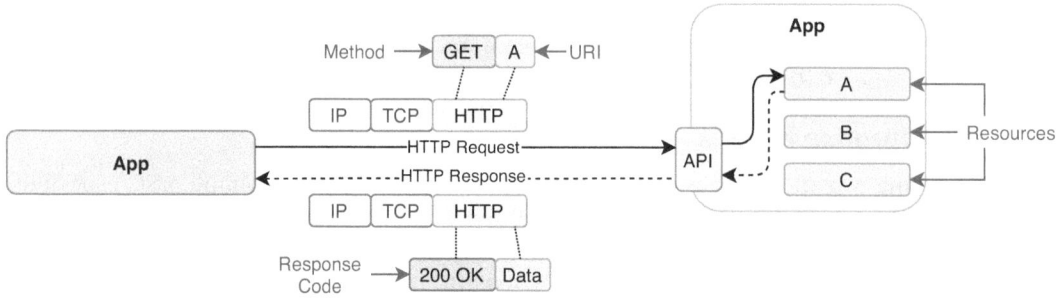

Figure 23.2   An API call in the form of an HTTP request receives a response in the form of an HTTP response. The HTTP request includes an HTTP method and a URI, and the response includes a response code and the relevant data.

HTTP is a natural choice for REST APIs due to its ubiquity on the web and its alignment with REST's architectural principles; we'll cover those in section 23.3. In this section, let's take a look at the various HTTP methods that define a request's desired action, and then we'll look at the response codes that can be sent in reply.

23.2.1 *HTTP requests*

HTTP uses a client-server architecture in which clients send requests and servers send responses. In an HTTP request, the client specifies the Uniform Resource Identifier (URI) of the resource it wants to access. But specifying the resource's URI isn't enough for the server to take action; the client needs to tell the server exactly what action it wants the server to take on the specified resource. Consider what kinds of actions can be taken on a resource:

- *Create*—Create a new resource on the server
  - For example, create variable `"ip_address"`, and set the value to 10.1.1.1.
- *Read*—Retrieve a resource from the server
  - For example, what is the value of variable `"ip_address"`?
- *Update*—Modify an existing resource on the server
  - For example, change the value of variable `"ip_address"` to 10.2.3.4.
- *Delete*—Delete a resource from the server
  - For example, delete variable `"ip_address"`.

These four types of actions are called *CRUD (Create-Read-Update-Delete) operations*. CRUD isn't an HTTP-specific term but rather a general description of the four basic operations for manipulating and managing data. To specify exactly what action the client wants to perform on the specified resource, it includes an *HTTP method* in its request.

Figure 23.3 shows the format of an HTTP request message. It begins with a start line (containing the method, URI, and HTTP version of the request), optional headers that provide additional information, a blank link separating the headers from the body, and then the optional message body (which is only present in some request types).

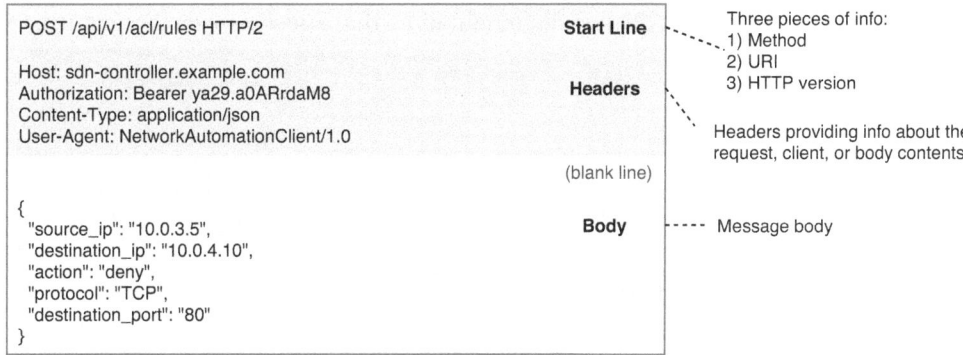

Figure 23.3   The format of an HTTP request, consisting of a start line, headers, a blank line, and a message body. This message is an API call requesting to create a new ACL rule.

NOTE   CCNA exam topic 6.5 specifically refers to *HTTP verbs*—another term for HTTP methods (although not all HTTP methods are verbs—some are nouns). I will use the more accurate term: method.

The HTTP method is key because it is how the client specifies what it wants to do with the resource it is trying to access. Table 23.1 lists common HTTP methods and their equivalent CRUD operations. The HTTP *POST* operation is most often used to create a new resource on the server. *GET* is used to retrieve a resource from the server (or read its contents); your PC sends a GET request to retrieve a web page from a web server. *PUT* and *PATCH* are used to update a resource; the difference between the two is that PUT replaces the specified resource, and PATCH modifies it. Finally, DELETE is used to—you guessed it—delete the specified resource.

Table 23.1   CRUD operations and HTTP methods

CRUD operation	Purpose	HTTP method
Create	Create new resource	POST
Read	Retrieve resource	GET
Update	Modify resource	PUT, PATCH
Delete	Delete resource	DELETE

NOTE   Although the mappings listed in table 23.1 are generally accepted, they are not 1:1 equivalents, and some can map to different CRUD operations in different situations. For example, the PUT method can also be used to create resources. Each API has documentation that specifies exactly how it uses the HTTP methods.

23.2.2 HTTP responses

The example HTTP request we saw in figure 23.3 was an API call to create (POST) a new ACL rule on an SDN controller. After receiving and processing the request, the server (the SDN controller) will send an HTTP response. Figure 23.4 shows the HTTP response message format.

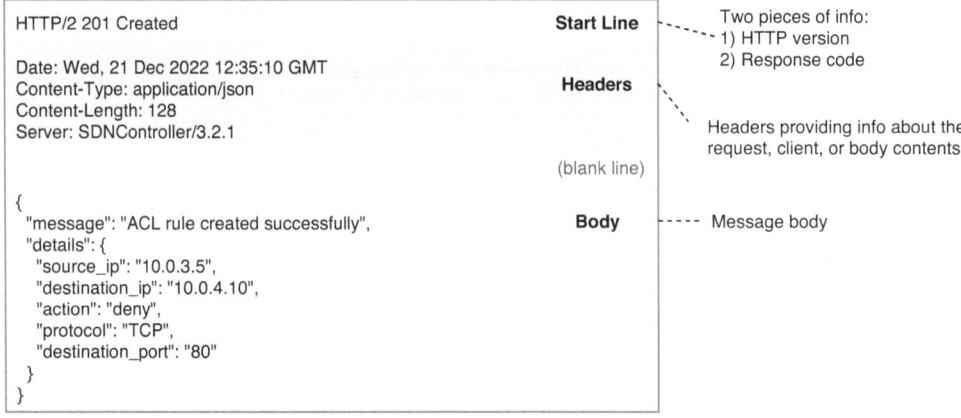

Figure 23.4   The format of an HTTP response. The response code `201 Created` indicates that the resource (the ACL rule requested in figure 23.3) was successfully created.

NOTE   Figures 23.3 and 23.4 both include the `Content-Type: application/json` header, indicating that the message body uses the JavaScript Object Notation (JSON) data format—foreshadowing! We'll cover JSON and other data formats in chapter 24.

The *response code* in the start line is the key element here; this code indicates the result of the request (i.e., success or failure). There are five main categories of response codes, indicated by their first digit:

- *1xx informational*—A provisional response. The initial part of the request has been received, and additional actions may be expected to follow.
- *2xx successful*—The request was received without problems, understood, and processed as expected.

- *3xx redirection*—Additional steps are required to complete the request.
- *4xx client error*—Points to an error on the client's part, either due to incorrect syntax or because the request is infeasible.
- *5xx server error*—Indicates that the server encountered an error and can't perform the request, even though the request appears to be valid.

Each response code consists of a three-digit numeric code and a short name. Table 23.2 lists and describes some common response codes (one or two from each category). For a complete list of HTTP response codes, check out this page from Mozilla: https://developer.mozilla.org/en-US/docs/Web/HTTP/Status.

Table 23.2 HTTP response codes

Code	Description
102 Processing	The server is processing the request, but the response is not yet available.
200 OK	The request succeeded.
201 Created	The request succeeded and a new resource was created.
301 Moved Permanently	The requested resource has been moved.
403 Forbidden	The client is not authorized to access the resource.
404 Not Found	The requested resource was not found.
500 Internal Server Error	The server encountered something unexpected that prevented it from fulfilling the request.

Figure 23.5 illustrates the client–server exchange that we saw in figures 23.3 and 23.4. The client sends a POST request to create a new ACL rule, and the server receives the request, processes it (creating the ACL rule), and sends a response with the code 201 Created.

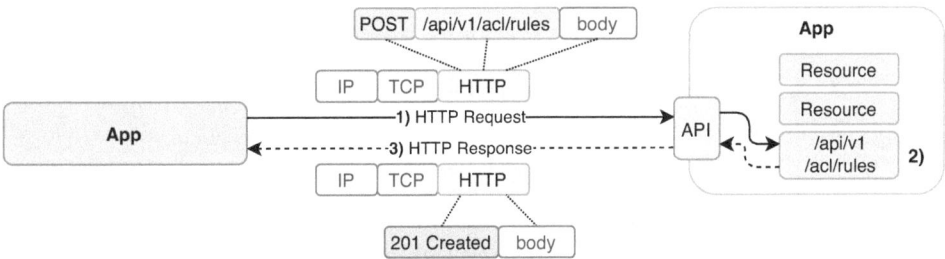

Figure 23.5 An HTTP exchange. (1) The client requests to create (POST) a new ACL rule. (2) The server creates the new rule. (3) The server sends a response with code 201 Created, indicating the ACL rule was created.

23.3 *REST APIs*

Representational state transfer (REST) is a type of software architecture that forms the basis of the World Wide Web. APIs that conform to REST architecture are called *REST APIs* or *RESTful APIs*. Most REST APIs are HTTP-based, using the various HTTP methods described in the previous section to interact with resources. In this section, we'll delve into REST architecture and make an API call to Cisco Catalyst Center.

23.3.1 *REST architecture*

REST architecture is defined by six constraints:

1 Uniform interface
2 Client-server
3 Stateless
4 Cacheable or noncacheable
5 Layered system
6 Code on demand (optional)

For the purpose of the CCNA exam, it's not worth digging into the details of all six constraints, but let's cover three to give you an idea of how REST APIs work.

REST: CLIENT-SERVER

REST APIs employ a client-server architecture. Clients use API calls (HTTP requests) to access resources on the server, which receives, processes, and responds to those requests. The strict separation between the client and server applications is essential; the client and the server must be able to change and evolve independently without breaking the interface between them (the API).

REST: STATELESS

REST API exchanges are *stateless*, meaning that each API exchange is a separate event, independent of all past exchanges between the client and server. We've covered a few stateful and stateless concepts previously:

- *Stateful*—Stateful firewalls, TCP
- *Stateless*—Access control lists (ACLs), UDP

Stateful firewalls and TCP are considered stateful because they remember and keep track of past interactions to make decisions about future interactions. Stateful firewalls don't just consider individual packets with no other context; they consider each packet's relationship to other packets when deciding whether the packet should be permitted or denied. And TCP, a connection-oriented protocol, keeps track of the state of connections and the delivery of packets.

ACLs and UDP do neither of those things and are therefore stateless; each message is its own event, independent of those before or after it. In the context of REST APIs, stateless means that the server does not store information about previous requests from the client to determine how it should respond to new requests.

> **NOTE** Although REST APIs use HTTP, which employs TCP (stateful) as its Layer 4 protocol, HTTP and REST APIs themselves are stateless. Don't forget that the functions of each layer of the TCP/IP model are independent!

One implication of REST's stateless nature is that if authentication is required, the client must provide authentication credentials in every single request. This can be done with a simple username/password that is included with each request, but a more robust approach is to require clients to generate an *access token* (also called an *authorization token*). We'll examine a few authentication methods in section 23.3.2.

REST: CACHEABLE OR NON-CACHEABLE

If a resource is *cacheable*, it means that it can be cached—temporarily stored for reuse. This can significantly improve efficiency; there's no need to retrieve the same resource repeatedly when accessing it multiple times. For example, frequently accessed web pages can be cached to improve load times.

However, not all resources should be cached; sensitive and frequently updated information should not be cached. For example, a user's personal dashboard showing a real-time account balance in a banking application is not a good candidate for caching. Caching the data could lead to outdated information being displayed, and it poses a security risk if the sensitive data is stored inappropriately.

In REST architecture, resources can be cacheable or noncacheable, but they must be marked as such, whether implicitly or explicitly. Cacheable resources must be marked as cacheable, and noncacheable resources must be marked as noncacheable.

> **NOTE** Check out https://restfulapi.net/rest-architectural-constraints/ for an explanation of all six REST architectural constraints.

23.3.2 *REST API authentication*

APIs provide access to an application and its data, so security is a major concern when designing and using APIs. Instead of responding to all requests, the server should properly authenticate and authorize clients. If the process is successful, the server fulfills the request. If the process fails (e.g., due to invalid credentials or insufficient permissions), the server refuses the request.

In this section, we'll examine a few common REST API authentication methods:

- *Basic authentication*—a simple username/password are provide for authentication
- *Bearer authentication*—a token the client obtains from an authentication server and then includes in its API calls

- *API key authentication*—a unique identifier assigned to a client application that allows it to access the API
- *OAuth 2.0*—an industry-standard framework that provides access delegation

BASIC AUTHENTICATION

Basic authentication is a simple method where a username and password are provided in the HTTP header for authentication. While simple and convenient to implement, basic authentication is not considered secure because it suffers from the same weaknesses as other simple username/password-based solutions: if a malicious user obtains the credentials, they can gain access to the API. If using basic authentication, it's critical to use HTTPS to encrypt the API calls; if using standard HTTP, the credentials are sent in unencrypted cleartext.

BEARER AUTHENTICATION

In *bearer authentication*, the client obtains a token (the "access token" mentioned in section 23.3.1) that it then provides for authentication in its API calls. This token can be obtained in various ways; often, the client obtains the token from an authorization server by first going through a separate authentication process, often using a username and password. Access tokens are typically valid for a limited time, requiring renewal for continued use.

Bearer authentication is generally considered more secure than basic authentication because the client does not have to repeatedly transmit the same username/password. However, like basic authentication, bearer authentication should only be used with HTTPS to ensure the token is transmitted securely. Even though the token itself doesn't contain sensitive information like a username/password, it grants access to API resources. Interception of the token could allow an attacker unauthorized access to the resources.

Figure 23.6 shows an example of bearer authentication; the client obtains a token from an authorization server and then uses the token to access the API of the server that hosts the desired resource.

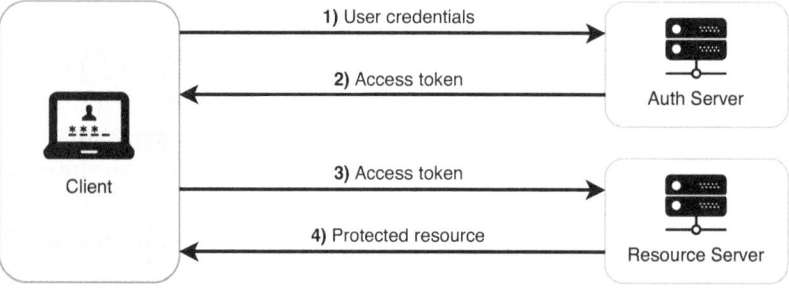

Figure 23.6   REST API bearer authentication. A client obtains an access token from an authorization token and uses the token to access the desired resource on the resource server.

NOTE In some cases, the same server might function as both the authorization server and the resource server in bearer authentication. We'll see an example of this in section 23.3.3.

API KEY AUTHENTICATION

API key authentication involves the use of a unique identifier assigned to each client application. The client application includes this key in its API calls, similar to an access token used in bearer authentication. However, it's important to note that an API key identifies an application, not a user; for user-based authentication and authorization, access tokens are more appropriate.

Unlike access tokens, which are generally short-lived and expire after a set period of time, API keys typically do not automatically expire (unless revoked by the server). This makes them less secure if not managed properly, as they can be used indefinitely if compromised.

API keys are usually easier to implement and use, but they lack the fine-grained control and security features offered by more sophisticated authentication methods. And once again, if security is a concern, always use HTTPS to encrypt API calls; otherwise, the API key can easily be intercepted in transit.

OAUTH 2.0

Open Authorization 2.0 (OAuth 2.0) is an industry-standard framework that is widely used in modern web applications. OAuth 2.0 provides *access delegation*, allowing third-party applications to access resources (i.e. via a REST API) on behalf of a user without sharing the user's credentials. You've almost certainly used OAuth 2.0 before. Some common examples you might be familiar with are:

- *Logging in with Google*—Many websites and apps offer the option to log in using your Google account instead of creating a new account on the website itself. OAuth 2.0 allows the website or app to access your basic Google profile information without sharing your password with the third-party service.
- *Connecting apps to social media accounts*—When you connect apps to your account on Instagram, Facebook, LinkedIn, or other social media platforms, OAuth 2.0 is used to grant these tools permission to read your social media data or post on your behalf.
- *Calendar integration*—A third-party tool might request access to your Google Calendar to check your availability and schedule meetings. When you authorize this, Google provides an access token to the tool, which allows it to view and manage your calendar without needing your Google account password.

There are countless other examples. Figure 23.7 gives a high-level overview of how OAuth 2.0 works. To make sense of the diagram, consider the third example listed previously: a third-party tool requesting access to Google Calendar on your behalf. The *client* in figure 23.7 is the third-party tool requesting access. The *resource owner* is you—the person who owns the Google account associated with the calendar and is, therefore, capable of granting access to the calendar. The *auth server* is Google's authorization server, and the *resource server* is Google's server that hosts the information relevant to your Google Calendar.

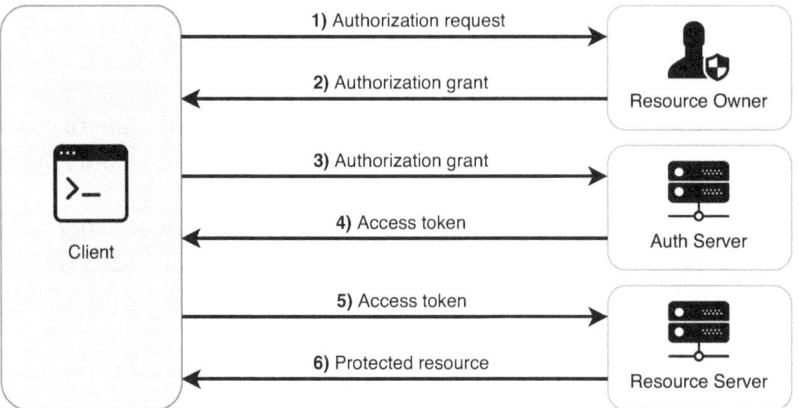

Figure 23.7   The basic OAuth 2.0 process. Through access delegation, the client application is able to access the resource owner's protected resources on behalf of the owner.

Let's walk through the basic process as illustrated in figure 23.7:

1 The client (third-party tool) requests authorization from the resource owner (you) to access the resource (your Google Calendar data).
2 The resource owner grants the authorization by logging into their account and giving permission.
3 The client exchanges the authorization grant for an access token from the auth server (Google's authorization server).
4 The auth server provides an access token to the client.
5 The client uses the access token to request the protected resource from the resource server (Google's server).
6 The resource server validates the access token and provides the requested resource (calendar data) to the client.

The access token granted in step 4 of the process functions just like the access token used in bearer authentication, as covered previously. The token grants access to the specified resources within the appropriate scope of access and is typically valid only for a limited period, requiring regular renewal. This could require the user to manually grant authorization again, or the client might receive a *refresh token* from the authorization server that allows it to automatically refresh its access token multiple times within a longer period of time.

NOTE   The access token granted to the client has a specific *scope* that dictates exactly what resources the client can access and what actions it can perform; this scope is enforced by the resource server. It's best to be cautious about granting third-party apps access to your accounts beyond what is necessary.

23.3.3 *Making REST API calls to Catalyst Center*

In this section, we'll make a couple of API calls to Cisco's always-on Catalyst Center sandbox that I introduced in the previous chapter. To do so, we'll use Postman, a versatile platform for building, testing, and using APIs.

NOTE   You can access Postman at https://www.postman.com/. You'll have to make a Postman account if you want to follow along (it's free). Another option is Insomnia, available at https://insomnia.rest/, but I will use Postman for this demonstration.

Our objective is to retrieve Catalyst Center's inventory list—the list of devices it manages. First, we need to generate an access token. After logging in to Postman, click Workspaces, and then open My Workspace, as shown in figure 23.8.

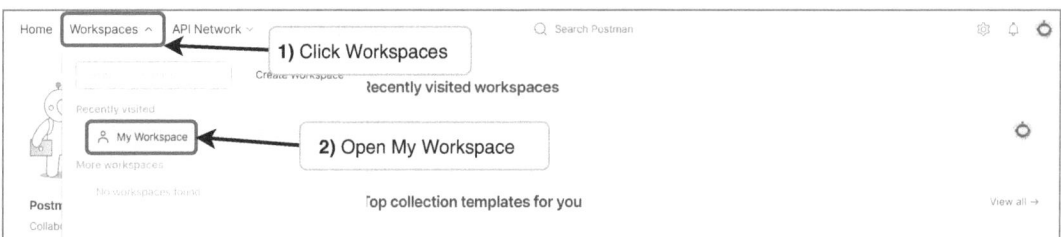

Figure 23.8   Accessing My Workspace in Postman to make an API call

From My Workspace, click New and then HTTP, as shown in figure 23.9; we are going to send HTTP requests to Catalyst Center's REST API.

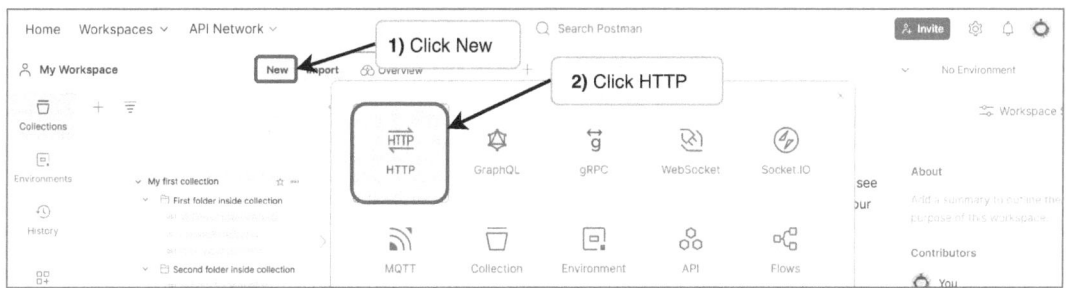

Figure 23.9   Click New and HTTP to send HTTP requests to Catalyst Center's REST API.

Now it's time to make the first API call: a POST request to generate an access token that we will use in the next API call. Figure 23.10 shows how to do this:

1   Specify the POST method and URI https://sandboxdnac.cisco.com/dna/system/api/v1/auth/token.
2   Click Authorization, and select Basic Auth.
3   Enter the username devnetuser and password Cisco123!.
4   Click Send to send the API call to Catalyst Center.
5   Copy the token from the response.

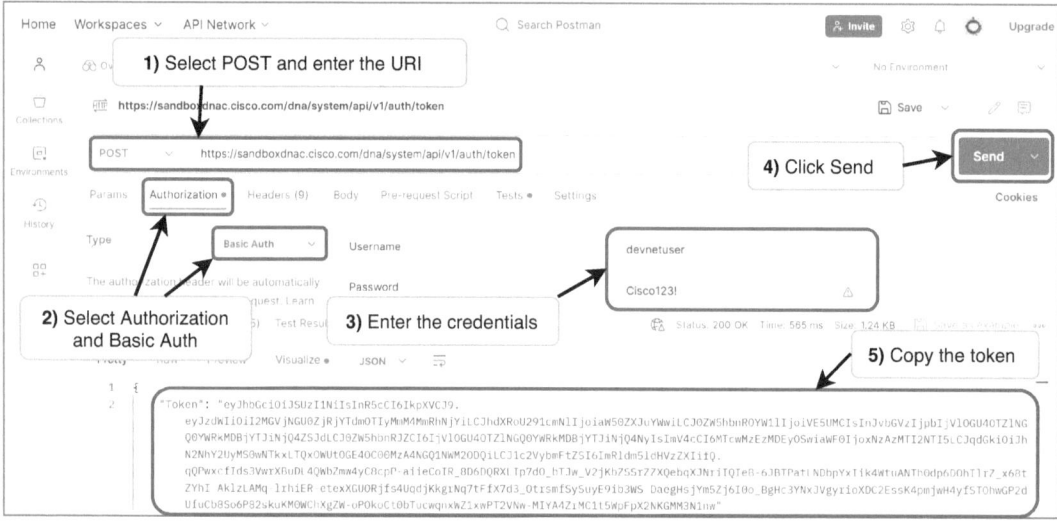

Figure 23.10   Generating an access token with a POST request to Catalyst Center

After sending the POST, you should receive a response with code 200 OK (you can see Status: 200 OK under the user credentials in figure 23.8) and the token itself. The following output shows the access token generated from my POST request; your token will be different:

```
{
"Token": "eyJhbGciOiJSUzI1NiIsInR5cCI6IkpXVCJ9.eyJzdWIiOiI2MGVjNGU0ZjRjYTdmOTIyMmM4M
mRhNjYiLCJhdXRoU291cmNlIjoiaW50ZXJuYWwiLCJ0ZW5hbnROYW1lIjoiVE5UMCIsInJvbGVz
IjpbIjVlOGU4OTZlNGQ0YWRkMDBjYTJiNjQ4ZSJdLCJ0ZW5hbnRJZCI6IjVlOGU4OTZlNGQ0YWR
kMDBjYTJiNjQ4NyIsImV4cCI6MTcwMzEzMDEyOSwiaWF0IjoxNzAzMTI2NTI5LCJqdGdiOiJhN2
NhY2UyMS0wNTkxLTQxOWUtOGE4OC00MzA4NGQ1NWM2ODQiLCJ1c2VybmFtZSI6ImRldm5ldHVzz
XIifQ.qQPwxcfIds3VwrXBuDL4QWbZmw4yC8cpP-
aiieCoIR_8D6DQRXLIp7dO_bTJw_V2jKbZSSrZZXQebqXJNriIQIeB-
6JBTPatLNDbpYxIik4WtuANTh0dp6DOhIlrZ_x68tZYhI-AklzLAMq-lrhiER-
etexXGUORjfs4UqdjKkgrNq7tFfX7d3_OtrsmfSySuyE9ib3WS-
DaegHsjYm5Zj6I0o_BgHc3YNxJVgyrioXDC2EssK4pmjwH4yfSTOhwGP2dUfuCb8So6P82skuKM
0WChXgZW-oPOkoCt0bTucwqnxWZ1xwPT2VNw-MIYA4ZrMC1t5WpFpX2NKGMM3N1nw"
}
```

NOTE The token is the long string of characters inside of double quotes; don't copy the double quotes themselves. The output is JSON-formatted, and the double quotes indicate a JSON string—more on that in the next chapter!

Now that we have an access token, let's make a second API call to retrieve Catalyst Center's inventory list. Figure 23.11 shows the process:

1 Specify the GET method and URI https://sandboxdnac.cisco.com/dna/intent/api/v1/network-device.
2 Select Header to add an additional HTTP header to the API call.
3 Add the key X-Auth-Token, and paste the token you generated previously as the value.
4 Click Send to send the API call to Catalyst Center.

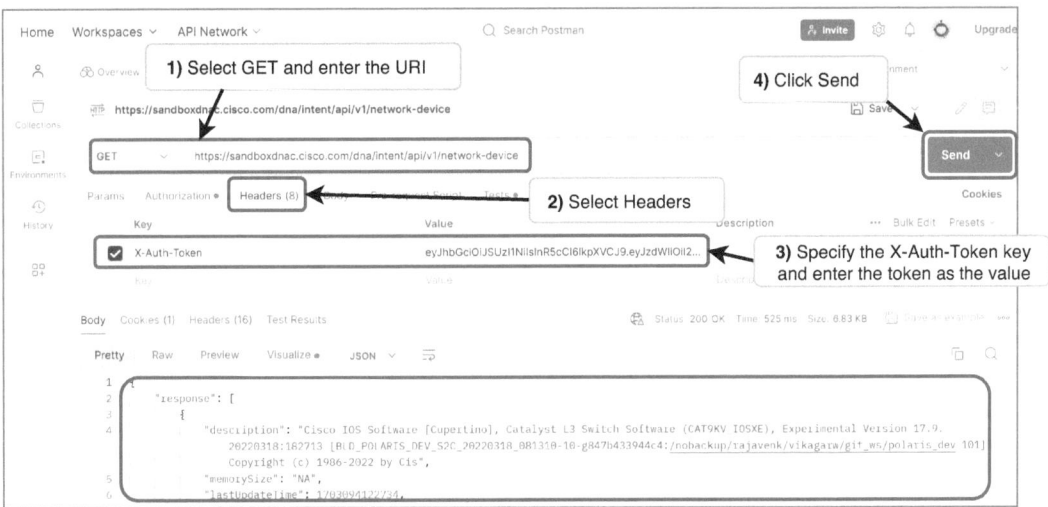

Figure 23.11   Sending a GET request to Catalyst Center to retrieve its inventory list

The Catalyst Center sandbox only manages four devices, but the message body of the response is 193 lines in length—too long to include all of it here. The following output shows a portion of the first device's information, including details like its MAC address, software version, hostname, and serial number. Once again, this data uses the JSON format:

```
{
    "response": [
        {
. . .
            "lastUpdateTime": 1703094122734,
            "bootDateTime": "2023-12-19 17:25:02",
            "macAddress": "52:54:00:01:c2:c0",
```

```
"apManagerInterfaceIp": "",
"deviceSupportLevel": "Supported",
"softwareType": "IOS-XE",
"softwareVersion": "17.9.20220318:182713",
"hostname": "sw1",
"serialNumber": "9SB9FYAFA2O",
```

. . .

In summary, we made two API calls to Catalyst Center: a POST request to generate an access token and a GET request to retrieve Catalyst Center's inventory list. For a more detailed walkthrough and further resources on Catalyst Center, you can check out this guide on Cisco DevNet: https://mng.bz/WE6a.

Cisco DevNet

DevNet is a program by Cisco to support developers and other IT professionals looking to create applications and integrations using Cisco's suite of products and APIs. It provides resources such as documentation, courses, learning labs, and sandbox platforms for experimentation. If you want to dive deeper into network automation, DevNet is an invaluable resource. Check it out at https://developer.cisco.com/.

Summary

- *Application programming interfaces* (APIs) are software interfaces that open up an application's data in a way that allows other applications to access it in a uniform manner, facilitating communications between applications.

- To access an application's internal data, other applications can simply make an *API call* (request) to the application's API. The API interprets and fulfills the request, returning the relevant information in a response.

- For applications on different machines to communicate over a network, a communication protocol is required. For most REST APIs, HTTP is the protocol of choice.

- HTTP uses a client–server architecture in which clients send requests and servers send responses.

- The essential actions that can be taken on a resource are called *CRUD (Create-Read-Update-Delete) operations.*

- An HTTP request can include various pieces of information. The two key elements are the *HTTP method* (also called the *HTTP verb*), which defines the request's desired action (CRUD operation), and the Uniform Resource Identifier (URI), which indicates the target of the request.

- HTTP methods can generally be mapped to one of the four CRUD operations: create (POST), read (GET), update (PUT, PATCH), and delete (DELETE).

- An HTTP response uses a similar format to an HTTP request. The key element is the *response code*, which indicates the result of the request.

- There are five main categories of HTTP responses, indicated by their first digit:
  - 1xx informational
  - 2xx successful
  - 3xx redirection
  - 4xx client error
  - 5xx server error
- Some common response codes are 102 Processing, 200 OK, 201 Created, 301 Moved Permanently, 403 Forbidden, 404 Not Found, and 500 Internal Server Error.
- *Representational State Transfer* (REST) is a type of software architecture that forms the basis of the World Wide Web. APIs that conform to REST architecture are called *REST APIs* or *RESTful APIs.*
- REST architecture is defined by six constraints:
  - Uniform interface
  - Client-server
  - Stateless
  - Cacheable or noncacheable
  - Layered system
  - Code on demand (optional)
- REST APIs employ a client-server architecture. The client and server applications must be able to change and evolve independently without breaking the interface between them (the API).
- REST API exchanges are *stateless*, meaning that each API exchange is a separate event, independent of all past exchanges between the client and server.
- The server does not store information about previous requests from the client to determine how it should respond to new requests.
- If a resource is *cacheable*, it means that it can be cached—temporarily stored for reuse. This can significantly improve efficiency because there's no need to retrieve the same resource repeatedly when accessing it multiple times.
- Frequently updated and sensitive information should not be cached. Caching such data could lead to outdated information being displayed, and it poses a security risk if sensitive data is stored inappropriately.
- In REST architecture, resources can be cacheable or noncacheable, but they must be marked as such, whether implicitly or explicitly.
- REST APIs can use a variety of methods to authenticate requests. Some common authentication types include basic authentication, bearer authentication, API key authentication, and OAuth 2.0.

- *Basic authentication* uses a username and password (provided in the HTTP header) for authentication. While simple and convenient to implement, it is not considered secure.

- In *bearer authentication*, the client obtains an access token from an authorization server, which it then uses to access the desired resource. The token is typically valid for a limited time, requiring renewal for continued use.

- *API key authentication* involves the use of a unique identifier assigned to each client application. The client application includes this key in its API calls, similar to an access token used in bearer authentication. The API key uniquely identifies an application, not a user.

- Unlike access tokens, API keys typically do not automatically expire, making them less secure if not managed properly.

- *Open Authorization 2.0* (OAuth 2.0) is an industry-standard framework that provides *access delegation*, allowing third-party applications to access resources (i.e., via a REST API) on behalf of a user without sharing the user's credentials.

- The client application requests authorization from the resource owner, receives an authorization grant, and then uses the authorization grant to obtain an access token from the authorization server. It then uses the access token to access the desired resource on the resource server.

Data formats

This chapter covers

- Why data serialization formats are needed
- JSON's primitive and structured data types
- Interpreting JSON-formatted data
- Other data serialization formats: XML and YAML

In the previous chapter, we established that communication between software applications on different devices is essential for network automation. We also covered one essential part of making that possible: application programming interfaces (APIs). APIs open up an application's data to allow external applications to access it in an efficient and uniform manner.

In this chapter, we'll cover the second half of the puzzle. For successful communication between applications, it's not enough for App A to be able to access App B's data; the data itself must be in a format that App A understands. That's the role of data serialization formats—standardized data formats that allow applications to communicate data in an agreed-upon format that both parties understand. With regard to the CCNA exam topics, we will cover topic 6.7: Recognize components of JSON-encoded data.

24.1   *Data serialization*

When we covered the TCP/IP networking model in chapter 4 of volume 1, I emphasized the importance of standardized protocols to enable communications between devices over a network. This doesn't just apply to the communication protocols used to carry messages; it applies to the contents of those messages as well. Applications, which can be developed in many different programming languages, store and interpret data in different ways. Figure 24.1 shows what happens when different applications attempt to communicate without using a data serialization format.

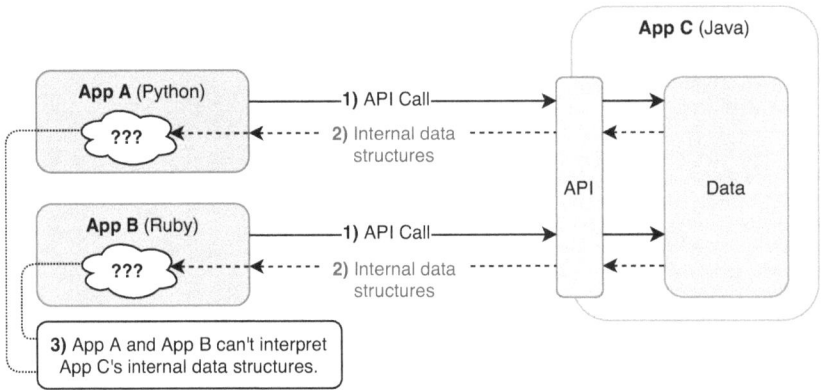

Figure 24.1   Communicating between applications without a data serialization format. Apps A and B, written in Python and Ruby, can't interpret App C's internal data structures.

Data serialization is the process of converting data into a standardized format for the purpose of storage or transmission. The data serialization process takes an application's data structures from a computer's memory and converts them into a series of bytes (hence the term *serialization*) that can be stored in a file or transmitted over a network. This process enables the data to be later reconstructed (i.e., by a different application). Data formats used for this purpose are called *data serialization formats*. In this chapter, we'll cover three:

- JavaScript Object Notation (JSON)
- Extensible Markup Language (XML)
- YAML Ain't Markup Language (YAML)

Data serialization enables an application to communicate its data to another application in a format both parties understand. Figure 24.2 shows how it works: App C's API converts its data structures into JSON-formatted data, allowing Apps A and B to interpret and reconstruct the data in their own languages.

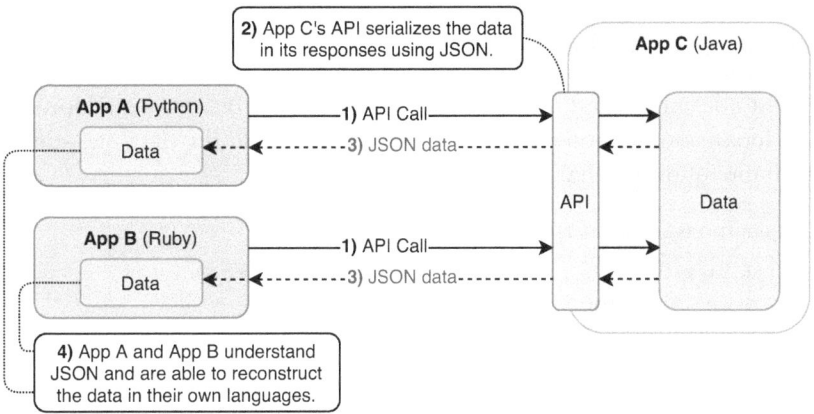

Figure 24.2 Data serialization formats like JSON allow applications to communicate data in a format understood by both parties.

NOTE   The term *data serialization* might sound complex, but it just means converting data into a format that's easy to store or transfer. JSON, XML, and YAML are all standard data formats that many applications can understand, making them common choices for sharing data among different applications.

24.2 JSON

JavaScript Object Notation (JSON) is an open-standard data serialization format. It was originally derived from JavaScript, but is language independent; applications in many programming languages can generate and interpret JSON-formatted data. REST APIs often support JSON, which is likely why Cisco chose to include JSON as a CCNA exam topic.

One of JSON's main characteristics is its human readability. Although it is designed for communication between computer applications, properly formatted JSON data is easy for us to read, too. To prove that, here's an example of JSON-formatted data:

```
{
  "interface_name": "GigabitEthernet1/1",
  "is_up": true,
  "ip_address": "192.168.1.1",
  "netmask": "255.255.255.0",
  "speed": 1000,
  "description": null
}
```

Even if you don't know anything about JSON yet, I'd bet that you can read and understand that data. It's composed of a series of *variables*—logical containers for values—and the values they hold. For example, the variable `"interface_name"` holds the value `"GigabitEthernet1/1"`.

NOTE   A variable and its value are often called a *key-value pair.* We'll examine JSON key-value pairs in this section.

You might not understand the significance of the curly braces or the double quotes in the previous example, but you can probably deduce that the data pertains to an interface with the following characteristics:

- Its name is GigabitEthernet1/1.
- Its status is up.
- Its IP address is 192.168.1.1.
- Its netmask is 255.255.255.0.
- Its speed is 1000 (Mbps).
- It currently has no description.

In this section, we'll explore the different JSON data types and practice interpreting JSON-formatted data by looking at some examples.

EXAM TIP   JSON is explicitly mentioned in exam topic 6.7: Recognize components of JSON-encoded data. Make sure that you can differentiate between the different data types we cover and interpret simple JSON-formatted data.

24.2.1 *JSON primitive data types*

JSON data is represented using four fundamental forms called *primitive data types.* Here are the four primitive data types and some examples of each:

- *String*—An alphanumeric text value. JSON strings are always enclosed in double quotes. Examples:
  - `"Hello."`
  - `"5"`
  - `"true"`
  - `"null"`
- *Number*—A numeric value. Examples:
  - `5`
  - `101.25`
- *Boolean*—A data type with only two possible values: `true` and `false`.
- *Null*—A data type that represents the intentional absence of a value and is always represented as `null`.

Take a close look at the examples I gave for strings: `"5"` is a string, not a number; `"true"` is a string, not a Boolean; `"null"` is a string, not null. Any value enclosed in double quotes is a string (a text value), even if it would be a different data type without double quotes.

EXAM TIP   Remember that point for the exam! Don't be fooled by a numeric value in double quotes; with regard to JSON data types, it's a string, not a number.

Take another look at the previous example of JSON data. The key of each key-value pair is a string, and each of the four primitive data types is present in the values:

```
{
  "interface_name": "GigabitEthernet1/1",
  "is_up": true,
  "ip_address": "192.168.1.1",
  "netmask": "255.255.255.0",
  "speed": 1000,
  "description": null
}
```

"GigabitEthernet1/1" is a string.

true is a Boolean.

"192.168.1.1" is a string.

"255.255.255.0" is a string.

null is a null value.

1000 is a number.

NOTE   The Boolean and null data types must be lowercase: `true`, `false`, and `null`.

24.2.2 *JSON structured data types*

While primitive data types in JSON represent singular values, *structured data types*, as the name implies, are used to organize information into more complex structures. JSON has two structured data types:

- *Object*—An unordered set of key-value pairs
- *Array*—An ordered set of values

JSON OBJECTS

A JSON *object* is an unordered set of key-value pairs. *Unordered* means that the order of the key-value pairs in the object is insignificant; they can be reordered without affecting the meaning of the object. The example of JSON data that we already looked at a couple of times is an object: curly braces enclosing six key-value pairs. Here it is once again:

```
{
  "interface_name": "GigabitEthernet1/1",
  "is_up": true,
  "ip_address": "192.168.1.1",
  "netmask": "255.255.255.0",
  "speed": 1000,
  "description": null
}
```

An opening curly brace indicates the start of an object.

A closing curly brace indicates the end of an object.

Here are some important points about objects in JSON:

- Objects are enclosed in curly braces.
- The key of each key-value pair must be a string.

- The value of each key-value pair can be any valid JSON data type: string, number, Boolean, null, or even another object (or array—the next data type).
- The key and value of each key-value pair are separated by a colon.
- If there are multiple key-value pairs, each pair is separated by a comma.
- There must not be a trailing comma after the final key-value pair.

In all of the previous example's key-value pairs, the value is a primitive data type: string, number, Boolean, or null. However, structured data types are also valid values for an object's key-value pairs. These "objects within objects" are called *nested objects*. The following example shows an object that contains two key-value pairs. The two keys are `"device"` and `"interface_config"`, and the value of each of those keys is a nested object with its own set of key-value pairs:

```
{
  "device": {
    "name": "R1",
    "vendor": "Cisco",                    Nested object 1
    "model": "1101"
  },
  "interface_config": {
    "interface_name": "GigabitEthernet1/1",
    "is_up": true,
    "ipaddress": "192.168.1.1",
    "netmask": "255.255.255.0",           Nested object 2
    "speed": 1000,
    "description": null
  }
}
```

Figure 24.3 shows that same object, highlighting the keys and values to illustrate the nested objects.

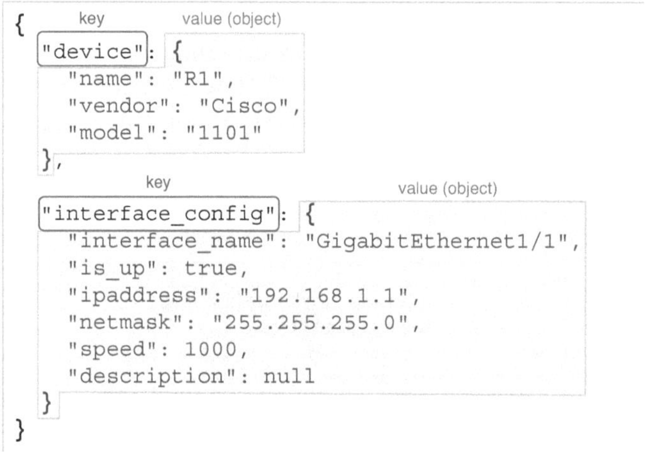

Figure 24.3   An object consisting of two key-value pairs. The value of each key-value pair is a nested object with its own set of key-value pairs.

Now is a good time to introduce another key point about JSON: *whitespace*—including spaces, line breaks, and tabs—is insignificant in terms of data interpretation. All of the examples shown so far have used whitespace to enhance their readability, but that whitespace has no actual meaning in JSON. Here's that previous example with all whitespace removed:

```
{"device":{"name":"R1","vendor":"Cisco","model":"1101"},"interface_config":
{"interface_name":"GigabitEthernet1/1","is_up":true,"ipaddress":
"192.168.1.1","netmask":"255.255.255.0","speed":1000,"description":null}}
```

Although it makes no difference to the application interpreting the data, I'm sure you'll agree that the previous examples are more human readable.

> **NOTE** We won't cover the general best practices regarding whitespace for making human-readable JSON; the CCNA exam just requires you to interpret JSON-formatted data, not write it yourself.

JSON ARRAYS

The previous examples of key-value pairs showed one value for each key. However, a key can hold multiple values using the array data type. A JSON *array* is an ordered set of values.

> **NOTE** Unlike JSON objects, arrays are *ordered*. The order of the object's values is significant, so changing their order would change the meaning of the array.

The following example is a JSON object with two key-value pairs; the value of each is an array containing multiple values. The "interfaces" array contains three strings, and the "random_values" array contains four values of different data types: a string, a number, a Boolean, and null:

```
{
  "interfaces": [
    "GigabitEthernet1/1",              An array containing
    "GigabitEthernet1/2",              three string values
    "GigabitEthernet1/3"
  ],
  "random_values": [
    "Hi",
    42,                                An array containing four
    false,                             values of different data types
    null
  ]
}
```

Here are the key points about arrays:

- Arrays are enclosed in square brackets.
- The values can be of any valid JSON data type.
- The values don't have to be of the same data type.

- The values are separated by commas.
- There must not be a trailing comma after the final value.

24.2.3 *Identifying invalid JSON*

The previous examples all showed valid JSON-formatted data. In this section, we'll look at a few examples of invalid JSON. This is useful practice for "trick questions" on the CCNA exam and for checking your understanding of JSON syntax. Here's the first example:

```
{
  "routerConfig": {
    "hostname": "Router01",
    "interfaces": [
      "GigabitEthernet0/0",
      "GigabitEthernet0/1"
    ],
    "enabled": TRUE,
    "ipAddress": "192.168.1.1",
    "subnetMask": "255.255.255.0"
    "gateway": NULL
  }
}
```

There are three issues with this example:

- Booleans must be lowercase: `true`, not `TRUE`.
- Null must be lowercase: `null`, not `NULL`.
- There is a missing comma after the value of `"subnetMask"`. There must be a comma between each of an object's key-value pairs.

> **NOTE** If you want to validate JSON data, you can use a website like https://jsonlint .com/. Paste the data and click Validate JSON; it will indicate whether the data is valid or not. Try it with the examples in this section.

The following example is also invalid JSON, but for different reasons than the previous example:

```
{
  "switchSettings": {
    "model": "WS-C2960C-8PC-L",
    "ports": 8,
    "management": {
        "accessMode"-"ssh",
        "port": 22
    },
    "firmwareVersion": "15.2(7)E7",
    "location": "Data Center A",
  }
}
```

Here are the two issues with the second example:

- There is an invalid character (-) separating the `"accessMode"` key from its value `"ssh"`. A key-value pair's key and value must be separated by a colon.
- There is a trailing comma after `"location"`'s value. An object's key-value pairs must be separated by commas, but there must not be a trailing comma after the final pair.

Let's look at one more example, again with two new issues that render it invalid:

```
{
  "firewallConfig": {
    "rules": [
      {
        "id": 1,
        "action": "allow",
        "sourceIp": "10.0.0.0/24"
      },
      {
        "id": 2,
        "action": "deny",
        "sourceIp": "10.0.1.0/24"
      }
  },
  "defaultAction": "deny"
```

This example's issues are related to closing objects and arrays:

- The final closing curly brace (to close the opening curly brace at the start of the example) is missing.
- The value of `"rules"` is an array, but it has no closing square bracket.

You now know (almost) all of JSON's rules! JSON is fairly simple, and there's not much to it beyond what we've covered here. JSON is defined in RFC 8259, and you can read it for free at https://datatracker.ietf.org/doc/html/rfc8259 for more details. Compared to most RFCs, it's a relatively simple read, but it goes beyond what you need to know for the CCNA. Feel free to check it out for reference, but you don't have to read all of it.

Exam scenario

The following question illustrates how you might be tested on your knowledge of JSON on the CCNA exam.

Q: Examine the JSON-formatted data below. Which of the following statements is true?

```
{
  "deviceName": "Switch-01",
  "location": "Office Building B",
  "deviceType": "Switch",
  "firmwareVersion": "4.5.7",
  "uptimeHours": 1023,
```

(continued)

```
"managementAccess": {
  "enabled": true,
  "port": "22"
},
"allowedIPs": ["192.168.1.100", "192.168.1.101", "192.168.1.102"],
"lastUpdated": null
}
```

    A The value of `"allowedIPs"` is a JSON object.

    B The value of `"port"` is a JSON number.

    C There is one nested object.

    D It is invalid JSON data.

Let's examine each statement to determine which is true:

- The value of `"allowedIPs"` is an object.
  - False. It is an array, not an object.
- The value of `"port"` is a number.
  - False. It is enclosed in double quotes, so it is a string, not a number.
- There is one nested object.
  - True. The entire example is an object consisting of various key-value pairs, and the value of `"managementAccess"` is a nested object.
- It is invalid JSON data.
  - False. After identifying that the previous statement is true, you can rule out this one through the process of elimination. There are no missing or extra curly braces or square brackets, no trailing or missing commas, or any other elements that would render the data invalid.

24.3   *XML and YAML*

The CCNA exam topics list only explicitly mentions JSON. However, it's worth taking a brief look at two other popular data serialization formats: XML and YAML. In this section, we'll cover their basic characteristics and compare them to JSON.

24.3.1   *XML*

Extensible Markup Language (XML) is a data serialization format with syntax similar to HyperText Markup Language (HTML), which is the standard markup language for web pages. A *markup language* is used for annotating documents (i.e., web pages), specifying structure, and formatting. XML has become a popular choice to format data for storage and transmission, although it is less common than JSON or YAML. Like JSON, XML is commonly supported by REST APIs.

    XML uses HTML-like tags for its key-value pairs, with an opening and closing tag: `<key>value</key>`. Interestingly, many Cisco IOS **show** commands can be displayed in XML format by adding | **format** to the end of the command. The following example shows the partial output of **show ip interface brief** on a router, in the standard IOS format and in XML format:

```
R1# show ip interface brief
Interface               IP-Address      OK?   Method   Status    Protocol
GigabitEthernet0/0      192.168.1.1     YES   manual   up        up
GigabitEthernet0/1      unassigned      YES   unset    down      down
. . .
R1# show ip interface brief | format
<?xml version="1.0" encoding="UTF-8"?>
<ShowIpInterfaceBrief xmlns="ODM://built-in//show_ip_interface_brief">
  <SpecVersion>built-in</SpecVersion>
  <IPInterfaces>
    <entry>
      <Interface>GigabitEthernet0/0</Interface>        ◄──  Beginning and end
      <IP-Address>192.168.1.1</IP-Address>                  of R1's G0/0 interface
      <OK>YES</OK>
      <Method>manual</Method>
      <Status>up</Status>
      <Protocol>up</Protocol>
    </entry>                                           ◄──
    <entry>                                            ◄──  Beginning and end of
      <Interface>GigabitEthernet0/1</Interface>             R1's G0/1 interface
      <OK>YES</OK>
      <Method>unset</Method>
      <Status>down</Status>
      <Protocol>down</Protocol>
    </entry>                                           ◄──
. . .
  </IPInterfaces>
</ShowIpInterfaceBrief>
```

XML is generally considered less human readable than JSON, but you can probably decipher the meaning of that output. Like JSON, whitespace in XML is insignificant, but it's usually formatted to make it more readable. The following example shows the same output with whitespace removed—easy for a computer to read, but not so readable for a human!

```
<?xml version="1.0" encoding="UTF-8"?><ShowIpInterfaceBrief xmlns="ODM://
built-in//show_ip_interface_brief"><SpecVersion>built-in</SpecVersion>
<IPInterfaces><entry><Interface>GigabitEthernet0/0</Interface><IP-Address>
192.168.1.1</IP-Address><OK>YES</OK><Method>manual</Method><Status>up
</Status><Protocol>up</Protocol></entry><entry><Interface>GigabitEthernet0/1
</Interface><OK>YES</OK><Method>unset</Method><Status>down</Status>
<Protocol>down</Protocol></entry></IPInterfaces></ShowIpInterfaceBrief>
```

24.3.2　*YAML*

YAML Ain't Markup Language (YAML—it rhymes with "camel") is another popular data serialization format. YAML originally stood for "Yet Another Markup Language," but it was officially renamed to the recursive acronym "YAML Ain't Markup Language" to emphasize its purpose as a data serialization format rather than a document markup language.

YAML is quite readable; of the three formats we have covered, it is perhaps the most human friendly. One of the notable differences between YAML and JSON/XML is that whitespace is significant in YAML. Proper indentation in YAML is not just about readability; it defines the structure and hierarchy of the data. Take a look at the following YAML-formatted data:

```
---
wirelessAccessPoint:
  name: AP350
  location: Office Floor 3
  operatingMode: dual-band
  ssids:
    - name: OfficeWiFi-2G
      band: 2.4GHz
      maxClients: 30
    - name: OfficeWiFi-5G
      band: 5GHz
      maxClients: 50
```

Compared to JSON and XML, YAML-formatted data looks quite minimalistic, contributing to its readability. In YAML, the structure of the data is defined through indentation levels without the need for many additional markers like those found in JSON (like commas and curly braces) or the tag structure of XML. For comparison, here's the same data represented in JSON:

```
{
  "wirelessAccessPoint": {
    "name": "AP350",
    "location": "Office Floor 3",
    "operatingMode": "dual-band",
    "ssids": [
      {
        "name": "OfficeWiFi-2G",
        "band": "2.4GHz",
        "maxClients": 30
      },
      {
        "name": "OfficeWiFi-5G",
        "band": "5GHz",
        "maxClients": 50
      }
    ]
  }
}
```

And finally, the same data in XML format. I think you'll probably agree that, of the three, the YAML data is the easiest to read.

```
<wirelessAccessPoint>
  <name>AP350</name>
  <location>Office Floor 3</location>
  <operatingMode>dual-band</operatingMode>
  <ssids>
```

```
  <ssid>
    <name>OfficeWiFi-2G</name>
    <band>2.4GHz</band>
    <maxClients>30</maxClients>
  </ssid>
  <ssid>
    <name>OfficeWiFi-5G</name>
    <band>5GHz</band>
    <maxClients>50</maxClients>
  </ssid>
  </ssids>
</wirelessAccessPoint>
```

Summary

- Data serialization is the process of converting data into a standardized format suitable for storage or transmission. This process enables the data to be later reconstructed (i.e., by a different application).

- Data serialization formats like JSON, XML, and YAML enable an application to communicate its data to another application in a format that both parties understand.

- JavaScript Object Notation (JSON) is a human-readable data serialization format. Applications in many programming languages can generate and interpret JSON-formatted data, and REST APIs often support JSON.

- A variable is a logical container for values. A variable and its value are often called a *key-value pair.*

- JSON data is represented using four fundamental forms called *primitive data types.*

- A JSON string is a text value that is enclosed in double quotes, such as `"Hello."`, `"5"`, `"true"`, and `"null"`.

- A JSON number is a numeric value, such as `5` or `101.25`.

- The JSON Boolean data type has only two possible values: `true` and `false`.

- The JSON null data type represents the intentional absence of a value and is always represented as `null`.

- Any value enclosed in double quotes is a string (a text value), even if it would be a different data type without double quotes (i.e., `"5"`)

- The JSON Boolean and null data types must be lowercase: `true`, `false`, and `null`.

- JSON structured data types (object and array) are used to organize information into more complex structures.

- A JSON *object* is an unordered set of key-value pairs. *Unordered* means that the order of the key-value pairs in an object is insignificant.

- Important points about objects:
  - Objects are enclosed in curly braces.
  - The key of each key-value pair must be a string.

- – The value of each key-value pair can be any valid JSON data type.
- – The key and value of each key-value pair are separated by a colon.
- – If there are multiple key-value pairs, each pair is separated by a comma.
- – There must not be a trailing comma after the final key-value pair.
- Structured data types (object/array) are valid values for an object's key-value pairs.
- An object within an object is called a *nested object.*
- Whitespace—spaces, line breaks, and tabs—is insignificant in JSON. Whitespace is often used to enhance readability, but it doesn't affect the data's meaning.
- A JSON array is an ordered set of values. Important points about arrays:
  - – Arrays are enclosed in square brackets.
  - – The values can be of any valid JSON data type.
  - – The values don't have to be of the same data type.
  - – The values are separated by commas.
  - – There must not be a trailing comma after the final value.
- A single error like a misplaced comma will render JSON data invalid, so precision is essential.
- *Extensible Markup Language* (XML) is a data serialization format with syntax similar to HyperText Markup Language (HTML), which is the standard markup language for web pages.
- XML is a popular choice as a data serialization format used to format data for storage and transmission. Like JSON, it is commonly supported by REST APIs.
- XML uses HTML-like tags for its key-value pairs, with an opening and closing tag: `<key>value</key>`.
- Many Cisco IOS commands can be displayed in XML by adding | **format** to the end of the command, such as `show ip interface brief` | `format`.
- Whitespace in XML is insignificant.
- YAML Ain't Markup Language (YAML)—formerly "Yet Another Markup Language"—is a popular data serialization format known for being human friendly.
- Whitespace is significant in YAML. Proper indentation is not just important for readability; it defines the structure and hierarchy of the data.

Ansible and Terraform

This chapter covers

- Configuration management and its challenges
- Template-based configuration
- Automating configuration management with Ansible and Terraform

Configuring devices in the CLI is something many network engineers grow to love, but it simply doesn't scale well. As networks grow in size and complexity, the manual, one-by-one configuration of devices makes managing each individual device's configuration infeasible. Not only is configuring each device time-consuming and prone to human error, but tracking configuration changes and enforcing standards across numerous devices becomes unmanageable. Many modern networks require more efficient solutions.

In this chapter, we'll cover CCNA exam topic 6.6: Recognize the capabilities of configuration management mechanisms such as Ansible and Terraform. These tools, which embody the principles of infrastructure as code (IaC), play a crucial role in automating and standardizing device configurations, ensuring accuracy and consistency. Automating configuration management tasks is essential in many modern networks, which are increasingly large and complex. We'll begin by examining configuration management and its difficulties and then consider how automation tools like Ansible and Terraform help to solve those problems, streamlining and enhancing the process of configuration management.

25.1   Configuration management

Configuration management in networking involves various tasks aimed at maintaining, controlling, and documenting the configurations of network devices. Proper configuration management is important in networks of all sizes but becomes especially critical in larger networks. This section will discuss some key aspects of configuration management, including establishing standards, traditional configuration management techniques, and the importance of maintaining configuration consistency across devices in the network.

25.1.1   Establishing configuration standards

Although no two devices in a network will have identical configurations, they also shouldn't be completely unique. To ensure the security and consistent operations of devices in a network, most elements of a device's configuration can and should be standardized. The following are some examples of configurations that can be shared among most or all devices in a network:

- *DNS servers*—All network devices should use the same DNS servers for consistent name resolution.
- *NTP servers*—To maintain consistent time across all devices in the network, they should query and sync to the same NTP servers.
- *Routing protocols*—Routers should use the same routing protocols with standardized configurations to ensure consistent and efficient routing decisions across the network.
- *QoS policies*—To ensure consistent treatment of different types of traffic, QoS policies should be standardized.
- *AAA servers*—Centralized AAA (RADIUS/TACACS+) servers should be used to control access to network resources and the network devices themselves.
- *Security policies*—Uniform security policies, such as defining which traffic should be permitted or denied, are essential in maintaining a consistent security posture.
- *Logging and monitoring settings*—Syslog messages should be sent to centralized servers to provide a complete and consistent view of network activities. This aids in troubleshooting and security monitoring.

This list is not comprehensive, but I think you get the idea. Key configurations like IP addresses and hostnames will vary per device, but standardizing the aforementioned core aspects is vital for managing large-scale environments, maintaining security, and ensuring operational consistency. Figure 25.1 shows partial output of two routers' configurations; aside from hostnames and interface IP addresses, their configurations are identical, as they follow established standards.

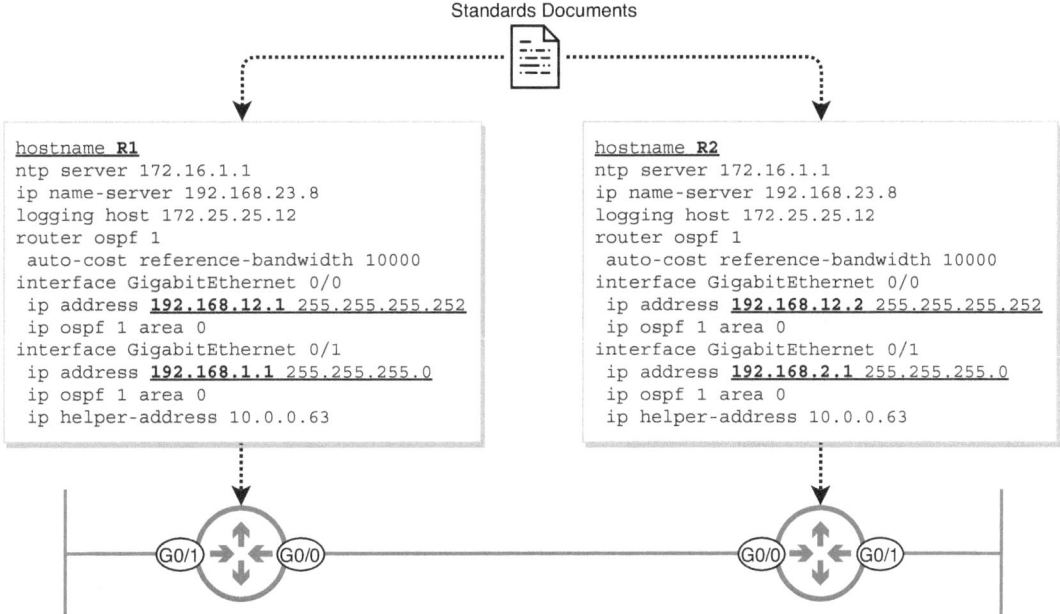

Figure 25.1 Device configurations should be derived from standards, ensuring consistent operations across all devices. Although each device will have some unique configurations, most should be consistent across devices.

Developing these standards involves understanding the network's needs, aligning with industry best practices, considering security and performance, and involving key stakeholders such as IT security teams, management, server teams, and external consultants or vendors. Typically, this is a task for more senior staff. If you're new to networking, your role will likely focus on implementing, operating, and maintaining the network as per these established standards, which are equally important in the network lifecycle.

25.1.2 *Configuration drift*

Maintaining consistent configurations according to organizational standards is essential for the security and reliability of the network. However, it's common for network configurations to gradually diverge from these standards over time. This phenomenon is called *configuration drift*, and it can pose significant challenges to network security and operational efficiency. Figure 25.2 illustrates the concept.

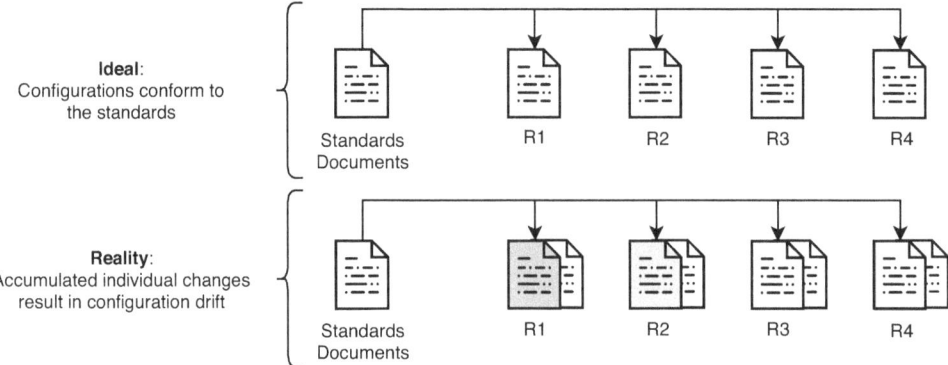

Figure 25.2 Accumulated individual changes result in deviation from standard configurations, called configuration drift.

Configuration drift typically arises from the traditional method of managing network configurations—the manual, device-by-device approach. Configuring each device individually often leads to inconsistencies due to human error, differing interpretations of the standards, and small ad hoc configuration changes that accumulate over time. As networks grow and become more complex, this manual approach proves increasingly inadequate, with implications like the following:

- *Inconsistency*—Manual configurations can vary slightly from each change, especially when performed by different network admins or engineers. Over time, these small variations can lead to significant inconsistencies across the network.
- *Error-prone*—The manual process is susceptible to human error. A mistyped command or overlooked configuration can create security vulnerabilities or performance problems that may go unnoticed until problems arise.
- *Not scalable*—As the network expands, manually ensuring that every new device or update adheres to the standard configurations becomes infeasible.
- *Difficult to monitor and correct*—Continuously monitoring each device for adherence to configuration standards is challenging. Correcting deviations can be impractical, as it often involves manually checking and adjusting the configurations of each device.

Even with the best of intentions to follow established standards, some degree of configuration drift is almost inevitable when managing a large and complex network manually. In the next section, we'll look at how configuration management tools use automation to enforce configuration consistency, reducing the risk of configuration drift for more reliable and secure network operations.

NOTE The basic point to remember from this section is that as a network grows in size and complexity, manual configuration management can result in configuration drift, negatively affecting the reliable and secure operation of the network.

25.2 Configuration management tools

Configuration management tools use software to automate various tasks related to configuration management, from deploying initial configurations and configuration changes to enforcing configuration standards. Device configurations are centrally managed from a server, instead of individually managed on the devices themselves. Figure 25.3 gives a tool-agnostic overview of how configuring devices with one of these tools generally works.

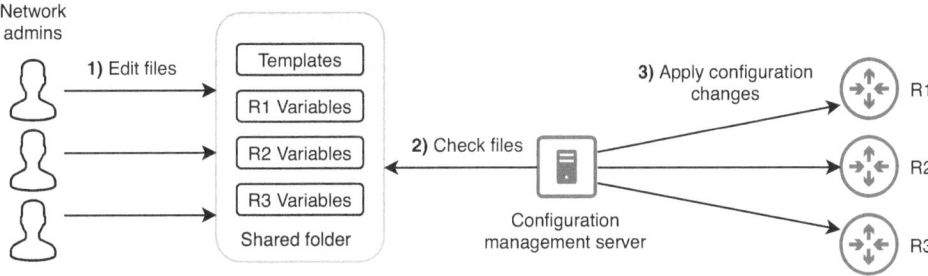

Figure 25.3   Configuring devices with a configuration management tool. Configurations are centrally managed from a shared folder. A server running a configuration management tool applies configuration changes to devices.

Instead of configuring devices individually, configurations are centrally managed from a shared folder. A configuration management server is responsible for applying any changes to the appropriate devices.

Device configurations aren't simply stored as is on the server; instead, a variety of files are used, each with a different purpose—the types of files and their names depend on the tool. However, two key elements are configuration templates that define the desired state of device configurations using a standardized format and variables that store specific values unique to each device.

Using the example of two routers with near-identical configurations that we saw in figure 25.1, the following example shows how a configuration template can be formatted to generate those two separate configurations, replacing the unique per-device configurations with variables:

```
hostname {{hostname}}
ntp server 172.16.1.1
ip name-server 192.168.23.8
logging host 172.25.25.12
router ospf 1
```

A variable for each router's hostname

```
auto-cost reference-bandwidth 10000
interface GigabitEthernet 0/0
 ip address {{g0/0addr}} {{g0/0mask}}
 ip ospf 1 area 0
interface GigabitEthernet 0/1
 ip address {{g0/1addr}} {{g0/1mask}}
 ip ospf 1 area 0
 ip helper-address 10.0.0.63
```

← **Variables for the router's
G0/0 IP address and netmask**

← **Variables for the router's
G0/1 IP address and netmask**

This single template can be used for all routers that require similar configurations, with a separate file listing the variable values for each router. The following example shows R1's values; by inserting the appropriate values in the configuration template, the server can assemble R1's configuration. A change to the configuration template or variable files will result in the server applying the changes to the appropriate devices:

```
---
hostname: R1
g0/0addr: 192.168.12.1
g0/0mask: 255.255.255.252
g0/1addr: 192.168.1.1
g0/1mask: 255.255.255.0
```

**Key:value pairs that provide
values for the configuration
template's variables**

In addition to configuring devices from a central server, configuration management tools can enforce conformity to the standards defined in the configuration files on the server. As shown in figure 25.4, the configuration management server is able to detect any deviations from the standard templates. It compares the active configuration on a device like R1 against the expected configuration as defined by the templates and variables. This comparison can be scheduled to occur at regular intervals or triggered manually by an administrator. If a discrepancy is found, the server alerts the administrators, who can then take appropriate action, ensuring that the network remains secure and operates as intended.

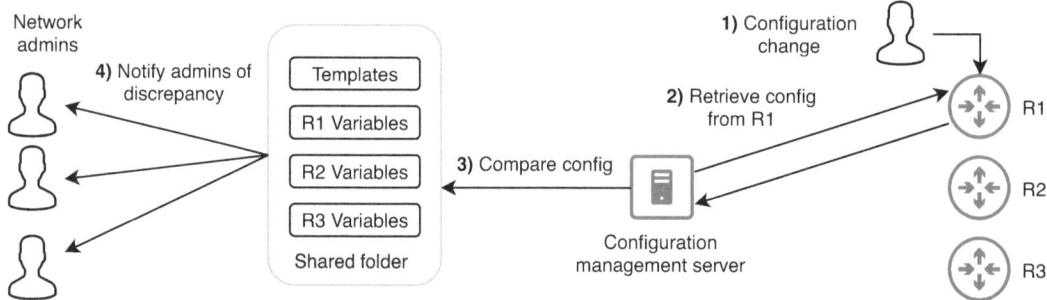

Figure 25.4   The configuration management server compares device configurations to the standards defined in the configuration files and notifies admins of a discrepancy.

The CCNA exam topics list mentions two configuration management tools and Terraform. Table 25.1 summarizes some key details about each of these tools, such as the programming language each is written in, the names of their key files and the file formats they use to store configurations. In addition to Ansible and Terraform, table 25.1 also lists Puppet and Chef—two other configuration management tools that we will briefly touch on in this section.

The table identifies each tool as *agent-based* or *agentless*; agent-based tools require a software "agent" on managed devices, and agentless tools don't. It also lists each tool as being mainly procedural or mainly declarative; a *procedural* approach involves defining a series of steps to configure the target system, and a *declarative* approach involves defining the desired end state of the system and letting the tool figure out how to achieve that desired state. Finally, it also differentiates between *push* and *pull* models; in a push model, the server sends the configuration to the client, while in a pull model the client requests the configuration from the server. In the rest of this section, we will examine these points in greater detail.

Table 25.1 Configuration management tools

	Ansible	**Terraform**	**Puppet**	**Chef**
Language	Python	Go	Ruby	Ruby
Configuration file format	YAML	HashiCorp Language (HCL)	Puppet DSL	Ruby
Communication protocol	SSH, NETCONF	HTTP (API)	HTTP (API)	HTTP (API)
Agent-based/agentless	Agentless	Agentless	Agent-based	Agent-based
Procedural/declarative	Procedural	Declarative	Declarative	Procedural
Push/pull	Push	Push	Pull	Pull

Infrastructure as code

Ansible, Terraform, Puppet, and Chef are all examples of *infrastructure as code* (IaC). Rather than the traditional method of provisioning and managing IT infrastructure through manually configuring servers and network devices, IaC provisions and manages infrastructure through code—configuration files that describe the desired state of the infrastructure and how to configure the available resources to achieve that desired state. By treating infrastructure as code, organizations can version control their infrastructure configurations, apply consistent settings across environments, and automate the entire lifecycle of infrastructure provisioning, management, and decommissioning.

25.2.1 Ansible

Ansible is a configuration management tool that was acquired by Red Hat (the creators of the popular Linux distribution Red Hat Enterprise Linux). Ansible itself is written in Python, although most of the files it employs are written in YAML. One of Ansible's defining features is that it is *agentless*, meaning it doesn't require any special software (an "agent") to run on the managed devices. Instead, the Ansible *control node*—a server on which you have installed Ansible—uses SSH to connect to managed devices and push configuration changes to them.

> **NOTE**   In addition to SSH, Ansible can use NETCONF—a protocol developed to address some of SNMP's limitations—to configure devices.

This is called a *push model*; instead of managed devices connecting to and pulling (retrieving) configuration information from the control node, the control node connects to and pushes (sends) configurations to its managed devices. Ansible primarily uses a procedural approach, where you define a sequence of steps or tasks to be executed on the managed devices in a specific order. Terraform, which we'll cover next, takes a different approach. Figure 25.5 gives a high-level overview of how Ansible works.

> **NOTE**   The Ansible control node connects to TCP port 22 on the managed devices—the standard port used by SSH.

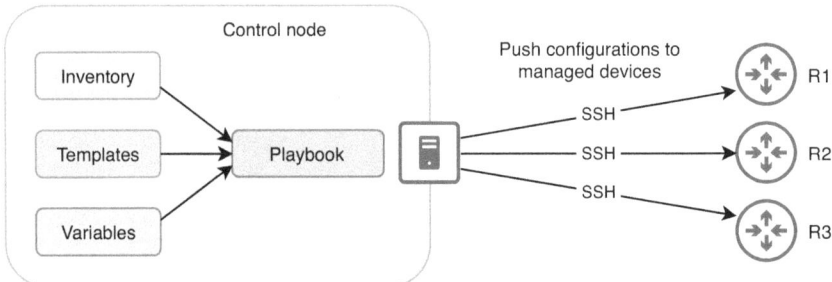

Figure 25.5   Basic Ansible operations. Inventory, template, and variable files define configurations, and playbooks define actions. The control node uses SSH to connect and push configurations to managed devices.

Push or pull?

The push model and the pull model each have their own advantages. The main advantages of a push model are centralized control and immediate updates. For example, if you need to send a critical configuration update to devices, you can configure the changes on the server, which can immediately push the changes to the managed devices.

On the other hand, the pull model tends to distribute the workload across the network, as each managed device independently checks for and applies updates. However, this can introduce delays, as you have to wait for devices to check in, rather than immediately pushing new configurations from the server. Neither approach is the correct answer in all situations; it depends on which suits your organization and network.

Ansible uses four main types of files:

- *Inventory*—A file (usually in YAML format) that lists the hosts Ansible manages, optionally organizing them into groups. It can include variables specific to each individual host or group.
- *Template*—Files containing configuration syntax and variables that are processed by Ansible to produce final configuration files for hosts. Templates use the Jinja2 templating language.
- *Variables*—YAML files that list variables and their values. These values are inserted into the templates to create complete configuration files.
- *Playbook*—A YAML file that outlines tasks and procedures to manage configurations on the managed devices defined in the inventory.

In addition to these four file types, there are two additional terms you should know:

- *Module*—A discrete unit of code that can be used by a playbook to perform a specific task. Modules are essentially plugins or components of the Ansible application itself.
- *Task*—A single operation or action as defined in a playbook.Of the tools we cover in this chapter, Ansible is the one that is most often used for managing network device configurations. Thanks to Ansible's agentless design, no additional software is required on the managed devices; they just need to accept SSH connections from the control node. For this reason, Ansible is generally considered the simplest to set up and use to configure your network devices.

25.2.2 *Terraform*

Terraform is an IaC tool developed by HashiCorp. Whereas Ansible is primarily focused on configuration management, Terraform is primarily a *provisioning tool*, focused on deploying and provisioning new infrastructure (servers, databases, networks, etc.) rather than managing the configurations of existing infrastructure. While CCNA exam topic 6.6 refers to Terraform as a configuration management tool, that is typically not its main use case.

> **NOTE** While Ansible and Terraform can both perform both roles (provisioning and configuration management), they are sometimes used together to take advantage of the strengths of each: Terraform to provision infrastructure and Ansible to manage its configuration.

Figure 25.6 gives a high-level look at how Terraform can be used to provision resources on various platforms.

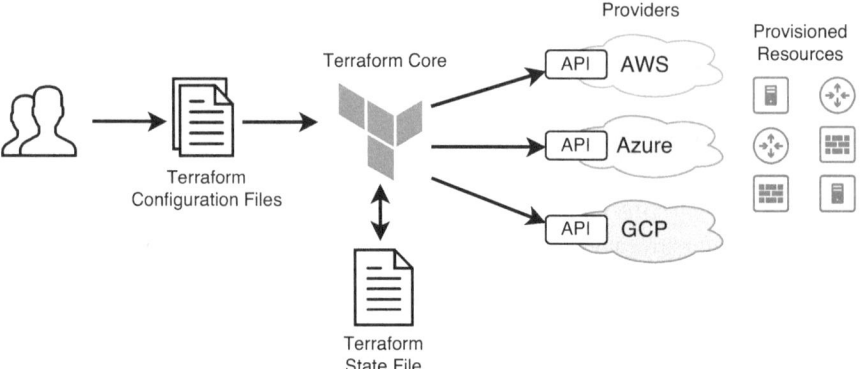

Figure 25.6   Provisioning resources with Terraform. Configuration files are processed byTerraform Core to interact with various providers (i.e., public cloud providers) and manage infrastructure resources while maintaining state information in the state file.

> **NOTE**   Like Ansible, Terraform uses a push model and also doesn't require a software agent to be installed on the devices it provisions or manages; it takes an agentless approach.

The basic Terraform workflow consists of three main steps:

1 *Write*—Define the desired state of your infrastructure resources in configuration files using HCL.
2 *Plan*—Verify the changes that will be executed before applying them.
3 *Apply*—Execute the plan to provision and manage the infrastructure resources according to the configuration files.

At the heart of Terraform is *Terraform Core*, the central part of Terraform that processes configuration files, manages the state of the infrastructure, and communicates with various providers to provision resources. Unlike Ansible's procedural approach, Terraform employs a more *declarative* approach in which you define the desired end state for the infrastructure using *configuration files* rather than specifying the step-by-step instructions for how to achieve that desired state. Terraform Core compares the desired end state defined in the configuration files to the current state in the Terraform *state file* and takes the necessary steps to bring the infrastructure in line with the desired end state.

Terraform Core communicates with various *providers* to provision infrastructure resources; for example, public cloud providers like Amazon Web Services (AWS), Microsoft Azure, and Google Cloud Platform (GCP). It does so via each provider's APIs, allowing Terraform to interact with and manage a wide array of resources. Beyond public clouds, Terraform also supports on-premises infrastructure providers such as VMware vSphere and OpenStack, and container orchestration platforms like Kubernetes.

NOTE Most importantly for a CCNA candidate, Terraform can interact with a variety of Cisco platforms to provision and manage infrastructure. For example, there are Terraform integrations with Cisco Catalyst Center, Application-Centric Infrastructure (ACI—Cisco's data center automatization solution), and IOS XE (a modern version of IOS that is run by many Cisco network devices, such as their Catalyst switches).

While Terraform itself is written in *Go* (a programming language developed by employees at Google), Terraform defines and provisions infrastructure using a configuration language called *HashiCorp Configuration Language* (HCL). HCL is an example of a *domain-specific language* (DSL)—a type of computer language that is specialized to a particular purpose (unlike general-purpose languages such as Python and Go).

The main benefits of a DSL such as HCL stem from its specialization; it's designed specifically for its intended purpose and can often perform complex tasks with much less effort than a general language would require. However, it does mean you have to learn another language specifically for the purpose of using Terraform, which can be considered a downside.

25.2.3 *Puppet and Chef*

Puppet and Chef are two other prominent IaC tools that, like Ansible, are primarily used for the purpose of configuration management. Puppet and Chef were both included as topics in version 1.0 of the current CCNA exam (exam code 200-301), but were removed in version 1.1. However, it is worth taking a brief look at these two tools to compare and contrast them with Ansible and Terraform. There are two key differences:

- In contrast to Ansible and Terraform's push model, Puppet and Chef primarily use a *pull* model.
- Whereas Ansible and Terraform use an agentless architecture, Puppet and Chef use an *agent-based* architecture.

PUPPET

Puppet is an IaC tool for configuration management that is written in the Ruby programming language. It uses an *agent-based* architecture, meaning that a software agent needs to be installed on each managed device. Each device's agent periodically connects to a central server, known as the *Puppet master*, to retrieve configuration information. This is known as a *pull model*. Instead of the management server connecting to managed devices to push configurations, the manage devices connect to the server to pull their configurations.

Like Terraform, Puppet uses a declarative DSL called *Puppet DSL* to define the desired state of the infrastructure. The Puppet master sends configuration instructions to the agents, which then apply the necessary changes to bring the devices into compliance with the defined state. The following example shows the simplicity of Puppet's DSL.

```
service { 'ssh':
  ensure => running,
}
```

> **Ensures that the SSH service is running on the device**

NOTE   For an explanation of the reasoning behind Puppet's use of a DSL, you can go straight to the source—Puppet's founder wrote a short blog about it at https://www.puppet.com/blog/puppet-language. It's an interesting read to learn about the benefits of a DSL.

While a popular tool for managing the IT infrastructure configuration, its level of adoption is relatively low compared to Ansible when it comes to managing networks; not all network devices support a Puppet agent, so Puppet is often not a viable choice.

CHEF

Chef is another IaC tool for configuration management that bears some similarity to Puppet. Like Puppet, Chef is written in the Ruby programming language. Chef also uses an agent-based approach, requiring a Chef client to be installed on each managed device; this agent connects to the Chef server to pull and apply the latest configurations.

However, unlike Puppet, Chef uses a procedural approach. In Chef, you define a sequence of steps or tasks, known as *recipes*, which outline the specific actions needed to configure the system. These recipes are grouped into *cookbooks*, which can include additional components such as templates, files, and metadata. When the Chef client runs, it executes the recipes in the specified order to bring the managed device into the desired state.

Like Puppet, Chef doesn't have the popularity of Ansible in the context of managing networks. This is likely why Puppet and Chef were removed from the CCNA exam topics list. However, I recommend knowing their basic characteristics. Specifically, you should understand how a pull model differs from a push model, and the difference between an agentless and agent-based approach.

Which tool to use?

We've explored some basic characteristics of these four tools, but which should an organization use? The choice depends on the needs of the particular organization. For example, if an organization's network devices don't support a Puppet or Chef agent, Ansible is the natural choice for configuration management. But even if device support isn't an issue, the simplicity of Ansible's agentless approach makes it the preferred tool in many networks.

Another key consideration is the operational mode: push or pull? Depending on the organization's workflows and specific needs, Ansible may be favored for its push model. If a pull model is preferred, the choice is between Puppet and Chef. Of the two, Puppet's declarative nature allows you to define the desired end state without specifying the specific steps to get there. Chef, on the other hand, takes a procedural approach, which may be preferred for those who want detailed control over the configuration process.

Terraform is primarily used for infrastructure provisioning rather than configuration management. If your primary need is to deploy infrastructure across various platforms, including cloud and on-premises environments, Terraform's declarative approach and support for different providers make it an excellent choice. Terraform excels in provisioning complex multi-cloud environments and ensuring that the infrastructure remains consistent and reliable by maintaining the desired state through its configuration files.

Ultimately, the decision on which tool to use should be based on the specific requirements of your infrastructure and the workflows of your organizaon process.

Summary

- Configuration management in networking involves various tasks aimed at maintaining, controlling, and documenting the configurations of network devices.
- Although no two devices in a network will have identical configurations, they also shouldn't be completely unique. To ensure the security and consistent operations of devices in a network, most configurations can be standardized.
- Some configuration elements that can and should be standardized include DNS servers, NTP servers, routing protocols, QoS policies, AAA servers, security policies, and logging and monitoring settings.
- Maintaining consistent configurations according to organizational standards is essential for the security and reliability of the network.
- It's common for network configurations to gradually diverge from standards due to human error, differing interpretations of the standards, and small ad hoc changes that accumulate over time. This is called *configuration drift*.
- Configuration drift can pose significant challenges to network security and operational efficiency but is almost inevitable when managing a large and complex network manually.
- Configuration management tools use software to automate various tasks related to configuration management, from deploying initial configurations and configuration changes to enforcing configuration standards.
- Configuration management tools manage device configuration from centralized servers instead of on the devices themselves.
- Configuration files are stored on the server, and the configuration management server is responsible for applying any changes to the appropriate devices.
- Configuration management tools employ configuration templates that define the desired state and structure of device configurations using a standardized format and variables that store specific values unique to each device.
- Configuration management tools can also monitor managed devices to enforce conformity to the standards defined in the configuration files on the server.

- Ansible is a configuration management tool written in Python. One of its defining features is that it is agentless, meaning it doesn't require any special software (an agent) to run on the managed devices.
- The Ansible control node—a server on which you have installed Ansible—uses SSH to connect to managed devices and configure them.
- Ansible uses a push model. Instead of managed devices connecting to and pulling configuration information from the control node, the control node connects to and pushes configurations to the managed devices.
- Ansible primarily uses a procedural approach, where you define a sequence of steps or tasks to be executed on the managed devices in a specific order.
- Ansible uses four main types of files:
  - *Inventory*—A YAML file that lists the managed hosts
  - *Template*—Jinja2 files containing configuration syntax and variables that are processed to produce final configuration files for hosts
  - *Variables*—YAML files that list variables and their values
  - *Playbook*—A YAML file that outlines tasks and procedures to manage configuration on the managed devices
- Two other key terms are module—a discrete unit of code that can be used by a playbook to perform a specific task—and task—a single operation or action as defined in a playbook.
- *Terraform* is an infrastructure as code (IaC) tool developed by Hashicorp. Whereas Ansible is primarily focused on configuration management, Terraform is primarily a *provisioning tool*, focused on deploying and provisioning new infrastructure.
- Like Ansible, Terraform uses a push model and also doesn't require a software agent to be installed on the devices it provisions or manages; it takes an agentless approach.
- *Terraform Core* is the central part of Terraform that processes configuration files, manages the state of the infrastructure, and communicates with various providers to provision resources.
- Terraform employs a *declarative* approach in which you define the desired end state for the infrastructure using *configuration files* rather than specifying the step-by-step instructions for how to achieve that desired state.
- Terraform Core compares the desired end state defined in the configuration files to the current state in the Terraform state file and takes the necessary steps to bring the infrastructure in line with the desired end state.
- Terraform is written in the programming language Go, but defines and provisions infrastructure using a language called *HashiCorp Configuration Language* (HCL). HCL is an example of a *domain-specific language* (DSL)—a type of computer language that is specialized to a particular purpose.

- *Puppet* and *Chef* are two other prominent IaC tools that, like Ansible, are primarily used for the purpose of configuration management. Puppet and Chef are both written in Ruby.

- In contrast to Ansible and Terraform's push model, Puppet and Chef primarily use a *pull* model in which the managed devices connect to the management server to retrieve their configurations.

- Whereas Ansible and Terraform use an agentless architecture, Puppet and Chef use an *agent-based* architecture. A software agent must be installed on managed devices.

- Like Terraform, Puppet uses a declarative DSL called *Puppet DSL* to define the desired state of the infrastructure.

- In contrast to Puppet's declarative approach, Chef uses a procedural approach, similar to Ansible.

Exam topics reference table

The following table lists the CCNA exam topics and the chapters in this book that cover each of them. However, keep in mind that Cisco occasionally (but rarely) makes minor, unannounced changes to the exam topics, so I recommend going straight to the source to verify the official list: https://learningnetwork.cisco .com/s/ccna-exam-topics.

Furthermore, Cisco publishes its Certification Roadmaps at https:// learningnetwork.cisco.com/s/cisco-certification-roadmaps. I recommend book-marking that page; it will give you information about Cisco's yearly certification review process and any scheduled changes coming to the CCNA exam (and Cisco's other exams).

The first time you read this book, I recommend following the chapters in order. However, it's important to carefully examine the CCNA exam topics and make sure you know all of them before taking the CCNA exam. This resource should be helpful in that process; if there are any exam topics that you don't feel confident about, refer to the table to know which chapters you should review.

Exam topic	Chapter(s)
1.0 Network fundamentals—20%	
1.1 Explain the role and function of network components	2 (vol. 1)
1.1.a Routers	2 (vol. 1)
1.1.b Layer 2 and Layer 3 switches	2 (vol. 1), 12 (vol. 1)
1.1.c Next-generation firewalls and IPS	2 (vol. 1), 11 (vol. 2)
1.1.d Access points	18 (vol. 2)
1.1.e Controllers	19 (vol. 1), 22 (vol. 2)
1.1.f Endpoints	2 (vol. 1)
1.1.g Servers	2 (vol. 1)
1.1.h PoE	10 (vol. 2)
1.2 Describe characteristics of network topology architectures	15-17 (vol. 2)
1.2.a Two-tier	15 (vol. 2)
1.2.b Three-tier	15 (vol. 2)
1.2.c Spine-leaf	15 (vol. 2)
1.2.d WAN	16 (vol. 2)
1.2.e Small office/home office (SOHO)	15 (vol. 2)
1.2.f On-premises and cloud	17 (vol. 2)
1.3 Compare physical interface and cabling types	3 (vol. 1)
1.3.a Single-mode fiber, multimode fiber, copper	3 (vol. 1)
1.3.b Connections (Ethernet shared media and point-to-point)	3 (vol. 1), 8 (vol. 1)
1.4 Identify interface and cable issues (collisions, errors, mismatch duplex, and/or speed)	8 (vol. 1)
1.5 Compare TCP to UDP	22 (vol. 1)
1.6 Configure and verify IPv4 addressing and subnetting	7 (vol. 1), 11 (vol. 1)
1.7 Describe private IPv4 addressing	9 (vol. 2)
1.8 Configure and verify IPv6 addressing and prefix	20 (vol. 1)
1.9 Describe IPv6 address types	20 (vol. 1)
1.9.a Unicast (global, unique local, and link local)	20 (vol. 1)
1.9.b Anycast	20 (vol. 1)
1.9.c Multicast	20 (vol. 1)
1.9.d Modified EUI 64	20 (vol. 1)
1.10 Verify IP parameters for Client OS (Windows, Mac OS, Linux)	4 (vol. 2)
1.11 Describe wireless principles	18 (vol. 2), 20 (vol. 2)
1.11.a Nonoverlapping Wi-Fi channels	18 (vol. 2)
1.11.b SSID	18 (vol. 2)
1.11.c RF	18 (vol. 2)
1.11.d Encryption	20 (vol. 2)
1.12 Explain virtualization fundamentals (server virtualization, containers, and VRFs)	17 (vol. 2)

1.0 Network fundamentals—20% *(continued)*	
1.13 Describe switching concepts	6 (vol. 1)
1.13.a MAC learning and aging	6 (vol. 1)
1.13.b Frame switching	6 (vol. 1)
1.13.c Frame flooding	6 (vol. 1)
1.13.d MAC address table	6 (vol. 1)
2.0 Network access—20%	
2.1 Configure and verify VLANs (normal range) spanning multiple switches	12 (vol. 1), 13 (vol. 1)
2.1.a Access ports (data and voice)	12 (vol. 1), 13 (vol. 1)
2.1.b Default VLAN	12 (vol. 1)
2.1.c InterVLAN connectivity	12 (vol. 1), 13 (vol. 1)
2.2 Configure and verify interswitch connectivity	12 (vol. 1), 13 (vol. 1)
2.2.a Trunk ports	12 (vol. 1), 13 (vol. 1)
2.2.b 802.1Q	12 (vol. 1), 13 (vol. 1)
2.2.c Native VLAN	12 (vol. 1)
2.3 Configure and verify Layer 2 discovery protocols (Cisco Discovery Protocol and LLDP)	1 (vol. 2)
2.4 Configure and verify (Layer 2/Layer 3) EtherChannel (LACP)	16 (vol. 1)
2.5 Identify basic operations of Rapid PVST+ Spanning Tree Protocol	14 (vol. 1), 15 (vol. 1)
2.5.a Root port, root bridge (primary/secondary), and other port names	14 (vol. 1), 15 (vol. 1)
2.5.b Port states and roles	14 (vol. 1), 15 (vol. 1)
2.5.c PortFast	14 (vol. 1), 15 (vol. 1)
2.5.d Root guard, loop guard, BPDU filter, and BPDU guard	14 (vol. 1), 15 (vol. 1)
2.6 Compare Cisco Wireless Architectures and AP modes	19 (vol. 2)
2.7 Describe physical infrastructure connections of WLAN components (AP, WLC, access/trunk ports, and LAG)	19 (vol. 2), 21 (vol. 2)
2.8 Describe network device management access connections (Telnet, SSH, HTTP, HTTPS, console, TACACS+/RADIUS, and cloud managed)	19 (vol. 2), 21 (vol. 2)
2.9 Interpret the wireless LAN GUI configuration for client connectivity, such as WLAN creation, security settings, QoS profiles, and advanced settings	21 (vol. 2)
3.0 IP Connectivity—25%	
3.1 Interpret the components of routing table	9 (vol. 1), 17 (vol. 1), 21 (vol. 1)
3.1.a Routing protocol code	9 (vol. 1), 17 (vol. 1)
3.1.b Prefix	9 (vol. 1), 21 (vol. 1)
3.1.c Network mask	9 (vol. 1), 21 (vol. 1)
3.1.d Next hop	9 (vol. 1), 21 (vol. 1)
3.1.e Administrative distance	17 (vol. 1)
3.1.f Metric	17 (vol. 1)
3.1.g Gateway of last resort	9 (vol. 1), 21 (vol. 1)

3.2 Determine how a router makes a forwarding decision by default	9 (vol. 1), 17 (vol. 1), 21 (vol. 1)
3.2.a Longest prefix match	9 (vol. 1), 17 (vol. 1), 21 (vol. 1)
3.2.b Administrative distance	17 (vol. 1)
3.2.c Routing protocol metric	17 (vol. 1)
3.3 Configure and verify IPv4 and IPv6 static routing	9 (vol. 1), 17 (vol. 1), 21 (vol. 1)
3.3.a Default route	9 (vol. 1), 21 (vol. 1)
3.3.b Network route	9 (vol. 1), 21 (vol. 1)
3.3.c Host route	9 (vol. 1), 21 (vol. 1)
3.3.d Floating static	17 (vol. 1), 21 (vol. 1)
3.4 Configure and verify single area OSPFv2	17 (vol. 1), 18 (vol. 1)
3.4.a Neighbor adjacencies	18 (vol. 1)
3.4.b Point-to-point	18 (vol. 1)
3.4.c Broadcast (DR/BDR selection)	18 (vol. 1)
3.4.d Router ID	18 (vol. 1)
3.5 Describe the purpose, functions, and concepts of first hop redundancy protocols	19 (vol. 1)
4.0 IP Services—10%	
4.1 Configure and verify inside source NAT using static and pools	9 (vol. 2)
4.2 Configure and verify NTP operating in a client and server mode	2 (vol. 2)
4.3 Explain the role of DHCP and DNS within the network	3 (vol. 2), 4 (vol. 2)
4.4 Explain the function of SNMP in network operations	6 (vol. 2)
4.5 Describe the use of syslog features including facilities and severity levels	7 (vol. 2)
4.6 Configure and verify DHCP client and relay	4 (vol. 2)
4.7 Explain the forwarding per-hop behavior (PHB) for QoS such as classification, marking, queuing, congestion, policing, shaping	10 (vol. 2)
4.8 Configure network devices for remote access using SSH	5 (vol. 2)
4.9 Describe the capabilities and functions of TFTP/FTP in the network	8 (vol. 2)
5.0 Security fundamentals—15%	
5.1 Define key security concepts (threats, vulnerabilities, exploits, and mitigation techniques)	11 (vol. 2)
5.2 Describe security program elements (user awareness, training, and physical access control)	11 (vol. 2)
5.3 Configure and verify device access control using local passwords	5 (vol. 1), 5 (vol. 2), 11 (vol. 2)
5.4 Describe security password policy elements, such as management, complexity, and password alternatives (multifactor authentication, certificates, and biometrics)	11 (vol. 2)
5.5 Describe IPsec remote access and site-to-site VPNs	16 (vol. 2)
5.6 Configure and verify access control lists	23 (vol. 1), 24 (vol. 1)

5.0 Security fundamentals—15% *(continued)*	
5.7 Configure and verify Layer 2 security features (DHCP snooping, dynamic ARP inspection, and port security)	12-14 (vol. 2)
5.8 Compare authentication, authorization, and accounting concepts	11 (vol. 2)
5.9 Describe wireless security protocols (WPA, WPA2, and WPA3)	20 (vol. 2)
5.10 Configure and verify WLAN within the GUI using WPA2 PSK	21 (vol. 2)
6.0 Automation and Programmability—10%	
6.1 Explain how automation impacts network management	22 (vol. 2)
6.2 Compare traditional networks with controller-based networking	22 (vol. 2)
6.3 Describe controller-based and software defined architecture (overlay, underlay, and fabric)	22 (vol. 2)
6.3.a Separation of control plane and data plane	22 (vol. 2)
6.3.b Northbound and Southbound APIs	22 (vol. 2)
6.4 Explain AI (generative and predictive) and machine learning in network operations	22 (vol. 2)
6.5 Describe characteristics of REST-based APIs (authentication types, CRUD, HTTP verbs, and data encoding)	23 (vol. 2)
6.6 Recognize the capabilities of configuration management mechanisms such as Ansible and Terraform	25 (vol. 2)
6.7 Recognize components of JSON-encoded data	24 (vol. 2)

CLI command reference table

Most chapters of this book introduce several Cisco IOS CLI commands—totaling about 300. Being proficient with these commands is essential for success on the CCNA exam. The following table lists the various commands covered in this volume, organized by chapter, and gives a brief description of each. For a more complete explanation of a command's purpose and its usage, refer back to the relevant chapter.

Several commands are covered in multiple chapters in this book. In most cases, I have listed the command only under the chapter in which it was covered first or covered in greatest depth. Furthermore, a few commands in this book were introduced for demonstration purposes rather than as commands you need to know for the CCNA exam; for completeness, I include these commands in the table as well.

Mode	Command	Description
Chapter 1: Cisco Discovery Protocol and Link Layer Discovery Protocol		
(config)#	[no] cdp run	Globally enable/disable CDP.
(config)#	cdp timer *seconds*	Set the CDP advertisement timer.
(config)#	cdp holdtime *seconds*	Set the CDP holdtime.
(config)#	[no] cdp advertise-v2	Enable/disable CDPv2 advertisements.
(config-if)#	[no] cdp enable	Enable/disable CDP on an interface.
#	show cdp	View basic CDP status and information.
#	show cdp neighbors [detail]	View information about CDP neighbors.
#	show cdp entry *name*	View detailed information about the specified CDP neighbor.
#	show cdp interface [*interface*]	View information about CDP interfaces.
#	show cdp traffic	View CDP traffic statistics.
(config)#	[no] lldp run	Globally enable/disable LLDP.
(config)#	lldp timer *seconds*	Set the LLDP advertisement timer.
(config)#	lldp holdtime *seconds*	Set the LLDP holdtime.
(config)#	lldp reinit *seconds*	Set the LLDP reinitialization timer.
(config-if)#	[no] lldp transmit	Enable/disable LLDP Tx on the interface.
(config-if)#	[no] lldp receive	Enable/disable LLDP Rx on the interface.
#	show lldp	View basic LLDP status and information.
#	show lldp neighbors [detail]	View information about LLDP neighbors.
#	show lldp entry *name*	View detailed information about the specified LLDP neighbor.
#	show lldp interface [*interface*]	View information about LLDP interfaces.
#	show lldp traffic	View LLDP traffic statistics.
Chapter 2: Network Time Protocol		
#	show clock [detail]	View the time of the software clock.
#	clock set *hh:mm:ss month day year*	Set the time of the software clock.
#	show calendar	View the time of the hardware calendar.
#	calendar set *hh:mm:ss month day year*	Set the time of the hardware calendar.
#	clock update-calendar	Sync the calendar to the clock's time.
#	clock read-calendar	Sync the clock to the calendar's time.
(config)#	clock timezone *name hours-offset minutes-offset*	Set the device's time zone.
(config)#	clock summer-time *name* recurring *start-date-time end-date-time*	Enable summer time (daylight saving time).
(config)#	ntp server *ip-address* [prefer]	Configure this device as an NTP client of the specified server.
(config)#	ntp update-calendar	Use NTP to regularly update the calendar.

(config)#	**ntp source** *interface*	Set the interface used to send NTP messages.
(config)#	**ntp master** [*stratum*]	Make this device a primary NTP server with its own clock as the reference clock.
(config)#	**ntp peer** *ip-address*	Configure a symmetric active NTP relationship on two devices.
(config)#	**ntp authentication-key** *key-number* **md5** *key*	Configure an NTP authentication key.
(config)#	**ntp trusted-key** *key-number*	Specify an NTP trusted authentication key.
(config)#	**ntp server** *ip-address* **key** *key-number*	Configure this device as an NTP client of the specified server and authenticate it with the specified key.
#	**show ntp associations**	View a list of NTP associations (time sources).
#	**show ntp status**	View the device's NTP status.

Chapter 3: Domain Name System

(config)#	**ip domain lookup**	Enable the device to send DNS queries.
(config)#	**ip name-server** *ip-address*	Configure the DNS server(s) to send DNS queries to.
(config)#	**ip dns server**	Configure the device as a DNS server, allowing it to respond to DNS queries.
(config)#	**ip domain name** *domain-name*	Set the device's default domain name.
(config)#	**ip host** *hostname ip-address*	Create a manual name-to-IP mapping.
#	**show hosts**	View all name-to-IP mappings.

Chapter 4: Dynamic Host Configuration Protocol

(config)#	**ip dhcp excluded-address** *low-ip high-ip*	Specify a range of addresses that the device won't lease to DHCP clients.
(config)#	**ip dhcp pool** *name*	Create/configure a DHCP pool.
(dhcp-config)#	**network** *address* {**/***prefix-length* | *netmask*}	Set the range of IP addresses to lease to clients.
(dhcp-config)#	**default-router** *ip-address*	Set the pool's default gateway.
(dhcp-config)#	**dns-server** *ip-address*	Set the pool's DNS server.
(dhcp-config)#	**domain-name** *domain-name*	Set the pool's domain name.
(dhcp-config)#	**lease** *days hours minutes*	Set the pool's lease time.
#	**show ip dhcp binding**	View addresses leased to DHCP clients.
#	**clear ip dhcp binding** {***** | *ip-address*}	Clear DHCP leases.
#	**show ip dhcp conflict**	View DHCP conflicts.
#	**clear ip dhcp conflict** {***** | *ip-address*}	Clear DHCP conflicts.
(config-if)#	**ip address dhcp**	Configure the interface as a DHCP client.
(config-if)#	**ip helper-address** *ip-address*	Configure the interface as a DHCP relay agent.

Chapter 4: Dynamic Host Configuration Protocol *(continued)*

(Windows)	`ipconfig`	View basic IP information.
(Windows)	`ipconfig /all`	View more detailed IP information.
(Windows)	`netstat -rn`	View the routing table.
(macOS)	`ifconfig`	View interface information.
(macOS)	`netstat -rn`	View the routing table.
(Linux)	`ifconfig`	View interface information (net-tools).
(Linux)	`route`	View the routing table (net-tools).
(Linux)	`ip addr`	View interface information (iproute2).
(Linux)	`ip route`	View the routing table (iproute2).

Chapter 5: Secure Shell

(config)#	`username` *username* `secret` *password*	Create a local user account.
(config)#	`line console 0`	Configure the console line.
(config)#	`line vty 0 15`	Configure all 16 VTY lines.
(config-line)#	`password` *password*	Configure a line password.
(config-line)#	`login`	Require a user to provide the line password to access the line.
(config-line)#	`login local`	Require a user to log in with a local user account to access the line.
(config-line)#	`exec-timeout` *minutes*	Set the inactivity logout timer.
(config-line)#	`transport input {telnet	ssh	all	none}`	Set the protocols that can be used to connect to the line.
(config-line)#	`access-class` *acl* `in`	Apply an ACL to limit access to the line.
(config)#	`ip default-gateway` *ip-address*	Set the Layer 2 switch's default gateway.
#	`show ip default-gateway`	View the Layer 2 switch's default gateway.
#	`show ip ssh`	View SSH settings and information.
(config)#	`crypto key generate rsa`	Generate an RSA key pair (for SSH).
(config)#	`ip ssh version 2`	Allow only SSH version 2 connections.

Chapter 6: Simple Network Management Protocol

(config)#	`snmp-server community` *password* `ro`	Configure a read-only community string.
(config)#	`snmp-server community` *password* `rw`	Configure a read-write community string.
(config)#	`snmp-server enable traps`	Enable SNMP traps.
(config)#	`snmp-server host` *ip-address* `[version 2c]` *community-string*	Specify the NMS to send traps to.

Chapter 7: Syslog

#	`terminal monitor`	Enable real-time logging to the VTY lines for the current session.
(config)#	`logging console` `[severity]`	Configure logging to the console line.

(config)#	**logging monitor** [*severity*]	Configure logging to the VTY lines.
(config)#	**logging buffered** [*bytes*] [*severity*]	Configure logging to the logging buffer.
(config)#	**logging trap** [*severity*]	Configure logging to a Syslog server.
(config)#	**logging** [**host**] *ip-address*	Specify the Syslog server to send logs to.
(config)#	**service timestamps log datetime** [**localtime**] [**msec**]	Timestamp log messages with the current date and time.
(config)#	**service timestamps log uptime**	Timestamp log messages with the device's current uptime.
(config-line)#	**logging synchronous**	Automatically reprint the current command on a new line if cut off by a log message.
#	**show logging**	Show Syslog settings and the logging buffer.
#	**show memory**	Show device memory usage.
#	**debug** *command*	Display detailed real-time information about various operations/events.

Chapter 8: Trivial File Transfer Protocol and File Transfer Protocol

#	**show file systems**	View the device's file systems.
#	**dir** *file-system*	View the contents of a file system.
#	**more** *file-name*	View the contents of a file.
#	**show flash:**	View the contents of flash memory.
#	**copy** *src-file-path dst-file-path*	Copy a file.
#	**copy tftp: flash:**	Copy a file from a TFTP server to flash.
#	**copy ftp: flash:**	Copy a file from an FTP server to flash.
(config)#	**ip ftp username** *username*	Set the default FTP username.
(config)#	**ip ftp password** *password*	Set the default FTP password.
#	**copy ftp://***username:password*@*server-ip* **flash:**	Copy a file from an FTP server to flash, specifying the authentication credentials.
#	**show version**	View information about the IOS version.
#	**show boot**	View information about the boot image.
(config)#	**boot system** *image-path*	Set the IOS image that will be loaded on the next boot.

Chapter 9: Network address translation

(config-if)#	**ip nat inside**	Configure an inside interface.
(config-if)#	**ip nat outside**	Configure an outside interface.
(config)#	**ip nat inside source static** *inside-local inside-global*	Configure a static NAT mapping.
(config)#	**ip nat pool** *pool-name start-ip end-ip* **prefix-length** *length*	Create a NAT pool.
(config)#	**ip nat inside source list** *acl* **pool** *pool-name*	Configure a dynamic NAT mapping of an ACL to a NAT pool.

Chapter 9: Network address translation

(config) #	`ip nat inside source list` *acl* `pool` *pool-name* `overload`	Configure a dynamic PAT (NAT overload) mapping of an ACL to a NAT pool.
(config) #	`ip nat inside source list` *acl* `interface` *interface* [`overload`]	Configure a dynamic PAT mapping of an ACL to an interface IP address.
#	`show ip nat translations`	View the NAT translation table.
#	`show ip nat statistics`	View NAT translation statistics.

Chapter 10: Quality of service

(config-if) #	`switchport voice vlan` *vlan-id*	Configure the port's voice VLAN.
(config-if) #	`power inline auto`	Enable PoE on the port, and automatically detect and power devices.
(config-if) #	`power inline static` [`max` *milliwatts*]	Enable PoE on the port with a static power reservation.
(config-if) #	`power inline police`	Enable power policing on the port.
(config-if) #	`power inline never`	Disable PoE on the port.
#	`show power inline`	View PoE status and ports.
#	`show power inline police`	View power policing status and ports.

Chapter 11: Security concepts

(config) #	`enable algorithm-type` {`md5` | `sha256` | `scrypt`} `secret` *password*	Configure an enable secret using the specified hashing algorithm.
(config) #	`enable secret` *type hash*	Configure an already-hashed enable secret.
(config) #	`username` *username* `algorithm-type` {`md5` | `sha256` | `scrypt`} `secret` *password*	Configure a user account, and hash the password using the specified algorithm
(config) #	`username` *username* `secret` *type hash*	Configure a user account with an already-hashed password.

Chapter 12: Port Security

(config-if) #	`switchport port-security`	Enable Port Security on the port.
(config-if) #	`switchport port-security maximum` *number*	Limit the maximum number of MAC addresses that can be learned on the port.
(config-if) #	`switchport port-security mac -address` *mac-address* [`voice vlan`]	Configure a static secure MAC address.
(config-if) #	`switchport port-security violation` {`shutdown` | `restrict` | `protect`}	Set the Port Security violation mode of the port.
(config-if) #	`switchport port-security aging time` *minutes*	Enable aging, and set the aging time for secure MAC addresses learned on the port.
(config-if) #	`switchport port-security aging type` {`absolute` | `inactivity`}	Set the Port Security aging type.
(config-if) #	`switchport port-security aging static`	Enable static secure MAC address aging.

(config-if)#	`switchport port-security mac -address sticky`	Enable sticky secure MAC address learning.
#	`show port-security`	View a list of Port Security-enabled ports.
#	`show port-security interface` *interface*	View Port Security settings for a port.
#	`show mac address-table secure`	View secure MAC addresses.
(config)#	`errdisable recovery cause psecure-violation`	Enable ErrDisable Recovery for ports disabled by Port Security.
(config)#	`errdisable recovery interval` *seconds*	Set the ErrDisable Recovery interval.
#	`show errdisable recovery`	View ErrDisable Recovery settings.

Chapter 13: DHCP Snooping

(config)#	`ip dhcp snooping`	Enable DHCP Snooping.
(config)#	`ip dhcp snooping vlan` *vlans*	Activate DHCP Snooping on VLANs.
(config)#	`no ip dhcp snooping information option`	Disable option 82 insertion.
(config-if)#	`ip dhcp snooping trust`	Configure the port as a DHCP Snooping trusted port.
(config-if)#	`ip dhcp snooping limit rate` *pps*	Rate-limit DHCP messages on the port.
(config)#	`errdisable recovery cause dhcp-rate-limit`	Enable ErrDisable Recovery for ports disabled by DHCP Snooping rate limiting.
#	`show ip dhcp snooping`	View DHCP Snooping status and settings.
#	`show ip dhcp snooping binding`	View the DHCP Snooping binding table.

Chapter 14: Dynamic ARP inspection

(config)#	`ip arp inspection vlan` *vlans*	Enable DAI on the specified VLANs.
(config)#	`ip arp inspection validate {[src-mac] [dst-mac] [ip]}`	Enable optional DAI checks.
(config-if)#	`ip arp inspection trust`	Configure the port as a DAI trusted port.
(config-if)#	`ip arp inspection limit rate` *pps* `[burst interval` *seconds*`]`	Rate-limit ARP messages on the port.
(config)#	`errdisable recovery cause arp-inspection`	Enable ErrDisable Recovery for ports disabled by DAI rate limiting.
#	`show ip arp inspection`	View DAI status and information.
#	`show ip arp inspection interfaces`	View DAI interface status and settings.

Chapter 17: Virtualization and cloud

(config)#	`ip vrf` *name*	Create a VRF instance.
(config-if)#	`ip vrf forwarding` *vrf*	Assign the interface to a VRF.
#	`show ip vrf`	View a list of VRFs and their interfaces.
#	`show ip route vrf` *vrf*	View the specified VRF's routing table.
#	`ping vrf` *vrf ip-address*	Ping a host from the specified VRF.

Chapter 21: Wireless LAN configuration		
(dhcp-config)#	**option 42 ip** *ip-address*	Set the DHCP pool's NTP server address.
(dhcp-config)#	**option 43 ip** *ip-address*	Set the DHCP pool's WLC address (to help LWAPs identify their WLC).
Chapter 24: Data Formats		
#	**show** *command* **| format**	Display the output in XML format (only works for some commands).

Chapter quiz questions

This appendix includes several quiz questions for each chapter of this volume. The goal of these questions is not necessarily to simulate real CCNA exam questions, but simply to test your knowledge of each chapter's contents. With that said, many of these questions are similar to what you might find on the CCNA exam; these questions target the CCNA exam topics and aim for a similar level of detail.

In any case, these questions will help you evaluate your readiness for the exam and identify some of your weak points—topics that you should focus on before taking on the CCNA exam itself. For the correct answers and a brief explanation of each question, refer to appendix D. I recommend attempting each chapter's questions after you have studied the chapter, and then once more for review after you have finished the book.

Chapter 1: Cisco Discovery Protocol and Link Layer Discovery Protocol

1 A Cisco switch and a Juniper switch use a Layer-2 discovery protocol to share information about each other. Which protocol are they likely using?

   A CDP

   B LLDP

   C FHRP

2 Which of the following commands doubles the frequency at which a device sends CDP messages?

   A `cdp timer 30`

   B `cdp hello-interval 30`

   C `cdp timer 15`

   D `cdp hello-interval 15`

3 By default, how many LLDP messages can a device miss from its neighbor before removing the neighbor from its LLDP neighbor table?

   A 1

   B 2

   C 3

   D 4

4 Which command allows the device to control how long its LLDP neighbors wait before removing its entry from their neighbor tables?

   A `lldp timer`

   B `lldp holdtime`

   C `lldp reinit`

   D `lldp receive`

5 Which command globally enables CDP on a device?

   A `cdp enable`

   B `cdp transmit`

   C `cdp run`

   D `cdp receive`

6 You issue `show cdp neighbors` on R1. SW1's entry shows `Local Intrfce: Gig 0/0` and `Port ID: 0/1`. Which of the following statements is true?

   A R1 G0/0 is connected to SW1 G0/1.

   B R1 G0/1 is connected to SW1 G0/0.

7 Which of the following statements about LLDP is false?

   A An interface must have an IP address to send LLDP messages.

   B LLDP Tx and Rx can be controlled separately.

   c LLDP is disabled on Cisco devices by default.

   d Any vendor can implement LLDP on its devices.

8 Which command(s) can be used to disable LLDP on an interface?

   A `no lldp run`

   B `no lldp enable`

   c `no lldp transmit` and `no lldp receive`

   D `lldp disable`

Chapter 2: Network Time Protocol

1 The output of **show clock** shows an asterisk (*) before the time. What is the significance of this asterisk?

   A The device's clock was manually configured.

   B The time was learned via NTP.

   c The time is considered trustworthy.

   D The time is not authoritative.

2 Which command manually configures a Cisco device's clock?

   A R1# `clock set 12:45:00 January 19 2024`

   B R1(config)# `clock set 12:45:00 January 19 2024`

   c R1# `clock time 12:45:00 January 19 2024`

   D R1(config)# `clock time 12:45:00 January 19 2024`

3 Which kind of NTP server operates as both an NTP client and server?

   A Reference server

   B Primary server

   c Secondary server

4 Which of the following commands configures a Cisco device in NTP client/server mode?

   A `ntp master`

   B `ntp server`

   c `ntp client`

   D `ntp peer`

5 R1 is an NTP client. The output of **show ntp associations** on R1 shows st: 3. What does this output mean?

   A R1 has a total of three NTP associations.

   B R1's NTP stratum is 3.

   c R1 learns the time from a server whose NTP stratum is 3.

6 Which command allows a Cisco device to function as an NTP server without being an NTP client?

A `ntp master`

B `ntp server`

C `ntp primary-server`

D `ntp primary`

7 Which commands are necessary to configure a Cisco IOS device as an NTP client, authenticating the server it learns the time from? (select three)

A `ntp authentication`

B `ntp server 10.0.0.1 authenticate`

C `ntp authentication-key 1 md5 P3sSw!rd`

D `ntp trusted-key 1`

E `ntp server 10.0.0.1 key 1`

8 What is the default NTP stratum level of a Cisco router that has been configured with `ntp master`?

A 5

B 6

C 7

D 8

Chapter 3: Domain Name System

1 Which part of the URL "https://www.jeremysitlab.com/ccna-resources" is the authority?

A https

B www.jeremysitlab.com

C /ccna-resources

D www.jeremysitlab.com/ccna-resources

2 What is the TLD of "mail.google.com."?

A mail

B google

C com

D .

3 Which kind of DNS server holds the definitive set of records for a specific domain?

A Domain DNS server

B Authoritative DNS server

C Definitive DNS server

D Root DNS server

4 Which kind of DNS query asks for a definite answer (the IP address or an error message)?

   A Iterative DNS

   B Definitive DNS

   C Authoritative DNS

   D Recursive DNS

5 A recursive resolver receives a query for a domain name that does not exist in its cache. What kind of DNS query does the recursive resolver send to the root server to resolve the domain name?

   A Iterative DNS

   B Definitive DNS

   C Authoritative DNS

   D Recursive DNS

6 Which of the following DNS record type descriptions are correct? (select three)

   A A: Points to an IPv6 address

   B CNAME: Points to another domain name

   C PTR: Used for reverse DNS lookups

   D NS: Specifies the domain's mail server(s)

   E AAAA: Points to an IPv4 address

   F SOA: Provides administrative information such as admin contact

7 Which command allows a Cisco IOS device to respond to DNS queries?

   A `ip domain-lookup`

   B `ip name-server`

   C `dns-server`

   D `ip dns server`

8 Which configuration is needed on a Cisco router for it to forward DNS request packets between a PC and a DNS server?

   A `ip dns server`

   B `ip domain-lookup`

   C `ip name-server 8.8.8.8`

   D No DNS configuration is needed.

Chapter 4: Dynamic Host Configuration Protocol

1 Which of the following DHCP messages are sent by a DHCP server? (select two)

   A ACK

   B DISCOVER

   C REQUEST

   D OFFER

2 When configuring a DHCP pool, which of the following DHCP settings is configured in global configuration mode?

   A The range of addresses to assign to clients

   B The excluded address range(s)

   C The default gateway

   D The DNS server

3 Which of the following commands configures a Cisco router as a DHCP client?

   A `R1(config-if)#` **`ip address dhcp`**

   B `R1(config-if)#` **`ip dhcp client`**

   C `R1(config)#` **`ip address dhcp`**

   D `R1(config)#` **`ip dhcp client`**

4 Which command displays the list of clients that a Cisco router, functioning as a DHCP server, has leased addresses to using DHCP?

   A **`show ip dhcp table`**

   B **`show ip dhcp binding`**

   C **`show ip dhcp server`**

   D **`show ip dhcp database`**

5 R1's G0/1 interface is connected to the WAN and G0/2 is connected to a LAN with DHCP clients. Where should the **`ip helper-address`** command be configured to make R1 function as a DHCP relay agent?

   A Interface configuration mode for G0/1

   B Interface configuration mode for G0/2

   C Global configuration mode

   D DHCP configuration mode

6 Which command shows detailed information about a Windows host's network configuration?

   A **`ipconfig`**

   B **`ipconfig /detail`**

   C **`ipconfig /verbose`**

   D **`ipconfig /all`**

7 Which command can be used to clear all of a router's DHCP bindings?

   A **`clear ip dhcp binding all`**

   B **`clear ip dhcp binding`**

   C **`clear ip dhcp binding *`**

   D **`clear ip dhcp binding dynamic`**

8 Which of the following DHCP messages are always broadcast? (select two)

   A OFFER

   B REQUEST

    c DISCOVER

    d ACK

Chapter 5: Secure Shell

1 Which command, when applied to a console or VTY line, requires login with a local user account to access the line?

    A `login local`

    B `login`

    c `local login`

    D `login user`

2 Which command can be used to configure a Layer-2 switch's default gateway?

    A `ip default-gateway 10.0.0.1`

    B `ip route 0.0.0.0 0.0.0.0 10.0.0.1`

    c `ip default-router 10.0.0.1`

    D `default route 10.0.0.1`

3 The output of **show ip ssh** states `SSH Enabled - version 1.99`. What does this output mean?

    A The device accepts SSHv1.99 connections only.

    B The device accepts SSHv1 and SSHv1.99 connections.

    c The device accepts SSHv2 connections only.

    D The device accepts SSHv1 and SSHv2 connections.

4 Why is a domain name needed to generate an RSA key pair with the **crypto key generate rsa** command?

    A Each RSA key pair is domain-specific.

    B The domain name is used as part of the key pair's name.

    c The domain name determines the size of the key pair.

    D Each RSA key pair requires a unique domain name.

5 When generating RSA keys, what is the minimum modulus size required to support SSHv2?

    A 512 bits

    B 768 bits

    c 1024 bits

    D 1536 bits

6 Which of the following commands can be used to allow only SSH connections?

    A `R1(config)# transport input ssh`

    B `R1(config-vty)# transport input ssh`

    c `R1(config-if)# transport input ssh`

    D `R1(config-line)# transport input ssh`

7   Which command can be used to apply an ACL to the VTY lines?

  A `access-class 1 in`

  B `access-group 1 in`

  C `access-list 1 in`

  D `ip access-group 1 in`

8   In addition to a domain name, what configuration might be required to generate RSA keys with `crypto key generate rsa`?

  A A VTY line password

  B A management interface

  C A non-default hostname

  D A DNS server

Chapter 6: Simple Network Management Protocol

1   Which SNMP message type is an unacknowledged notification from a managed device to the NMS?

  A Inform

  B Trap

  C Set

  D Notify

2   Which SNMP message type allows the NMS to retrieve a large amount of information from a managed device without specifying each individual OID?

  A Get

  B GetNext

  C GetBulk

  D GetRange

3   Which message type triggers a response from the NMS?

  A Get

  B Inform

  C Set

  D GetNext

4   Which SNMP version(s) use community-string authentication? (select all that apply)

  A SNMPv1

  B SNMPv2

  C SNMPv2c

  D SNMPv3

5 Which of the following statements are true? (select two)

   A The RO community string allows the NMS to send Get/GetNext/GetBulk and Set messages.

   B The RW community string allows the NMS to send Get/GetNext/GetBulk and Set messages.

   C The RW community string allows the NMS to send Set messages only.

   D The RO community string allows the NMS to send Get/GetNext/GetBulk messages only.

6 Where does an SNMP managed device store OIDs?

   A The RIB

   B The IMDB

   C The MIB

   D The OIDB

7 Which of the following statements are true? (select two)

   A SNMP managers listen on UDP port 161.

   B SNMP managers listen on UDP port 162.

   C SNMP agents listen on UDP port 161.

   D SNMP agents listen on UDP port 162.

8 Which SNMP versions support a user-based security model? (select all that apply)

   A SNMPv1

   B SNMPv2

   C SNMPv2c

   D SNMPv3

Chapter 7: Syslog

1 Which command enables logging to an external Syslog server with the informational severity level and higher?

   A `logging host 5`

   B `logging host 6`

   C `logging trap 5`

   D `logging trap 6`

2 Which of the following Syslog severity level and IOS keyword pairs are correct? (select three)

   A `informational` = 6

   B `warnings` = 3

   C `errors` = 4

   D `alerts` = 2

   E `critical` = 1

F `emergencies` = 0

G `notifications` = 5

3 Which command is necessary to enable real-time logging to the VTY lines for the current session?

   A `R1# logging monitor`

   B `R1# terminal monitor`

   C `R1(config)# logging monitor`

   D `R1(config)# terminal monitor`

4 Which of the following statements accurately describes the effect of the `logging buffered notifications` command?

   A Logs of severity level 5 and numerically higher will be logged.

   B Logs of severity level 5 and numerically lower will be logged.

   C Logs of severity level 5 will be logged.

5 What is the facility of the Syslog message `Jan 20 08:05:52: %LINK-3-UPDOWN: Interface GigabitEthernet0/2, changed state to up`?

   A `LINK`

   B `3`

   C `UPDOWN`

   D `Interface GigabitEthernet0/2, changed state to up`

6 What is the mnemonic of the Syslog message `Jan 20 08:36:29: %SYS-5-CON-FIG_I: Configured from console by jeremy on vty3 (192.168.1.224)`?

   A `SYS`

   B `5`

   C `CONFIG_I`

   D `Configured from console by jeremy on vty3 (192.168.1.224)`

7 Which command specifies an external Syslog server to send log messages to?

   A `logging server 10.0.0.10`

   B `logging trap 10.0.0.10`

   C `logging external 10.0.0.10`

   D `logging host 10.0.0.10`

8 Which severity levels will be logged to the console line as a result of the `logging console 2` command? (select three)

   A Alerts

   B Errors

   C Warnings

   D Emergencies

   E Notifications

   F Critical

Chapter 8: Trivial File Transfer Protocol and File Transfer Protocol

1 Why does TFTP use UDP, not TCP?

   A TFTP is a real-time application that is sensitive to delay.

   B TFTP is a simple query/response protocol that doesn't need the overhead of setting up a connection.

   C TFTP provides its own reliability and doesn't need TCP's overhead.

   D TFTP only sends trivial files that don't need reliable data delivery.

2 Which type of IOS file system is used to represent external FTP/TFTP servers?

   A Opaque

   B File

   C External

   D Network

3 Which of the following is a characteristic of TFTP?

   A Requires user credentials

   B Clients can only issue read or write requests

   C Establishes two connections between the client and server

   D Clients can navigate through a server's file directories

4 Which command can be used to transfer a file from the local device to an external FTP server?

   A `copy ftp: flash:`

   B `copy flash: ftp:`

   C `transfer ftp: flash:`

   D `transfer flash: ftp:`

5 Which of the following are characteristics of FTP? (select two)

   A Provides reliable delivery at the Application Layer

   B Establishes two connections between the client and server

   C Uses TCP ports 20 and 21

   D Provides encrypted file transfers

6 Which command can be used to specify which IOS file will be loaded upon the next system reboot?

   A `R1(config)# boot file`

   B `R1(config)# boot system`

   C `R1# boot file`

   D `R1# boot system`

7 Which commands configure the default FTP user credentials? (select two)

   A `ip ftp login jeremy`

   B `ip ftp username jeremy`

    c `ip ftp password password123`

    D `ip ftp secret password123`

8 Which connection does an FTP client use to send commands to the server?

    A The control connection

    B The command connection

    c The data connection

    D The transfer connection

Chapter 9: Network Address Translation

1 Which of the following NAT types provide one-to-one translations only?

    A Static NAT and dynamic PAT

    B Static NAT

    c Dynamic NAT

    D Static NAT and dynamic NAT

2 Which Cisco NAT term describes the IP address of a host in the internal network from the perspective of hosts in the external network?

    A Outside global

    B Inside global

    c Outside local

    D Inside local

3 In a typical inside source NAT scenario, which of the following addresses is usually a private address?

    A Outside global

    B Inside global

    c Outside local

    D Inside local

4 R1 must use NAT to allow hosts in its connected LAN to communicate over the internet. Which of the following commands should be used to enable this? (select two)

    A `ip nat inside` on the LAN-facing interface

    B `ip nat outside` on the internet-facing interface

    c `ip nat internal` on the LAN-facing interface

    D `ip nat external` on the internet-facing interface

5 Which of the following NAT types provides many-to-one translations?

    A Static NAT

    B Dynamic PAT

    c Dynamic NAT

6 In a typical inside source NAT scenario, which of the following addresses should be identical in the output of `show ip nat translations`? (select two)

   A Inside local

   B Inside global

   C Outside local

   D Outside global

7 Which of the following commands creates a pool for dynamic PAT?

   A `ip nat pool POOL1 203.0.113.1 203.0.113.10 netmask 255.255.255.248`

   B `ip nat pool POOL1 203.0.113.1 203.0.113.10 netmask 0.0.0.15`

   C `ip nat pool POOL1 203.0.113.1 203.0.113.10 prefix-length 28`

   D `ip nat pool POOL1 203.0.113.1 203.0.113.10 prefix-length 29`

8 ACL 1 only permits packets sourced from the 10.0.0.0/24 subnet. After issuing the `ip nat inside source list 1 gigabitethernet0/0` command on R1, what action will it take on packets denied by ACL 1?

   A It will forward them without translation.

   B It will discard them.

   C It will buffer them until they can be translated.

   D It will translate their source IP to GigabitEthernet0/0's IP.

9 Which of the following commands configures dynamic PAT?

   A `ip nat inside source list 1 pool POOL1 overload`

   B `ip nat inside source list 1 pool POOL1`

   C `ip nat inside source list 1 pat POOL1`

   D `ip nat inside source list 1 203.0.113.1 overload`

10 When PAT is configured, what happens when two pre-translation messages use the same source port number?

   A The second packet is dropped.

   B The second packet is buffered until the port number becomes available.

   C The second packet's port number is translated to a new number.

   D The second packet is forwarded without translation.

Chapter 10: Quality of service

1 What does traffic shaping do?

   A Buffer traffic that exceeds the configured rate limit

   B Drop traffic that exceeds the configured rate limit

   C Decide the order in which queued packets are transmitted

   D Categorize packets according to their markings

2 Which of the following often leads to TCP global synchronization?

  A WRED

  B RED

  C Tail drop

  D Jitter

3 Which QoS feature modifies specific fields in the Layer-2 and Layer-3 headers to facilitate the categorization of messages?

  A Classification

  B Scheduling

  C Marking

  D Queuing

4 Which feature would an ISP's customer likely implement to avoid exceeding the ISP's rate limit?

  A Marking

  B Policing

  C Scheduling

  D Shaping

5 Which QoS feature involves identifying the traffic type of a particular packet?

  A Identification

  B Classification

  C Queuing

  D Marking

6 Which of the following markings indicates a high priority and a high drop precedence?

  A AF11

  B AF13

  C AF41

  D AF43

7 Which QoS feature drops or re-marks traffic that exceeds the configured rate limit?

  A Policing

  B Shaping

  C Marking

  D Buffering

8 Which scheduling method combines a priority queue with a weighted round-robin scheduler?

  A CBWFQ

  B PQ

    c EF

    d LLQ

9 Which marking is typically used for voice call traffic?

    A EF

    B DF

    c AF4x

    d CS6

10 Which marking is typically used for best effort traffic?

    A EF

    B DF

    c CS1

    d AF3x

11 Which concept refers to the variation in delay?

    A Latency

    B Jitter

    c Loss

    d RTT

12 Which command guarantees power to a PoE-enabled device connected to the port?

    A `power inline auto`

    B `power inline static`

    c `power inline police`

    d `power inline port`

Chapter 11: Security concepts

1 Which element of the CIA triad aims to protect systems and data from unauthorized access?

    A C

    B I

    c A

2 A malicious user who intends to harm the security of an organization's systems is an example of what?

    A Threat

    B Exploit

    c Vulnerability

    d Mitigation technique

3 A DHCP exhaustion attack is an example of which attack types? (select two)

   A Spoofing

   B DoS

   C Man-in-the-middle

   D Reflection

4 Which of the following are examples of social engineering? (select three)

   A Backdoor

   B Whaling

   C Trojan horse

   D Phishing

   E Tailgating

   F Ransomware

5 Which of the following are examples of physical access control? (select two)

   A MFA door locks

   B User education programs

   C Phishing awareness email campaigns

   D Security cameras

   E Secure device passwords

6 Which of the following are common advantages of using a password manager? (select three)

   A Integrated physical access control

   B Stronger passwords

   C Auto-fill

   D Encrypted storage

   E Integrated anti-malware

   F Protection against social engineering

7 Which of the following commands configures an enable secret using type-9 hashing?

   A `enable algorithm-type scrypt secret AcingTheCCNAExam!`

   B `enable algorithm-type md5 secret AcingTheCCNAExam!`

   C `enable algorithm-type sha256 secret AcingTheCCNAExam!`

   D `enable algorithm-type md9 secret AcingTheCCNAExam!`

8 Which of the following is an example of MFA?

   A Entering a username/password and a PIN

   B Performing a fingerprint scan and a retina scan

   C Scanning a badge and entering a PIN

   D Scanning a badge and tapping a phone notification

9 Which of the following provides PNAC?

   A NGFW

   B NGIPS

   c 802.1X

   D AAA

10 Which AAA element consists of granting a user or device appropriate access?

   A Accounting

   B Authentication

   c Authorization

   D Access

11 Which AAA protocol combines authentication and authorization into a single operation?

   A ISE

   B RADIUS

   c TACACS+

   D AAA+

12 Which of the following is an example of stateless packet filtering?

   A NGFW

   B An ACL applied to a router interface

   c NGIPS

   D UDP

13 Which component of 802.1X is the network device that the client connects to?

   A Supplicant

   B Gateway

   c Authentication server

   D Authenticator

Chapter 12: Port Security

1 After configuring `switchport port-security` on a port, how many MAC addresses can be learned on the port by default?

   A 0

   B 1

   c 2

   D Unlimited

2 You issue `switchport port-security` on a port and receive the following error message: `Command rejected: FastEthernet0/1 is a dynamic port.` What is the cause for this error?

   A The port uses dynamic MAC address learning.

   B The port uses a dynamic routing protocol.

   C The port's operational mode is determined by DTP.

   D The port is a DHCP client.

3 Which of the following actions does a switch take by default when a Port Security violation occurs? (select three)

   A Discard the violating frames

   B Increment the violation counter

   C Disable dynamic MAC address learning

   D Re-enable previously disabled ports

   E Error-disable the port

4 Which of the following is a difference between secure MAC addresses and regular MAC addresses in a switch's MAC address table?

   A Secure MAC addresses can be statically configured.

   B Static secure MAC addresses age out by default.

   C Dynamic secure MAC addresses don't age out by default.

   D Only one secure MAC address can be learned per port.

5 Which command can be used to automatically re-enable a port disabled by Port Security?

   A `errdisable recovery cause port-security`

   B `errdisable recovery cause psec-shutdown`

   C `errdisable recovery cause psec-disable`

   D `errdisable recovery cause psecure-violation`

6 Which of the following commands causes dynamic secure MAC addresses to be saved in the device's running-config?

   A `SW1(config)# switchport port-security mac-address sticky`

   B `SW1(config)# switchport port-security sticky`

   C `SW1(config-if)# switchport port-security mac-address sticky`

   D `SW1(config-if)# switchport port-security sticky`

7 Which of the following MAC addresses will be removed from the MAC address table if the corresponding port goes down? (select all that apply)

   A Sticky secure MAC addresses

   B Dynamic secure MAC addresses

   C Static secure MAC addresses

   D Dynamic MAC addresses

8 Which of the following commands configure a port to block frames from invalid MAC addresses without affecting valid traffic? (select two)

   A `switchport port-security violation guard`

   B `switchport port-security violation protect`

   C `switchport port-security violation restrict`

   D `switchport port-security violation shutdown`

Chapter 13: DHCP Snooping

1 Which DHCP messages are always discarded when received on a DHCP Snooping untrusted port?

   A ACK, REQUEST

   B DISCOVER, OFFER

   C ACK, OFFER

   D REQUEST, DISCOVER

2 Which table is used by DHCP Snooping to inspect client DHCP RELEASE and DECLINE messages?

   A The DAI table

   B The DHCP binding table

   C The DHCP Snooping binding table

   D The ARP table

3 Which command disables option 82 insertion on untrusted ports?

   A `no ip dhcp snooping option 82`

   B `no ip dhcp snooping information option`

   C `no ip dhcp snooping insert 82`

   D `no ip dhcp snooping information insert`

4 Which of the following statements is true?

   A DHCP Snooping doesn't work when a relay agent is used.

   B DHCP Snooping inspects messages received on trusted ports.

   C DHCP Snooping is enabled by default if DHCP is used.

   D DHCP Snooping must be enabled globally and per-VLAN.

5 How does DHCP Snooping treat a DHCP message received on a trusted port?

   A It allows the message.

   B It allows the message if it is a DHCP server message.

   C It allows the message if it is a DHCP client message.

   D It inspects the message to decide which action to take.

6 Which of the following messages are sent by DHCP clients? (select four)

   A NAK

   B REQUEST

     c ACK

     d OFFER

     e RELEASE

     f DISCOVER

     g DECLINE

7 What does DHCP Snooping provide in addition to DHCP message inspection?

     A Automated DHCP pool configuration

     B Rate-limiting of DHCP messages

     c Inspection of standard data frames

     D Client credential authentication

8 Which two fields does DHCP Snooping inspect in client DISCOVER and REQUEST messages?

     A Source MAC and chaddr

     B Source MAC and source IP

     c Source MAC and destination MAC

     D Destination MAC and destination IP

Chapter 14: Dynamic Address Resolution Protocol Inspection

1 Which table does DAI use to inspect messages received on untrusted ports?

     A The ARP table

     B The MAC address table

     c The DHCP Snooping binding table

     D The DHCP binding table

2 How does DAI treat ARP messages received on trusted ports?

     A It allows them.

     B It allows ARP replies.

     c It allows ARP requests.

     D It inspects them to determine the appropriate action.

3 Which of the following statements about DAI is false?

     A DAI must be enabled globally and per-VLAN.

     B DAI validates ARP messages using the DHCP Snooping binding table.

     c DAI rate limits ARP messages on untrusted ports by default.

     D All ports are untrusted by default.

4 What kind of ARP reply is sent without receiving an ARP request?

     A Unprompted ARP

     B Spoofed ARP

c Gratuitous ARP

d Poisoned ARP

5 Which of the following commands are necessary for a basic DAI configuration? (select two)

A `ip arp inspection`

B `ip arp inspection vlan 10`

C `ip arp inspection trust`

D `ip arp inspection validate src-mac`

6 What is the default DAI rate limit on trusted ports?

A 10 pps

B 15 pps

c 25 pps

D Unlimited

7 Which command enables automatic recovery of ports disabled by DAI rate-limiting?

A `errdisable recovery cause arp-inspection`

B `errdisable recovery cause dai-violation`

c `errdisable recovery cause dai-rate-limit`

D `errdisable recovery cause dai`

8 Which command causes the switch to inspect ARP messages for suspicious IP addresses?

A `ip arp inspection validate src-ip`

B `ip arp inspection validate dst-ip`

c `ip arp inspection validate ip`

D `ip arp inspection validate src-dst-ip`

Chapter 15: LAN architectures

1 Which layer of a three-tier LAN is most likely to implement security services such as Port Security, DHCP Snooping, and DAI?

A Access

B Distribution

c Core

2 Which layers are combined in a two-tier LAN? (select two)

A Access

B Distribution

c Core

3 In a three-tier LAN, where is the border between Layers 2 and 3 usually located?

   A Access

   B Distribution

   C Core

4 In a three-tier LAN, which switches are most likely to support PoE?

   A Access switches

   B Distribution switches

   C Core switches

5 In a three-tier LAN, which layer is focused on speed and reliability, avoiding CPU-intensive operations?

   A Access

   B Distribution

   C Core

6 In a three-tier LAN, where is QoS marking most often performed?

   A Access

   B Distribution

   C Core

7 Which of the following statements about spine-leaf architecture is true?

   A Every leaf switch is connected to every other leaf switch.

   B Every leaf switch is connected to every spine switch.

   C Every spine switch is connected to every other spine switch

   D End hosts connect to spine switches.

8 Which of the following are benefits of spine-leaf architecture? (select two)

   A Consistent and predictable latency between servers

   B More efficient north-south communication

   C Simple scalability by adding more leaf switches

   D Reduced need for east-west communication

9 Which type of network is most likely to benefit from spine-leaf architecture?

   A Small-to-medium enterprise LANs

   B Large enterprise LANs

   C Data center LANs

   D SOHO LANs

10 Which of the following statements about SOHO networks is true?

   A SOHO networks typically use a two-tier architecture.

   B SOHO networks require redundant internet connections.

   C SOHO networks require separate WAN and internet connections.

   D SOHO networks' needs are often met by a single wireless router.

Chapter 16: WAN architectures

1 In which type of MPLS VPN do CE routers form neighbor relationships directly with other CE routers (i.e. with OSPF)?

   A L2VPN

   B L3VPN

2 In which type of MPLS VPN do CE routers form neighbor relationships with PE routers?

   A L2VPN

   B L3VPN

3 In an MPLS WAN, which of the following routers run MPLS? (select all that apply)

   A P

   B PE

   C CE

4 Where is the MPLS label inserted into a message?

   A Before the Ethernet header

   B Between the Ethernet and IP headers

   C Between the IP and TCP/UDP headers

   D After the TCP/UDP headers

5 Which technology facilitates a full mesh of IPsec VPN tunnels with minimal manual configuration?

   A MPLS

   B DSL

   C TLS

   D DMVPN

6 Which type of VPN establishes a tunnel between an end host and a corporate firewall or router?

   A Site-to-site VPN

   B Host-based VPN

   C Remote-access VPN

   D Secure-access VPN

7 Which of the following protocols is most often used for site-to-site VPNs?

   A IPsec

   B TLS

   C GRE

   D CAPWAP

8 Which VPN technology is often used for its combination of broadcast/multicast support and security?

  A GRE

  B IPsec

  C GRE over IPsec

  D PPP

9 Which of the following statements accurately describes tunneling?

  A Tunneling is the process of encapsulating a packet inside of another packet, creating a virtual pathway for the internal packet.

  B Tunneling is the process of encrypting data for secure transmission across a network.

  C Tunneling is a technique that limits the number of broadcast messages in the network.

  D Tunneling is the process of encapsulating a TCP segment in an IP header for transmission across a network.

10 Which internet connection design offers one connection to each of two or more ISPs?

  A Dual-homed

  B Multi-homed

  C Single-homed

  D Dual multi-homed

Chapter 17: Virtualization and cloud

1 Which of the following virtualization technologies is installed directly on server hardware?

  A Type 1 hypervisor

  B Type 2 hypervisor

  C Container

2 Which of the following statements about type-2 hypervisors is true?

  A The hypervisor interacts directly with the hardware resources.

  B VMware ESXi is a popular type-2 hypervisor.

  C The hypervisor is installed on a host OS.

  D VMs running on a type-2 hypervisor don't need to run their own OS.

3 Which of the following statements about VRF is true?

  A VRF enables the creation of virtual interfaces in a router.

  B VRF creates multiple routing tables on a router.

  C By default, hosts in different VRFs can communicate with each other.

  D All interfaces are assigned to VRF 1 by default.

4 Which of the following cloud service models provides the most control to the customer?

   A PaaS

   B SaaS

   C IaaS

5 Which cloud service model offers a complete software product to the customer?

   A PaaS

   B SaaS

   C IaaS

6 AWS, Azure, and GCP are examples of what cloud deployment model?

   A Commercial cloud

   B Private cloud

   C Public cloud

   D Hybrid cloud

7 Which of the following are advantages of cloud computing? (select two)

   A Reduced CapEx

   B Reduced OpEx

   C Greater control over infrastructure

   D Simplified global scaling

8 In the context of cloud computing, what is rapid elasticity?

   A Measuring and charging based on each customer's use of resources

   B The ability to deploy cloud resource with a self-service model

   C The ability to flexibly scale infrastructure according to need

   D The ability to flexibly connect to cloud infrastructure via a variety of connection methods

9 In which model do customers rent space, cooling, electricity, etc, in a shared data center?

   A SaaS

   B IaaS

   C Colocation

   D On-prem

10 Which of the following virtualization technologies is more lightweight, using fewer hardware resources?

   A A container

   B A VM running on a type-1 hypervisor

   C A VM running on a type-2 hypervisor

Chapter 18: Wireless LAN fundamentals

1 Which term refers to the phenomenon of an electromagnetic wave bending when it passes from one medium to another one with a different density?

   A Diffraction

   B Refraction

   C Reflection

   D Scattering

2 Which term refers to the erratic spreading out of an electromagnetic wave as the result of encountering a surface or medium with irregularities?

   A Diffraction

   B Refraction

   C Reflection

   D Scattering

3 Which kind of service set consists of multiple APs' coverage areas, integrated into a coherent whole offering connectivity for clients?

   A BSS

   B IBSS

   C MBSS

   D ESS

4 Which frequency bands used by 802.11 wireless LANs offer many non-overlapping channels? (select two)

   A 2.4 GHz

   B 5 GHz

   C 6 GHz

5 Which 2.4 GHz channel pattern is generally recommended to avoid interference between adjacent APs?

   A 1-5-9

   B 1-6-11

   C 1-7-13

   D 1-6-13

6 Which of the following uniquely identifies each AP in an ESS?

   A SSID

   B BSSID

   C APID

   D Roaming ID

7 Which of the following 802.11 standards offer many non-overlapping channels? (select two)

  A 802.11g

  B 802.11a

  C 802.11ac

  D 802.11b

8 Which of the following identifiers is the MAC address of the AP's radio?

  A SSID

  B BSSID

  C ESSID

  D Channel ID

9 Which of the following AP modes functions as a wireless client on behalf of a device without wireless capabilities?

  A Repeater

  B Outdoor bridge

  C Workgroup bridge

  D Mesh

10 Which 802.11 standards support both the 2.4 GHz and 5 GHz bands? (select three)

  A 802.11be

  B 802.11a

  C 802.11g

  D 802.11n

  E 802.11ac

  F 802.11ax

11 What is the term for a wireless LAN's non-unique, human-readable name?

  A BSS

  B SSID

  C BSSID

  D APID

12 Which type of AP in an MBSS connects to the DS?

  A RAP

  B MAP

  C DAP

  D DSAP

Chapter 19: Wireless LAN architectures

1 When a wireless client sends a frame to another client associated with the same AP, what is the RA of the frame when the client transmits it?

   A The destination client's MAC

   B The sender's MAC

   C The AP's MAC

2 Which of the following messages are used in passive scanning?

   A Beacon messages

   B Discovery messages

   C Advertisement messages

   D Probe messages

3 Which of the following are not 802.11 management messages?

   A CTS/RTS

   B Probe request/response

   C Authentication request/response

   D Association request/response

4 Which kind of AP is managed by a WLC?

   A Autonomous AP

   B Managed AP

   C Lightweight AP

   D Controller AP

5 Which of the following APs typically connects to the DS via an access link?

   A Cloud-based AP

   B Autonomous AP

   C LWAP in local mode

   D LWAP in FlexConnect mode

6 Which LWAP mode captures 802.11 frames for analysis in Wireshark?

   A Monitor

   B Sniffer

   C SE-Connect

   D Rogue detector

7 When FlexConnect local switching is enabled for a WLAN, which device is responsible for switching traffic between the 802.11 and Ethernet networks?

   A The LWAP

   B The WLC

   C The switch

   D The router

8 Which LWAP mode is dedicated to analyzing traffic on the wired LAN?

   A Monitor

   B Sniffer

   C SE-Connect

   D Rogue Detector

9 In Cisco Meraki's cloud-based AP solution, which traffic is tunneled to the Meraki cloud?

   A Management traffic

   B Data traffic

   C All traffic

10 Which WLC deployment option uses a dedicated hardware appliance?

   A Embedded

   B Autonomous

   C Cloud

   D Unified

11 Which of the following functions are centrally controlled in a split-MAC architecture? (select two)

   A Client authentication and association

   B RF management

   C Beacon transmission

   D RF signal transmission and reception

12 Which statement about CAPWAP is true?

   A The CAPWAP control tunnel is encrypted by default.

   B The CAPWAP data tunnel is encrypted by default.

   C Both CAPWAP tunnels are encrypted by default.

13 Which of the following is not a benefit of cloud-based network management?

   A Rapid deployment with ZTP

   B Highly customizable to meet complex networking requirements

   C Simplified management via a web-based dashboard

   D Enhanced visibility and analytics

Chapter 20: Wireless LAN security

1 Which 802.11 security protocol was developed to overcome the vulnerabilities of WEP?

   A CCMP

   B GCMP

   C TKIP

   D RC4

2   Which authentication methods are available in WEP? (select two)

   A PSK

   B Open System

   C Shared Key

   D 802.1X

3   Which WPA3 feature protects the PSK against brute-force attacks?

   A PMF

   B FS

   C EAP

   D SAE

4   Which of the following use AES counter mode encryption? (select all that apply)

   A CCMP

   B GCMP

   C TKIP

   D WEP

5   Which protocol is used to carry EAP messages between a supplicant and authenticator?

   A 802.1X

   B EAPoL

   C RADIUS

   D EAP-FAST

6   Which WPA3 feature ensures that a compromised PSK cannot be used to decrypt past communications?

   A PMF

   B FS

   C EAP

   D SAE

7   Which of the following uses 802.1X authentication?

   A WEP

   B TKIP

   C WPA-Enterprise

   D WPA-Personal

8   Which of the following employs SAE?

   A WPA2-Enterprise

   B WPA2-Personal

   C WPA3-Enterprise

   D WPA3-Personal

9 Which protocol does the original WPA standard employ for data encryption and integrity?

A TKIP

B WEP

C PSK

D EAP

10 Which protocol does the WPA3 standard employ for the most secure data encryption and integrity?

A TKIP

B CCMP

C GCMP

D AES

Chapter 21: Wireless LAN configuration

1 Which of the following methods can be used to connect to the GUI of a Cisco WLC? (select all that apply)

A Telnet

B SSH

C HTTP

D HTTPS

E Console port

2 Which WLC port type is used to carry user data traffic?

A Distribution system port

B Data port

C Service port

D Dynamic port

3 Which WLC port type is used for OOB management of the WLC over the network?

A Distribution system port

B Data port

C Service port

D Console port

4 Which WLC interface type is used to establish CAPWAP tunnels with LWAPs?

A Virtual interface

B Dynamic interface

C Management interface

D AP-manager interface

5   Which WLC interface type is used for OOB management of the WLC over the network?

   A Virtual interface

   B Service-port interface

   C Management interface

   D AP-manager interface

6   Which advanced WLAN feature encourages clients to associate with less-busy LWAPs?

   A Client Autoconfig

   B Client Override

   C Client Load Balancing

   D Client Band Select

7   When configuring a hexadecimal WPA2 PSK in the Cisco WLC GUI, how many characters must the PSK be?

   A 8 characters

   B 32 characters

   C 64 characters

   D 256 characters

8   Which QoS level is assigned to a WLAN by default, offering best-effort treatment of traffic?

   A Bronze

   B Silver

   C Gold

   D Platinum

9   Which advanced WLAN feature delays responses to 2.4 GHz probes to encourage clients to use 5 GHz instead?

   A Client Autoconfig

   B Client Override

   C Client Load Balancing

   D Client Band Select

10   Which of the following are Layer-3 security settings? (select two)

   A 802.1X

   B Passthrough

   C PMF

   D Conditional Web Redirect

11   Which WLC interface type is used to map WLANs to VLANs?

   A Virtual interface

   B SVI

c WLAN interface

D Dynamic interface

12 Which tab of the Cisco WLC GUI allows you to configure settings related to the LWAPs managed by the WLC?

A Wireless

B Management

c WLANs

D Controller

13 If you enable LAG on a Cisco WLC, which ports are included in the LAG?

A All ports

B All DS ports

c All DS and redundancy ports

D All service ports

Chapter 22: Network automation

1 Which logical plane is responsible for routers exchanging BGP messages with each other to share routing information and build their routing tables?

A Management Plane

B Control Plane

c Data Plane

2 Which logical plane is responsible for a switch examining the source MAC address of each frame it receives and creating MAC address table entries?

A Management Plane

B Control Plane

c Data Plane

3 Which logical plane is responsible for a switch examining the destination MAC address of each frame it receives and making a forwarding/flooding decision?

A Management Plane

B Control Plane

c Data Plane

4 Which of the following planes are distributed in a traditional (non-SDN) network? (select all that apply)

A Management Plane

B Control Plane

c Data Plane

5 Which of the following statements about SDN architecture are true? (select two)

A The Data Plane is distributed

B The Control Plane is distributed

    C The Data Plane is centralized

    D The Control Plane is centralized

6 Which type of API is most common in the NBI of SDN architecture?

    A OpenFlow

    B REST

    C NETCONF

    D OpFlex

7 Which SDN interface is used to communicate with the managed devices?

    A NBI

    B SBI

    C HTTP

    D Application

8 Which SDN architecture layer contains the network devices responsible for forwarding messages across the network?

    A Application Layer

    B Transport Layer

    C Control Layer

    D Infrastructure Layer

9 Which Cisco SDN solution takes advantage of spine-leaf architecture?

    A ACI

    B SD-Access

    C SD-WAN

    D SD-DC

10 Which of the following are Management Layer protocols? (select two)

    A SSH

    B NTP

    C STP

    D ARP

11 Which of the following is not a benefit of network automation?

    A Reduced human error

    B Reduced time to configure devices

    C Reduced OpEx

    D Reduced CapEx

12 Which type of machine learning involves labeled data sets?

    A Supervised learning

    B Unsupervised learning

    C Reinforcement learning

13 Which of the following can be provided by predictive AI?

   A Device configuration generation

   B Automated network diagrams

   C Network traffic forecasting

   D Automated network design

14 Which Catalyst Center AI feature can be used to automate troubleshooting?

   A Machine reasoning

   B AI endpoint analytics

   C AI enhanced RRM

   D AI remediation

Chapter 23: REST APIs

1 Which HTTP method is generally equivalent to a CRUD "create" operation?

   A PUT

   B PATCH

   C POST

   D GET

2 Which HTTP methods are generally equivalent to a CRUD "update" operation? (select two)

   A PUT

   B PATCH

   C POST

   D GET

3 Which HTTP method is used to replace the specified resource?

   A PUT

   B PATCH

   C POST

   D GET

4 Which HTTP response code indicates that the request resource was not found?

   A 200

   B 201

   C 403

   D 404

5 Which of the following HTTP response code classes are correct? (select three)

   A 2xx = successful

   B 4xx = server error

   C 5xx = client error

    D 1xx = informational

    E 3xx = redirection

6 Which of the following statements about REST APIs are true? (select two)

    A REST APIs are stateful.

    B REST APIs are stateless.

    C REST uses a client-server architecture.

    D REST uses a peer-to-peer architecture.

7 Which statement about caching is accurate with regard to REST APIs?

    A Resources must be marked as cacheable or non-cacheable.

    B Resources are never cacheable.

    C Resources must be cacheable.

8 Which of the following HTTP response codes indicates a successful request?

    A 102

    B 200

    C 301

    D 500

9 Which REST API authentication method allows a client to access a resource on a server on behalf of the resource's owner?

    A OAuth 2.0

    B Basic authentication

    C API key authentication

    D Bearer authentication

10 In which REST API authentication method does a client authenticate with an authorization server to receive a token that the client includes in its API calls?

    A OAuth 2.0

    B Basic authentication

    C API key authentication

    D Bearer authentication

11 What is the primary advantage of using OAuth 2.0 for accessing resources?

    A OAuth 2.0 requires no client-side implementation.

    B OAuth 2.0 allows third-party applications to access resources without sharing the user's credentials.

    C OAuth 2.0 tokens do not expire.

    D OAuth 2.0 is easier to implement than basic authentication.

Chapter 24: Data formats

1   In which data serialization language is whitespace significant?

  A XML

  B YAML

  C JSON

2   Which data serialization language uses HTML-like tags?

  A XML

  B YAML

  C JSON

3   What is the JSON name for an unordered set of key-value pairs?

  A Array

  B List

  C Item

  D Object

4   Which statements are true about the following JSON data? (select two) `{"interface_name":"GigabitEthernet1/1","is_up":"true","speed":1000}`

  A The value of "is_up" is a JSON boolean.

  B The value of "speed" is a JSON number.

  C The data is a JSON object.

  D The data is a JSON array.

5   Which of the following statements about JSON arrays are true? (select two)

  A Arrays are enclosed in square brackets.

  B There can be a trailing comma.

  C The values don't have to be of the same data type.

  D The value can be of any valid JSON data type except another array.

6   Which of the following statements about JSON objects are true? (select two)

  A The key of each key-value pair must be a string.

  B The value of each key-value pair can be any valid JSON data type except another object.

  C There must not be a trailing comma.

  D Objects are enclosed in square brackets.

7   Which statement about the following JSON data is true? `{"device":"Switch01","location":"DataCenterA","uptime":"72 hours","ports_active":24}`

  A It is valid JSON data.

  B A comma is missing.

   c The whitespace formatting is invalid.

   d There is an extra colon.

8 Which of the following are valid JSON strings? (select all that apply)

   A `'Hello.'`

   B `"Acing The CCNA Exam"`

   c `"true"`

   D `True or false`

   E `"1000"`

   F `null`

Chapter 25: Ansible and Terraform

1 Which of the following statements about Ansible are true? (select two)

   A Ansible is written in Python.

   B Ansible uses an agent-based model.

   c Ansible uses a pull model.

   D The Ansible control node connects to port 22 of managed devices.

2 Which of the following statements about Puppet are true? (select two)

   A Puppet is written in Ruby.

   B Puppet is written in Python.

   c Puppet uses a pull model.

   D Puppet uses a push model.

3 Which language are most Ansible files written in?

   A Python

   B YAML

   c JSON

   D Ruby

4 Which of the following statements about Chef are true? (select two)

   A Chef is written in Python.

   B Chef uses a pull model.

   c A Chef client must be installed on managed devices.

   D Chef uses an agentless model.

5 Which of these IaC tools are primarily used for configuration management? (select three)

   A Ansible

   B Chef

   c Terraform

   D Puppet

6 Which statements about HashiCorp Configuration Language are true? (select two)

   A It is more flexible than a language like Python or Go.

   B It can perform complex tasks with less effort than general languages.

   C It is a declarative language.

   D It is a procedural language.

7 Which of the following configuration management tools use an agent-based model? (select two)

   A Puppet

   B Ansible

   C Chef

   D Terraform

8 Which Ansible file defines automation tasks to manage configuration on managed devices?

   A Template

   B Module

   C Playbook

   D Run-list

9 Which of the following statements about Terraform are true? (select two)

   A Terraform uses a pull model.

   B Terraform primarily uses a declarative approach.

   C Terraform requires a software agent on managed devices.

   D Terraform is written in Go.

10 What are the three steps in the basic Terraform workflow?

   A Write, execute, review

   B Write, plan, apply

   C Create, apply, troubleshoot

   D Plan, write, execute

Chapter quiz answers

This appendix lists the answers to the chapter quiz questions in appendix C and gives explanations for each answer. The explanations are brief (one or two sentences); for more thorough explanations of the concepts, refer back to the relevant chapter.

Chapter 1: Cisco Discovery Protocol and Link Layer Discovery Protocol

1. A Cisco switch and a Juniper switch use a Layer-2 discovery protocol to share information about each other. Which protocol are they likely using?
B: LLDP
Link Layer Discovery Protocol (LLDP) is a vendor-neutral Layer-2 discovery protocol used by various networking devices, including those from Cisco, Juniper, and most other vendors. Cisco Discovery Protocol (CDP), on the other hand, is Cisco proprietary (although it has been implemented by a few other vendors).

2. Which of the following commands doubles the frequency at which a device sends CDP messages?
A: `cdp timer 30`

The **cdp timer** command sets the frequency at which CDP messages are sent. The default timer is 60 seconds, so setting it to 30 seconds would double the frequency.

3. By default, how many LLDP messages can a device miss from its neighbor before removing the neighbor from its LLDP neighbor table?

D: 4

The default hold time for LLDP is 120 seconds, and LLDP messages are sent every 30 seconds by default. Therefore, a device can miss up to 4 LLDP messages (120 seconds / 30 seconds per message) before it removes the neighbor from its table.

4. Which command allows the device to control how long its LLDP neighbors wait before removing its entry from their neighbor tables?

B: **lldp holdtime**

The **lldp holdtime** command sets the amount of time a device's neighbors should hold information before discarding it. This time is communicated in LLDP messages sent by the device.

5. Which command globally enables CDP on a device?

C: **cdp run**

The **cdp run** command—issued in global config mode—globally enables CDP on a Cisco device. This command is required to activate CDP if it has been previously disabled (although CDP is globally enabled by default).

6. You issue **show cdp neighbors** on R1. SW1's entry shows Local Intrfce: Gig 0/0 and Port ID: 0/1. Which of the following statements is true?

A: R1 G0/0 is connected to SW1 G0/1.

In the output of **show cdp neighbors**, the Local Intrfce column indicates the interface of this device (R1), and the Port ID column indicates the interface of the neighboring device (SW1).

7. Which of the following statements about LLDP is false?

A: An interface must have an IP address to send LLDP messages.

LLDP doesn't require an IP address on an interface to send (or receive) messages—the same applies to CDP. CDP and LLDP are Layer-2 discovery protocols; they function even on interfaces that don't have Layer-3 IP addresses.

8. Which command(s) can be used to disable LLDP on an interface?

C: **no lldp transmit** and **no lldp receive**

To completely disable LLDP on an interface, both transmission and reception of LLDP messages must be turned off. You can do this with the **no lldp transmit** and **no lldp receive** commands in interface config mode.

Chapter 2: Network Time Protocol

1. The output of show clock shows an asterisk (*) before the time. What is the significance of this asterisk?

D: The time is not authoritative.

An asterisk before the time, such as *08:56:18.831 UTC Mon Aug 28 2023, means that the clock's time is not authoritative—not considered to be accurate. This disappears after manually setting the time or syncing to an NTP server.

2. Which command manually configures a Cisco device's clock?

A: `R1# clock set 12:45:00 January 19 2024`

The command to set the software clock is `clock set` *hh:mm:ss month day year*. Note that the *month* and *day* arguments can be reversed: `January 19` and `19 January` are both valid.

3. Which kind of NTP server operates as both an NTP client and server?

C: Secondary server

A secondary NTP server operates both as an NTP client (synchronizing its time with a more authoritative server) and as a server (providing the time to clients of its own).

4. Which of the following commands configures a Cisco device in NTP client/server mode?

B: `ntp server`

The `ntp server` *ip-address* command configures a Cisco device in NTP client/server mode. The device will become an NTP client of the server specified in the command. It will also function as an NTP server, capable of providing the time to clients of its own. This makes the device a secondary NTP server.

5. R1 is an NTP client. The output of `show ntp associations` on R1 shows `st: 3`. What does this output mean?

C: R1 learns the time from a server whose NTP stratum is 3.

The `show ntp associations` command lists the device's NTP associations—NTP servers that it learns the time from. The `st` column lists the association's NTP stratum. In this case, the value of 3 means that R1 learns the time from a server whose NTP stratum is 3.

6. Which command allows a Cisco device to function as an NTP server without being an NTP client?

A: `ntp master`

The `ntp master` command can be used to make the device function as an NTP server even if it isn't an NTP client of another server. This command can be useful in isolated environments where an external NTP server isn't available. It can also function as a backup; if the device loses connectivity to its NTP servers, it can still function as an NTP server and provide the time to its own clients.

7. Which commands are necessary to configure a Cisco IOS device as an NTP client, authenticating the server it learns the time from? (select three)

C: `ntp authentication-key 1 md5 P3sSw!rd`

D: `ntp trusted-key 1`

E: `ntp server 10.0.0.1 key 1`

The `ntp authentication-key` *key-number* `md5` *key* command is necessary to create an authentication key. Then, `ntp trusted-key` *key-number* is necessary to identify the key as "trusted". Finally, `ntp server` *ip-address* `key` *key-number* is necessary to specify that the key should be used to authenticate the specified server. The `ntp authentication` command is not necessary in this case, although some sources incorrectly state otherwise.

8. What is the default NTP stratum level of a Cisco router that has been configured with ntp master?

D: 8

When a Cisco router is configured with **ntp master** without specifying a stratum level, it defaults to stratum 8.

Chapter 3: Domain Name System

1. Which part of the URL "https://www.jeremysitlab.com/ccna-resources" is the authority?

B: www.jeremysitlab.com

In a URL, the authority specifies the domain name or IP address of the server where the resource is hosted. In this case, "www.jeremysitlab.com" is the authority.

2. What is the TLD of "mail.google.com."?

C: com

Domains that are immediately under the root (which is represented by ".") are called top-level domains (TLDs). In this URL, the TLD is "com". Other common TLDs include "net", "org", "edu", etc.

3. Which kind of DNS server holds the definitive set of records for a specific domain?

B: Authoritative DNS server

The DNS server that holds the definitive set of records for a specific domain is called an "authoritative DNS server".

4. Which kind of DNS query asks for a definite answer (the IP address or an error message)?

D: Recursive DNS

A recursive DNS query expects a definite answer from the DNS server. If the DNS server does not have the answer, it will query other DNS servers until it finds the answer, or reply with an error message if it can't.

5. A recursive resolver receives a query for a domain name that does not exist in its cache. What kind of DNS query does the recursive resolver send to the root server to resolve the domain name?

A: Iterative DNS

When a recursive resolver sends a query to a root server, it typically performs an iterative query. The root server responds with a referral to a TLD server, and the recursive resolver continues querying down the DNS hierarchy to find the answer.

6. Which of the following DNS record type descriptions are correct? (select three)

B: CNAME: Points to another domain name

C: PTR: Used for reverse DNS lookups

F: SOA: Provides administrative information such as admin contact

A CNAME record maps a domain name to another domain name. PTR records are used for reverse DNS lookups and map an IP address to a domain name. SOA records provide administrative information such as admin contact details, a serial number, etc. The others are incorrect: An A record points to an IPv4 address, an NS record specifies the domain's authoritative DNS server(s), and a AAAA record points to an IPv6 address.

7. Which command allows a Cisco IOS device to respond to DNS queries?

D: `ip dns server`

The `ip dns server` command enables a Cisco router to act as a DNS server, allowing it to respond to DNS queries.

8. Which configuration is needed on a Cisco router for it to forward DNS request packets between a PC and a DNS server?

D: No DNS configuration is needed.

For a Cisco router to forward DNS requests, no specific DNS configuration is needed. The router will simply forward these packets based on its routing table. The `ip dns server`, `ip domain-lookup`, and `ip name-server` commands are used for different DNS functionalities on the router itself, not for forwarding DNS requests.

Chapter 4: Dynamic Host Configuration Protocol

1. Which of the following DHCP messages are sent by a DHCP server? (select two)

A: ACK

D: OFFER

In the standard Dynamic Host Configuration Protocol (DHCP) DISCOVER, OFFER, REQUEST, ACK (DORA) exchange, the DISCOVER and REQUEST messages are sent by the client, and the OFFER and ACK messages are sent by the server.

2. When configuring a DHCP pool, which of the following DHCP settings is configured in global configuration mode?

B: The excluded address range(s)

When configuring a DHCP pool on a Cisco router, most settings are configured in DHCP configuration mode (accessed with `ip dhcp pool` *name*). However, any ranges of excluded addresses—addresses that should not be leased to clients—must be configured in global configuration mode with `ip dhcp excluded-address` *low-ip high-ip*.

3. Which of the following commands configures a Cisco router as a DHCP client?

A: R1(config-if)# `ip address dhcp`

To configure a Cisco router interface to obtain its IP address via DHCP, use the `ip address dhcp` command in interface configuration mode. The router will send DHCP DISCOVER messages out of the interface to attempt to lease an IP address.

4. Which command displays the list of clients that a Cisco router, functioning as a DHCP server, has leased addresses to using DHCP?

B: `show ip dhcp binding`

The `show ip dhcp binding` command displays the current address bindings and lease times for a Cisco router operating as a DHCP server.

5. R1's G0/1 interface is connected to the WAN and G0/2 is connected to a LAN with DHCP clients. Where should the `ip helper-address` command be configured to make R1 function as a DHCP relay agent?

B: Interface configuration mode for G0/2

To configure R1 as a DHCP relay agent, the **ip helper-address** *ip-address* command should be applied to the LAN-facing interface (G0/2). This command forwards clients' broadcast DHCP messages received on the interface to the DHCP server specified in the command.

6. Which command shows detailed information about a Windows host's network configuration?

D: **ipconfig /all**

The **ipconfig /all** command in Windows displays detailed information about the host's network configuration, including IP address, subnet mask, default gateway, DNS servers, and DHCP status.

7. Which command can be used to clear all of a router's DHCP bindings?

C: **clear ip dhcp binding ***

The **clear ip dhcp binding *** command is used to clear all dynamic DHCP bindings from a Cisco router's DHCP server database.

8. Which of the following DHCP messages are always broadcast? (select two)

B: REQUEST

C: DISCOVER

In the DHCP DORA exchange, messages sent by clients (DISCOVER and REQUEST) are always broadcast. Messages sent by the server can be either unicast or broadcast, depending on what the client indicates in its messages.

Chapter 5: Secure Shell

1. Which command, when applied to a console or VTY line, requires login with a local user account to access the line?

A: **login local**

The **login local** command on a console or VTY line configures the device to require users to log in with a username and password in the device's local user database.

2. Which command can be used to configure a Layer-2 switch's default gateway?

A: **ip default-gateway 10.0.0.1**

The **ip default-gateway** *ip-address* command is used to set the default gateway on a Layer-2 switch, which is necessary for the switch to communicate with devices outside of its local subnet (for example, when connecting to the switch remotely with SSH).

3. The output of **show ip ssh** states SSH Enabled - version 1.99. What does this output mean?

D: The device accepts SSHv1 and SSHv2 connections.

There are two versions of SSH: version 1 and version 2. "Version 1.99" isn't a separate version of SSH; instead, it means that the device accepts both SSH version 1 and version 2 connections.

4. Why is a domain name needed to generate an RSA key pair with the **crypto key generate rsa** command?

B: The domain name is used as part of the key pair's name.

A domain name is required for generating RSA key pairs because it is combined with the device hostname to name the key pair.

5. When generating RSA keys, what is the minimum modulus size required to support SSHv2?

B: 768 bits

The modulus of the RSA keys must be at least 768 bits in size to support SSHv2. Otherwise, only SSHv1 can be used. However, in newer software versions, SSH can't be used at all with modulus sizes smaller than 2048 bits.

6. Which of the following commands can be used to allow only SSH connections?

D: `R1(config-line)#` **`transport input ssh`**

The **`transport input ssh`** command, when applied to VTY lines (using **`line vty 0 15`**), specifies that only SSH connections are allowed to the device—no Telnet.

7. Which command can be used to apply an ACL to the VTY lines?

A: **`access-class 1 in`**

Use **`access-class`** `acl` **`in`** to apply an ACL to the VTY lines to control remote access to the device. This filters incoming connections, limiting which hosts can connect to the device.

8. In addition to a domain name, what configuration might be required to generate RSA keys with **`crypto key generate rsa`**?

C: A non-default hostname

In some devices, in addition to a domain name, a non-default hostname is also required to generate RSA keys with **`crypto key generate rsa`**.

Chapter 6: Simple Network Management Protocol

1. Which SNMP message type is an unacknowledged notification from a managed device to the NMS?

B: Trap

A Simple Network Management Protocol (SNMP) trap is an unacknowledged message sent from a managed device to a Network Management Station (NMS). Traps are used to notify the NMS of significant events or conditions on the managed device, but the NMS doesn't acknowledge them with Response messages.

2. Which SNMP message type allows the NMS to retrieve a large amount of information from a managed device without specifying each individual OID?

C: GetBulk

The GetBulk message type is used to retrieve large amounts of data from a managed device. It allows the NMS to request a range of OIDs in a single message, making it more efficient than specifying each OID individually.

3. Which message type triggers a Response message from the NMS?

B: Inform

An Inform message is similar to a Trap, but it requires an acknowledgment from the NMS. After receiving an Inform message, the NMS sends a Response message back to the managed device.

4. Which SNMP version(s) use community-string authentication? (select all that apply)

A: SNMPv1

C: SNMPv2c

SNMP versions 1 and 2c use community-string authentication; a community string is basically a password. SNMPv2 (no "c") is not widely implemented; it doesn't use community strings. SNMPv3 uses a more advanced user-based security model.

5. Which of the following statements are true? (select two)

B: The RW community string allows the NMS to send Get/GetNext/GetBulk and Set messages.

D: The RO community string allows the NMS to send Get/GetNext/GetBulk messages only.

The read-only (RO) community string only allows the NMS to read information from the managed device with Get, GetNext, and GetBulk; it can't modify the managed device with Set messages. The read-write (RW) community string, on the other hand, allows Get, GetNext, GetBulk, and Set messages.

6. Where does an SNMP managed device store OIDs?

C: The MIB

Object Identifiers (OIDs) in SNMP are stored in a database called the Management Information Base (MIB) of a managed device. Each OID is a variable containing a value, and SNMP works by interacting with these variables and their values.

7. Which of the following statements are true? (select two)

B: SNMP managers listen on UDP port 162.

C: SNMP agents listen on UDP port 161.

SNMP agents, running on managed devices, listen on UDP port 161 for incoming SNMP messages from the SNMP manager, running on the NMS. The SNMP manager listens on UDP port 162 for messages from the SNMP agents running on the devices it manages.

8. Which SNMP versions support a user-based security model? (select all that apply)

D: SNMPv3

SNMPv3 is the only version of SNMP that supports a user-based security model, which provides a more secure framework than the simple community-string authentication used in SNMPv1 and SNMPv2c.

Chapter 7: Syslog

1. Which command enables logging to an external Syslog server with the informational severity level and higher?

D: `logging trap 6`

The `logging trap` [*severity*] command can be used to control the severity level of messages logged to a Syslog server. "Informational" is severity level 6, so the `logging trap 6` command enables logging to an external Syslog server with the informational severity level and higher.

2. Which of the following Syslog severity level and IOS keyword pairs are correct? (select three)

A: `informational` = 6

F: `emergencies` = 0

G: `notifications` = 5

Here are the Syslog severity levels in order:

- `emergencies` = 0
- `alerts` = 1
- `critical` = 2
- `errors` = 3
- `warnings` = 4
- `notifications` = 5
- `informational` = 6
- `debugging` = 7

3. Which command is necessary to enable real-time logging to the VTY lines for the current session?

B: R1# `terminal monitor`

The command `terminal monitor` is used in the command-line interface to enable real-time logging to the VTY lines for the current session. Although the `logging monitor` command enables/disables logging to the VTY lines, `terminal monitor` must be used to enable it for the current session.

4. Which of the following statements accurately describes the effect of the `logging buffered notifications` command?

B: Logs of severity level 5 and numerically lower will be logged.

`logging buffered notifications` enables logging at severity level 5. However, it doesn't only enable logging of messages of severity level 5; it enables logging of all messages with a severity level of 5 and numerically lower (more severe). So, the command enables logging of messages of severity levels 0–5.

5. What is the facility of the Syslog message `Jan 20 08:05:52: %LINK-3-UPDOWN: Interface GigabitEthernet0/2, changed state to up`?

A: `LINK`

The format of a Syslog message is `seq:timestamp: %facility-severity-mnemonic: description`. In this case, `LINK` in the facility, indicating the service, application, or other component of the device that generated the message.

6. What is the mnemonic of the Syslog message `Jan 20 08:36:29: %SYS-5 -CONFIG_I: Configured from console by jeremy on vty3 (192.168.1.224)`?

C: `CONFIG_I`

`CONFIG_I` is the mnemonic of this Syslog message, a short text string providing a brief description of the event that triggered the Syslog message. In this case, we know it is something related to the configuration of the device.

7. Which command specifies an external Syslog server to send log messages to?

D: `logging host 10.0.0.10`

Although the `logging trap` command is used to enable/disable logging to external Syslog servers, the `logging host` *ip-address* command is used to specify a Syslog server to send log messages to.

8. Which severity levels will be logged to the console line as a result of the `logging console 2` command? (select three)

A: Alerts

D: Emergencies

F: Critical

The `logging console 2` command configures the console to log messages with a severity of critical (level 2) and numerically lower, which includes alerts (level 1) and emergencies (level 0).

Chapter 8: Trivial File Transfer Protocol and File Transfer Protocol

1. Why does TFTP use UDP, not TCP?

C: TFTP provides its own reliability and doesn't need TCP's overhead.

Although file transfer protocols typically use TCP to provide reliable delivery of messages, the TFTP protocol itself uses lock-step communication to provide its own reliability. For that reason, it can use the lightweight UDP as its Layer-4 protocol instead of TCP.

2. Which type of IOS file system is used to represent external FTP/TFTP servers?

D: Network

Cisco IOS uses the `ftp:` and `tftp:` file systems to represent external FTP/TFTP servers. Both file systems use the "network" file system type.

3. Which of the following is a characteristic of TFTP?

B: Clients can only issue read or write requests

Unlike FTP, which provides more robust capabilities, TFTP is a simple protocol that only allows clients to send read requests (to download a file) and write requests (to upload a file) to the server.

4. Which command can be used to transfer a file from the local device to an external FTP server?

B: `copy flash: ftp:`

The IOS command to transfer files is `copy` *source destination*. To transfer a file from the local device to an external FTP server, the *source* should be a file or directory on the local system (i.e. **flash:**) and the *destination* should be **ftp:**.

5. Which of the following are characteristics of FTP? (select two)

B: Establishes two connections between the client and server

C: Uses TCP ports 20 and 21

FTP establishes two connections between the client and server. The first is the control connection (TCP port 21), through which the server authenticates the client and the client sends commands to the server. The second is the data connection (TCP port 20), through which file transfers occur. With a single control connection, the client can establish multiple data connections with the server.

6. Which command can be used to specify which IOS file will be loaded upon the next system reboot?

B: R1(config)# **boot system**

The **boot system** *file-path* command, used in global configuration mode, is used to specify the IOS file that the device should load upon the next reboot.

7. Which commands configure the default FTP user credentials? (select two)

B: **ip ftp username jeremy**

C: **ip ftp password password123**

The commands **ip ftp username** *username* and **ip ftp password** *password* are used to configure the default username and password for FTP connections initiated from the device.

8. Which connection does an FTP client use to send commands to the server?

A: The control connection

The client uses the FTP control connection to send commands to the server. One example is RETR (retrieve), which is used to download a copy of a file from the server.

Chapter 9: Network Address Translation

1. Which of the following NAT types provide one-to-one translations only?

D: Static NAT and dynamic NAT

Static NAT provides a permanent one-to-one translation between an inside local address and an inside global address. Dynamic NAT also provides one-to-one translations but assigns inside global addresses dynamically from a pool.

2. Which Cisco NAT term describes the IP address of a host in the internal network from the perspective of hosts in the external network?

B: Inside global

In Cisco NAT terminology, an inside global address is an IP address assigned to a host on the internal network, as seen from the external network. This address is usually a public IP address.

3. In a typical inside source NAT scenario, which of the following addresses is usually a private address?

D: Inside local

In a standard inside source NAT setup, the inside local address is usually a private IP address. This address is not routable on the internet and needs to be translated to a public (inside global) address for communication over the internet.

4. R1 must use NAT to allow hosts in its connected LAN to communicate over the internet. Which of the following commands should be used to enable this? (select two)

A: **ip nat inside** on the LAN-facing interface

B: **ip nat outside** on the Internet-facing interface

To enable NAT, use **ip nat inside** on the LAN-facing interface(s) and **ip nat outside** on the internet-facing interface(s). These commands define the interfaces' roles in the NAT process.

5. Which of the following NAT types provides many-to-one translations?

B: Dynamic PAT

Dynamic PAT, also known as NAT overload, maps multiple private IP addresses to a single public IP address, using unique port numbers to keep track of each session.

6. In a typical inside source NAT scenario, which of the following addresses should be identical in the output of **show ip nat translations**? (select two)

C: Outside local

D: Outside global

When performing inside NAT, only inside addresses are translated (inside local to inside global); the outside local and outside global addresses should be identical in the output of **show ip nat translations**.

7. Which of the following commands creates a pool for dynamic PAT?

C: **ip nat pool POOL1 203.0.113.1 203.0.113.10 prefix-length 28**

The command to create a NAT pool is **ip nat pool** *name start-ip end-ip* {**prefix -length** *length* | **netmask** *netmask*}. Options A, C, and D use correct syntax, but options A and D specify a /29 prefix length (netmask 255.255.255.248). This only encompasses the range from 203.0.113.0 to 203.0.113.7, meaning that the commands will fail; the prefix length must be sufficient to encompass all of the addresses included in the *start-ip* to *end-ip* range.

8. ACL 1 only permits packets sourced from the 10.0.0.0/24 subnet. After issuing the **ip nat inside source list 1 gigabitethernet0/0** command on R1, what action will it take on packets denied by ACL 1?

A: It will forward them without translation.

In the context of NAT, an ACL is used to determine which packets are eligible for NAT; it isn't used to decide which packets will be forwarded or discarded. Packets denied by the ACL are not translated, but will be forwarded as normal according to the router's routing table. However, this will likely result in those untranslated packets being discarded by the ISP's router due to their private addresses.

9. Which of the following commands configures dynamic PAT?

A: **ip nat inside source list 1 pool POOL1 overload**

This command configures dynamic PAT using the specified access list and pool, with the **overload** keyword enabling multiple inside local addresses to share one inside global address.

10. When PAT is configured, what happens when two pre-translation messages use the same source port number?

C: The second packet's port number is translated to a new number.

In PAT, if two packets have the same source port, NAT will assign a unique port number for the second packet. The inside global IP address of each packet will be identical after translation, so a unique source port number is needed for identification.

Chapter 10: Quality of service

1. What does traffic shaping do?

A: Buffer traffic that exceeds the configured rate limit

Traffic shaping buffers excess traffic to conform to a configured rate limit, smoothing out the rate at which packets are sent.

2. Which of the following often leads to TCP global synchronization?

C: Tail drop

Tail drop, which occurs when packets are dropped from the end of a full queue, can lead to TCP global synchronization, where multiple TCP flows reduce their window sizes simultaneously, leading to network underutilization. This can lead to a global TCP window size increase, leading to congestion and tail drop again—a vicious cycle. Random Early Detection (RED) and Weighted RED (WRED) are techniques to avoid tail drop, not causes of it.

3. Which QoS feature modifies specific fields in the Layer-2 and Layer-3 headers to facilitate the categorization of messages?

C: Marking

Marking modifies fields in Layer-2 (CoS) and Layer-3 (DSCP) headers, making the classification of messages for QoS much simpler.

4. Which feature would an ISP's customer likely implement to avoid exceeding the ISP's rate limit?

D: Shaping

Traffic shaping is often used to control traffic rates to comply with ISP-imposed rate limits, buffering and delaying excess traffic. The ISP, on the other hand, often uses policing to strictly enforce the configured rate limit.

5. Which QoS feature involves identifying the traffic type of a particular packet?

B: Classification

Classification identifies the traffic type of a packet based on defined criteria, such as the marking in the DSCP field of the IP header.

6. Which of the following markings indicates a high priority and a high drop precedence?

D: AF43

AF43 (Assured Forwarding class 4, drop precedence 3) indicates high priority but also a high likelihood of being dropped in times of congestion. AF defines four priority classes (1–4) and three drop precedence values (1–3).

7. Which QoS feature drops or re-marks traffic that exceeds the configured rate limit?

A: Policing

Policing drops or re-marks traffic that exceeds a configured rate limit, enforcing a strict bandwidth limit without buffering.

8. Which scheduling method combines a priority queue with a weighted round-robin scheduler?

D: LLQ

Low Latency Queuing (LLQ) combines a strict Priority Queue (PQ) for high-priority traffic with Class-Based Weighted Fair Queuing (CBWFQ) for other traffic classes, using a weighted round-robin scheduler.

9. Which marking is typically used for voice call traffic?

A: EF

The Expedited Forwarding (EF) marking is typically used for voice traffic to ensure low delay, jitter, and loss by treating these packets with high priority. When using LLQ, packets marked with EF are typically queued in the priority queue.

10. Which marking is typically used for best effort traffic?

B: DF

Default Forwarding (DF) is the default marking for best effort traffic, indicating no special treatment or priority.

11. Which concept refers to the variation in delay?

B: Jitter

Jitter refers to the variation in delay between packets, which can negatively affect user experience in real-time apps like voice and video calls.

12. Which command guarantees power to a PoE-enabled device connected to the port?

B: `power inline static`

The `power inline static` command reserved a fixed amount of power for the specified port, ensuring the device connected to the port receives power.

Chapter 11: Security concepts

1. Which element of the CIA triad aims to protect systems and data from unauthorized access?

A: C

The "C" in the CIA triad stands for "Confidentiality", which aims to protect systems and data from unauthorized access, ensuring that sensitive information is only accessible by authorized entities. The "I" stands for "Integrity", and the "A" stands for "Availability".

2. A malicious user who intends to harm the security of an organization's systems is an example of what?

A: Threat

A malicious user intent on harming an organization's systems is an example of a threat—the real possibility of a vulnerability to be exploited.

3. A DHCP exhaustion attack is an example of which attack types? (select two)

A: Spoofing

B: DoS

A DHCP exhaustion attack involves spoofing DHCP requests to exhaust the IP address pool of a DHCP server, leading to a Denial of Service (DoS) for legitimate users who cannot obtain IP addresses.

4. Which of the following are examples of social engineering? (select three)

B: Whaling

D: Phishing

E: Tailgating

Phishing involves tricking users into revealing sensitive information, and whaling is phishing targeted at high-profile individuals (i.e. a CEO). Tailgating is the act of following someone into a secured area. These are all forms of social engineering, which manipulates people into breaking normal security procedures.

5. Which of the following are examples of physical access control? (select two)

A: MFA door locks

D: Security cameras

Multi-factor authentication (MFA) door locks and security cameras are examples of physical access controls. They are used to secure physical premises by controlling entry and monitoring physical activities.

6. Which of the following are common advantages of using a password manager? (select three)

B: Stronger passwords

C: Auto-fill

D: Encrypted storage

Password managers allow users to generate and store long, complex, and unique passwords for each account without having to remember each one, encouraging stronger passwords. The ability to automatically fill in usernames/passwords can protect against keylogger malware. Furthermore, password managers encrypt stored passwords, protecting the passwords even if the device is compromised.

7. Which of the following commands configures an enable secret using type-9 hashing?

A: **enable algorithm-type scrypt secret AcingTheCCNAExam!**

The command to configure an enable secret with a specific hashing algorithm is **enable algorithm-type** *algorithm* **secret** *secret*. The **scrypt** algorithm (Cisco's recommendation), is type 9.

8. Which of the following is an example of MFA?

C: Scanning a badge and entering a PIN

MFA involves verifying a user's identity via at least two "factors": knowledge (something you know), possession (something you have), and inherence (something you are). A badge is an example of something you have, and a PIN is an example of something you know.

9. Which of the following provides PNAC?

C: 802.1X

802.1X is a security protocol that provides port-based network access control (PNAC), ensuring that only authenticated devices can access network resources.

10. Which AAA element consists of granting a user or device appropriate access?

C: Authorization

AAA stands for Authentication, Authorization, and Accounting. Authentication is the process of verifying identity, authorization is the process of granting appropriate access, and accounting is the process of keeping track of activities.

11. Which AAA protocol combines authentication and authorization into a single operation?

B: RADIUS

Remote Authentication Dial-In User Service (RADIUS) is an AAA protocol that combines authentication and authorization into a single operation, unlike Terminal Access Controller Access-Control System Plus (TACACS+), which keeps all three AAA components separate.

12. Which of the following is an example of stateless packet filtering?

B: An ACL applied to a router interface

Stateless packet filtering, such as an ACL applied to a router interface, filters packets on a per-packet basis without considering other context such as the packet's relation to other packets.

13. Which component of 802.1X is the network device that the client connects to?

D: Authenticator

802.1X defines three roles: the supplicant (the client device that wants to connect to the network), the authenticator (the network device that the supplicant connects to), and the authentication server (the server that verifies the supplicant's credentials).

Chapter 12: Port Security

1. After configuring `switchport port-security` on a port, how many MAC addresses can be learned on the port by default?

B: 1

By default, when port security is enabled, a switch port is allowed to learn only one MAC address. If a frame from another MAC address arrives on the port, a Port Security violation is triggered.

2. You issue `switchport port-security` on a port and receive the following error message: `Command rejected: FastEthernet0/1 is a dynamic port`. What is the cause for this error?

C: The port's operational mode is determined by DTP.

To enable Port Security on a port, you must manually configure it as an access or trunk port with `switchport mode {access | trunk}`. If the switch's mode is `dynamic auto` or `dynamic desirable` (meaning it uses DTP to determine its operational mode), the `switchport port-security` command will be rejected.

3. Which of the following actions does a switch take by default when a Port Security violation occurs? (select three)

A: Discard the violating frames

B: Increment the violation counter

E: Error-disable the port

The default Port Security violation mode is "shutdown". This means that, if a Port Security violation occurs on a port, the switch will discard violating frames, increment the violation counter, and error-disable the port—effectively shutting it down.

4. Which of the following is a difference between secure MAC addresses and regular MAC addresses in a switch's MAC address table?

C: Dynamic secure MAC addresses don't age out by default.

One key difference between secure MAC addresses and regular MAC addresses in a switch's MAC address table is that dynamic secure MAC addresses configured for Port Security do not age out by default, while regular dynamic MAC addresses do age out after a certain period of inactivity.

5. Which command can be used to automatically re-enable a port disabled by Port Security?

D: `errdisable recovery cause psecure-violation`

The command to enable ErrDisable Recovery is `errdisable recovery cause` *cause*, and the keyword to enable it for ports disabled by Port Security is `psecure-violation`.

6. Which of the following commands causes dynamic secure MAC addresses to be saved in the device's running-config?

C: SW1(config-if)# `switchport port-security mac-address sticky`

The `switchport port-security mac-address sticky` command in interface config mode enables the sticky learning feature, which saves dynamically-learned secure MAC addresses in the device's running-config.

7. Which of the following MAC addresses will be removed from the MAC address table if the corresponding port goes down? (select all that apply)

B: Dynamic secure MAC addresses

D: Dynamic MAC addresses

Both dynamic secure MAC addresses and regular dynamic MAC addresses are removed from the MAC address table when the corresponding port goes down. Sticky and static secure MAC addresses are not removed.

8. Which of the following commands configure a port to block frames from invalid MAC addresses without affecting valid traffic? (select two)

B: `switchport port-security violation protect`

C: `switchport port-security violation restrict`

The protect and restrict modes both drop packets with invalid source MAC addresses but continue to forward traffic from known MAC addresses.

Chapter 13: DHCP Snooping

1. Which DHCP messages are always discarded when received on a DHCP Snooping untrusted port?

C: ACK, OFFER

DHCP Snooping always discards DHCP server messages received on untrusted ports. In the DHCP DORA (DISCOVER, OFFER, REQUEST, ACK) exchange, the OFFER and ACK messages are sent by the server, and will always be discarded if received on a DHCP Snooping untrusted port.

2. Which table is used by DHCP Snooping to inspect client DHCP RELEASE and DECLINE messages?

C: The DHCP Snooping binding table

The DHCP Snooping binding table holds information about successful DHCP leases that were observed by the DHCP Snooping-enabled switch. This table is then used to inspect and validate DHCP RELEASE and DECLINE messages received on untrusted ports.

3. Which command disables option 82 insertion on untrusted ports?

B: `no ip dhcp snooping information option`

The `no ip dhcp snooping information option` command disables the insertion of DHCP option 82 into messages received on untrusted ports. This is often necessary when configuring DHCP Snooping to allow clients to successfully lease addresses.

4. Which of the following statements is true?

D: DHCP Snooping must be enabled globally and per-VLAN.

Enabling DHCP Snooping requires two commands: `ip dhcp snooping` to enable it globally, and then `ip dhcp snooping vlan` *vlans* to enable it on each VLAN. Without both commands, DHCP Snooping won't function on the switch.

5. How does DHCP Snooping treat a DHCP message received on a trusted port?

A: It allows the message.

DHCP Snooping allows all DHCP messages received on trusted ports; it only inspects messages received on untrusted ports.

6. Which of the following messages are sent by DHCP clients? (select four)

B: REQUEST

E: RELEASE

F: DISCOVER

G: DECLINE

In addition to the DISCOVER and REQUEST messages sent in the DORA exchange, DHCP clients can also send RELEASE and DECLINE messages. OFFER, ACK, and NAK are server messages.

7. What does DHCP Snooping provide in addition to DHCP message inspection?

B: Rate-limiting of DHCP messages

DHCP Snooping provides rate-limiting of DHCP messages to prevent DHCP starvation attacks. It can be enabled on a per-port basis with `ip dhcp snooping limit rate` *pps*.

8. Which two fields does DHCP Snooping inspect in client DISCOVER and REQUEST messages?

A: Source MAC and chaddr

DISCOVER and REQUEST messages are sent before the client has successfully leased an IP address, so the client doesn't have an entry in the DHCP Snooping binding table yet. To inspect and validate these messages, the switch ensures that the Ethernet source MAC address and the "chaddr" (client hardware address) field of the DHCP message match.

Chapter 14: Dynamic Address Resolution Protocol Inspection

1. Which table does DAI use to inspect messages received on untrusted ports?

C: The DHCP Snooping binding table

DAI uses the DHCP Snooping binding table to validate ARP messages received on untrusted ports. This table contains mappings of IP addresses to MAC addresses that DAI refers to when validating ARP messages.

2. How does DAI treat ARP messages received on trusted ports?

A: It allows them.

ARP messages received on trusted ports are allowed without inspection in DAI; this is similar to DHCP Snooping's behavior.

3. Which of the following statements about DAI is false?

A: DAI must be enabled globally and per-VLAN.

Unlike DHCP Snooping, there is no separate command to globally enable DAI. It only needs to be enabled per-vlan with `ip arp inspection vlan` `vlans`.

4. What kind of ARP reply is sent without receiving an ARP request?

C: Gratuitous ARP

Gratuitous ARP (GARP) is an ARP reply sent without a preceding request. Although there are many legitimate uses for GARP, it can also be used in ARP poisoning attacks.

5. Which of the following commands are necessary for a basic DAI configuration? (select two)

B: `ip arp inspection vlan 10`

C: `ip arp inspection trust`

Basic DAI configuration requires you to enable DAI on each VLAN with `ip arp inspection vlan` `vlans`, and then trust the necessary ports with `ip arp inspection trust`.

6. What is the default DAI rate limit on trusted ports?

D: Unlimited

Although DAI limits ARP messages on untrusted ports to 15 pps (packets per second) by default, trusted ports do not have a default rate limit.

7. Which command enables automatic recovery of ports disabled by DAI rate-limiting?

A: `errdisable recovery cause arp-inspection`

The `errdisable recovery cause arp-inspection` command enables ErrDisable Recovery for ports disabled by DAI rate-limiting, allowing them to automatically recover without manual intervention.

8. Which command causes the switch to inspect ARP messages for suspicious IP addresses?

C: `ip arp inspection validate ip`

Use the `ip arp inspection validate` `checks` command to enable optional DAI checks. The `ip` keyword makes the switch check for suspicious IP addresses in the ARP Sender IP or Target IP fields. The other options are `src-mac` and `dst-mac`.

Chapter 15: LAN architectures

1. Which layer of a three-tier LAN is most likely to implement security services such as Port Security, DHCP Snooping, and DAI?

A: Access

The access layer in a three-tier LAN is usually responsible for implementing security services like Port Security, DHCP Snooping, and Dynamic ARP Inspection (DAI). This layer directly interacts with end-user devices, making it a critical point for enforcing security policies.

2. Which layers are combined in a two-tier LAN? (select two)

B: Distribution

C: Core

In a two-tier (collapsed core) LAN architecture, the distribution and core layers are collapsed into a single layer. This simplifies the architecture and is commonly used in smaller LANs where a separate core layer is not necessary.

3. In a three-tier LAN, where is the border between Layers 2 and 3 usually located?
B: Distribution
In a three-tier LAN, the distribution layer usually serves as the border between Layers 2 and 3 of the TCP/IP Model. End hosts use SVIs on the distribution switches as their default gateways, and the distribution switches use a routing protocol like OSPF to share routing information with each other and the core switches.

4. In a three-tier LAN, which switches are most likely to support PoE?
A: Access switches
The access layer is where end hosts that might require Power over Ethernet (PoE), such as IP phones and wireless access points, connect to the network. Therefore, access switches are most likely to support PoE.

5. In a three-tier LAN, which layer is focused on speed and reliability, avoiding CPU-intensive operations?
C: Core
The Core layer in a three-tier LAN is focused on providing fast and reliable transport of packets across the LAN. Core switches typically don't implement CPU-intensive operations like security features and QoS marking that would slow down the forwarding of packets.

6. In a three-tier LAN, where is QoS marking most often performed?
A: Access
QoS marking should generally be performed close to a packet's source, simplifying the classification process for the rest of the packet's journey. The access layer is where end hosts connect to the network, so marking is often performed at this layer.

7. Which of the following statements about spine-leaf architecture is true?
B: Every leaf switch is connected to every spine switch.
In a spine-leaf architecture, every leaf switch connects to every spine switch, but leaf switches don't connect to other leaf switches, and spine switches don't connect to other spine switches. End hosts—typically servers—connect to leaf switches, not spine switches.

8. Which of the following are benefits of spine-leaf architecture? (select two)
A: Consistent and predictable latency between servers
C: Simple scalability by adding more leaf switches
Different servers in a spine-leaf architecture are a consistent number of hops away from each other, providing consistent and predictable latency between servers. Scaling a spine-leaf LAN is simple: just add more leaf switches and connect each new leaf switch to each spine switch.

9. Which type of network is most likely to benefit from spine-leaf architecture?
C: Data center LANs
Data center LANs are most likely to benefit from spine-leaf architecture due to its high scalability, predictable latency, and efficient handling of the east-west traffic that is common in modern data centers.

10. Which of the following statements about SOHO networks is true?

D: SOHO networks' needs are often met by a single wireless router.

Small Office/Home Office (SOHO) networks are typically simple, and their networking needs can often be met with a single wireless router that combines several functions such as routing, switching, stateful packet filtering, and wireless access.

Chapter 16: WAN architectures

1. In which type of MPLS VPN do CE routers form neighbor relationships directly with other CE routers (i.e. with OSPF)?

A: L2VPN

In a Multiprotocol Label Switching (MPLS) Layer-2 VPN (L2VPN), CE (customer edge) routers form neighbor relationships directly with each other. The service provider's WAN network is transparent to the CE routers, functioning like a giant switch.

2. In which type of MPLS VPN do CE routers form neighbor relationships with PE routers?

B: L3VPN

In an MPLS Layer-3 VPN (L3VPN), CE routers form neighbor relationships with provider edge (PE) routers. Unlike in MPLS L2VPNs, the PE routers actively participate in the customer's routing domain.

3. In an MPLS WAN, which of the following routers run MPLS? (select all that apply)

A: P

B: PE

In an MPLS WAN, only the service provider's routers run MPLS: the P and PE routers. The CE routers connect to the PE routers, but don't run MPLS themselves.

4. Where is the MPLS label inserted into a message?

B: Between the Ethernet and IP headers

The MPLS label is inserted between the Ethernet and IP headers. For this reason, MPLS is sometimes called a "Layer 2.5" protocol.

5. Which technology facilitates a full mesh of IPsec VPN tunnels with minimal manual configuration?

D: DMVPN

DMVPN allows the creation of a dynamic full mesh of IPsec VPN tunnels with minimal manual configuration, simplifying the VPN setup for networks with many sites.

6. Which type of VPN establishes a tunnel between an end host and a corporate firewall or router?

C: Remote-access VPN

A remote-access VPN establishes a secure tunnel between an end host (like a remote employee's device) and a corporate firewall or router, allowing secure access to internal network resources.

7. Which of the following protocols is most often used for site-to-site VPNs?

A: IPsec

IPsec is commonly used for site-to-site VPNs, providing secure tunnels between routers or firewalls at the edge of their respective LANs.

8. Which VPN technology is often used for its combination of broadcast/multicast support and security?

C: GRE over IPsec

Generic Routing Encapsulation (GRE) over IPsec is used for its ability to encapsulate a variety of network layer protocols and support broadcast/multicast traffic while providing the security of IPsec.

9. Which of the following statements accurately describes tunneling?

A: Tunneling is the process of encapsulating a packet inside of another packet, creating a virtual pathway for the internal packet.

Tunneling involves encapsulating one packet within another to create a virtual pathway through a network. Tunnels are not necessarily encrypted (for example, GRE is unencrypted), but encryption is often used to create a secure VPN tunnel over a shared network.

10. Which internet connection design offers one connection to each of two or more ISPs?

B: Multi-homed

Single-homed offers one connection to one ISP. Dual-homed offers two connections to one ISP. Multi-homed offers one connection to each of two (or more) ISPs. Dual multi-homed offers two connections to each of two (or more) ISPs.

Chapter 17: Virtualization and cloud

1. Which of the following virtualization technologies is installed directly on server hardware?

A: Type 1 hypervisor

A type 1 hypervisor is installed directly on server hardware, interacting directly with the physical hardware. Examples include VMware ESXi and Microsoft Hyper-V. Type 2 Hypervisors run on a host OS and are less efficient, suitable for testing or development. Containers offer OS-level virtualization, sharing the host's kernel, but are not installed on server hardware directly.

2. Which of the following statements about type-2 hypervisors is true?

C: The hypervisor is installed on a host OS.

A type-2 hypervisor runs on a host operating system rather than directly on the hardware. This makes it less efficient compared to a type-1 hypervisor, as it needs to go through the host OS to access hardware resources.

3. Which of the following statements about VRF is true?

B: VRF creates multiple routing tables on a router.

Virtual Routing and Forwarding (VRF) allows a router to create multiple routing tables. In effect, this divides the router into multiple virtual routers, with each virtual router isolated from the others.

4. Which of the following cloud service models provides the most control to the customer?

C: IaaS

The infrastructure as a service (IaaS) model provides the most control to the customer. The cloud service provider offers the underlying infrastructure, on top of which customers can install virtual machines (VMs), install OSs, run applications, etc, customizing the CPU, RAM, and storage for each VM and configuring their interconnections to form a network.

5. Which cloud service model offers a complete software product to the customer?

B: SaaS

Software as a Service (SaaS) offers a complete software product to customers over the Internet. The software is hosted on cloud infrastructure, and users can typically access it through a web browser. Common examples are Microsoft 365 and Google Workspace.

6. AWS, Azure, and GCP are examples of what cloud deployment model?

C: Public cloud

Amazon Web Services (AWS), Microsoft Azure, and Google Cloud Platform (GCP) are examples of public cloud providers. They offer cloud resources over the internet, available for open use by the public (for a fee).

7. Which of the following are advantages of cloud computing? (select two)

A: Reduced CapEx

D: Simplified global scaling

Cloud computing offers reduced capital expenditure (CapEx)—upfront costs—as it minimizes the need for physical hardware investments. Additionally, cloud computing simplifies global scaling, allowing businesses to quickly expand their computing resources over the globe as needed.

8. In the context of cloud computing, what is rapid elasticity?

C: The ability to flexibly scale infrastructure according to need

Rapid elasticity is a key feature of cloud computing, enabling businesses to quickly scale their IT resources up or down based on their current requirements.

9. In which model do customers rent space, cooling, electricity, etc, in a shared data center?

C: Colocation

In colocation services, customers rent space, cooling, electricity, and other data center resources in a shared facility. They typically own the hardware and are responsible for managing their equipment within the data center.

10. Which of the following virtualization technologies is more lightweight, using fewer hardware resources?

A: A container

Containers are more lightweight and use fewer hardware resources compared to Virtual Machines (VMs). They share the host system's kernel and do not require a full operating system for each instance, which significantly reduces their overhead.

Chapter 18: Wireless LAN fundamentals

1. Which term refers to the phenomenon of an electromagnetic wave bending when it passes from one medium to another one with a different density?

B: Refraction

Refraction is the bending of an electromagnetic wave as it passes from one medium into another with a different density. This can affect wireless signals as they pass through various materials.

2. Which term refers to the erratic spreading out of an electromagnetic wave as the result of encountering a surface or medium with irregularities?

D: Scattering

Scattering occurs when an electromagnetic wave encounters a surface or medium with irregularities, causing the wave to spread out erratically. This can lead to signal degradation in wireless networks.

3. Which kind of service set consists of multiple APs' coverage areas, integrated into a coherent whole offering connectivity for clients?

D: ESS

An extended service set (ESS) consists of multiple access points (APs) with overlapping coverage areas, integrated into a single network to provide continuous connectivity for clients as they move across different APs' coverage areas.

4. Which frequency bands used by 802.11 wireless LANs offer many non-overlapping channels? (select two)

B: 5 GHz

C: 6 GHz

The 5 GHz and 6 GHz frequency bands used by 802.11 wireless LANs offer many non-overlapping channels, simplifying the channel selection process compared to the 2.4 GHz band. These channels can be combined to create wider channels, enabling greater data transfer rates.

5. Which 2.4 GHz channel pattern is generally recommended to avoid interference between adjacent APs?

B: 1-6-11

In the 2.4 GHz band, the 1-6-11 channel pattern is generally recommended as it uses three non-overlapping channels, reducing interference between adjacent APs. However, most countries outside of the US and Canada can use other patterns as well, such as 1-5-9-13.

6. Which of the following uniquely identifies each AP in an ESS?

B: BSSID

Each AP in an ESS is uniquely identified by its basic service set identifier (BSSID), which is the AP's MAC address.

7. Which of the following 802.11 standards offer many non-overlapping channels? (select two)

B: 802.11a

C: 802.11ac

802.11a and 802.11ac operate exclusively in the 5 GHz band, which offers many non-overlapping channels.

8. Which of the following identifiers is the MAC address of the AP's radio?

B: BSSID

The BSSID is the MAC address of the AP's radio and is used to uniquely identify the AP in a wireless network.

9. Which of the following AP modes functions as a wireless client on behalf of a device without wireless capabilities?

C: Workgroup bridge

An AP in workgroup bridge mode functions as a wireless client for devices without wireless capabilities, allowing those wired devices to connect to the wireless network.

10. Which 802.11 standards support both the 2.4 GHz and 5 GHz bands? (select three)

A: 802.11be

D: 802.11n

F: 802.11ax

802.11be (Wi-Fi 7), 802.11n (Wi-Fi 4), and 802.11ax (Wi-Fi 6) are standards that support operations in both the 2.4 GHz and 5 GHz frequency bands. Furthermore, 802.11ax and 802.11be also support the 6 GHz range.

11. What is the term for a wireless LAN's non-unique, human-readable name?

B: SSID

The service set identifier (SSID) is the human-readable name of a wireless LAN. It is broadcast by APs and used by clients to identify and connect to the network. However, unlike each AP's BSSID, SSIDs don't have to be unique.

12. Which type of AP in an MBSS connects to the DS?

A: RAP

In a mesh basic service set (MBSS), root access points (RAPs) are the APs that connect directly to the distribution system (DS)—the wired network.

Chapter 19: Wireless LAN architectures

1. When a wireless client sends a frame to another client associated with the same AP, what is the RA of the frame when the client transmits it?

C: The AP's MAC

When a wireless client sends a frame to another client associated with the same AP, the receiver address (RA) is set to the AP's MAC address when the client transmits the frame. The AP then forwards the frame to the destination client.

2. Which of the following messages are used in passive scanning?

A: Beacon messages

In passive scanning, a wireless client listens for beacon messages broadcasted by APs. These beacon messages contain information about the network, such as the SSID and supported data rates.

3. Which of the following are not 802.11 management messages?

A: CTS/RTS

Clear to Send (CTS) and Request to Send (RTS) are 802.11 control messages, not management messages. Management messages include Probe request/response, Authentication request/response, and Association request/response.

4. Which kind of AP is managed by a WLC?

C: Lightweight AP

A lightweight access point (LWAP) is managed by a wireless LAN controller (WLC). The LWAP relies on the WLC for management functions, configuration, and control.

5. Which of the following APs typically connects to the DS via an access link?

C: LWAP in local mode

An LWAP in local mode typically connects to the DS via an access link. Because all data traffic is tunneled to the WLC using Control and Provisioning of Wireless Access Points (CAPWAP), the LWAP's connection to the distribution system (DS) typically only needs to support the management VLAN.

6. Which LWAP mode captures 802.11 frames for analysis in Wireshark?

B: Sniffer

In Sniffer mode, an LWAP captures 802.11 frames, which can be exported and analyzed using tools like Wireshark.

7. When FlexConnect local switching is enabled for a WLAN, which device is responsible for switching traffic between the 802.11 and Ethernet networks?

A: The LWAP

When FlexConnect local switching is enabled, the LWAP is responsible for switching traffic between the 802.11 wireless and Ethernet wired networks; it doesn't tunnel data traffic to the WLC.

8. Which LWAP mode is dedicated to analyzing traffic on the wired LAN?

D: Rogue detector

In Rogue Detector mode, the LWAP is dedicated to analyzing traffic on the wired LAN to detect rogue devices connected to the network. The LWAP's radios are disabled.

9. In Cisco Meraki's cloud-based AP solution, which traffic is tunneled to the Meraki cloud?

A: Management traffic

In Cisco Meraki's cloud-based AP solution, management traffic is tunneled to the Meraki cloud. This includes configuration and monitoring data, while user data traffic is handled locally on the AP.

10. Which WLC deployment option uses a dedicated hardware appliance?

D: Unified

A unified WLC is a dedicated hardware appliance. Various hardware models are available, supporting anywhere from a few hundred LWAPs to as many as 6000.

11. Which of the following functions are centrally controlled in a split-MAC architecture? (select two)

A: Client authentication and association

B: RF management

In a split-MAC architecture, functions like client authentication, association, and RF management are centrally controlled by the WLC. This central control allows for consistent policy enforcement and network management. The LWAPs handle real-time operations like transmitting and receiving RF signals.

12. Which statement about CAPWAP is true?

A: The CAPWAP control tunnel is encrypted by default.

Only the CAPWAP control tunnel is encrypted by default. The data tunnel, however, is not encrypted by default; it must be enabled separately. CAPWAP encryption uses Datagram Transport Layer Security (DTLS)—a type of TLS that uses UDP instead of TCP.

13. Which of the following is not a benefit of cloud-based network management?

B. Highly customizable to meet complex networking requirements

While cloud-based network management provides a variety of benefits such as rapid deployment with zero-touch provisioning (ZTP), simplified management via a web-based dashboard, and enhanced network visibility and analytics, it might not be suitable for organizations with highly specialized or complex network requirements.

Chapter 20: Wireless LAN security

1. Which 802.11 security protocol was developed to overcome the vulnerabilities of WEP?

C: TKIP

Temporal Key Integrity Protocol (TKIP) was developed as an interim solution to overcome the vulnerabilities of Wired Equivalent Privacy (WEP). TKIP was implemented as part of the original Wi-Fi Protected Access (WPA) standard to provide improved security compared to WEP. TKIP uses the same underlying mechanism as WEP but includes additional features to secure wireless data transmission.

2. Which authentication methods are available in WEP? (select two)

B: Open System

C: Shared Key

WEP supports two authentication methods: Open System and Shared Key. Open System Authentication allows any device to authenticate and attempt to connect to the network. Shared Key Authentication uses a WEP key for authentication, requiring the client device to have the correct key before it can connect.

3. Which WPA3 feature protects the PSK against brute-force attacks?

D: SAE

Simultaneous Authentication of Equals (SAE) is a WPA3 feature that allows the client and AP to verify that they have matching PSKs without rendering the PSK vulnerable to brute-force attacks.

4. Which of the following use AES counter mode encryption? (select all that apply)

A: CCMP

B: GCMP

Both Counter Mode with Cipher Block Chaining Message Authentication Code Protocol (CCMP) and Galois/Counter Mode Protocol (GCMP) use Advanced Encryption Standard (AES) in counter mode for encryption. CCMP is used in WPA2 for secure data encryption, while GCMP, which offers enhanced performance and security, is utilized in WPA3.

5. Which protocol is used to carry EAP messages between a supplicant and authenticator?

B: EAPoL

EAPoL (EAP over LANs) is the protocol employed by 802.1X to carry EAP (Extensible Authentication Protocol) messages between a supplicant and an authenticator.

6. Which WPA3 feature ensures that a compromised PSK cannot be used to decrypt past communications?

B: FS

Forward Secrecy (FS), also called Perfect Forward Secrecy (PFS), is a feature of WPA3 that ensures that a compromised PSK cannot be used to decrypt past communications. This is because the encryption keys used for each session are unique and not solely derived from the PSK.

7. Which of the following uses 802.1X authentication?

C: WPA-Enterprise

WPA-Enterprise uses 802.1X authentication, which provides a more robust security framework than simple PSK-based authentication. It is typically used in enterprise environments (hence the name).

8. Which of the following employs SAE?

D: WPA3-Personal

WPA3-Personal employs SAE for authentication. SAE enhances the security of the authentication process, protecting against brute-force attacks on the PSK.

9. Which protocol does the original WPA standard employ for data encryption and integrity?

A: TKIP

The original WPA standard employs TKIP for data encryption and integrity. TKIP was designed to provide a more secure alternative to WEP while being able to run on existing hardware.

10. Which protocol does the WPA3 standard employ for the most secure data encryption and integrity?

C: GCMP

The WPA3 standard employs GCMP for the most secure data encryption and integrity. GCMP uses the AES counter mode encryption and Galois Message Authentication Code (GMAC) for data integrity.

Chapter 21: Wireless LAN configuration

1. Which of the following methods can be used to connect to the GUI of a Cisco WLC? (select all that apply)

C: HTTP

D: HTTPS

The graphical user interface (GUI) of a Cisco wireless LAN controller (WLC) can be accessed via HTTP or HTTPS in a web browser. Telnet and SSH are used for remote access to the command-line interface (CLI), and the console port can be used to access the CLI with a console cable.

2. Which WLC port type is used to carry user data traffic?

A: Distribution system port

A WLC's distribution system (DS) ports are the standard network ports that connect to the DS—the switched Ethernet LAN. User data traffic is sent from and received on these ports.

3. Which WLC port type is used for OOB management of the WLC over the network?

C: Service port

The service port on a Cisco WLC is used for out-of-band (OOB) management—connecting to and managing the WLC via a dedicated connection that is separate from the DS ports.

4. Which WLC interface type is used to establish CAPWAP tunnels with LWAPs?

D: AP-manager interface

The AP-manager interface on a Cisco WLC is used to establish CAPWAP tunnels with LWAPs. By default, the management interface acts as the AP-manager interface, but you can optionally configure a separate AP-manager interface. For this reason, option D is more correct than option C; although the management interface sometimes acts as the AP-manager interface, that is not always the case.

5. Which WLC interface type is used for OOB management of the WLC over the network?

B: Service-port interface

The service-port interface corresponds to the physical service port and is used for OOB management. The management interface, on the other hand, is the default interface for in-band management via the DS ports.

6. Which advanced WLAN feature encourages clients to associate with less-busy LWAPs?

C: Client Load Balancing

If a client tries to associate with a busy LWAP, the Client Load Balancing feature makes the WLC encourage the client to seek a less-busy AP.

7. When configuring a hexadecimal WPA2 PSK in the Cisco WLC GUI, how many characters must the PSK be?

C: 64 characters

The WPA2 PSK can be configured as 64 hexadecimal characters. Alternatively, it can be configured as 8–63 ASCII characters.

8. Which QoS level is assigned to a WLAN by default, offering best-effort treatment of traffic?

B: Silver

The Silver QoS level is the default and is used for best-effort treatment of traffic. The other levels are: Platinum (voice), Gold (video), and Bronze (background).

9. Which advanced WLAN feature delays responses to 2.4 GHz probes to encourage clients to use 5 GHz instead?

D: Client Band Select

Client Band Select is a feature that delays responses to 2.4 GHz probe requests to encourage clients to connect to the 5 GHz band, which is usually less crowded.

10. Which of the following are Layer-3 security settings? (select two)

B: Passthrough

D: Conditional Web Redirect

Passthrough and Conditional Web Redirect are both Layer-3 WLAN security settings. Passthrough allows the user to access the network after accepting certain terms and conditions or viewing a mandatory message. Conditional Web Redirect redirects the user to a specific web page under certain conditions (i.e. their password is expired).

11. Which WLC interface type is used to map WLANs to VLANs?

D: Dynamic interface

Dynamic interfaces on a Cisco WLC are used to map WLANs to VLANs. Each dynamic interface is mapped to a VLAN on the wired network and a corresponding WLAN on the wireless network.

12. Which tab of the Cisco WLC GUI allows you to configure settings related to the LWAPs managed by the WLC?

A: Wireless

The Wireless tab in the Cisco WLC GUI is where you configure settings related to the LWAPs managed by the WLC.

13. If you enable LAG on a Cisco WLC, which ports are included in the LAG?

B: All DS ports

When you enable link aggregation group (LAG), all DS ports are included in the LAG. However, not all DS ports need to be active; as long as there is one functioning physical port in the LAG, it will be operational.

Chapter 22: Network automation

1. Which logical plane is responsible for routers exchanging BGP messages with each other to share routing information and build their routing tables?

B: Control Plane

The Control Plane is responsible for the exchange of routing protocol messages, like BGP, between routers. This plane handles the logic needed to build and maintain routing tables and other tables necessary for forwarding messages.

2. Which logical plane is responsible for a switch examining the source MAC address of each frame it receives and creating MAC address table entries?

B: Control Plane

The Control Plane in a switch is responsible for examining the source MAC addresses of incoming frames and creating MAC address table entries, which are used for making forwarding decisions. The forwarding decisions themselves are the role of the Data Plane.

3. Which logical plane is responsible for a switch examining the destination MAC address of each frame it receives and making a forwarding/flooding decision?

C: Data Plane

The Data Plane (or Forwarding Plane) in a switch is responsible for examining the destination MAC addresses of incoming frames and making forwarding or flooding decisions based on this information. Any activities related to the actual forwarding of messages are the responsibility of the Data Plane.

4. Which of the following planes are distributed in a traditional (non-SDN) network? (select all that apply)

A: Management plane

B: Control plane

C: Data plane

In a traditional network architecture, all three planes are distributed. Each network device is managed individually, builds its own tables for forwarding traffic, and makes independent forwarding decisions.

5. Which of the following statements about SDN architecture are true? (select two)

A: The Data Plane is distributed

D: The Control Plane is centralized

In software-defined networking (SDN) architecture, the Data Plane remains distributed; each network device is responsible for forwarding messages across the network. The Control Plane, on the other hand, is centralized in the SDN controller, which is responsible for providing instructions about how to forward messages to the network devices.

6. Which type of API is most common in the NBI of SDN architecture?

B: REST

In the northbound interface (NBI) of an SDN controller, representational state transfer (REST) APIs are commonly used, allowing applications to programmatically interact with the controller.

7. Which SDN interface is used to communicate with the managed devices?

B: SBI

The southbound interface (SBI) of an SDN controller is used to communicate with the managed devices. The name comes from how SDN architecture is usually illustrated, with the Application Layer at the top, the Control Layer in the middle, and the Infrastructure Layer (where the managed devices are located) at the bottom.

8. Which SDN architecture layer contains the network devices responsible for forwarding messages across the network?

D: Infrastructure Layer

The Infrastructure Layer in SDN architecture contains the physical and virtual network devices responsible for forwarding messages across the network. This layer is where the Data Plane's forwarding of messages takes place.

9. Which Cisco SDN solution takes advantage of spine-leaf architecture?

A: ACI

Cisco's Application-Centric Infrastructure (ACI) uses a spine-leaf architecture, optimizing east-west communication between servers in a data center.

10. Which of the following are Management Layer protocols? (select two)

A: SSH

B: NTP

Secure Shell (SSH) and Network Time Protocol (NTP) are protocols used in the management layer of network systems. SSH provides secure access to the CLI of network devices, and NTP ensures accurate time synchronization across the network.

11. Which of the following is not a benefit of network automation?

D: Reduced CapEx

While network automation can lead to reduced operating expenses (OpEx) through efficiency and reduced human error, it doesn't directly lead to reduced (capital expenses (CapEx). CapEx is typically associated with investments in equipment and infrastructure.

12. Which type of machine learning involves labeled data sets?

A: Supervised learning

Supervised learning is a type of machine learning (and deep learning) that involves labeled data sets. This is highly effective when clear and accurate labels are available, enabling precise predictions and classifications.

13. Which of the following can be provided by predictive AI?

C: Network traffic forecasting

AI models can analyze network traffic to predict future network load, allowing for proactive provisioning of additional resources or QoS policy optimization.

14. Which Catalyst Center AI feature can be used to automate troubleshooting?

A: Machine reasoning

Catalyst Center's Machine reasoning (MR) engine automates network troubleshooting, performing a root cause analysis when issues arise and potentially resolving problems without requiring manual intervention.

Chapter 23: REST APIs

1. Which HTTP method is generally equivalent to a CRUD "create" operation?

C: POST

The HTTP POST method is generally equivalent to a CRUD "create" operation. It is used to create a new resource on the server.

2. Which HTTP methods are generally equivalent to a CRUD "update" operation? (select two)

A: PUT

B: PATCH

The HTTP PUT and PATCH methods are generally equivalent to a CRUD "update" operation. PUT is used to replace a resource, and PATCH is used to modify a resource.

3. Which HTTP method is used to replace the specified resource?

A: PUT

The PUT HTTP method is generally used to replace the specified resource entirely. If the specified resource does not exist, it may be created using PUT.

4. Which HTTP response code indicates that the request resource was not found?

D: 404

The 404 "Not Found" HTTP response code indicates that the requested resource was not found on the server.

5. Which of the following HTTP response code classes are correct? (select three)

A: 2xx = successful

D: 1xx = informational

E: 3xx = redirection

1xx codes are informational, 2xx codes indicate successful responses, and 3xx codes indicate that further action needs to be taken to complete the request. The remaining classes are 4xx for client errors and 5xx for server errors.

6. Which of the following statements about REST APIs are true? (select two)

B: REST APIs are stateless.

C: REST uses a client-server architecture.

REST APIs are stateless, meaning that each request is a separate event, independent of all past exchanges between the client and server. Each request from the client must contain all the information needed to understand and process the request. REST is based on a client-server architecture in which the client and server are independent of each other.

7. Which statement about caching is accurate with regard to REST APIs?

A: Resources must be marked as cacheable or non-cacheable.

In REST APIs, resources can be cacheable or non-cacheable, but they must be explicitly or implicitly marked as such.

8. Which of the following HTTP response codes indicates a successful request?

B: 200

The 200 "OK" HTTP response code indicates a successful request. This response code is commonly used to indicate that a GET, PUT, POST, or PATCH request was successfully processed.

9. Which REST API authentication method allows a client to access a resource on a server on behalf of the resource's owner?

A: OAuth 2.0

OAuth 2.0 is designed to allow third-party applications to access resources on behalf of the resource owner without sharing the owner's credentials. The resource owner grants authorization to the third-party client application, which uses the authorization grant to obtain an access token. This token allows the client to access the resource on behalf of the owner.

10.   In which REST API authentication method does a client authenticate with an authorization server to receive a token that the client includes in its API calls?

D: Bearer authentication

In bearer authentication, the client authenticates with an authorization server to obtain an access token, which it includes in its API calls to access protected resources. The access token is typically short-lived, requiring regular renewal for continued access.

11. What is the primary advantage of using OAuth 2.0 for accessing resources?

B: OAuth 2.0 allows third-party applications to access resources without sharing the user's credentials.

OAuth 2.0 provides a secure way to delegate access to resources by issuing tokens, thereby eliminating the need to share the user's credentials with third-party applications. OAuth 2.0 is a key component of many modern web applications.

Chapter 24: Data formats

1. In which data serialization language is whitespace significant?

B: YAML

In YAML (YAML Ain't Markup Language), whitespace (specifically, indentation) is significant and is used to denote structure of the data. In XML (Extensible Markup Language) and JSON (JavaScript Object Notation), whitespace is not significant for the structure of the data.

2. Which data serialization language uses HTML-like tags?

A: XML

XML uses HTML-like tags to indicate key-value pairs: `<key>value</key>`.

3. What is the JSON name for an unordered set of key-value pairs?

D: Object

In JSON, an unordered set of key-value pairs is known as an "object". It is enclosed in curly braces, with keys and values separated by colons.

4. Which statements are true about the following JSON data? (select two)
`{"interface_name":"GigabitEthernet1/1","is_up":"true","speed":1000}`

B: The value of `"speed"` is a JSON number.

C: The data is a JSON object.

The value of `"speed"` is a numeric value that is not enclosed in double quotes, so it is a JSON number. The data as a whole is a JSON object—a set of key-value pairs enclosed in curly braces.

5. Which of the following statements about JSON arrays are true? (select two)

A: Arrays are enclosed in square brackets.

C: The values don't have to be of the same data type.

A JSON array is an ordered set of values enclosed in square brackets. The values can be of any valid JSON data type (including another array), but don't all have to be of the same data type. The values are separated by commas, but there must not be a trailing comma.

6. Which of the following statements about JSON objects are true? (select two)

A: The key of each key-value pair must be a string.

C: There must not be a trailing comma.

A JSON object is an unordered set of key-value pairs enclosed in curly braces. The key of each pair must be a string, and the value can be any valid JSON data type (including another object). The key and value of each pair are separated by a colon, and each pair is separated by a comma, but there must not be a trailing comma.

7. Which statement about the following JSON data is true? `{"device":"Switch01",` `"location":"DataCenterA","uptime":"72 hours","ports_active":24}`

A: It is valid JSON data.

There are no missing commas, extra colons, or any other elements that would make this data invalid; it is valid JSON data.

8. Which of the following are valid JSON strings? (select all that apply)

B: `"Acing The CCNA Exam"`

C: `"true"`

E: `"1000"`

A JSON string is an alphanumeric text value enclosed in double quotes. This applies to values that would otherwise be of a different data type without quotes: `"true"` would be a JSON boolean without double quotes, and `"1000"` would be a JSON number.

Chapter 25: Ansible and Terraform

1. Which of the following statements about Ansible are true? (select two)

A: Ansible is written in Python.

D: The Ansible control node connects to port 22 of managed devices.

Ansible is written in Python and employs an agentless model in which it uses SSH (TCP port 22) to connect to managed devices. Unlike Puppet and Chef, Ansible uses a push model; the Ansible control node pushes configurations to managed devices, instead of managed devices retrieving configurations from the control node.

2. Which of the following statements about Puppet are true? (select two)

A: Puppet is written in Ruby.

C: Puppet uses a pull model.

Puppet is written in Ruby. Unlike Ansible and Terraform, Puppet is agent-based and employs a pull model in which the Puppet agent on managed devices connects to the REST API on the Puppet master to retrieve configurations.

3. Which language are most Ansible files written in?

B: YAML

Most Ansible files, including inventory and playbook files, are written in YAML , which is popular for its readability and ease of use.

4. Which of the following statements about Chef are true? (select two)

B: Chef uses a pull model.

C: A Chef client must be installed on managed devices.

Like Puppet, Chef is agent-based and requires an agent called the "Chef client" to be installed on managed devices. It also uses a pull model, in which the Chef client connects to the Chef server's REST API to retrieve configurations.

5. Which of these IaC tools are primarily used for configuration management?

A: Ansible

B: Chef

D: Puppet

Of these four infrastructure as code (IaC) tools, Ansible, Chef, and Puppet are primarily used for configuration management, whereas Terraform is primarily used as a provisioning tool.

6. Which statements about HashiCorp Configuration Language are true? (select two)

B: It can perform complex tasks with less effort than general languages.

C: It is a declarative language.

Terraform uses HashiCorp Configuration Language (HCL), a domain-specific language (DSL)—a type of computer language specialized for a particular purpose, unlike general-purpose languages like Python or Go. HCL is declarative, meaning that it specifies the desired outcome rather than the specific procedures to achieve that outcome. It can often perform complex tasks with much less effort than a general language would require.

7. Which of the following configuration management tools use an agent-based model? (select two)

A: Puppet

C: Chef

Both Puppet and Chef use an agent-based model where agents installed on managed devices communicate with a central server (Puppet master or Chef server) to retrieve configuration information and apply it.

8. Which Ansible file defines automation tasks to manage configuration on managed devices?

C: Playbook

In Ansible, playbooks are the primary files where automation tasks are defined. Playbooks are written in YAML and describe the configurations of managed devices.

9. Which of the following statements about Terraform are true? (select two)

B: Terraform primarily uses a declarative approach.C: Terraform is written in Go.

Terraform is an IaC tool written in the Go programming language. It primarily uses a declarative approach, in which you define the desired end state for the infrastructure rather than specifying the step-by-step instructions for how to achieve that desited state.

10. What are the three steps of the basic Terraform workflow?

B: Write, plan, apply

The basic Terraform workflow consists of three main steps. The first is *write*, in which you define the desired state of your infrastructure resources in configuration files using HCL. The second is *plan*, in which you verify the changes that will be executed. The third is *apply*, in which you execute the plan to provision and manage the infrastructure resources.

index